Global Connections

VOLUME I

The first textbook to present world history via social history, drawing on social science methods and research. This interdisciplinary, comprehensive, and comparative textbook is authored by distinguished scholars and experienced teachers, and offers expert scholarship on global history that is ideal for undergraduate students. Volume 1 takes us from the origin of hominids to ancient civilizations, the rise of empires, and the Middle Ages. The book pays particular attention to the ways in which ordinary people lived through the great changes of their times, and how everyday experience connects to great political events and the commercial exchanges of an interconnected world. With 68 maps, 47 illustrations, timelines, boxes, and primary source extracts, the book guides students easily from specific historical incidents to broader perspectives, enabling them to use historical material and social science methodologies to analyze the events of the past, present, and future.

JOHN COATSWORTH is Professor of History and of International and Public Affairs, and Provost at Columbia University.

JUAN COLE is Richard P. Mitchell Collegiate Professor of History at the University of Michigan.

MICHAEL P. HANAGAN is Visiting Scholar, Vassar College.

PETER C. PERDUE is Professor of History at Yale University.

The late CHARLES TILLY was formerly the Joseph L. Buttenwieser Professor of Social Science at Columbia University.

LOUISE TILLY is Emeritus Professor, New School University.

Global Connections: Politics, Exchange, and Social Life in World History

VOLUME I

JOHN COATSWORTH
JUAN COLE
MICHAEL P. HANAGAN
PETER C. PERDUE
CHARLES TILLY
LOUISE TILLY

CAMBRIDGE
UNIVERSITY PRESS

CAMBRIDGE
UNIVERSITY PRESS

University Printing House, Cambridge CB2 8BS, United Kingdom

Cambridge University Press is part of the University of Cambridge.

It furthers the University's mission by disseminating knowledge in the pursuit of education, learning, and research at the highest international levels of excellence.

www.cambridge.org
Information on this title: www.cambridge.org/9780521145183

© John Coatsworth, Juan Cole, Michael P. Hanagan, Peter C. Perdue, Charles Tilly, and Louise Tilly 2015

First published 2015

Printed in the United States of America by Sheridan Books, Inc.

A catalog record for this publication is available from the British Library

ISBN 978-0-521-19189-0 Hardback
ISBN 978-0-521-14518-3 Paperback

Cambridge University Press has no responsibility for the persistence or accuracy of URLs for external or third-party internet websites referred to in this publication, and does not guarantee that any content on such websites is, or will remain, accurate or appropriate.

CONTENTS

ILLUSTRATIONS

Source information for all illustrations in this textbook can be found online at www.cambridge.org/globalconnections1.

MAPS

Source information for all maps in this textbook can be found online at www.cambridge.org/globalconnections1.

ACKNOWLEDGEMENTS

Global Connections looks at the cultures, states, and empires of world history and at the interrelationships among societies on the peripheries or in the interstices of these formations. Many commentators on the contemporary world and academic historians now agree that students need a comprehensive overview of the human experience from a global perspective. After many years of teaching regional and national histories, we have combined our individual expertise to make our own contribution to this exciting and growing field. It has been a stimulating experience. We hope that our readers share the same sense of excitement in reading it as we felt in writing it.

One of the strengths of this project was the participation of colleagues of the caliber of Charles and Louise Tilly. Alas, Charles Tilly died shortly after his share of the project was completed, and Louise Tilly, who initiated the project, was unable to finish for medical reasons. But the spirit of Charles and Louise Tilly informs the entire book through the many discussions and even arguments that went into its making.

We are grateful to the many seminars and the conference that gave us a venue to rehearse various aspects of our work. An MIT World History Workshop in Boston in June 2003 was an important inspiration in moving the project forward. Over the course of the project we discussed and debated it in several public venues where we received invaluable criticism. In New York, participants in the New School's seminar on state formation and Columbia University's Workshop on Contentious Politics were sympathetic and helpful. We are especially grateful to Cassandra Cavenaugh, Ali Ferdowsi, David Kelly, Anne McCants, Jeff Ravel, Jennifer Spock, and Rui Wang.

At every stage in the process of writing this book we have benefited from the advice, good counsel, and criticism of friends, colleagues, and fellow historians. We are indebted to Behrooz Moazami, Sidney Tarrow, Elizabeth Wood, and Wayne Te Brake. Miriam Cohen read many chapters of this manuscript and patiently suggested many changes. We would also like to thank the dozens of anonymous scholars who reviewed draft chapters of the manuscript. Their invaluable experience in teaching world history in the classroom has helped us to make this a readable story.

We also particularly wish to thank the staff at Cambridge University Press, ideal collaborators and co-workers, particularly Deborah Gershenowitz, senior commissioning editor, Valerie Appleby, development editor, Dana Bricken, editorial assistant, Charles Howell, textbook and digital project co-ordinator, and Catherine Flack, textbook development manager.

INTRODUCTION: THE HUMAN STORY FROM PREHISTORY TO 1500

About two and a half million years ago, on a medium-sized planet of a relatively insignificant star in one of fifty billion galaxies in the universe, our ancestral species, *Homo erectus*, made stone tools in Africa. About 200,000 years ago *Homo sapiens sapiens*, our species, emerged, also in Africa. Now, over 7 billion members of this species cover every spot on the globe, and a few of them have landed on the moon. This species shares the planet with millions of other species, thousands of which are disappearing every year, mostly because of human impact. This book tells the story of the human world, from the beginning to the present. It is an analytic narrative about the human processes that cross continents and order time on a global scale.

On the universal scale, we still don't matter much, but since this is our story, we care greatly about it. We respond more to the needs of other humans than to those of plants, animals, and insects. Likewise, we care more about our family and friends than about millions of other humans who live far away. And yet we are connected to them all. Every day, in the news, we hear much more about what affects our own country here and now than we do about long gone peoples of the past. But we are still immersed in the achievements of our distant ancestors. We need to know what they did for us in order to know where we are, and where we are going.

Narrowness can be dangerous. If we only focus on what seems to affect us personally, we miss the less obvious impulses that shape our lives, and we ignore the long-term trends that guide our fate. This history traces the expansion of humans' awareness of each other and of the world around them over time. As humans moved out of Africa to cover the rest of the globe, many groups kept in touch with each other, even over vast distances. A new idea – a better pot, a stronger axe, a more powerful god – caught on when others found it useful. Once humans began to speak, they told others about new ideas and things. Sooner or later, technological, cultural, and economic innovations covered the world. Global connections are the essence of the human story.

Since the years in which our species, *Homo sapiens sapiens*, spread from Africa to settle East Asia, human history has always been global history, but the pace and even direction of global change has not been constant. The human wave did not always advance; it sometimes contracted. The initial settlements of Britain by hominids, the biological family that includes humans and the great apes, may have begun as early as 200,000 years ago. But the rise and fall of temperatures, linked to the growth and contraction of glaciers, allowed human settlements to advance or forced them to retreat. For thousands of years hominids, including *Homo sapiens* and *Homo sapiens sapiens* (us), crossed the land bridges that periodically tied Ireland and Britain to the continent. The migrants from the continent who permanently settled Britain entered the country only 12,000 years ago. When temperatures again permitted human habitation, between 12,000 and 9,500 years ago, new human cultural groups, different from the original settlers, were there to take advantage.

Such an example reminds us that globalization has never been a one-way process. Globalization occurs when community life is affected by actions, events, and relations at an increasingly greater distance from the locality. The expansion of groups across territory, such as in continental migration to Britain, is an example of globalization. In pre-ice-age Britain, bands and tribes of peoples from the European continent entered an unoccupied land and spread across it, extending human linkages across a wide territory.

Contrary to some common usages, globalization does not mean that a process comprises the entire globe. It refers to the *expanding* of processes and movements across territory. Deglobalization is its opposite: It refers to the *shrinking* geographic influence of processes and movements.

In the case of the settlement of Britain and Ireland, at any given time and place globalization and deglobalization were usually happening simultaneously; small bands of hunter-gatherers left the old settlements on the continent to take advantage of new hunting grounds to the north, while a group of pilgrims returned to the south to participate in ancient ceremonies at traditional religious sites. It is the net balance that counts. Is the society globalizing *more* than it is deglobalizing? Is its territory expanding? Are important events or actions increasingly influenced by distant groups or happenings?

If somehow we could measure the geographic frequency and territorial consequences of all these decisions in any one period for a given region and add them up, we would be able to provide a definitive response to the question of whether globalization or deglobalization was occurring. Alas, we can seldom provide a precise answer to this question, but informed estimates of main trends are possible.

In the period covered by the first volume of this book, the years from the agricultural transformation to 1500, we argue that the world globalized more than it deglobalized. We do not argue that the global is good, the deglobal bad. Many of us have primary loyalties in small communities based on church, or kin, or family. Nor do we lament the fall of exploitative and oppressive global empires. We study an important phenomenon, one that entails both good and bad, that has both costs and benefits.

This book claims that in respect to politics, commerce, and social life, the main course of human history has been a globalizing one. Globalization occurred not just at the beginning and end of our period but all along the way. Despite periods of deglobalization, including such major events as the breakup of the Roman empire, the collapse of the Han empire in China, the abandonment of the Mayan city of Copán, the world globalized with respect to politics, commerce, and social life more than it deglobalized. This is an enormous claim, one that we will spend a good part of the next five hundred pages explaining and defending. By the end we hope to have provided a convincing picture of the main trends at work.

Politics globalized in the years between the advent of the agricultural revolution and 1500 CE. City-states continued to be important, and large parts of the world, particularly in Africa, the Americas, and Southeast Asia, remained largely stateless, dominated by village associations and kin groups. But the salient characteristic of political change over the long haul between the Akkadian empire, discussed in Chapter 2, and the Ottoman empire, discussed in Chapter 14, was the rise in the size and power of empires and the extent to which they filled the available political space. Empires were heterogeneous political units linked to central power by indirect rule. The Achaemenid empire that occupied much of the territory of today's Iran contained kingdoms annexed in one fell swoop by conquest and governed directly by the emperor, as well as areas ruled by subordinate kings who paid tribute, as well as tribal societies that gave the merest nod to the emperor's authority. By 1500, particularly in Eurasia, we can talk about a world of empires. Containing diverse groups of people, they frequently abutted other empires, inciting inter-imperial competition and further extending imperial globalism.

At the very beginning of our period, city-states pursuing the course of empire lacked an adequate system of transportation and bureaucratic techniques for provisioning troops at home; early empires maintained powerful armies by annual plundering expeditions and prolonged stays in subject cities at municipal expense. Sargon of Akkad, one of the world's first empire builders, who ruled in Mesopotamia around 2500 BCE, used plundering and forced hospitality to maintain his army.

But the Akkadian empire ruled by Sargon, the very epitome of a powerful state in his era, would have been considered puny by his imperial successors in the Ottoman empire that controlled the territory of the old Akkadian empire in 1500. Sargon's army of 5,000–6,000 men struck contemporaries with awe but would not long have withstood an Ottoman army that could mobilize 250,000 in a single campaign. But for both Akkadians and Ottomans, to build a mighty empire required a countryside rich enough and agricultural classes sufficiently numerous to support large armies. It would have needed an administrative regime able to compute and levy taxes, and a military sufficiently large to defend these resources from rivals and to defeat and expropriate the wealth of rival empires. The increasing spread and diversity of agriculture in the Near East provided the agricultural resources. The development of written language and the growth of bureaucratic professions created a generalized technology – global technologies really – that allowed states to count and record everyone's resources based on uniform language understandable by tax collectors. Later imperial rulers developed techniques for provincial administration. Professional imperial administrators also perfected the techniques of rule across long distances. Provincial governors, road systems, and government granaries were all used by rulers in Persia, Han China and the Inka highlands to rule diverse groups of people. The invention of money also figured large: what invention was more global than money? It could circulate in areas where no one recognized the figure on the coin or the country of its origin.

Finally, empires depended on their ability to wage war. Like any aspirants for empire, Sargon's Akkadian empire was in the forefront of military technology. Unlike its poorer neighbors, the empire could field disciplined professional armies. Sargon was one of the pioneers of the composite bow in military affairs, a revolutionary new technology. The composite bow used specially reinforced materials to create greater tension and thus greater ability to penetrate the leather jackets worn in battle.

Empires were global in their ability to expand and to integrate disparate cultures. Being products of military conquest and political co-optation, empires could rise extremely rapidly, incorporating pre-existing political units and administrative bureaucracies. Imperial defenders lauded their diversity. In eleventh-century Hungary St. Stephen is said to have recommended "guest and foreign peoples" to his son and heir because "they are very useful, they bring varied values and customs, weapons and knowledge with them, all of which ornament the royal Court and make it splendid, while frightening the haughty foreigners. For weak and defenseless is a country which has but a single language and uniform customs."[1]

If St. Stephen's Hungary could find a place for many peoples, it could – and did – just as easily collapse with the same rapidity. Subordinate political units took advantage of regional discontent or military weakness and departed empire with the same territorial boundaries and subordinate rulers as they had entered it. When empires expanded incorporating disparate polities, the political world globalized; when they collapsed into their component parts, it deglobalized. No empire lived forever but some lasted much longer than others. Trying to understand why some empires were able to balance contending religions, ethnic groups, and political traditions and last for centuries while others proved unable to maintain such a balance and collapsed after decades is one of the central themes of this volume.

While empires occupy the center of our attention, commercially oriented city-states were sometimes important political actors. City-states survived lacking agricultural hinterlands because they were centers of trade and had access to ready cash. They formed in the interstices between empires where they served as trade intermediaries across extensive borderlands. The extensive commercial connections of city-states, sometimes extending across vast areas, made them important global players. When an empire confronted military challenge it went to the countryside to recruit soldiers; city-states used their wealth to buy mercenaries. In the third century CE, the strength of Palmyra (in modern Syria) was based on its nobles' role as desert tribesmen willing to protect the caravan routes, an openness to foreign merchants, and a strategic position on the Silk Road. City-states also acquired power as entrepôt towns; these were particularly important along the Indian coast where the monsoon season often required merchants to unload their cargoes and wait until the winds favored further transit. And Southeast Asian city-states such as Srivijaya in Sumatra acquired their power from their strategic riverine locations as port cities controlling the luxury goods produced in the hinterland and selling them to foreign nations.

Commerce also globalized in the years before 1500. The most striking example of long-distance trade in the pre-1500 period was undoubtedly the so called Silk Road, discussed in Chapter 8. It flourished for centuries, connecting Chinese silk and luxury goods with the eastern Mediterranean and all the regions along the way. The rise and fall of Central Asian kingdoms determined the state of the trade, as well as circumstances in the Chinese and western Mediterranean ports that were the end points of so much trade. When the road opened wide for merchants, Eurasian trade globalized; when it closed to them, Eurasian trade deglobalized.

Spanning continents, the Silk Road was the creation of commercial enterprise escorted by military forces. Merchants shepherded their precious commodities through vast spaces inhabited by bandits and hostile tribesmen, encountering floods and sandstorms and intermediary rulers who tried to impose confiscatory tolls. There was no real terminus or starting point to the Silk Road; sometime it was in the Black Sea ports, other times in Jordan, and at other times in Egypt, depending on local conditions and opportunities. Production too occurred at various sites along the road. Experts recognize dozens of silk products that originated in areas from Baghdad to Chang'an, Bukhara, and Kashgar.

From a global perspective, the Silk Road depended on governments farsighted enough to promote international trade and to recognize the need to treat foreign merchants fairly. The fall of strong Chinese dynasties such as that of the Han (206 BCE – 220 CE) and Tang (618–907) regimes and the ensuing chaos closed the road for a generation. At its high point during the Pax Mongolica (Mongol Peace, 1206–1368 CE), the trade flourished under the protection of rulers who imposed a strong government throughout the entire Eurasian Plain. The Mongols even contributed to production by settling communities of silk workers in East and Central Asia.

The growing involvement of Europeans in the silk commerce, making the Silk Road all the more global, is shown in the extraordinary efforts European monarchs and city-states made to reopen the road when it closed in the fifteenth century. Together the breakup of Mongol rule, the descent of Central Asia into political chaos, and the xenophobia of the Ming dynasty effectively interrupted Eurasian commerce. This was a classic example of deglobalization. In despair, European rulers financed expensive expeditions down the coast of Africa, searching for alternative routes. Eventually this search yielded another path to the east. One of its side benefits was the discovery of the Americas and the beginning of another global era.

But when the Silk Road was operating, it depended not only on governments but on diasporic, close-knit communities yet with transnational ties binding them together over enormous spaces. Global trade required that mercantile commitments made in one distant portion of the world be honored in another. Between Palmyra in modern-day Jordan and Chang'an in China there were many different currencies, laws, and customs. Even within empires, tolls and legal regulations varied. Local people were required to solve local problems but they had to be trustworthy in financial matters. These communities had to be large enough to thrive at crucial locations throughout Eurasia but small enough to vouch for the honor of all members and to punish them by exclusion if they violated their faith. The diasporic religious or ethnic community served these purposes.

Diasporic communities were vital to the operation of the Silk Road. Every member of the community had a vested interest in a reputation for integrity. Those who violated this trust were resolutely banished; exclusion from the community meant a degree of total isolation that few could endure. Historically language, religion, and ethnicity have been the bases for constructing community, but these identities were invariably reinforced by intermarriage of diaspora members and the adoption of common cultural characteristics. Armenians, Greeks, Gnostic Christians, Gujaratis, Jews, Lebanese, and Nestorian Christians are only a few of the diasporic traders who have played key roles in global trade. Social life and politics together with markets made the Silk Road work.

Finally, social life also globalized. The world's major religions emerged in this period. We define a major religion as one that attempted successfully to convert millions of followers, perhaps even entire societies. The major religions in today's world were all founded before 1500, although the distribution of believers would change significantly after that date. In the world before 1500, religion was more central to social life than for most people in the modern world. It was not simply a question of personal devotion, but religion and social institutions were more deeply intertwined than today. Religious identities entailed obligations of solidarity toward fellow believers but often they inspired distrust and suspicion of those outside the faith. In many societies a particular religion enjoyed a preferred position within the state and responsibility for providing basic education, alms, and shelter; non-believers were sometimes excluded from these services. The spread of major religions and the blending of religious faith with everyday social institutions that tightened connections was a globalizing phenomenon. On the other hand, minority religions excluded from state services that gave pride of place to members of state-sponsored religions failed to get the benefits of this globalization. Inclusion and exclusion went hand in hand.

If we recognize the globalism of the dissemination of religious ideas throughout whole societies, let us not forget the globalism of minority religious communities whose social relations encompassed huge spaces. The mercantile diaspora, discussed above, often originated in religious missions. Social life sometimes coincided with economic interest. Having been rejected by the dominant Christian orthodoxies, Nestorian Christianity spread east as missionaries followed the Silk Road looking for converts. But Nestorian Christians soon established a position for themselves as merchants and traders that further reinforced their presence on the road. Nestorian religious convictions gave them a distinctive identity, one that marked them off from others. This in turn gave small communities an internal solidarity and reputation for integrity. Theirs too was a globalizing experience.

Monarchs and religious hierarchs often espoused universal religions that attempted to convert or enforce obligations on all members of society. Emperors, shahs and kings believed that empire would be still stronger if everyone accepted the same beliefs. In their efforts to impose religious centralization, rulers and religious leaders met with resistance along pre-existing fault lines. The Roman pope and the Byzantine emperor disagreed over religious practices, but their differences emerged against a background of political and social antagonism. Roman Catholics and Greek Orthodox religious leaders represented not just religious differences but very different geographic and political constituencies, as political ties between Rome and Constantinople weakened. Orthodox efforts to impose doctrine on Egyptian Christians created new divisions but also recalled long-held ill will based on previous bitter controversies over religious jurisdiction and intolerance. As Byzantine emperors increased taxes to build armies to repel their foes, the hard-pressed taxpayers of Egypt and the Near East found emperors' efforts to impose religious orthodoxy all the more intolerable. Their resistance would significantly weaken the empire's ability to respond to the Islamic challenge. Thus the globalizing efforts of empires produced deglobalizing local revolts. At the end of the day politics, commerce, and social life came together to produce new social identities.

Besides politics, commerce, and social life, two other central themes join with the three outlined above: technology and gender relations. Technology is the use of human, natural, and mechanical power over the non-human world, for human ends. Humans have always had to get their food, clothing, and shelter from the natural world, and they have constantly tried to improve the conditions under which they live. Superior productive power created goods that were profitable for trade, and often (in the form of weaponry) superior in war. How people gain their living from nature defines a significant portion of their culture, uniting them around a common mode of existence and separating them from others. The oldest division of this kind is that between the nomadic pastoralist, who moves constantly with his herds, and the settled agriculturalist. The use of technology thus shapes relations of power, exchange, and community, without totally determining them. Although the environment has strongly affected how humans live, we should avoid assuming that natural changes directly determine their development: human social decisions have always inflected the way in which the natural world's processes make an impact on the collective whole.

Of all the ways of acting on nature that humans use for their benefit, communication and transportation technology deserve special attention. The movement of messages and goods between peoples separated by large distances is the key theme of this story of interconnections. Whether by speech, smoke signals, writing, the telegraph, or the internet, people have always sent information to each other in order to co-ordinate their activities for mutual gain, to warn their enemies, or just to express their love for each other. How fast the messages travel, how far, how often, and in what medium (oral or visual, handwritten or printed) certainly affect the density and quality of communication, but all express the underlying, irrepressible urge to tie one person to another. Contrary to what you might have heard, global communication did not begin with the internet; networks of trade and information have covered the globe since the human story began. Likewise, the movement of commodities over distances short and long, on human backs, on animals, on carts, railroads, or airplanes, serves the goals of commerce and community. All things have social lives.

Gender relations have shaped the human story in ways both public and private. Humans, like other mammals, belong genetically to two biological sexes, but gender, which means the social expression of biological sex, has varied greatly over time and space. Men and women have taken on highly diverse roles depending on their relationship to hierarchies of power, relationships of exchange, and social structure. Still, in general, men have dominated power hierarchies through all of human history, as they still do. Male dominance originated in physical strength, but ideologies of rule that justified male supremacy through reference to divine power, and the fact that men wrote nearly all the histories, kept domination going over the long term. In commercial relations, women had more nearly equal positions. Although they did not become the richest people in a society, they often controlled small-scale trade, and as artisans or textile producers they took on important economic roles within the household. In small communities like the family, women usually held subordinate but vital positions: they did the cooking, the housekeeping, and childrearing that made it possible for human social life to continue. Sometimes powerful women emerged in the historical records at the top of their societies, as wives or mothers of rulers; then we can tell their stories in more detail. Until recent times, most individual women have remained nearly invisible, but they were an essential part of the processes that enable humans to survive. We can tell their collective story even if we cannot find out much about their individual lives.

This is a world history, but it is also a regional history. Although common processes spanned the entire world, they did not have equal strength or develop at the same rate everywhere. To tell the global story coherently, we must divide the world into regions. Regions are large geographic divisions of the globe, considered as intense fields of political, economic, and cultural interaction. Sometimes these regions have sharp geologically defined boundaries, like oceans and high mountains, but usually they do not. For centuries, humans have found ways to cross deserts, climb mountains, and sail on all the world's oceans. Geological barriers have slowed down their movements, but never stopped them entirely. Sometimes these regions coincided fairly closely with large empires or civilizations, but often they spanned several political or cultural units. Eurasia, Africa, and the Americas are the largest of these regional units, but we often refer to smaller units like Central Eurasia, the Middle East, East Asia, Southeast Asia, Europe, or South America.

In this story, we explicitly compare political institutions, production and exchange, and social groups within and across regions; we focus on how contacts and connections constructed (and destroyed) relationships among these societies; and we look at large-scale processes of structural change that shaped the shifting regional divisions. Bear in mind, however, that few of these regions have a very sharp natural boundary: where does Europe stop and Asia begin, for example? Regions are only useful ways to think about the geographic concentration of certain cultural and economic processes in certain times.

For every period and major geographic region, within the limits of available sources, we will describe basic settlement patterns, political and military organizations, how people produced and exchanged goods, and social relations (including gender, family, and religious communities). After reading our story of political events, the emergence of religious beliefs, and socio-cultural practices, you should be able to discuss subjects like forms of military organization or marriage rituals and to compare them across regions and over time.

Modern-day historians no longer rely exclusively on written sources. Collaboration with archaeologists has allowed them to extend their knowledge more deeply into the past to learn about ancient social practices and power structures. For many of these subjects, especially the lives of poor people, women, or mobile peoples, we have far fewer sources than for the settled, male, wealthy power-holders. If we have less to say about these people it is not because they mattered less; it is because we have much less information. In our story, we will discuss the sources historians use to obtain reliable information about the past.

Yet even a few basic facts can support important comparisons. Often the only thing we know about many people in the past is when they were born, when they died, when they married, if they did, and how many children they had. These basic demographic facts still help us to imagine what it meant to live in a world in which people had far more children, many of whom died in infancy, and much shorter life spans than today.

For examining interactions between regions, we also must use indirect evidence. Only a few traders, pilgrims, or spies left direct accounts of their travels, but we still know about transmission routes of many goods and organisms. Some, like gunpowder, taken from China to Europe by Muslim and Mongol warriors, were brought intentionally from one place to another; others were unwanted hitchhikers. For example, in the fourteenth century CE, as trade grew, bubonic plague spread along land and sea trade routes from Eastern Eurasia into the Mediterranean and Europe, taking millions of lives. On the other hand, inter-regional contact could also yield health benefits. Mediterranean authorities discovered that quarantining ships from plague-struck areas was an effective way of limiting the spread of plague and soon the practice was adopted by most ports. Foods, germs, and weapons all moved long distances because other people brought them along on their travels, whether they wanted to or not.

The globalization of the years before 1500 culminated in the discovery of the Americas and the conquest of the Aztec and Inka empires. After that, a river of silver, caravans of sailing ships, and hordes of armies moved across both the Old and New Worlds, inextricably

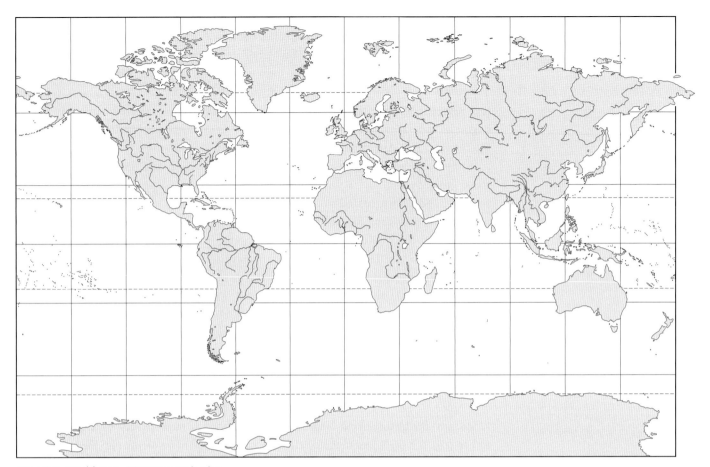

Map 0.1 World map, Mercator projection

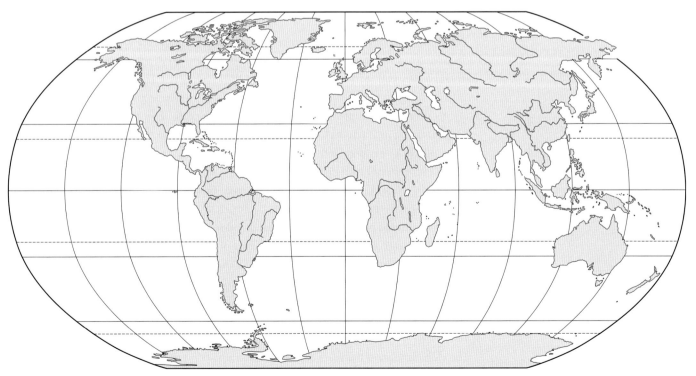

Map 0.2 World map, equal area projection

connecting them together. For the first time since they had left Africa years ago, all the major populations of the human race were in contact with one another. At a terrible cost in disease, death, murder, war, and exploitation, the year 1500 would provide the basis for a new kind of global history.

Note 1 John A. Armstrong, *Nations before Nationalism* (Chapel Hill: University of North Carolina Press, 1982), p. 114.

World map: prehistory and agriculture

Tehuacan

Five largest cities *000s*

1. Hao

3. Babylon

5. Nimrud

100

100

100

50

50

2. Nineveh

4. Thebes

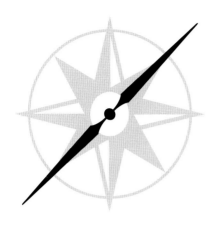

PART I

5000–600 BCE: The rise of cities, states, and pastoralism

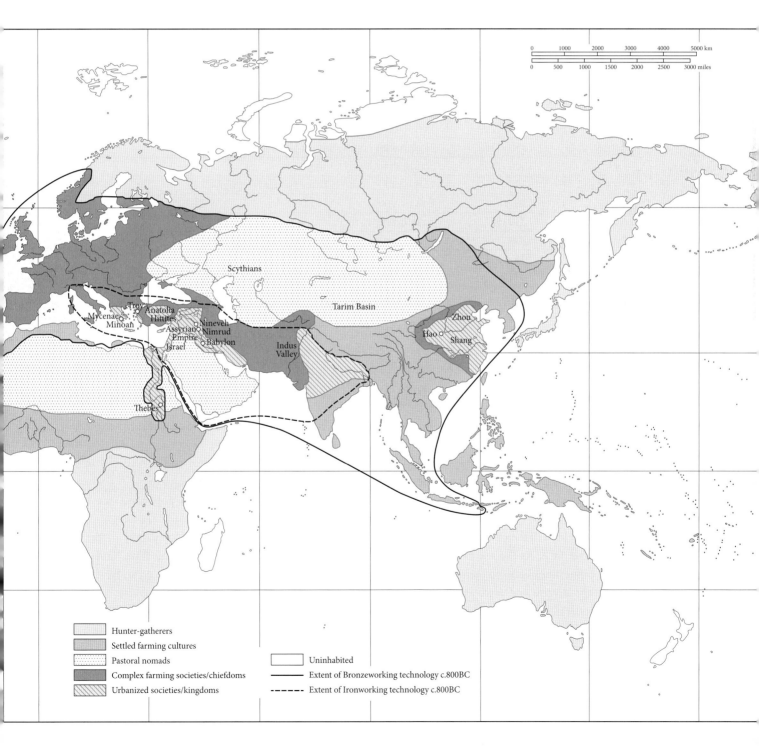

Scythians

Tarim Basin

Troy
Anatolia
Mycenae Hittites
Minoan
Nineveh
Assyrian Nimrud
Empire Babylon
Israel
Indus
Valley

Zhou
Hao
Shang

Thebes

	Hunter-gatherers
	Settled farming cultures
	Pastoral nomads
	Complex farming societies/chiefdoms
	Urbanized societies/kingdoms

	Uninhabited
——	Extent of Bronzeworking technology c.800BC
- - - -	Extent of Ironworking technology c.800BC

Prehistory	
200,000–100,000	*Homo sapiens sapiens* (our species of human beings) first appears in Africa.
100,000–40,000	Humans migrate from Africa, traces found throughout Eurasia.
15,000	Last ice age ends with new warming trend; humans cross to western hemisphere.
10,000	Agricultural transformation begins in Southwest Asia, eventually spreads to every continent.
First City-States and Empires	
3000	Cities and states present in Mesopotamia; state develops in Egypt; Minoan culture in Crete; pastoralist societies in western Iran, Central Asia, the southern Ukraine.
2500	Writing systems develop; alphabets by 1500 BCE.
2500–1600/1200	Indus Valley civilization.
2300	First pastoralists (Amorites) invade Mesopotamia.
2000–1700	Chariot invented; chariot warriors from Central Asia invade the Middle East, Egypt, and China.
Age of the Chariot-Driven Empires	
1650–1200	Hittite empire.
1550–1100	Mycenaean civilization in Greece.
1500–1045	Shang dynasty in China.
1285	Battle of Qadesh (Hittites versus Egyptians).
1260	Fall of Troy.
1230–587	Israelite states in Palestine.
1200	"Sea People" invasions of eastern Mediterranean.
1045–771	Zhou dynasty in China.
1000	First evidence of horseriding warriors.
665	Assyrian empire.

History is about how people change their world and themselves over time. After fortuitous mutation produced the first human beings in Africa in about 200,000 BCE, people changed very slowly at first. Their numbers increased a few at a time as they moved about looking for food and shelter. They left behind pitifully few traces of who they were, what they believed, and how they survived. This is why the first chapter of our book can cover 99 percent of the time since humans first walked the earth and fit most of what's left in just two more chapters that stop in 600 BCE.

Though 99 percent of human time is covered in our first three chapters, 99 percent of the roughly 110 billion humans who have ever lived were born after 600 BCE. As the number of human beings increased, and the connections between them intensified, human history became more diverse and fascinating, and the pace of historical change accelerated. That is why this book starts out at lightning speed covering multiple millennia, but devotes more and more pages to smaller and smaller time periods as it

continues. More people have been making more changes in less time in each new era of our history.

During the first 190 millennia of human history, a tiny number of humans accomplished extraordinary things, never before achieved by any of the earth's countless other creatures: they made languages, tools, fire, weapons, painting, clothing. Some of them moved out of Africa and spread out in small bands and tribes across the Eurasian land mass. A few reached Alaska and then moved south, thinly populating the western hemisphere.

By 10,000 BCE, the total human population of the globe numbered less than 10 million. At about this time, humans were just discovering, after millennia of trial and error, how to make their food supplies steadier and more predictable by planting seeds or seedlings and domesticating animals. This farming transformation made it possible for more people to survive in a given territory than had been possible when food supplies depended on collecting and foraging. The human population began to increase a tiny bit faster, from 0.0015 percent per year to as much as 0.0045 percent, still very slow but three times as fast as ever before. The total population of human beings on earth increased from less than 10 million in 10,000 BCE to perhaps 100 million in 600 BCE.

At the same time, faster-growing populations sometimes outstripped harvests. Climate changes could now mean famine. Sedentary farmers often fell victim to marauding foragers, whose hunting skills made them skillful warriors. Although the farming revolution proved to be a huge technological advance for humankind, it was not a happy experience for many of the people who pioneered it, as Chapter 1 shows.

Agriculture also made it possible for people to come together in much larger communities, beginning by about 3000 BCE. The rise of towns and cities represented a huge step forward in social organization. In areas where agriculture proved to be especially productive, large numbers of people could be freed to specialize in other jobs, from making useful objects to communing with the gods. Specialization made people more skillful. Writing systems first developed in cities, vastly increasing people's ability to communicate over great distances and to learn from their own past. Cities became centers of economic exchange, social differentiation, and political power.

Like the farming revolution, city life also had drawbacks. High population density spread disease. City people suffered from malnutrition and even starvation when harvests failed. Politics (from the Greek word *polis*, meaning city) meant power, usually concentrated in the hands of a ruler claiming to be divine, or to have divine approval, and the ruler's extended family, clan, or lineage. Cities, by making human life more unequal, inspired envy of those with wealth, making them vulnerable to rebellions from below and attacks from outside. States emerged when city elites came together to create more effective and therefore complex and specialized military forces, capable of suppressing revolt, subduing other cities, and extending the sway of a single ruler over larger and larger territories. Chapter 2 explores these themes and describes the earliest and most important city-states and empires.

Just as the farming revolution was taking hold in the Fertile Crescent and spreading elsewhere, a pastoral alternative emerged. Agricultural communities concentrated on growing crops and raised livestock to supplement their diet, while pastoralists relied for food mainly on their herds of sheep, goats, or cattle. Agricultural communities were mostly sedentary, while pastoralists migrated as the seasons changed in search of new pastures for their herds. Pastoralists from the Eurasian steppe first domesticated horses, then camels. They developed military skills protecting herds and muscling out rivals to keep the best pastures.

Beginning in about 2000 BCE, some pastoralists turned from raiding farming villages on the periphery of ancient empires to attacking cities. Their weapon of choice was the horse-drawn chariot, which spread throughout the Middle East. By 1700 BCE, many of the ancient cities and empires throughout Southwest Asia had suffered defeat and either collapsed entirely or succumbed to new rulers. By 1000 BCE, pastoralists had learned the key military technique of riding on horseback. Chapter 3 shows how repeated waves of mounted pastoralists, viewed as rough barbarians by city people, destroyed or took over ancient cities and empires. In some notable cases, the invaders eventually succumbed to the attractions of city life and installed themselves as rulers and overlords.

By 600 BCE many of the enduring patterns of economic and social life, the key institutions of political power, the modes of artistic expression, and even the great legends that have shaped religious creeds down to modern times, had already made their appearance on the human stage.

1 From human origins to agricultural transformation

Timeline	
200,000–100,000 BP (Before the Present)	Evolution of *Homo sapiens sapiens* in Africa.
100,000 BP	*Homo sapiens sapiens* begin to spread out of Africa.
40,000 BP	*Homo sapiens sapiens* traces found from Europe to New Guinea.
30,000 BP	Elaborate rock engravings and cave paintings.
15,000 BP	End of the last ice age – global warming.
11,000–10,000 BP	*Homo sapiens sapiens* traces found from Alaska to Nova Scotia.
10,000 BP	Oldest agricultural community: residents of Abu Hureyra in the Middle Euphrates Valley begin raising domesticated sheep and goats and growing einkorn.
9,500 BP	City of Jericho in the Jordan Valley: walled agricultural community occupying nine acres.
9,000 BP	Rice cultivated along the Middle Yangtze River valley.
8,000 BP	Emmer and einkorn wheat and domesticated animals introduced into Southeastern Europe and Greece; wheat and barley farmed along the Nile and the Indus.
7,500 BP	Sorghum and millet farmed in North China.
5,500 BP	Cattle-herding in the Sudan.
4,759 BP	Maize cultivated in the Tehuacán Valley in Southern Mexico.
4,500 BP	American Midwestern Native Americans living in river valleys plant goosefoot and marsh elder and sunflowers.
4,000 BP	Sorghum, millet, and yams cultivated in Central Africa.
1,000 BP	Agriculture comes to La Plata region of Southwest USA from Mexico.
1788 CE	British settlers bring agriculture to Australia.

About one and a half million years ago, a young boy left home and did not return. Whether his family knew about his fate or whether he just disappeared, we will never know. He may have died from blood poisoning consequent upon losing his baby teeth. In 1984 the nearly complete skeleton of this 11–13-year-old was discovered by a team of paleoanthropologists working at a site around Narioko-tome River near the shores of Lake Turkana in Kenya. "Nariokotome Boy," as he has become known, was a species of **hominid** (two-legged primate) known as ***Homo ergaster*** ("working man"), the immediate predecessor of the human species *Homo sapiens* ("wise man") and our own subspecies ***Homo sapiens sapiens***. Nariokotome Boy belonged to a society that made crude tools, thus the name. Long-limbed and tall (he would have stood 6 foot 1 when mature) he was well prepared for a life roaming the equatorial grasslands looking for animals to scavenge. He was powerfully built, much stronger than his human descendants.

Long-distance traveling on the African plains produced the first primates to walk on two feet. Walking on two feet, bipedalism, involved important changes in the hominid body and equally important changes in society. In order to balance themselves on their feet, the hominid pelvis narrowed and the rib cage constricted. Women with such narrow pelvises would have found it difficult to accommodate babies' growing brain size. Over many hundreds of thousands of years the interplay of genetic mutations with death and survival rates resulted in an accommodation of growing brain size to bipedalism. It came at a price. Babies of chimpanzees are born with mature brains but babies of the new hominid species were born with immature brains – a characteristic inherited by human babies. Of living primates, human babies are alone in their accelerated brain development in the first year after birth. Like human babies, Nariokotome Boy would have been absolutely helpless for a long time after birth. This new species, *Homo erga-ster*, required a more complex social structure than any yet existing. Their mothers would need help to take care of these helpless babies and some form of support, perhaps by a partner, perhaps by a band. Raising Nariokotome Boy would not have been easy.

Such enhanced social co-operation would have required great effort because in Nariokotome Boy's society, communication probably involved gestures and a few sounds. The boy's vertebral canal is insufficiently developed to give him the control over breathing necessary for complex speech; the areas of the human brain that control speech are not fully developed. As Alan Walker, one of Nariokotome Boy's discoverers, has remarked: "he remains an animal in a human body."

Developing toolmaking skills, walking on two feet, and living in an increasingly complex society, Nariokotome Boy was on the verge of humanity. His species proved remarkably successful; originating in Africa, their bones have been found as far as Indonesia.

This chapter deals with what happened when *Homo ergaster* stepped over the line, developing more complicated speech, better tools, and more sophisticated social organization. It focuses on the history of *Homo sapiens sapiens*, thinking men and women, the sole surviving members of the genus *Homo*, the readers of this book. It begins with an examination of earliest human society up to and including the origins of agriculture – still, after language, the greatest and most consequential trans-formation of human society.[1]

Between 10,000 and 3,500 years ago human beings in much of the world began cultivating crops and domesticating plants and animals. While agriculture was discovered independently in different regions of the world, the key discoveries were made within a few thousand years of one another, relatively close together given the long period (between 100,000 and 200,000 years) that our species has existed on this globe. Approximately 10,000 years ago, wheat was first cultivated in the Near East; 7,000 years ago, maize in Mexico; 6,500 years ago, rice and varieties of millet in East Asia; 6,000 years ago, potatoes in Peru; and 4,000 years ago, sorghum in sub-Saharan Africa. Within a thousand years of the introduction of potatoes in Peru, most humans had become agriculturalists, although there were still parts of the human world untouched by agricultural transformation. Agriculture first came to Australia with European colonists in the late eighteenth century, although Australian aborigines had been modifying their landscape with fire and waterworks in order to enhance the populations of the wild animals and plants they depended upon for a long time before the Europeans arrived.

This chapter focuses on the origins, character, and results of this initial agricultural transformation. It makes several points.

- Long before the agricultural transformation human beings like ourselves (*Homo sapiens sapiens*) had mastered a whole series of prerequisites for agricultural development; some, like firemaking and elementary toolmaking, were inherited from their hominid ancestors, including Nariokotome Boy's contemporaries; others, like the acquisition of sophisticated language skills, were their own achievements.
- Agricultural transformation evolved among societies of collectors who lived in resource-rich environments with access to a variety of food sources. Before the advent of agriculture these societies possessed plant-processing technologies, were increasingly sedentary, and lived much of the year in relatively densely populated agglomerations.
- Agricultural transformation involves the domestication of both plants and animals. It occurred both by separate invention in various areas of the world and by spreading from areas of invention to other areas.

- Agricultural transformation yielded a labor-intensive society far more productive and predictable than any hitherto existing. It created a new agricultural "way of life" practiced by the majority of humankind until very recently.
- Agricultural transformation led to increased trading among specialized communities, and farming and exchange together made possible more complex forms of cultural interaction, and also the growth of new forms of hereditary social inequality, as embodied in institutionalized kinship and class systems. It may have intensified some pre-existing forms such as gender inequality and turned episodes of sporadic violence into systematic warfare.
- Agricultural transformation also provoked rebellion and resistance. While agriculture provided the basic framework of social life for much of the world until last century, large numbers of people in areas of the world where it was feasible continued to practice pastoral and nomadic ways of life, and some more isolated populations continued to forage for wild foods. Conflict between agriculturalists and non-agriculturalists has provided one important theme of human history.

1.1 THE HOMINID HERITAGE AND *HOMO SAPIENS*

The agricultural transformation was one of the most important steps in human development, but as our discussion of Nariokotome Boy has suggested, it built on a long history of accomplishment. In terms of human evolution, agriculture represents a relatively recent innovation, yet it could not have come into existence without the existence of tools, without the mastery of fire, and without the ability to co-operate in relatively complicated ways toward a distant end. Invented two and a half million years ago, the earliest known stone tools were the work of hominids, a family of creatures that includes our ancestor Nariokotome Boy (*Homo ergaster*). *Homo ergaster* mastered the use of fire, which enabled him to warm himself, to cook, and to fend off wild animals. *Homo ergaster* was also the first hominid to leave Africa, where hominids first evolved. Moving into adjacent regions with similar climate and physical terrain to those of their African homeland, they crossed the then-existing land bridge connecting Africa and Arabia at the edge of the present Red Sea. *Homo ergaster* reached Asia about 1.7 million years ago, the Near East 1.5 million, and Southern Europe 1.2 million years ago.

Some 200,000 to 100,000 years ago our own species, *Homo sapiens sapiens*, emerged in African forests and grasslands. For the longest time, from anywhere between 6,000 and 12,000 generations, humans got along without agriculture, surviving mainly as foragers. At most, some 600 human generations have been farmers. Millennia of foraging generally promoted flexible human dietary requirements, allowing the consumption of many varieties of plants and animals and thriving on fiber, fruits, and low-fat, low-salt foods.

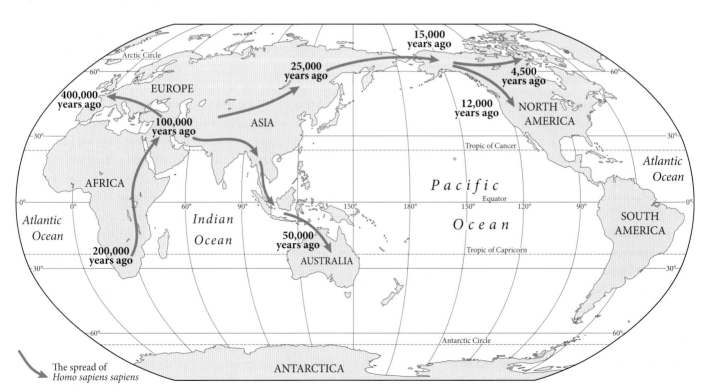

Map 1.1 The spread of *Homo sapiens sapiens*

Some 100,000 to 50,000 years ago humans followed their hominid predecessors and spread out from the African forests and grasslands. Between 60,000 and 50,000 years ago most migrating humans, like their hominid ancestors, moved toward South Asia, following the path shown in Map 1.1. Initially, bands of *Homo sapiens sapiens* took the same routes for the same reasons as *Homo ergaster*: the road east led to familiar climates and featured the easiest and most convenient terrain. The basic unit of *Homo sapiens sapiens* society was the **band** of between 15 and 50. The size of the band was limited by the spatial distribution of the resources it required, and hunting and foraging usually demanded a relatively large amount of space. About 40,000 years ago, such small human bands entered Europe, about the same time that they arrived in North China and Indonesia.

In Africa and outside of Africa, *Homo sapiens sapiens* encountered other *Homo sapiens*, descendants of *Homo ergaster*. The precise relationships among these members of the human species and our ancestors and the differences among the groups is unclear. These other members of the species *Homo*, for example **Homo neanderthalensis** ("Neanderthal man") in Europe and Southwest Asia and *Homo erectus* ("upright man") in East and Southeast Asia, were products of previous migrations and earlier adaptations to local conditions. There is much debate about the extent to which these other groups had evolved along parallel lines; some scholars, for example, believe that Neanderthals also made complex tools and buried their dead. We do know that after millennia of contact with other members of the genus *Homo*, *Homo sapiens sapiens* emerged the sole survivor. How *Homo sapiens sapiens* triumphed – whether by violence, by outbreeding their competitors, or by out-organizing them, and whether the different hominid species interbred – are still topics of fierce debate.

1.2 WHAT HAPPENED TO *HOMO SAPIENS SAPIENS* BETWEEN 75,000 AND 35,000 YEARS AGO?

In any case, sometime between 75,000 and 35,000 years ago, *Homo sapiens sapiens* began to display some extraordinary qualities that differentiated them from all their hominid predecessors. Minor physical changes occurred. The basic human body changed as the brain enlarged but the skeleton became less sturdy, the chin more prominent, the teeth smaller. The human capacity for making things increased dramatically. Humans acquired new technologies, including both more effective cutting tools and a wider array of specialized tools. They began to develop more effective weapons such as the bow and arrow

and the throwing stick, increasing their ability to hunt the larger herd mammals safely, from a distance. They lived in larger concentrations, and interacted more intensively across regions. They produced garments: the oldest known form of clothing, skirts of twisted fabrics, can be seen on works of prehistoric art dating to this period. Also, humans began to demonstrate new cultural propensities. They made music and produced remarkable stone drawings, statues, and carved objects. They began to deliberately bury some of their dead, with increasingly elaborate grave goods, perhaps indicating the presence of some form of religious belief.

Among the most striking and distinctive characteristics of this new type of hominid, *Homo sapiens sapiens*, are the works of prehistoric stone art that have survived in so many areas of the world. Most of our knowledge is confined to articles fashioned in stone or bone. Because so little of it has survived, we have only occasionally any idea of the extent or richness of art produced on wood and hides or on tattooed human bodies. More typically, survivals are found in more enduring materials. Baked clay figures of animals made more than 26,000 years ago have been found in the Czech Republic. Small figurines of women in stone, ivory, bone, and clay were fashioned in Central and Eastern Europe 25,000 years ago. Remarkable cave drawings were produced in Siberia, North Africa, and the French Pyrenees 18,000 years ago.

What Do the Drawings on the Rocks Mean?

Many aspects of prehistoric art still mystify scholars. The walls of the Lascaux caves in southern France and the Spear Hill complex in northwest Australia, the rock surfaces of the Petrified Forest in Arizona and the Wadi Telisaghé in Libya, seem to urgently bombard the visitor with messages. In southwest France and along the Pyrenees between France and Spain, 18,000 years ago highly skilled artists crawled their way to obscure portions of caves and labored in physically awkward positions to create magnificent drawings which included realistic portraits of animals, imaginary drawings of half-human half-animal figures, and non-figurative repertoires of repeated designs. In some cases, generation after generation of artists labored over centuries in the same caves, elaborating on pictorial themes or slightly modifying earlier designs. As can be seen in the Lascaux cave drawings of southern France, some of these works show a technical and artistic mastery of drawing that have influenced modern artists. As Figure 1.1 shows, there is nothing "primitive" about these paintings. They reveal a profound knowledge of animal life and body shape.

Numerous attempts have been made to interpret this prehistoric art. One anthropologist builds his argument from

Figure 1.1 Paleolithic cave painting, Lascaux, France. These images, discovered in caves in southwestern France, are estimated to be over 17,000 years old. They mainly depict humans and large animals that lived in this region at that time.

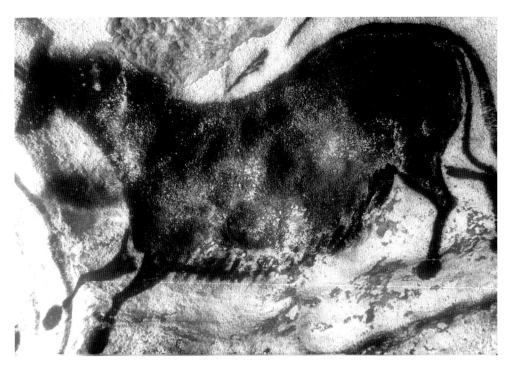

the evidence of children's palm prints on cave walls. From youthful foot prints on cave floors and from analogies with hunter-gatherer societies in the American Northwest, he argues that the prehistoric caves of southern France and the Pyrenees were used for secret initiation rituals for elite youth. Another scholar has argued that a system of dots found in several rooms is an elementary star chart. For clues about the meanings of these paintings and symbols, scholars have examined the practices of contemporary peoples who create rock art, such as the Khoi of southern Africa, and anthropologists have located indigenous populations prepared to interpret these inscriptions. These interpretations reveal elaborate cultural beliefs, showing that even depictions whose understanding seems obvious may be overlaid with recondite symbolism. Some argue that an important theme of cave art is that of religious figures, shamans, who enter into drug-induced trance states at rock surfaces seen as portals between worlds. Perhaps the most important conclusion of many experts is that there is not one message on the rocks but many. Prehistoric artists portrayed rituals, marked fertility rites, recorded significant contemporary events, testified to dreams and sacred visions, charted the skies, and sketched impressions for their own sake.

Did *Homo Sapiens Sapiens* Communicate in New and Complex Ways?

Recognizing these drawings on the wall as new efforts to communicate on a more sophisticated level than previously may be the most important lesson that we can learn from the only

hominids to master complex language. With their language skills, they were able to develop their own distinctive cultures and interact more easily with other humans across cultures.

A plausible explanation of this sudden flourishing of culture may be the development of more sophisticated language structures than **protolanguage** – the limited language capabilities that so far have been elicited by human trainers from gorillas and chimpanzees. This protolanguage, consisting largely of proper and common nouns and their juxtaposition to convey meaning, may have been a characteristic feature of earlier hominids. Hominid development of protolanguage had progressed for a long time and advances were embodied in the growing capacity of hominid brains and throats to communicate in more structured and concise ways. Between 2,500,000 and 250,000 years ago brain capacity was enlarging in areas of the brain that deal with language, and a modern larynx, capable of a wide range of sounds, developed.

Between 75,000 and 65,000 years ago *Homo sapiens sapiens* escaped the bonds of protolanguage. Before leaving Africa, *Homo sapiens sapiens* went beyond the use of words to describe real entities and developed the capacity to form coherent sentences and to use grammatical rules to express relationships. This achievement gave humans the ability to develop ideas literally unthinkable before this linguistic change. A vervet monkey in East Africa possesses some linguistic capacity. Different vervet calls warn the group of the presence of predators, specific calls even indicating the nature of the predatory menace, whether pythons, martial eagles, or leopards. The vervet's loud shrill cry – those who have heard it do not forget it – is probably more immediately effective than a human cry in connecting a perceived threat to an immediate situation, the coming of a python, and attaining an end, the quick dispersal of the potential victims. For many other purposes, the linguistic capacity of the vervet fails. While effective in indicating "python coming," the vervet lacks the ability to impart a complex variety of meanings by reordering words to give new meanings. Vervets cannot convey caution, "the python may come"; give reassurance, "the python is not coming"; or intensify a warning, "many pythons are coming." Such distinctions require grammar.[2]

Grammatical abilities associated with some of the most important aspects of human symbolic communication are lacking in the protolanguage of chimpanzees and gorillas. Such a new capacity would have enabled *Homo sapiens* to conceive of new tools without examples before them and to understand abstract ideas. The distinctive feature of our direct ancestors may have been the acquisition of essentially modern language capabilities; the symbolic and cultural systems produced by these new language capacities are recorded on cave walls. In turn, mastery of language may have been one important factor in our ancestors' success in competition against animals with sharper claws, larger teeth, and, in the case of the Neanderthals, bigger brains.

Developed language capacities promoted higher levels of communication among different human bands. If these bands did not speak the same language they did share a similar complicated symbol-making ability, and this promoted inter-group communication. During this same period, beginning between 75,000 and 65,000 years ago, as we shall see, technologies became more sophisticated and religious rituals more elaborate. Our ancestors sought and acquired items only available at long distances. Obsidian and flint were central to the expanded tool-making capacities, while seashells and amber were used in religious rituals or as prestige items. Many of these items were not locally available and were likely acquired by some form of exchange.

Early on, our ancestors exhibited a capacity for making tools, creating complex cultural symbols, negotiating among diverse human groups. These capacities proved decisive in human development.

1.3 WHAT IS A FORAGER?

Before the agricultural transformation humans survived by hunting and gathering – a description that encompasses a great variety of human activity. Hunter-gatherers include small groups of no more than thirty to fifty people moving over a large area, as well as the first inhabitants of villages whose population numbered in the hundreds. Hunter-gatherers range from **foragers** to **collectors**. The great majority of hunter-gatherers in prehistoric times were foragers. Foragers are more mobile than collectors; they hunt and fish and gather wild fruits, leaves, and tubers, consuming what they gather within a few hours or days. Their pattern of settlement becomes diverse or aggregated according to their foods and the season. In contrast, collectors – among whom were the people who invented agriculture – are more sedentary, remaining in favored localities and sending out smaller groups to bring back resources to the larger collectivity. Societies of collectors are often referred to as "complex hunter-gatherer societies."

Foraging is a "way of life": for foragers the search for food is so encompassing that it defines many aspects of the life of the entire group and of the individuals that compose it. Foraging possibilities are crucially shaped by the character of available game and plant resources and these, in turn, are powerfully influenced by climate. Box 1.1 discusses our current theories of the determinants of long-term climate change. As the Box explains, they have followed cyclical patterns that are relatively well understood. Nonetheless, there have been significant departures from these overall trends. Because the era that witnessed the beginning of the transition to agriculture was a period of climatic change, many scholars have sought to portray climatic change as the moving force behind agricultural transformation. But the ending of the last glacial period, 13,000 years ago, opened a very unstable period, one of great climate fluctuation rather than the smooth development of warmer weather. The thousand years of warming that followed the glacial period were interrupted by a severe cold snap – labeled the Younger Dryas stadia – that lasted for over a millennium (12,800–11,500 BP). The alternation of warming and cooling periods influenced the migratory behavior of animal herds and those who hunted these herds. Colder periods witnessed the increased formation and movement of glaciers, i.e. **glaciation**. Glaciation promoted the formation of land routes from continents to outlying islands, even to other continents. Ice bridges connected Great Britain and Ireland to the European continent and linked Asia and North America, enabling human settlement of areas that would later become less accessible.

During the last glacial period steppes and tundra predominated over much of the subcontinent and supplied an ideal environment for hoofed animals. Migratory herds – reindeer, red deer, steppe bison, elk, now extinct aurochs, wild horses, asses, and woolly mammoths – provided a rich array of game. Pursuing large herd animals or using nets to catch migratory fish and seals, humans honed their hunting skills. Although dogs provided help as guards and a source of food during hard times, their use in hunting explains why they were the first domesticated animals. Foragers invented effective methods of

Box 1.1 Ice Ages

At least since the eighteenth century, thinkers have looked at glaciated valleys and huge boulders in the midst of fields (moraines) and speculated on the existence of eras when average temperatures were very different from their own. An "ice age" refers to a long-term reduction in the temperature of the earth's surface. Cooling periods within an ice age are referred to as "glacial periods," while warming periods within an ice age are called "interglacials." The most widely accepted theory of long-term climate change is that of the Serbian scientist Milutin Milanković (1879–1958), who traced it to variations in the earth's orbit. According to Milanković, ice ages are determined by three orbital cycles due to (1) the obliquity of the earth's axis, (2) the eccentricity of the earth's orbit, and (3) the precession of the earth's orbit. "Obliquity" refers to the measure

of our planet's tilt; it completes a full cycle every 42,000 years. "Eccentricity" refers to the elliptical orbit of the earth with a period of oscillation of approximately 96,000 years. And "precession" describes the gyration caused by the earth's oblate shape which completes a cycle every 21,000 years. While affected by great volcanic activity or dramatic change in the earth's water currents, Milanković's theory, although corrected to take account of these factors, is the most plausible current interpretation of long-term climate change. Much work remains to be done. Recent and still highly tentative research has discovered a warming period between 100 BCE and 200 CE that roughly correlates with the rise and fall of the Roman empire. Evidence for a "medieval warming period" between 800 and 1300 CE, and a "Little

Ice Age" from 1350–1850 CE, is more solid but is not well documented outside Europe and North America, and the starting and ending dates of these periods is a matter of controversy.

Beginning in the 1900s, however, and accelerating with great rapidity after 1980, the cooling effects predicted by Milanković have been replaced by a powerful warming trend which has little past parallel. Climatologists are almost universally convinced that an important cause of this warming is increased levels of carbon dioxide and other gases in the earth's atmosphere, mainly a product of human agency, particularly the spread of the First and Second Industrial Revolutions. Human agency and pollution have more than cancelled out the natural forces that have hitherto determined ice ages.

killing, such as the bow and arrow, enabling them to hunt and kill large animals from a distance. Early hunters often specialized in a single species such as the red deer or mammoth, whose bones dominate the dumps near campsites. In such cases, foragers followed the migratory animal herds. In other cases, they might sequentially practice separate and geographically diverse activities, having discrete summer and winter camps where they pursued distinctive activities, such as fishing in the summer, hunting in the winter. Moving between summer and winter encampments, foragers might make half a dozen shorter stops to gather maturing grass seeds or to hunt small animals. Early humans also used fire to clear the land and for hunting animals; for better or worse, the use of fire began humanity's long quest to reshape the environment.

We imagine the end of the glacial period and ensuing periods of climatic warming as beneficial to human life, but initially the warming trend created a scarcity of resources and a dietary deficit. Climatic warming raised sea levels and many rich coastal areas, favorite habitats of foragers, returned to the sea. Warming also brought the expansion of dense forests that supported less efficient food sources for humans than the great herds of large animals that had roamed tundra and steppe. It forced foragers to

diversify their diet and to search for alternative sources to the diminishing migratory herds.

One result of climatic change with enormous consequences for human history was increased human efforts to diversify their diet. As the world warmed, hunters and gatherers, including both foragers and collectors, played a crucial role in the evolution of agriculture; they identified the small handful of plants whose domestication was critical to societal growth. While many domesticated plants have contributed to a varied diet, almost all of the complex and large societies that have existed in human history have been based on just six families of edible plants: wheat, barley, millet, rice, maize, and potatoes.[3] The identification and selection of certain plants as worthy of cultivation and not others were fateful decisions. Human society has been profoundly shaped by foragers' decisions to turn toward particular grains. Imagine Europe without wheat, China without rice, Mesoamerica without maize!

Were there Gender Divisions among Foragers?

Little is known about gender divisions and gender hierarchies among societies of prehistoric foragers. Were the early cave artists, the first weavers, or the first potters men or women? Was there a strict division of labor between male hunters and female gatherers in foraging societies? Did men have power over women? We do not know for sure but there are clues. In societies of modern foragers, precise demarcations between male and female work are often difficult to find. Neither should we make too fine a distinction between hunting seen as male work involving outdoor activity and distant journeying and gathering seen as women's work and centered on the home. Both could involve long journeys bearing heavy burdens. The content of hunting and gathering depended on the character of regional resources and was subject to great variation. While we can find societies where bone development among adult males indicates sustained use of the bow and arrow and adult female skeletons with bones twisted to the demands of grinding grains, it is unwise to make blanket assertions about the character of either hunting or gathering.

Even if men may have predominated as hunters and women as gatherers and food preparers, it is not necessarily the case that separate roles gave men greater power. In many contemporary foragers' societies the female contribution to food production is vital and in some cases more important than that of males. The relative contribution of male hunters and female gatherers varies today among foraging populations, and it probably varied in the past with the climate and the character of the plant and animal populations. In many foraging societies, young male hunters contribute the most high caloric foods but the yield of hunting is highly erratic and hunting ability declines with age. In contrast, female contributions tend to be steadier and levels of female productivity remain constant with age. Gathering became even more important in the warming periods after 13,000 BP as migratory herds became scarcer; female gatherers and food preparers may well have been the initiators of the agricultural transformation.

Were there Other Important Social Divisions among Foragers?

If gender divisions of social power were not very well developed, neither were other social divisions, such as differences in economic or personal status. Much of what we know about social relations among prehistoric peoples comes from analysis of grave contents. The grave shown in Figure 1.2 is relatively intact; it has escaped the greed of robbers and the plows of farmers but not the curiosity of scholars. Box 1.2 discusses how archaeologists use material from the past, in this case grave contents, to imagine the societies that interred the deceased. This grave contained a woman with a newborn baby. Beside the skull is a series of pendants, maybe a necklace, made from the teeth of red

deer and wild pig. Burial customs suggest that most foragers lived in societies with relatively low levels of social differentiation: excavations find little distinction in the grave deposits of foragers' graves, in part because there was little surplus to distribute in such groups. In rich environments, as foragers settled down, grave contents changed. The elaborate burial of children is taken to be a sign of the origins of hereditary power. A powerful leader might merit a grand send-off but the elaborate burial of a child suggests ascribed power. Judged by these criteria, individuals were honored and respected but most foraging societies did not transmit status by heredity from parent to child.

Additional insight into the behavior of prehistoric foragers may be obtained from analogies with contemporary foragers, but such comparisons must always be made with reservations. For one, modern foragers like the Khoi of the bleak Kalahari Desert in southern Africa are often groups that survive mainly because they have been consigned to hostile terrain that other groups do not wish to settle. In contrast, 10,000 years ago foragers had all the world's rich resources at their disposal. At the same time, most modern foragers possess tools such as metal knives or shovels that are products of industrial societies and unknown to prehistoric foragers. There is no reason to think that these differences counterbalance one another and we must beware of too quick comparisons between ancient and modern foragers. Keeping these cautions in mind, contemporary foragers may offer insights into the behavior of prehistoric foragers.

In fact, today as in the past, weak social differentiation was probably both cause and effect of the character of foraging society. Contemporary foraging societies discourage inequality by putting a high premium on leisure-time activities such as sleeping, dreaming, and storytelling. When sufficient surplus is obtained for survival, little effort is made to accumulate more. In any case, moving from place to place in small groups, individuals have little opportunity to accumulate material resources on a scale that would strongly differentiate them from their fellows. Foragers go where food is available, and as natural resources are unreliable, foragers must be flexible. In regard to territorialism, contemporary foragers often have a sense of traditional hunting grounds but are usually quite flexible in opening their lands to other foragers in exchange for access to theirs. Sometimes foragers have to choose among a variety of alternative resources but other times they must try new expedients when all established resources fail.

Did Foragers Wage War?

Ancient foragers were also less likely than their descendants to engage in that collective conflict between groups that we call war. Of all the stone art that survives, remarkably few drawings

Figure 1.2 A Stone Age burial. Suppose that you are an archaeologist in Denmark and have just discovered the grave below. What might the burial tell you about the society in which these people lived? What might you want to study next?

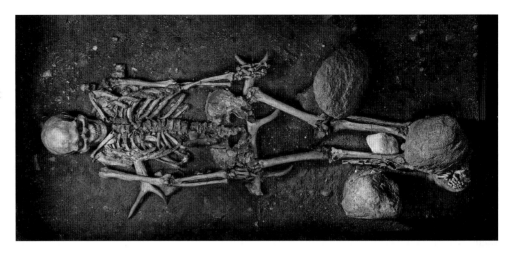

Box 1.2 How Do We Know What We Know?

In most of the world the agricultural transformation occurred before the invention of writing. How can historians and archaeologists know about events in such societies? The following shows how archaeologists can use physical evidence such as burial grounds to deduce characteristics of past societies.

The cemetery of Oleneostrovski Mogilnik in Karelia has evidence for the most complex social organization currently known from the period between the end of the last glacial period to the introduction of agriculture. Hereditary social positions and economic ranking were prevalent. The 170 graves excavated – roughly a third of the total number in the cemetery – showed marked variability in the quantity of grave goods: 20 percent of the graves had no items while others had more than 400 items. Much of this variability can be accounted for by horizontal social differentiation, that is, by reference to age and sex alone, conforming to the pattern found elsewhere in Mesolithic Europe. For instance, there were few child burials, suggesting that the inheritance of wealth was limited. Males and females were regularly associated with different types of grave goods: bone points, slate knives, and bone pins with males and carved beaver incisors with females.

Cross-cutting this horizontal social differentiation are patterns which suggest that certain individuals had social positions independent from achieved social status. Nine graves contained carved effigies of snakes, elks, and humans, suggesting that these individuals had some special social position. In addition there were four shaft graves in which the deceased assumed a standing position. These are likely to be the graves of shamans. A third type of social distinction at Oleneostrovski Mogilnik is division of the entire cemetery into two grave clusters, probably reflecting a bipartite division of the society, perhaps into two clans. Elk effigies were restricted to graves in the northern cluster, whereas snake and human effigies predominated in the southern cluster.

unambiguously depict warlike scenes. The small size of forager bands hardly enabled them to perpetrate massive bouts of killing, but an analysis of prehistoric burials reveals that hunter-gatherers sometimes met violent death from other humans. European archaeologists have uncovered mass graves of men, women, and children, dispatched violently, that may indicate the slaughter of one band by rivals. Foraging covers a great variety of social and environmental conditions and, while hunters and gatherers were notably less murderous than the people of the city-states and kingdoms who would succeed them, they were not inherently pacifistic.

Certainly, foragers had non-violent options unavailable to their agricultural descendants. Bitter disagreements among tribesmen could always be resolved by secession, and quarrels between different bands could be settled by the weaker group's departure. Indeed the fissure of larger bands into smaller was the central dynamic of forager society. Once they reached a certain size, groups of foragers naturally tended to hive off and move elsewhere. The tens of thousands of years preceding the introduction of agriculture were marked by great migrations as hunter-gatherers spread to unoccupied portions of the globe capable of supporting human habitation. Attempts to impose hierarchical power within a band or of one band over another could always be rejected by moving out further into the wilderness. Everyone was doing it.

But climatic change, the global warming which initially put new strains on foragers' resources, probably encouraged conflict. Warming strained existing resources and forced foragers to re-evaluate their relationship to the land and to other foragers. This may have been the world's first population crisis. It seems absurd to speak of world population pressure fifteen thousand years ago when less than nine million people inhabited the entire globe but population pressure expresses a relationship between resources and population. Foragers required large spaces in which they could roam and hunt. With only elementary technologies, mobile bands need a very large amount of space to support themselves. Modern foragers with basic technologies require about one square mile of territory for each individual in the band and the ratio for ancient foragers was probably not very different. Constricting resources forced foragers to take a new look at environments that were especially rich in resources and to seek to mark them for their own and maintain their presence near them.

1.4 THE TRANSITION TO AGRICULTURE

Foraging did not suddenly give way to agriculture, and many of the features that we associate with an agricultural way of life were already present, in embryo, in those complex hunter-gatherer societies that pioneered agricultural transformation. Foragers gradually became more sedentary collectors, and sedentism encouraged the development of village society. The rise of societies of collectors preceded agricultural transformation and prepared the way for it: many of the features that we associate with agriculture as a way of life – year-round settled communities and routinized labor on the land – were already fore-shadowed among more sedentary collectors.

For a long time scholars sought to link the emergence of agriculture to climatic changes or wrenching population strains that threatened groups with starvation and forced them to search for new types of food. Increasingly, however, our understanding of these events has become more complex: attention has been focused on human dispersion across continents, the growth of human populations, and the emergence of territorialism. Bruce D. Smith has argued that while population growth and climatic change were important to the spread of agriculture, it was the wealthier and more prosperous regions that made the first step, not the most famished.[4] As populations spread throughout the globe, some groups occupied particularly strategic, resource-rich sites. In parts of Southwest Asia, North China, and Mesoamerica,

agriculture originated in relatively prosperous, densely populated, fixed communities strategically situated close to rivers, lakes, marshes, and springs that could provide important food supplements. Inhabitants of strategically well-located communities settled down and established control over particular sites, sending out smaller bands to supplement nearby resources. Instead of spinning off groups toward less populous areas, some collectors turned to more intensive population of the lands in which they were already established.

Southwest Asia Leads the Way

Southwest Asia presents the earliest and the best-documented case of how agriculture developed among collectors who lived in areas with rich and various resources. Sedentism in Southwest Asia was particularly encouraged by the presence of grasses that had high yields and could be quickly harvested. Not only did these grasses provide important back-up foods, but their preparation also trained residents in food-processing technologies – winnowing, threshing, grinding, and cooking. Knowledge of food-processing technologies smoothed the transition to greater dependence on grains when collectors' continued presence in a favored locality depleted animal populations. To counterbalance these losses, local dwellers increased their access to edible crops by eliminating weeds, scrub, and other obstacles to harvesting. In so doing, they were creating a local environment more suitable for human needs. In time, the presence of cultivated plants nearby constituted a further reason for continuing to inhabit a region.

A good example of the situation in which agriculture first evolved is that of Abu Hureyra, one of the earliest farming communities in Southwest Asia so far discovered.[5] Founded by collectors, Abu Hureyra is typical of sites in which agriculture emerged in Mesoamerica and East Asia. It was a site selected to provide access to a wide variety of different resources. Abu Hureyra was located near the Euphrates River valley flood plain, close to streams that fed dense forests, and adjacent to northern steppe lands. Outside the flood plain with its rich plant life, the river flowed into swamps and meanders where water-loving plants and animals flourished, and created a rich soil that supported deep forests where cattle, pigs, and deer ran free, with a rich cover of annual plants, shrubs, and nut-bearing trees. The steppe was the home of migrating flocks of gazelle that were a major food source; hunters killed gazelles in large numbers during the animals' annual migration, dried the meat, and ate it throughout the year. Gradually as human populations grew, the ever-larger slaughter of gazelle decreased the size of the migratory herds and forced the inhabitants of Abu Hureyra to look elsewhere to supplement their diet.

To maintain themselves, collectors in Abu Hureyra brought plants and seeds that they had previously gathered elsewhere to favorable locations nearer their settlement; this transfer of plants to new environments, away from wild ancestors, enormously facilitated the process of genetic selection that was the essence of plant domestication. By planting selected wheat or rye seeds in areas where they had never before been grown, agriculturalists subjected them to new selective pressures. Around Abu Hureyra, rainfall was erratic and practically non-existent from July to September so the first fields grew up next to wadis, dry streams that collected water during the rainy season and retained moisture for long periods. Centuries after the beginning of agriculture, the residents of the growing village again adjusted to the continuing decline in the wild gazelle flocks by integrating sheep and goats already domesticated by neighboring communities. While sheep and goats contributed meat to the population, they gradually became more important in providing milk, cheese, yogurt, and wool.

The Evolution of Territorialism

With the domestication of plants and animals, the sense of territorialism developing among collectors took ever firmer hold. Territorialism formed the bases for the growth of city, empire, and modern state. As bands settled down, territory was no longer a space defined by religious sites where band members congregated periodically to celebrate seasonal rituals such as the commemoration of the summer solstice or the beginning or ending of the growing season, or by foraging zones that gave groups particular access to fishing streams, groves of nut trees, or hunting grounds. Instead, ideas of territory became embodied in the permanently occupied mud-walled family dwellings in the village and in a specific plot of nearby land subject to daily labor whose specific characteristics were known to their smallest details.

By daily living within an enduring settled community and next to stable neighbors and by unremitting labor on the soil, individual, kin group, and tribe acquired a new title of possession to the land and a new notion of property. In villages such as Jericho or Çatal Hüyük, decapitated bodies and decorated skulls have been found buried in the foundations of homes or interred in the equivalent of the family living room. Archaeologists believe that these skulls belonged to celebrated ancestors or the founders of family groups. Ceremonial burial may have been intended to give some kind of cosmic protection or community identification to the dwellings in which they were deposited. The close presence of ancestors consecrated village homes, further tying men and women to the location.

For early generations of hunter-gatherers accustomed to mobility and small numbers, living together permanently with larger numbers of people must have been hard to endure and required new types of social skills. As bands became attached to a given site, it became more important to distinguish between those bands of foragers who were one's own people, although often engaged in distant trips in search of resources, and other forager groups that lived in nearby areas. Thus, as territorialism became more encompassing, decisions about social identity and entitlement also emerged. Assertions of identification with a settled group may be found in the common designs carved on tools and the shared rituals used in interments. Living side by side over long periods of time also entailed more attention to neighbors' wants and community needs. With the growth of territorialism, the **tribe** emerged, a more complex form of society with recognized political leaders. By and large these positions were not hereditary and rested on the leader's continuing ability to perform services recognized as such by the community.

1.5 AGRICULTURE

What is meant by agricultural transformation? Scholars formerly spoke of an agricultural revolution but have come increasingly to realize that agricultural transformation comprised a whole series of changes which occurred at various rates and in different contexts. **Farming** involves selecting plants and animals and modifying their environment so as to increase their productivity and utility to humans. Saving and planting selected seeds, bulbs, and shoots and weeding, watering, and draining plants are all ways of modifying the environment to serve human purposes. Selecting certain animals for breeding represents a similar process. One distinctive feature of agriculture was that, within very broad limits, ever greater efforts devoted to the soil increased its productivity and, while it did not produce the kind of windfall involved in killing a mammoth, agriculture produced more reliable returns than other food-producing activities.

Although China and Mexico were not far behind, Southwest Asia has the best claim to having first developed agriculture both as technique and as way of life. The first farmers created a sustainable, balanced agricultural economy in Southwest Asia combining both domesticated animals and crops that was firmly in place about 8,200–8,700 years ago. **Emmer** wheats and **einkorn** wheats and barley were native grasses on the western edge of the Fertile Crescent which became the first domestic grains. As mentioned above, saving seeds for future planting and controlling animal breeding was the essence of agriculture. Luckily for Southwest Asian farmers, wheat and barley plants were particularly easy for early harvesters to manipulate.

Map 1.2 The emergence of agriculture

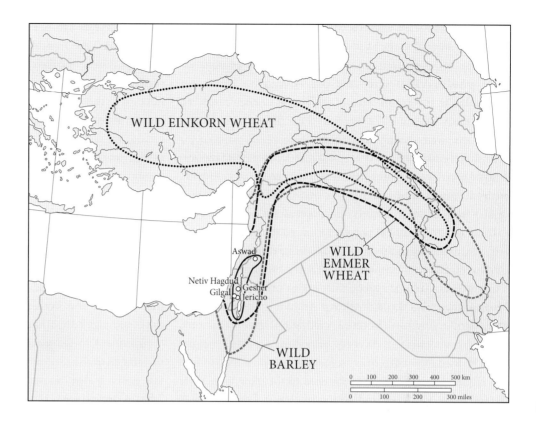

How Did *Homo Sapiens Sapiens* Learn to Domesticate Plants and Animals?

Take the case of emmer wheat, the direct ancestor of modern wheat and one of the first domesticated plants. Like many grasses, wild wheat ears are brittle, disseminating their seeds gradually to the winds. Cutting the wheat grasses with sickles during a brief harvest period, early collectors were more likely to accumulate less brittle kernels (the more brittle kernels had already broken off). The saving of the less brittle kernels favored the perpetuation of these characteristics in the crops planted from these seeds at the next planting. As a result, wheat kernels gradually became less brittle and more easy to harvest. Fortunately brittleness in wheat kernels responded easily to selection. This important genetic transition – away from the brittle kernels – maybe controlled as few as two genes.

When grains responded so quickly to selection, at a certain point unconscious selection may have given way to conscious. Saving large seeds that were more easily retained and handled encouraged the development of plants with larger seeds. Wild wheat and barley have two rows of kernels but domesticated plants have six. Early cultivators, by planting kernels from rare six-rowed plants rather than the standard two-rowed plants, created a large population of these more productive mutants. As a result of such selection processes, many seed crops

exclusively rely on farmers for their propagation. Without farmers, modern corn, banana, and taro could not reproduce. In the sixteenth century the crops of some Caribbean islands became extinct when the human populations who knew how to cultivate them died off from exposure to Western diseases.

Southwest Asians applied the same kind of selective process to animals. In the wild, male sheep and goats developed large horns because males fight with their horns to breed and the victorious – most often larger-horned – males went on to reproduce themselves. But large-horned beasts are hard to handle. When humans began to regulate the breeding of domestic animals, they reversed the process, keeping smaller males with less dangerous horns for breeding purposes and eating the larger-horned males. As a result, most domesticated animals such as sheep and pigs are smaller and less fierce than their wild predecessors. Sheep and alpacas were selected for their ability to retain wool and thus are woolier than their wild ancestors. Because farmers were more likely to retain and breed strong milk-producers, domesticated cows give much more milk than their ancestors.

Balanced Agriculture

Built on the domestication of both plants and animals, a balanced agricultural economy emerged in Southwest Asia that, in main outlines, has survived into the present day. About 10,000 years ago, wild barley, wild rye, wild emmer and einkorn wheats were domesticated in the western portion of the Fertile Crescent along the Mediterranean coast, while the herding of domesticated goats and later sheep and pigs emerged in the Zagros Mountains in the eastern area of the Fertile Crescent, between the Caspian Sea and the Persian Gulf. The abundant and dependable water supply made this whole region suitable for agricultural experiments. As Map 1.2 shows, the partial overlapping of a variety of grains, many of which could be cultivated, enabled farmers to develop grains that could be farmed in a similar manner but in a variety of temperatures and soils.

Combining agricultural practices from their eastern and western neighbors, agriculturalists in the central area of modern Turkey joined cereal cultivation and animal breeding to produce a balanced agricultural regime that was to prove viable for the Mediterranean world and Southwest Asia for millennia. Associating stock-raising with cereal cultivation gave embryonic farming communities a diversity of resources; animal manure could be used to fertilize crops, some of which were used to feed animals, and animals could be fastened to the plow to increase the extent of cultivation. Indeed the Southwest Asian emphasis on herding had a longstanding influence on the dietary habits of all those who adapted their farming methods, making dairy products a larger component of the diet than in most other agricultural societies and giving animal fertilizers a larger role in agriculture. Dairy products were high in energy yield and an important source of calcium, while animal fertilizer increased agricultural productivity without exhausting the soil.

Between 10,000 and 8,000 years ago, an agricultural way of life came to dominate society in Southwest Asia. Agricultural developments here were of especial significance because of its strategic geographic location. Southwest Asia is on the main line of the temperate zone that links Mediterranean Europe to North India; crops that grew in one area might grow in the other. Agricultural innovation traveled step by step along the great east–west corridor of human migration and civilization that linked the Atlantic coast of Ireland to the Pacific coast of Japan. Over millennia pastoral invaders (like the Huns), plague bacilli (like the Black Death), and costly products (like silk) followed the same great Eurasian road as the knowledge of the cultivation of wheat and of the domestic chicken.

1.6 HOW DID AGRICULTURAL TRANSFORMATION SPREAD?

Agriculture brought with it a complex pattern of changes and each receiving area modified this pattern according to its own needs. Agriculture reached southern Italy and the Indus Valley at least 7,000 years ago, Scandinavia and the British Isles 6,000 to 5,000 years ago. Agriculture spread throughout Europe in a variety of ways, through colonization by migrant farmers, the adoption of agriculture by indigenous inhabitants, and some mixture of the two. Instances of folk migration, elite adoption, popular diffusion, and colonization all occurred. Agriculture first spread to Greece, which was adjacent to and shared the Mediterranean climate of the Levantine coast. Where they found empty space, as in the Aegean islands and portions of Southeastern Europe, farmers moved in and established their own agricultural communities. Both colonization and the adaptation of local populations were important along the southern Mediterranean. The spread of farming involved adaptation of Southwest Asian techniques to different conditions in various regions. For example, Europeans found emmer wheat particularly suitable to their climate, and similar considerations led farmers to favor cattle and pigs rather than sheep and goats.

No subject in European prehistory has provoked more controversy than the identity of those outsider groups or processes that disseminated innovations across the continent. In the early days of archaeology, scholars associated each style of pottery with a particular ethnic group and concluded that the spread of pottery styles indicated the expansion of a conquering people. A later generation of archaeologists has pointed out that pottery styles and other innovations could also be propagated by trade expansion and by religious conversion, or created by interaction between natives and outside settlers. Some traces of the past practices of indigenous peoples can be found in the case of almost every current of cultural expansion. Sorting out the role of outside colonization and of other social processes presents an extremely challenging task.

In the very important case of the pioneers of agriculture in Central and Western Europe, whose earliest traces are found in Transdanubian Hungary and Bohemia and whose influence ultimately extended toward the Rhine and into northern France, the case for colonization from the Black Sea area or Anatolia is a strong one, particularly in the later phases of its expansion. This group of agricultural colonizers, the **Linear Band peoples**, named after the incised line patterns on the their pottery, spread rapidly across the north central loess European Plain (see Map 1.3). Their settlements tended to follow rivers and they picked particularly fertile places in European forest lands where they established small farming plots. The Linear Band peoples brought pottery-making with them as well as their distinctive single longhouse, chipped stone tools, domestic animals, and placement of cemeteries adjacent to settlements.

While still only a very tentative hypothesis, it could be that the Linear Band peoples were the first to bring the Indo-European languages to Europe. The Indo-European languages are that

Map 1.3 The distribution of Linear Pottery culture

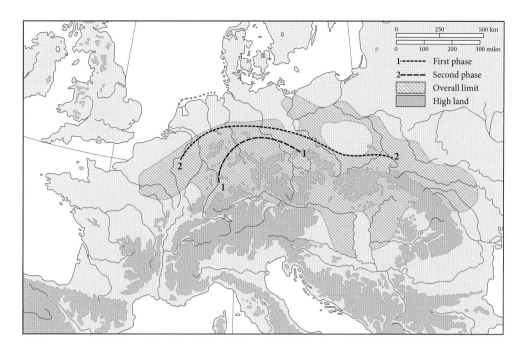

family of languages which includes most European languages as well as Persian and Sanskrit. If they were the first carriers of Indo-European, the Linear Band peoples were not the last. Having established a base of Indo-European speakers, other variants of the language may have spread with succeeding waves of agricultural and cultural innovation from outside Europe.

Both in Southwest Asia and in Europe, agriculture was still in its beginning stages. The plow, horses, wheeled carts, metalworking, and irrigation – essential elements of peasant agriculture in these parts of the world – were as yet unknown, and their invention and dissemination in succeeding millennia were to have great impact, making it possible to bring into cultivation large quantities of land previously considered unsuitable to agriculture.

Why Did So Many Peoples Invent Agriculture?

In North Africa, agriculture spread unchanged from the Near East but sub-Saharan Africans developed their own crops. The desertification of what would become the Sahara Desert was already in progress and, about 6,500 years ago, Africans in the central savannas and grassland regions adopted drought-resistant local plants: millet, sorghum, and African rice. African rice belongs to the same genus as Asiatic rice but it was developed separately and comes from different wild plants. As in Europe, domesticated cattle played a very important role in most of African agriculture. In Central Africa, cattle were domesticated independently and herds gradually migrated toward West Africa and southern Africa; some native breeds gradually developed immunity to trypanosomiasis (sleeping

sickness). The drying up of North Africa may have promoted the expansion of balanced agriculture into West Africa by contracting the regions in which tse-tse flies flourished (see Chapter 4). Still, the prevalence of trypanosomiasis, fatal to most domestic animals, spread by the tse-tse fly, slowed the spread of cattle in West African agriculture. West African agriculturalists were denied the full effects of a balanced agriculture but they developed innovative practices and their own array of domesticated plants.

Unlike the great east–west oriented Eurasian temperate zone, Africa is a north–south oriented continent whose temperate zones are separated from one another by desert and tropical forest. In the case of agricultural transformation, this north–south longitudinal orientation meant that while Africa, like Eurasia, encompassed a great variety of climatic regimes, in Africa desert, savanna, and rain forest prevented the spread of domesticated plants and animals from Mediterranean to southern Africa. They made the transmission of agricultural innovations to climatically similar regions much more difficult than in the case of the great latitudinal transition belt that linked Southwest Asia to Europe, Central Asia, and India. Map 1.4 reveals the Central Eurasian highway which accelerated the spread of agricultural transmission while many of Africa's agriculturally richest areas remained on the periphery. Water-loving wheat and barley were not well adapted to the dry savannas and grassland regions and never spread south from North Africa and so never reached the more temperate lands of southern Africa where they now thrive. In contrast the eastward journey of wheat from Southwest Asia to Persia, India, and North China encountered fewer geographic obstacles.

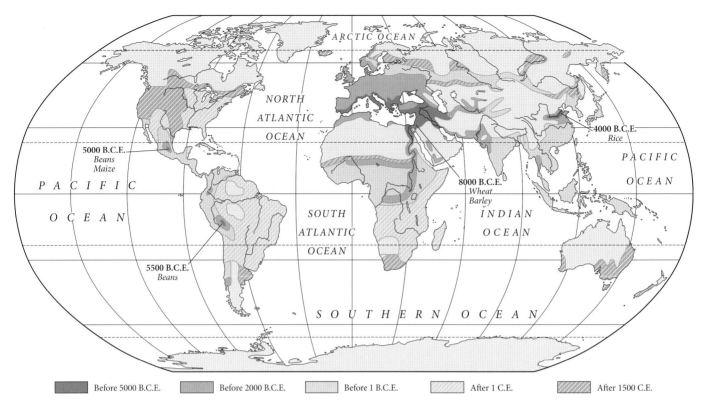

| Before 5000 B.C.E. | Before 2000 B.C.E. | Before 1 B.C.E. | After 1 C.E. | After 1500 C.E. |

Map 1.4 Early agriculture

East Asia

At least 6,500 years ago, perhaps one or two thousand years earlier, East Asia developed the variety of rice that today provides 21 percent of the calories consumed by our species. Rice most likely developed in the middle and lower Yangtze Valley in central China at a time when warmer climates allowed the wild ancestor to thrive in places where rice is not grown today. At roughly the same time, agricultural transformation also occurred in the Yellow River area of China and in its northeast. As in Southwest Asia, varieties of millet and soybean were domesticated in the Yellow River region of North China by sedentary villagers who had initially engaged in hunting and gathering. The two Chinese river valleys were in communication and gradually exchanged information about farming and domestication of animals but the specific innovations probably originated separately in the different regions. The rich soybeans, supplemented by pork, enabled Chinese agriculturalists to obtain a diet nutritionally rich enough to dispense with dairy products from cattle or goats. Because they had alternative nutritional resources, modern Chinese populations, like many modern African and Amerindian populations, never developed the lactose tolerance of European and to a lesser extent of Southwest Asian agriculturalists. Pigs, chickens, and water buffalo were also domesticated in East Asia although their origins are still largely unknown.

Southeast Asia developed a host of important crops: taro and yams, coconuts, sago palms, and citrus trees. So far, investigators have been unable to agree on the specific regions that first produced these crops, although they have uncovered what appear to be irrigation canals that go back 9,000 years in New Guinea.

Middle and South America

Middle and South America contributed an even greater variety of crops to modern agriculture; later on in the sixteenth and seventeenth centuries, the introduction of American plants was to profoundly influence Eurasian agriculture, bringing potatoes to Ireland, tomatoes to Italy, and sweet potatoes to China. The three central crops of the Mesoamericans were maize, beans, and squash. About 7,000 years ago, maize appeared in the Tehuacán Valley of Mexico, evolving from a local plant, teosinte, and spreading into both North and South American continents. Maize took much longer to domesticate than did wheat and barley. Considerably more genetic changes were necessary to increase cob size and so improve maize productivity than to reduce kernel brittleness and improve wheat productivity. New research indicates that maize was first cultivated for the sugar in its stalks, with focus on the nutritious kernels coming later. Due to lack of suitable candidates for draught animals and the

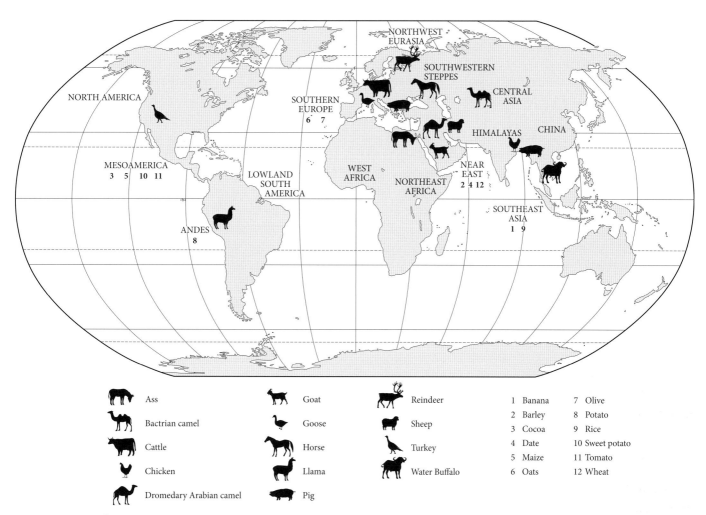

Map 1.5 Origin of crops and domestic animals

absence of sheep in close proximity to areas of agricultural transformation, North America did not produce large domesticated animals; this lack of draught animals imposed serious burdens on Mesoamerican agriculture. Map 1.5 lays out the large animal candidates for domestication in the years after the spread of agriculture. The presence of so many larger mammals in Eurasia and their dearth in the Americas may have constrained the growth of balanced agriculture in the Americas.

In the tropical lowlands of South America hunter-gatherers developed manioc and sweet potatoes. Common beans such as kidney, red pinto, and lima beans also originated in the Americas: beans were simultaneously domesticated in Mexico and the South American Andes. About 5,000 to 4,000 years ago, potatoes and quinoa (a grain crop that grows well in high elevations) emerged in the Andes along with domestic animals such as llamas, alpacas, and guinea pigs. The Andes were the only place in the Americas where domesticated animals played an important role in the food supply. The North American Midwest and Southwest also developed domestic crops. Goosefoot, sunflower, marsh elder, and gourds played an important role in the

Mississippi Valley. These were the main staples of Amerindian populations in the valley before the relatively late arrival of maize a little more than two thousand years ago.

1.7 HOW DID THE SPREAD OF AGRICULTURE AFFECT THE DAILY LIFE OF ORDINARY PEOPLE?

In the two thousand years after the discovery of farming and domestication, a distinctive agricultural way of life began to take shape and to spread from the Fertile Crescent to Turkey and western Iran. A similar transformation of food technologies into a way of life also occurred in China, India, Mesoamerica, and the Andes – indeed in every region affected by agricultural transformation. Surveying this large expanse of time we can identify some long-run trends that stand out, while recognizing that they often took centuries to become fully visible. The most distinctive aspects of the triumph of agriculture as a way of life were the emergence of large numbers of small-scale settled communities, new forms of communal solidarity, and increased interaction among these settled communities. On the eve of agricultural transformation, sedentary communities of collectors had been privileged, relatively stable oases in a world of foragers, human agglomerations that formed only in the richest and most well-endowed areas.

The cultivation of a particular plot of land and the saving of seeds combined with sedentism to produce a society of villages with increased social differentiation within the village and growing linkages among groups of villages. In Southwest Asia some elements of this new way of life came together quickly while others took more time. But within a couple of thousand years of the first domestication of plants and animals a new agricultural way of life emerged there. Ultimately this new lifestyle involved the widespread use of pottery, the plow and irrigation, wheeled transport, the horse, metalworking, and the spread of weaving. It produced population growth and increased exchange among communities. An agricultural "way of life" emerged that integrated daily life with the practices of a balanced agriculture. Right up until the nineteenth century, small agricultural communities provided the food, the tax revenue, and the population that were the lifeblood of the world's empires and great cities.

The study of housing plans uncovered by archaeological excavations suggests that from the beginning of agricultural transformation, in Southwest Asia and East Asia, the individual farming households played the key role in village society although lineage groups, groups of kinsmen, probably also played a significant role. In Southwest Asia characteristic features of agricultural village society included mud-wall cottages, two-storey wood structures, and brick-making. Each village maintained its own shrines and altars that could capture religious feelings in intimate and personal ways.

Agricultural transformation made possible a great expansion of small communities. These could thrive not only in especially favored areas with access to multiple resources but in any environment with arable land. Farming also instituted a new demographic regime permitting greater population density. Hunter-gatherers had relatively low fertility rates. A migratory lifestyle discouraged high fertility, and primitive forms of birth control may have been practiced. Among foragers, children born during a period of migration had low survival rates. In contrast, farmers had more use for child labor than hunter-gatherers did, while sedentism removed old fertility bars.

One of the aspects of agricultural transformation was a storage revolution. In agricultural societies pottery flourished as never before and in such quantities that archaeologists use pottery styles to trace the movement of cultures. Pottery – a fired ceramic work of clay – was first invented by foragers in Japan and North China almost 13,000 years ago. But pottery was too cumbersome and fragile for wide use by foragers, who were unable to benefit from some of its most important uses. Pottery was particularly useful in cooking and storing the plant products that were becoming a more important dietary element among collectors. It played an even more important role for farmers who had to store their harvests and next year's seeds. In Southwest Asia, pottery developed slowly; gourds, skins, baskets, and ground stone bowls served the same purposes. But once pottery had been re-invented in Southwest Asia, somewhere around 8,000 years ago, it quickly became an integral part of the agricultural way of life. It was more fuel-efficient than stone boiling, and soaking and cooking increased the nutritional value of plants. The great expansion of storage allowed accumulation on an unparalleled scale. Never before had anyone, either family or group, controlled such vast stocks of resources.

The domestication of plants and animals gave humans access not only to more reliable nutritional sources but to better clothing and also stimulants. The cultivation of flax, cotton, jute, and hemp yielded new textile materials, as did the raising of goats and sheep. Box 1.3 discusses the development of textiles and garment manufacture and their classification as "women's work." Interestingly enough, textiles seem always to have served as much for decoration and display as for cover and protection against the elements. As Andrew Sherratt has argued, mind-altering drinks and drugs were another product of the agricultural transformation.[6] Agriculture provided the grains for alcoholic drinks, both fermented and distilled, and for the growth of narcotic plants. The Bell Beaker peoples, one of the important successors to the Linear Band peoples, likely used their beakers for drinking some form of alcoholic beverage, either beer, mead, or fermented milk. The distinctive Cord Ware pottery may have been used in religious rituals that involved drugs. Both drugs and alcohol may have been initially confined to religious specialists and used in their rites, but their consumption gradually spread to elites. The spread of Bell Beaker drinking sets across Europe may be a classic case of how new lifestyles spread among Indo-European-speaking elites.

Commerce

By encouraging the spread of lifestyles based on pottery, textiles, and stimulants, village society encouraged the growth of commerce. The more securely settled the majority of the population, the more necessary was heightened mobility among a minority that promoted exchange. If bands of people no longer moved toward resources, then these had to be brought to them. Population density permitted greater specialization among farmer-craftsmen who produced higher quality items than the average tribesman who had to make his own tools, weapons, and decorations. These time-intensive products might easily be valued

Box 1.3 Textiles, Garments, and Agricultural Transformation

Spinning is the oldest garment-making craft and string skirts have been found depicted on stone carvings more than 20,000 years old. Weaving – which involves two operationally different sets of elements: a pre-arranged and more or less fixed warp, and an inserted weft – dates back to the agricultural transformation. The domestication of sheep that produced wool and the cultivation of crops such as flax, hemp, and nettle that produced fibers encouraged textile production. Our very first pictures of garment-making show women at work and it looks as if Neolithic garment-making was women's work. As migratory populations settled down permanently, women spent more time at home childbearing and rearing children and may have found more time to weave. Our first evidence of actual garments in cities such as Nahal Hemar in the Judean Desert and Çatal Hüyük in Anatolia shows garments with complex patterns, designed for display as much as for use. Some were almost certainly colored, although traces of actual colors have vanished. Some of these patterns have had a surprising longevity, passing from generation to generation and people to people who have lived in a certain region. Very distinctive dress patterns that originated in the Hallstatt culture of Central Europe, 2,500 years ago, were found worn by mid-twentieth-century Hungarian peasant women.

outside the tribe and become objects of trade. Hunter-gatherers sometimes made use of copper nuggets and meteoric iron but more advanced metalworking was the product of village society. As networks of exchange intensified across villages within a region, specialization among village producers naturally increased. On the peripheries of village societies were the rare small communities of miners or axe-makers who took advantage of local ore deposits or quarries to engage in forms of specialization that went well beyond the normal features of village society. Such diversified production would become more typical with the emergence of the city (see Chapter 2).

While trade increased in agricultural societies, we know nothing about how trade was negotiated or the auspices under which it occurred. It could have taken the form of ritual exchange in which a parcel of valuable goods was collectively presented to neighboring kinsmen with the understanding that either then or later they would reciprocate. Alternatively trade may have occurred in the payment of bridewealth – the husband's family's payment for receiving the bride's labor – or in the form of tribute or it might have involved bargaining and negotiating between individuals from neighboring villages.

Trade typically emerged not as a separate sphere of activity but as part of new material and cultural developments. The previously discussed Linear Band peoples introduced cattle-herding, but the advancing settlements in Western Europe did not have the resources or security to stock large herds and must have depended on trade with older established settlements to maintain their stock. The culture associated with Bell Beaker Ware pottery introduced alcohol consumption to Europe, probably as part of cultic rites for religious elites, but these celebrations entailed new and often costly drinking vessels that became objects of exchange. In sustaining trade they also maintained their social and cultural links with the initial region of settlement from which they had sprung.

Gender Relations

Some scholars believe that since women gatherers were primarily responsible for tending plants, they were very likely the initiators of the agricultural transformation. Although the argument is plausible it is probably impossible to corroborate. Nevertheless, we do know that the spread of agriculture affected women in complicated ways. Caught between the increased childbearing that was a characteristic feature of agricultural life and increased demand for their labor in plant-processing and food preparation engendered by agricultural transformation, women's position in the agrarian family economy may have deteriorated more often than it improved. While their new centrality in agriculture gave women's roles in tending plants, processing grains, and cooking food a heightened social value, it also condemned them to particularly boring and tedious forms of labor.

In considering the effect of agriculture on gender relations let us look at the case of Pueblo Amerindians living in La Plata in the Southwest United States nearly a thousand years ago. In La Plata the advent of agriculture resulted in a great increase in brutality against women and children and probably to attacks on other tribes to kidnap women for agricultural labor. Permanently watered, with plentiful wild game and turkey and a productive agriculture, the region where the Pueblo Indians lived was generally healthy, yet skeletal evidence reveals systematic violence toward women and children. Women carried a disproportionate part of the burden in agriculture and the settled life that it entailed; they ground corn, prepared food, gathered wood, built and mended houses, made pottery and clothing, while men were responsible for planting and tending corn, occasional hunting, and religious and ceremonial services. Prosperity in La Plata also led to higher fertility and increased migration. Higher fertility meant that women were pregnant over a longer proportion of their married life and this may have increased tension at a time when the spread of agriculture increased women's workload. In turn, increased demand for female labor was associated with the presence of an underclass of immigrant women who were routinely battered and their young children killed.

Some have suggested that the greater involvement in war characteristic of agricultural transformation – to be discussed shortly – was key to the greater pressure on women in farming societies. This may be the case but we should not assume that warfare necessarily created societies where males ruled in unquestioned fashion. The relationship between female social power and warfare is just as complicated as that between female social power and agriculture. Extremely warlike practices such as those of the North American Iroquois confederation produced societies in which women had considerable social and some political authority. The absence of warriors from the village for long periods of time left affairs in the hands of women and gave them considerable experience and authority in ruling.

Social Differences

New demands for women's labor and greater compulsion in its extraction were only one element of a new regime of social inequality that began to develop with agricultural transformation. Unequal social relations existed in all known foraging and collecting societies. Age, health, and ability had long provided bases for unequal treatment, but with agricultural society these inequalities tended to become more systematic and embodied in class or kin institutions. In a variety of ways, territorialism and agricultural transformation encouraged the growth of social inequality. Claims on land, the ability to store agricultural products, the growth of population, and increased commerce all promoted social differentiation. If small-scale agrarian societies in the modern world offer an analogy, early agrarian society and social differentiation were probably expressed in the language of kinship.

The new centrality of farming did not bring new prestige to its practitioners, either men or women. Quite the opposite. Those who performed the tedious but indispensable work of tending crops and preparing food were looked down upon and dominated by newly prosperous kin groups who asserted a special relationship to the gods as well as by chiefs who exerted growing power over their lives. Agricultural transformation created a new social surplus and a variety of groups in collecting society struggled to extract this new wealth.

New political and religious leaders arose who sought to control this new social wealth. **Chiefdoms** – hierarchical political orders – arose that exercised new types of collective power. Archaeologists have documented the rise and fall of chiefly systems in many regions of the world. Where chiefdoms were successful in establishing themselves over a prolonged period of time, it was because chiefs were able to transform personal success into control over institutions and resources. As scholars such as Timothy Earle have shown, chieftains used a variety of strategies to increase their power, and the result was a whole series of different kinds of polity. In Denmark (2300–1300 BCE) war chiefs consolidated their power by bringing craftsmen under their control and monopolizing local weapons production as well as by controlling the cattle trade. Earle examines three economies that had undergone agricultural transformation, the Andean, the Hawaiian, and the Danish. Increased warfare benefited skilled warriors: in the Andes (500–1534 CE) chiefs engaged in direct military competition with other local groups which produced a never-ending cycle of internecine conflict. In Hawaii (800–1824 CE) chiefs also used warfare to increase their power but they did so by annexing lands on which they then installed their own retainers. This proved a more enduring basis for power than simple reliance on force. Finally, the growth of exchange gave new power to those who could use supralocal connections to control trade, especially trade in elite prestige items or in religious goods.

Once established, strong chiefdoms often reinforced the growth of farming by enforcing agricultural activity on most members of society, on men as well as on women. Competing with rival chiefdoms either militarily or for the possession of prestige goods, chiefdoms sought to extract ever more resources from the farming population. The reliability of agricultural production and its responsiveness to intensification allowed chiefs to routinely extract resources from farmers. To increase their extractions, chiefs put agriculturalists under their own surveillance, in so far as they could, or that of their retainers. As far as the climate permitted and as much as chiefs could oversee, agricultural work became year-round and unceasing.

Because of its greater prosperity and larger populations, agricultural society was also able to carry out more sustained levels of collective conflict; its increased emphasis on territorialism also increased the likelihood of war. The inhabitants of Jericho had been peaceful farmers for centuries when about 5,000 years ago the village was burned down and settled by a new population. The new settlers themselves may have been refugees from the chaos and warfare that marked the emergence of the distant Babylonian state. The village's new inhabitants drew the lesson from their predecessors and built a wall around the settlement. But in an age of increasing warfare, walls were not inviolable. Jericho's walls would tumble down half a dozen times before the site was finally abandoned 2,700 years ago.

Conflicts between foragers and farmers also occurred. Western and Central Europe's first agriculturalists, the Linear Band peoples, constructed fortified border villages in Germany and the Low Countries and in Belgium a no-man's-land of approximately 12 to 18 miles separated advancing agriculturalists from foragers. In one village situated in modern-day Belgium all the first houses were destroyed by fire. In Western Europe Linear Band peoples practiced an extensive form of agriculture and constructed permanent settlements, thus bringing them into conflict with pre-existing foragers. Together these may explain the greater need for fortification in these areas.

If agriculture represented a new way of life, it certainly was a complicated new lifestyle. It introduced some of the most important features – both for ill and for good – of modern human societies.

1.8 WAS THE AGRICULTURAL TRANSFORMATION WORTH IT?

While scholars refer to an agricultural transformation, they sometimes forget that pastoralism always dominated some regions of the world and it was never a unilinear process; agricultural transformations were sometimes reversed. European introduction of the horse on the American Great Plains led the Crow Amerindians to abandon agriculture and become hunters. Faced with the colder climate characteristic of the Little Ice Age, the Norse inhabitants of medieval Greenland gave up farming for hunting and fishing. Some evidence suggests that Eurasian pastoral herders originated as practitioners of a balanced agriculture who adapted themselves to the conditions of the steppes and became herders. Certainly on the steppe-land edges of the Chinese empire lived hundreds of thousands of marginal cultivators who turned to pastoralism when farming conditions became difficult or the Chinese state too oppressive. Chinese peasants who opted for pastoralism had counterparts in the Ottoman, Russian, and Iranian empires. As we shall see in Chapter 3, for millennia pastoralism constituted an alternative to agriculture for those living on the periphery of agricultural land. Why did people remain hunter-gatherers or pastoralists? Why did millions of villagers opt for a mobile pastoralism?

While we rightly laud the agricultural transformation of hunter-gatherers into agriculturalists as one of the great changes in human history, we seldom consider the devastation it brought on humankind. If agriculture is the source of many of humankind's greatest achievements, these achievements have been won at great cost.

Had agriculturalists not been driven to maintain their hold over strategic campsites, or been tied to land by territorial loyalties, or been compelled to labor by dominant chiefs, it is difficult to know whether many would have freely chosen an exclusive reliance on agriculture. Research on Eurasia has recently been supported by work on the transition to agriculture in the Americas. It shows that, compared to hunting-gathering and foraging in general, agriculture is associated with shorter life expectancies, higher infant disease rates, smaller body size, and chronic hunger.

Agricultural communities are liable to a wider range of killer diseases than hunter-gatherer societies. Hunter-gatherers are particularly susceptible to such diseases as rabies, tularemia, and hemorrhagic fevers that result from too close contact with wild animals. Most murderous diseases, such as anthrax and salmonella, more typically spread to humans from domesticated animals. The terrible killer, malaria, thrives in the stagnant water produced by human farming communities, and schistosomiasis is endemic to man-made ponds and irrigation trenches in many areas of the world. Some of the most murderous epidemic diseases can only be passed from one human to another and confer immunity on those who survive the disease. Hunter-gatherer societies are generally too small to support such diseases. Diseases such as influenza, mumps, rubella, and smallpox and possibly diphtheria and pertussis are diseases that require the existence of large human societies in order to exist. Sunlight kills many disease vectors that thrive in the darkness of human habitations and seasonal mobility minimizes diseases associated with sewage-contaminated water.

The diet of hunter-gatherers is also typically healthier than that of agriculturalists. Meat-eating combined with a diet of fish and vegetables provides a very healthy diet compared with one based on stored cereals, which are generally poor sources of proteins, vitamins, and minerals. Serious dietary deficiency results among populations that rely too exclusively on cereals. Rice is poor in proteins, wheat diets lack zinc, and maize is deficient in several amino acids and in niacin.

Agriculture can feed more people than hunting and gathering and farmers have, as discussed earlier, higher fertility rates. As a result of the new technology and political regime, farmers focused their energies on a very limited number of crops and animals. They had more monotonous diets and often suffered from the lack of fresh food. Comparison of the rare burial grounds of ancient hunter-gatherers with the more frequently found cemeteries of agricultural populations shows that while the skeletons of hunter-gatherers have heavy dental wear, they were generally healthier than farmers. Also, while agriculture is more dependable and regular than hunting-gathering, agriculturalists have less recourse when disruptions do occur, such as the devastation of their crops. Average height of men and women – a useful indicator of dietary adequacy – dropped by five or six inches with the spread of the agricultural revolution in Greece five thousand years ago.

Agriculturalists were less able to preserve their autonomy because they lacked arms. As rulers asserted their sway over settled populations they also disarmed them. Farming supported professional armies and a disarmed peasantry made it easier to extract taxes to support the military. In contrast, the distinction between soldiers and male producers was almost unknown among pastoralists and hunter-gathers. Arms were necessary to hunting and herding and pastoralists were often skilled horsemen. The ability of pastoralists to militarily resist tax levies and government edicts, and their armed enforcers, made them extremely difficult for dictatorial miltary leaders to govern. But, again and again, charismatic leaders who imposed their rule over pastoralists could easily mobilize them into mighty armies able to challenge the power of agrarian empires.

When living conditions deteriorated and political authorities demanded more grain, poorer farmers in marginal farmlands might decide to return to hunting or take up pastoralism. When the farm was located near steppe land, there was little that landlord or ruler could do to prevent agrarian escapees. At the same time as they rejected village society, pastoralists still often envied farmers their securely stored larders and grain bins as well as the high quality goods produced in village workshops. When large numbers fled agriculture and became pastoralists, it was a sign of a crisis within village society, a crisis that pre-existing, mobile pastoralists might use to their advantage.

Writing in 1377 CE, the great historian Ibn Khaldun asserted that all of human history could be seen as a struggle between agrarian-based sedentary societies and desert-based pastoralists. Indeed, desertions from agriculture and invasion by pastoralists were constant themes of all ancient imperial history. Empires fell as pastoralists rode over the village fields. Sooner or later, however, pastoral rulers found it necessary to restore village boundaries, for empires required agricultural surpluses to survive.

While most historians would not see this conflict as the single dynamic of world history, it remains nonetheless one of its great themes, and this great dynamic of world history began with the invention and spread of agriculture.

Conclusion

The agricultural transformation discussed in this chapter was more a product of plenty than of poverty. The heartland of agricultural development was fertile land and a diverse habitat that gave hunter-gatherers access to year-round food supply that enabled a core of people to settle down permanently. Such an environment encouraged the domestication of plants and animals. The agricultural transformation developed in tandem with a whole series of innovations that encouraged it and, in turn, were influenced by it. Pottery, textiles, and an intensified gendered division of labor combined with new ideas of territorialism and political hierarchy to create a new way of life. Agriculture permitted concentration and population growth; it also permitted social inequality and conflict on an unparalleled scale.

Today, we all live in societies based on the agricultural transformation. Although the number of agriculturalists and their proportion within the world population is dropping rapidly, all modern life continues to rest on agriculture. The huge populations of our globe, our cities, and all our civilizations depend on farmers who produce our daily bread, or our daily rice, or our daily tortillas. Without agriculture we could not maintain our orchestras, our scientific laboratories, or our libraries. Neither could we mobilize millions of men and women in our great wars or support the administrative apparatuses of repressive dictatorships. For good or for ill, almost all the events discussed in the remainder of this book rest on the broad back of the agricultural transformation.

Study Questions

(1) What was the nature of the communications revolutions thought to have occurred 75,000–30,000 years ago? What is "protolanguage" and how does it differ from human language?

(2) What do we mean by foraging, by collecting, by farming? What do we mean by "balanced agriculture"?

(3) Describe some characteristic features of foraging as a way of life. Compare and contrast these features with agriculture as a way of life.

(4) Discuss the pros and cons of the agricultural transformation. If you were in the Near East 10,000 years ago, would you have been in favor of the agricultural transformation? In the long run has humanity benefited from this transformation?

Suggested Reading

Paul G. Bahn, *Prehistoric Art* (Cambridge University Press, 1998). This is a wide-ranging and well-informed survey.

Elizabeth Wayland Barber, *Women's Work: The First 20,000 Years: Women, Cloth, and Society in Early Times* (New York: W.W. Norton, 1994). The large historical range of this study puts women's work and its evolution in perspective.

Luigi Luca Cavalli-Sforza, Paolo Menozzi, and Alberto Piazza, *The History and Geography of Human Genes* (Princeton University Press, 1994). This book integrates demography and recent genetic research in the debate over Indo-European origins and development.

David Christian, *Maps of Time: An Introduction to Big History* (Berkeley: University of California Press, 2011). World history begins with the "Big Bang" in this biologically oriented approach.

Jared Diamond, *Guns, Germs, and Steel: The Fates of Human Societies* (New York: W.W. Norton, 1997). Diamond's book is a fascinating and suggestive study of human evolution.

TIMOTHY EARLE, *How Chiefs Come to Power: The Political Economy of Prehistory* (Stanford University Press, 1997). Earle provides a comparative analysis of the growth of social differences in a variety of prehistoric societies.

JOYCE MARCUS AND KENT V. FLANNERY, *Zapotec Civilization: How Urban Society Developed in Mexico's Oaxaca Valley* (London: Thames & Hudson, 1996). This is an innovative study of the evolution of agriculture in Mesoamerica.

STEVEN MITHEN, *After the Ice: A Global Human History, 20,000–5,000 BC* (London: Weidenfeld & Nicolson, 2003). A history of the world from the last ice age until the origins of agriculture, based on archaeological case studies, this book is a wonderful depiction of day-to-day human life and its great variety.

ANDREW SHERRATT, *Economy and Society in Prehistoric Europe: Changing Perspectives* (Princeton University Press, 1997). Sherratt offers an innovative and suggestive perspective on prehistoric Europe.

BRUCE D. SMITH, *The Emergence of Agriculture* (New York: Scientific American, 1998). This is a well-argued and important survey of the agricultural transformation worldwide.

Glossary

band: Basic unit of hunter-gatherer societies. Band members spend most of their lives in groups of between fifteen and forty, most often living on wild plants and animals. The division of labor in bands is generally along age and sex lines. Money is not used and most exchange takes place along kinship or friendship lines show a very limited division of labour.

chiefdom: Regionally organized society with a centralized decision-making hierarchy that co-ordinated activities among several village communities. The essential aspect of chiefdoms is hierarchy and rank that extend across geographic space. Hereditary succession is an aspect of almost all known chiefdoms.

collectors: They are more sedentary than foragers. They remain in favorite locales and send out smaller groups to bring back resources to the larger collectivity.

emmer *and* einkorn: Native grasses on the western edge of the Fertile Crescent that became the first grains to be domesticated.

farming: Involves selecting plants and animals and modifying their environment so as to increase their productivity and utility to humans.

foragers: They hunt and fish and gather wild fruits, leaves, and tubers, consuming what they gather within a few hours or days. Their pattern of settlement becomes diverse or aggregated according to their foods and the season.

glaciation: The covering of the earth with glaciers or masses of ice. During an ice age, periods of glaciation alternate with warmer interglacial periods during which the glaciers retreat toward the poles.

hominid: A primate of the family *Hominidae*, of which the modern human *Homo sapiens sapiens*, chimpanzees, gorillas, and orangutans are the only surviving species.

***Homo ergaster*:** Literally "working man." This species developed about one and a half million years ago. The first hominid species to leave Africa, they roamed grasslands from Africa to the Middle East and China. They tamed fire and brought it into routine use, and at least some of them made tools. There seems to have been an increased cranial capacity over their ancestor *Homo habilis*, i.e. they had larger brains.

***Homo neanderthalensis*:** Neanderthals are an extinct species of human, named after Neander Valley in Germany where their bones were first discovered. Heavily built and low browed, they occupied Europe and the Middle East 100,000–30,000 years ago.

Homo sapiens sapiens: The first anatomically modern humans, now the only surviving human species.

Linear Band peoples: Agricultural colonizers, named after the characteristic incised lines on their pottery, who spread across Northern and Central Europe in the Neolithic period.

protolanguage: Language ability consisting largely of proper and common nouns and their juxtaposition to convey meaning. The limited language capabilities so far elicited by human trainers from gorillas and chimpanzees may have been characteristic of this form of hominid communication.

tribe: A group larger than a band, with a recognized leader whose power rests on popularity and the ability to render services, including the performance of ritual observances.

Notes   1 Alan Walker and Pat Shipman, *The Wisdom of the Bones: In Search of Human Origins* (New York: Vintage, 1997).

2 Derek Bickerton, *Language & Species* (University of Chicago Press, 1990).

3 Jared Diamond, *Guns, Germs, and Steel: The Fates of Human Societies* (New York: W.W. Norton, 1997).

4 Bruce D. Smith, *The Emergence of Agriculture* (New York: Scientific American, 1998).

5 A.M.T. Moore, G.C. Hillman, and A.J. Legge, *Village on the Euphrates: From Foraging to Farming at Abu Hureyra* (Oxford University Press, 2000).

6 Andrew Sherratt, *Economy and Society in Prehistoric Europe: Changing Perspectives* (Princeton University Press, 1997).

2 Cities and states

Timeline	
5000 BCE	Grain farming already widespread in Fertile Crescent and North China.
3000 BCE	Cities and states already established in Mesopotamia, states (and perhaps still undiscovered cities) in Egypt, Minoan civilization in Crete.
2500 BCE	Indus Valley civilization thriving up to collapse between 1600 and 1200 BCE; by this time, different writing systems in use not only in Indus, but also around the Fertile Crescent, in adjacent regions of Asia and Europe as well, maybe also in China.
1700 BCE	Chariot-using warriors, probably from Central Asia, begin invading and conquering in Middle East, Egypt, China.
1600–1046 BCE	Shang cities and states in North China.
1580 BCE	Mycenaean civilization in Greece.
700–500 BCE	Hindu and Buddhist religions developing in South Asia, roughly contemporaneous with Zoroastrianism and monotheistic Judaism in Middle East, Confucianism in China.
665 BCE	Consolidation of Assyrian empire.

The small Iraqi city of Warka lies about 185 miles south of Baghdad, not far from where the joined Tigris and Euphrates rivers empty into the Persian Gulf. The Bible calls the place Erech, but five millennia ago local people knew it as Uruk. For centuries Uruk dominated the area of southern Mesopotamia then known as Sumer. At some time between 2800 and 2500 BCE a great king named Gilgamesh ruled Uruk. Soon after Gilgamesh's time, the region's people were remembering him as a god and reciting vivid stories about him. Scribes eventually recorded those stories on clay tablets as different versions of the Gilgamesh epic.

The first texts of the epic that archaeologists have – literally – unearthed date from around 2100 BCE, some 500 years after Gilgamesh actually ruled Uruk. The stories pit their flawed hero Gilgamesh against the anti-hero Enkidu, against the monster Humbaba, and against the avenging Bull of Heaven.

The Gilgamesh epic mixes myth and deep historical truth. Above all, it records the new and growing mastery of city (Gilgamesh) over country (Enkidu). A settlement existed at Uruk from at least 5000 BCE, with substantial buildings showing up a thousand years or so later. After another thousand years, toward 3000, Uruk had become a major center of Mesopotamia, the region of today's Syria and Iraq lying between the Tigris and the Euphrates (in Greek, Mesopotamia means "between the rivers"). About the same time, people in or near Uruk started writing; they began making regular inscriptions of standard **pictographs** – word-pictures – on wet clay tablets, which then dried into permanent records. That was a first in human history. As we reconstruct human experience from that point forward in time, we can analyze written texts to supplement the pictures, physical artifacts, skeletons, genetic traces, surviving languages, and alterations of landscapes that provide our major evidence on humanity up to then.

The **Fertile Crescent** forms an arc from the Persian Gulf through what is now southern Turkey, down through Palestine, and over to Egypt. Between about 9000 and 7000 BCE, humans created the world's first major zone of agricultural villages in the Crescent. As a crude shorthand, we can call the southern part of that zone Mesopotamia, the northern part Assyria, and the western part Egypt. By 7000 BCE the whole region's people had learned how to cultivate field grains and legumes. They had also domesticated dogs, goats, sheep, pigs, cattle, and cats, but not yet the donkeys, horses, and camels that would later play large parts in the region's history. People of the great agricultural arc were also building houses, streets, walls, and towers of mud bricks, which they made by mixing earth, water, and straw or gravel in rectangular molds, then leaving the mixture to dry in the sun for several weeks.

The Fertile Crescent soon produced the world's first cities: good-sized towns with well-defined public spaces, massive buildings, plenty of non-agricultural activity, and clear signs of social differentiation. By 5000 BCE cities had multiplied in Mesopotamia and nearby areas. With cities grew up both long-distance trade and military domination based on warring and conquering city-states. (The round, spiked royal crown so familiar to Europeans descends from the Assyrian portrayal of queens with hats mimicking city walls.) Middle Eastern cities of the earliest historical era depended on agriculture for their survival, but they also stimulated agricultural intensification in their hinterlands. City-based civilization developed over the next five millennia through much of Eurasia and North Africa; urban centers in the Americas arose independently and are surveyed in Chapter 4.

As compared to the previous million years of human existence, change came with startling rapidity. Nevertheless, the transformations described in this chapter took plenty of time. The 4,400 years reviewed here, after all, occupied more than half of all the time between the initial development of cities and the day on which you are reading this book. Since the years are many, the portion of the earth's surface involved vast, and the record still very fragmentary, this chapter often leaps centuries as if they were single days.

All together, the changes we take up here produced one of humanity's greatest transformations since the very emergence of *Homo sapiens*. To describe and explain how that great transformation occurred, this chapter centers on the following historical changes:

- After 5000 BCE fragmented bands and villages that had long engaged in the hunting, fishing, gathering, herding, and cultivation described in Chapter 1 came under the influence of expanding, competing cities and states across significant stretches of Southern Eurasia and North Africa, notably in the Middle East, in and around the Mediterranean, in the Indus Valley, and in China.
- Within the same zones, village agriculture, urban crafts, military organization, centralized political administration, and literacy all expanded mightily, and to some extent reinforced each other.
- As a consequence, unprecedented connections of economic activity, political power, and culture grew up among scattered human settlements.
- Each region formed its own distinctive kinds of cities and states with varying balances of economic activity, political power, and culture; those models then powerfully shaped each region's later history.
- Eventually all these regions influenced each other, but archaeologists and historians are still sorting out how early and deep that mutual influence ran.

2.1 TRADE, POLITICAL POWER, AND CULTURE

How and why did these far-reaching changes occur? It helps to distinguish three general forms of human connection: trade, political power, and culture.

Trade

Trade includes the production and transfer of goods and services. Sometimes trade operates through markets, but often people produce and transfer inside kinship groups, villages,

Map 2.1 Areas of city and state development in Eurasia

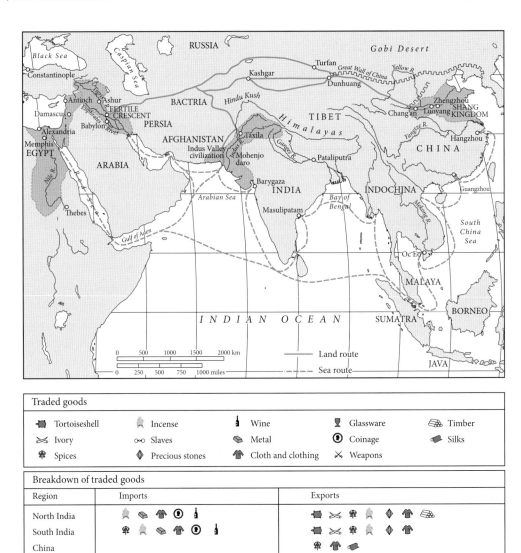

Traded goods				
🐢 Tortoiseshell	🪔 Incense	🍶 Wine	🍷 Glassware	📚 Timber
✂ Ivory	∞ Slaves	🧱 Metal	⊙ Coinage	🧣 Silks
🌳 Spices	◈ Precious stones	👕 Cloth and clothing	✕ Weapons	

Breakdown of traded goods					
Region	Imports		Exports		
North India	🪔 📚 🧣 ⊙ 🍶		🐢 ✂ 🌳 🪔 ◈ 👕 📚		
South India	🌳 🪔 📚 👕 ⊙ 🍶		🐢 ✂ 🌳 🪔 ◈ 👕		
China			🌳 👕 🧣		
Arabia	🌳 🍶 🧱 👕 ⊙ 📚		🐢 ✂ 🌳 🪔 ∞ ◈ 🍶 🧱 👕		
East Africa	🐢 ✂ 🧱 👕 🍷 ⊙ ✕		🐢 ✂ 🌳 🪔 ∞ 🍶 🧱 👕 🍷 ⊙		

military units, and other sorts of organization without using money or markets. Whether market-mediated or not, trade typically promotes communication, interdependence, and divisions of labor; people in different sites specialize in one product or another, transfer some of that product to people elsewhere, and get from others goods and services they do not produce. When the flow of goods and services connects two sites in ways that are mutually beneficial, we can reasonably talk about "exchange." But in the ancient world many transfers took the form of tribute, offerings, taxes, and confiscations for which producers received little or no return. See Box 2.1 for an example of ancient tax-collecting.

As kingdoms and empires settled into place, however, economic activity managed by merchants generally became more crucial to a regime's prosperity. Long-distance trade depended especially on middlemen who organized caravans or voyages and

created systems of credit to underwrite them. Prominent commercial changes over the whole period 5000–600 BCE included great increases in agricultural productivity, expansion in the variety and volume of urban crafts, proliferation of economic activity in both regards, and sharpening rural–urban economic differentiation.

Political Power and Coerced Labor

Political power helps explain one-way transfers of goods and services. When people apply concentrated means of harm, or threats of harm, to each other they are exercising political power. Political power creates connections among people both by establishing governmental control over whole populations and by introducing defensive or offensive boundaries between populations. Interactions across those boundaries, however friendly or

Box 2.1 Tribute and Trade

Throughout the ancient world of cities and states, large-scale transfers of goods and services typically began as tribute rather than as merchant-to-merchant exchange. A few years before 1750 BCE, Hammurabi, a famous law-giving king of Babylon, sent this instruction to his tax collector:

The moment you see this tablet of mine, send to Babylon Šep-Sin, the Overseer of the Merchants, with his 1,800 gur [bushels] of grain and his arrears of 19 minas [1 mina = about 500 grams] of silver, and Sin-muštal, the Overseer of the Merchants, with his 1,800 gur of grain and his arrears of 7 minas of silver,

and together with them a reliable servant of yours.

Hammurabi was collecting tribute, not exchanging goods and services. By collecting debts in silver as well as grain, he was establishing a crude sort of money without stamping coins or printing bills.

---

hostile, also create connections – solidarity on the one hand, division on the other. Note the ferocity of this message of about 1800 BCE from the king of Aleppo (now in Syria) to his faithless former ally the king of Der (east of the Tigris, near the Zagros Mountains):

May Šamas [the god of justice] investigate my conduct and yours, and render judgment! I behave to you like a father and brother and you behave to me like an ill-wisher and enemy . . . I swear to you, by Addu, the god of my city, and Sin my personal god, I shall not rest until I have destroyed your land and yourself! Now I shall come at the beginning of spring, and I shall advance to the doors of your city gate, and shall acquaint you with the bitterness of the weapons of Adad and Yarim-Lin.

Armies, navies, militias, police forces, guards, bandits, pirates, and thugs all specialize in using political power to create or maintain connections and divisions. When governments and military organizations grow, political power becomes a more prominent connector. Sometimes that happens at the expense of trade, as when rulers commandeer rural men, animals, and food for pursuit of war. But sometimes political power and economic activity reinforce each other, as when rulers coerce rural people to build roads or dig canals that then carry goods and people between country and city.

Some coerced labor went neither into war nor into commercial infrastructure, but into monumental display. Temples, funeral buildings, statues, fortresses, castles, walls, and other monuments provided sites for public worship, ceremonies, defense, and residence of the powerful. But as today's sports stadia, civic centers, and skyscrapers advertise the power and wealth of the municipal leaders who have them built, the monuments of ancient times broadcast the importance of priests, kings, and urban ruling classes. Uruk stood out from earlier settlements for its great walls.

Similarly massive walls rose at Mohenjo-daro in the Indus Valley. The rammed-earth walls of China's Zhengzhou, an early Shang capital, stood about 60 feet wide, 30 feet high, and 4,000 feet long; they would have taken 10,000 workers ten or twenty years to build. Whatever their value for defense and containment, those walls announced the power of Shang emperors to mobilize vast amounts of labor – or military force. Those same emperors commanded the construction of massive, wealth-filled royal tombs. Egyptian pyramids and Sumerian **ziggurats** (monumental towers) likewise announced their builders' might. As these examples suggest, political power changed every bit as much as economic activity during the period 5000–600 BCE; during those four and a half millennia, previously autonomous villages and nomadic bands fell under the sway of powerful city-states, kingdoms, and empires through important parts of Eurasia and North Africa.

Toward the end of that period, furthermore, began a counter-current that continued for another two millennia. On the vast Eurasian steppe, people had domesticated horses – first for food, then for transportation – some time around 4000 BCE. They took to herding sheep on a large scale, moving with their flocks from pasture to pasture. They soon invented forms of warfare centering on mounted bowmen. After 1000 BCE, nomads originating outside the zones of agrarian empires and city-states began to invade those zones from the steppe, raiding, burning, and looting their more prosperous neighbors. Some of them then settled as soldiers and landlords at the edges of empire. Others made it their business to remain mounted, armed, and mobile as they extracted tribute from sedentary populations.

Scythians arrived in the Black Sea steppe from the Volga basin between 750 and 700 BCE, and for a time held the great Persian empire hostage. They were simply the first major nomadic wave in a series of westward movements. Invaders eventually included Parthians, Sarmatians, Huns, Avars, Bulgars, Magyars, Turks, Mongols, and Tatars. These mounted warriors fixed in place

THE RISE OF CITIES, STATES, AND PASTORALISM

the European idea of barbarians as people who not only lacked civilization (as the original Greco-Roman version of the word "barbarian" implied) but also lived from hunting, gathering, herding, and preying on civilized peoples rather than settling down meekly in cities and villages. Of course their European victims exaggerated: although armed nomadic people did not run agrarian empires from fixed capital cities, they created sophisticated systems of communication and co-ordination, established royal hierarchies of their own, and regularly returned to sites where they buried their rulers in spectacular tombs containing finely wrought jewelry.

Culture and the Origins of Writing

Because people tend to take culture for granted, its changes play a less obvious historical role than economic activity or political power. But it connects people in ways that economic activity and political power do not. Culture creates bounded ties among social locations: individuals, households, communities, and organizations. Its local structure varies as dramatically as do structures of economic activity and political power. Culture's ties include the full array of creative production: shared beliefs, practices, symbols, and self-representations. They can take the form of shared religion, common ethnicity, trading partnerships, friendship, work-based solidarity, communities of taste, and political movements. Each relation of culture involves not only such common properties, but also a boundary separating insiders from outsiders. Culture's ties form the basis of **trust networks**, those webs of connection on which people rely when engaging in long-term, high-risk, socially contingent activities such as marriage, personal sponsorship, long-distance trade, and credit.

Like economic activity and political power, culture has its own specialists, for example priests, intellectuals, artists, heads of kin groups, village elders, and matchmakers. In Babylon one study of 3,060 scribes who wrote on clay tablets in the Semitic language called Akkadian (for the empire of Akkad, or Agade, founded by the great conqueror Sargon of Agade around 2300 BCE) showed that 2,681 worked for private individuals, 368 for religious temples, and only 11 for the royal palace. Most of all, scribes were handling contracts, shipments, and correspondence, including those of temples and governments. Their writings did more than record transactions; they cemented social ties. Scribes served not only as readers, writers, and recorders, however, but also as **diviners** (future-tellers), poets, and interpreters of the classics. As with economic activity and political power, our period brought enormous changes in culture to Eurasia and North Africa. Major developments included formation of far-flung ethnic trading networks, elaboration of kinship ties among scattered ruling classes, emergence of large-scale monotheistic

religions, invention of writing as means for recording or communication, and the resulting establishment of religious and secular literati.

Assuming that no one "invented" spoken language as such, writing may be the single most influential human invention of all time. Writing profoundly affected human life because it so greatly facilitated record-keeping and long-distance communication. Although it certainly created ties among literate people, it also produced a profound new boundary between the literate and the illiterate. Middle Easterners have a claim to the first invention of writing, although exactly when, where, and how it happened remains a matter of definition and dispute. By 9000 BCE, people in southern Mesopotamia were using clay tokens of different shapes to represent counts of various objects; some of those shapes reappeared in almost identical form when scribes began pressing wedges into soft clay tablets to produce standard symbols toward 3000 BCE. Since the scribes made their impressions in the clay with wedge-shaped sticks, we call the tablets **cuneiform**, from *cuneus*, Latin for wedge. Archaeologists have recovered more than three thousand written tablets from Uruk alone, and tens of thousands from elsewhere in Mesopotamia.

Beginning as pictographs, one simplified picture per object, Mesopotamian characters rapidly became abstract representations. By 2000 BCE, Mesopotamian scribes were using about 500 characters with great regularity. Somewhere between 9000 and 2000 BCE, then, Mesopotamians invented writing more or less as we know it. Not exactly as we know it, however: Mesopotamian scribes continued to use modified pictographs with hundreds of characters rather than the radically simplified alphabets with their twenty-odd characters that Westerners now usually employ for their writing. Although Egyptians wrote a kind of alphabet between 2000 and 1800 BCE, the ancestor of Middle Eastern alphabets only emerged between 1500 and 1000 BCE, when Phoenicians of what is now Lebanon may have invented it, and certainly began using it widely.

So who invented writing, and when? We step into a minefield of priority claims. By 3000 or so, for example, Egyptians were using brilliant pictographs, and appear to have begun both codifying the signs and assigning standard sounds to some of them. By 2700 they had developed representations for all sounds in their spoken language; that did not happen in Mesopotamia until relatively late. Who came first? In China, the first hard evidence of writing comes from the divining bones and shells of late Shang around 1200 BCE (see Box 2.4 below). Yet some scholars argue that earlier writing on silk and bamboo has simply disappeared, some have claimed that signs on turtle shells from five thousand years earlier (6600–6200 BCE) qualify as steps toward writing, and still others have identified marks on pottery from about 4500 BCE onward as early versions of later Chinese characters.

China does not offer Mesopotamian writing its only possible competition. Starting around 2600 BCE, the Indus Valley civilization left soapstone seals combining pictures with a script no one has deciphered so far. Specialists cannot actually read any South Asian writing from before about 500 BCE. In Central America, traces of writing – almost certainly an independent invention – date back to about 650 BCE. For the time being, then, we know neither which region first produced a full-fledged writing system nor whether that first invention influenced all the rest. Whatever the answers to the questions of when and where it emerges, writing accompanied and helped cause huge alterations. Although writing played significant roles in economic activity and political power, it especially fostered culture; it promoted taking account of and responding to others in distant times and places.

Interactions of Trade, Political Power, and Culture

Exchange, political power, and culture obviously interact. Pure forms of these connections rarely appear; even a mainly coercive relation between kings and their subjects typically involves some mutual trade and culture. Chinese kings of the Shang period not only ran armies and extracted tribute, but also served as priests of the high god Di and of the cult that honored royal ancestors. Those ancestors had themselves become semi-divine through their sustained contact with the high god both before and after death. Shang kings employed diviners to prepare animal bones or turtle shells whose cracks, supposedly produced by the same ancestors, foretold the weather and the human future. Kings frequently interpreted those cracks on their own. They also conducted ceremonies and sacrifices, including sacrifices of human beings. At the later Shang kings' deaths, their followers buried them in pits with chariots, horses, dogs, weapons, precious objects, and people. Excavators of those tombs have often found human skeletons beheaded and arranged in regular ranks. Tombs of early Egyptian kings likewise contain ceremoniously arranged bodies of executed humans. Although the kings' priestly role surely backed up their political power with threats of supernatural power, it probably also made them key figures in cultures cemented by popular religion.

Economic activity, political power, and culture do not just overlap in the same persons and places. They also affect each other, as when expansion of long-distance trade provides new opportunities for bandits to rob merchants, or when formation of a new religion threatens rulers' control over their subjects. (The rise of Hebrew monotheism – the patriarch Abraham is supposed to have grown up in Haran, northern Mesopotamia, around 1500 BCE – posed just such a threat to surrounding empires. That threat helps explain the persecution of Jews in ancient times.) As cities and states increased their dominance, connections began to operate on larger and larger scales. During their heyday of 2600 to 1900 BCE, for example, craftsmen of Indus Valley cities worked raw materials – especially copper and precious stones – from other regions of South Asia, from Central Asia, and from the Persian Gulf. Their products reached as far as the Mediterranean and Mesopotamia. In fact, jewel-makers from the Indus Valley civilization formed a distinctive minority among Mesopotamian craftsmen. In such cases of shared religion, kinship, and geographic origin, trade and culture reinforce each other so well that specialized trades operate effectively with little political power. In such cases, ostracism by your group simultaneously removes your livelihood, your credit, and your social standing.

Relations of economic activity, political power, and culture take both equal and unequal forms. Merchants and artisans sometimes treat each other as rough equals, but exploit their workers, clerks, and servants mercilessly. Urban militias and gangs often compete with each other on fairly level fields, but take their place in very unequal relations with fellow citizens. Communities of believers and members of the same lineages may well experience solidarity with each other, but that does not keep priests and patriarchs from behaving like despots. In the period from 5000 to 600 BCE, unprecedented systems of inequality based on large organizations and widespread connections grew up in all regions of city and state expansion. On the whole, priests and kings collaborated in maintaining the privileges of tiny ruling classes supported by tribute from most of the population.

Yet relative predominance of economic activity, political power, and culture as sources of connection varies significantly over space and time, with significant consequences for the texture of social life. In periods of rapid political expansion, coercive power loomed larger than in the routine operation of agrarian empires. Predatory states such as the Scythians built more of their structure around force than did cult-based states such as most Egyptian regimes. On the whole, it looks as though a combination of political power and culture, with less space for economic activity, distinguished Chinese cities and states of our period from those further west. To put it crudely: local life differs depending on whether soldiers, merchants, or priests have the upper hand. Compared to our own mercantile time, the period from 5000 to 600 BCE was an age of soldiers and priests.

2.2 CITIES AND STATES

Cities figured centrally as intersections of political power, economic activity, and culture. Throughout Eurasia, cities generally lived within defensive walls, and built new walls as they expanded. Indeed, the old Chinese word *cheng* means both "city" and "wall." Priests, kings, and priest-kings concentrated their coercive forces within city walls, exercised surveillance over spaces and activities within the walls, monitored movements through city gates, and ventured out through the gates in force to exercise more intermittent control over the hinterland. But cities also served both as crucial junctions for economic activity and as major consumers of rural products; they provided the pivots of trade. Finally, temples, sacred spaces, memorials, and literati all concentrated in cities, which became the major sites for public events producing or confirming culture.

Relative to political power and culture, economic activity generally looms larger in cities than it does in rural areas. Artisans, manufacturers, merchants, and producers of commercial services concentrate in urban areas and wield disproportionate influence within them. Not always and everywhere: some cities (as in Egypt) seem to have served chiefly as sites for cultural ceremonies. Rulers established others (notably in China's periods of imperial expansion) as military outposts. Still, the sheer concentration of specialized non-agricultural populations within walled settlements generally made trade crucial to urban activity. They had to get food from elsewhere.

Babylon

Take the case of Babylon, a metropolis that grew up in the same region as Uruk, but a thousand years later. First laid out around 2000 BCE, the city followed a very regular plan of boxes within boxes: an inner walled citadel open only to priests, kings, and their retainers; a surrounding city of some 400 hectares (roughly 1,000 acres, or 1.5 square miles) bisected by the Euphrates, contained by a rectangular wall, with geometrically arranged buildings and streets; and an outer wall surrounding an area about twice that size. In the center, side by side, stood the royal fortress and the temple of Ishtar. Unsurprisingly, the one Mesopotamian world map that survives shows Babylon at its very center.

Although Babylon served at first as a base for political conquest and control, the city soon developed extensive industry and trade. Babylonians made fine textiles, shipping them far and wide. Particular kinds of manufacturing clustered together within Babylon. The city had streets named for particular crafts, for example the makers of a certain kind of dipping vat. Since some textile workshops had many female workers, certain of those streets probably teemed with women. In Babylonian documents from after 1000 BCE, we find names of trades – tanner, seal-cutter, potter, builder, smith, and so on – used as rough equivalents of family names. If some of the city's great wealth came from its control over a rich agricultural hinterland, its own manufacturing and trade also contributed mightily to the city's importance.

Its wealth made Babylon an object of respect, but also of envy and attack. As Babylon became the dominant city of southern Mesopotamia toward 1000 BCE, its patron god Marduk rose to the top of the region's divine hierarchy. Babylonians marked the year's end by moving Marduk's statue to a special house outside the city gates, then returning it in triumph as the new year began. When King Sennacherib of the Assyrian empire (704–681 BCE) first conquered Babylon, he removed the divine statue, and thus symbolically degraded the city. When his forces sacked Babylon in 689, Sennacherib boasted that "The hands of my people took hold of the gods' dwellings there and smashed them." A Babylonian literary text of the time described the effects of the god's departure in these terms:

People's corpses block the gates. Brother eats brother. Friend strikes friend with a mace. Free citizens stretch out their hand to the poor [to beg]. The scepter grows short. Evil lies across the land. Usurpers weaken the country. Lions block the road. Dogs go mad and bite people. Whoever they bite does not live, he dies.

Like their contemporaries elsewhere in Eurasia, Babylonians wrote their forms of connection – including their protective connections with the gods – on their cityscapes. Their great ceremonial towers, or ziggurats, entered the Hebrew Bible in the form of the Tower of Babel (see Figure 2.1).

Cities without Walls

Egypt is the great exception. Although Egyptians built great ceremonial centers such as Memphis from 2900 BCE onward, archaeologists digging along the Nile Valley have not uncovered inhabited, walled cities comparable to the royal citadels of Mesopotamia, the Indus Valley, or China. That could be because the narrow fertile valley, surrounded by barren land, operated as the equivalent of a single city. Or it could be that ruins of old cities lie hidden beneath the mud of the valley itself, which has supported dense populations for thousands of years and is therefore not an easy site for excavations. Tell-el-Amarna, the new capital established by Pharaoh Amenhotep IV between 1370 and 1350 BCE, had a compact structure similar to those of Middle Eastern cities, but clung to the Nile and lacked surrounding walls. Along the Nile's flanks, in any case, Egypt's rulers built monuments – especially great pyramids, obelisks, and sphinxes – to rival any erected in the cities of other urban regions.

Figure 2.1 Babylonian ziggurat. The ziggurat was a terraced step pyramid of successively receding stages. It was commonly used by Iranian and Mesopotamian religious figures about four thousand years ago. The original ziggurats may have possessed small chapels at the top. The tower top was not used for public religious ceremonies as it was the place where gods came into contact with priests. It was a private place, not a public stage.

Cities and Trade

In Babylonia, Assyria, Egypt, and elsewhere, cities only survived because they drew food and raw materials from surrounding rural regions while supplying their specialized goods and services to people from outside. Although urban temples seem at first to have controlled Mesopotamia's long-distance trade, as that trade expanded private merchants took it over. In fact, Mesopotamians may well have originated an urban pattern that persists to our own day: the enclave of merchants from one city who establish themselves in another city, purveying goods from their place of origin. Such settlements often formed on a river or road outside the city walls.

During the late nineteenth century, scholars were surprised to see a new kind of cuneiform tablet showing up in sales of antiquities from central Turkey. Eventually they identified more than 10,000 such tablets. The texts later turned out to be written in an Akkadian dialect used in Ashur, the city from which Assyria got its name. The inscriptions dated mainly from the century after 1880 BCE. Ashur was 1,000 miles from the central Turkish site where scavengers and archaeologists dug up the tablets. Here lay a puzzle: what connected the distant site to Ashur? Solution to the puzzle: merchants from Ashur had organized faraway trading colonies in Anatolia, most often creating enclaves near a city's castle wall. The trading system brought tin and textiles from Assyria across the Taurus Mountains on donkeyback, returning gold and silver to Ashur. Rulers at both ends of the long itinerary had an interest in maintaining

the trade; officials in Ashur levied a 5 percent tax at a shipment's departure, while officials at the destination collected another 3 percent. The taxes, of course, made it profitable to smuggle goods past customs posts or bribe customs officers, subverting political power by means of trade.

An Ashur merchant's clay note to partners in another trading center shows us the interplay of economic activity and political power:

As to the purchase of Akkadian textiles, about which you wrote to me, since you left the Akkadians have not entered the City [of Ashur]. Their country is in revolt. If they arrive before winter, and there is the possibility of a purchase which allows you profit, we will buy for you and pay the silver from our own resources. You should take care to send the silver.

Merchants and their cities depended on states for the maintenance of order that made trade safe. But states depended on merchants and cities for revenue.

Organizing Political Power

Egyptians, Babylonians, and other peoples of 5000–600 BCE did not simply build cities. They also created states. If all we mean by government is relatively stable, spatially organized power in whatever form it occurs, governments existed throughout the human world at least from the development of village-based agriculture onward. But the special form of government we call a **state** involved (and still involves) four distinctive elements:

(1) major concentrated means of coercion, especially an army
(2) organization that is at least partly independent of kinship and religious relations
(3) a defined area of jurisdiction
(4) priority in some regards over all other organizations operating within that area

All of these are, of course, relative. In the period we are examining here, for example, kings always played key religious roles, and priests often wielded exceptional power within states. Nor did any city-state or empire ever establish stable control over its outer boundaries for very long. Still, the conjunction of concentrated coercion, partly independent organization, territorial jurisdiction, and priority over other organizations distinguished the sorts of government that grew up after 5000 from the villages, clans, religious cults, and armed bands that preceded them.

States centered on political power, but could not survive without substantial support from economic activity and culture. They required economic activity – both production and distribution – to sustain their specialized personnel and activities, including armies, officials, and royal households. They required culture to back up their threats, to make their promises credible, and to provide connections within the subject population that facilitated negotiating taxes, conscription, and more general support for governmental activity. No city-based ruler could build major monuments or expand armed forces significantly without commandeering massive labor from villages in the hinterland. When either economic activity or cultural influence fell away, state authorities might survive for a while by means of intensified political power, but eventually brute force failed.

Across the ancient world, rulers and their subjects created three main kinds of state: city-states, empires, and military predators. **City-states**, such as Uruk, based their administration in a single capital but controlled enough rural territory to supply food for their non-agricultural populations, taxes in precious metal or kind for governmental activity, and manpower for renewal of armies and urban services. **Empires**, such as those of Shang China, sometimes centered on a single capital and sometimes rotated their central administration among cities, but they always relied heavily on regional power-holders who enjoyed considerable autonomy just so long as they delivered resources and compliance to the center. Empires of the time rarely managed to control more than 100,000 square miles (about the size of today's Arizona) for very long. Such states look small compared to the nearly 4 million square miles occupied by today's mainland China. Still, empires covered vastly

Figure 2.2 Descendant of Sargon of Akkad.

larger territories than the typical city-state's 2,000–4,000 square miles; you could have fitted thirty or forty city-states into a single major empire. Forming around 2300 BCE, Sargon's Akkadian realm has a claim to be the world's first empire. One of his descendants is shown in Figure 2.2. But the imperial model of rule eventually multiplied in all the major regions of city-state development.

Meanwhile, **military predators**, such as the Scythians, sometimes had no durable capital city at all, but moved their central authority as defense and conquest dictated. Mounted warriors wielding bows, arrows, lances, and swords constituted their shock troops and enforcers. States moved among the types, notably as conquest of substantial territories transformed city-states (for example, Babylon) or military predators (for example, the Shang's predecessors) into empires. For short periods, a fourth kind of state, the **federation** of city-states, occasionally formed as a defensive measure. But in this period federations always fell apart as the shared threat declined or internal rivalry intensified.

Relations between cities and states varied among the four types of rule. In city-states the city's ruling apparatus ran the whole state, tight integration between urban and rural activity prevailed, while the chief threats to continued rule consisted of external attacks and of splits within the urban ruling class. Empires typically established more contingent, hard-bargained relationships among rulers, urban populations, and the rural peoples of their domains. That made overcoming resistance to central decrees, bargaining with regional power-holders, and putting down peripheral rebellions a larger part of state activity. Military predators fed on cities and their dependent territories, often extracting tribute by threats of sacking, burning, rape, and massacre. Temporary federations always had to deal with the divergent interests or outright competition of their cities' priests, merchants, landlords, and military leaders.

Through all of human history since 5000 BCE, cities and states have carried on a kind of love-hate relationship. On one side, merchants, manufacturers, bankers, and workers have tried to evade governmental control and taxes while still demanding government-backed security for their own enterprises. On the other side, soldiers, priests, and officials have preferred not to contend with unruly city-dwellers but have depended on manufacturing and trade for the revenues to support state activities. Where cities had developed early and widely, aspiring state-builders typically made broad concessions to merchants and manufacturers, if not to workers; the city-state run not by a king but by a council of rich citizens represents an extreme version of that trade-intensive bargain. Where conquest came first, cities grew up in precarious interstices, remaining vulnerable to confiscation and pillage; the predatory state based on nomadic forces represents an extreme version of a political power-intensive bargain. In between, varying balances between economic activity and political power yielded very different systems of rule, as well as significantly different relations between city and country.

2.3 CITY AND COUNTRYSIDE IN THE ANCIENT WORLD

In regions where city-based states dominated the landscape, every city depended on generating and capturing an agricultural surplus in its immediate vicinity. With field grains, such a surplus typically depended on methods that reliably produced yields of at least three times the seed sown: a third or more for the next season's seed, a third or more for local consumption, and up to a third for distribution elsewhere. Agricultural historians often speak of **yield/seed ratios**: if you sow a bushel of wheat and reap three bushels, your ratio is 3:1. Before

the European agricultural revolution that became visible in England and Holland during the seventeenth century, typical yield/seed ratios for barley, wheat, oats, and rye in that already highly productive region ran in the vicinity of 7:1. In Eastern Europe at the same time, ratios remained around 4:1. With the varieties of rice, millet, wheat, and barley grown in the regions of city and state expansion between 5000 and 600 BCE, it is unlikely that yield/seed ratios much exceeded 3:1.

Remember that farmers can't eat or sell all the grain they grow, since they have to save enough as seed for the next season. At ratios of three to one, sheer arithmetic means that a grain-eating population must remain predominantly agricultural. The vast majority of households must raise their own food, and produce small surpluses for transfer to others. Before food reaches the city, furthermore, it disappears into feeding the countryside's non-agricultural population, into wastage, and into the very effort of transporting it to consumers. Once food enters city walls, the rich and privileged take more than their numerical share, but if the rest of the population do not receive an average of 1,500 calories or so per day they do not survive. At low yield/seed ratios, the energy cost of producing and delivering a surplus equal to more than 1,500 calories per day per non-agricultural person radically limits any agricultural region's urban population. These circumstances help explain the combination of heavy dependence of cities and states on productive agricultural regions with high proportions of total population – typically 90 percent or more – in agriculture.

In the ancient world, rivers and canals made the shipping of food from rural to urban areas easier, cheaper, and safer than overland transportation, which helps account for the early concentration of urban development in the Tigris–Euphrates region, the Nile Delta, and river basins of South and East Asia. In all our regions, however, people engineered water flow as cities and states expanded. Canals, irrigation channels, and well-banked rivers became crucial for transportation, watering of crops, sewage disposal, and human water consumption. This helps explain elaborate systems of water regulation and extensive urban controls over nearby farmers.

At least in Mesopotamia, city and country interacted even more intensively than this description implies. Richer and more powerful households commonly included workers who moved back and forth between urban locations and the same households' estates in the surrounding region, engaging in farming, trade, and domestic service depending on the season. In the state of Lagash, a neighbor of Uruk, the ruler's wife maintained her own rural–urban household including gardeners, brewers, cooks, craftsmen, fishermen, herders, and farmers. Household members traded goods from her personal estate far and wide across the Middle East. Just as modern magnates have often maintained city houses and country estates, their Mesopotamian counterparts connected city and country through their own personal activity. Most likely, similar arrangements occurred in Egypt, the Indus Valley, China, and other regions of urban expansion.

This tight interdependence of rural and urban did not, however, keep urbanites from viewing rural people with contempt. In all the ancient world's urban regions, city people anticipated the distinction Romans later made between civilized (city-dwelling) and pagan (country-dwelling). Rural–urban contrasts remained sharp, with literacy, royalty, public ritual, temples, palaces, monuments, and even gods largely situated inside city walls. A cultural boundary grew up between rural and urban people, with distrust across the boundary.

Note the urban and elite slants of the available evidence. Over the three to seven millennia that separate us from the events described in this chapter, the materials that survive with traces of those events are disproportionately stone, hardened clay, bone, or metal rather than paper, wood, cloth, plants, flesh, or packed earth. Urban structures and artifacts have therefore left far more traces than their rural counterparts. What is more, the crucial importance of writing – not only concentrated in cities but focused on urban affairs – imparts a further bias toward cities. Unsurprisingly, archaeologists themselves have flocked to urban sites when they can find them. The resulting historical record greatly underrepresents rural experience. Rural social processes were surely more complex and varied than the way city-dwellers saw and reported them. They certainly involved different intersections of economic activity, political power, and culture. Most likely, for example, rural people maintained their own local religions in addition to – or instead of – worshipping the high gods of cities and kings. But for the time being we must settle for concentrating on connections among cities and states.

Even within cities, the survival of big structures, metal objects, jewelry, and glazed ceramics biases the record toward rich and powerful people. Women and children, furthermore, rarely show up in the available material: fleeting mentions of royal women, priestesses (themselves commonly royal women), royal children, female officials, female merchants, or female parties to lawsuits, and occasional paintings, carvings, or sculptures of women and children in portrayals of daily life. At this distance, we can only imagine the voices of ordinary people, especially women and children. We hear even fewer voices from outside of well-excavated cities.

Still, the evidence that has survived from cities allows us to see important ways in which the lives of cities and states between 5000 and 600 BCE differed from those of our own time. Let us look more closely at the major regions of city and state development before reviewing connections among their histories.

Mesopotamia

Within Mesopotamia, a southeastward shift of innovation and organization seems to have occurred between 7000 and 4000 BCE. Receding waters of the Persian Gulf left a rich alluvial plain and people who already knew how to manage water. By 6000, settled agricultural villages had sprung up over the parts of Mesopotamia, Assyria, Anatolia, and the Mediterranean's eastern end that had access to abundant fresh water from rainfall or nearby rivers. The Middle East's earliest known mud brick village, Jericho, does not lie in Mesopotamia, but in the Jordan Valley above the Dead Sea; its first well-dated remains come from around 9000 BCE. Jericho had a wall, a tower, and enough diversified crafts that some archaeologists consider it to be a city – the world's oldest. Other complex villages from before 6000 BCE have come to light in southern Turkey, Syria, and northeastern Iraq.

Many of the village sites contain crafted objects far from the geographic origins of their raw materials, for example, semiprecious stones, copper, and the volcanic glass called obsidian. These objects provide evidence of extensive connections, and perhaps of well-developed trading systems, across the Middle East's northern and western tiers. By 5000 BCE, however, the region's cultural, political, and economic center of gravity was moving toward southern Mesopotamia. Mesopotamia had the great advantage of intensive agriculture watered by rivers and canals. That meant it could support substantial cities and non-agricultural populations more easily than neighboring regions could. Mesopotamians may also have invented the plow, crucial for efficient production of crops grown from sown seed, some time between 6000 and 5000 BCE. They were certainly using ox-drawn plows widely in the time of Uruk.

Scholars debate whether the substantial towns of Mesopotamia's Ubaid culture (from 5900 BCE onward), such as Eridu and Ur, count as full-fledged cities – as big settlements containing well-defined public spaces, massive buildings, plenty of non-agricultural activity, and clear signs of social differentiation. So long as partial excavations of inhabited sites (rather than written texts) provide our major evidence for urban history, we run the risk of mixing up different periods; later inhabitants commonly built new structures on old foundations, salvaging material from older buildings as they did so. Even radiocarbon dating, for that reason, leaves wide margins of uncertainty. The crucial transition toward city-dominated regions, in any case, occurred in the time of Uruk. People lived continuously at Uruk from around 5000, but the first ruins of major buildings excavated there date from a thousand years or so later, in the temple complexes of Ishtar (goddess of love and war) and of An (god of the sky). Those ruins include splendid pictures of deities, rulers, priests, and ceremonies on walls, seals, and pottery.

Map 2.2 Ancient Mesopotamia

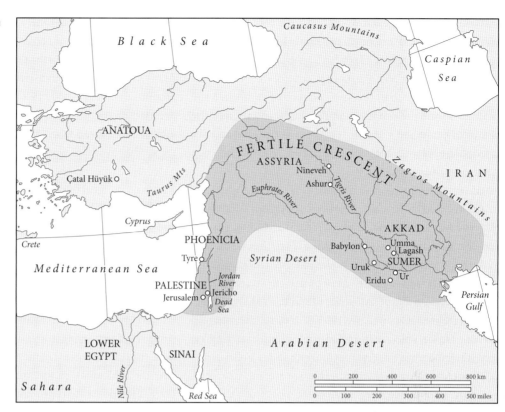

After 5000, southern Mesopotamia combined increasing political influence with expanding commercial connections. No large empire originated in the region; rivalries among prosperous cities blocked that sort of internal unification. But centers such as Uruk, Nippur, and Babylon controlled their immediate surroundings, formed unequal alliances with nearby cities, and exercised political influence far beyond those surroundings. Take, for instance, the little Lagash kingdom, 60 miles or so northeast of Uruk. The state included not only the city of Lagash, but also nearby Girsu and Nina. Although much more extensive empires – Egyptian, Assyrian, Hittite, and others – rose and fell to the north and west of Mesopotamia, in general the rich, urban region between the Tigris and Euphrates produced temporary clusters of city-states and resisted incorporation into externally based empires.

Like Italian city-states of the European Renaissance, such clusters wielded much greater power than their compact size suggests. They often exercised influence, for example, through trading colonies at considerable distances from their capitals. Again like Italian city-states, Mesopotamia's centers unceasingly formed alliances, conquered, lost ground, and warred over intermediate territories. As a result, the political map changed constantly. Not until Sargon of Agade started his conquests in the region toward 2330 BCE did any king succeed in uniting all of Mesopotamia in a single state. Sumerian legend later described Sargon as a foundling. Prefiguring Moses, he floated down the Euphrates in a reed basket, became a gardener, attracted the love of the goddess Ishtar, and became king through her influence. The very myth marked Sargon as an outsider. Mesopotamians resisted him as they did all outside conquerors.

The Akkadian empire endured about a century and a half before disintegrating. Its successor, the Third Dynasty of Ur, dominated much the same territory for another century or so. Kingdoms centered on Babylon – but not all ruled by the original Babylonians! – then waxed and waned from around 2000 to 1150 BCE or thereabouts. Greater unification did not occur until another Sargon (known as Sargon II) incorporated Babylon and Babylonia into his Assyrian empire after his accession in 722 BCE. Even that annexation generated rebellion after rebellion, which in turn incited Assyrian emperor Sennacherib's sacking of Babylon in 689. Assyrian control over Babylonia ended in Assyria's own disintegration within another sixty years. King Nabopolassar of Babylon then boasted:

I slaughtered the land of Assyria, I turned the hostile land into heaps and ruins. The Assyrian, who since distant days had ruled over all the peoples, and with his heavy yoke had brought injury to the people of the Land, his feet from Akkad I turned back, his yoke I threw off.

His successor Nebuchadnezzar of biblical fame conquered Jerusalem in 597 BCE and extended Babylon's political writ elsewhere, but his successors only kept his fragile empire going until the Persian invasion of 539. Persia kept control over the region for two centuries after that. (Persian conquerors authorized the return of Jews from their captivity in Babylonia, and decreed the rebuilding of Jerusalem's Jewish temple at their government's expense.) Mesopotamia was long balanced uneasily between fragmentation and unification.

United or not, the region as a whole spread its influence far and wide. Eventually the cultural styles of southern Mesopotamia prevailed through a much larger region, including Susa in present-day Iran, and Nineveh, across the Tigris from Mosul in today's northern Iraq. Through trade and emulation, pottery, seals, and tablets in southern Mesopotamian styles became familiar to people in Egypt, Anatolia, the Indus Valley, and the eastern Mediterranean as well. By 1900 BCE or so, the southern kingdom of Larsa, which then included Uruk, was carrying on extensive exchanges via the Persian Gulf with Indus Valley cities. Its rich agriculture, opulent cities, extensive trading networks, and splendid crafts made Mesopotamia the object of recurrent, but always temporary, efforts to capture its riches for empires based elsewhere.

Assyria

The name "Assyria" does not apply properly to northern Mesopotamia before the conqueror Ashur-uballit – note his name – built a new empire based on the city of Ashur after 1363 BCE. Ashur overlooked the upper Tigris not far north of where Baghdad stands today. Agriculture developed in Assyria well in advance of southern Mesopotamia. Naturally watered portions of the zone we are calling Assyria – the plains and foothills of today's northern Iraq and Syria – nurtured many grain- and cattle-raising agricultural villages before 9000 BCE. By 7000, villagers of the region inhabited rectangular buildings of packed mud and made sophisticated decorated pottery.

Nothing like cities formed in Assyria, however, until after 5400. The Ubaid culture of southern Mesopotamia then began extending its influence northward. From that date onward, temples, other large buildings, public spaces, and artifacts suggesting urban crafts begin showing up in archaeologists' digs. Even then, the region urbanized more slowly than southern Mesopotamia, and under Mesopotamian influence. At Habuba Kabira on the upper Euphrates, for example, archaeologists have uncovered a religious acropolis ("upper city" in Greek), a fortification wall, and a settlement extending more than half a mile along the river; the site dates from toward 3000 BCE, and contains artifacts very similar in style to those found further

south. About the same time, nearby Tell Brak and Nineveh also showed strong signs of cultural contact with southern Mesopotamia. Further to the northwest, and not far from the Mediterranean, the Mesopotamian-style city of Ebla flourished from around 2500 to 1600 BCE, leaving behind great palaces, temples, tombs, golden sculptures, and thousands of cuneiform tablets. From those tablets, we learn of a wool-processing industry at Ebla in which women did a major part of the production.

In the same era began conquests that shifted the Middle Eastern political balance northward. Sargon of Agade (2334–2279 BCE by one count) began his conquests with Uruk and other parts of southern Mesopotamia. But his troops reached out in all directions: down the Persian Gulf, into the mountains of Iran, and across much of Assyria. His successors expanded the Akkadian empire. King Naram-Sin (2254–2218), for example, boasted that he had sacked Ebla. He left a large building at Tell Brak built with bricks inscribed with his name, a stone relief portraying him in southeastern Turkey, and a victory stele (upright stone monument) in western Iran. With Naram-Sin, the Akkadian empire reached its geographic maximum. Over the next two centuries, it then slowly disintegrated in battles with other ascendant powers from the north, west, and east.

Nomadic Amorites, who probably moved in from Arabia, eventually conquered significant parts of Assyria as well as Mesopotamia, settling into cities and villages as they did so. Shamshi-Adad I, an emperor likely of Amorite origins who ruled the region including Ashur around 1810 to 1780 BCE, left an inscription boasting "a stele inscribed with my great name I set up in the country of Laban [Lebanon] on the shores of the Great Sea." His successor Hammurabi, who died in 1750, left another stele, this one inscribed with the first great code of laws we have from the Middle East. A few centuries later, a first wave of invaders from the steppe beyond the Black Sea and Caspian Sea seems to have helped form the Mittani and Hittite empires that successively dominated important parts of Anatolia and the eastern Mediterranean between 1650 and 1300 BCE. Predatory bands of armed horsemen repeatedly swept in to pillage Assyrian cities only to establish themselves as more sedentary rulers. Through their influence the horse-drawn chariot became a standard royal armored vehicle in the region after 1600 BCE.

As political unification became more common (although still intermittent) in Assyria, trade expanded as well. Judging both from written records and from geographic distributions of traded goods, by not long after 2000 BCE Ashur had become a central location in trading networks extending from the Persian Gulf to Troy, at the very western end of Anatolia, and on into Europe. Trading connections among cities often remained in place longer than the city-states, kingdoms, and empires through which they passed; except for nomadic predators, no one could long sustain a war-waging state without drawing revenues from commercial populations. The Hittite capital of Hattusas in central Anatolia, for example, contained a major colony of merchants from Ashur, located within the city walls close to the Great Temple; the city thrived on its trade until about 1200 BCE. Ashur itself became the base of a major empire, and a barrier to the Hittites' southeastward expansion, after 1500 BCE. Ashur-uballit (1363–1328 BCE) established a kingdom running from the Euphrates into Iran's mountains. Although the period from 1200 to 1000 brought imperial disintegration, Assyria again grew to dominate a large arc of the agricultural area and trading network from present-day Lebanon to southern Mesopotamia. Box 2.2 recounts an Assyrian victory celebration. During that same period, the united monarchy of Israel and Judah was forming in Palestine. Over the next century or so, Israel and Judah repeatedly fought off the Assyrians, generally keeping those easterners from dominating the trading cities that by then ringed the eastern Mediterranean.

Within their territory, Assyrian military men repeatedly built states whose organizational principles stood halfway between the prosperous city-states of southern Mesopotamia and the predatory armies that swept into the Middle East from its peripheries. These states seem to have been more warlike and male-dominated than their neighbors and their predecessors; at least in the laws of the time we find the world's earliest written requirements that aristocratic women wear veils and restrict their social contacts. Perhaps such restrictions reflected a prevailing military culture. Assyrian rulers also practiced deportation of local populations on an unprecedented scale. Scholars estimate that they displaced 4.5 million people in three centuries pivoting on 700 BCE.

Assyria's emperors conducted annual military campaigns that combined conquest and quelling of rebellion with collection of tribute to supply the men, animals, and equipment consumed by their armies. Ultimately the men, animals, and equipment, or the gold and silver to buy them, came from ordinary workers, farmers, merchants, and manufacturers. Assyrian states depended on cities and their trade, but gave political power more weight than their trading neighbors. In all three kinds of state, however, connections of culture as embodied in religion, legend, kinship, and language provided indispensable glue for social relations.

Egypt

If Mesopotamia offered large scope for connections based on economic activity while Assyria gave the edge to political power, Egypt offers a sensational opportunity to watch cultural connections at work. For millennia Egyptian kings not only acted as friends of the gods like their Assyrian and Mesopotamian counterparts, but also claimed to join the company of gods when they died. Later kings actually identified themselves as gods on earth. They and their followers built a significant part of public life around cults of death and ancestors. Kings, queens, and princesses often served simultaneously as priests and rulers. As compared with Assyria and Mesopotamia, Egypt accorded substantial power and visibility to women.

Box 2.2 Ashurbanipal the Assyrian Conqueror

In 877 BCE Ashurbanipal II of Assyria conquered Mount Lebanon and reached the Mediterranean coast. Of these victories he boasted:

I washed my weapons in the Great Sea and made sacrifices to the gods. I received tribute from the kings of the sea coast, from the lands of the men of Tyre, Sidon, Byblos, Mahallata, Maiza, Kaiza, Amurru, and Arvad which is in the sea: gold, silver, tin, bronze, a bronze cauldron, linen garments with multi-colored trimmings, a large female ape and a small female *ape, ebony, boxwood, ivory, and sea-creatures.*

Some of the tribute items surely reflected trading connections of the conquered cities to Africa, via Egypt. When Ashurbanipal founded a new imperial capital at Kalhu (the biblical Calah) on the northern Tigris, he built a huge palace featuring doorways flanked by large stone bulls with human heads. Elsewhere in the palace he placed stone blocks boasting of his hunting prowess: he claimed to have killed 450 lions and 390 wild bulls while hunting from his chariot, not to mention trapping ostriches, bulls, lions, and elephants. Ashurbanipal also had his craftsmen make a stele bearing his portrait and an inscription recounting the emperor's personal exploits, the rebuilding of Kalhu, the palace's construction, and the feast that celebrated its completion. The feast lasted ten days for 69,574 male and female guests who consumed 14,000 slaughtered sheep and 10,000 skins of wine. Kalhu survived until its destruction by the combined force of Medes and Babylonians that smashed Assyria in 612 BCE.

Map 2.3 Ancient Egypt and the Nile

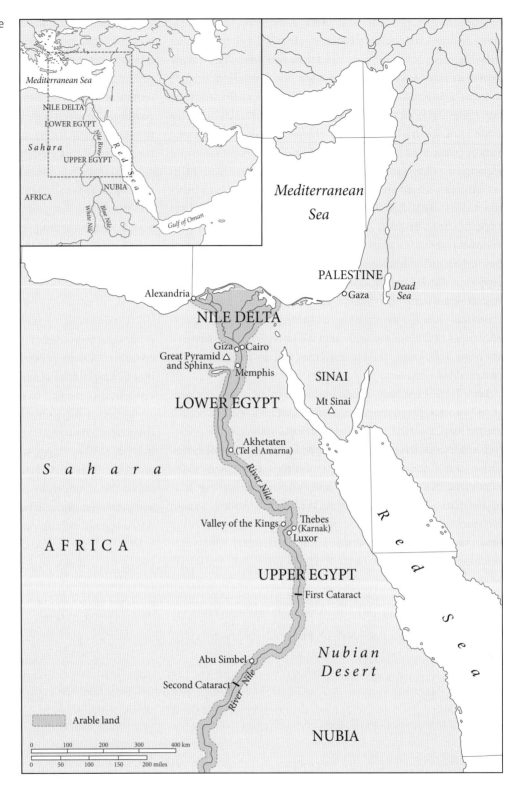

Egypt's physical environment profoundly shaped its history. Ninety-five percent of Egypt's present territory consists of forbidding desert, and the proportions were not much different in 5000 BCE. The Nile flows approximately south to north from origins in present-day Sudan and Ethiopia to a delta on the Mediterranean; within Egypt, it runs for about 1,000 miles.

Historians distinguish Upper Egypt (to the south) from Lower Egypt (including the delta, and to the north). The two regions competed, and recurrently broke into rival kingdoms, one based upstream, the other downstream.

The Nile still dominates Egypt, bringing water and nutrients from far to the south. In prehistoric times, annual summer floods produced a startling contrast between a narrow strip of jungle along the watercourse and broad expanses of barren land on either side. Only in the delta did fertile land widen into more than one or two miles across. As a result, people who learned how to clear heavy brush, dig good wells, build dikes, create irrigation canals, and adjust growing seasons to the river's ebb and flow could produce grains with high yield/seed ratios. The earliest known pictures of Egyptian daily life include people chopping away thick vegetation and kings opening canals. Desert expanses, furthermore, meant that Egyptian settlements were less vulnerable to encroachment and invasion from outside than were the grain-growing city-states of Assyria and Mesopotamia.

Assyria and Mesopotamia have their historical revenge: the flowing Nile destroyed or buried most residues of the ways that Egyptians lived their daily lives on and close to the river. A disproportionate share of the available evidence comes from preserving desert sands. While archaeologists of Assyria and Mesopotamia have dug directly into the central sites of economic activity, political power, and culture, their colleagues in Egypt have concentrated on tombs and memorials built outside the Nile Valley's fertile land. We therefore run the risks both of exaggerating the centrality of death to Egyptian culture and of underestimating the importance of urban settlements in that culture.

The first known signs of farming villages in Egypt date from about 4400 BCE, the first traces of urban settlements from 3100 or so. Both of them concentrated in the narrower portions of the Nile Valley south of today's Cairo. With the development of agriculture came pottery depicting river animals such as hippopotami, crocodiles, lizards, and flamingoes. With the development of cities we begin to see stone portraits of kings, priests, and priest-kings. By that time, unmistakable traces of overland trade with Palestine via the Sinai peninsula show up in the archaeological record.

The timeline shown in Box 2.3 places the development of cities and states in Egypt, which corresponded approximately to the first dynasties, at least a thousand years after similar changes in Mesopotamia. As of 3000 BCE, nevertheless, a unified state controlled the Nile Valley from the delta to the Nile's first cataract at Aswan, some 600 miles up the river. The so-called Palermo Stone, part of an Old Kingdom stele, describes the god Horus as giving the Egyptian throne to King Menes, the first great unifier; that First Dynasty started Egypt's long succession some time between 3100 and 3000 BCE. Menes established his capital in a place called White Wall, most likely near the site of the later pyramids.

If Mesopotamia's political, economic, and cultural center of gravity moved southward toward the Persian Gulf during the first few millennia of cities and states, in Egypt the comparable movement ran from south to north, toward the delta and the Mediterranean. During periods of centralized rule the Egyptian capital, or at least the royal residence, shifted from dynasty to dynasty, but generally settled somewhere near the Nile in the region south of today's Cairo.

By the time of Pharaoh Djoser (2667–2648 BCE), Egyptian rulers had begun building the massive stone pyramids tourists still find awesome today. Those pyramids not only broadcast royal power, but also demonstrated the capacity of the Egyptian state to mobilize and discipline vast amounts of labor. Aligned north and south with startling precision, the placement of pyramids relied on the Egyptians' close observation of sun, moon, and stars to chart the earth, divine affairs, human decisions, and seasons of the Nile. Djoser's pyramid at Saqqara was the world's first large, completed stone building. After Djoser, the custom caught on. Less than a century later, Pharaoh Khufu (2589–2566 BCE) built the largest pyramid of all at Giza. It contains roughly 2.3 million blocks of stone averaging 2.5 tons each. In a nearby pit Khufu's followers placed a huge boat, most likely to carry the deceased king across the sky in the company of gods. The pharaohs of Djoser's and Khufu's times ran a highly centralized state in which all land, goods, and labor theoretically belonged to the pharaoh. Through internal taxation and external conquest the state commandeered vast resources for royal projects.

Spectacularly effective centralization continued for about 500 years, then weakened after 2200 BCE. During later phases of the Old Kingdom, for example, regional administrators began to inherit their offices and exercise direct control over resources

Box 2.3 Periods of Egyptian History

Historians of Egypt commonly divide the ancient historical record into nine periods:

1   Predynastic (5300–3100 BCE)
2   First and Second dynasties (3100–2686)
3   Old Kingdom (2686–2125)
4   First Intermediate (2160–2055)
5   Middle Kingdom (2055–1650)
6   Second Intermediate (1650–1550)
7   New Kingdom (1550–1069)
8   Third Intermediate (1069–664)
9   Late Period (664–332)

Some scholars also locate a Zero Dynasty between 3200 and 3000.

produced within their regions. By then kings could no longer redistribute land, labor, and goods at will. With the declining Old Kingdom began an alternation between periods of state fragmentation (the Intermediate Periods) and new eras of unification (the Middle Kingdom, New Kingdom, and Late Period in Box 2.3 above). During Intermediate Periods, regional rulers often arose and waged war against each other. Ankhtifi, who ruled a region in southern Egypt around 2100 BCE, left a stele declaring that:

> I am the hero without equal; one who spoke freely while people were silent on the day when fear was spread and Upper Egypt did not dare to speak . . . As long as this army of Hefat is calm, the whole land is calm, but if one steps on its tail like that of a crocodile, then the north and south of this whole land tremble with fear.

Ankhtifi did not claim to be king, but he did claim autonomous power in his region, including the power to wage war on his own. Our knowledge of Ankhtifi is exceptional: Because centralized regimes generally produced more abundant and better-kept records, alternation of fragmentation with newly centralized control means that we know much less about what happened during periods of fragmentation.

Still, for ancient Egypt we always know more about political power and culture than about economic activity. Later Egyptian kings often trumpeted their conquests and even claimed to be gods, but they did not boast much about trade and craft production. Because so much of the early Egyptian evidence comes from royal funerary monuments, their contents, and their art, we must infer early trading patterns from two sorts of residues: objects and raw materials in tombs that clearly came from elsewhere, and Egyptian-origin objects found outside of Egypt.

In Egyptian tombs there appear wood, oil, copper goods, jewelry, and pottery revealing exchanges with Lebanon, Palestine, Anatolia, Assyria, Crete, Cyprus, Mesopotamia, and Nubia (the far reaches of the Nile). Egyptian goods likewise show up in all those locations. Turquoise and copper, for example, came from mines worked by Canaanite slaves in the Sinai peninsula. Silver arrived from Anatolia. Malachite and myrrh (respectively a coppery green mineral and a gum resin used in incense or perfume) came from Punt, a country somewhere near today's Eritrea. Punt also supplied slaves, gold, ebony, ivory, monkeys, and baboons, some of which no doubt reached Punt from further down the African coast or across the Red Sea. The brilliant blue stone lapis lazuli arrived all the way from Badakh- shan in northeastern Afghanistan, some 2,500 miles from the Nile. Egypt maintained especially active trade with, or via, the Sinai peninsula and the Phoenician port of Byblos. By the time of the Middle Kingdom (2055–1650 BCE), Egyptians, like their

Mesopotamian neighbors, were using silver as a form of money as well as a decorative metal; that fact in itself indicates extensive trade.

Within Egypt itself, production and exchange of manufac- tured goods such as decorative pottery and tools seem to have prospered in periods of royal decline. The potter's wheel came into use around 2400 BCE, and moved into mass production two centuries later. Although they served as political capitals, cities such as Memphis and Thebes were large enough to generate extensive flows of goods and to sustain specialized populations of craft workers.

Despite the Nile's self-containment, Egyptian rulers warred intermittently with their neighbors, for example rulers of Nubia to the south and of Libya to the west. They also fought off the forces they called Asiatics, a general name for kingdoms to their east and northeast. A mysterious people Egyptians named the Hyksos, probably invaders from Palestine or Lebanon, actually ruled much of the Delta region between 1650 and 1550 BCE, before being driven out by Ahmose, founder of the New King- dom. The term Hyksos simply means "rulers of foreign coun- tries." With the Hyksos, chariots and horses entered Egyptian warfare, a fact that may connect the Asiatics and the Hyksos to predatory bands from the Eurasian steppe that were beginning to invade the Middle East during the half-millennium after 2000 BCE. Later Egyptian kings prided themselves on horsemanship; they paraded, warred, and hunted in horse-drawn chariots.

King Ahmose and his successors not only conquered import- ant parts of Nubia but also carried on extensive military exped- itions in Palestine and Lebanon. A court poet from the time of Pharaoh Merenptah (1213–1202 BCE) composed these triumph- ant lines:

> The princes are prostrate, saying: "Mercy!" Not one raises his head among the Nine Bows [captives]. Desolation is for Tehenu; Hatti is pacified; plundered is Canaan with every evil; carried off is Ascalon; seized upon is Gezer; Yanoam is made as that which does not exist; Israel is laid waste, his seed is not; Palestine is become a widow for Egypt! All lands together, they are pacified. Everyone who was restless has been bound by Merenptah.

Although the poet greatly exaggerated Egyptian power, Gaza and parts of the Mediterranean coast did remain under Egyptian rule until around 1150.

By that time, the so-called Sea Peoples, originating in the Aegean and the eastern Mediterranean, had repeatedly invaded Egyptian territory. During the Third Intermediate Period (1069–664 BCE), chiefs from Libya also frequently ruled parts of the Nile Delta. The eastern Mediterranean was becoming a well-connected, if rarely unified, economic and political system. In that setting, Egypt was never again able to maintain the splendid isolation of its early millennia. For most of the century after 700 BCE, in fact, various Egyptian rulers (especially kings of Kush, in the south) were battling for control of the territory with the ascendant Assyrians, who only lost their overlordship toward 610. Between then and the conquest of Egypt by Alexander the Great (332–323 BCE), Egypt acquired a degree of internal unity, but at the cost of incessant military engagement with Persians and other conquering powers.

Indus Valley

The early civilization of South Asia's Indus Valley poses important puzzles, especially how people co-ordinated their activities, what they believed, and why the civilization disappeared so rapidly. As the British explored India and built railroads during the nineteenth century, they came on mounds full of baked bricks from old cities, which they tried unsuccessfully to identify with places named by earlier travelers. Excavations of those mounds in the 1920s uncovered remains of Harappa, Mohenjo-daro, and other

systematically planned great cities from around 2600 BCE. Eventually, geologists and historians realized that the main axis of the civilization did not follow the present path of the Indus, just below the mountains that separate Pakistan from Afghanistan, but a bygone system centered on the Ghaggar and Saraswati rivers, which then carried water from the Himalayas down to the Arabian Sea near present-day Karachi, Pakistan. The Indus civilization of 2600 to 1900 BCE produced stone seals in a script of 400 to 450 standardized signs that scholars have still not deciphered. They also manufactured beautiful stoneware ceramics and superb bronze implements by processes still poorly understood.

In contrast with Assyria, Mesopotamia, and Egypt, the peoples of the Indus left no signs of large-scale warfare or captive-taking. Nor did they build the great temples and funerary monuments that usually represent priestly power and royal cults. The civilization stressed connections of economic activity and culture, apparently with less political power than prevailed in other early city-state systems. While it flourished, that civilization connected more than 1,500 settlements across an area twice the size of

Map 2.4 Ancient Harappan civilization

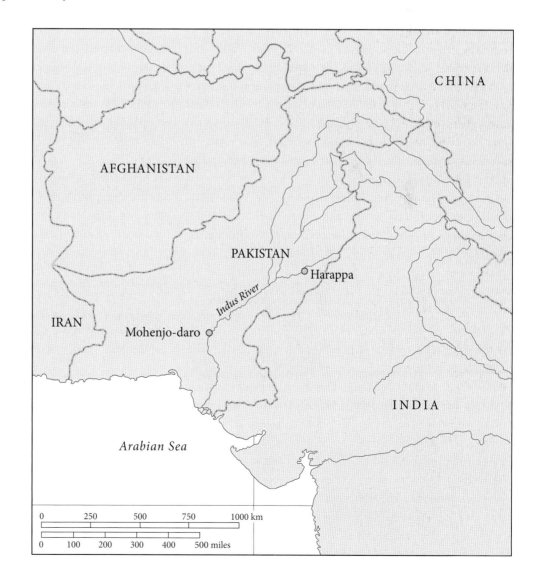

Mesopotamia. Outside of the Indus Valley itself, it extended into today's Afghanistan on the west and covered much of present-day Gujarat to the east. Indus artisans traded goods with Mesopotamians via the Persian Gulf, but worked in styles distinctly their own. After 1900 BCE, many cultural traits persisted, but cities and inter-regional connections declined. In another two centuries, the distinctive Indus script had disappeared as well. No new large-scale urban civilization grew up in South Asia until the formation of the Mauryan empire around 300 BCE.

Signs of settled agriculture first show up in the Indus archaeological record about 6500 BCE, and by 5000 archaeologists find clear evidence of craft production in metal, stone, bone, ivory, and ceramics, as well as trade in craft objects among distant regions. During the spring of 2001, for example, scientists doing water surveys in the Bay of Cambay, Gujarat, discovered foundations of a significant settlement on a former riverbank some 100 to 130 feet beneath the sea. Artifacts recovered from the site included stone tools, semi-precious stones, and pottery fragments. Preliminary dating of the artifacts placed the settlement between 6100 and 5700 BCE. Walled settlements, not yet obviously qualifying as cities, grew up in the Indus Valley and adjacent regions after 3000 or so. They were concentrated heavily along rivers and seacoasts. Toward 2600 writing appeared on seals. By analogy with the Middle East, of course, we should find it unsurprising that the next phase should be a well-connected network of specialized cities, each surrounded by a region of intensive agriculture. But exactly what process created the crucial connections remains unclear.

The Indus people built substantial cities of mud brick, kiln-baked brick, wood, straw, and (more rarely) cut stone. Mohenjo-daro covered 250 hectares, Harappa 150, Rakhigarhi, Ganweriwala, and Dholavira more than 80. Their planners must have used close astronomical observation to lay out major walls, streets, and buildings in neat rectangles oriented north and south. Most likely they aligned their cities to the constellation called the Pleiades, which still occupies the first position in South Asia's traditional astrology. Within cities, the distribution of artifacts indicates the existence of specialized craft neighborhoods for jewelry, ceramics, and other forms of production. At their edges, near city gates, stand spaces for markets and for lodging of caravans. Extensive systems of baths, latrines, sewers, and drainage ditches make Indus cities exceptional among early urban civilizations – and it is tempting to identify them with the ritual bathing that still occurs widely in South Asia.

Standardized weights and measures, as well as widespread use of similar seals in conjunction with long-distance shipments, provide evidence of centralized control over trade within and among Indus cities. The special prominence of animal symbols, notably the ubiquitous unicorn, suggests mediation of trade by networks of merchants linked through kinship, religious ritual, or shared devotion to a totem. The frequent representation of females as powerful, independent figures in Indus art similarly suggests that women occupied relatively significant positions in Indus public life. Altogether, the remains of Indus civilization fit a picture of well-connected, merchant-dominated city-states organized in overlapping trading networks, matrilineal kin groups, and ritual communities.

China

Ancient China offers us two dramatic contrasts with the histories of cities and states we have reviewed so far. First, available literary texts date from much later than the events they relate, but take their

Box 2.4 The Shang Speak with Their Ancestors

The Shang period (roughly 1600–1050 BCE) yields China's first archaeological evidence of substantial cities, centralized states, big armies, chariot warfare, writing, and massive inequality. Judging from excavations of cities and royal tombs, a significant share of Shang public ritual and belief centered on communication with ancestors. One way people communicated with the dead was to place offerings on their graves. Another was to distinguish a royal burial by sacrificing humans, slaughtering animals, laying out riches, and supplying such useful items as chariots and weapons, all to accompany the departed ruler into another world. In both these sorts of one-way communication, Shang people seem to have hoped that ancestors would help them from their positions in the company of gods. A third form of conversation produced more direct answers. Professional diviners applied hot pokers to turtle shells or cattle shinbones to produce cracks, which kings then interpreted as answers to questions they had posed: for example, whether the ancestors were causing a king's current illness, what sorts of offering the ancestors needed, and whether ancestors would intercede with the gods to ask for rain, abundant harvests, or victory in battle. On these "oracle bones" priests often wrote accounts of what happened, and how the ancestors responded. Heat-cracked bones from the Shang period thus become our earliest evidence of Chinese writing.

Map 2.5 Ancient China: a. China in the late Shang Dynasty (c.1600–1046 BCE), b. China in the Zhou Dynasty (1046–256 BCE).

(a)

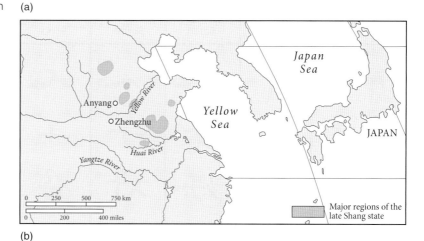

(b)

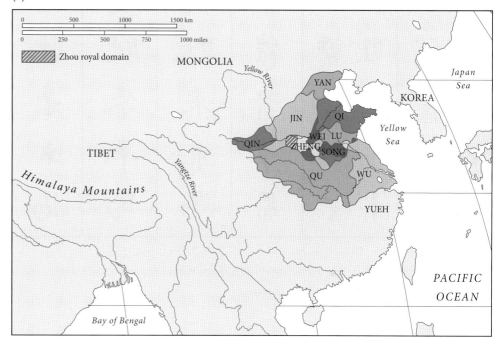

accounts much further back in time than any excavated archaeological sites containing significant residues of city and state activity (see Figure 2.3). In contrast, while waiting for someone to decode Indus texts, we must reconstruct South Asia's ancient history entirely from archaeological remains. Second, political power backed by ritual figures even more prominently in early Chinese civilizations – or at least in the current evidence concerning them – than in Assyria or Egypt. In a region of war and conquest, we must tease information on economic activity and culture from between the lines of soldierly communications, mostly self-serving.

Village-based agriculture developed first in the eastern half of what we now know as China. To the north and west pastoral people prevailed into modern times. Even today, pastoral Mongolia lies just across the Great Wall to the north of today's capital, Beijing. Agricultural villages formed in the Yellow River basin some time between 5000 and 4000 BCE. By 3000 BCE,

rice-growing villages in Shandong (near today's Shanghai and the Yellow Sea) were raising pigs, dogs, cows, goats, horses, and chickens, using wooden plows, and producing pottery. But cities and states were yet to come.

The early Chinese history of cities and states currently sets historians and archaeologists at odds. Later literary texts include extensive accounts of a city-building Xia dynasty running from roughly 2200 to 1600 BCE, but so far well-dated remains only begin with the later Xia period, after 1900 BCE. The later writers created a story of continuity from China's most ancient period to the time of unified empire by beginning with a legendary Yellow Emperor, then continuing through Xia and Shang dynasties to the Zhou and Qin. (We have seen a similar search for continuity in Egypt, where the god Horus was supposed to have put the First Dynasty in place by making Menes king.) In fact, no archaeological evidence so far confirms the existence of the Xia

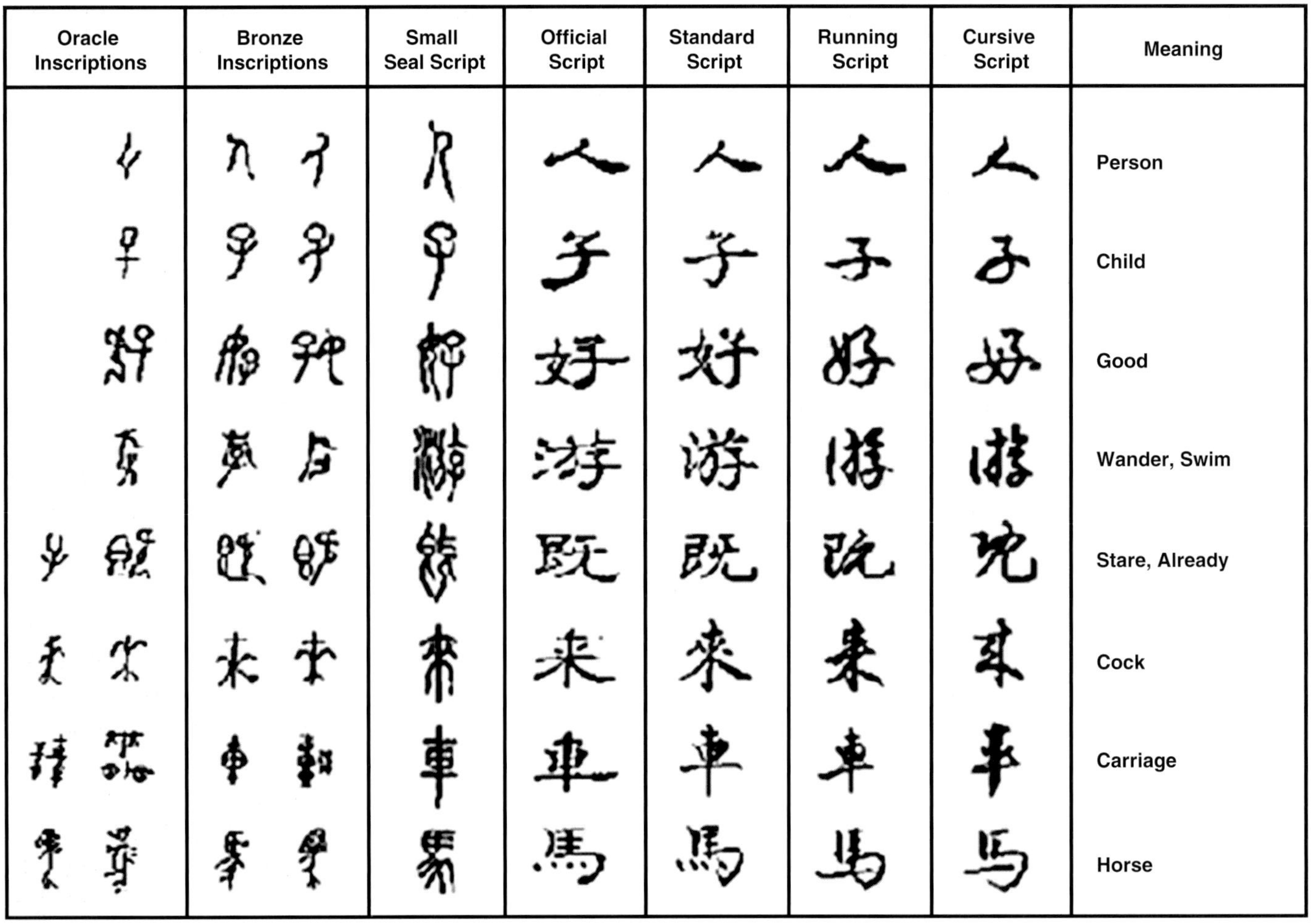

Oracle Inscriptions	Bronze Inscriptions	Small Seal Script	Official Script	Standard Script	Running Script	Cursive Script	Meaning
							Person
							Child
							Good
							Wander, Swim
							Stare, Already
							Cock
							Carriage
							Horse

Figure 2.3 Evolution of Chinese writing. Chinese is one of the world's oldest languages. It has two major dialects: Cantonese and Mandarin. It is based on a system of symbols that represent a complete word or phrase. Over the years spoken Chinese has changed dramatically but written Chinese has undergone much less change.

dynasty, even though today's People's Republic has launched a major project to discover it.

Although classic texts treat Xia as the earliest of the great dynasties that unified much of China, if it existed the kingdom surely had multiple competitors close at hand. According to the texts, the Xia realm formed in the Yellow River's alluvial plain. Like their Mesopotamian, Egyptian, and Indus counterparts, the Xia are supposed to have created extensive water-control systems backed by astronomically based calendars. Legend says that they also developed methods for working bronze into containers, tools, armor, and weapons. Finally, goes the story, King Jie oppressed people so badly that numerous tribes resisted his rule, until Shang Tang carried out the rebellion that ended the Xia dynasty. At that point, archaeological evidence begins to intersect with the literary record.

Literature records the names of thirty-one Shang kings over six centuries, but the extent of their realms surely varied greatly over time. Later historians created a myth of a unified Shang

empire centered in Anyang (modern Henan province) that exacted tribute from surrounding states. Recent Chinese excavations, however, have revealed a great diversity of regional cultures that were quite distinct from Anyang. For a brief period, one northern state may have conquered many outlying regions, but it soon lost control to competing power-holders. China during most of the Shang period now looks more like the interconnected city-states of Mesopotamia than the strongly centralized empires of Egypt. Extraordinary bizarre bronze statues found in two pits of Sichuan show that remarkably different cultures flourished at the same time independently of Anyang. Political power played a smaller role in connecting the Shang than commercial and cultural exchange.

Identifiable Shang artifacts are concentrated in the area of northeast China west of the Yellow Sea, between the Yellow and Yangtze rivers. The artifacts include elegant bronzes and pottery, plus the divining bones and shells that contain the first known examples of Chinese writing. The Shang region contains large, well-watered plains of fine soil, which made farming possible without deep plows and heavy draught cattle. Shang farmers raised rice, millet, wheat, flax, and mulberry trees, the latter for silkworms. But many parts of the Shang countryside swung between flood and drought, which gave an advantage to states that could somehow control water, stock food, and redistribute it over large territories. The Shang apparently improved on Xia practice in all these regards. In the process, they built large cities and formidable armies. By 1200 BCE, they were equipping their armies with horse-drawn wheeled chariots, which probably came to China from nomadic warriors of Central Asia.

Surviving remains of Shang cities include thick walls of packed earth containing palaces, temples devoted to ancestors, and shops producing weapons and sacrificial vessels under centralized supervision. Abundant Shang bronze vessels reflect sophisticated metalworking crafts, considerable concentrations of wealth, and public rituals involving ceremonial use of the vessels. The rituals included human and animal sacrifices in honor of royal ancestors. Shang royal families built splendid tombs, filled them with precious objects, and conducted impressive funerals. Some excavated Shang tombs contain decapitated human bodies as well as chariots apparently buried with their live horses attached; in Tomb 1001 at the Shang capital Anyang, archaeologists have uncovered the remains of seventy-four humans, twelve horses, and eleven dogs, all sacrificed for the burial ceremony.

As compared with the art of the Middle East and the Indus Valley, Shang bronze decorations stand out for their featuring of stylized wild animals rather than domesticated animals, plants, or people; those animals could well represent totems for the male-headed lineages around which the Chinese elite long organized their kinship. As far back as records go, members of those lineages married out. The practice meant that women usually joined their husbands' lineages when they married, and that rulers of adjacent kingdoms often had extensive kinship ties with each other. It also meant that women (who generally left home at marriage) made bigger geographic moves in their lifetimes, on average, than men did.

Around 1050 BCE, warriors of a kingdom called Zhou defeated their Shang overlords and became East China's dominant power. The earliest evidence of Chinese armies including massed infantry with small numbers of horse-drawn chariots dates from this period; the model for that sort of army probably arrived in China via Central Asia. The new style of military organization may well have underlain Zhou's victories over Shang. For their definitive battle against Shang, later texts reported that the Zhou put into the field 300 chariots, 3,000 "tiger warriors" on horseback, and 45,000 armored infantrymen.

Later transcriptions of Zhou texts (perhaps just as mythical as the Gilgamesh epic) describe them as occupying the world's very center, enjoying the **Mandate of Heaven** for their rule. The Mandate of Heaven is a very old Chinese belief that the gods bestowed a right to rule on leaders so long as they governed justly. The widespread acceptance of this reveals the remarkable homogeneity of Chinese cultural belief at an early stage. The texts call their kings Sons of Heaven. Those texts also show kings conquering nearby kingdoms, taking large numbers of slaves, building fortified towns, and incorporating Shang nobles into their own governing structure. From 841 BCE onward, Zhou regimes prepared annual chronicles of events for transmission to posterity, a practice that continued through centuries of Chinese history. In classic imperial style, Zhou rulers parceled out regional control to family members and co-operative local magnates. Inscribed bronzes from their time show kings actively rewarding their followers. By 800 BCE, the system had settled into domains of about 200 lords, perhaps 25 of them major vassals – and potential rivals – of the Zhou king. Where the Shang had been great hunters, the Zhou expanded village agriculture to support their substantial cities.

Both archaeological and textual evidence become much richer for the period 770–256 BCE. Historians often call regimes of that period Eastern Zhou because Zhou rulers, under attack by barbarians in the west, shifted their base closer to the Yellow Sea. The Eastern Zhou never controlled all of North China, and faced increasing competition from adjacent kingdoms as time went on. Within the Zhou regime, partly independent city-states warred incessantly with each other. But like their belligerent contemporaries in Mesopotamia, they also traded increasingly and built up their urban populations.

To the Zhou's south, in the Yangtze Valley, the state of Chu grew up as a rich, powerful competitor with the Zhou. In fact, Chinese tradition treats the years from 403 to 221 BCE (when one of the rival kingdoms, the Qin, completed its conquest of the others) as the Warring States period. In Zhou times, large disciplined armies of infantry, cavalry, and crossbowmen served the greater lords, guaranteeing incessant warfare and frequent rebellion. In order to support the increasingly burdensome military establishment, the more successful lords built up central administrations, installing regular systems of taxation and conscription. They also supported literati who recorded their exploits, handled their correspondence, wrote poetry, and composed distillations of wisdom. Confucius (551–479 BCE) was the most famous in a long series of sages. He was also one of the last apologists for the Zhou order.

Conclusion   Our tales of Mesopotamia, Assyria, Egypt, the Indus, and China have repeatedly overflowed into adjacent areas of Africa, Europe, and Asia. Today's Iran, Turkey, Syria, Lebanon, Jordan, Palestine, and Israel hosted some of the world's earliest agricultural villages and trading towns. By 4500 BCE, village agriculture flourished not only in the regions we have examined, but also in other significant parts of Europe, North Africa, South Asia, and East Asia. Despite its huddling along the Nile, Egypt exchanged goods, cultural forms, and military engagements with all of its surrounding peoples. We have encountered multiple empires based in adjacent territories: Mittani kings dominated the territory northwest of Assyria for a century after 1480 BCE, as Hatti kings northwest of the Mittani, and conquering Hittites later occupied the western half of the Mittani space. Medes made northern Iran their base for conquest after 675 BCE. By 560 they dominated a territory from the Indus to Anatolia, far more than any previous Middle Eastern empire. Nor should we forget the mounted Libyans, Amorites, and Scythians who roared in repeatedly from nearby desert and steppe.

On Crete, Minoan civilization produced its cities and sumptuous art between 2000 and 1400 BCE, with a genuine empire extending its power through much of the eastern Mediterranean and Aegean during the last two centuries. An overlapping Mycenaean civilization flourished in Greece from around 1580 to 1120 BCE, most likely until destroyed by Greek-speaking Dorian invaders from the north. We have seen smaller kingdoms such as Judah and Israel rise and fall along the eastern Mediterranean after 1250 BCE. The leader Moses led his people from Egypt to Palestine some time after 1300 BCE, and his followers created two different kingdoms. Once King David (1006–966 BCE) united the two realms, his forces conquered the remaining city-states of Canaan. His successor Solomon formed a fairly centralized state that lasted until 926 BCE. Phoenicians never established an empire, but after 1000 BCE they established trading colonies as far away from their capital, Byblos, as southern Spain. Dealing with long periods, volatile peoples, and multiple forms of political organization, we cannot possibly contain the history of cities and states within neat regional boundaries.

Commercial connections likewise refused to respect political boundaries. People living somewhere around the Mediterranean's eastern end, for example, learned how to work iron toward 1200 BCE, and within four hundred years artisans were making iron implements from southern France to central Iran and southern Arabia. Extensive trade, probably both seaborne and overland, linked Indus cities and Mesopotamia. Amber from Scandinavia, tin from Spain, and ivory from East Africa all made their way to Lebanon. Workshops in both the Middle East and the Indus Valley used lapis lazuli from upland Afghanistan. After its establishment by Phoenicians in 814 BCE, the Tunisian port of Carthage maintained extensive trading relations with West Africa. By 600 BCE, the region from India and Iran to Greece and North Africa had established an intricate network of economic activity, political power, and culture.

At that point, the Chinese of Zhou were not only battling their neighbors, but also exchanging goods extensively with the populations of Mongolia to the north, with agricultural regions to their south, and very likely with people in Korea and southern Japan as well. Since village agriculture was underway in the Philippines, Indonesia, and other parts of Southeast Asia before 3000 BCE, it is possible that Chinese traders were already establishing their presence in the Pacific and Indian oceans well before 600 BCE. When the Asian archaeological record has received as much attention as has gone into the Middle East, much more extensive commercial connections will surely come to light.

The greatest mystery, however, concerns possible connections among all the early civilizations across the Eurasian steppe. Recent archaeological digs in Turkmenistan and Uzbekistan have turned up evidence of city life in the regions north of Iran before 2200 BCE; the unknown inhabitants of those Central Asian cities may even have had their own system of writing. Elsewhere on the steppe, mobile peoples from Manchuria to Hungary rarely built cities or left concentrations of artifacts for archaeologists to dig, yet their movements obviously affected all the agricultural populations to their south. Since the horse and chariot, originating in the steppe, had become part of military and royal displays in all the ancient civilizations by 1200 BCE, nomadic kingdoms clearly influenced their neighbors across the expanse of Eurasia and North Africa. Could they also have transmitted innovations in writing, crafts, and warfare? If city-based civilizations were beginning to form quite independently in the Americas, by 600 BCE their Eurasian counterparts had all established some connections, direct or indirect, with each other.

Study Questions

(1) Why and how should we pay attention to ancient myths such as the story of Gilgamesh?

(2) What were the biggest changes in human experience that occurred across Eurasia between 5000 and 600 BCE?

(3) Who built city walls, and what advantages did they get from the walls?

(4) Where and when would you place the invention of writing? Why there and then?

(5) What were the main obstacles to building big, unified states in Eurasia before 600 BCE?

(6) Where did horse and chariot warfare first develop, and what difference did it make?

(7) How did trade connect ancient cities and states? What major regional differences occurred in that connection?

Suggested Reading

PAUL G. BAHN AND COLIN RENFREW, *The Cambridge Illustrated History of Archaeology* (Cambridge University Press, 1999). Archaeology features here not as dusty specimens but as the lively history of human discovery.

JOHN BAINES AND JAROMIR MALEK, *Cultural Atlas of Ancient Egypt* (New York: Facts on File, 2000). This work provides beautifully illustrated summaries of art, artifacts, history, and geography, complete with exceptional maps.

CAROLINE BLUNDEN AND MARK ELVIN, *Cultural Atlas of China*, rev. edn. (New York: Facts on File, 1998). In the same series as the Baines and Malek book on ancient Egypt, this book locates Chinese history firmly in its geographic context.

JEAN BOTTÉRO, *Everyday Life in Ancient Mesopotamia* (Baltimore: Johns Hopkins University Press, 2001). These elegant, informative essays cover food, love, sex, sin, magic, medicine, and much more.

PATRICIA BUCKLEY EBREY, *The Cambridge Illustrated History of China* (Cambridge University Press, 2010). Not just early China, but all Chinese history, is lavishly described.

GORDON JOHNSON, *Cultural Atlas of India* (New York: Facts on File, 1996). Another book in the cultural atlas series (see Baines and Malek, and Blunden and Elvin), it situates South Asia's long history in its geographic and cultural settings.

Glossary

city-state: A state with its administration based in a single capital controlling enough rural territory to feed its non-agricultural population.

cuneiform: Mesopotamian wedge-shaped writing produced by writing with sticks in wet clay.

diviners: Future-tellers. In Shang China, for instance, they applied heat to cattle bones and turtle shells, producing cracks that kings read as communication with ancestors.

empire: A state with a central administration (sometimes centered on a single city) and subordinate regions, but relying heavily on regional power-holders.

federation: A league of city-states, formed for defensive purposes, and falling apart after the shared threat receded or under pressure of internal rivalry.

Fertile Crescent: Region of early agriculture from the Persian Gulf through Anatolia to Egypt.

Mandate of Heaven: A Chinese emperor's god-given right to rule. His mandate was valid so long as he governed well and fairly.

military predators: A people who had no durable capital city but moved their central authority as military contingencies dictated.

pictograph: A word-picture giving a stylized, standardized representation of an object.

state: A form of government with: means of coercion (usually an army); organization independent of kinship and religious relations; a defined area of jurisdiction; and priority over all other forms of organization in that area.

trust network: Webs of connection enabling sufficient trust for engaging in high-risk socially contingent activities such as long-distance trade.

yield/seed ratio: How much grain finally grows from the planting of a given amount of seed; for example, three bushels of grain from one bushel of seed is a yield/seed ratio of 3:1.

ziggurat: A kind of monumental tower built by rulers in Sumer.

3 People on the move

Western Eurasia	
c. 4000 BCE	In the steppes of the southern Ukraine, humans apply the bit to horses' teeth.
3500–3000 BCE	Horseriding people disperse from the southern Ukraine.
c. 3300 BCE	Date of "Ice Man," a prehistoric body found preserved in Alpine ice in 1991.
3100 BCE	First wheeled vehicles.
3000–1500 BCE	Abraham leads his people out of Ur in Sumer to Canaan (Palestine).
c. 2300 BCE	Amorite pastoralists seize Mesopotamian cities.
2000 to 1700 BCE	Charioteers from Central Eurasia called Aryans move into northern Iran, Afghanistan, the Indus Valley in modern Pakistan, and North India.
c. 2000 BCE	Date of oldest mummies of Tarim Basin. Oldest surviving chariot. Urban life begins to flourish in central Anatolia.
1750 BCE	Kassites attack Babylon.
1749 BCE	Amorite Shamshi-Adad I takes the throne of the Assyrian empire.
1700 CE	Hyksos use horse-drawn chariots to invade Egypt.
c. 1650–1200 BCE	Hittite empire in central Anatolia.
1600 BCE	Great palace built at Mycenae in southern Greece.
1400 BCE	Mycenaeans destroy Minoan civilization of Crete.
1375–1355 BCE	Suppululiumas I, Hittite king, receives marriage proposal from queen of Egypt.
1300–1250 BCE	Hebrew tribes leave Egypt to return to Canaan.
c. 1285 BCE	Hittites fight Egyptians in Battle of Qadesh.
1260 BCE	Collapse and burning of walls of Troy.
1230 BCE	Joshua leads Hebrews west across Jordan River.
1200 BCE	Sea Peoples attack Egypt.

1180 BCE	Troy sacked again.
1020–1000 BCE	Reign of Saul, first king of Hebrews.
c. 1000–900 BCE	First use of horseriding in battle.
1000–500 BCE	Compilation of Hebrew Bible.
965–931 BCE	Reign of Solomon, king of Israel.
c. 900 to 800 BCE	Cimmerians in steppes of southern Russia and the Ukraine.
c. 800 BCE	Final composition of Homeric epics.
723 BCE	State of Israel destroyed by Assyrians.
650 BCE	Scythians displace Cimmerians.
587 BCE	Babylonians eliminate state of Judah, in southern Palestine, and deport the population.
513 BCE	Darius, king of Persia, attacks Scythians.
Eastern Eurasia	
c. 1500–1100 BCE	Shang dynasty of China.
1200 BCE	Chariots appear in Anyang, capital of Shang.
1045 BCE	Zhou warriors conquer Shang from the West.
771 BCE	End of Western Zhou under barbarian invasion.
463–222 BCE	Era of Warring States.

"Call me the Ice Man, or Ötzi for short. Austrian mountain climbers found me under a glacier high up in the Alps in 1991. Now you can see me, big as life, preserved in a museum in Northern Italy. Don't I look like myself? What was I doing up there? I won't tell, and you can't know for sure. But from what I was carrying and how I died, you can find out what it was like to live in the fourth millennium BCE. Yes, I was born 5,300 years ago, and by good luck for archaeologists, my body is still around today."

If it had not been for global warming, which melted the high Alpine glaciers, we would never have found the Ice Man. But with modern scientific techniques, we can study the Ice Man's life, which was long before written documents appeared, in extraordinary detail. One thing we know is that he was on the move. No one could live in the high Alps permanently, then or now. Most intriguing, he died because someone shot him in the back. The flint arrowhead is still embedded in his shoulder. Was he a raider fleeing the law, a trader involved in a commercial dispute, a policeman killed by a thief, or a villager in a feud? We can't tell, but we can be sure that many others like him moved all across Eurasia for a whole variety of reasons from earliest times.

"Call me the Beauty of Loulan. My body was found in the desert sands of the **Tarim Basin** (deserts in Turkestan, Central Asia), and now I am in a museum in far western China. The extremely dry sands prevented my body from decomposing, so you can see me real as life, buried with my clothes, my jewels, my cap, and my little child. I am four thousand years old, but I can tell you, our people did not originate here. We came from the West, and we brought evidence of our home with us. Look at our big noses, our fair hair, our blue eyes, and our textile patterns, which look just like those of the Celtic peoples of Ireland! Where do you think we came from?"

This chapter argues that a new, mobile form of production, called **pastoral nomadism**, emerged as an alternative to settled agriculture when certain peoples in the grasslands and deserts learned to domesticate horses and camels and base their living mainly on herds of animals rather than food grains. It also examines the effects that population movements, by land and by sea, had on the settled societies around them.

The three great themes of this book – politics, exchange, and social life – all shaped these movements. Armies and states drew people in, organized them, and drove others out. Commercial links lured adventurous traders like Ötzi out on dangerous mountain paths in search of new markets and new goods. And social organizations, like the oasis societies of the Tarim, or the nomads of the steppes, decided whether some people would stay where they were born, or move on. The hunter-gatherers of Chapter 1 also moved across the continents, but in small groups, at a slower rate. In this period, as we approach the time of written records and urban society (see Chapter 2) and beyond, several things changed:

- Larger bands of people moved in more organized ways, and left bigger traces.
- These peoples brought with them their own languages and social practices, and mixed them with those of other peoples in the places they went.
- Some broke away from settled agriculture, to live mainly off herds of animals.
- Those who could domesticate the horse and attach it to carts gained tremendous advantages in mobility and military power over those who could not.
- By the end of our period, around 600 BCE, a full-fledged alternative social organization to cities and agriculture, nomadic pastoralism, had spread across the steppes of Eurasia. Nomadism would decisively shape the history of the entire continent for the next two millennia.

3.1 THE ICE MAN, THE MUMMIES, AND THE HORSEMAN

The Ice Man is one of the oldest preserved human bodies in the world. Archaeologists have examined intensively his clothing, the artifacts he carried, his DNA, and his body organs. Many mysteries remain, but the Ice Man has revealed an extraordinary amount about human life in the fourth millennium BCE. We can tell by the things he carried that he belonged to a society which produced textiles, medicines, and tools, and we know by the way he died that this society already contained conflict. The Ice Man literally embodies the central themes of this book: trade, mobility, violence, and the bonds of human societies across the planet. Box 3.1 describes how historians and archaeologists reconstruct past societies by combining textual, material, and human remains.

The mummies of the Tarim Basin tell us that humans can live in very inhospitable places (the weather was definitely much wetter there in the past than it is now, but it was just as hot). Not only that, but they have been looking for new places to live for millennia. Their bodies, clothing, jewelry, and goods tell us much. The "Beauty of Loulan," shown in Figure 3.1, lies beside a winnowing basket, used to separate wheat chaff from grain, and dyed woolen goods. The sheep and the wheat had to come from the Middle East. Amazingly enough, the bodies of the Tarim mummies look very similar to the Ice Man. The

weave of these mummies' clothing resembles most closely the very distinctive styles of the Celts of ancient Europe. Most intriguing of all, we have texts in an extinct **Indo-European** language from the very same oases dating from the seventh century CE, and this language shares features not with nearby Persian or Indian languages, but with Celtic and Latin. Could these be the same people who migrated there thousands of years ago, and could this be the language they spoke? It's tempting to think so.

Evidence of early drug use can be found in the **Oxus civilization** that flourished in the great Central Asian valley of the Amu Darya River, then known as the Oxus. These graves contained a fascinating item: twigs of the plant ephedra, the base of the modern drug ephedrine. In the temple complexes of the Oxus civilization in modern Turkmenistan there are special white plastered rooms close to the central shrine where jars of ephedra and hemp are found together. Smoking hemp (the same as modern marijuana), of course, creates hallucinations. Both ancient Iranian and Indian sources mention a sacred drink called **soma** or **haoma**, that gives access to the spirit world, a world more real than the world we live in. Ephedra was probably added to the drink to keep the ritualists awake while they had their visions. The Tarim Basin people didn't have hemp, but they kept the ephedra for symbolic purposes: it was their guide to the other world. This is another piece of evidence linking them to the west.

These tantalizing hints show that the human family has always been in motion, from when *Homo sapiens* first left Africa until our time of jet travel. Technological advances have made travel much quicker, but the essential motives have stayed the same: to trade goods and knowledge with others, to settle new lands, and, sometimes, to conquer others. Even those many people who stayed close to their villages or towns did not escape the influence of those who traveled far and wide. They bought goods from far away, heard stories from across the continent, and suffered from distant and nearby wars.

From almost the beginning of settled agricultural life in the ancient Near East, certain groups explored alternatives to remaining fixed to the soil, depending only on their plants. Some of them, called **pastoralists**, depended more on the products of their animals, mainly sheep and goats, than directly on the soil. They moved from place to place seeking pasturelands at the edges of village communities. Farmers might join them when severe drought struck their fields or armies forced them to flee. Later written accounts, by urban scribes, viewed these nomads as utterly alien, because they were beyond the state's control, but often the sedentary and nomadic life mingled together. Each group had unflattering things to say about the other, but they could not avoid mutual contact.

Box 3.1 How Do We Know What We Know: What Things Survive?

Before the invention of writing, we can only know about the peoples of many parts of the world by the artifacts they left behind: their houses, their pots, their clothing, their weapons, and, sometimes, their own bodies. Only a tiny fraction of any of these items will ever survive to our day. Nearly all human bodies decompose rapidly, because micro-organisms turn us back into dust. Only where the air is very dry, high in frozen glaciers, or deep in desert sands, will a body survive intact. Thus only very remote places preserve whole bodies from ancient times. (Egyptian "mummies" are actually not intact bodies: the internal organs were removed, and the embalming fluids did not completely prevent decomposition.)

Bones are easier to find, but often only the wealthiest people's bones survive, protected by deep tombs. The poor, in shallow graves, had their bones dug up and scattered. The lavish tombs of ancient nobles and kings tell us what the rich could do, but not nearly so much about ordinary people. City plans and old walls may include poor quarters as well as temples and palaces; trash heaps (called "middens") include many of the common objects that people threw away, usually broken in little pieces (called "shards").

Broken ceramics (potsherds) are the most abundant pieces of evidence at any site. They have the unique properties of being man-made objects which are long-lasting, but fragile, so they are frequently thrown away, soon after they are used. Unlike valuable metal objects, which can sit around as collectors' items for a long time, potsherds give quite precise sequences of dates. Carbon-14 analysis cannot date ceramics, but can assign dates to wood and other organic materials, if they survive. Flint arrowheads are great collectors' items now, but if they are taken from their original site, or counterfeited, scholars get confused. Metals get melted down much of the time. Only valuable ritual objects made of bronze tend to last (unless the tombs are looted). In the "Bronze Age" very few people actually used bronze, but it forms much of the evidence. Iron became much cheaper, much more widespread, but more often melted down. Wood, bamboo, etc., decompose very rapidly, except in very dry climates. Often we have the mistaken impression that "nothing happened" for a long time in tropical regions, but the main reason for this misunderstanding is that documents and tools decayed very rapidly in moist environments. Just as much "history" happened there as anywhere else, but we can't find it out.

Likewise with writing: What survives is never a random sample of what was written. Most writing in the past, as now, served practical, routine needs of administration and trade. We tend to think of ancient societies as highly ritualized, because little of the routine material survives, while the religious specialists carefully preserved their sacred texts. Ancient religion, however, was embedded in the ordinary practices of daily life.

For the mobile people of this chapter, traders and nomads, evidence is particularly hard to come by. They carried nearly everything they owned with them; they used it up; and they threw it away. But if a Chinese silk cocoon turns up in an Egyptian tomb, for example, we know that someone must have brought it there. Comparing different metallic alloys can show which mines produced different objects. Underwater archaeology in the deep sea, using robot-operated submersible vehicles and sonar, has brought ancient shipwrecks to light that show us where ancient traders went.

The global trends of the last few decades have made it possible for us to find out about the most distant human past. Without global warming, the hikers would never have found the Ice Man in the deep Alpine glaciers. Without the end of the Cold War, Russian, Central Eurasian, and American archaeologists could not co-operate in investigating the horseriders and mummies. Modern DNA analysis of ancient corpses will provide rich information about the complex linkages among human beings that are invisible in written records, just as genetic analysis of modern peoples reveals an amazing amount about ancient migrations. Like a circle turning back on itself, globalization today exposes the traces of motion and communication of long vanished peoples.

3.2 WHY DID SOME PEOPLE LEAVE AGRICULTURE TO BECOME PASTORALISTS?

By *c.* 3000 BCE substantial pastoral life had developed in the Zagros Mountains of western Iran, just as major cities and states were forming in Mesopotamia. Perhaps both styles of life grew together, as states extended irrigated agriculture to drier areas, and herders moving between dry and wet fields branched off to create an economy relying on animals alone. Even without the horse or the camel, these pastoralists, because of their mobility, could separate from city-states and move beyond their control, and the city-state rulers saw them as serious threats. Around 2300 BCE, the tent-dwelling Amorites, the earliest

Figure 3.1 The Beauty of Loulan. This female mummy, discovered in the desert of modern Xinjiang in West China, is at least four thousand years old. She has Caucasian features, and the winnowing basket beside her indicates that these people in West China ate foods closely resembling those of the wheat-eating populations of the Middle East and Europe.

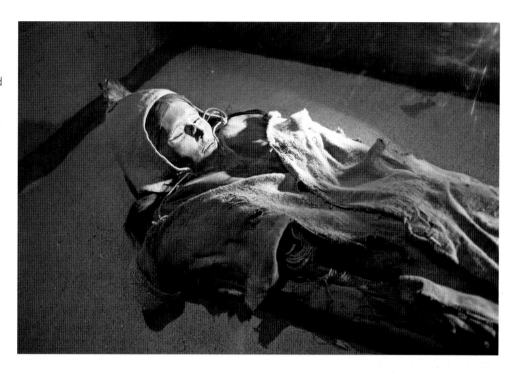

well-documented group of pastoralists, took control of several Mesopotamian cities, either by force or by invitation. In 1749 BCE the Amorite Shamshi-Adad I took control of the region of Ashur, which later became the core of the Assyrian empire. Even the famous Hammurabi of Babylon had tent-dwelling ancestors. The best-known now of these early settlers, since they have kept their identity to the present day, are, of course, the **Israelites**. They, too, were nomadic herdsmen who lived in tents and occupied poor hill country in the Holy Land.

When humans could only walk from one place to another, limited energy and food forced them to move slowly and carry very little with them. The first great leap forward in transport and communication occurred when humans learned to ride animals, especially the horse. We now know that as early as 4000 BCE, in the steppes of the southern Ukraine, humans applied the bit to horses' teeth. The people there depended heavily on horsemeat and domesticated animals, and they worshipped the horse in religious cults. From around 3500 to 3000 BCE, this group of horseriders began to disperse from their homeland, first to the east, then to the west. Having the horse made them very powerful. They could trade over vast distances and raid settled villagers with impunity.

At about the same time, the Arabs learned to domesticate the camel, allowing them to cross fierce deserts from oasis to oasis. They created trade routes for incense and spices from southern Arabia to Syria, Palestine, and Mesopotamia. By the ninth century BCE they were using one thousand camels in their armies.

The second vital technology was the invention of the wheeled vehicle, around 3100 BCE. Heavy wagons then took a long time to evolve into light chariots. The oldest surviving chariot dates from about 2000 BCE. It was buried in a tomb east of the Ural Mountains in Russia which connects it to fortified settlements, bronze implements, and the cult of the horse. The first people who hitched the domesticated horse to the wheeled chariot gained immense power. Now they could carry large loads of goods, brandishing heavy weapons, moving quickly across vast grasslands, dominating all before them. No wonder they buried entire horses and chariots in their graves to celebrate this resource, equivalent to possessing the nuclear weapon of their day.

Although horses, chariots, and warships made mobility possible, they were not its driving forces. These people moved into neighboring regions for many reasons: to gain power by conquest, to trade valuable goods, or to spread new religions. More often than not, they probably "oozed in" by making alliances with poweful local leaders who found them helpful. But the settled writers who created our documentary sources tended to see all of them as cruel invaders who only thought of battle. We have to look beyond the literal words of our sources to find out what they really wanted.

3.3 FINDING LANGUAGES WITHOUT WRITING

Dead bodies do not speak. Without written texts, we cannot be sure what language these people spoke. Unlike the settled civilizations of Mesopotamia and Egypt, which have left us the inscriptions of clerks and priests, the mobile peoples of Eurasia traveled light, without clay tablets. Yet the discipline of historical linguistics, by examining systemic linkages between modern and ancient languages, has indirectly reconstructed the structure and vocabulary of languages before the advent of writing. The one we know best is called **Proto-Indo-European**, the ancestor of English, Russian, Sanskrit, Iranian, Hindi, and many other modern languages. (Figure 3.2 charts the Indo-European language family.) From its vocabulary, we know that the speakers of this language were familiar with temperate fauna and flora, horses, sheep, and wheeled vehicles. Scholars still debate the location of the homeland, but the most likely candidates are Anatolia in central Turkey, the Caucasus, or the southern steppes of the Ukraine. Given what we know about the origins of the horse and the wheeled vehicle, it is most plausible to assume that the Proto-Indo-Europeans originated in the same place, the southern steppes of the Ukraine. They were the first pastoral nomads, living off animals, not fields of grain, moving constantly with their herds and possessions in search of better pastures. They may have moved there from the marginal agricultural regions to the south, or from the forests of the north, as early as the seventh millennium BCE. In the third millennium BCE they moved west into Europe and pushed east of the Urals. This is the most likely story of how the Caucasian mummies turned up in Turkestan.

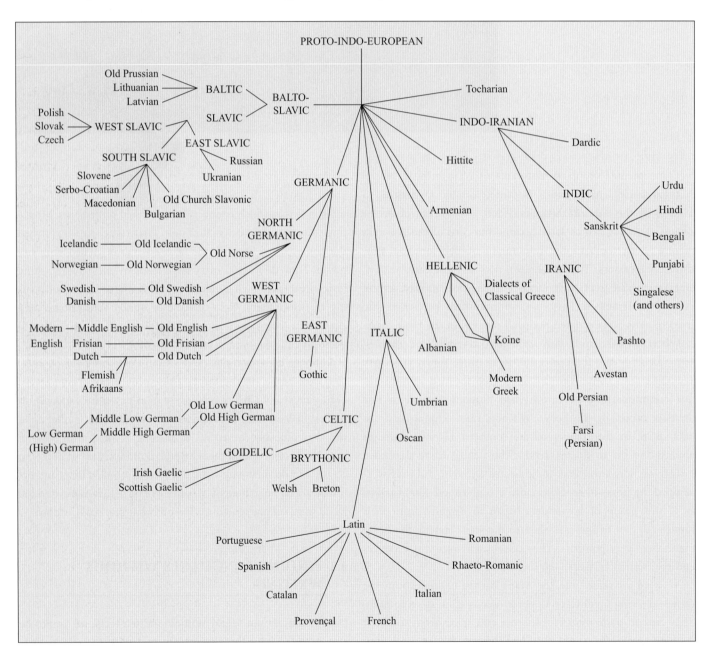

Figure 3.2 Over fifty modern languages, and many classical and extinct languages, descend from a single ancestral language, reconstructed with linguistic techniques as Proto-Indo-European. This chart shows the genetic relationships between the ancient and modern languages that belong to the Indo-European family.

The Indo-Europeans were a linguistic community, not a racial one. They spoke the same language, but they did not necessarily form a common ethnic or kinship group, any more than modern Americans do. It's especially important to keep this distinction in mind, because the nineteenth-century European scholars who discovered the common roots of the Indo-European languages misused their knowledge in damaging ways, to justify European imperial conquest of the "backward" non-Indo-European peoples, and later, under the Nazis, to assert the racial superiority of "Aryans" over all others. The Nazi **swastika**, a reversed version of an ancient Sanskrit symbol, shows how innocent religious emblems can be perverted to horrific ends.

3.4 THE CHARIOT CHANGES WARFARE

By 1750 BCE the horseriders appear in written records. In 1750 the Kassites attacked Babylon; in 1700 the Hyksos used horse-drawn chariots to invade Egypt. No one missed the importance of this invention: the chariot became the great fighting weapon of the Middle East, used by the Assyrians, the Hittites, and the Mycenaeans, Homer's warriors at **Troy**, a city on the northwest coast of Turkey, besieged by the Greeks in the *Iliad*. The invaders called "Aryans" came to India around the same time. When the Hittites fought the Egyptians in the great Battle of Qadesh, around 1285 BCE, over three thousand chariots fought on each side. China's mass chariot attacks came somewhat later.

The horseriders forced the settled civilizations to develop active responses to ward off attack. Their raids stimulated movements of peoples all around the ancient Middle East. These horseriders had discovered a new way of life, radically different in its principal features from the urban, settled societies which they attacked. Pastoral nomadism combined cultural elements in a distinctive fashion which remained remarkably powerful and consistent until the sixteenth century CE. The basic elements were:

- High mobility, made possible by the domestication of the horse.
- Liberation, at least in part, from the demanding labor of digging the ground and sowing plants. Instead, the nomads lived off herds of animals, which they drove from place to place regularly to find grass.
- A society of warriors, whose men were highly skilled at mobile, rapid attacks on horseback.

Such people terrified and mystified the peasant agriculturalists and kingdoms who were their victims. They left almost no written sources of their own, so we depend almost entirely on the biased accounts of their enemies, who saw them as nothing

but "barbarians" (both Greek and Chinese writers used this term for nomads, whom they saw as literally subhuman). Yet nomadism had its own powerful attractions for people who could survive the rigors of life in the grasslands. Pastoral societies tended to be more egalitarian than urban settlements, and probably healthier. Since the grasslands supported less dense populations, epidemic diseases could not spread as fast. Anyone who did not like the rule of one warrior-king in the steppe could set out on his own, with a little help from his friends, and establish his own tribe. The pure nomad, completely unattached to the land, was rare, but an ideal: he prized his freedom and despised the earthbound peasant, who in turn feared him as a savage.

Settled and Nomadic Interactions

The two ways of life could mix in practice: nomads often tilled small plots of land as insurance against loss of herds; and peasants on the edge of the steppe could abandon their poor fields and turn into nomads from time to time. Most pastoralists only wanted to raid settled societies, not rule them: they admired many goods produced in cities, and used them to create their most valuable artifacts, such as the fabulous golden carings of animals shown in Figure 3.3. Kings, in turn, recognized the value of their ultimate military weapon, the chariot, and tried to attract nomadic warriors into fighting for them.

Figure 3.3 Pastoral peoples depended entirely on animals for their livelihood, so their arts naturally featured horses and other powerful animals to symbolize their importance. They obtained gold and other metals by trading with and raiding settled civilizations, and their craftsmen produced small but highly refined carvings which could easily be carried from place to place.

The two styles of life, one mobile, one settled, confronted and mingled with each other over centuries. The "invasions" recorded so often in the texts could just as easily be commercial deals gone bad, or conflicts between two settled states employing nomad mercenaries, not necessarily wholesale invasions by the steppe peoples. There was often no one decisive battle, but an extensive series of engagements, including migrations, trade relations, and gradual cultural osmosis. Instead of reducing the pastoral–agrarian relationship to nothing but war and rapine, we would do better to see it as including all the means of human intercultural interaction, from the most violent to the most idealistic. These mobile chariot people brought new ideas with them as well as horses and warriors. Let us look at the some of the effects of these "invasions" in more detail.

3.5 THE INDO-ARYANS

From around 2000 to 1700 BCE, charioteers from Central Eurasia moved into northern Iran, Afghanistan, the Indus Valley in modern Pakistan, and North India. By *c.* 1000 BCE the invaders had reached Delhi. They described themselves as *arya*, meaning "noble" (the origin of the modern "Iran"), and they spoke an Indo-European language, the ancestor of Sanskrit, modern Persian, and North Indian languages. The old Harappan/Indus River cities had already declined under catastrophic attacks of flood and earthquake, and the invaders finished them off, replacing this culture with their own new beliefs. Through oral recitation, priests passed down the Aryan sacred hymns for centuries before they turned into written form as the most ancient Persian and Indian religious texts, the **Avesta** and the **Rig Veda**. These texts reflect the society of the early conquest period. The Vedic traditions include the worship of major gods of nature: Indra, the war and thunder god; Varuna, the lord of the sky and of waters; Agni, the fire god; and Soma, lord of the sacred juice. The Aryans practiced clearly pastoral rituals, including horse sacrifice, and loved chariot-racing, heavy drinking, singing, and gambling. Their hymns exalt patriarchal warriors and demean women. In India, they reinforced the division of people into four categories, or **varnas** (literally, "colors"): Brahmins (priests), Kshatriyas (warriors), Vaishyas (commoners), and Shudras (low-class "dark" peoples). Their great historical epic, the *Mahabharata*, in 100,000 lines (over six times the length of the *Iliad*), describes the battles, loves, and intrigues of gods and goddesses, kings and warriors. It probably refers to wars conducted in the tenth century BCE among these warrior castes.

Where did the Indo-Aryans come from and how did they get to India? Recent excavations of an entirely distinct, hitherto unknown Bronze Age civilization in modern Turkmenistan have provided a crucial key to this mystery. From 2200–1700 BCE, the Oxus civilization, centered on oases south of the Amu Darya (or Oxus) River, in modern Turkmenistan, created the classic institutions of the agrarian city-state: fortified settlements surrounded by up to three walls, irrigation agriculture, citadels, and graves with valuable goods made from copper, bronze, and precious stones. These included seal carvings of mythological figures arranged in a narrative form, images of narcotic plants, and a series of symbols connected to Indo-Iranian mythology. There is also evidence of the horse culture brought from the steppe nomads of the **Andronovo** region east of the Ural Mountains. One plausible scenario, then, is that the steppe nomads of Andronovo moved through the Oxus urban civilization, picking up and leaving cultural elements there, and then moved into India and Iran with their distinctive "Aryan" mythologies.

The pastoralist Aryans, despite their love of war, also appreciated city life. As they spread east and southward across the Ganges Plain, they created larger settlements, though not nearly the size of those in the Harappan civilization. New political units had formed by the sixth century BCE. India demonstrates the almost universal process of sedentarization of mobile nomads as they came in contact with the villages and towns of the lowlands. The Aryan peoples mixed their pastoral traditions with local cultures, laying down the fundamental religious and social components of ancient Iranian and Indian civilization. After the sixth century BCE, priests and writers in South Asia wrote down systematic versions of these doctrines, forming what we now call Hinduism.

3.6 THE HITTITES, *C.* 1650–1200 BCE

In the central Anatolian plateau of modern Turkey, urban life began to flourish around 2000 BCE. Even though rainfall was scarce and transportation difficult in this arid, mountainous country, these independent cities thrived on agricultural production combined with an extensive trade in bronze and copper. **Hattusas** (modern Boghazköy) was a major city that covered 50 to 70 acres, a huge expanse. Then nearly all of these cities collapsed around 1750 BCE. A century later a new people, with a powerful, aggressive ruler, revived the great cities and created a great empire, which lasted for nearly 500 years. This empire, the Hittite empire, vanished from sight for millennia until excavations revealed it in the early twentieth century. Like the Aryans, the Hittites were northern invaders on horseback who took over a pre-existing settled urban civilization in decline. But unlike the case of the Aryans, we have the contemporary documents of the Hittite state, in the form of 25,000 cuneiform tablets, which contain the oldest written Indo-European language.

Centered at Hattusas, the rulers engaged in constant warfare and international relations with neighboring powers, expanding to rival Egypt and Babylon. Hittite texts even mention a powerful kingdom to their west, called Akkhiyawa, which may well be the Mycenaean Greeks, or Achaeans, celebrated by Homer. The empire fell apart and revived in the fourteenth century BCE, extending its maximum reach over Palestine and as far as Babylon. Around 1285 BCE, the Hittite army won a major battle at Qadesh with the Egyptians, where the Hittites used 3,500 chariots and 45,700 men. By feeding disinformation to the Egyptian army, they lured the pharaoh into a trap, until he was nearly encircled and annihilated. He escaped only when Hittite troops lost military discipline while looting his camp. One of the largest military engagements in the ancient world, the Battle of Qadesh led to the first detailed peace treaties between two major powers. By 1200 BCE the unified empire had vanished under the pressure of peoples pushing in from the west.

The Hittites in their heyday had a highly efficient military machine based on horsemen driving two-horse chariots, which brought powerful archers quickly to the battlefield. They represent one of the most dynamic of the empires created by the rapidly moving horsemen who had come out of the steppes into the core of the ancient Near East.

The Hittites left behind extensive documentation of their kings' activities and ideology of rule. The king was the servant of the storm god, who brought him victory in battle. He stood between humans and god, with the obligation to defend his people against enemies and provide them with goods obtained from conquest. He created laws and a limited administration to distribute goods to his people, showing his compassion toward them, but when he conquered others he looted their cities and burned them to the ground, and deported their populations. His rivals would do the same to him. In this tempestuous, savage world, the men who drove horses to battle still gained all the prizes, even though they now occupied large settled regions and heavily fortified cities filled with traders and farmers.

The Hittite king Suppiluliumas I (1375–1355 BCE) became so powerful that he received a marriage proposal for his son from the queen of Egypt. She stated: "My husband has died, and not one son do I have. But of you it is said that you have many sons. If you will give me a son of yours, he could be my husband. For how may I take one of my slaves and make him a husband and honor him?" The king was skeptical, but sent his son to Egypt, where he was killed by rivals for the queen's affection. Diplomacy was family business in the Near East, close-knit but treacherous.

3.7 MOVING BY SEA: THE QUESTION OF TROY

Just as the Hittites were creating their kingdom in Anatolia, another group of Indo-European speakers was moving out of the steppe in two directions, west across Anatolia and down the Aegean peninsula, bringing the horse with them, occupying the Neolithic villages of the Peloponnesus. By 1600 BCE they had built a great center at **Mycenae**, featuring large walls, the dominating "Lion Gate," and characteristic beehive-shaped vaulted tombs. The boulders in the walls were so large that later Greeks thought only the race of giants, the Cyclops, could have moved them. The Mycenaeans built other large citadels, including Tiryns and "Nestor's Palace" at Pylos. They soon turned to the sea to increase their wealth, developing trade contacts across the Aegean. The elegant, wealthy, but unfortified Minoan civilization of Crete blocked their access to the riches of Egypt until these buccaneers of the sea took over Knossos and destroyed it in 1400 BCE. At Crete, they learned about writing on clay tablets and the advantages of a civil bureaucracy. These warrior-traders dominated the mainland of Greece, Crete, the islands, and the coast of the Aegean Sea from c. 1550–1100 BCE.

The heroes of Greek mythology – Agamemnon, Ajax, swift-footed Achilles, Hektor, Hecuba of Troy, and Odysseus of many tricks – lived in the Mycenaean Age. But how can we connect myth with material remains? **Heinrich Schliemann**, the brilliant, romantic, unscrupulous German merchant, speculator, treasure-seeker, and pioneering archaeologist, had dedicated his life since 1868 to finding the genuine site of Homer's Trojan war. He thought he had found it at a small hill called Hissarlik in the northwest corner of Turkey, in the region where, ever since ancient times, people had suspected the city of Troy to have been. He devastated the site with extensive diggings, but he did indeed find not just one great city, but at least seven of them, built on top of each other. Yet he still could not prove a definite link with the heroes of Homer's *Iliad*. The second level from the bottom, Troy II, which he thought was Homer's Troy, was too primitive and unimpressive to be the site of a glorious battle. He needed to dig at Mycenae to find definite evidence.

In 1876 at Mycenae he found a circular wall surrounding five shaft graves, which contained a spectacular treasure, including a marvelous gold mask which he naturally, but mistakenly, called the "Mask of Agamemnon." (Because of the great passion for ancient Greek civilization that drove the nineteenth-century excavators, and because archaeology as a discipline was only in its early stages, it is still difficult to sort out fact from fantasy in this part of the world.) He also found a distinctive kind of grey pottery that appeared after his death in later excavations at Troy, but at Level VI, not the unimpressive Level II. Level VI was the first to contain horse bones. Troy VI and Heroic Mycenae were clearly part of one linked culture, which also included the great palace of Knossos on Crete. Not until 1952, because of a magnificent job of decipherment of the Linear B tablets found at Knossos and Mycenae, could we be sure that the peoples who built all these palaces actually spoke Greek.

Independent kingdoms in the mountains of the Peloponessus, led by Mycenae, built great walls, burial grounds, and halls to display their wealth. They gathered warriors around them with promises of adventure and loot. Soon they expanded across the seas, conducting pirate raids in the Aegean and establishing colonies on the coast of Turkey. Mycenaeans often captured women when they razed and looted cities, bringing them back home to serve as slaves. Their greatest Greek rival was Troy, settled earlier from the east. Located on a high bluff overlooking the sea, dominating the trade route, it was an attractive target. The Trojans competed with the Mycenaeans over trade, and may even have battled with them over the huge schools of fish moving through the Dardanelles. This economic background of piracy and trade war lies behind the great epics of the *Iliad* and the *Odyssey*, the cornerstones of Western literature.

The *Iliad* and the *Odyssey*: Fact or Fiction?

Both poems describe the adventures of traveling warriors, telling first how they left home and then how one of them returned. The *Iliad* draws its material from the tale well known to the Greeks of how the assembled kings and warriors of the Achaeans sailed to Troy to capture a woman, Helen, who had been kidnapped by Paris with the gods' approval. The ten-year siege of Troy, won with the famous trick of the wooden horse, ended with the death of Achilles, the sack of the city, the killing of the male inhabitants, and the enslavement of all the women.

The *Iliad* focuses on the "wrath of Achilles," who at first refused to fight when his commander Agamemnon took away his mistress to satisfy the gods. When Patroklos, Achilles' closest friend, entered the battle wearing Achilles' armor and lost his life to the great Trojan warrior Hektor, Achilles had the gods make him new armor and revenged himself by killing Hektor and dragging his body back to the Achaean ships with his chariot. The poem ends with the burial of Hektor by the Trojans. The honor due to great warriors in the form of women and glorious death in battle is its central theme.

The *Odyssey* describes the tortuous journey home of Odysseus, designer of the wooden horse. After many fabulous adventures, he arrives at his palace of Ithaca to rejoin in disguise his son, his wife, and his dog, but he must kill all the suitors harassing his wife Penelope before his family and his estate are safe. Unlike Achilles, Odysseus regains his honor not through straightforward confrontation but by indirection and deceit.

Great singers, or bards, at the royal courts of Mycenae and elsewhere had passed on the components of these stories orally for centuries after the Heroic Age had ended, until they were put into final form around the eighth century BCE and written down c. 550 BCE. Many believe only a single genius, the blind poet Homer, could have created the powerfully unified themes and vivid personalities of both epics; others point to the many inconsistencies in the stories and even deny that Homer existed.

There are definite elements of the *Iliad* that are based on historical facts of the Mycenaean Age, including archaic place names and the famous boar-tusk helmets worn by the Achaeans. The later Greek trireme, shown in Figure 3.4, certainly derived from earlier models, which the Achaeans may have used. And Troy's walls collapsed and burned around 1260 BCE, a possible date for Homer's Trojan war. But was it from an earthquake or a great battle? Did the bards merely glorify a small skirmish, or did their epic of the Greek nation reflect a genuine all-Achaean war? A plausible case can be made that the *Iliad* does narrate, in essence, a real mobilization of the kings of the Mycenaean Age against the prosperous coastal city of Troy, although we may never know exactly the who, what, and when of the battle. Mythology, archaeology, and historical documents intersect very imperfectly, but they come from a common world.

Figure 3.4 This stone carving depicts a trireme, a military vessel propelled by three ranks of rowers stacked on top of each other. Phoenicians, Greeks, Romans, and other contending powers used it as their dominant warship in the Mediterranean for many centuries. The Achaeans featured in the Homeric epics may well have used an earlier model of this ship to carry their expedition against Troy.

3.8 THE DARK AGES BEGIN

"All at once the lands were on the move, scattered in war." So proclaims an Egyptian temple relief. Beginning around 1200 BCE, a tremendous movement of peoples inflicted great destruction on the major cities of the eastern Mediterranean. The pharaohs of Egypt twice fought off major coastal attacks by armed groups they called the "Sea Peoples," but these invaders surged through Syria and Palestine, and Hittite lands, demolishing cities as they went. Egypt noted the invasion, by "Philistines" from Crete, of the Gaza Strip and coastlands to its north. These **Philistines** gave their name to Palestine. Mycenae built its largest Cyclopean walls around this time; shortly thereafter all the major citadels of the Greek mainland, except for Athens, were completely destroyed. Then Hattusas fell, ending the Hittite empire; Minoan civilization on Crete ended, Babylon was sacked, and Troy was sacked again, for the final time, around 1180 BCE. The Sea Peoples could have been groups of pirates centered on the Aegean islands, perhaps aided by roving Mycenaean warriors pushed south by new migrants from the north. Climatic changes may have put all these people on the move. The Greeks later spoke of an invasion of "Dorians" from the north, who eliminated the Mycenaean citadels, and inaugurated nearly two centuries of blanks in the historical record of Greece. The Dorians have left no archaeological record; one theory holds that they were lower-class groups rebelling against exploitation by the Mycenaean elites. It was the revenge of the sea on the landed empires of antiquity. The Heroic Age, and the age of stable imperial bureaucracies, which produced writing, buildings, and organized armies, had given way to general mayhem.

3.9 THE ISRAELITES

"Now the Lord said to Abraham, 'Go from your country and your kindred and your father's house to the land that I will show you. And I will make of you a great nation, and I will bless you, and make your name great" (Genesis 12.1).

In the midst of these imperial conflicts, sometime between 3000 and 1500 BCE, Abraham, a chieftain of a small semi-pastoral tribe, led his people out of Ur, in Sumer, up the Euphrates River and into the land of Canaan (modern Israel and Palestine), "a land flowing with milk and honey" which his tribal God, Yahweh, had promised to him (Joshua 5.6). They brought with them the common myths of Sumer, including stories about the creation of the world, the great flood, and how the collapse of the Tower of Babel produced the many languages of the world. (Box 3.2 demonstrates the common features of the Sumerian flood myth and the flood described in the Hebrew Bible. Map 3.1

shows the territory of ancient Palestine.) When famine struck, as it often did, many of his tribe fled to Egypt, where they worked for the pharaoh on his great public works. Around 1300 to 1250 BCE, these tribespeople left Egypt to return to Canaan, and in the mountains of southern Palestine their god Yahweh promised the land of Israel to the twelve tribes who worshipped him.

The Hebrew books of Genesis and Exodus tell this as the story of one God's chosen people who are destined to rule the land of Israel. The story fits the general context of the region, when many tribal peoples were wandering through the area, but neither archaeology nor written documents of other civilizations give much distinctive evidence about the ancient Hebrews. The Hebrews were just one of many pastoral peoples who led their flocks of sheep and goats to the desert when water was available, and moved to settled lands in the summer. As the story of Cain and Abel demonstrates, pastoralists and agriculturalists could be mixed within the same family, but they did not always get along. In Box 3.3, other sources also describe this deep conflict between two kinds of way of making a living. Even when a number of pastoralists shared a common religious cult, they often fought against each other. The stories of the Bible were put together much later, from *c.* 1000–500 BCE, to create a coherent story of the formation of a single people who conquered the land of Israel with God's support. The twelve or so tribes who shared this God, however, probably did not fight as a unified force most of the time.

The Hebrew Pastoralists Expand their Kingdom

When Joshua led his tribe, the house of Joseph, west across the Jordan River around 1230 BCE, he began an extended period of battles against the other (and oldest) inhabitants of Palestine, the **Canaanites**, just as the old empires of the Near East were crumbling under attack from the Sea Peoples and associated migrations. Egyptian documents tell of constant plundering by the "Habiru," a generic name for restless nomads, military mercenaries, traders, and freed slaves who roamed in bands, threatening the city elites that had forced them into servitude. The Israelites were part of this general uprising, but by 1230 BCE the Egyptians had recognized them as an important political force in Palestine. Like other settled nomads, they connected themselves more closely with the land, establishing law codes and borrowing much from the existing Canaanite urban culture.

The Canaanites worshipped a fertility god called Baal, whose rites closely followed the agricultural cycle. Every year he died and was reborn in the spring. Baal was also the thunder god who conquered Chaos, subdued his enemies, and established an everlasting kingdom. The Hebrews adopted the theme of conflict with the turbulent waters of Chaos, but rejected the fertility cult. Yahweh did not die and revive annually; he was the single, eternal, unchanging God who directed the course of his people's history and established their moral order.

After subduing all the others, the Israelites confronted their greatest rival: the Philistines on the coast. Attacks by the Philistines convinced the Israelites that they needed unity in this armed struggle, so they chose the warlord Saul (r. 1020–1000 BCE) as their first king. Supporters of the customary tribal democracy warned that a king would only oppress his people with heavy burdens, but in this time of crisis, the people demanded a strong leader. This kingship was a gift by God to the Israelites in their time of need, under the condition that if the king violated his covenant with God and his people, he would be replaced. The Chinese would call this principle more impersonally the **Mandate of Heaven**.

Saul recruited professional soldiers to support his tribal armies, among whom the most impressive was David, who had defeated the great Philistine warrior Goliath in individual battle. Saul, however, fearing David's popularity, forced him to flee to the Philistines, but David returned and took the kingship, first by military force, later with Yahweh's approval. Unlike Saul, David and his descendants embodied the spirit of the people they ruled:

they were the "lamp of Israel, which could never be extinguished." Yahweh guaranteed to preserve the house of David forever: "the Lord will make you a house. When your days are fulfilled and you lie down with your fathers, I will raise up your son after you, who shall come forth from your body, and I will establish his kingdom. He shall build a house for my name, and I will establish the throne of his kingdom for ever" (2 Samuel 11–13). David built the great citadel at Jerusalem and led Israel's wars of conquest for forty years. At the same time, he began imitating the court ceremonies of neighboring states like Assyria and Egypt, building up his bureaucracy while generating resentment among the common people.

Solomon, his successor, relaxed the military demands of the kingship, but generated the greatest wealth the kingdom had seen. Coming from a merchant background, he exploited customs taxes on the trade routes controlled by his state to bring in luxury goods from Egypt and build himself a luxurious palace. Keeping up with the military demands of the day, Solomon introduced chariotry to the Israeli army, meaning fewer, but more specialized, expensive warriors. He greatly impressed the queen of Sheba with his magnificent court, and he became

Box 3.2 The Stories they Told: Sumerian and Hebrew Flood Myths

Ancient peoples shared stories of the origin of the world and the creation of kings and cities. These communal tales show remarkable similarities because of constant cultural interaction. Note how this Sumerian flood myth anticipates the main features of the biblical flood, including the king who becomes a leader chosen by God, the great boat, and the resettlement of the earth:

Give ear to my instruction:
. . . a flood will sweep over the cult-centers;
To destroy the seed of mankind . . .
Is the decision, the word of the assembly of the gods.
. . . All the windstorms, exceedingly powerful, attacked as one,
At the same time, the flood sweeps over the cult-centers,
After, for seven days and seven nights,
The flood had swept over the land,

And the huge boat had been tossed about by the windstorms on the great waters,
Utu came forth, who sheds light on heaven and earth.
Ziusudra opened a window of the huge boat,
The hero Utu brought his rays into the giant boat.
Ziusudra, the king,
Prostrated himself before Utu . . . [and]
Vegetation, coming up out of the earth, rises up.
. . . Anu and Enlil cherished Ziusudra,
Life like that of a god they give him,
Breath eternal like that of a god they bring down for him . . .

Noah was six hundred years old when the flood of waters came upon the earth. And Noah and his sons and his wife and his sons' wives with him went into the ark, to escape the waters of the flood . . .

The flood continued forty days upon the earth; and the waters increased, and bore up the ark, and it rose high above the earth . . . and all flesh died that moved upon the earth . . . He blotted out every living thing that was upon the face of the ground, man and animals and creeping things and birds of the air; they were blotted out from the earth. Only Noah was left, and those that were with him in the ark . . . In the six hundred and first year . . . the waters were dried from off the earth, and Noah removed the covering of the ark, and looked, and behold, the face of the ground was dry . . . Then God said to Noah, "Go forth from the ark, you and your wife, and your sons and your sons' wives with you. Bring forth with you every living thing that is with you of all flesh . . . that they may breed abundantly on the earth, and be fruitful and multiply upon the earth.

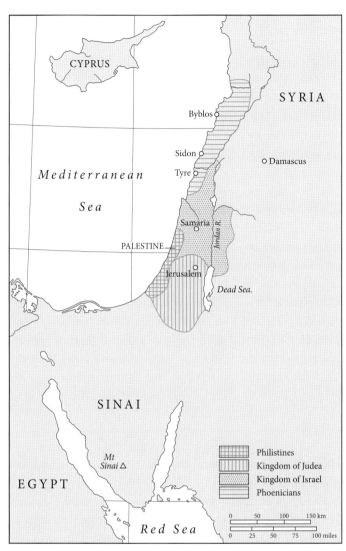

Map 3.1 Ancient Palestine

renowned as a literary person, author of the Song of Solomon and thousands of proverbs and poems. These tribal nomads had come a long way. Yet the kingdom he ruled was torn by rivalry between the north and the south. After Solomon's death, Israel split into two kingdoms which never again united. The Assyrians destroyed the northern state of Israel in 723 BCE; in 587 BCE the Babylonians eliminated the southern state of Judah, razed the temple in Jerusalem, and deported the population.

The political experience of the Israelites was short-lived, and rather typical of its time, but their religion, of course, was not. In the Hebrew Bible, the Jewish people created a great unifying moral message, one that lasted long after all the other ancient empires had vanished. The power of the divine revelation, the intense dedication of the kings and prophets, and the great value placed on the sacred texts, kept the Jewish identity alive when all their political power had vanished. For the Israelites, community bonds generated coercive power for a while, but commercial success

weakened them. When their kingdom collapsed and they were deported to Babylon, they once again had only their religion to bind them together against continual threats to their existence.

3.10 CHINA FROM SHANG TO ZHOU

Objects and people moved all the way to the eastern end of Eurasia. Even the earliest Chinese cultures show influence from the west. China's oldest bronze objects appear in tombs from *c.* 2000 BCE in the extreme northwest of China, where migrants across Central Eurasia could have introduced Near Eastern technology. China's first great urban civilization, however, the Shang (*c.* 1500–1100 BCE), was centered in the North China Plain, with its capital at Anyang, in modern Henan (see Chapter 2). The Shang kings developed the mass production of huge bronze vessels, using enormous quantities of the metal, in a highly distinctive fashion. Sacrifices using these ritual objects, which symbolized the authority of the king, linked the kings to heavenly forces. Around the king's capital were other subordinate rulers, who formed part of a loose confederation of states recognizing each other as part of a common culture. These kings constantly fought against each other, but they did not use chariots or horses.

Around 1200 BCE, the chariot suddenly appears in Anyang's remains, and its form closely resembles early chariots found in graves in Central Eurasia. Clearly, the idea of the chariot had arrived in China from the west around this time. But this rare chariot was too unstable to be a useful weapon of war, although it had high prestige value. It could have served as a mobile platform for the king to look over his troops. By around 1000 BCE, however, peoples in the northern and western regions of China began to use massed chariots in war. The chariot arms race continued until four to five thousand chariots were used in battle, just like the Hittite battles in Egypt.

In 1045 BCE, new invaders from the west, the Zhou rulers, conquered the Shang to create the second of China's great dynasties. Map 3.2 displays the extent of the new Zhou dynasty. As the poet described the battle, "The field of Muye was so broad. The sandalwood chariots were so gleaming. The teams of four were so pounding. There was the general Shangfu. He rose as an eagle, aiding that King Wu, and attacked the great Shang, meeting in the morning, clear and bright." Chariots gave the Zhou a decisive military edge.

The Zhou Justify their Rule

The Zhou conquerors did not explain it that way, however. They claimed that their god, Heaven (**Tian**), had decided that the

Box 3.3 Pastoralists, City-Dwellers, Horsemen, and Warriors

These texts vividly portray conflicting ideals of the peoples of this archaic age. In this Sumerian myth, the goddess Adnigkidu is warned not to marry the barbarian nomad god Martu: "He who dwells in the mountains ... having carried on much strife ... he knows not submission, he eats uncooked food, he has no house where he lives, he is not interred when he dies, my friend – how is it you would marry Martu!" Adnigkidu answers her friend: "I will indeed marry Martu."

The story of Cain and Abel shows that the hostility between pastoralists and agriculturalists could fester within the same family: "Now Abel was a keeper of sheep, and Cain a tiller of the ground ... Cain said to Abel his brother, 'Let us go out to the field.' And when they were in the field, Cain rose up against his brother Abel, and killed him." (Also note that here, it is the "civilized" farmer who kills the "barbarian" pastoralist. But Cain's curse is to wander the earth without rest, the worst fate of all for a settled person.)

A pastoralist shows contempt for the city-dweller, c. 1770 BCE: "You look forward to eating, drinking, and sleeping, but not to accompanying me? Sitting or sleeping will not redden you from the sun. As for me, if I keep myself inside just one day, until I leave the city walls behind to renew my vigor, my vitality ebbs away."

The Indo-Aryans praise the horse and bow: "With the bow let us win cows, with the bow let us win the contest and violent battles with the bow. The bow ruins the enemy's pleasure; with the bow let us conquer all the corners of the world. Neighing violently, the horses with their showering hoofs outstrip everyone with their chariots. Trampling down the foes with the tips of their hoofs, they destroy their enemies without veering away."

The Greeks follow their divinely supported impulses for war: "Zeus sent down in speed to the fast ships of the Achaeans the wearisome goddess of Hate, holding in her hands the portent of battle. She took her place on the huge-hollowed black ship of Odysseus ... and cried out a great cry and terrible and loud, and put strength in all the Achaians' hearts, to go on tirelessly with their fighting of battles. And now battle became sweeter to them than to go back in their hollow ships to the beloved land of their fathers."

Shang rulers were too wicked to deserve the central power and had transferred its support to the virtuous Zhou. Maybe they were right, but they also had the chariots to back up their philosophical point. This theory of "transferring the Mandate of Heaven" (**geming**) became the most important justification for resisting rulers in China, and the same word today means "revolution." But behind this revolutionary upheaval, past and present, lay the force of new technology just as much as moral theory.

As the Zhou, originally chariot-riding barbarians from the west, settled down in the cities of North China, they established a new political order. First, the "virtuous" King Wen established the alliances and rituals that bound the Zhou allies together, then his successor, the martial King Wu, led the military campaigns that overthrew the Shang. The most famous Zhou personage was not a ruler at all, but a minister, the duke of Zhou, who pronounced the Mandate of Heaven theory to the conquered Shang people, while promising that the new rulers would act with benevolence and sincerity. They would not oppress them with heavy taxes or condemn them for crimes unjustly, and would "attend even to the helpless and solitary, and even to pregnant women." The duke, however, was only an advisor to the king, who might have his own ideas of how to make decisions. The arguments between ministers like the duke of Zhou, Confucius' hero, and the actual ruler over the proper interpretation of Heaven's will would ring through Chinese philosophy and statecraft for centuries.

The Zhou expanded their military power eastward to control key areas of the lower Yellow River and North China Plain, creating a much more centralized administration than the Shang. For about two hundred years after the conquest, the Zhou gave China more peace and order than it had ever known. This era of stability gave the Zhou legendary status among later writers as the ideal human society, where people followed proper laws and rituals, and virtuous rulers listened to the advice of learned, honest scholars. We have so few genuine documents from the early Zhou that it is difficult to tell whether any aspects of this vision corresponded to reality, but at least for a time, the Zhou conquest brought peace, military strength, and prosperity.

The new Zhou deity, and the new theory of rule that they brought with them, however, did fundamentally transform the character of authority in China. The Shang deity, called **Di**, was a personal god, who expressed his will by answering questions inscribed on turtle shells and ox scapula (shoulder bones). Diviners interpreted the cracks created by heating these "oracle bones" in the fire. The Zhou deity, Heaven, was a universal, impersonal, cosmic force that stood above the ruler and his people. Heaven could judge the moral worth of a society as Yahweh did, but Heaven did not favor any particular ethnic group: anyone who practiced proper rituals could inherit

Map 3.2 Western Zhou China

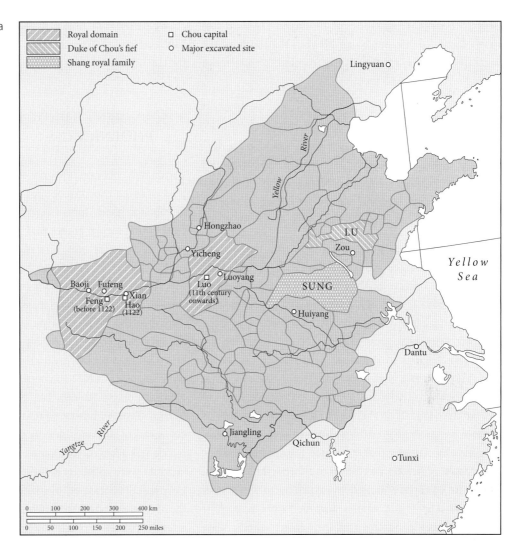

Heaven's mandate. There were, indeed, "barbarians" beyond the realm of human civilization who rejected the classical ideals, and they deserved to be eliminated, but within the emerging Sinitic culture centered in the North China Plain, all deserved Heaven's grace.

The legitimacy of a ruler depended on his ability to provide for his people by feeding them in time of need and protecting them against enemy attacks. The Zhou knew that "Heaven's mandate is difficult to maintain," and they knew that military force alone, though necessary, would not guarantee that their rule would continue. Thus, along with fourteen standing armies, the Zhou kings developed a rudimentary bureaucratic administration dependent on literate officials. These officials, called **shi** (meaning servitors, scribes, secretaries, or historians), wrote down orders and gave the ruler counsel dependent on written precedents. This was not a full bureaucracy in the modern sense, with salaried officials and a full set of job descriptions with carefully limited functions. The officials gained their income from fiefs, not salaries, and did not have clear responsibilities. But it did create stability and a written record to give policy continuity beyond the individual ruler.

Outside the capital, the kings delegated authority to relatives of the king by granting them landed fiefs. This form of "feudalism" had a few features in common with the medieval European model – the use of titles of nobility and the prestige of horseriding warriors – but many more differences. It was a city-based culture, where literate officials were gaining importance, chaotic internecine warfare was rare, and there were no heroic military epics or romantic poetry. China's classic texts, unlike those of Vedic India or Mycenaean Greece, do not glorify war, pillage, and horses; instead, they praise the careful administrator and the sober, benevolent ruler.

Zhou Decline Sparks Protest

Yet signs of decline inevitably appeared. In times of social unrest, people normally have three choices: exit (leave the state), voice (protest), or loyalty (keep quiet and obey). Chinese writers expressed all these options. From the ninth century BCE forward, poets lamented the tragic gap between the ideals of the founding rulers and the evidence of corruption, drunkenness, and cruelty they saw around them:

> *When guests are drunk, they howl and bawl, upset my baskets and dishes, cut capers, lilt, and lurch. For when people are drunk they do not know what blunders they commit. Cap on one side, very insecure, they cut capers lasciviously. If when they got drunk they went out, they would receive their blessing like the rest. But if they get drunk and stay, the power of the feast is spoilt. Drinking wine is very lucky, provided it is done with decency.*

In an indirect satire of greedy government, the poet threatens to leave the state where "huge rats" eat his grain: "Huge rat, huge rat, eat my millet no more, for three years I've fed you, yet you pay me no heed. I swear that I will leave you, and go to a happier land. A happy land, a happy land, and there I will find my place."

Some poets were even more direct: "Di [the term for the highest god] on High is so contrary; the people below are all exhausted. You utter talk that is not true, and make plans that are not far-reaching. There are no sages so reliable, and no substance at the altar. That the plans are not far-reaching is why I greatly remonstrate." To "remonstrate" meant to protest a ruler's policy by claiming that it violated the laws of Heaven. The goal of these protesters was not to overthrow the kingdom, but to help the ruler save himself by returning to the proper Way. Many brave poets and scholars lost their lives by protesting, but some succeeded in changing their rulers' minds. They would continue to remonstrate throughout all Chinese dynasties.

During a major drought in the ninth century, one poet concluded that "the great mandate is about at an end." Solar and lunar eclipses and violent storms all gave ominous indications of disaster to come. The arrogant King Li was driven out of the capital into exile in 842 BCE, the first truly reliable date in Chinese history. Efforts to restore some order lasted only a short time, and in 771 BCE the "Dog barbarians," who had been threatening the Zhou from the west for a century, sacked the capital, killed the king, and ended the Western Zhou.

The Zhou kings continued to rule in the east, but local lords built many new cities as they gained wealth and became more independent. The kings held less and less power, while their subordinate lords started to make war on each other. The second half of the Zhou looks more like the chaos of medieval "feudalism" than the first half. The peaceful kingdom was sliding into the outright massacres of the well-named Era of Warring States (463–222 BCE).

As invaders from the west who settled down, created a stable government, and developed a philosophy of rule, only to be driven out themselves by other invaders, the Zhou initiated the classic pattern of Chinese political evolution, later known as the "dynastic cycle." Their political institutions laid the cornerstone for later dynasties, and provided a model of virtuous rule.

3.11 ANCIENT TRADE ROUTES: METALS AND PHOENICIANS

Fortunately, not everyone moved just because of war. Commerce put just as many people on the road as coercion. Traders in search of valuable goods spread across the Mediterranean and inland, establishing regular routes that followed lines of geographic convenience. Metallic ores, rare and scattered, offered great opportunities for profit. Gold was the great prestige metal, which the Mycenaeans hoarded in their palaces and tombs, in the form of shields, drinking cups, and masks. Schliemann's most spectacular discovery, the "Mask of Agamemnon," certainly does not depict the great leader of the Achaeans, but it does demonstrate the power and wealth of a great king. But where did the Mycenaeans get their gold? Greece had very few minerals. The main source was Nubia (modern Sudan), but gold came from as far away as Ireland. Bronze, however, an alloy of copper and tin, was the key metal of this age, vital to all the great states. Finding these metals was a key motivation for the Mycenaean sea voyages. Tin deposits were quite rare: the main sources were in Syria and Cornwall. Tin traveled overland long distances to ports where the Mycenaeans could obtain it. A gold cup found in Cornwall has a similar pattern to one found in a Mycenaean grave. Via Rhodes, Cyprus, and Crete, the Mycenaeans gained access to Egypt, their most important trading relation, but they expanded westward to Sicily, Sardinia, and Italy too. The poor soils of Greece drove their populations out to sea to develop the first great maritime trading state, a strategy Venice would follow much later.

The Phoenicians Dominate the Mediterranean Trade Routes

But the Mycenaean Greeks were not the only great traders. Two shipwrecks dating from the fourteenth and late thirteenth centuries BCE, recently discovered off the coast of southern Turkey, now show that Canaanite traders rivaled the Mycenaeans in maritime power. These ships contained tons of copper and tin, cedar and ebony logs, Syrian cylinder seals, bronze tools and weapons, elephant and hippo ivory, and even remnants of the crew's fish dinner. They were carrying pottery vessels and scrap metal from Cyprus or Palestine to the Aegean. These sailors, later known as Phoenicians, were Semitic Canaanites with great urban centers at Tyre and Sidon on the east coast of the Mediterranean, in modern Lebanon. (Map 3.3 shows the Phoenician settlements around the

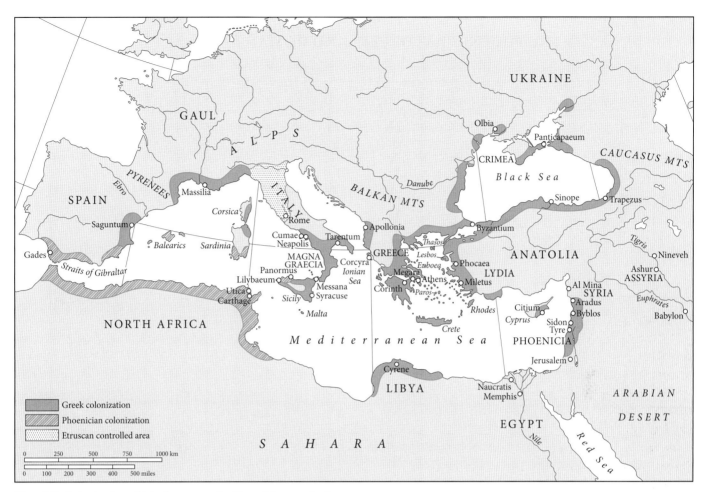

Map 3.3 Colonization of Mediterranean by Phoenicians and others

Mediterranean.) Pushed to the coast by Israelite expansion after the thirteenth century, they became the dominant traders on the Mediterranean, mingling with Mycenaeans and others. In search of raw materials for trade, they established merchant colonies in the major inland cities of the Near East. Then, along the coast of North Africa, they founded city-states like Carthage, Utica, Tripoli, and Gades (Cádiz) in southern Spain, and moved through the Straits of Gibraltar, down the coast of West Africa, and perhaps even across the Sahara. They exported the great cedar trees of Lebanon, and traded in tin, copper, purple dyes made from the murex snail (Phoenician means "purple" in Greek), and earned fame as architects, textile workers, woodworkers, and jewelers. Hiram, the Phoenician king of Tyre, sold to the Israelites the huge cedar timbers that built Solomon's temple, in exchange for wheat and oil. But the Greeks cursed them as greedy knaves, "a people full of bitterness and surly, submissive to rulers, tyrannical to those they rule, abject in fear, fierce when provoked, unshakable in resolve, and so strict as to dislike all humor and kindness."

The Phoenicians are most famous today as the "inventors," or at least popularizers, of the modern alphabet. Yet because they wrote down their language on perishable materials like papyrus or paper, and because the coastal cities were damp, we have almost no documents in the Phoenician language. Like the steppe nomads, we must rely on mainly hostile accounts by other peoples. Other societies had created alphabets as early as 1500 BCE. The coastal city of Ugarit had its own alphabet of thirty symbols, and the towns of southern Palestine had adapted Egyptian hieroglyphs into simple signs for use in routine transactions. But the Phoenician alphabet contained twenty-two consonants which fitted the sounds of the language well and, unlike cuneiform, could be written on many different media. Their shapes still resemble closely the modern Hebrew, Greek, and Roman alphabets. The multiple contacts of the seafaring Phoenicians induced them to create a means of communication applicable to many languages, and their cultural influence led others to copy them. The Hebrews and Greeks adapted the Phoenician alphabet to write down their sacred texts and national epics around the eighth century BCE. Figure 3.5 shows the relationship between these ancient alphabets and our modern Roman script.

THE PHOENICIAN, GREEK, AND ROMAN ALPHABETS

PHOENICIAN			GREEK			ROMAN	
Phoenician	Phoenician Name	Modern Symbol	Early Greek	Classical Greek	Greek Name	Early Latin	Classical Latin
𐤀	'aleph	’	Α	Α	alpha	A	A
𐤁	beth	b	Β	Β	beta		B
𐤂	gimel	g	Γ	Γ	gamma		C
𐤃	daleth	d	Δ	Δ	delta	D	D
𐤄	he	h	Ε	Ε	epsilon	E	E
𐤅	waw	w	Ϝ		digamma	F	F
							G
𐤆	zayin	z	Ι	Ζ	zeta		
𐤇	heth	h	Η	Η	eta	H	H
𐤈	teth	t	⊗	Θ	theta		
𐤉	yod	y	Ι	Ι	iota	I	I
𐤊	kaph	k	Κ	Κ	kappa	K	K
𐤋	lamed	l	Λ	Λ	lambda		L
𐤌	mem	m	Μ	Μ	mu	M	M
𐤍	nun	n	Ν	Ν	nu	N	N
𐤎	samek	s			xi		
𐤏	ayin	‘	Ο	Ο	omicron	O	O
𐤐	pe	p	Π	Π	pi		P
𐤑	sade	s	Ϻ		saw		
𐤒	qoph	o	Ϙ		qoppa		Q
𐤓	rěs	r	Ρ	Ρ	rho		R
𐤔	šin	sh/s	Σ	Σ	sigma	S	S
𐤕	taw	t	X		tau		T
				Υ	upsilon	V	V
				Χ	chi		X
							Y
				Ω	omega		Z

SOURCE: Andrew Robinson, *The Story of Writing* (London, 1995), p. 170.

Figure 3.5 This table shows the twenty-two original signs of the Phoenician alphabet, with their pronounciations, alongside the early and modern Greek and Roman alphabets derived from them. The close resemblance of symbols like "D," "M," and "O" shows that once invented, the alphabet became an extremely widespread writing device, adopted by many different types of language over great expanses. Russian Cyrillic and modern Hebrew, Arabic, and Persian alphabets also derive from Phoenician. The Sinitic and Sanskrit scripts have an independent origin.

3.12 A MAN'S WORLD?

What happened to relations between men and women during this time of warfare and movement? Some archaeologists have argued that the earliest settled civilizations, like Minoan Crete, worshipped primarily a mother goddess of fertility. Many small figurines do portray fertile women, but other archaeologists claim that these are not goddesses, but merely dolls. In any case, objects by themselves reveal little about a society's structure: brutal men can worship women in theory, but treat them badly in real life. Nineteenth-century social theorists held that early "matriarchal" societies turned into oppressive patriarchies when the horseriding conquerors arrived; now we are not so sure. Certainly the Vedic hymns praise fast horses, strong drink, and domination of beautiful women, and the Mycenaeans captured women to make them slaves. When the Greeks invaded Crete, they replaced the mother goddesses with the more domesticated goddesses Hera, guardian of the hearth, Demeter, patroness of the grain fields, and Artemis, patroness of the hunt. But life in the ordinary households of ancient cities was not favorable for women either, and in some ways the pastoral life offered them greater equality. Women took on the vital economic roles of herding the sheep and pitching the tents, while the men were out of sight on military expeditions. They could not be confined to walled houses like their settled sisters. Although we know little of the ordinary woman's life, certain women, like the queen of Egypt who wrote to the Hittite king, did gain great political power. Since dynastic politics depended on family connections, women had strong personal influence behind the scenes.

3.13 MOUNTED ARCHERS: THE ULTIMATE WEAPON

Domesticating the horse, controlling him with bit and bridle, and hitching him to a chariot was difficult enough. Actually mounting the horse and riding him into battle was far more challenging. Firm evidence of warriors who fought on horse in battle, as opposed to riding to the battle in chariots, does not appear until *c.* 1000–900 BCE. Men who could master this skill literally seemed superhuman, as they controlled the horse so closely that their bodies seemed welded to the animal. The Greek myth of the Centaurs portrays these mounted men as close to gods.

Once again, the primary source of innovation was the southern Russian steppe, particularly the area north of the Black Sea

between the Don and Danube rivers. A shadowy group called the Cimmerians roved about these lands in the ninth century BCE, but the Scythians displaced them around 650 BCE. The Greek historian **Herodotus** (490–425 BCE) gives us the first extensive discussion of these true horse nomads of the steppe. Herodotus grudgingly conceded that

the Scythian nation has made the most clever discovery among all the people we know – though for the rest I do not admire them much … No invader who comes against them can ever escape and … none can catch them if they do not wish to be caught. For this people has no cities or settled forts; they carry their houses with them and shoot with bows from horseback; they live off herds of cattle, not from tillage, and their dwellings are on their wagons. How then can they fail to be invincible and inaccessible for others?

When Darius, the Persian king, marched against them in 513 BCE, the Scythians simply vanished into the endless steppe, burning the grass and filling in the wells as they retreated. Darius called them cowards: "Why do you keep flying from me when you might make a choice of courses? If you think yourself strong enough to oppose my power, stop this wandering to and fro and stand and fight. If your mind tells you that you are the weaker, then, likewise, stop running away, give gifts to your master, and come to words with me." The Scythian king merely answered, "If you claim to be my master, you will be sorry you said so." The Scythians lured Darius deep into the steppe, then wheeled around with their fast cavalry and cut off his supply lines. The starving Persian army only barely escaped disaster. This pattern repeated itself again and again when agricultural armies marched against pastoral horsemen.

Herodotus described accurately the classic features of nomadism: the portable tent which we call a "yurt," their fondness for fermented mare's milk, or *kumyss*, and their interesting custom of making gilded cups out of the skulls of their enemies. The Scythians also collected a hoard of "sacred gold" from raids or from trade with their neighbors, with which they produced spectacular portable sculptures of animal figures. The Scythians and their successors had a highly developed technology perfectly suited to their grassland environment, an irresistible cavalry force, and a sophisticated religious and artistic culture. This unified nomadic culture, the culmination of several millennia of pastoralists, spread to span the entire Eurasian steppe, and for the next two thousand years would have decisive impacts on the settled empires around them, from Rome to Iran to India to China.

Conclusion

In this chapter we have surveyed the evolution of mobile peoples out of the settled societies of Eurasia. We have shown that sharp alternatives to settled urban and agricultural life could flourish in particular environments, on sea and on land, and attract populations with distinctive cultures. For the most part, the mobile peoples did not leave written records, and their archaeological remains are scarce, but recent discoveries, like the Ice Man and the mummies of the Tarim Basin, have allowed us to reconstruct more details of their lives. Settled peoples often feared these nomads, characterizing them as barbarians and pirates, but in fact the technology to support a mobile life was extremely sophisticated, and the nomads made great contributions to all of the cultures of Eurasia. These people on the move created tales of their origins, which developed into the founding mythologies of major civilizations. The Hindu *Mahabharata*, the stories of the Hebrew Bible, the Chinese political theory of the Mandate of Heaven, and the epics of the *Iliad* and *Odyssey* were products of this age of migration, conquest, and exchange. Most of our modern alphabetic writing systems derive from the records kept by traders who moved around the shores of the Mediterranean.

Pastoral nomadism, a distinct form of life reliant more on animals than on agriculture, evolved from densely settled regions, but the nomads, who were much more mobile than agriculturalists, spread out to cover the grasslands of the Eurasian continent. Seafarers also used their boats to found colonies, trade, and raid across the Mediterranean. These new technical achievements, mastering horses and building big ships, brought large-scale inter-actions between the mobile populations and settlers in cities and fields. Often the myths describe simple conquest of settled peoples by the new horseriders and seafarers, but the historical reality was more complex. They might struggle for power over each other, or trade with each other, or use each other in alliances against other rivals. Even within family groups, some might practice agriculture, while others tended sheep. The nomads' military skills made them a powerful tool for rulers of states, but these people were also difficult to control. Their migrations, invasions, and commercial relationships exasperated the rulers of settled civiliza-tions, but they could not be eliminated. When strong empires dominated the Middle East, India, and China, they constantly had to face threats of invasion from the rapid armies of the nomads of the Eurasian steppes. Nomads and seafarers certainly destroyed many cities and villages, but they also stimulated the growth of civilization by challenging settled societies to develop defenses against them. This military threat forced the settled civilizations to develop large armies, new military technologies, bureaucratic administration, and written records. Because of the mobile peoples, the major civilizations of the world came into much closer contact with each other, and this constant interaction would last until the nearly complete elimination of powerful nomadic states in the eighteenth century CE. The interaction between these two forms of life was a central feature of the history of Eurasia until the dawn of modern times.

Study Questions

(1) Why did pastoralists and settled agriculturalists have so much difficulty accepting each other? Explain the different principles of their ways of life. Why was mobility both attractive and threatening to settled people?

(2) Some peoples, like the Mycenaeans, Hebrews, or Phoenicians, moved long distances for trade or conquest, while others, like the Philistines, or Canaanites, tended to stay put. What would determine whether a group of people chose to become mobile traders or settled city-dwellers?

(3) Compare the different religious systems created by conquering peoples such as the Aryans, Hebrews, and Zhou Chinese. How did they invoke heavenly powers to promote their rule? What happened to the people who were conquered, and how did they respond to the newly arrived rulers?

(4) Would you rather be a farmer, or a horseman or horsewoman? Can farmers and pastoralists ever get along with each other?

Suggested Reading

DAVID W. ANTHONY, *The Horse, the Wheel, and Language: How Bronze-Age Riders from the Eurasian Steppes Shaped the Modern World* (Princeton University Press, 2007). Based on archaeological evidence for the origin of horseriding in the southern Ukraine, this book argues that chariot-riding evolved along with the horse in the steppes.

C.W. CERAM, *The Secret of the Hittites: The Discovery of an Ancient Empire* (London: Phoenix Press, 2001). This is a dramatic popular account of the discovery of Hittite civilization.

JOHN GRAY, *Archaeology and the Old Testament World* (London: T. Nelson, 1962). Gray discusses the relationship between biblical events and archaeological evidence.

DONALD HARDEN, *The Phoenicians* (New York: Praeger, 1962). This work is a basic synthesis of the available information.

MARK EDWARD LEWIS, *Sanctioned Violence in Early China* (Albany: State University of New York Press, 1989). This is an extended analysis of the important role of warfare, vengeance, and blood rituals in Shang and Zhou China.

J.P. MALLORY AND VICTOR H. MAIR, *The Tarim Mummies: Ancient China and the Mystery of the Earliest Peoples from the West* (New York: Thames & Hudson, 2008). The authors survey the evidence on mummies, horses, ancient migrations, and Indo-Europeans.

JAMES B. PRITCHARD AND DONALD P. FLEMING (eds.), *The Ancient Near East: An Anthology of Texts and Pictures* (Princeton University Press, 2010). This is a collection of basic primary sources and images from Babylonian and other traditions.

KONRAD SPINDLER, *The Man in the Ice: The Preserved Body of a Neolithic Man Reveals the Secrets of the Stone Age* (London: Weidenfeld & Nicolson, 1994). Analysis of the Ice Man's body continues to provide details of his life. Spindler's work gives the latest findings but there are certain to be more.

LORD WILLIAM TAYLOUR, *The Mycenaeans*, rev. edn. (London: Thames & Hudson, 2004). Taylour provices a basic synthesis of archaeological and textual information.

MICHAEL WOOD, *In Search of the Trojan War* (Berkeley: University of California Press, 1998). This entertaining provocative work explores the relationship between Homer's epics and the archaeology of Troy.

Glossary

Andronovo: Site of horse nomadic culture, east of Ural mountains in Russia.

Avesta: Ancient Persian sacred texts.

Canaanites: Oldest inhabitants of Palestine.

Di: Term for the god of the Shang people; later applied to Chinese emperors.

geming: Chinese term for "transfer of Mandate of Heaven," i.e. change of dynasties, or revolution.

Hattusas: A major city of central Anatolia in the ancient period, which collapsed around 1750 BCE.

Heinrich Schliemann: German businessman and archaeologist, discoverer of Mycenae and Troy.

Herodotus: Greek historian (490–425 BCE) who wrote about the nomads of Central Asia and about the Persian Wars.

Indo-European: A family of related languages, including Sanskrit, Greek, Latin, Hittite, Russian, and Celtic.

Israelites: A pastoral people who moved from Sumeria to Palestine; they worshipped a single god, Yahweh.

Mahabharata: Sanskrit historical epic referring to wars among Aryans in the tenth century BCE.

Mandate of Heaven: The principle of divine authority determining the survival and collapse of ancient Chinese dynasties.

Mycenae: Ancient palace and kingdom in southern Greece.

Oxus civilization: A newly discovered agrarian civilization south of Amu Darya River, in modern Turkmenistan.

pastoral nomadism: A form of life dependent on herding animals, mobility in grasslands, and a society of warriors on horseback.

pastoralists: People who depend for their livelihood more on herding mobile animals than on cultivating the soil.

Philistines: A coastal people of Palestine.

Proto-Indo-European: A language assumed to be the ancestor of modern Indo-European languages.

Rig Veda: Ancient Sanskrit sacred texts.

shi: Literally "scribes": officials who wrote down Chinese kings' orders, later called historians.

soma *or* haoma: Sacred hallucinogenic drink of ancient Iranians and Indians.

swastika: Ancient Sanskrit symbol of the Aryan people.

Tarim Basin: Deserts of Central Asia, where ancient mummies have been found buried.

Tian: Chinese term for Heaven, the supreme heavenly power.

Troy: City on northwest coast of Turkey, besieged by Greek warriors in the *Iliad*.

varnas: Categories of people among the ancient Aryans.

The world, *c.* 0 CE

Teotihuacan

Olmec

Niger
Valley

Moche
Chavin
Nazca
Wari

Five largest cities *000s*

1. Alexandria

3. Seleucia

5. Chang'an

| 1000 | 800 | 600 | 500 | 450 |

2. Rome

4. Antioch

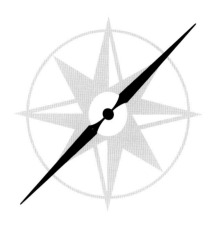

PART II

600 BCE – 600 CE: A world of regions

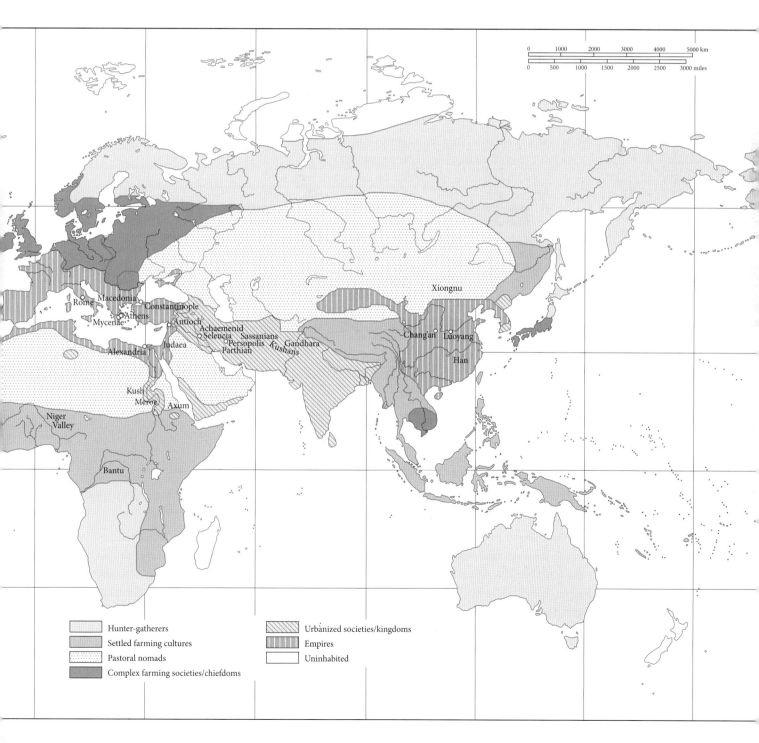

Hunter-gatherers		Urbanized societies/kingdoms	
Settled farming cultures		Empires	
Pastoral nomads		Uninhabited	
Complex farming societies/chiefdoms			

Rome
Macedonia
Mycenae
Athens
Constantinople
Antioch
Achaemenid
Seleucia
Persopolis
Parthian
Sassanians
Gandhara
Kushans
Alexandria
Judaea
Kush
Meroe
Axum
Niger
Valley
Bantu
Xiongnu
Chang'an
Luoyang
Han

Africa	
600 BCE – 600 CE	Civilizations flourish along Mediterranean and Nile Valley.
600 BCE	Start of Iron Age in sub-Saharan Africa.
591 BCE – 350 CE	Kingdom of Meroë on southern Nile.
100–500 CE	Migration of Bantu groups into southern Africa; Saharan camel caravans multiply.

Americas	
1400–200 BCE	Chavín culture in Andes.
1200–300 BCE	Olmec culture on Caribbean coast.
600 BCE – 900 CE	Mayan city-states in Central America.
150–550 CE	Teotihuacán empire in Mexico.
200–1000 CE	Tiwanaku Andean empire.
375–650 CE	Moche and Nazca empires on Andean coast.
400–1000 CE	Wari Andean empire.

South Asia	
700–500 BCE	Hindu and Buddhist religions develop in South Asia, roughly contemporaneous with Zoroastrianism and monotheistic Judaism in Middle East and Confucianism in China.
556–330 BCE	Persian empires.
247 BCE – 224 CE	Parthian empire in Iran.
78–180 CE	Kushan empire.
224–651 CE	Sasanian empire in Iran.
300–550 CE	Gupta empire in Ganges Valley.

East Asia	
771–221 BCE	Eastern Zhou, ending with Qin unification of China.
209–60 BCE	Wars of Chinese with Xiongnu, ending with submission to Han.
206 BCE – 8 CE	Former (Western) Han dynasty.
25–220 CE	Latter (Eastern) Han dynasty.
386–534 CE	Northern Wei dynasty.

Mediterranean	
800–500 BCE	Multiple invasions of eastern Mediterranean.
800–510 BCE	Greek Archaic period.
540–400 BCE	Height of Persian empires.
490–323 BCE	Greek Classical Age.
339–290 BCE	Rise of Rome to dominate Italy.
58–51 BCE	Roman conquest of Gaul.
476 CE	End of Roman empire in the west.

Although the Americas went their way separately for another thousand years, during the twelve centuries pivoting on the year 0 CE Asia, Africa, Europe, and the Americas all created civilizations of previously unequaled power and brilliance. In Africa, the great Egyptian kingdoms splintered, but the Nile Valley and the Mediterranean coast interacted even more intensely with the dynamic economies and empires to their north and east. Trade across the Sahara also expanded, and mass migrations occurred further south in Africa. In East Asia, Chinese military leaders finally ended centuries of warfare to create for the first time a unified empire that prevailed in one form or another over most of the next two millennia – although certainly not without warfare at the frontiers, periodic civil wars, occasional conquests, and plenty of vindictive violence on a smaller scale.

South Asia became even more of a crossroads than before, as kingdoms and civilizations either rose within the territory or reached into the subcontinent from West and Central Asia. The Mediterranean hosted Greek, Roman, and other civilizations that for Europeans became emblems of their historical origins. Meanwhile, Central and South America witnessed the spectacular rise and fall of empires and city-states based both in coastal regions and in the Andean highlands. Since the last of these great empires – the Aztecs – was still thriving when Europeans arrived in the Americas toward 1500, we can think of 600 BCE to 600 CE as the time when all the large continents laid the civilizational foundations of their later histories.

Foundations, literally as well as figuratively: a close look at the period in the next three chapters will show how much our historical knowledge owes to the archaeologists who dig up and interpret evidence of early civilizations. Almost all of the historical texts specialists can now read from that time became available through archaeology; the only exceptions are writings like the Greek classics or Indian and Greek oral myths, copied from one generation to the next. In many cases we can only place their evidence in context by examining the buildings, tombs, tools, weapons, clothing, and other material remains. Furthermore, new archaeological finds keep altering our historical understanding. The ancient past as we understand it is not static.

Take the case of Central America. Historians knew nothing of Mexico's Olmec civilization (roughly 1200–300 BCE), for example, until the 1930s. Until recently, most historians of Central America thought that the Mayan civilization, powerful and flourishing in today's Mexico, Guatemala, and Honduras for about fifteen centuries, maintained ceremonial centers, but lacked genuine cities, states, and armies. Excavations of areas adjacent to such centers and Tikal, combined with deciphering of Mayan script, has completely changed their minds: as with other major civilizations, they find strong evidence of centralized, coercive government, not to mention an elaborate system of canals that could not have operated without extensive central co-ordination. Current investigations will most likely reveal more extensive connections along the Andes' Pacific slopes and lowlands as well.

Central America is not the only frontier for archaeology. In Central Asia, future archaeologists will surely help historians get a clearer picture of the warlike, mobile peoples who operated in a great arc from the Middle East to China. It would not be surprising to learn of hidden cities and civilizations along what eventually became the Silk Road linking China to Europe. In short, the best we can do now for the period from 600 BCE to 600 CE is a historical summary subject to change as new evidence comes to light.

Yet some things are clear. None of the period's spectacular civilizations could have risen without agriculture that yielded a substantial surplus, and without some central apparatus that delivered agricultural products to soldiers, priests, officials, craft workers, servants, and other city-dwellers who did not herd or till for themselves. Despite variation in how warlike or commercial different civilizations were, they all depended on extensive systems of trade, political control, and cultural communication. Substantial armies required not only food, but also men, animals, weapons, armor, clothing, and shelter; civilian populations produced the military wherewithal. New, more elaborate religions often created substantial classes of priests, monks, and scholars who depended on others for their daily bread. Merchants could only thrive if they could buy their subsistence from other people.

Because such systems of control and co-ordination pushed available resources to their limits, they remained vulnerable to shifts in climate, external attacks, rebellion, and internal decay. New empires and dynasties rose rapidly only to fall even faster. Even massive China saw dramatic alternation between unification and fragmentation. The Eastern Zhou, the Qin, the early Han, the late Han, and the Northern Wei were only the most remarkable dynasties to come and go between 600 BCE and 600 CE. When empires fell, their capitals usually dwindled or collapsed into ruins. Humans were still experimenting with the dangerous work of constructing durable cities, states, and cultures.

4 Africa and the Americas: making history in challenging environments

Timeline	
30,000–10,000 BCE	A land mass surfaces between Siberia and Alaska as the last ice age causes oceans to shrink.
18,000–15,000 BCE	Earliest known migrations of humans from Siberia to Alaska.
12,000 BCE	Earliest carbon-dated human remains in the Americas at various sites.
9000–2500 BCE	Wet era in Africa; Sahara blossoms.
2000–1000 BCE	First agricultural transformations in the Americas (Mesoamerica) and sub-Saharan Africa (Nubia)
1400–200 BCE	Chavín culture in Andes.
1200–300 BCE	Olmec culture in Mexico.
1000 BCE – 500 CE	Bantu migrations in Africa.
c. 800 BCE – c. 300 CE	Kingdom of Kush (Nubia); takes over Egypt as Twenty-fifth Dynasty (751–636 BCE); retreats to new capital at Meroë in 593.
600 BCE	Iron production begins in sub-Saharan Africa near the bend in the Niger River; spreads with Bantu migrations.
c. 600 BCE – 950 CE	Kingdom of Axum; King Ezana (r. 320–50 CE) converts to Christianity.
c. 100 BCE	Camels begin crossing the Sahara; trade expands.
150–550 CE	Teotihuacán, city in the Valley of Mexico, builds first large empire in Mesoamerica.
200–900 CE	Mayan city-states flourish in Mesoamerica; collapse coincides with era of droughts, 800–1000.
200–1000 CE	Tiwanaku, city on Lake Titicaca, builds large tributary empire in southern Andes.
375–650 CE	Moche and Nazca states on Peruvian coast.
400–1000 CE	Wari, city-based empire in northern Andes, first to manage reciprocity and trade for state building.

Sickle cell anemia is a human blood disorder in which red blood cells called hemoglobin change shape from round to sickle-shaped (curved and pointed). The disease is transmitted genetically. Infants that receive the trait from both parents get the disease, which causes potentially debilitating anemia, clogging of small blood vessels with sometimes extreme pain in soft tissue and bones, kidney dysfunction, even heart attack and stroke. People who inherit the trait from only one parent can transmit it to their children, but seldom develop any of the symptoms of the disease.

Sickle cell anemia affects mainly people of African descent. About 20 percent of the population of sub-Saharan Africa have the trait. In the United States, approximately 8 percent (one in every twelve) African Americans have the trait, though only one in 500 have inherited it from both parents and suffer from the disease. Sickle cell was first identified by a Chicago physician, James B. Herrick, in 1910, but it took much longer for researchers to discover the connection between sickle cell anemia and malaria.

Malaria is one of the most serious health threats on the planet. It is spread in the saliva of the female **Anopheles mosquito**. It strikes some 400 million people every year, of whom two to three million die. Most of the victims it kills are children. Over 80 percent of all known cases of malaria occur in Africa. Not until recent times did medical researchers discover that sickle-shaped red blood cells help malaria patients survive the disease. In fact, we now know that the minute genetic mutation that created the sickle cell trait originated in tropical Africa where the disease has raged uncontrolled for tens of thousands of years. Unfortunately, only those who receive the sickle cell trait from *one* parent develop immunity to malaria. The minority who get the trait from both parents suffer double jeopardy – sickle cell anemia plus no immunity from malaria.

As the history of sickle cell anemia shows, environment shapes human history through the impact of the physical landscape, climate, vegetation, and other animal life, including the microscopic organisms that affect health. This chapter will explore the early history of two major world regions where the environment – including landscape, climate, and disease – played a crucial role in shaping human societies. The key points are:

- African and Native American societies were shaped by environmental conditions that favored low population density, delayed the agricultural transformation, and thus slowed or postponed the transition to city-states and empires.
- African geography is dominated by regions that run across the continent from east to west, impeding north–south migration and communication; and even in the regions most favorable to human survival, the environment imposed

limitations on the scale of human organization and hindered urbanization.

- The geography of the Americas is extremely diverse, but human migrants from Asia found vast regions where abundant wildlife favored hunting, gathering, and fishing; the small scale of social organization – bands and later chiefdoms – probably helped people adapt to new areas as successive generations moved south to people the hemisphere.
- In West Africa, the agricultural transformation occurred when bands of nomads, some with experience as pastoralists, fled from the Sahara into the Sahel region as the climate turned hotter and dryer; with iron implements, agriculture became easier. The new ironmaking technology spread east and south with Bantu-speaking peoples whose migrations transformed much of the continent.
- The agricultural transformation occurred in the Americas at roughly the same time as in Africa (2000–1000 BCE), but unlike Africa, it quickly led to the development of large-scale polities, first city-states and then empires.
- The emergence of city-states and empires in Mesoamerica and the Andes depended on the development of food production strategies that exploited local environments to the maximum; changing climatic conditions and overexploitation of ecological niches may have caused the collapse and abandonment of cities and contributed to the fall of great empires.

4.1 HISTORY AND ENVIRONMENT IN AFRICA AND THE AMERICAS

At the beginning of the Common Era, only about 10 to 20 percent of the world's 230 to 300 million people lived in Africa and the Americas. Africa's sparse population of perhaps 15 to 20 million people was probably due to the continent's relatively inhospitable environment. Since *Homo sapiens* originated in Africa and migrated to other regions over many thousands of years, conditions of life must have made it easier to bear and raise children outside of Africa than in Africa itself. In Latin America, the sparse population of perhaps 10 to 15 million resulted from the late arrival of humans in the western hemisphere. The first humans did not reach the Americas until between 18,000 and 15,000 BCE, at least 40,000 years after the first people migrated out of Africa into Asia and then later to Europe. Even though the natural environment in the Americas was more favorable than in Africa and the Native American population probably grew somewhat faster than early African populations, Africa benefited from a substantial head start.

In Africa (except for the Nile basin, covered in Chapter 2), the agricultural transformation began later than in Asia and Europe. Pastoralism also took longer to get started or proved unsustainable. Even after the agricultural transformation, people lived mainly in small settlements scattered across the landscape. They avoided building cities and kept their politics and their polities local, kin-based, and relatively egalitarian (though men from favored lineages tended to dominate in the larger communities and chiefdoms). In sub-Saharan Africa, most people shunned urbanization and state-making until after 600 BCE. In the Americas, the transition to agriculture also occurred later than in Asia and Europe, but in contrast to Africa, the first urban cultures and city-states appeared soon after. The first large city-states and territorial empires arose in Mexico and Peru just as the Roman empire was disintegrating.

The human geography of Africa is dominated by the continent's location astride the equator (see Map 4.1). Most of the African land mass consists of two huge areas that are exceptionally hostile to human survival – the Sahara Desert and the Central African tropical rain forest. In the Sahara, the world's largest desert, most plant and animal species cannot survive. Apart from its great salt deposits and occasional oases, the Sahara has little to recommend it to human beings. To the south, the tropical rain forest was equally inhospitable to human life. In the intense heat, steamy humidity, and constant rainfall, plant and animal species mature, multiply, and mutate at dizzying speeds. The tropical rain forest is full of killers, including diseases, parasites, and predators. Tropical soils are extremely poor in nutrients, covered by dense foliage, and difficult to farm. Pastoralism was also impossible because of the African tse-tse fly, which causes a debilitating illness (sleeping sickness) in humans and is deadly for horses, cattle, and other livestock. Even less arid or humid areas where agriculture and pastoralism were feasible proved to be riskier than in most of the rest of the world, because rainfall in Africa was (and still is) less reliable and predictable.

Similar conditions (deserts and tropical rain forests) exist in the western hemisphere. The migrants who crossed the land

Map 4.1 African regions and places

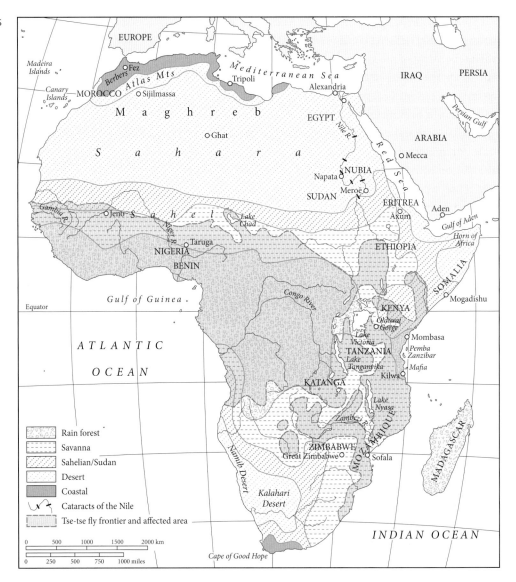

bridge from Siberia to Alaska between 18,000 and 15,000 BCE or migrated by sea much later (*c.* 6000 BCE) established themselves throughout the Americas. Like Africans, most avoided settling in deserts or rain forests. Unlike Africa, however, the western hemisphere also contains large areas of temperate climate and moderate rainfall, including most of North America and the "southern cone" of South America. Even more important for its early history, the Americas contained many mountain plateaus and valleys, even in areas near the equator, where temperatures remained moderate throughout the year, soils were rich in minerals, and rainfall proved to be fairly predictable for many years at a time. In Africa, only the highland regions of modern Ethiopia match these favorable conditions. Thus, in the Americas, the agricultural transition led quickly to the development of large towns and cities and even great empires, while in Africa towns and cities came later, tended to be smaller, and did not provide the manpower and resources for large territorial states.

4.2 AFRICAN ENVIRONMENTS

Africa is unique in many ways. Over three quarters of the African continent is located in the tropics near the equator – more than any other major land mass. This has negative consequences for the health of people, animals, and food crops. Unlike Latin America, Africa does not possess mountain ranges that rise high enough above the equatorial heat to provide temperate zones for human habitation. Africa also has more land mass per mile of coastline that any other continent. Most of the continent is landlocked, more isolated from contact with the rest of the world than any other continent except the Americas (up to 1492). Reinforcing that isolation is the African coast, which is unusually harsh and difficult to navigate, with few natural harbors anywhere outside the Mediterranean. Apart from the upper Nile, Africa's rivers cannot be navigated beyond short stretches, so internal communication and trade is also difficult.

African Regions

Africa is a continent of diverse regions that generally run east to west. The largest single feature is the **Sahara Desert**, now too dry to support human habitation except for isolated communities of traders and pastoralists clustered in tiny patches where wells tap underground pools or streams. South of the Sahara lies the **Sahel**, an arid steppe 120 to 250 miles in width, that stretches 4,000 miles in length from the Atlantic Ocean to the Red Sea, from whence it drops south to form a ring around the Ethiopian highlands. Between the Sahel and the tropical rain forest to the south is a vast **savanna** or plain, mostly grassland where it

touches the Sahel, but wooded to the south where it gradually gives way to a vast tropical rain forest. The area south of the rain forest repeats this pattern in reverse, with the Kalahari and Namib deserts replicating Sahara-like conditions.

Each of these strips acted as a barrier to migration. Moving south or north required humans to adapt their survival strategies to new and unfamiliar environments. The most daunting barrier of all was the huge tropical rain forest. Adaptations that succeeded in one zone could not easily be transported to the corresponding zone on the other side of the rain forest. Grain agriculture, which first developed in the Nile Valley and the Ethiopian highlands in ancient times did not reach similar temperate zones in southern Africa until modern times.

In the Sahel and savanna regions of West Africa, where sub-Saharan agriculture was first practiced, extreme variations in the timing and magnitude of rainfall add an additional element of risk and uncertainty that persists to the present. In the rain forest regions, where rain is abundant, soils are thin and lacking in nutrients; the abundant tropical foliage is possible only because short life cycles guarantee that decaying plants are constantly replenishing the soil. Agriculture requires felling trees, clearing patches of land, and planting crops that can withstand competition from the forest plants and weeds, constant rainfall, and a huge variety of hungry pests and foraging animals.

Disease in the Tropics

The greatest obstacle to African food production and trade today as well as in the past is disease. In hot, damp climates, there is no cold season to kill off microbes, viruses, parasites, insects, weeds, and other pests. Moreover, the reproduction of harmful organisms accelerates in the tropics. In temperate climates, for example, mosquitoes take weeks to mature after eggs are laid in water; in the tropics, this aquatic phase takes only a few days. For thousands of years, the most deadly tropical disease has been malaria (see above). Disproportionate numbers of Africans also suffer from parasitic infestations like hookworm (one billion sufferers today), tapeworm, ringworm, and many others. Until recently, the disease called "river blindness" (spread by blood-feeding black flies that thrive along riverbanks) affected millions. Today, the HIV-AIDs epidemic affects Africa more than any other continent.

The disease that has most affected Africa's history is **trypanosomiasis**, commonly called **sleeping sickness** or **nagana**. This disease kills both humans and their domesticated animals, especially horses and cattle. It is carried by the **tse-tse fly**, which thrives in areas of high annual rainfall (at least 20–28 inches) and mixed vegetation of trees, bushes, and grasslands. The tse-tse fly and sleeping sickness are absent from the Sahara and the Sahel, but form a barrier to raising horses and cattle that runs across the entire continent.

South of the tse-tse fly frontier (shown in Map 4.1 above), human porters had to carry all freight, animal-driven plows and other equipment could not be used in agriculture, and livestock-raising failed. Only thinly scattered sparse populations of hunters and gatherers could survive in such areas.

4.3 AFRICA TO 600 BCE

There is evidence of human habitation throughout Africa in Neolithic times. The entire continent may have had a population as large as one million inhabitants 100,000 years ago. The agricultural transformation based on Southwest Asian food grains began first in the lower (northern) Nile Valley of Egypt not long after 5000 BCE. By 2000 BCE, agriculture predominated in the upper (southern) portion of the Nile later called Nubia. The precocious development of agriculture, cities, and empires based on the amazing productivity of agriculture in the Valley of the Nile in Egypt has already been discussed in Chapter 2.

Nubia and Ethiopia

The Egyptian example exerted considerable influence in Nubia, the Nile Valley region south of Egypt between the first and fifth cataracts (waterfalls). In this upland region, the Nile flows for long stretches through deep gorges. Even where agriculture is feasible, the valley land on either side of the river runs in narrow strips. Much of Lower (northern) Nubia was so inhospitable that it remained virtually uninhabited as late as 1000 BCE. In Upper Nubia, from the third to fifth or sixth cataracts, the first major black African polities emerged based on farming (mainly **sorghum**, a tropical grass) and sheep-herding sometime after 900 BCE. The Kingdom of Kush with its capital at Napata derived its wealth mainly from the trade and tribute networks its rulers established with regions further south. Kush acted as entrepôt and go-between, sending gold, ivory, semi-precious stones, ebony, slaves, and other products to Egypt. The Kingdom of Kush was so successful that in 751 BCE it managed to exploit divisions among the rulers of Egypt to invade and establish a new Egyptian dynasty (called later the "Ethiopian" or Twenty-fifth Dynasty) that lasted until 636 BCE, when it fell to Assyrian invaders. Thereafter, the Kush retreated to the south and established a new capital at Meroë, where a new Nubian state flourished until the fourth century CE.

In the Ethiopian highlands to the south of Nubia, the unusually temperate climate, fertile soils, and ample rainfall attracted migrants from the north as well as from southern Arabia. The proximity of Red Sea ports along the Eritrean coast encouraged trading links to Arabia and the Indian Ocean. Archaeological evidence is sketchy, but it is likely that city-states and even larger territorial units developed in this region long before the establishment of the kingdom of Axum at the dawn of the Common Era (see below).

North Africa and the Sahara

Much of the North African shore of the Mediterranean from the Nile Delta to the Maghreb region consists mainly of inhospitable desert. By 5000 BCE, migrating bands possibly from the eastern Mediterranean had settled along the coast of modern Algeria and Morocco and in the Atlas-Aurès mountains behind it. They first developed foraging activities, combining fishing in the Mediterranean with hunting and gathering. These northern peoples, later called Berbers, were eventually subjugated by Greek colonists and Roman armies, but many in the interior avoided this fate. By 3000 BCE, this population had developed its characteristic nomadic pastoralism, herding goats and sheep; others on the coast cultivated a variety of food crops, as did the migrants and colonists who settled on oases in the Sahara.

West Africa

Between 9000 and 2500 BCE, it rained in the Sahara. The Saharan wet phase provided enough rainfall to attract migrants to its numerous lakes and streams. The first inhabitants were bands of hunters, gatherers, and fishermen. By 7000 BCE, the archaeological evidence confirms the presence of domesticated animals, including cattle, sheep, and goats. Evidence of cultivation is much sketchier and occurs 3,000 years later. Late in the wet phase, probably well after 4000 BCE, small bands of agriculturalists moved south into the Sahel and continued on to the savanna. As the desertification of the Sahara intensified in the second millennium BCE migration to the south probably increased. As the climate became drier, the tse-tse fly frontier moved south beyond the Sahel. Livestock herders and farmers from the Sahara mixed with or displaced the Sahel's sparse local population of hunters and gatherers, but the process was gradual and slow. There is no evidence of conquest or forced displacement.

One of the four major African language groups (see Map 4.2), the Niger–Congo group, which includes Arabic-influenced Swahili and the other Bantu languages, originated in West Africa among the pastoralists and farmers who moved into this region from the Sahara. The other three main language groups are the Afro-Asiatic (including Arabic, spoken in many varieties throughout North Africa and the Horn), the Nilo-Saharan,

Map 4.2 Africa's major language groups

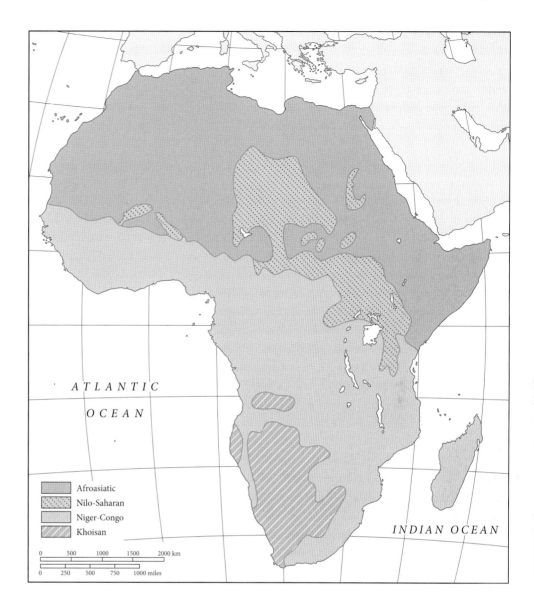

ATLANTIC

OCEAN

INDIAN OCEAN

Afroasiatic
Nilo-Saharan
Niger-Congo
Khoisan

0   500   1000   1500   2000 km

0   250   500   750   1000 miles

spoken mostly in and south of the Sahara, and the Khoisan (click) languages that originated among the hunter-gatherer peoples of southern Africa.

In contrast to the Nile Valley, Nubia, and Ethiopia, environmental conditions in sub-Saharan tropical Africa from the Sahara to the Kalahari made dense urban settlements difficult and even dangerous. Each hectare of land required more work and yielded less than in more favored areas. The prevalence of disease, including parasites, capable of wiping out or debilitating entire populations made it crucial for humans to live in small groups, so that if an infection or infestation devastated one band, others were not inevitably affected. By 900 BCE or so, walled villages of 500 to 1,000 inhabitants were established in Senegambia and the region where the Niger River turns southward. Though there is no evidence of any territorial state until much later, peace and security conditions must have improved substantially by 700 BCE when walls ceased to be built and open villages with smaller populations

proliferated. A century later, security must have declined again. Villages were relocated to less accessible sites, walls were built again, and evidence of raiding (possibly by Berber nomads from north of the Sahara) appears in some areas.

Central, Southern, and East Africa

The inhabitants of Central and southern Africa, and the interior of East Africa, lived in small bands of hunters, gatherers, and fishermen until the arrival of the Bantu migrants (see below).

4.4 IRONMAKING AND AGRICULTURE, 600 BCE TO 600 CE

Two great innovations profoundly affected Africa at the dawn of the Common Era. The first was the spread of ironmaking, which revolutionized both agriculture and warfare. The second was the introduction of the camel, which revolutionized trade, especially across the Sahara. As farm production grew, trade increased, and population rose, the great Bantu migration began. Eventually, cities and state-making with all their risks and hardships appeared for the first time in sub-Saharan Africa.

From Stone to Iron

The leap from stone implements to metal tools and weapons first occurred in Southwest Asia about 4000 BCE and spread west into Europe and east to China over the next millennium. Turning rocks into metal can only be done by heating the ore to a point where the metal becomes liquid and can be separated from other "impurities." Metal production started with the relatively soft metals that liquefy at the lowest temperatures: copper (which melts at 1,083 degrees Centigrade) followed by lead, gold, and silver. Mixing copper with tin produced the "Bronze Age." Iron melts at 1,540 degrees. Finding a way to produce that much heat took another three thousand years, until the Hittite empire (1500–1200 BCE). After the Hittite discovery, ironmaking techniques slowly spread to Europe, South Asia, and China over the next several centuries.

The spread of metallurgy, especially ironmaking, took place slowly for two reasons. First, many regions of the world lack readily accessible deposits of iron. Transporting heavy ores over long distances was costly, though less so by water than overland. Second, the furnaces consumed huge amounts of charcoal to produce the needed heat. Ironmaking, which needs 50 percent more heat than copper, required advances in furnace design and a huge increase in charcoal production. Ironmaking thus developed mainly in forested regions or in areas adjacent to extensive woodlands. The Egyptians made little use of iron, even after the technology became known to them, because the lower Nile lacked forests to cut down to make charcoal.

Unlike Southwest Asia and other regions, sub-Saharan Africa had no Bronze Age. Production of iron began simultaneously with that of the softer metals, especially copper, by about 600 BCE in two distant regions. The first was in West Africa, just below the Sahara, the second at Meroë in southern Nubia. Both regions have abundant iron ore and access to great forests.

Origins of African Ironmaking

Historians once thought that ironmaking was discovered and developed independently in Africa. Differences in the design of the West African furnaces lent plausibility to this hypothesis. African ironsmiths did introduce a number of variations and improvements, but the basic technology of ironmaking seems to have been imported. In West Africa, Berber tradesmen familiar with Phoenician ironmaking are most likely to have been the source of the new technology. In the east, ironmaking likely arrived with traders and artisans from Egypt or from Arabia across the Red Sea. The fact that ironmaking did not appear in sub-Saharan Africa after a long era of learning and experimentation with easier metals, but instead simultaneously, also argues against an independent African discovery.

Iron spread throughout sub-Saharan Africa mainly from West Africa. The best documented early site of West African ironmaking is at Taruga on the Jos Plateau near the Niger Bend in what is today central Nigeria, where at least thirteen iron furnaces were operating, the oldest dating from 600 BCE. From this region, ironmaking spread throughout sub-Saharan Africa. Though Taruga and other early sites belonged to the Nok culture, the main carriers of the new technology were Bantu-speaking people, who incorporated iron into a new model of agriculture (mixed with pastoralism where feasible), which they spread throughout the continent.

4.5 BANTU MIGRATIONS

The **Bantu migrations** – movements of diverse groups of agriculturalists, cattle-herders, artisans, and fishermen speaking a variety of Bantu languages – started when a first wave of settlers began moving south and east from their original homes along the Niger River sometime after 1000 BCE. In the Niger region, they grew yams, peppers, gourds, and various legumes, and supplemented these crops with hunting, gathering, and fishing. Population growth rewarded, but also endangered, their success. As communities grew, they sent out or expelled some of their friends and relatives to explore and eventually settle elsewhere. This strategy was perfectly suited to an environment that could not support dense populations and where the rapid spread of disease threatened population centers.

The Bantu migrants must have eventually numbered in the hundreds of thousands. They moved south over 1,000 miles through the Central African rain forest and into the savannas beyond it (see Map 4.3). They reached the East African uplands some 2,500 miles away a few centuries later. Then they turned south, reaching the Serengeti Plain by 500 CE. Remarkably, this vast migration was not organized by any single authority or institution. Migrating to new areas became integral to Bantu culture and identity. No outside or higher authority was needed to set them in motion.

The Bantu-speakers had two great advantages over the other cultures they met in their travels. First, they understood farming.

Map 4.3 Bantu migrations

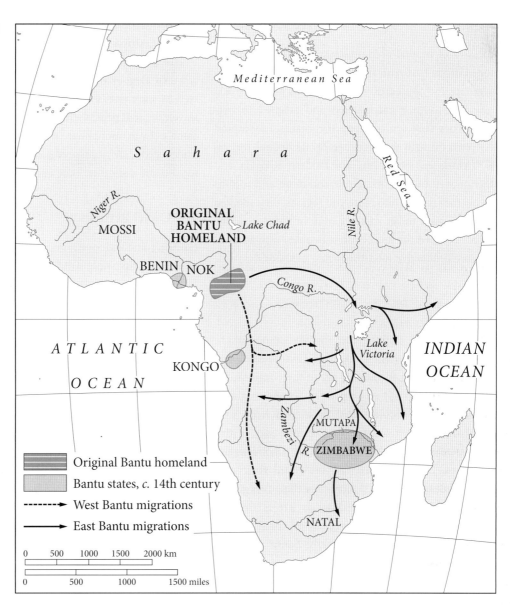

In most areas, they became the pioneer farmers, introducing agriculture for the first time. Second, iron became available early in the migrations. By 400 BCE, Bantu farmers were using iron axes to fell trees and iron hoes to plant crops and control weeds. The new iron implements made Bantu agriculture much more productive than ever before at an early stage in the migration process. The age of iron and the age of agriculture were synonymous with the arrival of Bantu-speaking peoples throughout sub-Saharan Africa.

Central Africa

Most Bantu migrants probably moved only once, walking for days, weeks, months, or even years before settling down permanently in a new place. The migrants applied the knowledge they brought with them to the new environments they encountered.

Since the migrations took place over many generations, migrating groups had time to adapt. In the Central African rain forest, the Bantu migrants adopted bananas and plantains as staples. There they encountered diverse groups of pygmoid hunters and gatherers, notable for their knowledge of the forest's plant and animal resources, their extraordinary skills as hunters, and their short stature (due mainly to childhood dietary deficiencies). Bantu farming bands settled on riverbanks and other favorable locations, using iron axes to clear small patches of land for crops. They usually left hunting to the natives of the area and traded yams, bananas, and other harvested crops along with iron tools, knives, and arrow points in exchange for game, animal skins, medicinal herbs, and other forest products. The influence of the Bantu settlements can be seen in the widespread adoption of Bantu languages by the pygmoid hunters and gatherers of the region.

East Africa

Similar processes of mutual accommodation, trade, and influence developed in the East African interior and southern Africa. The Bantu groups introduced diverse food crops and livestock, changing the mix as they encountered and adapted to new environments. They first settled along the chain of lakes and rivers that stretch through the more temperate upland regions from Lake Victoria in the north into modern Rwanda and Burundi, then moved into the less fertile and more arid regions of Tanzania. As they moved into more arid regions, they adopted cattle-herding and grew millet and sorghum. In these areas, the Bantu met and absorbed the local Cushite peoples, who adopted the Bantu's more productive food-producing methods.

Southern Africa

From about 100 to 500 CE, Bantu groups migrated into southern Africa, breaking into two streams south of Lake Malawi, one along the coast and another further inland. In these regions, the Bantu groups continued to rely on crops of millet and sorghum, along with cowpeas, but supplemented these food crops with small herds of sheep and goats. On the western edge of this migration, they encountered the click-speaking Khoikhoi and San ethnic groups, both of which had developed their own successful survival strategies. The languages of these two groups originated in the Zambezi Valley perhaps as late as the first century BCE, but divided sometime later as the Khoikhoi adopted sheep-herding (perhaps from early Bantu migrants) while the San continued as hunters and gatherers. Until the arrival of European settlers in the nineteenth century, the three groups coexisted more or less peaceably. Their different food strategies led them to settle in different areas.

4.6 EARLY AFRICAN CITY-STATES AND TRADING NETWORKS

Between about 100 and 500 CE, Saharan camel caravans grew steadily in number and importance. In this era, few caravans actually crossed the Sahara to the Mediterranean coast. Most brought salt from the Sahara to villages first in the Niger Valley and then to trading centers just below the Sahara throughout West Africa. Old trading networks linking Egypt to Nubia and East Africa also revived in this era. Along the East African coast, trade with Arabia and across the Indian Ocean to India and beyond also began to exceed earlier levels. By 600 CE, trade had led to the development of trading towns and entrepôts on the southern fringes of the Sahara and to the production of tradable commodities across sub-Saharan West and East Africa.

The caravan trade needed marketplaces where traders could sell their cargoes and buy goods to take back across the desert as well as warehouses to store goods, food, and drink for weary travelers, and pens with plenty of water and fodder for the camels. Even more than markets and entrepôts, the caravan trade needed African producers to supply goods to exchange for the salt and other trade goods the caravans supplied.

The Camel Revolution

Camels come with one hump or two, but only one prickly (some would say impossibly irritable) personality. The double-humped Bactrian camel has a thick coat that keeps it warm in temperate and even cold climates, but is ill-suited to the desert. The single-humped dromedary, however, thrives in the desert. It can carry heavy loads over long distances with little or no water and food. Camels can drink as much as 100 liters of water at a single sitting and then go up to nine days without drinking. Their speed and endurance are legendary. Walking along at 4 miles per hour for 12 to 16 hours per day is not unusual. These are feats that would kill any other pack animal.

Camels were domesticated later than horses, cattle, and the other herd animals. The first archaeological evidence dates from 3000 BCE in southern Arabia, but domesticated camels were not found in North Africa and the Sahara until the first century BCE. Introduced by the Berber predecessors of the modern Tuareg, they soon revolutionized long-distance trade across the Sahara, which had nearly vanished as the region became drier and drier. Because of the distances involved, the African exports to the trans-Saharan trade were limited to cargoes that could either walk across the desert (slaves and, on some routes, livestock) or fetch a high price in relation to their weight (palm oils, kola nuts, and later gold, ivory, gems, and spices). The most important product exported from the Sahara to sub-Saharan Africa was salt, mined from the beds of lakes that had dried up during the millennia after 2500 BCE.

Jenne-jeno

In West Africa, the agricultural transformation linked to the Bantu produced enough food to free up small numbers of people for work in mining, metallurgy, weaving, pottery-making, and other trade-related occupations. Regional trading centers developed in the Niger Delta that allowed people to specialize, some as farmers and fishermen, others as ironsmiths and goldsmiths, artisans, and marketers. To survive in the tropical heat, however, it was vital for Africans to resist the temptation to create population centers where disease could easily wipe out large numbers of people.

Jenne-jeno is the best studied of the early West African trading towns. It began as a farm village in the Niger Delta when it was first settled in about 250 BCE. By the second century of the Common Era, the village had grown into a sizeable market town. At its peak in about 800 CE, the population totaled 27,000, extremely large for the tropics. Three peculiarities, common to West Africa at this time, but rare in human history, characterized this town. First, the settlement pattern tended to minimize contagion. Instead of a single densely populated "city," Jenne-jeno consisted of a central place with twenty-seven satellite clusters located at an average distance of half a mile from the center. Second, though the central place was surrounded by a thick wall, there is no evidence of warfare or violence throughout its long history. The wall may have served to limit access to the market (for taxing or other purposes), but seems not to have been needed for defense. Third, there is no evidence anywhere in Jenne-jeno of the emergence of a privileged elite or of a centralized, hierarchical authority, no big palaces, monuments, pyramids, temples, or elaborate burial sites. Despite these peculiarities – or perhaps because of them – Jenne-jeno managed to survive as a trading center for some 1,600 years.

The town served as a marketplace both for local producers and for long-distance traders. Archaeological digging has turned up slag heaps from iron furnaces, weavers' quarters, and evidence of the work of other producers of tradable goods. The digs have also turned up many items that must have been imported from far away, including gold jewelry. The development of trade elsewhere in Africa (and later on in West Africa) sparked urban development, state-making, warfare, and inequality. The dispersed settlement pattern, peaceableness, and egalitarianism that seem to have characterized Jenne-jeno and many other large villages and towns in early West African history contrasts sharply with the Egyptian model of centralization and elite rule adopted in East Africa.

Kingdom of Kush (Nubia)

Far to the east in the Nubian region south of Egypt, the kingdom of Kush survived its fall from power in Egypt in 636 BCE. One reason for the Kushite defeat was technological. The invading Assyrians had iron weapons, but the Kushites had failed to change the Egyptian reliance on bronze. The Kushite rulers relocated their capital from Napata (following an Egyptian raid that sacked the city in 593 BCE) to the more easily defended "island" of Meroë, further south past the great bend in the Nile. This move precipitated two important changes in Kushite society. First, Meroë's rulers encouraged the development of iron

smelting. The area is rich in iron ore and wood for charcoal. Second, the White Nile does not flood extensive areas suitable for flood plain agriculture as the Nile does in Lower Nubia and Egypt, but the Meroë region does receive sufficient rainfall to grow tropical grains (millet and sorghum) using iron hoes. So the Meroitic rulers encouraged the development of a new kind of agriculture based on small producer communities rather than state co-ordination and control, closer to sub-Saharan practice than to the Egyptian model.

The arrival of the camel also helped Meroë become a key center of trade and tradable production by making it possible to ship goods north across the desert rather than up the difficult terrain of the Nile Valley through northern Nubia. By 200 BCE, Meroë was producing iron, cotton cloth, pottery, and other products for local trade while serving as an entrepôt for the export of ivory, gold, animal skins, fragrances, and oils produced in East Africa to the south. The Meroitic monarchs derived much of their wealth from controlling and taxing this trade. The pyramids at Meroë shown in Figure 4.1 illustrate this trade-based wealth.

In its Meroitic phase, the kingdom of Kush remained tied to the Egyptian model of a highly centralized state ruled by a monarch and a small, privileged elite. The changed environment caused some alterations in the system, however. Agriculture, now in the hands of farmers and sheep-herders dispersed in small villages throughout the "island," could no longer be controlled tightly (or even taxed effectively) by the state. The monarch's income came to depend more on trade than production and the state never developed the capacity to mobilize great armies of obligated workers to build huge monuments on the Egyptian scale.

Meroë declined rapidly in the third century CE. When Axumite invaders overran the "island" in 350 CE, the town had been abandoned for at least a generation. The causes of Meroë's collapse are not precisely known, but historians hypothesize that the economic decline of Roman Egypt and Axum's diversion of ivory and other goods from the south reduced opportunities for profitable trade and undermined Meroë's rulers. In addition, deforestation to make charcoal for iron smelting probably took a toll on the region's environment. Finally, overcropping to support the city's large population may have depleted the soil and made it impossible for the city's population to survive.

Axum in Ethiopia

The kingdom of Axum (or Aksum) originated with the arrival of Arab and Yemeni immigrants, who crossed the Red Sea sometime before 600 BCE and settled in the Ethiopian highlands.

Figure 4.1 The Meroë archaeological site, 186 miles north of the Sudanese capital Khartoum. The Meroë pyramids form one of the most spectacular sights in Sudan with about fifty small pyramids – the tombs of the rulers of Kush from about 250 BCE to 350 CE. The pyramids lie on the tops of two rocky ridges blanketed by sand dunes about three miles east of the Nile.

There they introduced agriculture and merged with the native population of Africans. Axum is to modern Ethiopia what the Roman empire is to modern Italy, a glorious ancient precursor that serves as a source of national pride. The Axumites spoke and wrote a Semitic language, called Ge'ez, a forerunner of the modern Amhara language of Ethiopia. They created the first written African culture outside of Egypt.

The Greeks and Romans knew Axum as a key trading city mediating between the Red Sea and Mediterranean routes and the ivory, furs, leather, gold dust, and incense of the interior of Africa. The Axumites established their own Red Sea port at Adulis, which also served as an entrepôt for Indian Ocean goods, including silks and spices, traveling north to Mediterranean markets. The Axumite state exacted tribute from farmers and herders, encouraged artisans to produce luxury goods (copper, bronze, glass, resin-based oils) for export, and taxed the African products that passed through Adulis. It minted valuable coins that preserve the names of its kings.

The Axumite kingdom warred with Meroë but never with Egypt. Egyptian influences were not excluded and even encouraged. When the Egyptian elite converted to Christianity under Roman tutelage in the fourth century CE, the Axumite King Ezana (r. 320–50 CE) followed suit early in his reign. Axumite Christianity soon came under the influence of the Egyptian Monophysite church, whose monks had played a key role in converting much of the Egyptian peasantry (aided by the Roman decision to exempt Christians from slavery and conscription). At some point the legend grew up that the kings were the descendants of Solomon and the queen of Sheba. The Axumite state declined in the eighth century, perhaps for environmental causes similar to those that doomed Meroë, but Christianity remained the region's dominant religion to modern times.

4.7 AMERICA'S TWO CONTINENTS

Like Africa, the physical geography of the Americas runs mainly in wide strips of similar climate and vegetation. Unlike Africa, however, the strips are cut by huge mountain ranges running from north to south. The African highlands that run south from Ethiopia are older, and like the Appalachian range in the eastern United States, never reach the heights of the Rockies or the Andes. A second contrast, but no less important, is the fact that most of the land mass of the western hemisphere (including virtually all of the North American continent) is located in temperate climate zones beyond the Tropics of Cancer and Capricorn. Because of their greater diversity in altitudes and in climate zones, the environments of the western hemisphere are more varied than those of Africa.

The Importance of Altitude

Comparing the African and American tropics, two differences stand out. First, a large portion of the American tropics north of the equator lies under the waters of the Caribbean Sea and the Gulf of Mexico. Second, a large portion of the tropical mainland both north and south of the equator is lifted out of tropical deserts and rain forests and into more temperate climates found in mountain plateaus and valleys by the Sierra Madre ranges in Mexico and Central America and the Andes mountains in South America. Map 4.4 shows these features for the northern hemisphere and for South America.

The effect of changing elevations can be seen by driving south into Mexico from the southwestern United States. The deserts and dry savannas of the Mexican north are close to sea level. To the south, as Mexico's two mountain chains come ever closer together, the central plateau rises slowly to over 10,000 feet above sea level. As the landscape rises, it becomes cooler and greener. Driving inland from the Atlantic or Pacific coast, the rise from sea level is even more rapid. The altitude change from the Pacific coast of South America into the Andean Mountains is equally abrupt.

As in Africa, tropical deserts and rain forests are the most difficult regions for human settlement, apart from the frozen arctic and the barren tops of high mountains. They cover a significant portion of the western hemisphere, more than in Europe and Asia, but much less than in Africa. Desert conditions exist in diverse locations: southern and Baja California, the southwestern United States and northern Mexico, the coast of Peru, and the Atacama Desert in northern Chile. All of these deserts would fit comfortably inside the Sahara, with plenty of room to spare. The tropical rain forests of the Caribbean and the Amazon basin are also smaller in size and as a proportion of total land area than the African tropical rain forest, even when measured at their fullest extent before the massive deforestation of the past hundred years.

In the pre-Columbian era, the largest and densest populations in the Americas lived in two main areas: **Mesoamerica** and the Andean region. Mesoamerica (or Middle America) is the region that extends from Central Mexico southward into Central America. Its northern boundary marks the limits of sedentary agriculture north of the Valley of Mexico (see Map 4.4). Its southern boundary extends down the Pacific coast to include Guatemala, Belize, and portions of Honduras and El Salvador. The region of dense population in the Andes extends down the Pacific Coast from southern Ecuador to southern Peru (see Map 4.4). The bulk of the human settlements in this region as in Mesoamerica were found in highland valleys and plateaus rather than on the coast.

Origin of the Native Peoples of the Americas

The first humans to reach the Americas probably came from Siberia during the last ice age when glaciers soaked up so much water that ocean levels throughout the world fell to low levels. About 30,000 BCE, the shrinking North Pacific had fallen enough to expose a large mass of land running from northeast Asia to what is today called Alaska. This land "bridge" was actually quite large, measuring up to 600 miles across for several millennia. Later called Beringia, after the Bering Strait that now covers it, the bridge stayed above water until about 10,000 BCE when global warming melted the glaciers enough to submerge it again.

Scholars and scientists are still uncertain about the arrival dates of the first immigrants, what languages they spoke, and even what to call them (see Box 4.1). Recent DNA studies have suggested that there were actually two separate migrations, one probably overland between 18,000 and 15,000 BCE and another that must have come in by water in about 6000 BCE. Some archaeologists still argue for earlier dates going back as far as 40,000 BCE, but the physical evidence of human habitation that can be dated by modern carbon dating techniques (some of it recently redated using better methods) is no older than about 12,000 BCE. By that date or shortly thereafter, humans had already reached the southern tip of South America.

The peopling of the Americas has inspired scholars, journalists, and adventurers of all kinds to hypothesize that other migrants might have reached the Americas centuries before Columbus from the South Pacific, West Africa, Egypt, Palestine, Europe, and even Outer Space. While there is archaeological evidence of Viking settlements in Newfoundland, the coast of Labrador, and on Baffin Island in the tenth century CE, no physical evidence of other migrations has ever been found.

Disease in the Americas

Until the late fifteenth century, when Europeans and Africans arrived in large numbers bringing Old World diseases with them,

Map 4.4 Physical features of the western hemisphere

Tropic of Cancer

Tropic of Capricorn

Unclassified highlands or ice-cap
Tundra and alpine tundra
Coniferous forest
Midlatitude deciduous forest
Subtropical broadleaf evergreen forest
Mixed forest
Midlatitude scrubland
Midlatitude grassland
Desert
Tropical seasonal and scrub
Tropical savanna
Tropical rain forest

the disease environment of the Americas was relatively benign. The tropical areas of the Americas were less healthy than other regions, but the tropics constituted a much smaller percentage of the total landmass than in Africa. As in Africa, people living in tropical areas lived in bands and chiefdoms scattered thinly across the landscape and avoided creating great population centers where diseases could spread and become endemic. Most of the indigenous population of the Americas, however, lived in temperate climate zones either north of the Tropic of Cancer or in mountain valleys and plateaus more than 5,000 feet above sea level.

The disease environment of the Americas may also have benefited from the accidents of geography. The first human inhabitants of the Americas passed through northern Siberia

Box 4.1 What Name for the "First Americans"?

The people who migrated to Alaska from Siberia left no written records, so we have no idea what they called each other. As they multiplied and moved, peopling the entire hemisphere, they divided and subdivided into new bands and communities, chose or acquiesced in new leaders, and adapted to the diverse environments they found. Their survival strategies, social relationships, religious practices, and even their language and speech patterns became more and more diverse as time passed. By 1500 CE, there may have been as many as a thousand mutually unintelligible languages and dialects spoken in the Americas (though scholars have grouped most of them into three to six language groups, comparable to the four main African language groups).

The first Europeans to arrive in the Americas thought they had found the "Indies," the name Europeans had given to the landmasses and islands that touch what they called the Indian Ocean. Spanish explorers referred to the people they encountered as "Indians" (indios in Spanish and Portuguese). The name stuck even after the Europeans learned more geography.

Mistaken geography was not the only problem with this name, however. "Indians" often suffered from oppression, persecution, and discrimination at the hands of the Europeans. The term "Indian" came to be associated with this history and the racial prejudice it embodied. In many parts of the Americas, the dominant Europeans and their ancestors used "Indian" as an insult.

This is why many writers, along with government agencies, newspapers, and businesses, avoid using the term "Indian" and now prefer other terms. In the United States, "Native American" is the term used by the government in official documents like the Census. In Latin America, the term "indigenous" (indigena in Spanish) is the most commonly used. The indigenous peoples of the hemisphere are also commonly referred to as the Native or aboriginal population of the Americas.

The Native American population is also commonly referred to by using the names associated with the many ethnic, cultural, and linguistic traditions represented among them. Thus the indigenous inhabitants of the region extending from the Yucatan peninsula and Southern Mexico to Belize, highland Guatemala, and northern Honduras are called the Maya.

Some cautions are in order, however. The names that have come down to the present are often those imposed by European conquerors, not the names used by the indigenous peoples themselves. Moreover, ethnic identities in the past, just like today, tended to be layered and overlapping. For example, we now refer to the powerful pre-Hispanic rulers of Central Mexico as the "Aztecs," a name invented in the late eighteenth century and popularized by Alexander von Humboldt, a German traveler and historian, who visited Mexico in the early 1800s. The "Aztecs" themselves were a Nahuatl-speaking people, who probably referred to themselves as the Mexica.

and Alaska where the long, frigid winters would have made it impossible for many disease-causing microbes and parasites to survive the journey. The disease environment in the Americas also benefited from the relative lack of domesticated animals. Many human diseases and parasites originated in livestock or other animals and spread to humans only after domestication. The list of such diseases is long and includes measles, smallpox, influenza, and many more. Other diseases are carried, incubated, and spread via blood-sucking insects to humans from domestic animals, including sleeping sickness and numerous parasites. The only large animals domesticated in the Americas were the Andean alpaca, llama, and vicuña, all of which were confined to mountainous regions where low temperatures during much of the year reduced the health dangers they represented. Native Americans also domesticated the turkey, the muscovy duck, the honeybee, and the dog, none associated with major human ailments.

4.8 THE AMERICAS TO 600 BCE

As in sub-Saharan Africa, but for quite different reasons, the transition from hunting and foraging to sedentary agriculture took place gradually over thousands of years and was not completed anywhere until after 2000 BCE, at least five millennia later than in the Fertile Crescent of Southwest Asia. While most of Africa made do without horses and other draft animals because of the tse-tse fly, Native Americans made do without draft animals because they did not exist in the western hemisphere. Unlike Africa, however, the agricultural transformation in the Americas occurred without iron and took place after migration had slowed or stopped altogether. The development of agriculture in the Americas also led to the rapid growth of city-states and empires, in contrast to Africa where iron tools and agriculture did not lead to the establishment of high-density population centers, but instead to the Bantu migrations that dispersed the farming population throughout the continent.

Late Transition to Agriculture

Glaciers covered the northern half of North America as far south as New Jersey until sometime after 8000 BCE. The retreat of the glaciers thereafter coincided with the extinction of many species of animal that humans had depended on for food. Mammoths and mastodons disappeared forever, while horses became extinct until reintroduced by Europeans in the sixteenth century. As Native Americans grew in number, they migrated less and devoted more attention to exploiting the ecological niches they or their ancestors had occupied. Hunting, gathering, and fishing predominated everywhere, but gradually people discovered how to make better use of plant life as well.

The main food crops of the Americas include maize, beans (frijol), and squash in Mesoamerica and potatoes, yucca, and other root crops in the Andes. Unlike the wheat, barley, and rye of Southwest Asia, which came from wild grasses and were relatively easy to breed selectively, the food staples of the Americas – maize and potatoes – were quite difficult and time-consuming to engineer. Cultivation developed, but initially the food crops served only to supplement the diet of bands and communities that continued to rely mainly on hunting and foraging. For example, in the Tehuacán Valley of Mexico by 5000 BCE, human foragers had found and exploited wild maize, gourds, chilies, and avocados. By 3500 BCE, there is evidence of cultivation of beans and squash. The archaeological evidence shows, however, that such groups did not settle in one place and thus did not depend on agriculture for the bulk of their food needs. Instead, they continued to move from one site to another during the year, a strategy that reduced the risk of over dependence on any single food source or location.

Sedentary agriculture required centuries of genetic engineering as well as the development of new techniques of cultivation. Farmers taught themselves to save the seeds or roots of plants with the highest yields for the following year's planting. The earliest successes came with fast-growing gourds and squash, whose seeds were easily stored. But the transition from part-time tending of wild plants to full-time dependence on food crops could not take place until high yields could be achieved growing staple crops like maize and potatoes. In the case of maize, for example, the yield had to reach 450 to 550 pounds per hectare reliably year after year before it made sense for the inhabitants of the Tehuacán Valley or anywhere else to abandon semi-nomadic foraging and settle on farms. Even with genetically selected seed, however, yields did not reach the threshold levels until cultivators discovered, through trial and error, how to

ensure that their crops got enough water and nourishment. Not until 2000–1500 BCE did sedentary farming communities appear in the Americas.

Foundational Cultures: The Olmecs (1200–300 BCE) and Chavín (1400–200 BCE)

Evidence of incipient cultural, commercial, and perhaps even political unity across large regions of Mesoamerica and the Andes appears in the archaeological record between 1500 and 1000 BCE. In Mesoamerica, this development is identified with the Olmec culture, which arose along the Caribbean coast in the modern Mexican states of Veracruz and Tabasco. In the Andes, the new development was initially identified with a major archaeological site in the Peruvian highlands known as Chavín de Huantar. In recent times, however, the pre-eminence of Chavín de Huantar has succumbed to new dating techniques that have shown that this site was constructed toward the end rather than the beginning of the spread of the "Chavín" culture.

The name given to the Olmecs comes from the Nahuatl language of the Aztecs, who referred to the later inhabitants of this area as Omecatl or "rubber people" (after one of the trade goods the Aztecs imported from them). The core area of the Olmecs is a gently rising alluvial plain that stretches from the sea to the foothills of the Sierra Madre Oriental. Beginning in about 1200 BCE, the Native peoples of this area began building a major population and political center known today as San Lorenzo, which held a maximum population of perhaps 7,000 inhabitants at its height some centuries later. Three other towns, La Venta, Laguna de los Cerros, and Tres Zapotes, developed later; all had populations of several thousand inhabitants.

Pre-Olmec agriculture used **slash-and-burn** (called **swidden**) methods, similar to Bantu farmers in the African rain forest. Farmers cleared forest or brush vegetation, burned the ground cover, and used planting sticks to make holes through the ashes into the soil. After one harvest or at most two, the field had to be abandoned for up to ten years before it had recovered sufficiently to plant again. The Olmecs introduced new methods, including irrigation canals, drained fields rescued from swamps, and **raised fields**, that is, fields raised above wetlands and river deltas to protect crops from flooding. This evolution facilitated a concentration of power in the hands of rulers who could organize or coerce co-operation for such projects.

The Olmecs may have pioneered the political transition from band organization to chiefdoms in the Americas. The huge Olmec stone heads, made from single blocks of stone transported on rafts and log rollers from quarries 90 miles away, now testify silently to the power of the Olmec chiefs. While there is evidence of fairly complex political organization elsewhere in this era, none provides clearer evidence of the transition than the Olmec sites.

From the Olmec core area, Olmec religious symbols, trade goods, and political organization spread far and wide. Olmec craftsmen produced small carved animals, especially jaguars, and various half-human creatures out of jade, serpentine, and clay, to trade for luxury goods not available locally. Olmec scribes developed the continent's first writing, using up to 500 distinct glyphs to record major events and celebrate the deeds of lords and chiefs. The Olmec rulers also controlled the external trade of their region and extracted taxes from traders. Olmec agricultural techniques, jade carving, religious symbols like the jaguar, and even artistic styles influenced later developments throughout Mesoamerica from the Maya to the Aztecs. By 300 BCE, however, the Olmec towns had been abandoned, never to revive.

Once considered the Andean counterpart to the Olmecs, the Chavín culture is now understood as but one of several foundational cultures to influence later developments in the Andes. Its uniqueness lay in the coherence and uniformity of the religious symbols and practices it exported (or imposed) throughout a vast region. Like the Olmecs, the Chavín craftsmen carved representations of animals, especially crocodiles, birds of prey, and cats of all kinds, including jaguars. They frequently combined animal and human features in terrifying combinations representing various gods. Chavín-style art and religious symbols, along with the distinctive U-shaped Chavín-style ceremonial centers, have been found mixed with other traditions in a large area of northern Peru from the Pacific coast to the highlands.

Now that Chavín de Huantar, the largest town (population 2,000–3,000) associated with Chavín-style artifacts is no longer seen as the origin of the new culture, other sites vie for designation. Some are located in highland regions near Chavín de Huantar, but other early Chavín sites have been found along the Pacific coast where permanent settlements had long exploited both fishing opportunities and the relatively fertile strips of land along rivers flowing down from the Andes. Little is known of political organization in this era, but the people of Chavín de Huantar, like the Olmecs at San Lorenzo before them, appear to have made the transition from large band to chiefdom and profited from their strategic location along trade routes running both north–south through the highlands and east–west between the highlands and the coast.

4.9 CITIES AND EMPIRES, 600 BCE – 600 CE

At the dawn of the Common Era, urbanization began almost simultaneously in Mesoamerica and the Andean region. The new cities left abundant evidence of hierarchical class structures, complex governing systems, and occupational specialization. They fed themselves by exploiting adjacent farmlands and forests with ever greater efficiency. They developed trade and tribute relations with their own hinterlands and with other cities and regions. A small number of these first cities managed to defeat rival towns and extend their dominance over extensive territories with large populations. By 600 CE, these two regions of the Americas had begun to look more like ancient Southwest Asia or Egypt of the pyramids than sub-Saharan Africa.

In the rest of the Americas, however, urbanization and state formation did not occur. People continued to avoid large population clusters, social organization remained relatively egalitarian, and political power gravitated to individuals in bands or to certain families or lineages in the numerous chiefdoms scattered across the landscape. In areas as different as temperate North America and the Amazonian tropics, the cultivation of food crops spread widely, but agriculture usually remained subordinate to hunting and gathering strategies.

Mesoamerica: The Mayan City-States (200–900 CE)

The ruins of Mayan pyramids and temples can be found throughout southern Mexico and northern Central America (see Map 4.5). They adorn mountain slopes in highland Guatemala, river valleys in Belize and Campeche (Mexico), dry savannas in Yucatan, tropical rain forests in northern Honduras and the Peten (Guatemala). Complex chiefdoms commanding several thousand people and capable of building small stone temples and monuments can be dated to as far back as 400 BCE. Not until about 300 CE, however, is there solid evidence of the new farming techniques on which the Mayan urban economy depended.

For many years up to the 1970s, archaeologists and historians believed that these ruins were the legacy of a unique civilization. The Mayan achievements in architecture, writing, artistic expression, astronomy, and mathematics were impressive. Unlike other societies with sophisticated high cultures, the Maya seemed to have managed these accomplishments despite their dependence on low-yield slash-and-burn farming methods that were practiced at the time of the Spanish conquest in the sixteenth century. Assuming that the ancient Maya used the same methods, archaeologists concluded that cities could not have existed. The pyramids and temples must have been ceremonial centers populated only by priests and their helpers. The priests would have been supported by contributions of food and clothing from the peasants who benefited from the priests' knowledge of matters both practical (the calendar, for planting) and spiritual. Somehow, the Maya had found a way to reap all of the benefits of urban

Map 4.5 Mesoamerican states and cultures; a. Mesoamerica c. 300 BCE, b. Mesoamerica c. 500 CE.

(a)

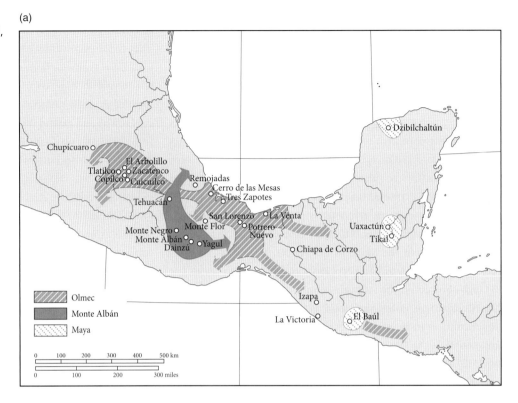

(b)

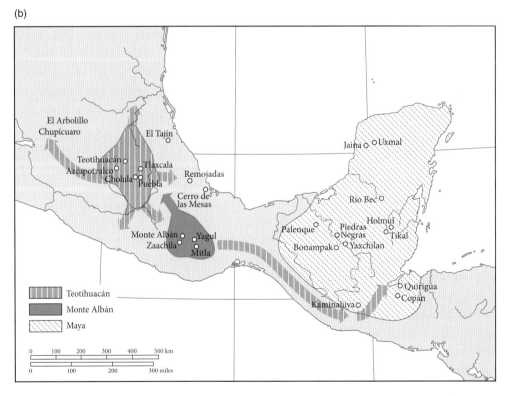

civilization while avoiding the tyranny, warfare, disease, and inequality that accompanied urban development and state formation elsewhere in the world.

This idyllic account of the Maya was false. Three scientific breakthroughs have yielded a more accurate though less flattering picture of Mayan society. First, archaeologists in the 1960s and 1970s began to turn their attention away from the pyramids and temple complexes to survey the areas surrounding them. What they found was astounding: the ruins of hundreds and even thousands of homes – entire cities they had not noticed. The ceremonial centers were actually constructed in the middle of large towns and cities, some with populations as large as 50,000–70,000 people. Second, archaeologists also discovered the remains of sophisticated drainage systems, raised fields, and irrigation canals on a scale much larger than anything the Olmecs had ever imagined. Satellite photography suggested that the Mayan area had been crisscrossed by hundreds of miles of canals. Then, finally, the Mayan hieroglyphic writing system was decoded with astounding results (see Box 4.2). Most of the inscriptions on stelae, monuments, and burial sites were not religious at all. Instead, they recorded the great achievements (mostly military victories) of local rulers and their dynasties.

The transition from chiefdoms to city-states probably occurred first among the southern Maya, who lived in fertile valleys inland from the Pacific coast of El Salvador and Guatemala. Instead of a small elite composed of a single chief and his family, the new states included multiple privileged lineages and elite functionaries such as war leaders, priests, provincial governors, engineers to design irrigation works and supervise other agricultural projects, architects, sculptors, muralists, scribes, and tax collectors. Artisans worked with local gems and metals (copper and gold) to make tools, ornaments, and religious objects. Important functions were performed by local traders and merchants specializing in long-distance luxury trades. The elites of the Mayan towns like Kaminaljuyu (Guatemala) and Copán (Honduras), for example, probably constituted 2 percent of the population. Their achievements and privileges rested on the backs of commoners engaged in farming and occasional corvée construction labor.

The southern Mayan city-states reach a high point between 100 and 250 CE. In the latter year, the Ilopango Volcano in central El Salvador erupted with terrifying violence, spreading thick ash over an area as large as 60 miles around. As a result, some areas became uninhabitable for more than a century. Survivors moved north, where Mayan culture flourished for another 600 years. Most of the Mayan city-states controlled territories in the range of 1,000 square miles or less, but the states centered at Tikal and Calakmul may have been much larger. Mayan hieroglyphic inscriptions give accounts of frequent wars, with graphic descriptions of the punishments meted out to the vanquished.

Box 4.2 Mayan Writing

The Maya were the only Mesoamerican people to devise a complete written language. Like the Sumerian and Egyptian scripts, the Mayan system was composed of a mixture of ideographs and phonetic symbols, which were written in double columns to be read from left to right and top to bottom. The language was rudimentary in many ways. It had few adjectives or adverbs, and the numbering system comprised only three symbols: a shell for zero, a dot for one, and a bar for five.

During the classical era from 300 to 900 CE, the Maya used the script to record dynastic statistics with deliberate precision, listing the date of the ruler's birth, his accession to power, and his marriage and death, while highlighting victories in battle, the capture of prisoners, and ritual ceremonies. The symbols were carved on stone panels, stelae, and funerary urns or were painted with a brush on folding screen books made of bark paper; only four of these books from the late period remain extant today.

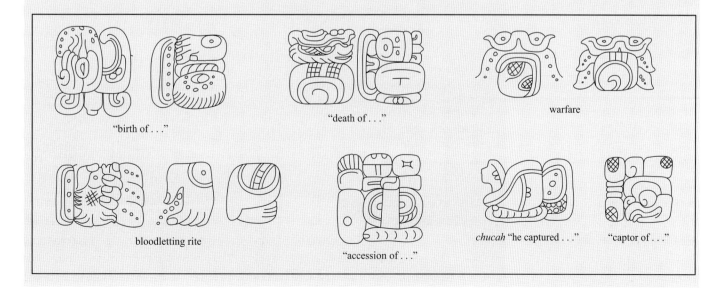

"birth of . . ."   "death of . . ."   warfare

bloodletting rite   "accession of . . ."   *chucah* "he captured . . ."   "captor of . . ."

On the collapse of states and the abandonment of urban places in the Mayan regions after 800 CE, see Chapter 9.

Mesoamerica: Teotihuacán Empire (150–550 CE)

In the Valley of Mexico, far to the north of the Mayan region, Native Americans built the great city of Teotihuacán, which grew from a small farming town in 150 BCE to an immense city of 100,000–200,000 inhabitants at its peak between 450 and 500 CE. As Figure 4.2 illustrates, the ruins of its pyramids and temples, located in the Valley of Mexico 25 miles northwest of Mexico City, constitute one of the most impressive archaeological zones in the world. The city covers more than 8 square miles. It was laid out in a dense grid pattern around an immense ceremonial center with massive temples and pyramids. The largest is the Pyramid of the Sun, which rises to a height of 200 feet above the Avenue of the Dead. Despite the size of the city and its monumental constructions, little is known about its rulers. In contrast to the Maya and most other Mesoamerican cultures, there are virtually no representations of rulers, victorious battles, or social hierarchies in the art and architecture of

Teotihuacán, though all were prominent features of the city's society and politics.

Teotihuacán seems to have begun its growth after 100 CE when the Popocateptl Volcano erupted and buried Cuicuilco, a rival town located at the southern end of the Valley of Mexico, under an immense lava flow. The rulers of Teotihuacán expanded the agricultural potential of their region through irrigation works and raised fields. They attracted or coerced most of the population of the entire valley to move to Teotihuacán. As other rulers in the ancient world had discovered, the size of the capital city and the wealth it controlled helped to determine how much territory it could aspire to control.

Teotihuacán's rulers also benefited from state-sponsored trading. Early in the city's development, they took control of the nearby obsidian mines at Pachuca and Otumba. Handcrafted obsidian weapons, tools, and statuary produced by artisans in over 400 workshops became the city's main export. Teotihuacán exports also included ceramics, shell ornaments, and textiles for elite consumers. The city's artisans produced pottery for local use, stone statuary and blocks for construction, rough cloth, and many other products. While the city acquired

Figure 4.2 The Pyramid of the Sun, constructed around 100 CE, is the third largest in the world. The urban complex that developed around it grew to a population of between 100,000 and 200,000, making it one of the largest cities in the world in its time. The city was abandoned by about 550. Nearly a thousand years later, the Aztecs gave it its name; we do not know what it was called at the time it was built to tower over the city of Teotihuacán.

its basic food supplies mainly from its immediate environs, the Teotihuacán elite imported large quantities of luxury products from distant areas, including feathers, gold, and the highly prized cacao beans from the Mayan city-states.

The empire of Teotihuacán may have been larger in territory and population than the Egypt of the pharaohs but fell far short of the Chinese or the Romans. In the absence of written records, historians have had to rely on indirect evidence to measure its size. Teotihuacán trade goods, emissaries, tribute collectors, and religious symbols and myths spread throughout Mesoamerica. Archaeological digs at virtually every Mayan city, for example, have turned up evidence of Teotihuacán influence extending over three centuries or more. Some hieroglyphic inscriptions suggest alliances between Mayan cities and Teotihuacán or even the establishment of Teotihuacán military colonies or trading settlements. Evidence of direct rule by Teotihuacán through provincial governors is much more limited, perhaps to an area of no more than 10,000 square miles in the Valley of Mexico and adjacent regions with a total population of less than one million. Beyond this core, however, the rulers of Teotihuacán probably exacted tribute from otherwise independent chiefdoms and city-states covering a much wider area. For much of its history, Teotihuacán maintained apparently peaceful relations with a rival but much smaller empire centered at Monte Albàn in the Valley of Oaxaca to the south.

In about 550, all of the buildings in the center of Teotihuacán, including temples and elite residences, were burned, their contents looted, and their religious statues and ceramics systematically smashed and destroyed. At about the same time, perhaps simultaneously, most of the homes throughout the city seem to have been abandoned. How and why this happened is debated by archaeologists.

Teotihuacán's collapse seems inescapably linked to food supply. Skeletal remains of city residents show unmistakable signs of famine episodes in the century or so preceding the collapse. Archaeologists have discovered a growing gap between the height of skeletons found in the elaborate graves of the city's elite and those of commoners. These differences in height demonstrate rising inequality in access to basic nutrition, with elites monopolizing some foods, especially scarce meat supplies.

Keeping population at Teotihuacán left some of the valley's best agricultural lands out of cultivation, even though some of the city's food supplies probably came from outlying areas by canoe across Lake Texcoco. Dispersing the population throughout the valley would have increased food production, but would also have encouraged the development of competing urban centers and potential rivals to power and dominance. Teotihuacán's collapse was thus due partly to its success in centralizing power, and too many people, in a single place.

Archaeologists still debate whether Teotihuacán's final destruction came from internal revolt or invasion. Teotihuacán's religious and political art, in contrast to the Maya, emphasized repetition and uniformity. Like Islamic decorative art, there are no human representations on any of the structures uncovered thus far, in contrast to the exuberantly individualistic stone carvings and hieroglyphic inscriptions of the Maya in this era. Though there are clear references to a hierarchy of power and status, nobles and commoners alike are depicted without recognizable individual characteristics. If Teotihuacán religious and political ideas were consistent with these artistic expressions, the sharp rise in inequality in the last century before the collapse might well have seemed especially shocking to a population in which people were expected to submerge their individual interests for the good of the society. With this background, the fact that Teotihuacán's center was destroyed and looted, apparently by people angry enough to take time out from looting to smash religious icons and statues, while the city's ordinary residences were not torched, lends further credence to the theory of revolt from below.

A second hypothesis holds that Teotihuacán fell to invaders. Weakened by too many mouths to feed, the city began losing population long before its center was destroyed. The city's decline after 500 is paralleled by the rise of other towns and cities in Central Mexico, such as Cholula to the south. Perhaps a rival city took advantage of Teotihuacán's weakness. Or perhaps the city was destroyed by "barbarian" invaders, forager nomads pushed into Central Mexico from the far north by drought and hunger. In Mesoamerican traditions, invading armies usually burned temples and ceremonial centers, looting and destroying the religious and political symbols of their vanquished rivals. The recent discovery of a life-sized marble death statue of a great personage shot through with arrows parallels representations of the ritual execution of defeated kings and rulers at other sites in Central Mexico.

However its rulers fell, the entire city was abandoned completely at about the same time. A century later, parts of Teotihuacán were reoccupied by people whose material artifacts mark them as culturally distinct from the Teotihuacános. The ceremonial center was never used again, as though somehow cursed.

Andean Coast – The Moche and Nazca (375–650 CE)

Andean geography made large cities and the empires based on them much more difficult to build than in Central Mexico, as Map 4.6 shows. Much of the Peruvian coast, for example, consists of a narrow strip of arid desert no wider than 30–60 miles. The Pacific Ocean produces clouds that blow in over the hot land but do not produce rain until they reach the cooler air of the

Map 4.6 Cities and empires of the Andes

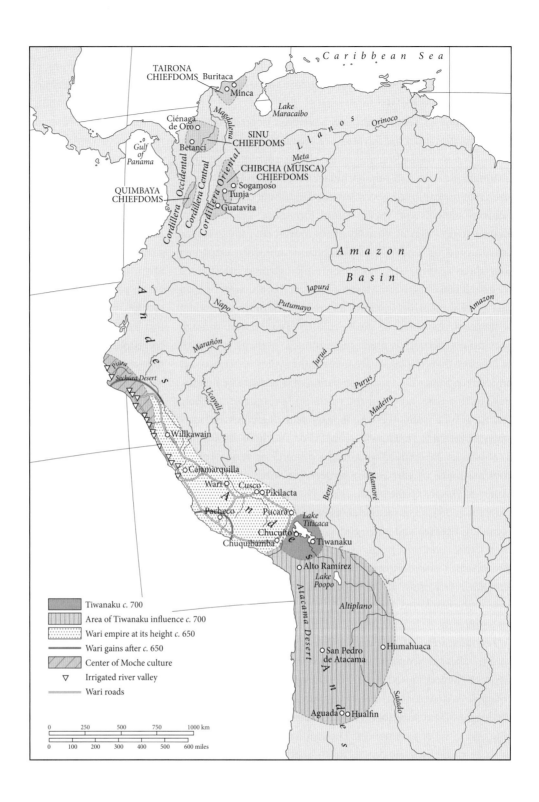

mountains. Rain and snow in the mountains feed rivers that descend to cut across the desert from east to west before reaching the ocean, where the cycle begins again. Agriculture developed along the coastal river basins. Large towns emerged in areas where irrigation canals made agriculture especially productive. The coastal areas were not unified, however, by a single great river system like the Nile, and the lack of natural harbors made coastal communication by boat extremely difficult. Since the coastal towns produced much the same food and craft products, they had little reason to develop economic ties; their trading interests pointed them toward the mountains rather than each other.

Nonetheless, both the Mochica state centered at Cerro Blanco on the Moche River on the north coast of Peru, and the Nazca state centered on the Rio Nazca 250 miles south of modern Lima, exerted some measure of control over large coastal territories. Both apparently subjugated highland territories adjacent to their principal cities. While both possessed the organizational capacity to mobilize large labor forces for canal-building and religious or funerary construction, neither could boast a city population to match the urban development occurring simultaneously in Mesoamerica. The Moche culture's most distinctive feature was its magnificently illustrated pottery bowls, vessels, and small statuary, which depicted every aspect of Mochica life, both real and imaginary. So much Mochica pottery depicts sexual activity that it had to be displayed in a separate museum in Lima open only to adults. Excavations at burial sites reveal a highly stratified society.

Nazca fame soared after a plane flew over a barren stretch of land between the Rio Nazca and the Rio Ingenio in 1926 and discovered large-scale human-made line drawings in the desert floor below that were visible only from the air. The lines were constructed by digging shallow trenches that exposed lighter-colored earth beneath the surface. Most of the lines are straight, arranged like spokes of a wheel centered on a water source, and may have had some utilitarian purpose. In one area, however, the straight lines give way to circles and curves that outline the shape of plants and animals. The Nazca lines have never been explained. Several imaginative writers have suggested that they were made by extraterrestrial visitors to mark landing places for spaceships. Because the dry air of the desert prevents decay, burial sites in the Nazca area have proved to be a treasure trove for archaeologists (but also for thieves). Richly embroidered cloth woven by the Nazca's predecessors, known as the Paracas culture, has been found in almost perfect condition more than 2,000 years after it was first woven.

Andean Highland Empires: Tiwanaku (200–1000 CE) and Wari (400–1000 CE)

Two major highland states also arose in this era and overlapped with those of the Peruvian coast. The first was centered in modern Bolivia at Tiwanaku (today's Tiahuanaco) on the south shore of Lake Titicaca. The second was centered at Wari (or Huari) in the Central Andes in the modern province of Ayacucho in Peru. (See Map 4.6 above.)

The Tiwanaku empire developed, like Teotihuacán, from the relatively secure foundation of a successful city-state. Lake Titicaca and Tiwanaku are located 12,600 feet above sea level in a cold area of scant rainfall and frequent frost. Tiwanaku's rulers developed and extended the irrigation systems and raised fields, that first appeared in the region centuries earlier, in an environment that presented many more challenges than Central Mexico. Tiwanaku's "raised fields" (shown in Figure 4.3) produced potatoes and other roots, but maize and most other food crops could not be grown in the cold climate with its short growing season. The lake, however, supplied fish and shellfish. On the surrounding arid, high-altitude savanna (called *puna*), Tiwanaku herdsmen tended large herds of llama and alpaca, but the natural vegetation is so sparse and stunted that each animal requires a large area to provide the food it needs.

The "raised fields" built by Tiwanaku's people were roughly 3–10 feet above the surrounding area and 15–50 feet long and

Figure 4.3 Warmed during the day by the sun, the water kept the crops from freezing during the cold Andean nights and even extended the growing season. Probably invented by farmers on the shore of Lake Titicaca, raised fields produced the food surpluses needed to support the city of Tiwanaku. Lost after the Spanish conquest, the system was rediscovered by archaeologists and revived by farmers in modern times. Studies show that land cultivated in this manner could yield 20 tons of potatoes per hectare.

wide. Between these fields, the people dug canals to bring water from the lake. The fields themselves were layered with rich soil on top and periodically fertilized by shoveling muck and sediment from the canals. Below the top soil were layers of stone and sand that allowed for drainage. Raising the fields protected them from flooding during the rainy season. The water in the canals acted as a heat reservoir that protected the crops from frost. The canals ensured a supply of water after the dry season began. The canals also attracted fish and wild fowl. This ingenious system of cultivating potatoes and other root crops was productive enough to support a population of 20,000–40,000 people at the apex of Tiwanaku's development. Archaeologists have discovered raised fields in many locations throughout the Americas, from the Mississippi Valley to the Amazon region and as early as the Olmecs in Mexico (1200–300 BCE). Nowhere did this technology do more to raise agricultural productivity than at Tiwanaku, which would have been nearly uninhabitable without it.

In its prime, Tiwanaku's influence penetrated an extensive territory. Its gods and symbols were accepted and revered, as evidenced in the pottery and temple art in a large area of the southern Andes. The state-building strategy followed by Tiwanaku's rulers aimed at securing their city access to food and raw materials not available in their core area. They used two main mechanisms to achieve this goal. The first was colonization. They sent out agricultural colonists to produce maize, cotton, squash, peppers, and other vegetables that could only be grown at lower altitudes. Tiwanaku's rulers then taxed the colonists by taking a portion of their harvests. The second was state-sponsored trade. Tiwanaku (like Teotihuacán) promoted the development of artisan products to be exchanged for food and other goods. The city's rulers devoted much of their military resources to creating and protecting trade routes for llama caravans that extended throughout the southern Andes to the Pacific coast and as far south as the Atacama Desert of modern Chile.

The economic complementarity that characterized the Tiwanaku realm appears to have made it unnecessary for its rulers to develop a highly centralized system of governance. Archaeologists have found no evidence that Tiwanaku ever developed an elaborate governing structure for the areas over which it held sway. In the provinces of the Tiwanaku empire, where abundant evidence testifies to Tiwanaku's economic, religious, and cultural influence, there were no residences for provincial governors or storehouses for tribute goods, in contrast to the Wari state in the northern Andes.

Unlike Tiwanaku, the Wari state prospered mainly through military conquest and highly centralized rule. The Wari expanded from a less productive economic base than most other empires. With modest rainfall and no major water source to be controlled or managed co-operatively, Wari agriculture was based on low-yield dry-land farming with occasional small-scale terracing and irrigation. Llama and alpaca herding at higher elevations provided meat, wool, and pack animals. The Wari state overcame these local environmental limitations through conquest, state-sponsored artisan manufacturing, road-building, and state-sponsored trade, but it could only do so by creating a highly centralized governing structure.

The Wari first conquered regions where farming was more productive, from Cusco (the later Inka capital) in the south to Cajamarca in the north, adding adjacent coastal territories as they could. To make this system work, they had to build roads, push other regions to produce more food (or at least export more), and control the trade to make sure Wari exports monopolized markets. The Wari state developed extensive craft industries producing export goods, which it put to use in a state-regulated trading network. In their capital, the Wari rulers organized artisan workshops producing pottery, cloth, ornaments, and religious objects from semi-precious stone such as lapis lazuli, obsidian, and turquoise as well as imported shells and other materials. To facilitate both trade and conquest, the Wari, besides improving or building roads, used khipus (knotted string devices) for record-keeping. More importantly, the Wari state was probably the first to seize upon Andean traditions of mutual aid and reciprocity to build a novel system for extracting resources from the populations it conquered. Instead of crudely seizing crops at harvest time along with other tribute goods, the Wari rulers required communities to farm plots designated for the state and the state religion, stored their harvests locally, and then staged elaborate festivities at which local producers and their chiefs were feted with food, drink, and craft products in return. Some of the stored products were kept to be used in case of future crop failures and famines. The rest went to the Wari ruler, governors, and military.

Conclusion

The people who inhabited sub-Saharan Africa and the Americas at the beginning of the Common Era confronted quite different environments. The first transitions from foraging to full dependence on agriculture and pastoralism occurred in Africa and the Americas 6,000–7,000 years after their first appearance in Southwest Asia. In Africa, agriculture and pastoralism confronted exceptionally hostile conditions. In the Americas, a more benign environment and low population density made hunting, fishing, and foraging a viable strategy long after the disappearance of megafauna at the end of the ice age.

The exceptional challenges posed by the African environment help explain why the agricultural transformation of sub-Saharan Africa did not quickly lead to urbanization and state formation, except in the Nile Valley and the Ethiopian highlands. The agricultural transformation began at the end of a long dry cycle, and was pioneered by people migrating out of the Sahara as its lakes and rivers turned to sand. Iron tools carried by Bantu migrants spread the benefits of low-yield farming, mixed whenever possible with fishing, foraging, and pastoralism, throughout much of sub-Saharan Africa. But even with iron tools, Bantu agriculture never produced enough surplus to support large urban populations or high-living elites. Moreover, the exceptionally unfavorable disease environment in much of tropical Africa posed the threat of epidemics.

More auspicious environmental conditions in the Americas may have delayed the agricultural transition by rewarding hunters and gatherers with abundant game and food gathered from wild plants. But once the transition to agriculture had been achieved, these favorable conditions also facilitated a much more rapid transition from small bands to increasingly complex chiefdoms, city-states, and empires in Mesoamerica and the Andes. The flourishing of Native American societies, from foraging bands to great cities and empires, was also linked to climatological changes. The transition to agriculture began after 2000 BCE at the close of a long period of abundant moisture that had begun 2000 years earlier. From 1800 BCE to 1 CE a dry trend set in, but from the dawn of the Common Era to about 800 CE, the climate became wetter again, though with increasing seasonal fluctuations in rainfall. The archaeological record of these later centuries is extraordinarily rich in the Americas.

When we return to these two vast regions of the globe in Chapter 9, we will examine how sub-Saharan Africans overcame incredible odds to create city-states and empires. And we will see that what nature nourished in the Americas, it could also destabilize and destroy.

Study Questions

(1) How did environmental conditions delay the agricultural transformation in Africa and the Americas?

(2) Describe how the Bantu migrations began and their impact throughout Africa.

(3) Why did urbanization and state formation occur later in sub-Saharan Africa and the Americas than in other parts of the globe?

(4) Why did urbanization and state formation occur so quickly after the agricultural transition in the Americas, but more slowly in Africa?

(5) Compare Africa's Jenne-jeno to the Mayan city-states.

(6) Compare the kingdoms of Kush and Axum to Teotihuacán and Tiwanaku.

(7) What impact did environmental change have on the rise and fall of city-states and empires?

Suggested Reading

ELIZABETH P. BENSON, *The Worlds of the Moche on the North Coast of Peru* (Austin: University of Texas Press, 2012). This is an excellent study of the rise of the Moche, their society, economy, politics, and culture, and the collapse precipitated by uncontrollable changes in the environment.

MICHAEL D. COE, *Breaking the Maya Code* (London: Thames & Hudson, 2012). This is a fascinating account of the academic debates and struggles over the organization of Mayan society, and the breakthroughs in decoding the Mayan hieroglyphs that revolutionized our knowledge of Mayan culture and politics.

GRAHAM CONNAH, *African Civilizations: An Archaeological Perspective* (Cambridge University Press, 2001). Connah surveys African cultures and states from earliest times, based on archaeological evidence of settlement patterns, agricultural activities, and cultural changes.

WILLIAM L. FASH, *Scribes, Warriors, and Kings: The City of Copán and the Ancient Maya* (New York: Thames & Hudson, 1991). This is a copiously illustrated account of a major Mayan city by the Harvard archaeologist who led the work of uncovering and understanding it.

MARJORIE M. FISHER, PETER LACOVARA, SALIMA IKRAM, AND SUE D'AURIA, *Ancient Nubia: African Kingdoms on the Nile* (Cairo: American University in Cairo Press, 2012). In this lavishly illustrated collection of essays, experts on Nubian history and culture from ancient times give detailed accounts of the major cities as revealed by modern archaeological discoveries.

RICHARDSON BENEDICT GILL, *The Great Maya Droughts: Water, Life, and Death* (Albuquerque: University of New Mexico Press, 2000). This book explores the environmental history of the Mayan collapse.

JOHN WAYNE JANUSEK, *Ancient Tiwanaku* (Cambridge University Press, 2008). Janusek's work is a major survey of the pre-Inka Tiwanaku empire, including the archaeological discoveries of recent years.

JOHN READER, *Africa: A Biography of the Continent* (New York: Knopf, 1999). This is a lively account by a leading historian and scholar of Africa.

HELAINE SILVERMAN AND DONALD PROULX, *The Nasca* (Oxford: Blackwell, 2002). This is an engaging, well-illustrated, and comprehensive survey of the mysterious people who made immense sand drawings visible from the air above.

JOHN H. TAYLOR, *Egypt and Nubia* (Cambridge, MA: Harvard University Press, 1991). This is a richly illustrated short survey of the Nubian cities and kingdoms of the upper (southern) Nile.

Glossary

Anopheles mosquito: Female mosquitoes of this species commonly carry malaria.

Bantu migrations: Slow migration of peoples speaking Bantu languages from origins in Senegambia throughout West and Central Africa from roughly 1000 BCE to 500 CE. Bantu migrants introduced iron tools and agriculture to many areas.

camels: Bactrian (two humped, colder climate); dromedary (single hump, ideal for deserts); dromedary camels made trans-Saharan trade possible, beginning in first century CE.

Mesoamerica: Also called Middle America, this is the region in North America where agriculture and urbanization developed after 2000 BCE; it extends from Central Mexico to northern Central America.

nagana: See trypanosomiasis.

raised fields: Farming technique that involves creating earthen platforms above the level of the surrounding countryside for growing crops.

Sahara Desert: The world's largest desert, covering most of North Africa and stretching from the Red Sea to the Atlantic Ocean.

Sahel: Arid steppe (flat plain) 120 to 250 miles in width, stretching 4,000 miles in length from the Atlantic Ocean to the Red Sea.

savanna: An extensive area of grassland with occasional bushes and trees.

sickle cell anemia: Genetically transmitted disease common in Africans and in descendants of Africans; originally developed as an adaptation that helped many Africans to resist malaria.

slash-and-burn: See swidden.

sleeping sickness: See trypanosomiasis.

sorghum: Tropical grass that is grown as a grain food and for animal fodder.

swidden: Agricultural technique used in forest areas where soils are thin; also known as slash-and-burn agriculture. Farmers cut down trees and undergrowth ("slash"), burn off the remaining plants, sow crops for a year or two, then leave the land fallow for up to ten years.

trypanosomiasis: Commonly called sleeping sickness or nagana; carried by African tse-tse fly; causes death in hoofed animals like horses and cattle and serious illness in humans.

tse-tse fly: The African tse-tse fly, which thrives in areas of high annual rainfall (at least 20–28 inches) and mixed vegetation of trees, bushes, and grasslands, spreads trypanosomiasis (sleeping sickness).

5 East, Central, and South Asia: the religious foundations of empires

South Asia

c. 600 – *c.* 300 BCE	Magadha kings
c. 550 BCE	Achaemenid Persians take Gandhara.
c. 543 – *c.* 491 BCE	Reign of King Bimbisara, who conquers eastern Bihar.
c. 400 BCE?	Mahavir, founder of Jain sect.
c. 368 BCE?	Death of Gautama Siddartha, founder of Buddhism.
343–321 BCE	Nanda dynasty.
327 BCE	Alexander of Macedonia enters Gandhara and marches into the Panjab.
c. 325 BCE	Chandra Gupta, founder of Mauryan dynasty.
322–184 BCE	Mauryan dynasty.
c. 265–232 BCE	Reign of Ashoka, third king of Mauryans.
247 BCE–224 CE	Parthian empire in Iran.
c. 78 CE	Reign of Kaniska, Kushan ruler, begins.
c. 100–300 CE	Kushans dominate North India and Central Asia.
224–651 CE	Sasanian empire in Iran.
c. 300–550 CE	Gupta empire in Ganges.

East Asia

1045–771 BCE	Western Zhou dynasty.
771–221 BCE	Eastern Zhou.
c. 771–476 BCE	Spring and Autumn period.
551?–479 BCE	Kong Qiu, or Confucius.
c. 475–221 BCE	Warring States period.
480–390 BCE	Mozi.
c. 300s BCE?	Text of Laozi recorded.
c. 371–289 BCE	Mencius.
c. 369–286 BCE	Zhuangzi
310–215 BCE	Xunzi.

307 BCE	The king of Zhao tells his army to ride horses.
221 BCE	Qin emperor reunifies China.
221–210 BCE	Reign of Qin Shihuang.
209–174 BCE	Modun first chieftain of Xiongnu.
206 BCE – 8 CE	Former Han dynasty.
206–195 BCE	Reign of Liu Bang, first emperor of Han dynasty.
198 BCE	Peace treaty between Han and Xiongnu.
145–90 BCE	Sima Qian.
141–87 BCE	Reign of Han Wudi.
60 BCE	Xiongnu leader submits to Han.
45 BCE – 23 CE	Wang Mang.
25 CE – 220 CE	Latter Han dynasty.
148 CE	Anshigao begins translation of Sanskrit texts into Chinese.
149 CE	Han emperor founds temple to Laozi.
155–220 CE	General Cao Cao.
311 CE	Xiongnu sack Luoyang.
386 – 534 CE	Northern Wei dynasty.

The great Indian king Ashoka came to the throne in the middle of the third century BCE, after a two-year-long war of succession, in which at least one of his brothers died. He fought a series of bloody wars, both before and after coming to power. About seven years after becoming king, he became a pro forma Buddhist, probably adopting this religion's rites but not really understanding its doctrines. Soon after, he conducted a major campaign against the strategic town of Kalinga in what is now Orissa, on the Bay of Bengal. He won after inflicting enormous numbers of casualties, with 100,000 killed and 150,000 taken prisoner.

A little over a year later, Ashoka wrote: "I have been a Buddhist layman for more than two and a half years, but for a year I did not make much progress. More than a year has passed since I visited the monastery, and I have become more ardent." In a long inscription, he wrote:

On conquering Kalinga, the Beloved of the Gods felt remorse, for when an independent country is conquered, the slaughter, death, and deportation of the people is extremely grievous to the Beloved of the Gods and weighs heavily on his mind . . . any sons or great-grandsons that I may have should not think of gaining new conquests, and in whatever victories they may gain should be satisfied with patience and light punishment. They should only consider conquest by dhamma to be a true conquest, and delight in dhamma should be their whole delight, for this is of value in both this world and the next.[1]

By dhamma (or dharma) Ashoka meant understanding the essential Buddhist doctrines about the order of the world. This story of Ashoka's conversion to Buddhism out of remorse over the massive bloodshed at Kalinga may be legendary, but he did have a genuine conversion experience. He probably did not stop being a conquering king, but he did change his internal and external policies. All his wars now had to be "just wars." He treated religious men respectfully, Brahmins, ascetics, and Buddhist monks alike. He spoke of universal compassion, love, and the nurturing of fellow human beings. He stopped slaughtering great numbers of animals at the imperial kitchens. He was the first monarch to build Buddhist monasteries and shrines on a large scale. He sent Buddhist missionaries out to spread the new religion, both in his own realms and in neighboring ones to the north and the south.

In the twelve centuries between 600 BCE and 600 CE, India and China erected a series of impressive centralized kingdoms. As the story of Ashoka demonstrates, military power, economic resources, and religious convictions all affected the construction of these kingdoms. India was much more fragmented than China. India's kingdoms did not cover the entire subcontinent, and they were relatively short-lived, while China's two great Han dynasties covered most of the core of modern China and lasted a total of four hundred years. India's social structure, based on hereditary castes, lacked the mobility China allowed between its basic occupations. Yet the trade routes of the Silk Road connected them together, and the societies shared many common trends:

- Iron tools allowed peasants to increase their production of food. The surplus food in turn allowed the development of larger and more complex cities. The kingdoms promoted agriculture in order to tax the peasants to support their standing armies.
- Military security in turn encouraged extensive international trade networks, including the beginnings of the Silk Road from East Asia to the Roman empire.
- Both India and China developed a classical language for religion and bureaucracy. Both produced thinkers consumed by the quest to understand the reasons for human existence, and the nature and origin of the world. Philosophical religions like Buddhism and Confucianism expressed this turn toward a more ethical vision of life, but so did more popular forms of emotional devotion, like the worship of Krishna or the Buddhist bodhisattvas (saints).
- In summary, the centralized kingdoms which rose and fell in China and India consolidated political power, created literate bureaucracies, and fostered the growth of enduring religious and philosophical systems.

5.1 SOUTH ASIA

The first large centralized states grew in South Asia after 600 BCE. One of them almost unified the subcontinent by the third century BCE. These empires stimulated new sophisticated schools of philosophy and religion, literary works, and advanced studies of medicine, optics, astronomy, and mathematics. A radical new philosophical religion, Buddhism, challenged the hierarchy of social castes in South Asia's Vedic, Hindu heritage, and gained substantial support from rulers and masses.

Indian society was traditionally divided into four main hereditary **castes** (varnas): the **Brahmins** or priests, the **Kshatriyas** or warriors, the **Vaishyas** or farmers, merchants, and artisans, and finally the **Shudras** or laborers. The priestly and warrior castes were considered noble. Even today, Kshatriya men and, to a lesser extent, Brahmins, share a few genetic markers with modern Europeans. These new tests support the theory, based on ancient legends, that Sanskrit-speaking warriors invaded India from Central Asia some three to four thousand years ago (see Chapter 3). The lower-caste men, and all Indian women, have stronger markers for Asian descent. Over time genes tend

to get mixed around, and there are no pure castes or races, so that these results are only statistical tendencies. Also, caste was not always a rigid barrier to changing one's status. Ideally everyone should follow his ancestors' occupation, but in times of rapid social change many people seized the opportunity to take new jobs.

Small groups of hunters and gatherers had spread through most of South Asia, which was thick forest or jungle. By the sixth century BCE, however, larger units had emerged in two main areas: along the Gangetic Plain in the east, where Buddhist sources speak of fourteen "great states," or warrior-clan federations, and in the upper reaches of the Indus Valley, the heartland of the Gandharan state. When the Achaemenid Persians took over Gandhara in the sixth century BCE, they introduced new Middle Eastern techniques of centralized bureaucratic administration into South Asia. Persian imports of wood, ivory, and other Indian goods caused trade to flourish.

The First Indian States

The strongest state, Magadha, began in what is now southern Bihar but came to rule much of the Gangetic Plain. Their first capital, located in Pataliputra, modern Patna, Bihar, had a fortress surrounded by a deep defensive moat. The Magadha empire's economy relied on control of shipping on the Ganges River and on a sort of agricultural revolution. The new state benefited from the great agricultural fertility of this region, which had both rainfall agriculture and irrigation works. In the fifth and fourth centuries, moreover, peasants improved their agricultural techniques, as heavy iron tools increased productivity. Magadha also profited from an extensive trading nexus that extended from the Bay of Bengal up to Taxila in the far north, and from western India to the east. The kingdom constantly struggled against neighboring clan confederacies. Central, monarchical rule did not always easily displace the more decentralized clan-based realms, but it gradually gained ascendancy, after King Bimbisara (r. c. 543 – c. 491 BCE) added eastern Bihar to the Magadha realm through conquest. Shifting clan confederacies and rapidly changing village religious cults were giving way to more institutionalized forms of society.

Magadha fitted the model of a Kshatriya-dominated state expressed in ancient epics. These legends and scriptures, however, described ideal rulers, not imperial practices. Indian history, as opposed to legends, shows us a messier reality, found in the two dynasties, the Nanda (343–321 BCE) and the Mauryan (321–185 BCE), which took over the Magadha realm. The Nandas replaced the Magadhas with a very different kind of ruling group. Dhana Nanda, a mere barber, mobilized a rebellion of Shudras against the Magadha. He defeated provincial barons who objected to the rule of a Shudra, ruled for about a decade, and conquered many smaller states ruled by clan warriors.

The Nandas had a huge army, including 200,000 foot-soldiers, 20,000 cavalry, 2,000 charioteers and 3,000–4,000 elephants. They employed their might to tighten administrative control of the empire and to raise taxes. By extending irrigation, they increased tax revenue from agriculture. Having been poor Shudras, they were determined to live richly as rulers, but the sullen Brahmins viewed them as irreligious. The Nandas appear to have departed from brahminical orthodoxy, and several of their rulers leaned to the Jain sect. The Nandas showed that the new agricultural resources of the Iron Age in eastern India could support the very large army and bureaucratic administration of a huge empire. The Mauryans learned these lessons well. They overthrew the Nandas and went on to rule India for nearly two centuries.

When Alexander of Macedonia, the great Greek conqueror of the Achaemenid empire, invaded India, he helped the Mauryans rise to power. In 327 Alexander entered Gandhara and marched into the Panjab. He was opposed by local warrior clans and by the Nandas' formidable army, which frightened Alexander's troops so much that they threatened to mutiny. Seeking local allies, Alexander met with an ambitious adventurer, Chandra Gupta. He came from a humble family in Magadha, but after resisting the Nandas, he fled to Taxila, a great Gandharan city in the north. Later on he raised an army in Magadha and attacked the Nandas, but was defeated, apparently because he had not secured the Panjab and so left himself open to a strike by loyalists from his rear. Chandra Gupta failed to persuade Alexander to join him in an assault on Magadha. Alexander, having reached the limits of what he could accomplish in the east, withdrew. He left behind a significant Greek force, however, and deputed authority in Gandhara and the Panjab to **satraps** or governors.

The Mauryan Empire

Because the Greeks in the north upset established social hierarchies and lines of authority, lower-caste Panjabis revolted against them. Chandra Gupta used these rebels in his army, seized Panjab, and used it as a base to launch a new war on the Nandas. He crushed the Nandas, pushed the Greek satraps north into what is now Afghanistan, and established the new Mauryan dynasty.

The Indian king Ashoka (r. c. 265–238 BCE), Chandra Gupta's grandson, was the greatest of the Mauryan rulers. Map 5.1 shows the extent of his empire. We know about his reign mainly from later Buddhist chronicles and legends but also from surviving stone inscriptions that date from his own time. As the opening

story shows, Ashoka was a conqueror who became a devout Buddhist. He may have calculated that conversion to Buddhism would naturally bring the people to develop a loyalty to the greatest Buddhist monarch of the day, himself. He also emphasized that his officers in conquered areas such as Kalinga should not engage in gratuitous cruelty, but rather should treat his new subjects, especially members of local elites and the religious classes, with respect. He attempted to institute a form of the rule of law in the conquered areas. He also ordered that good relations be cultivated with jungle and border tribespeople. Ashoka was among the first rulers in history to have endorsed an ideological state, which spread and supported an established religion as a bulwark to governmental authority and an asset in foreign relations. Unlike previous rulers, he wrote inscriptions on pillars to communicate with his subjects by explaining his views publicly. (China's Han dynasty would do the same with Confucianism a few decades later.) Ashoka's conquests and patronage of Buddhism brought much of India under his sway, nearly uniting the subcontinent for the first time. He did tolerate other sects, but also angered them by giving special favors to Buddhists.

Some sources indicate that toward the end of his life, Ashoka's excessive generosity to Buddhist leaders and institutions threatened to bankrupt his state. In a time of slow transportation and communication, provincial elites in places like Taxila could easily stage revolts. Alarmed, his council of ministers stepped in and left the king with little power or authority. For a while, his powerful chief queen, Karuvaki, appears to have issued edicts in his name.

The Mauryan dynasty went into political decline soon after Ashoka's death in 232 BCE. At least one of Ashoka's descendants abandoned Buddhism altogether. The last king was murdered in 185 BCE by his chief general, a Brahmin. The usurper established a new dynasty, the Sunga, but it held sway only over the center of India, and then only for about a hundred years. In the third and second centuries BCE, North India and at times even the Gangetic Plain were successfully invaded from Central Asia, by Greeks based in what is now Afghanistan. Greeks ruled in Gandhara and the Panjab, and gradually adopted Buddhism, but mixed it with their own beliefs. Figure 5.1 gives an example of this Bactrian Buddhist sculpture.

The economic prosperity of the Mauryan period was underpinned by key technological developments and by the spread of agriculture. Iron tools made land clearance possible. Iron, known to Indians for some time on a small scale, became the most popular metal for the making of tools, utensils, and weapons. At the city of Taxila, archaeologists have found iron hoes, axes, and arrowheads in large numbers. The Greeks prized Indian steel swords. Textual sources refer to the use of iron plowshares drawn by oxen in this period.

Map 5.1 Ashoka's empire

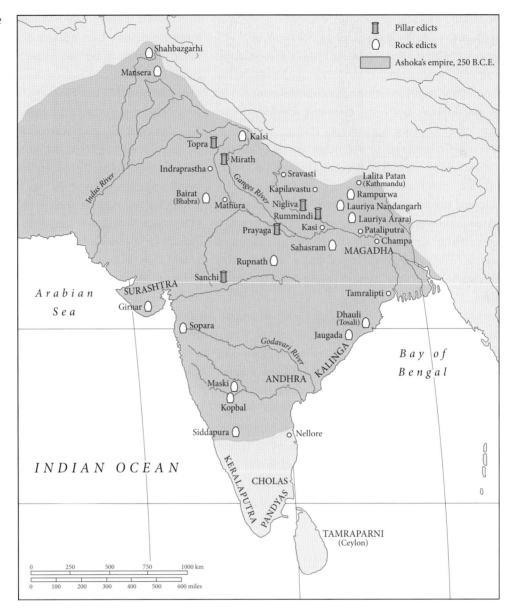

The Mauryan state encouraged farmers to clear and settle new land. Indian farmers grew wheat, barley, millet, and rice on different soils, but the staple food of North India was rice porridge. The main administrative manual to come out of the Mauryan empire, Kautilya's **Arthashastra**, stipulates that lands should be confiscated from those who neglected to cultivate them and given to others, farmers who paid their taxes easily should be rewarded by government help with seed grain and cattle, and rulers should take care of widows and orphans.

The advance of agriculture allowed the growth of walled cities. The *Arthashastra* called them the backbone of the state. Their specialized populations, such as metalworkers and weavers of cotton and silk textiles, formed craft organizations with hereditary leaders. City councils set prices for daily goods. Pataliputra, the capital, grew to 10 square miles in size, twice the extent of Rome in the same period. It had

60 gates and 570 towers, and the royal palace, with its hall of a hundred pillars, was classed among the wonders of the ancient world.

The Mauryan elites owned household slaves, but the *Arthashastra* insists that slaves from good backgrounds should not be made to do demeaning work, and that owners should not take advantage of female slaves sexually. Even if these provisions reflect an ideal more than the reality, their existence even with regard to slaves suggests a new sort of ethical thinking.

Indian Culture in the Axial Age

As Indo-Europeans, the warriors who began arriving in North India in the second millennium BCE brought with them a mythology very similar to that of the Greeks, Romans, and Norse. They had a god of war and of lightning and thunder

Figure 5.1 The Greek invasion of Persia, Afghanistan, and India, begun by Alexander the Great, left colonists in the region called Bactria, in northern Afghanistan, who mixed Buddhist and Hellenistic themes in their sculpture. This statue of the Buddha combines the Hellenistic focus on detailed portrayal of the folds of clothing and the rounded contours of the body with the meditative pose of the Buddhist deity. The deity's face has Greek features, but his topknot derives from the Buddhist tradition in which it indicates superior intelligence.

called Indra, a god of the sky and seas called Varuna, a high creator-god named Prajapati, and so forth. The **Rig Veda**, the oldest Hindu text, does not mention reincarnation or release from the cycle of birth and death. Rather, it imagines a divine world beyond this one, and urges ritual sacrifice to the gods. This system of ritual and myth interacted with local Indian beliefs and changed over time. The indigenous population, probably mostly speaking Dravidian languages, had its own pantheon, including the high god Siva and his son Ganesa (the elephant-headed god), and the monkey god Hanuman. The notion that human beings are reincarnated over and over again until they attain release through meditation and good morals could also have been indigenous to South Asia. Sanskrit religious texts included these local gods and ideas and spread across South Asia. In the Magadha period in North India, Hindus do not appear to have erected stone temples for worship. There may have been wooden temples, preferred because the region is plagued by frequent earthquakes, but if so they have not survived. Although the synthesis that emerged is often called Hinduism, there is no such single, unified religion. The word rather refers to a large number of loosely related, constantly changing beliefs and practices.

From the ninth to the fifth century BCE Indian thinkers began developing a different sort of speculative philosophy that did not depend on myths, sacrifices, and narratives about deities. The German philosopher Karl Jaspers, who noted similarities of consciousness across different civilizations during this period, called it the "Axial Age" (see Box 5.1). These new texts, the **Upanishads**, speak of God or Brahma as pure being and pure consciousness, as identical with ultimate reality. Brahma or

Box 5.1 The Axial Age

The German philosopher Karl Jaspers referred to the period from about 800 to 200 BCE as the "Axial Age," a time when the pivotal ethical and religious systems of the world formed in Greece, Palestine, Iran, China, and India. He wrote of India in this period that it "produced the Upanishads and Buddha and, like China [which gave us Confucius and Lao-Tse], ran the whole gamut of philosophical possibilities down to scepticism, to materialism, sophism and nihilism."

What impressed Jaspers as new about the religions and philosophies of this period was "that man becomes conscious of Being as a whole, of himself and his limitations. He experiences the terror of the world and his own powerlessness. He asks radical questions. Face to face with the void he strives for liberation and redemption." Writers and philosophers moved away from purely mythological forms of thinking and toward systems of thought that were grounded in individual ethics and in attempts to understand the workings of the universe without primary reference to unpredictable gods.

The term "Axial Age" is a convenient way to categorize this period of world history, as long as we do not take it too literally. Mythological thinking never disappeared; the great philosophers did not really reject it, but incorporated local versions into their doctrines. Greek mythology, Hindu epics, and Chinese rituals differ greatly, as do Plato, the Buddha, and Confucius. Still, looking at comparisons and connections between these writers is a stimulating way to study the eternal questions that all humans ask.

God is present everywhere in the world, just as salt is in salt water. They assert the identity of Brahma with the human soul or **atman** in a famous, if cryptic, saying: "You are that!" (*Tat twam asi*).

Unlike the older **Vedas** (sacred texts of Indian tradition), the new teachings reinterpret sacrifice symbolically. The Upanishads state that each individual has an eternal, unchanging soul, which is doomed to a cycle of rebirth and suffering. It can only awaken and achieve release (**moksha**) by recognizing its identity with Brahma. To that end, some advise the seeker after truth to focus his mind on a repeated word or phrase, called a **mantra**. The favorite mantra word was **aum**, or **om**. They use parables and paradoxes to shake believers out of their ordinary ways of thinking, and advise self-denial and contemplation as the means to escape rebirth.

Although the Upanishads became popular with intellectuals, for many Indians religion still revolved around the Vedic gods and the large-scale animal sacrifices of the Brahmin priests. Villagers most often worshipped local fertility goddesses and the spirits inhabiting caves and forests.

Revolts against the Brahmins: Jains and Buddhists

The popularity of the Upanishads instigated two major sectarian revolts against the Brahmin priestly tradition: Jainism and Buddhism. Jains followed the sage Mahavir (*c.* 400 BCE?), who abandoned his family at the age of thirty and wandered as an ascetic monk for twelve years. As in the Upanishads, Mahavir believed that human beings must free themselves from an endless cycle of painful rebirths and wretched lives. The key to doing so, he thought, was non-violence, truthfulness, refusing to steal, sexual abstinence, and detachment from material possessions as well as from other people. He rejected the caste system, but divided the Jain community into monks and nuns on the one hand, and laypersons on the other. The monks and nuns were expected to give up wealth, sex, and harming others (even animals and insects), while the laity lived an upright life. Mahavir may not have been the first sage to preach the ideals that became associated with Jainism, but he was probably the first great institution-builder of the religion, leaving behind 14,000 monks and 36,000 nuns, along with monasteries and lay followers.

The Life of the Buddha

The other challenger of Hindu orthodoxy was Gautama Siddartha (died *c.* 368 BCE?), who became known as the **Buddha** or enlightened one. He lived in the time of the Magadha kingdom. He was from the Kshatriya warrior class, the son of a minor dynasty ruling the area now on the Indian and Nepali border.

Ancient legends depict him as a spoiled prince who married and had a young son. When Gautama reached the age of 29, he began going out of the palace and noticing the afflictions that beset his humbler subjects. Deeply upset by the old age and sickness he saw, he experienced a spiritual crisis. He gave up the comfortable world of a royal householder to become an ascetic in order to search for the meaning of life. He joined thousands of other young men who pursued a life of self-denial and spiritual exercises, eating little and begging for a living. Later stories have him saying, "I was unclothed, indecent, licking my hands . . . I took food only once a day, or once in two or seven days . . . I subsisted on the roots and fruits of the forest, eating only those which fell."

Six years later, Gautama concluded that this extreme self-denial had no spiritual value in and of itself. He turned to a more moderate style of life, called in Buddhism the Middle Path, trying to understand the causes of pain instead. His circle of five friends left him, believing that he had become less serious in his quest.

Gautama spent the afternoon and evening meditating. Soon, after much struggle with his demons, he had revelations at the foot of a tree, known as the Bodhi (enlightenment) tree. Gautama now became the Buddha, the enlightened one. His mystical experience was not easy for him to express in words at first, but it did involve awakening to the nature of the world and the spiritual laws that govern it. Unlike Western private revelations, however, this law of life or ultimate truth (**dharma**) could be shared with others. Those who gained enlightenment by following his teaching were called **arahat**, or later, **bodhisattvas**.

The Buddha tracked down his five former friends near Benares (Varanasi), and preached to them this truth. They became his first followers. Thereafter his new religion spread quickly, with thousands of monks and nuns giving up their daily pleasures (good food, sex, and alcohol) in order to follow the Middle Path. They tended to move around in groups, and were satisfied with humble accommodations, even sleeping in caves. Eventually the monks established monasteries, creating communities of Buddhists called the **sangha**. Laypersons could also meditate and study his writings, even though they married and led ordinary lives. They could not hope for the same enlightenment as a devoted monk or nun, but their sober and ethical lives did contribute to their spiritual progress and hopes for release from the cycle of pain and suffering in the future. Soon the Buddha attracted some wealthy and powerful patrons, such as a famous courtesan who repented of her past life of sin.

The cornerstone of Buddhist teaching is that everything in the world is impermanent. We fall in love, however, with these impermanent things. We enjoy our houses; but earthquakes might knock them down. A beloved spouse or child might suddenly die. Although humans are constantly buffeted by change, they close their eyes to the tragedies brought on them by impermanence. They embrace the illusion that the people and things they love will last forever. They even think their own souls and their own personalities are unchanging and immortal. We can see logically that these are basic errors, but we have difficulty accepting the emotional consequences.

The Buddha's philosophy is summed up in the Four Noble Truths. First, ordinary existence is characterized by pain and suffering (**duhkha**). Second, we suffer because we desire things that we cannot have or that do not last. Third, attaining enlightenment (**nirvana**) allows a person to put away those desires and to stop suffering. Fourth, there is a method for becoming enlightened. It requires following the Eightfold Path: right views, right thought, right speech, right action, right livelihood, right effort, right mindfulness and right concentration. These methods help the believer to understand the nature of the world, to live a life of moderate self-denial, and to practice meditation.

The Buddhist conviction that all things are impermanent leaves no place for God or for deities. Divine beings exist, but they are impermanent and temporary, like everything else, though perhaps on a longer timescale. Buddhist salvation is not granted by a benevolent deity, but rather something individuals have to earn, by living a righteous life, putting away sinful thoughts, and regularly meditating. There is no individual, eternal human soul. The human person consists of five aggregates: the body, feelings, perceptions, mental formations, and consciousness. These are all constantly changing themselves, and only seem to be a permanent unity. This compound personality is doomed to go on suffering, dying, and being reborn over and over again unless the individual can attain enlightenment. At that point, the cycle of birth, death, rebirth, and suffering is broken and the person attains release or salvation.

Critics (including Catholic popes) have attacked Buddhism as a negative view of the world. Are we merely doomed to repeat again and again a wild and painful ride through a nightmarish, deceptive landscape? Buddhists, however, admit that there is good and beauty in the world. They simply think it is a mistake to become too dependent on it. Enlightened Buddhists can smile at death.

After the Buddha's death, his religion gained the patronage of some major rulers, but his community gradually split into two major schools. The Theravada, now practiced in Sri Lanka, Burma, Thailand, and Cambodia, retained the austere and abstract character of the Buddha's teachings. They saw the impermanent world and the world of nirvana as complete opposites. A later school, the Mahayana or "great vehicle," venerated people of great compassion, or bodhisattvas, who after attaining nirvana voluntarily returned to this world to help others. The more austere Theravada tradition objected to this worship of human figures, but Mahayana mystics insisted that the material world and the world of nirvana were only two sides of the same coin. Human and abstract realms could merge.

The Kushans and the Guptas

In the first through the third centuries of the Common Era, the Kushans created the first sustained state linking China and India, supporting the profitable trade across Central Asia known as the Silk Road. This network of trade routes (not a single road) allowed China, which monopolized silk production, to export the valuable, lightweight fabric by caravan in return for animals and gold. Silk Road merchants needed strong armed protectors like the Kushans, while the Kushan rulers accumulated gold coins from empires to the west in exchange for silk coming from the east. Buddhist pilgrims followed the merchants from India through Kushan territory into China, Central Asia, Afghanistan, and eastern Iran, while nomadic warriors protected or raided the precious caravans. We will examine this trade at its high point in Chapter 8.

The Kushans were Central Asian nomads who had developed good relations with the Chinese state until other tribal federations forced them to migrate west. They were the first to discover a very useful method of controlling horses in battle: the stirrup. By supporting a warrior's foot with a wooden bar or metal or leather strap, stirrups gave him much greater stability, allowing him to charge with large lances and shoot powerful bows. Stirrups spread west to Europe and east to the nomads on the Chinese border, increasing the speed and impact of nomadic attacks.

Over time, the Kushans and their tribal allies flooded into Afghanistan, and in the first century CE they went through the Khyber pass down into Gandhara and the Panjab. They placed their capital at Purushapura, modern Peshawar (now in northern Pakistan). The Kushan was one of only four large empires that dominated all of Eurasia in the opening centuries of the first millennium CE, along with the Roman, the Parthian (247 BCE – 224 CE) in Iran, and the Han Chinese. They profited greatly from their position in between these three, and controlled contact with India as well.

Archaeological findings indicate that the Kushan empire in North India was a time of great economic prosperity, extensive international trade, and flourishing cities. They appear to have melted down the gold coins they received in trade and reminted them. The remarkably consistent weight and purity of thousands of surviving Kushan coins are products of a strong, secure economy.

The empire's dominion extended at some points deep into the Gangetic Plain as far as Benares (Varanasi). Later coins of the dynasty give the kings Indian titles and depict the god Siva on the other side, suggesting that they became Indianized over time.

Like so many Central Eurasian newcomers, Kushan rulers were remarkably tolerant religiously, giving patronage to Zoroastrianism, Buddhism, and the worship of Siva within Hinduism. While in Afghanistan, they picked up the Greek culture of some of the remnants of Alexander's army, and at times used a Greek-derived script. The third Kushan ruler, Kaniska, who came to power about 78 CE, called a significant Buddhist council, had the Buddhist scriptures translated into Sanskrit from their original dialect, and supported missionary efforts in Central Asia. Gandharan Buddhist sculpture in this period shows both Indian and Greek influences in the depiction of the Buddha, who often adopts a Greek posture and wears Greek-style robes with many pleats.

During the 200s, Kushan political power in India declined. By about 250 CE they only held the far north, and by about 300 CE they had been reduced to vassals of a new Iranian, Zoroastrian empire, the Sasanian (224–651). Even after this period there were eras of Kushan resurgence until the nomadic Hun invasions of North India in 450.

In the period 300 to 550 CE, the Gangetic Plain threw up yet another successor to Magadha, the Gupta empire, showing that under the right conditions this region continued to have the potential to support a centralized state. Like the Mauryans, the Gupta rulers made Pataliputra their capital, and brought what are now southern Panjab, Uttar Pradesh and Bihar, and points west under their authority. The Guptas ruled a smaller state than the Mauryans and from all accounts were less centralized and less prosperous. Their cities do not appear to have been as big and thriving as those of the preceding Kushan era. Unlike the centralized and controlling Mauryans, the Guptas ruled by farming out many functions to other groups. Rural intermediaries were given land grants that sometimes became hereditary. Merchant guilds in the cities were exempted from certain taxes and in return provided many services to the urban population through a city council.

They benefited from continued, but probably less extensive, international trade with Central Asia and the Middle East. Yet merchants also began long voyages to Southeast Asia, as far as the Malay peninsula and the islands of Indonesia, so that Chinese silk could now come to India by both the maritime and the overland routes.

Even though most Gupta kings were Hindus, Buddhism continued to be important during this era. The kings patronized and tolerated Hindus, Jains, and Buddhists. At the grassroots level, there were new developments in Hinduism, and the Brahmin priestly caste grew in importance, but a true Hindu revival only occurred after the Guptas had fallen.

New Religious Cults: Siva, Vishnu, and Krishna

After the fall of the Mauryans, the minority or at least less powerful Brahmin schools became invigorated by the popularity of new deities not mentioned or barely mentioned in the ancient Vedas. Rather than speaking of a whole pantheon, devotees tended to stress allegiance to one of these gods over all the others, a development called "nenotheism". Those Hindus who came to feel that all the gods were just forms of their one, favorite deity came close to a sort of monotheism. The Vedic god Rudra was thought responsible for disease and natural disasters. He came to be identified with the Indian figure, Siva. Siva may have been worshipped in India as early as the ancient Indus Valley civilizations. Figure 5.2 shows Siva conducting the Dance of Life. Siva was depicted in the epics as a god of wrath and death

Figure 5.2 The Indian god Siva, derived from the Vedas, indicated a power who brought disaster and disease but also cured human ills and saved humans from harm. He was both destroyer and creator of the universe. In this statue Siva, surrounded by flames, dances to destroy the world and prepare its new creation by Brahma. He holds a cobra, and he stands on the demon of ignorance, whom he crushes into submission.

wielding a trident, but he was also a god of forgiveness and salvation. His followers were called Saivites, and became especially numerous in South India, but he was worshipped in the north as well. His stories appear in the *Mahabharata*, the great Hindu epic poem. Some of the later Kushan emperors depicted him on their coins, and some Gupta rulers seem to have favored him. Indian religion tended to be syncretic, which is to say that it allowed various elements to be mixed together. Thus, Saivites also read the Vedas and favored a particular Upanishad, and honored other Hindu gods as well.

Another local Indian god was identified with a Vedic god called Vishnu, who is rather obscure in the old Sanskrit texts. Vishnu came to be seen as a compassionate god, who incarnated himself in this world from time to time. His followers came to be known as Vaisnavites, and they conducted something of a rivalry with the Saivites. Two of Vishnu's incarnations, as the ancient king, Rama, and as the spiritual teacher, Krishna, emerged as beloved figures in popular religion. Some time between 200 BCE and 200 CE, Indian sages produced a book of religious teachings attributed to Krishna, called "The Divine Song" (**Bhagavad Gita**). This book, unlike the rational, abstract philosophy of the Upanishads, appealed to the heart and to the emotions. It stimulated a devotional form of Hinduism known as **bhakti**. Box 5.2 describes the primary features of the Krishna cult.

The story of Krishna was tacked on to the ancient epic, the *Mahabharata*. The action in the *Mahabharata* is depicted as occurring before the rise of the Maghada kingdom, perhaps three thousand years ago. It is the story of two ancient warrior clans that fought one another in a civil war until one of the clans wiped out the other. The epic stresses the need for human beings to fulfill the obligations laid on them by the varna or caste into which they were born. It is therefore part of the general ethical turn that Indian religion made in the second half of the first

millennium BCE, away from Vedic notions of ritual sacrifice to a pantheon of gods as the way to salvation.

The Bhagavad Gita puts forth Krishna as an avatar or incarnation of Vishnu, and shows him giving ethical and spiritual advice to the warrior Arjuna on the battlefield of Kuru where the two warring clans face one another. Arjuna has developed doubts about going into battle, wondering why he should kill his cousins and what difference it would make which side won. The battlefield is also identified by the sage as a symbol for the cosmic arena of right and wrong. Krishna advises Arjuna that he must fight because that is his caste duty as a warrior. He tells him not to worry about the killing, since souls are immortal, and each soul is an expression of Brahma, of God. The Bhagavad Gita sets out a path of spiritual discipline, including meditation, suppression of unhealthy passions, love for all creatures, and devotion to Krishna. The goal of these practices is to allow the soul to escape the unpleasant cycle of rebirth, and to enter heaven permanently. Unlike Buddhism, it recognizes the immortality of the individual and does not seek extinction. In an indirect reference to the Upanishads and Buddhism, it admits that wise persons might make spiritual progress by thinking of the divine in abstract terms, but says that this path is extremely difficult.

By combining adoration for a spiritual teacher, clear simple doctrines, techniques of meditation, and a moderate life of love and compassion, the Bhagavad Gita incorporated into Hinduism many of the elements that had probably contributed to Buddhism's popularity. It was more accessible to most ordinary folk than was Buddhism, however, and offered the hope of personal immortality. By not completely displacing the Brahmins and their rituals, it gained their allegiance in a way Buddhism never could. Yet Buddhism still remained centrally important and perhaps ascendant in India during the first centuries of the Common Era.

Box 5.2 Krishna in the Bhagavad Gita

The Bhagavad Gita depicts Lord Krishna as a loving savior, adored by his followers, and as an incarnation of the supreme God. The divine is described this way: "If in heaven, together should arise the shining brilliance of a thousand suns, then would that perhaps resemble the brilliance of that God so great." This emphasis on personal love and devotion to God appealed to common people in the succeeding centuries. In contrast to the Brahmins' worship of the Vedas, Krishna seems to be openly dismissive of the Vedas at one point, and in another passage he claims actually to be the Vedas. He is described as the ageless object of all real worship, who comes into human history from time to time: "For whenever the law of righteousness withers away and lawlessness arises, then do I generate myself on earth. For the protection of the good, for the destruction of evil-doers, for the setting up of the law of righteousness, I come into being age after age." Yet Krishna obtains "the supreme perfection of non-action" through renunciation of the world.

Secular culture also advanced in these centuries. It was probably in the Gupta period that India's greatest classical playwright, Kalidasa, arose. Kalidasa's most important work is **Recognizing Shakuntala**, which is renowned for its humor and love poetry, as well as its sensitive depictions of nature. In this play, a king falls in love with a beautiful girl of low station, Shakuntala. He weds her, and they live contentedly for a time. Then the girl accidentally offends a holy man, who puts an evil spell on her, making the king forget her completely. The holy man later regrets the harshness of his action and tells Shakuntala how to bring the monarch's memories of her back. She has to return to him a ring that he had given her. However, she loses the ring while bathing. She becomes desperate when she finds that she is pregnant. In the end, a fisherman finds the ring and returns it to the king, restoring his memory.

Women in Indian Texts

In contrast to the prudish Buddhists, secular Indian civilization was uninhibited in talking about and depicting sex. On the other hand, frank discussion is not the same as women's equality. Ancient India was a patriarchal society (that is, a society where men were dominant and the elder male head of the household most respected). The advent of heavy iron weapons and tools gave men an advantage and a primacy in war and agriculture that made women less important than they had been in hunting and gathering societies.

The **Kama Sutra**, written in the Maurya or Gupta period, is, however, more than merely a sex manual. It is full of advice on marriage and human relationships. Respect for women was mandated in the Rig Veda, and it is urged that daughters-in-law who go to live with their husbands' families be well treated. A heroine of the *Mahabharata*, Draupadi, at one point throws a male assailant to the ground and then gives her husband a tongue-lashing for not protecting her himself.

On the other hand, among the primary models for women's behavior in the *Ramayana* was Sita, the queen of Lord Rama, who was said to be so obedient that she literally walked in his footsteps. Women in the ancient texts are depicted ideally as wives, mothers, and managers of the household. Their social skills and activities are thought to help knit together the community. She is the provider of hospitality, and is responsible for performing a key Vedic ritual. Ordinarily, marriage was a sacrament and not just a contract, though short-term marriages by contract were allowed. According to the *Arthashastra*, she could be punished for neglecting to do her duty to her husband, for being rude to him, or for dallying with other men. Women were sometimes exploited, with prostitution apparently common. Girls could be married as young as 12.

Polygamy, the custom of one man taking several wives, was permitted. Women had no right to initiate a divorce, and they did not own property. Unlike in subsequent Hinduism, the *Arthashastra* permitted widows to remarry. Indeed, a woman was allowed to take another husband if she had been abandoned for several years or if her husband became a traitor.

Religious Coexistence

During these critical centuries, India abounded in very distinct religious doctrines, but they coexisted with each other. Buddhists significantly challenged many of the older practices now called Hinduism, but they modified others, like the belief in reincarnation. The rulers of centralized states found it useful to patronize some religious sects for their own purposes, but unlike Chinese rulers, they did not impose one orthodox practice systematically over the entire region, and they never unified the entire subcontinent. The rulers of China's larger empire, the Han dynasty, attempted to impose more uniformity than the South Asian kings.

5.2 CHINA

The Western Zhou

The Western Zhou dynasty (1045–771 BCE), which lasted 274 years, was China's longest-lived unified state located in a single capital. Its center was in the valley of the Wei River, near modern Xian. In 771 BCE, after a century of decline, this dynasty collapsed when an invasion forced the Zhou kings to move east to a new capital, near modern Luoyang. They still called themselves kings, but they had no real political power. The Chinese realm remained divided for more than 500 years thereafter into hundreds of small states. During this time, known as the Eastern Zhou (771–221 BCE), divided into the Spring and Autumn period (c. 771–476 BCE) and the Warring States period (c. 475–221 BCE), in the midst of constant warfare and intrigue, Chinese scholars expounded the basic doctrines that defined the classical tradition, while rulers and warriors put in place the fundamental institutions of the bureaucratic state. When the Qin emperor reunified China into an empire in 221 BCE, he put together the building blocks shaped by this half millennium of disunity. For this reason, we call it the Axial Age of Chinese civilization.

The Western Zhou kings had expanded their control by sending out colonists led by relatives of the imperial family. These colonists were given control of territories in return for military and administrative service, and received ranks that recognized their merit, like dukes, marquises, and princes. Because of this practice of enfeoffment and the use of noble titles, built on top of an agrarian society, the Western Zhou political structure looks somewhat like medieval European feudalism, although it lacked other key elements like oaths of vassalage or mounted armor-clad warriors, not to mention an organized church. "Feudal" China of this period was also united by the kinship ties between the colonists and the Western Zhou kings. Each of the colonists had a military garrison, housed in a walled town called a **guo**, or state, supported by the grain and labor of farmers.

The Zhou rulers and their colonists defined themselves as part of a single culture centered in the valley of the Yellow River. They called themselves the Hua, or Xia, in distinction to the "barbarians" to their north, east, west, and south. They fought wars to expand against these rivals, and settled the newly conquered lands. The Zhou king, who had claimed to inherit the Mandate of Heaven when he conquered the Shang, still claimed ritual supremacy over his relatives. After military victories, he had large bronze cauldrons cast, with inscriptions recording his appointment of lords to rule the new regions. The new local ruler celebrated with rituals of drinking and animal sacrifice. Box 5.3 gives one example of this kind of ritual.

At its maximum size, the Zhou state only controlled an area of about 125 miles on each side. Larger regions beyond the core territories in the Wei River valley and North China Plain had distinct cultures, but we have little literary evidence of their activities, except as threats to the Zhou king. In 957 BCE the Zhou royal army was destroyed in a major battle, and the Zhou domain began to fragment. The colonists paid their respects at court less often, and rival states in the northwest invaded and plundered the eastern lands, until they were driven off. These blows stimulated reform of the Zhou state, to increase its control over its shrunken central territory. Professional military officers received appointments instead of nobles, and the scribes who wrote down the king's commands gained influence. Most of China's earliest written records no longer survive, because they were inscribed in bamboo, not baked clay tablets, but the Zhou state created rudimentary archives of legal decisions about property, maps, and appointments.

The Western Zhou Dissolves into Warring States

After the Zhou king lost his capital in 771 BCE, each of the guo acted autonomously, although paying nominal respect to the king. The feudal structure broke down into competition between fifteen major powers. Unlike the earlier periods, for which we have only oracle bones and brief bronze inscriptions, this "Spring and Autumn period," named after its chief chronicle, produced abundant written sources about the states' intrigues, and is yielding a still expanding archaeological record. This time of intrigue, warfare, and diplomacy produced China's first true intellectuals – men who thought beyond the policy of a particular ruler and elaborated general principles of strategy.

The rulers and their advisors, however ruthless, still searched for community: a way to keep together the Zhou order without a truly powerful king. The Zhou king could designate an "alliance chieftain" (**ba**), the most powerful leader among the multiple states, to protect the Zhou realm against barbarian attack. In the seventh century, the other states agreed to name as *ba* the state of Qi, centered in modern Shandong. Guan Zhong, the first great statesman, strategist, and reformer named in the classic texts, advised its ruler. With his death in 645 BCE, Qi lost its dominance, and a true multi-state balance of power emerged among four states, all on the edges of the Zhou cultural sphere. Qi held on to Shandong, Jin controlled Shanxi in the north, Qin expanded in the west, and Chu held the south. These four negotiated peace agreements to prevent warfare for nearly forty years, but the underlying rivalry for dominance could not be stopped. As one ruler put it, "territory is defined by battle . . . where is the constancy?"

Coercion was not the only constant element, however. In the midst of warfare, commerce grew and peasants increased their output. In Western Zhou, peasants delivered the crops they could not consume directly to the lords of their estates. Land and labor were the only sources of wealth. In the Spring and Autumn period, iron entered China from Central Eurasia and was attached to wooden plows, making it possible to clear tougher soils and plow them deeper. North China's primary

Box 5.3 An Inscription from a Zhou Bronze Vessel

When the guests first approach the mats,
They take their places on the left and the right in an orderly manner.
The dishes of bamboo and wood are arranged in rows,
With the sauces and kernels displayed in them.
The liquor is mild and good,
And they drink, all equally reverent . . .
But when they have drunk too much,
Their conduct becomes light and frivolous,
They leave their seats and go elsewhere,
They keep dancing and capering . . .
Their deportment becomes indecent and rude . . .
They lose all sense of orderliness.

crop was millet, a tough plant that withstood drought better than wheat, and different varieties could adapt to varying conditions of soil, water, and temperature. The first coins appeared in this period, in the form of spade-like bronze objects or the rare cowrie shells which rulers gave to each other as gifts. The rulers built roads and dikes to increase the output of their domains and allowed individuals to trade in agricultural products across their borders, once they had paid customs taxes.

The Warring States period intensified to an extreme the military competition of the Spring and Autumn period, but this coercive mobilization also generated great commercial, techno-logical, and intellectual dynamism. Jin split into three states, and a new state of Yan arose in the northeast, increasing the number of contenders to seven. Each of the rulers now declared himself a king (**wang**), abandoning even the pretense of subordination to Zhou. They all knew that a life-and-death struggle must end with only one victor. Each ruler focused on concentrating all power within the state in his own hands, by crushing the independence of the nobility and hiring loyal bureaucrats. They attracted intellectual servants, or **shi**, who were totally dedicated to increasing their master's power.

The Art of War and Qin Unification

Sun Bin, the famous military strategist, wrote his text *The Art of War* to show his master how to win without fighting. He had brains not brawn to offer. But none of the *shi* were loyal to a single master; they peddled their intellectual wares to the highest bidder. Some got rich by collecting gold, silver, and official positions for their brilliance; others got themselves killed for being too clever by half. Yet even the most ruthless warrior needed these men: they taught him the techniques of statecraft that ensured his wealth and power. Later the most brilliant of these advisors earned a negative reputation as "**Legalists**." They did design law codes and administrative procedures, but not to defend the people's rights. Severe punishments would maintain order and ensure the extraction of the maximum from the populace. Shang Yang carried out the most thorough Legalist reforms in the Qin state in the mid fourth century, including the imposition of universal military service on young men, strict law codes, rewards for those who excelled in battle graduated according to the number of severed heads taken, and the organ-ization of the population into units of five and ten households who were obliged to spy on each other and subjected to collective punishment in case any one of them stepped out of line. He introduced to Qin the **xian**, the basic administrative unit origin-ating in the seventh century BCE that tied the peasant producer directly to a state official.

Other states soon copied Qin, but it became clear by the third century BCE that Qin's power was inexorably rising. Qin had conquered large territories in the northwest; its culture was poor, but it learned military tactics from the horseriders of the steppe; it was a pioneer in the use of mass peasant infantry and in forging new weapons. Other strategists promoted alliances to balance against Qin, but these did not last. The scale of battles, the size of armies, and the destructive power of weaponry increased steadily. The crossbow, introduced from South China, vastly increased infantry firepower. Defensive walls sprouted up everywhere, not just along the steppe frontier, but on interior borders between contending states. Cavalry came in from the steppe in the fourth century as a useful supplement to mass infantry. By 251 BCE, the state of Yan claimed to put 600,000 men in the field. In the culmination of a steadily increasing trend of mass violence that had lasted for centuries, Qin "unified" the Chinese realm in 221 BCE by brute force. Map 5.2 shows the vast extent of its conquests, which endured through the Han dynasty.

Philosophers, Strategists, and Kings

Yet in the midst of mayhem, China developed the most dynamic intellectual climate it would see for many centuries. Wandering "knights" (**shi**), members of the lower nobility, expounded an astonishing diversity of doctrines as they attempted to gain state support. These "Hundred Schools" contended with each other in an environment of unprecedented openness. Many of the *shi* offered specific, practical advice to rulers, but others promoted more abstract theories of cosmology and morality.

Confucius Tries to Set the World Right Kong Qiu (551?–479 BCE), or Confucius, and his disciples set the basic parameters of philosophical debate to which all his rivals had to respond. He came from the lower nobility of the state of Lu, a politically insignificant state which prided itself on carrying on the rituals of the Zhou kings. Confucius believed strongly that the early Zhou kings had created universal peace because they had followed the proper rituals that aligned the human and natural orders. He called this ideal order the Way, or **Dao**. Yet in his time, "the Way no longer prevailed in the world"; men fought each other continually because they had forgotten the value of ritual restraint and moral feeling. His mission was to teach everyone how to recover the ideal past world by following these social rituals, or **li**. As simple as a handshake, or as complex as a banquet or funeral, *li* were what held human society together. Yet no one could simply go through the motions; he had to infuse all his activities with intense dedication to make these rituals convincing. As in music or archery, anyone could tell the skilled from the unskilled practitioner of moral behavior.

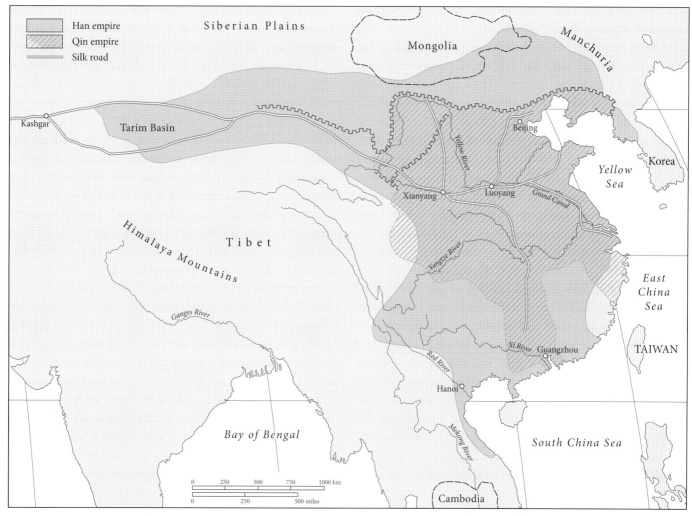

Map 5.2 Qin and Han empires

The true master was the **junzi**, or superior man, and his essential moral excellence was the powerful virtue of **ren**, weakly translated as "benevolence." *Ren*, whose written form combines the characters for "human" and "two," was the essential social glue binding humans together. Confucius described it in many ways, but its essence was common humanity. Anyone could learn to practice *ren*, whether a commoner or a noble, but it took both personal dedication and learning to carry it out seriously.

The charismatic Confucius attracted disciples who recorded his instructions in the book known as the **Analects**, or "discussions." He did not argue his points. Although he engaged in dialogue with his students, these were not Socratic inquiries into the nature of truth, but a search for the fundamental order of nature reflected in the human world. Beyond his disciples, few people were interested. Rulers and strategists wanted advice on immediate action, not elusive discussion of principles. Confucius spent his life looking for an enlightened ruler, but he never held an important political position, and he died in obscurity.

Many of his disciples, however, did gain government jobs, and they ensured that the Confucian school continued.

Mencius and Xunzi Carry On the Search for the Way Confucius lived at the turning point between the Spring and Autumn period and the Warring States, when the rituals of Zhou still served as models. A century later, when all Zhou power had vanished, Confucius' followers faced even more desperate conditions. Mencius (*c.* 371–289 BCE) carried on the Confucian program of attempting to convince vicious rulers to favor benevolence over brute force. Unlike Confucius, he spent a good deal of time at court pleading his case. Sometimes he could convince a ruler to lower taxes and treat his subjects well, because good government would attract a large population and make the state stronger. Mencius also had practical economic programs: he recommended returning to the "well-field" system of landholding, in which eight peasant households each farmed their own land and farmed one plot in common, the surplus of which they gave to the state. Then everyone had enough, and the ruler got what he needed. But to most hardheaded warring statesmen, Mencius looked too idealistic.

Mencius had rivals, within the Confucian school and outside it, who disputed his basic assumptions, forcing him to argue extensively for Confucian principles. In a famous debate over human nature, Mencius argued that humans were essentially good: they all had the sprouts of compassion for others. Anyone would feel a rush of pity on seeing a child fall down a well. Faulty upbringing and ignorance obscured our basic goodness, but it could be recovered through introspection and study. Like water, which innately flows downhill, the disposition to do good can be dammed up, but eventually it will break through. Even a mountain stripped of its trees could recover its natural resources with careful nourishment. The moral sense came from deep in the heart; it could not be imposed from outside. Mencius analyzed the psychology of moral sentiments more subtly than any other Chinese thinker. In the Mencian vision of the future, rulers and subjects who discovered their deep-seated compassion would exert virtuous power over others. Then the world would be peaceful and prosperous. Mencius' faith in original goodness and his Utopian vision of the future sound much like the eighteenth-century Frenchman Jean-Jacques Rousseau. But Mencius also warned that the people would justly overthrow abusive rulers who lost the Mandate of Heaven. Combining high idealism with common sense, Mencius attempted to persuade warrior-statesmen to enact good government.

His rival, Xunzi (310–215 BCE), who actually served in government, saw the world quite differently. For Xunzi, humans were essentially selfish, and the original state of society was one of disorder. The great sages of the past created social order by enforcing strict punishments and moral training, bending weak humans to their will. Order depended on strong-willed exertion of authority from above. Heaven's constant course was indifferent to human woes: they should not expect any encouragement from omens, or follow deluded fortune-tellers and shamans. Yet anyone could fix his mind on moral goals and pursue them actively, if properly trained. Xunzi followed Confucian tradition in respecting rituals, the authority of the classics, and the importance of education, but his disabused view of human nature aligned him closely with the harsh Legalists, who thought that only ruthless repression could keep people in line. Paradoxically, Mencius' sunny view of human potential became the orthodox position, even though in practice many officials had to act covertly on the assumptions of Xunzi and the Legalists.

Mozi Rejects Confucian Ritual Beyond the Confucian school, many other thinkers disputed the meaning of the Dao. Mozi (480–390 BCE), the most influential thinker of his time, rejected all Confucius' stress on ritual as wasteful. He took a strictly utilitarian approach: all that mattered to people was gain and loss. Keep order, feed the people, eliminate extravagant ceremonies, and all would be well. Mozi also rejected the Confucian moral hierarchy: instead of requiring each person to carry out his social role properly (as Confucius said, "Let the father be a father, let the son be a son"), Mozi advocated "impartial caring": treat everyone with the same compassion, regardless of personal connections. Western Christians who read Mozi in the nineteenth century were delighted to discover in him an equivalent to "universal love," and even called Mozi a "Christian socialist." But Mozi's advocacy of caring for all humanity came only from cold logic, not from inner compassion. His vision of life before the creation of the state corresponded closely to that of the seventeenth-century English political theorist Thomas Hobbes: a war of all against all. Only a firm ruler could impose a single standard.

Mozi gave Heaven a much more active role in enforcing moral norms than Confucius, making Heaven look more like a personal God than a natural force. He attacked the Confucians for being too fatalistic: they waited for Heaven's will to reveal itself instead of plunging into action. The Mohists also developed practical techniques of defensive warfare to show rulers that they could end war without aggression. They developed the closest analogue to Greek principles of logical reasoning, since they viewed philosophical debate as equivalent to intellectual warfare. The Mohists gained great influence in their time, but they died out with the unification of the empire. Their simplistic psychology, radical egalitarianism, and hostility to ritual and art fitted poorly with the formal, hierarchical world of the empire, and their defensive military techniques failed to stop the Qin military juggernaut.

Daoists Advocate Non-Action The "Daoists" had much longer, though indirect influence. The cryptic, fascinating text attributed to the shadowy figure Laozi, the **Daodejing** (*Classic of the Way and its Power*) collected mystical revelations, political theory, and arresting epigrams in a text of uncertain date (*c.* fourth century BCE) that has fascinated Chinese and Westerners for millennia. Box 5.4 points out the remarkable parallels between the *Daodejing* and the mystical texts of ancient India. It is, next to the Bible, the book with the largest number of English translations, nearly all of them different. It begins, "The Way [Dao] that can be spoken is not the eternal Way; the Name that can be named is not the constant Name." What does this mean? Unlike the Confucian Dao, which can be studied in historical texts, the Daoist Dao seems to be beyond words. It is "dim, dark," yet very simple, like an uncarved block with no

Box 5.4 The *Classic of the Way and its Power (Daodejing)*

Note the curious parallels between the mystic doctrines of Laozi, and the Bhagavad Gita and Indian Buddhism. Both the Chinese and Indian texts emphasize meditation, spiritual discipline, and the search for an indescribable sense of unity with all of creation, but the Indian writers put more emphasis on dedication to a single god, like Krishna, while the Chinese writers describe the eternal Way as an unnameable force, not a human deity.

The ways that can be walked are not the eternal Way;
The names that can be named are not the eternal name.
The nameless is the origin of the myriad creatures;
The named is the mother of the myriad creatures.
Therefore
Always be without desire in order to observe its wondrous subtleties;

Always have desire, so that you may observe its manifestations.
Both of these derive from the same source;
They have different names but the same designation.
Mystery of mysteries,
The gate of all wonders!

ornamentation. The mystical *Daodejing* hints at an indescribable reality that generates all the tangible objects of the material world. "Born before heaven and earth – silent and void – it stands alone and does not change. Pervading all things, it does not grow weary. You cannot keep it close. You cannot keep it far off. You cannot benefit it, nor can you name it … you cannot ennoble it or debase it." The Dao is all of nature, acting spontaneously, "of itself" (**ziran**). The goal of the Daoist sage is to merge with this transcendent force by abandoning all artificial activity (**wei**), including the ruler's stratagems and the philosopher's argumentation and moral preaching. "Practice non-action (**wuwei**), and there is nothing that will not be done."

The Daoist discards Confucian moral introspection and fussing about ritual: "cut off *ren*, abandon righteousness, and the people will return to filiality and kindness; cut off skill and abandon utility and robbers and thieves will disappear." He aims to be the dancer who cannot be distinguished from the dance, the butcher who carves without effort because he knows instinctively where all the joints are. In the duality of male action and female passivity, the Daoist favors darkness, stillness, and passivity: "The gateway of the mysterious female is the root of heaven and earth." He discards the trappings of civilization in order to achieve a primitive state, in which he can look with indifference on wealth, ornament, culture, or power. Sometimes the Daoists sound very much like Buddhists. The ten thousand things of the material world become as worthless as sacrificial straw dogs, burnt on the altar and discarded.

Yet the *Daodejing* is also a political text, addressed to rulers. Its discussion of **de**, or virtue, uses the same Confucian concept of moral power in a radically different way. Confucius would agree with Laozi that the ideal king should only look south, radiating his moral power without burdening the people with unnecessary action. But the Daoist ruler aims to keep his subjects ignorant and isolated from the outside world, as if his kingdom were a remote village which no one wanted to leave. Knowledge and technological progress injure this pristine state, and only cause oppression and frustration. The Daoist ideal of non-action stands at the furthest end of the spectrum from the incessant purposive activity of the Mohist ruler, who tries to give his people as much wealth and order as possible. The soft ruler, like the judo practitioner, will overcome the strong one by cunning.

No ruler took the Daoists' advice literally, any more than they did that of Confucius, but the Daoist concept of a state that would run itself had curiously broad impact. The harshest Legalist philosopher, Han Feizi, who praised despotic enforcement of laws, also told his ruler to step back and let his state run itself, once he had set up the legal machine. A perfect despotism would control the people so perfectly that, like the Daoist village, they could not even think of breaking the law.

Zhuangzi (*c.* 369–286 BCE), the wildest and funniest Chinese philosopher, took the Daoist ideals to extremes. Not only did he reject moral codes, laws, and civilized arts; he rejected all efforts to divide the world into sensible parts. He achieved a trance-like state in which he could not tell whether he was Zhuangzi dreaming of a butterfly, or a butterfly dreaming of Zhuangzi. He viewed everything relatively, rejecting all absolute standards: a huge mountain could be tiny, or the tip of a hair could be huge, depending on the situation. One debater could defeat another, but that didn't prove he was right. All fixed positions had truth only relative to each other. Constant transformation was the only regularity in Nature. Zhuangzi used ridicule, irony, fantasy, and logic in remarkably original combinations to jolt his audience out of their common-sense understandings, so as to draw them into his inverted world. If they understood him, even death would carry no sting, because human life itself merely dissolved into Nature's eternal rounds.

Popular Beliefs Are Less Philosophical

In this incredibly fruitful period, the philosophers were not the only occupants of intellectual terrain. They competed with other world views, which they often scorned as superstitious. Astrologers predicted policy outcomes from the positions of stars, or by observing eclipses and comets. Shamans claimed to contact the other world directly through mystical trances; healers invoked spells and used herbs to harmonize bodily functions with wider cosmic trends. Divination, using milfoil plant stalks, produced the mysterious and now popular text **Book of Changes** (*Yijing*), used to interpret the sixty-four hexagrams that expressed the structure of the universe. Figure 5.3 shows a chart of these hexagrams. Subsuming all of these was the division of the world into the two principles of Yin and Yang and the effort to describe the course of history in terms of the succession of five natural phases: earth, wood, metal, fire, water. Specialists in each of these "dark arts" wrote technical texts, but Daoists, Confucians, and Legalists all invoked their principles. The fundamental assumption of correlations between nature and the human world encouraged increasingly systematic and diverse attempts to bring all of the known world into orderly patterns.

Despite the abundance of sources for this period compared with earlier times, we still know almost exclusively about the mental worlds of elite Chinese men. Yet it is plausible to assume that commoners, and especially women, were more deeply immersed in the world of phases, geomancy, and astrology than in the philosophical speculations of the masters. This realm of correlative thinking linked the different classes of Chinese with

shared understandings that were just as important in binding the society together as the virtue and power of the sovereign.

In the end, the Legalists won the political debate, the Confucians captured the orthodox philosophical high ground, Daoists inspired art, poetry, and the enjoyment of nature, and the "correlative thinkers" influenced everybody. These tendencies did not coexist harmoniously. Any literate Chinese person involved in public affairs faced great tensions pulling him in different directions: toward the repression required by imperial law, or the humanity that tempered severe punishment, while favoring his own family, or the urge to get away from it all by dropping out of politics. At the same time, he might consult an almanac to check his star chart, cast divination with hexagrams, and see doctors who gave him potions and acupuncture. Chinese policymakers faced the same dilemmas as statesmen in India and Central Asia. Box 5.5 compares the policy prescriptions of Chinese, Central Asian, and ancient Indian texts.

The Unified Empire

All the scholars, strategists, and statesmen had longed to bring the **Hua** people (the term used by the Zhou to define their own culture) together, but the unification came in a form that few of them wanted. The state of Qin, in the far west, hemmed in by mountains and backed by the Yellow River, had developed superior economic and military strength by the third century. It had learned military skills from the northwestern barbarians, and it had carried out radical reforms to increase its wealth. Other states accused Qin of being avaricious and crude, but they

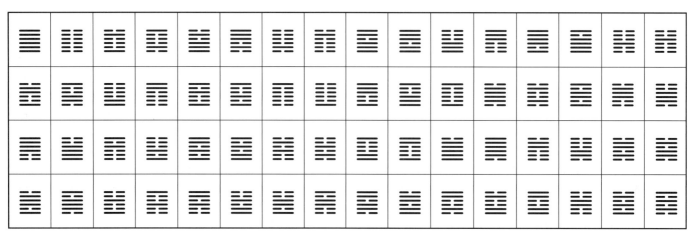

Figure 5.3 The *Book of Changes* is an ancient Chinese divination text used to foretell cosmic and human events. By pulling straws or throwing dice, the diviner chooses one of the sixty-four hexagrams formed out of combinations of broken and solid lines. He then interprets the symbol as a response to his questions. The solid lines represent yang forces (male, sun, and strong) and the broken lines represent yin (female, moon, and weak) forces, but the combination of both processes determines the multiple evolutionary directions of the heavens, the earth, and human life.

Box 5.5 What Should a Ruler Do?

Chinese, South Asian, and Central Asian rulers all had their own ideas of how to run a good government. They agreed on many basic principles: Keep peace and order, reward your supporters, try to expand your territory, promote agriculture or herding, take advantage of profits from trade. Beyond these basic principles, they all debated intensively over specific policy decisions. The philosophers and statesmen gave them advice on how to apply basic understandings of humans and nature to concrete decisions.

The Confucian Mencius had the clearest answers. He told rulers to lower taxes, avoid wasteful wars, and ensure that their people lived in peace and prosperity. Then their states would be strong, and they would have unrivaled reputations for virtue. His opponents, the Legalists, were a bit more skeptical. They thought that humans usually acted out of fear, not out of gratitude. The first thing a state needed was a strong army and high amounts of revenue, to put down enemies within and without. The people's suffering mattered less than the security of the state.

The Xiongnu had their own philosophy of government, too: Try to obtain the maximum amount of revenue by raiding, or trading with the wealthy Han empire to their south. They used Chinese advisors to tell them the best ways to get the goods they needed. The Xiongnu chieftain had to reward his warriors with prestigious goods in order to keep their support. Unlike Chinese bureaucrats, his followers could just move away and live without him if they saw no gain from submitting to him. On the other hand, they had to beware of the softening effect of Chinese luxuries. These could make them weak and vulnerable to Chinese invasion.

Indian political philosophy, as summarized in the *Arthashastra*, combines many strands of common sense with a stress on the need of the ruler to keep power at all costs. It assumes that the ruler's main occupation will be war and diplomacy with other states. "The king who is weaker than the other should keep the peace; he who is stronger should make war." The stress on war makes the *Arthashastra* sound much like

Chinese Legalist and military manuals. The Indian king should be very busy in working for his kingdom. The energetic Indian king was not at all like the Daoist ideal ruler, who merely faced south. An Indian king, after listening to reports, consulting with ministers, inspecting the army, and conducting rituals, had only three hours left to sleep. But the king could not think only of himself: "In the happiness of the subjects lies the happiness of the king; in their welfare, his own welfare. The welfare of the king does not lie in the fulfillment of what is dear to him; whatever is dear to the subjects constitutes his welfare." Kautilya, the practical author of the *Arthashastra*, did not invoke Heavenly Mandates to back up his king's authority, unlike Mencius, but he recognized the importance of managing the economy well and keeping subjects happy.

All the state-builders of Asia relied on practical experience and theories of human behavior to develop a science of policy, designed to keep the state secure and its subjects prosperous.

could not unite against it. In 221 BCE the Qin ruler conquered all the other states with overwhelming force, giving himself a new title: **Huangdi**, or "August Emperor." As Qin Shihuangdi, he was the first emperor of a united China.

Decisive changes during Qin Shihuang's short reign (221–210 BCE) marked the rest of China's imperial history. The key architect of these reforms was not the emperor, but his Legalist chief minister Li Si. Li extended to the entire empire the centralizing measures begun by the warring states, particularly the local administration based on xian, or counties, which abolished the power of the feudal lords and states and put all subjects directly under central control. The xian unit was remarkably stable: if the Qin empire had about 1,000 xian, China today has about 1,500, many with nearly the same boundaries. Li Si also imposed standardized weights and measures, extending even to the width of carriages (so that ruts in North China's muddy roads would

be the same size); he abolished the diverse writing systems of the states, replacing them with the standard script that all Chinese used until the twentieth century; and he ensured cultural uniformity by burning hundreds of classic texts and executing hundreds of scholars. Box 5.6 illustrates the savage intellectual repression inflicted by Li Si's measures.

Yet the ruthless Qin emperor brought peace. He melted down thousands of weapons, tore down hundreds of local walls, built grand imperial highways of a total length of 3,700 miles, greater than imperial Rome, and promoted agricultural production. He constructed long walls along the northwest frontier to keep out invaders, joining together many of the separate walls of the divided states. He presented himself as a sage, benevolent emperor, concerned for his people's welfare. He prepared for himself a huge tomb to celebrate his achievements, mobilizing 700,000 **corvée** laborers to build it. He had many of the builders

Box 5.6 The Qin Emperor on Academic Freedom

Li Si and the Qin emperor particularly detested the Confucian scholars who invoked the ideals of the past to criticize the present: "There are some men of letters who do not model themselves on the present but study the past in order to criticize the present age. They confuse and excite the ordinary people … It is expedient that these be prohibited." They preserved useful texts on medicine, forestry, and divination, but banned philosophy, rituals, history, and music. Their aim was not to eliminate learning but to ensure that the state monopolized it. "Those who want to study, let them learn from the officials," said Li Si.

killed after its completion to conceal its dimensions, and he brought much of his army with him into the next world. Few believed these fantastic accounts in the texts until the real tomb was excavated in 1974. Now thousands of tourists know that much of what historians wrote about the Qin emperor's tomb was true.

Li Si was a cold, calculating rationalist, but the emperor himself had a very different personality. He believed more strongly in the Five Phases scheme than in Legalism, for example. Since the Zhou represented the fire phase, Qin claimed water, which overcomes fire, as his symbol. Water was associated with the color black and the number six, so all flags had to be black, chariots six feet wide, and contracts six inches long. The emperor sent thousands of young boys and girls out into the eastern seas to find the blessed isles, the source of the elixir of immortality. They never returned (or perhaps they made it to Japan). He tried to have one of his sons succeed him, but at his death, mass revolts against severe corvée labor impositions broke out, and after a decade of civil war, a peasant leader named Liu Bang established the Han empire. Confucians under the new dynasty attacked the Qin for ignoring principles of benevolence and ritual, but even they had to admit that the endurance of the imperial system under which they served owed a great deal to the first founder.

The Han Dynasties, 206 BCE – 220 CE

Liu Bang (r. 206–195), the first peasant emperor, was not particularly fond of literati: he once urinated into a Confucian scholar's hat. Yet the dynasty he founded chose Confucian teachings as its orthodox tradition, and it lasted, with one interruption, for over four hundred years – a record of longevity that compares favorably with the western Roman empire. What was

the key to the Han's endurance? The Han rulers and their elites eliminated the crucial obstacles that had prevented unity for 500 years:

- They preserved and extended the uniform bureaucratic system of officials, laws, and language established by the Qin.
- They maintained sufficient coercive power to ward off invasions from the northwest frontier, and to put down internal revolt.
- They facilitated the growth of commerce and agriculture by keeping peace, and extracting relatively small amounts from a large population.
- They maintained the common cultural norms of the Axial Age, allowing multiple traditions to flourish and compete within the bounds of imperial orthodoxy.

Han government followed closely the model of the Qin. The territorial boundaries of the Han were almost the same, except for Han expansion into Central Eurasia. Twelve hundred counties at the lower level were subordinate to a hundred commanderies and thirteen circuits, ruled at the center by nine chief ministers, a Chief Counselor, and the Emperor. These officials collected regular salaries from taxes paid in grain or cloth. They ruled a population determined by census to be nearly 60 million people, comparable in size to the Roman empire.

Unlike the Qin, however, the Han rulers supported Confucianism as the official ideology of the empire. Scholars convinced the emperors that an education in the Confucian classics would provide loyal, talented men to run the administration out of a sense of duty rather than fear. The *shi*, or scholar-officials, could now be integral parts of the imperial state instead of just roving advisors. On the other hand, the scholars reserved the right to criticize rulers who deviated from the principles of the sages, and some lost their lives for speaking up too openly. This cooperative but tense relationship between dynastic rulers and the scholar-official class became one of the key features accounting for the longevity of all succeeding dynasties. The scholar-officials maintained the continuity of administrative procedure and proposed reforms, while the rulers pursued their goals of wealth, power, and glory.

Since this was the largest bureaucratic system ever created, it did not work perfectly. The bureaucracy did not cover the entire country; the feudal principle returned when Liu Bang created a new nobility to reward his brothers and sons and gave them control of two thirds of the territory. A tomb excavated in South China in 1975 displays the high life of this nobility (see Figure 5.4). The body of this woman, Lady Dai, was perfectly preserved, wrapped in twenty coats of embroidered silk brocade, encased in four interlocking coffins. Her beautiful silks, lacquer

Figure 5.4 The funeral cloth wrapping the body of this aristocratic woman, buried in Hunan in South China in the second century BCE, is an elaborately woven silk brocade indicating great wealth and power. Images of birds and animals surround her portrait in the center. Heaven is above her and two giant sea serpents dominate the underworld below. Messengers and offerings by her descendants help her on her path to heaven.

Agriculture and Trade Support the Han Empire The expanding economy, landed and commercial, supported the top-level officials and the nobles. Han peasants were the first to use widely the genuine iron plow, making possible clearance of tougher soils and greater yields on old lands. They grew the same "five grains" (two kinds of millet, beans, hemp, and wheat) as in the Warring States, but cultivated them more intensively. They knew about the nitrogen-fixing properties of soybeans, so they introduced legumes into crop rotations. Since the densest population lived in the cold and dry north, rice was not yet a major crop, although the sparse population of the south had begun to grow a little bit of it. The population probably grew rapidly until the first century BCE, when it hit a ceiling of 60 million and remained there for the next 700 years, limited by the agricultural regime. The government supported this population's livelihood with irrigation works, famine relief programs, and tax breaks that encouraged poor families to migrate to unsettled frontiers.

Private landowners drove much of the growth of the landed economy, but they threatened state revenues by bribing local officials to let them evade taxes and by encroaching on independent peasant holdings. The collapse of the Former Han dynasty in 8 CE was a result of growing inequality of landholding and deficits in tax collection. Wang Mang, a powerful state minister, briefly established a new dynasty, vowing to crack down on landowner evasion. He was a Utopian Confucian who tried to restore Mencius' ideal well-field landholding system, where all farmers have equal amounts of land. But powerful families and peasant rebels overthrew him, re-establishing the dynasty, now called the Latter Han, in 25 CE. After that, the state made few efforts to control landed property, and ultimately the inequalities created by land encroachment brought down the dynasty.

China's commerce flourished despite Confucian disapproval of the pursuit of profit. Farmers marketed a substantial percentage of their crops, and merchants profited by trading agricultural goods for urban products. The expanded empire provided many opportunities to make money: for example, in iron smelting, foreign trade, credit loans, fish peddling, grain storage, and trading cattle, sheep, and silk. Some officials resented merchants who flaunted their wealth, so they forbade them to wear silk or ride in carriages, and levied abusive taxes on them. Other officials, however, made profit from joint ventures. Merchants had no guaranteed property rights: the state could confiscate their wealth, just as it attacked wealthy landowners. Their best options were to buy official allies, invest profits in land, or get one of their sons into officialdom. Han China did not have an independent "bourgeois" class, but neither did anywhere else. Chinese merchants knew well how to work the system for their benefit.

vessels, fresh food, 300 gold pieces, and 100,000 bronze coins, show that she expected to enter the next life in style.

At the center of power, factional rivalries broke out between members of the "inner court," the emperor's personal favorites, and the "outer court," the representatives of bureaucratic routine. The emperors brought in eunuchs, castrated young men, as advisors so that they would have supporters totally dependent on them, but the eunuchs themselves divided into factions allied with the outer court officials. The emperor could not be the perfect autocrat: he had to attend court conferences and adjudicate conflicts among his advisors. The Han state did not run like the smooth machine envisioned by the Legalist-Daoist theorists, but somehow it muddled through for four hundred years.

Foreign trade was equally tied to politics. Under the notion of "tribute" (**gong**), the emperor graciously accepted "gifts" from inferior "barbarians" who "submitted" to China's superior culture. In return, the emperor gave gifts to the tributary envoys out of his benevolent intentions to "cherish visitors from afar." Thus the Chinese elite kept its distance from the vulgar pursuit of profit while using trade to secure diplomatic relations. The "barbarians," of course, had a different view of these transactions. They profited greatly from exchanging poor horses for valuable Chinese silks, and they extorted opportunities for greater tribute gifts by threatening to raid the frontiers. These profits were well worth a few kowtows. Through the language of tribute, these two vastly different cultural systems were sometimes able to communicate and trade for mutual benefit. But as we shall see, the Han's relations with its northern neighbors were turbulent and violent.

Han Scholars Write Synthetic Philosophy and Universal History Han intellectual culture carried on the tendencies of the Axial Age. The ruling elite learned one lesson from the fall of the Qin: too much brutality ensured your dynasty a short life, because it provoked universal revolt. Liu Bang announced that he would soften the harsh punishments of the Qin legal code, although he kept most of its provisions. His successor, Han Wudi (r. 141–87 BCE), determined to put Confucians, not Legalists, in charge of the orthodox doctrine of the state. Because they wanted to insert the Han into the lineage of approved dynasties, the emperors needed the Confucians to advise them on how to run their great bureaucracy predictably. Scholars diligently recovered the burned books and restored classical studies; the early Han imperial library contained 677 books.

Nearly all the scholars supported the imperial project, but the greatest of them continued to use the past to criticize the present. Sima Qian (145–90 BCE), China's greatest historian, came from a distinguished scholarly family, dedicated to learning moral lessons from the Spring and Autumn annals and from Confucius' teaching. But when he made the mistake of supporting a loyal general unfairly accused of treason, he suffered castration. Although he could have no descendants, he decided, as a "mere remnant of the knife and saw," to leave a comprehensive history of the world to posterity. His *Historical Annals* cover the entire history of the Chinese world from its origins to his own time, including chapters on imperial reigns along with treatises on rituals, economics, the calendar, and biographies of merchants and even righteous assassins. No officials sponsored his work, and he carefully evaluated his sources and gave his independent opinions. Sima Qian combined breadth of vision, recognizing the ceaseless change of societies over the long term, with sensitive insight into individuals living through these great changes, to provide a general history that none of his successors equaled. After him, official histories took a narrower view.

Besides state-sponsored Confucian ritual, Han thinking mingled different philosophies together. The Han scholars, putting together the *Spring and Autumn Chronicle* with the *Book of Documents*, the *Book of Rites*, the *Book of Odes*, and the *Book of Changes*, made these books the Five Classics of Confucian thought. These were the public documents distinct from the private philosophers, which presented the basic elements that all scholars had to work with. Han Wudi, besides Confucianism, supported the Five Phases theory, identifying the Han with earth and the color yellow. Yellow became the imperial color from then on. The philosopher Dong Zhongshu created a grand synthesis of Five Phases, dynastic cycle, and correlative thinking, with Daoist elements out of this mix. He was the social scientific-philosophic counterpart to the historian Sima Qian. Both aimed to summarize and synthesize large-scale processes in the newly unified universal empire.

Central Eurasian Cultures: A "Barbarian" Frontier?

The vast steppes, deserts, and forests of Central Eurasia supported a radically different kind of culture from the settled farmers of the core of China or South Asia. The settled writers always referred to these peoples as "barbarians," and almost always saw them as nothing but greedy, violent invaders of the heartland. Yet these peoples, especially the mounted nomad warriors, brought many innovations to both regions. They were not just looters and bandits, but had their own forms of military, commercial, religious, and political organization, which we can dimly recognize through the hostile texts and through recent archaeological investigations.

Central Eurasia extends from Manchuria, northeast of the North China Plain, westward across modern Russia and Mongolia to the grassy plain of Hungary. In the north, it includes the Siberian forests, and in the south, it extends to the high mountains of the Tibetan plateau, northern Iran, and the Caucasus. Three major geographic zones define the eastern half of Central Eurasia: the Manchurian Plain, Mongolia, and Xinjiang. Manchuria contains river basins, forests, and fertile fields that supported small populations of hunters, fishermen, and farmers. These tribal populations did not have a powerful effect on China until the tenth century CE. Mongolia, now divided into an independent country and the Inner Mongolian region of China, contains huge grasslands, the Gobi Desert, small forests, and rivers. For centuries it was the primary source of nomadic peoples who moved with their herds across the steppes, but also combined herding with agriculture and hunting. Modern Xinjiang, generally called the "Western Regions" by the Chinese, contains a huge desert (the Taklamakan) at its center, bordered by high mountain ranges, the Tianshan and Kunlun. Most of its people lived in oases on the edge of the desert, and they obtained water for their fields from canals that brought melted snow down from the mountains. As we saw in Chapter 3, the mummies discovered there show that people had moved into Xinjiang from the west by the second millennium BCE.

Across the northern and northwestern zone of China, from Manchuria through Mongolia, mixed economies of agriculture and pastoral nomadism gradually developed in the first millennium BCE. The essential elements of **pastoralism** – the domestication of the horse, the use of chariots, and the reliance on herds – had developed much earlier, in the Middle East and western Central Eurasia. The famous bronze figure of a flying horse in Figure 5.5 shows how this way of life had influenced Han Chinese later on. The first "true" nomads in written sources, the Sakas or Scythians, had appeared in the south Russian steppe in the tenth to ninth centuries BCE. By the ninth to seventh centuries, elements of the pastoral culture appear in tombs on the north Chinese frontier. By the sixth to fourth centuries, the appearance of the "Scythian triad" of animal art, weapons, and horse harnesses shows that pastoral nomads had arrived in the Ordos region of northwest China. Iron metallurgy, a key component of both nomadic and settled societies, came to China from the west, appearing first in the Ferghana Valley of Xinjiang, then moving into the northwest, reaching the Warring States in the sixth century BCE. Mounted warriors on horses then created a military elite, probably dominating mixed populations of

farmers, herdsmen, and hunters. They were not united in a single confederation, and they often coexisted symbiotically with farming communities.

Chinese writers knew that a very different culture lay beyond the passes to the north, and little more. Yet the Zhou people did not sharply divide the "civilized" Chinese realm to the south from a "barbarian" realm in the north. The peoples they called Rong and Di in the north were militarily powerful, and not part of the Zhou king's cultural sphere, but each of the competing rulers found them politically useful. Rong and Di soldiers could join Zhou military units, and the non-Zhou peoples often allied with Zhou states against other Zhou rivals. Disregarding the philosophers' abstractions, the statesmen dealt with anyone who could help them. Peace with the Rong and Di was often cheaper than war, and the Rong and Di could observe treaties, make oaths, and form alliances just as reliably, or unreliably, as the other states.

The Warring States period, as it intensified interstate competition, also intensified contacts between the Chinese and the northern peoples. Now there were genuine mounted warriors, called Hu, across the frontier, and they had a vital resource to offer: horses. In 307 BCE, the king of Zhao proposed a radical innovation: he told his troops to learn to ride horses like the Hu, creating China's first cavalry units. This meant not only learning new skills, but dressing in nomadic costume, with trousers and leather boots instead of robes. Some objected that this would turn them into barbarians, but the king insisted that he was only following his ancestors' recommendations to adopt useful foreign techniques. We will see again and again this argument

Figure 5.5 This magnificent bronze sculpture of a flying horse comes from northwest China, where the pastoral nomads strongly influenced local culture. The horse is 14 inches high, and it rides on a swallow, indicating that it gallops faster than the wind.

that China must learn from the outside world in order to save itself. These cavalry were used mainly against other warring states, not the nomads themselves. The adoption of nomadic military tactics greatly increased the Chinese troops' mobility, but now China needed to trade with the steppe to obtain horses. Gold and silver appear in great quantities in northern frontier tombs in the fourth century BCE, showing that nomadic leaders were getting rich from frontier trade. Commerce with the steppe thus supported coercion in the interior.

But a second dynamic territorial expansion brought further conflict with the nomads. As the Qin, Yan, and Zhao states pushed outward into the grasslands in order to clear new lands and graze their horses, they built many new walls. These walls were not really defenses against nomadic attacks; they were expansionist moves by these competitive states to build up resources to use against each other. When Qin Shihuang connected these walls into the Great Wall, he enclosed many pastoral peoples inside them; he was not just defending settled fields but increasing the size of his state.

We have seen how in India mounted horsemen from Iran and Afghanistan occupied the Indus Valley, stimulating the formation of new states in the Ganges Valley. Nomads on the Chinese frontier had similar effects, because they provided new military techniques and powerful allies for ambitious state builders. South Asians and Chinese looked down on these rude peoples, but they learned a great deal from them.

The Xiongnu Confederacy Preys on the Han Dynasty

We discussed the basic forms of pastoralism in Chapter 3. These nomads continued to move across Central Eurasia as China and India formed their first dynastic states. Beginning in the third century BCE, interactions between the Chinese and their northern neighbors generated the first great nomadic empire in East Asia: the Xiongnu. Map 5.3 shows how the Xiongnu spread across Central Eurasia. Throughout most of the Han dynasty, the Xiongnu occupied much of the territory beyond the Great Wall. They were Han China's only serious military rival. We do not know their ethnicity or the language of their rulers; most likely they were a confederation of many different peoples. They were nomadic warriors with a powerful chieftain, the Shanyu, who dominated the other tribes and collected tribute from

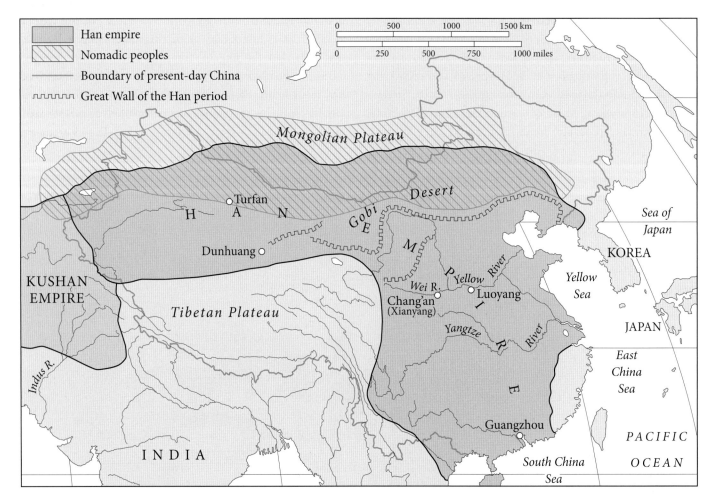

Map 5.3 Han empire and nomadic confederation of Xiongnu

the oasis peoples, while constantly raiding the Chinese frontier. Chinese military campaigns into the Ordos in 215 BCE touched off a crisis that led to the centralization of the nomadic warriors under a single chieftain. In 209 BCE Modun assembled a loyal band of warriors, assassinated his father, and made himself the supreme chief, acclaimed by all, forcing other tribes to give him tribute. The first Han emperor launched a major campaign against Modun, but suffered an embarrassing defeat, forcing him to sign a peace treaty in 198 BCE recognizing the Xiongnu as an equal state. Under this "policy of friendship," the Han agreed to send large quantities of goods to the Xiongnu if they would stop their border raids. The two powers agreed to regard each other "as brothers." The Han sent princesses to marry the Xiongnu chief, and once the chief even asked for the Han empress's hand in marriage. The Han aimed to corrupt the Xiongnu with wealth, so as to reduce their military power, while encouraging them to follow more Chinese customs. The Xiongnu chief, however, used the goods obtained from China to centralize his own state. Han officials clashed with each other over the need to establish state monopolies of salt and iron to support their military campaigns. Box 5.7 describes this policy debate.

Peace held for sixty years, but the policy of friendship came under strain. On the Chinese side, warmongers argued that it was humiliating to send money to those who were utterly foreign to Chinese ways, especially since the frontier raids had not stopped. On the Xiongnu side, the Shanyu chief benefited from the official trade, but he could not control his subordinate commanders, who continued to attack the frontier. The Han had meanwhile built up a much more powerful military force,

complete with cavalry, crossbows, and ironclad armor. Emperor Han Wudi launched a large military campaign that obtained surprisingly early success, and developed into an all out effort to exterminate the Xiongnu state. He drove back the Xiongnu from the frontier, and established new commanderies that were joined to the Han.

At the same time, he sent an envoy named Zhang Qian far away into the Western Regions to seek allies in the Xiongnu's rear. Zhang Qian failed to get his alliance, but he returned with valuable information that opened Chinese eyes to the prosperous cultures in the depths of Central Eurasia. A century later, the new opportunities for trade and diplomacy revealed by Zhang Qian's voyages led to the development of regular caravan trade along the silk routes. By 60 BCE, the Han had succeeded in depriving the Xiongnu of their economic base in the Western Regions, and the Xiongnu leader asked for peace. He submitted to the Han, which allowed him to pay tribute on generous terms. With the collapse of the Former Han, however, the Xiongnu recaptured control of the Western Regions, and rejected tribute ties with China. By the first century CE, the revived Latter Han had succeeded in splitting the Xiongnu empire into two parts, drawing the southern tribes into close dependence on China. New expeditions into the Western Regions established military colonies, where Chinese troops cultivated the land and garrisoned the oases.

In this seesaw struggle, the Han showed that they could drive back nomadic warriors, at very heavy cost, and they could win over the chieftains and oasis settlements with skillful diplomacy. Sima Qian made this struggle into a key theme of his history,

Box 5.7 Should the Government Own Industries? A Chinese Debate

An interesting debate held in 81 BCE illustrates the close connections of state power, commerce, and national security. Han officials imposed monopolies of salt and iron production so as to fund ambitious programs of expansion on the northwest frontier. The use of iron in everything from plows to cooking pots, and the daily need for salt, made these monopoly prices very burdensome. Literati scholars at court protested that the state should have nothing to do with commerce, and it should not fight expensive wars. It should abolish the monopolies, lower taxes, and advise the people

to limit their desires. Tough-minded officials responded that the barbarian threat to national security required increasing the arms budget; the monopolies supplied vital extra income: "The Xiongnu, savage and wily, boldly push through the barriers and harass the Middle Kingdom … they long deserve punishment for their unruliness and lawlessness … Our critics here, who demand that these monopolies be abolished, at home would have the treasury entirely depleted, and abroad would deprive the border of provision for its

defense." The literati, known as the *ru*, or soft-liners, lost this debate, and the monopolies stayed. The ru resembled advocates of laissez-faire government, except that they did not promote economic growth. Their opponents took the mercantilist position, favoring commerce protected by the state. Both points of view would continue to define the alternatives of Chinese political economy hereafter. Debates over taxation and defense in the Song dynasty echoed these earlier positions (see Chapter 11).

but he portrayed it as a unilateral defense of China against nomadic invaders. Like his contemporaries, he saw correlations between natural forces and human affairs, and he focused only on what the confrontation meant for China: did it indicate that Heaven was on the emperor's side? The ultimate victory of the Han, in his view, showed that it did. A more balanced perspective would see both the Xiongnu and the Han as states contending for control over a vast region, using commercial, coercive, and cultural appeals to win allies and mobilize resources. These interactions between China and Central Eurasia decisively affected the history of the entire continent until the eighteenth century CE, when nomadic military power finally vanished.

The Fall of Han China Begins a New Period of Division, 220–589 CE

By the second century CE, the Han central government began to lose control of much of the country. As the local elites accumulated land and shifted tax burdens to the poorer peasantry, they looked more to their own interests than to the central government. At the same time, the Confucian stress on loyalty to superiors lost conviction, as new Daoist sects drew mass congregations. The new Daoists had little but their name in common with the authors of the *Daodejing* and Zhuangzi. The Daoist church offered its followers not obscure mystical visions, but concrete benefits: cures for illness, and even eternal life. Their ceremonies did not stress quiet meditation, but passionate mass conversions, in which the followers rolled in the mud, confessed their sins, sang group hymns, and swore loyalty to the sect leader. Repeating the exhausting rituals several times a day, dazed by hunger, fatigue, incense, and noise, they sought to break through to ecstatic unity with the Dao.

The Han emperor himself had founded a temple to Laozi in 149 CE, but the Daoist followers did not obey him. The Five Pecks of Rice sect, a healing cult centered in Sichuan, essentially took over the province for thirty years, with an apocalyptic vision of sweeping away the old society by violence to inaugurate the millennium. The Yellow Turbans, peasant rebels in East China, half a million strong, revolted directly against the dynasty. Since the helpless emperors were captives of eunuch factions who fought each other, only the vigorous general Cao Cao could put down the revolt, but how loyal was he to the dynasty? Cao Cao became famous in novel and drama as a brilliant but unscrupulous leader, "a villain in times of order; a hero in times of disorder." He could win battles, but not restore a legitimate order. At his death, the Han dynasty fell, and China remained disunited for the next three and a half centuries.

Yet great changes occurred during this period of division, even though no single ruler could proclaim a Mandate of Heaven. Two more or less separate and distinct societies formed in North and South China. Most important, Buddhist missionaries arrived from India via Central Asia, inspiring Chinese to translate a huge quantity of foreign scriptures and to embed this foreign religion deeply into their culture. The Chinese pilgrim Faxian, described in Box 5.8, was very impressed with the wealth and happiness of the Buddhist Indian state which he visited. By 600 CE, China appeared to be a thoroughly Buddhist country, and Confucian official ideology seemed to have disappeared.

The division of the empire allowed the Xiongnu to penetrate deeply into North China. They sacked Luoyang in 311 CE. A Persian merchant in the city reported the shocking news to his friend in Samarkand, showing that foreign merchant communities spanned the Silk Road even in this time of upheaval. Buddhist missionaries had already used this commercial route to

Box 5.8 A Chinese Pilgrim Visits India

The Chinese Buddhist monk Faxian (399–413), who visited Pataliputra in the early 400s CE, visited two large Buddhist monasteries near the tomb of Ashoka, one Mahayana and one Theravada, which supported about 700 monks between them and were well administered. Modern historians share Faxian's impression that subjects of the Guptas were lightly taxed and administered. Faxian wrote:

The people are numerous and happy; they have not to register their households, or attend to any magistrates and their rules; only those who cultivate the royal land have to pay (a portion of) the grain from it. If they want to go, they go; if they want to stay on, they stay. The king governs without decapitation or (other) corporal punishments. Criminals are simply fined, lightly or heavily,

according to the circumstances (of each case). Even in cases of repeated attempts at wicked rebellion, they only have their right hands cut off. The king's bodyguards and attendants all have salaries. Throughout the whole country the people do not kill any living creature, nor drink intoxicating liquor, nor eat onions or garlic.

move out of India, so the Parthian monk Anshigao had been translating Sanskrit texts into Chinese in Luoyang since 148 CE. The new Xiongnu conqueror was not so interested in metaphysics, but he was impressed when the monk Fotudeng caused blue lotus flowers to sprout magically in his begging bowl, called down rainstorms, and cured the ill. Magic spells impressed the Xiongnu warriors, and looked attractive because they were not of Chinese origin. The Tabgach nomads, who established the Northern Wei dynasty in North China, from 386 to 534 CE, sponsored the building of over nine hundred monasteries and great Buddhist projects like the huge cave statues at Yungang in Shanxi province. These giant statues proclaimed the unity of imperial power with the religious establishment.

In South China, Buddhism also prospered, in somewhat gentler fashion, under sponsorship from Emperor Wu of the Liang dynasty, a scholar who converted from Daoism to Buddhism. He threatened to leave the throne to become a monk, and returned to rule after his ministers paid large contributions to the monastery. Then he held a feast for fifty thousand monks and lay believers. Like Christianity, Buddhism had evolved from a religion of withdrawal from the world into a large institution that profited from and supported state power. Both Jesus and the Buddha would have been astonished and dismayed at what happened to their teachings.

Parallels to the fall of Rome easily leap to the eye, when we note the growth of large landed estates, the rise of new religions, and the incursions of "barbarian" military warriors into empires that had lost central control. Both the Han and Roman projects were simply too far-reaching to be sustained by the underlying agrarian productive base, and they both faced serious rivals in the mobile warriors of the forests and steppes on their peripheries. Western Europe, of course, despite several abortive attempts, never successfully regained its unity (until the late twentieth century), but China did reconstruct its empire in the sixth century under the Sui and Tang. Yet the imperial ideal at both ends of Eurasia never disappeared; they shared the same nostalgic visions of a time of peace, expansion, and prosperity under unified rule.

Conclusion During these 1,200 years, from roughly 600 BCE to 600 CE, East and South Asia built powerful states in their core agricultural regions. These settled regimes used iron technology, crop specialization, and extensive trade to support their bureaucracies and armies. At the same time, in Central Eurasia, nomadic pastoralists created large confederations under charismatic rulers, relying for resources on grasslands, animals, horsemanship, trade, and raiding of the empires surrounding them, especially China. Both Chinese and Indian states adopted military technology from the pastoralists to strengthen their armies. Chinese regimes, after a tumultuous period of competition from 600 to 221 BCE, became a series of unified empires – the Qin, Former Han, and Latter Han – before fragmenting again. Indian states, with a more limited duration, never controlled the entire subcontinent.

The Central Eurasian nomads left us no written records, but the new agrarian states supported priests, bureaucrats, and intellectuals, who have left us the classic philosophical and religious writings of each civilization. Chinese writing, developed at least as early as 1200 BCE, transmitted fundamental philosophical thinking as well as popular beliefs in magic and the elements of bureaucratic culture. Indian alphabetical writing in Sanskrit recorded oral epics in massive detail and generated the original Buddhist texts, which were later translated into many languages, including Chinese. Neither culture was pure: both mixed many elements from local and imported sources. Cultural influences in general flowed from the Persian and Greek realms into India, out of South Asia through Bactria into China, from Central Eurasia into northwest China, and from China outward into Korea, Japan, and Southeast Asia.

By the end of this period, large empires had risen and fallen, but Buddhism endured in both China and India as the most dominant, established cultural institution for elites and commoners. The Buddhists, however, contested with many rivals. Daoists and Confucians in China asserted the primacy of native Chinese forms over foreign imports, but Buddhist translators adapted the original Sanskrit and other texts to fit into Chinese cultural norms. Hindus, Jains, and others in India actively competed for influence with Buddhism, and eventually succeeded in driving Buddhism out of its homeland.

Specific ecologies, historical trajectories, and cultural formations marked these three regions as distinctive centers of Eurasian ways of life. Nomadic pastoralism spread widely across the Eurasian plains, steppes, and desert, linking distant agrarian regions with the impact of war and trade. The "silk routes" were primarily military routes, with small amounts of luxury trade, but they also disseminated paper documents and religious imagery. South Asia, in general a receptor of pastoral invasions from the north, contained broad plains and river valleys, tropical coastal regions in the south, jungles, and mountain regions, but its dominant cultural centers were the basins of the Ganges and Indus rivers in the north. The three major states of this period – the Mauryans, Kushans, and Guptas – controlled only part of the subcontinent, but each lasted about two hundred years. China, also a vast expanse of diverse ecologies, was united three times under a single empire, each of which spanned northern arable lands, partial steppe lands, tropical, mountainous, and coastal zones in the south. Perhaps the superior unifying power of the Chinese states compared to the Indian ones is due to the combined influence of Central Eurasian military technologies and the cultural power of the Chinese logographic script. The Indian caste system, a product of conquest elites, also divided status groups within Indian society much more rigidly than the Chinese social hierarchy. On the whole, China became more mobile, socially and geographically, and more culturally uniform, while India continued to proliferate new religious and cultural movements. The contrast of Chinese tendencies toward unity with South Asian attraction to diversity has remained a distinctive feature of these two dominant Asian civilizations.

Study Questions (1) Centralized states developed in China, India, and Central Eurasia during this period. Which of them lasted the longest, and why? Discuss the role of ecology, military technology, religion, commerce, and leadership in ensuring the longevity of dynastic rule.

(2) Why did some writers of this period look beyond immediate concerns of wealth and strategy to discuss large philosophical questions? What was distinctive about the issues they discussed in this period, compared to earlier times? Which elements of the religious and philosophical works of this time continued as basic cultural features of the later civilizations?

(3) How can we find information about the relationship between elite philosophies and the lives of ordinary people in this period? Discuss how writers and rulers dealt with popular cults of religious devotion and protest movements.

(4) You are a Chinese or Indian king. Which religion suits you best? How will you make it dominate the other faiths?

Suggested Reading

South Asia EDWARD CONZE, *Buddhism: Its Essence and Development* (Birmingham: Windhorse, 2002). Conze discusses in detail the theology of Buddhism.

AINSLEE T. EMBREE AND ROBIN JEANNE LEWIS (eds.), *Sources of Indian Tradition*, vol. I: *From the Beginning to 1800*, 2nd edn. (London: Penguin, 1992). This is a collection of translated primary sources from ancient mythological texts through the colonial period.

BARBARA STOLER MILLER (trans.), *The Bhagavad-Gita: Krishna's Counsel in Time of War* (New York: Bantam Books, 2004). This readable translation also includes notes.

R.K. NARAYAN, *The Mahabharata: A Shortened Modern Prose Version of the Indian Epic* (London: Heinemann, 1978). One of India's best-known modern novelists gives an engaging abridged version of this enormous epic text.

STANLEY WOLPERT, *A New History of India*, 8th edn. (Berkeley: University of California Press, 2009). This is an authoritative survey of Indian history over the past 4,000 years.

East Asia THOMAS J. BARFIELD, *The Perilous Frontier: Nomadic Empires and China* (Oxford: Blackwell, 1989). This book provides an overview of the Xiongnu and other nomadic empires' relations with China.

WILLIAM THEODORE DE BARY, IRENE BLOOM, AND JOSEPH ADLER (eds.), *Sources of Chinese Tradition* (New York: Columbia University Press, 2000). This is a collection of basic sources in translation.

LAO TZU, *Tao Te Ching*, trans. VICTOR MAIR (New York: Bantam Books, 2012). Based on recently discovered texts, this work argues for close connections between Indian yogic traditions and Daoism.

MARK EDWARD LEWIS, *The Early Chinese Empires: Qin and Han* (Cambridge, MA: Harvard University Press, 2010). Lewis's volume is now the standard synthesis on the early Chinese empires.

BENJAMIN SCHWARTZ, *The World of Thought in Ancient China* (Cambridge, MA: Belknap Press, 1985). This book is a superb survey of Chinese thought.

Glossary   **Analects:** Text containing Confucius' discussions with his disciples.

arahat: Those who gain enlightenment by following Buddhist teachings.

The Art of War: Chinese text by Sun Bin describing how to win without fighting.

Arthashastra: Administrative manual describing ideal practices of Mauryan empire.

atman: Sanskrit word for human soul.

aum: Favorite mantra word in brahminical religion.

ba: An "alliance chieftain," a military leader of the Zhou period.

Bhagavad Gita: "The Divine Song," a book of religious teachings attributed to Lord Krishna.

bhakti: An emotional form of Hinduism involving devotion to Krishna.

bodhisattva: An enlightened being who chooses to help others achieve salvation; they are venerated by Mahayana Buddhists.

Book of Changes (***Yijing***): This divination text of ancient China was used to interpret sixty-four hexagram figures.

Brahmins: The Indian caste of priests.

Buddha: The enlightened one, an epithet for the Indian prince Gautama Siddartha.

castes (varnas): Hereditary occupational groups in ancient Indian society.

corvée: Forced labor.

Dao: Ideal social and natural order of Chinese philosophy.

Daodejing: This mystical text attributed to Chinese sage Laozi is a core text of Daoism.

de: Chinese term for virtue.

dharma: Ultimate truth, or order of nature.

duhkha: Pain and suffering, in Buddhist teaching.

gong: Chinese term for tribute in the form of gifts from barbarians to the Chinese emperor.

guo: Chinese term for a state in the Zhou period

Historical Annals (***Shiji***): Chinese universal history written by Sima Qian in the first century BCE.

Hua (Xia): Term used by Zhou people to define their culture, centered in the Yellow River region of China.

Huangdi: "August Emperor," a name given to himself by the Qin conqueror of China in the third century BCE.

Jains: An ascetic Indian sect.

junzi: The "superior man" of Confucian thought, who deserves to rule by moral excellence.

Kama Sutra: Indian text of Mauryan or Gupta period describing sexual techniques and marital relationships.

Kshatriyas: Indian hereditary caste of warriors.

Legalists: Chinese scholars who advised rulers how to increase the power of their state.

li: Rituals necessary in Chinese philosophy to ensure social order.

Mahabharata: Ancient Sanskrit epic describing battles of warrior clans.

mantra: Repeated words and phrase used by meditators.

moksha: In Sanskrit, release from cycle of rebirth and suffering.

nirvana: State of enlightenment, achieved in Buddhist teaching by suppressing desire.

om: Favorite mantra word in brahminical religion.

pastoralism: mode of life depending on herds of animals instead of cultivated fields.

Recognizing Shakuntala: Humorous love story by Kalidasa, Indian playwright of the Gupta period.

ren: "Benevolence," a fundamental moral principle of Confucian philosophy.

Rig Veda: The oldest Hindu sacred text.

sangha: Community of Buddhist monks.

satraps: Governors appointed by Alexander to rule Gandhara and Panjab.

shi: Wandering knights, philosophers, and strategists of Zhou period; later, a term for Chinese literati holding degrees in the examination system.

Shudras: The Indian caste of laborers.

Upanishads: Sanskrit texts of speculative philosophy.

Vaishyas: The Indian caste of farmers, merchants, and artisans.

Vedas: sacred texts of Indian tradition.

wang: "King," term for ruler of a state in the Zhou period.

wei: "action"; in Daoist thought, activity which obstructs recognition of the Way. See *wuwei*.

wuwei: "non-action"; in Daoist thought, spontaneous behavior in accord with the Way.

xian: Basic low-level administrative unit of Chinese bureaucratic state.

ziran: "of itself"; Daoist term for spontaneous action, and modern Chinese term for "nature."

Note 1 Romila Thapar, *Aśoka and the Decline of the Mauryas* (London: Oxford University Press, 1961), p. 256.

6 The ancient Mediterranean

Timeline	
1400–1200 BCE	Height of the Mycenaean Age; the great Lion's Gate at Mycenae is built. Large palaces at Tiryns and Pylos.
800–500 BCE	Greek Dark Ages. Eastern Mediterranean invaded by northern peoples who create swathe of destruction in their wake.
800–510 BCE	Greek Archaic Age: the *Iliad* and the *Odyssey*, attributed to the blind poet Homer. Homer probably collected and reorganized centuries old tales that had been orally recited by bards.
510 BCE	Athenians overthrow aristocratic oligarchy and, under the leadership of Cleisthenes, institute democratic reforms.
509 BCE	Expulsion of kings and foundation of the Roman republic.
490–323 BCE	Classical Age of Greece.
490 BCE	Battle of Marathon, in which Athenians defeat a Persian invading army.
447–432 BCE	Construction of the Parthenon at Athens.
432–404 BCE	Second Peloponnesian War, ending in defeat of Athens by a Spartan-led coalition.
429 BCE	Death of Pericles.
399 BCE	Trial and death of Socrates
339–290 BCE	Samnite Wars, in which Rome establishes itself as the dominant power in Italy.
338 BCE	Defeat of Athens by Macedonia at the Battle of Chaeronea signals the rise of Macedonian power.
336–323 BCE	Reign of Alexander the Great.
331 BCE	Alexander defeats the Persian king Darius and occupies his capital Persepolis.
323–30 BCE	Hellenistic Period.

218–202 BCE	Second Punic War, Rome's great conflict with Carthage, ending in victory of Rome.
133, 121 BCE	Tiberius and Gaius Gracchus killed.
91–87 BCE	Italian War (the revolt of Italians against Rome).
58–51 BCE	Gallic Wars (conquest of Gaul).
48 BCE	Caesar defeats Pompey to become dictator.
44 BCE	Assassination of Julius Caesar.
27 BCE – 14 CE	Rule of Augustus, the first Roman emperor. Originally known as Gaius Octavius (Octavian in English), he was the adopted son and heir of Julius Caesar.
c. 29–30 CE	Crucifixion of Jesus; foundation of the Christian church.
66–73 CE	Major revolt in Judea and destruction of the Second Temple.
74–100 CE	Gospels composed.
286–93 CE	Emperor Diocletian establishes tetrarchy; major reorganization of the empire.
312 CE	Battle of Milvian Bridge establishes Christian-sympathizer Constantine as western emperor.
330 CE	Establishment of Constantinople by Emperor Constantine.
395 CE	Augustine becomes bishop of Hippo in North Africa.
476 CE	Deposition of Romulus Augustus: end of the Roman empire in the West.
493–526 CE	Theoderic the Ostrogoth establishes a state in Italy.

Around 10 or 12 CE, sword and shield in hand, responding to alarms that the Sarmatian nomads who roamed the northern steppes were about to attack, P. Ovidius Naso stood on the walls of Tomis, a Black Sea town. A proud Roman, he was admittedly terrified at the prospect of confronting Sarmatian horsemen, famed for their ability to shoot poison arrows from horseback. A direct encounter between one of Rome's greatest literary masters and border nomads was only narrowly avoided. As the poet Ovid, P. Ovidius Naso shines in literary history, and his principal work, *Metamorphoses*, influenced writers from Chaucer and Dante to Spenser and Shakespeare. The Sarmatians themselves would clash with both Germans and Romans and, in the end, be vanquished by another nomadic people, the Huns, who would play a role in the destruction of the western Roman empire.

Ovid resided in Tomis, now the town of Constanta on the Black Sea in modern-day Romania, exiled there by an angry Emperor Augustus. Augustus' wrath was provoked in part by the badly timed publication of Ovid's witty manual on the art of seducing married women. At the moment of publication Rome had been shaken by a sexual scandal involving Augustus'

daughter Julia. Publication also occurred as the emperor was in the midst of a moral purity crusade. Augustus had created the new position of emperor from the wreck of the Roman republic and, like so many bold revolutionaries, the more he innovated the more he stressed his adherence to traditional values.

Ovid's place of exile must have been chosen by heartfelt enemies. They sent him where no one could read his Latin poetry. Located in the eastern empire, Greek was the dominant language in Tomis and many of the inhabitants spoke a dialect of Sarmatian. An exchange of letters between Tomis and Ovid's beloved Rome took about a year. And how he hated the weather! Although spring and summer were pleasant, Ovid, a Mediterranean man, was horrified by winters when the rivers froze; frozen rivers had the further disadvantage of making the city vulnerable to attacks across the ice.

In exile, Ovid gained an appreciation of the limits of Roman power. Peasants outside his city's walls were subject to nomadic incursions that destroyed crops and enslaved the survivors. As we have seen, Tomis itself was not safe from the threat of nomad invasion. Situated comfortably at Rome, writers such as Horace, Livy, and Virgil addressed elites throughout the Mediterranean world and praised Augustus as bringer of peace. At Tomis, Ovid knew the tenuous and precarious nature of peace on the imperial borders.

Ovid was writing at a time when Rome dominated a Mediterranean world that offered men and women a sense of common identity from Gades in Spain to Antioch in modern-day Turkey. Yet this identity was always fragile and continually contested. The twelve hundred years between 600 BCE and 600 CE witnessed the rise and fall of the Mediterranean as an integrated cultural, economic, and political unit. In 600 BCE the eastern Mediterranean was dominated by a ring of extremely dynamic city-states surrounded by vast agrarian peripheries that they only incompletely controlled and by an innovative and expanding Persian empire. By the middle of our period, roughly the years of Augustus' rule in Rome (27 BCE – 14 CE) and the period covered by the Gospels, a western Mediterranean power, Rome, had imposed a degree of unity on this world. The cosmopolitan religious interaction that developed out of this produced exceptionally rich and creative religious cultures. By 600 CE Mediterranean unity had collapsed, political elites retreated to their great rural estates, and the pace of urban life slowed or ceased altogether. In the eastern Mediterranean the great city of Constantinople inherited the mantle of Rome and remained the shining symbol of urban life for a beleaguered West.

This chapter emphasizes the interplay of economic, military, and cultural forces within an expanding Mediterranean world. It argues that:

- A series of military innovations that occurred in city-states provided one important impetus to Mediterranean unity. Military transformation was bound up with the institution of citizenship – the right to participate in political life. Military innovations were separable from the city-state and used to build great land empires. Contact with the Achaemenid empire of Persia provided Greeks with models of rule and new ideas that would echo through the Mediterranean for centuries.
- The wave of innovation sweeping the Greek world was matched by a wave of creativity in the Persian empire and a political unification encouraging the growth of a new society blending together diverse cultures.
- Commercial expansion tied to the growing chain of port cities provided another important dynamic force. Initially the eastern Mediterranean was the major center of commercial activity, and it always remained predominant, but over time and particularly focused on Rome, western Mediterranean commerce also expanded. The conquest of a Mediterranean-wide empire by the Roman city-state and the long peace that ensued provided an unparalleled period of commercial prosperity to the cities of the Mediterranean coast. Trade brought distant urban cultures into close contact. At the high point, commerce linked the Mediterranean to the Indian Ocean world and even to China.
- Starting out as a monarchy, Rome developed into a republic – a city-state that proved remarkably willing to expand political rights and participation to non-Romans. But the Roman republic was poorly equipped to cope with the vast wealth that poured into the city and influenced the policies of the master of the Mediterranean. As the Roman republic collapsed, no coherent model of political legitimacy emerged to unite troops, political elites, or imperial citizens. Succession crises were frequent and weakened Roman resources.
- Cultural interaction and political clashes in the eastern Mediterranean world produced an amazing florescence of religious beliefs. Jewish communities spread and found converts and sympathizers throughout the eastern Mediterranean. Christianity's growth was greatly encouraged by its selection as the imperial religion – although there were good reasons why a series of emperors selected Christianity for this purpose.
- Rome's unification of the Mediterranean world brought the empire into endemic conflict with the great Persian empires on its eastern borders and the non-state populations on its northern and southern borders. Increasingly, in order to keep political unity, rulers were forced to destroy the commercial unity that had once underwritten the Mediterranean world.
- As pressure on the empire grew, the strain was greatest in the western empire where the threats from non-state northern peoples proved particularly challenging and where the urban economy was weakest. Beset by foes, the Roman empire collapsed in the West but would survive for another thousand years in the East.

6.1 THE CHANGING MEDITERRANEAN

The Mediterranean region may be defined in many ways. Climatically it is an area of hot dry summers and mild rainy winters where wheat, the olive, and the vine thrive. Its shallow rivers, dry most of the year, its mountainous coastlines, and its characteristic light soils make much of the land difficult or impossible to cultivate. The arable land that does exist is particularly susceptible to drought and flooding.

On three sides the Mediterranean region is surrounded by mountains and on its south by desert. Ties between mountain and desert and more fertile lowland areas, between pastoralists, seasonal herders, and farmers, were fundamental relationships throughout the region. In terms of communication, its maritime nature defined a sense of place; over the twelve-hundred-year period studied here, seaborne transportation was much, much quicker than land transportation. Although the winter months saw an increased risk of storms, long-distance transportation emerged from a dense coastal trade. Urban dwellers in port cities such as Rome, Athens, and Alexandria were more speedily and reliably in contact with one another than with their countrymen in interior areas except where they were linked by Roman roads. Even with these roads, quantities of grain could be shipped from the eastern to the western Mediterranean at a time when such transport was technically impossible by land; the slow pace of land transportation would have required the bulk of grain to be fed to the animals that hauled it.

The Mediterranean may be seen as an area of small regions whose inhabitants sought to use varying local resources – soil types, altitude, proximity to trade routes, and drinkable water – to counterbalance a pronounced climatic instability. Susceptibility to summer drought and winter floods made the Mediterranean economy extremely precarious. Although the growth of large port cities encouraged regional specialization for urban markets, specialization increased susceptibility to periodic famine. When they could, Mediterranean agriculturalists tried to diversify their economy, depending not on monoculture or even on multiculture but on combining agriculture with fishing, trading, foraging, cattle raising, banditry, soldiery, and manufacturing. The existence of small micro-regions favored the growth of small states that initially expanded to fill up small geographic niches; their boundaries stopped at the nearest mountain crest or unfordable stream.

Climate Change in the Mediterranean World

While we refer to a "Mediterranean climate," as if it were a stable and constant feature of the region, recent evidence indicates that the climate changed over time and that these changes accelerated the region's climatic instability. Climatic instability in turn affected the course of empire. Recent scholarship has discovered long-term patterns of climate change which at times favored agriculturalists and at other times produced catastrophe. Climatologists associate the prosperity of the late republic and early empire, the years between 100 BCE and 200 CE, the period of most rapid Roman expansion, as the "Roman Optimum," a period of extraordinary climate stability. Rain was regular, temperature reliable, and the Nile floods favorable. Romans established vineyards in Britain. Between 200 CE and 900 CE, perhaps due to increased volcanic activity and to flare-ups of solar radiation, the climate of the Mediterranean and the European continent became less stable and more subject to draught. The land affected varied. Sometimes it is necessary to distinguish separate and contrasting weather regimes for the eastern and western Mediterranean; at other times the Mediterranean and all of continental Europe shared these patterns. A cooling trend dominated the last centuries of Roman history. Climate instability not only decreased the resources of the empire but, when it affected Central and Eastern Europe, accelerated the tribal migrations that ultimately brought the empire down.

6.2 THE ARCHAIC AGE TO THE HELLENIC AGE

Compiled and given definitive shape during the Greek **Archaic Age** (800–510 BCE) the Greek epics the *Iliad* and the *Odyssey* are the beginning of European literature. Five hundred years before Homer, **Mycenaean Age** Greece flourished. Its rich kingdoms and powerful rulers bore legendary names such as Mycenae, Pylos, and Tiryns, names that resounded in Homer's *Iliad*. By the time the *Iliad* had been written down, though, these powerful walled fortresses had been long abandoned; their great palaces had been burned in a great wave of devastation that occurred around 1200 BCE and included scenes of mass destruction in the eastern Mediterranean and as far away as Sicily and southern Italy. While the causes of this destructive rampage are uncertain, its results are not. The invaders who burnt cities did not simply replace previous rulers, they destroyed societies. Population decreased, settlements were abandoned or destroyed, written language disappeared, no large monuments were erected, luxury goods and metals, including bronze, vanished.

The very extent of Greek collapse provided abundant raw materials for the cultural and political rebuilding of new societies. Much of the distinctiveness of its society and politics after 750 BCE stemmed from Greece's intermediary role of bringing together the eastern and central Mediterranean world by trade and colonization, a role it shared with the Phoenicians who colonized Carthage in North Africa as one of a series of trading ports on their route to Spain. As mentioned in Chapter 2, Greeks adopted the Phoenician alphabet, and it may have been in the trading ports that they first picked it up from their rivals. Phoenician religious myths followed. Greece and Phoenicia linked the established empires and trading states of the Near East with the chiefdoms and city-states of Sicily and southern Italy. Less subject to control by a divine ruler and his palace than more bureaucratic Mycenaean Greece, Archaic Greek society emerged in closer cultural contact with Near Eastern society. When the Assyrians conquered Phoenician coastal cities in the

Near East, many Phoenician artisans may have fled to Greece, for their influence on Greek pottery is clear.

Emergence of the City-State in Greece and the Growth of Citizenship

Between 750 and 490 BCE city-states emerged in Archaic Greece. Our word "politics" is derived from **polis**, the Greek word for the city-state. Mountains covered almost three quarters of Greece. Shoaly rivers and craggy mountains made land communication difficult. As in the ancient Near East, Greek city-states established themselves in micro-regions where soil and access to the sea varied greatly over small distances.

Although land travel was often difficult, there were always points of contact between micro-regions and communication among the Greek lands. These linkages helped produce both a sense of shared cultural identity – as Greeks – and an even stronger sense of membership in a particular city-state – as Athenians, Corinthians, or Spartans.

Already in Homer's time, the city-state was central to religious rituals and occupied a sacred space in political thought; even the greatest Homeric rulers were really chieftains whose power was fragmentary. Departing for the Trojan wars, the great warrior Achilles, said to be the son of a goddess, was advised by his father King Peleus, "Be both a speaker of words and a doer of deeds." Rhetorical skill and military prowess were the supreme virtues

Map 6.1 Classical Greece

of successful chieftains during the Archaic Age when chiefs were losing their predominance to urban aristocratic factions.

Eligibility for military service was key to defining Greeks' relationship to their state. Armies admitted only taxpayers to their ranks. The close connection between taxpaying and soldiering originated in the training and weaponry required by new military tactics. Only men with resources could afford the military equipment and the time to learn how to use it; at the same time, men who fought in arms to defend the polity began to claim the right to participate in its direction. Their weapons gave them the means to assert their rights. Few political figures in the ancient world reached powerful positions without leading troops in the field.

Why Did Changes in Military Technology lead to the Expansion of Citizenship? Taxpaying soldiers who assumed responsibility for state affairs in city-states originated our modern concept of **citizenship**, which originally meant "having a share in the public life of the polis." The Greek conception of citizenship did not imply equality; in the early Greek city-states, many impoverished males, non-noble males, and all women were inferior citizens. Pressure to expand and equalize citizenship, at least for males, occurred as commercial growth enlarged the taxpaying population and as military innovations reduced the expense and skills required of soldiers. Increasingly, successful new military tactics enabled city-states to dispense with the aristocratic charioteers

who had dominated warfare in Mycenaean Greece, and even relegated the cavalry to a supporting role. Mass formations first in the infantry and later in the navy gave the less wealthy a key military role.

Once described as a "military revolution," historians have come to realize that these tactics came together over several centuries. The early evolution of the new warfare – called "**hoplite** warfare" after the Greek word for the new fighting man – is even observed in the *Iliad* although only as background to the individual combats between heroes that Homer presents as the main events. Perfected hoplite warfare was characterized by heavily armed foot-soldiers fighting in dense mobile formations. Soldiers lined up next to one another carrying large shields that overlapped with the shield of the adjacent man on the left of his comrade. Marching together in deep ranks of wall-like shields, Greek soldiers carried a long heavy spear for thrusting and a short sword for close-up fighting. In battle, serried lines of shielded armored soldiers ran at one another until one group began to give way or was outflanked, i.e. attacked from its unprotected sides. The body of closely linked fighters was called a **phalanx**. A good example of hoplites in battle can be seen in the seventh-century BCE vase in Figure 6.1. A piper can be seen leading another line of soldiers into battle.

A surplus-producing agriculture undergirded military innovation. The phalanx required money, discipline, and agricultural surplus: money to outfit the soldier with standardized shield

Figure 6.1 Mid-seventh-century wine pitcher in the Corinthian manner or style. Found in an Etruscan tomb in Italy, this vase shows a battle between hoplite formations. Note the serried ranks with their overlapping shields. The artisan potter has captured these formations at the very moment of impact when the front lines feel the first clash of contact.

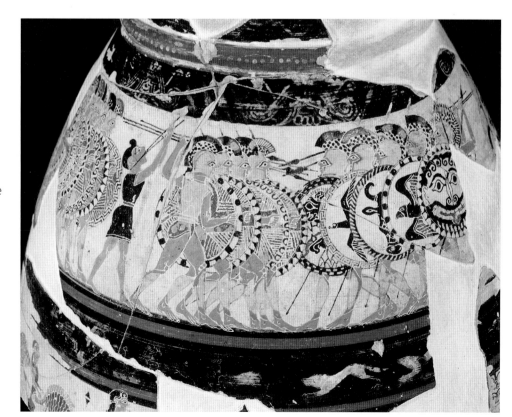

and weaponry, discipline to maneuver in unison, and grain and dried meat to feed the troops. Much of the grain and dried meat came from the small peasant farmers who provided the agricultural bases for the city-state. But during long campaigns when local farmers were continuously fighting and local resources fell short, city-states turned to trade to supply their troops. The new military tactics relied on commerce.

Hoplites were drawn from better-off farmers and prosperous craftsmen who had found cavalry too expensive and demanding but could afford the new weaponry as well as the time to practice its use. By itself, their new military importance did not necessitate any dramatic change in the political organization of the city-state. Prosperous farmers and comfortable craftsmen were often political conservatives. Only under the pressure of events did these groups look lower down the social arena for political allies and create institutions that could actively involve poorer groups in political life.

Why Did Military Participation Encourage Democracy? The expansion of male military participation and citizenship produced new democratic institutions where aristocratic predominance had already been undermined and where commercial elites saw opportunities to expand their power. Athens provides the model. A series of Athenian reformers had weakened the traditional kinship groupings and aristocratic families that were once the bulwark of elite rule. Dissension among aristocrats combined with the growing numbers of wealthy non-aristocrats created the opportunities for reforms that extended citizenship and brought poorer citizens actively into political life. Decisions were made by an assembly open to all citizens, some offices were determined by lot and thus open to the humblest citizens, and state payment for jurors meant that poor citizens were not only eligible but could actually afford to participate in judicial decision-making. The shards shown in Figure 6.2 were pieces of broken pottery used by Athenians as ballots to write down the name of their favorite. Votes were made in open assemblies where voters and candidates confronted each other face-to-face.

Athenian participatory democracy was based on this face-to-face encounter of citizens. At the public gym, the market, or on the battlefield, male Athenians spent much of their lives under the scrutiny of their male fellow citizens. Impassioned rhetoric in the assembly was most effective coming from a man of standing. Family honor counted in a small-scale Athenian society where so much of life went on in public and where families jealously prized memories of the athletic achievements or heroic battlefield behavior of earlier generations. Athens took away the citizenship of traitors' descendants.

Athens and Sparta: Limits of the Greek City-State

Both the leading Greek states, Athens and Sparta, showed the effects of military transformation on citizenship. Spartan citizenship displayed a single-minded concentration on militarism, while Athenian citizenship combined militarism with the encouragement of commercial activity and an enlarged conception of civic life. Athens was a great commercial power whose elite used their resources communally, even if their purpose was to assert their own power. Dramatists such as Euripides, Sophocles, and Aristophanes wrote their plays for municipal festivals, and sculptors such as Phidias sculpted for the great urban monument, the Pantheon. Athenian democracy's most bitter critics, philosophers such as Socrates and Plato, would never have been tolerated in the Spartan state they sometimes admired. Mature Sparta produced no philosophers of note or men of letters. All of Spartan life was devoted to preparing a restricted number of citizens to militarily dominate non-citizens and rival city-states. Sparta's cultivation of a relatively equal citizenship with little class distinction among its small elite, inured to hardship and skilled in warfare, exerted a fascination on Western thinkers fully as great as that of Athenian democracy.

Figure 6.2 Shards from broken clay pots provided the Athenian citizen with ballots. This citizen scratched the name "Xanthippos" on the shards to indicate his electoral preference.

In Athens as in Sparta, citizens' participation in military training and in political discussion was based on the unfree labor of men and women who were unarmed and silenced. Both Athens and Sparta had large unfree populations, slaves in Athens, and in Sparta the helots, an indigenous people who served as unfree harshly treated laborers.

Although women were normally noncombatants, women's position varied among the Greek city-states. To obtain soldiers, Sparta sought to promote fertility among its tiny elite and encouraged elite women to participate in athletic exercises so that they would raise healthy children. The absence of Spartan men on campaigns allowed Spartan women some initiative in economic and political affairs. In Athens, a small number of great courtesans such as Pericles' consort Aspasia, celebrated for her wit, played a limited role in public life. Nonetheless, women were more absent from the public arena in democratic Athens than in authoritarian Sparta – or Achaemenid Persia.

The subordination of women in the Greek city-states was maintained by marital customs, daily experience, and the rigors of a high-mortality demographic regime. Women married early, average age 15, to much older husbands, average age 30. At this age, a bridegroom's mother (but not his father) would likely still be alive and the bride's mother-in-law often presided over the home, training the younger woman in household skills and ruling the household in her son's name. The world of work in the Greek city-state was highly segregated. The vase in Figure 6.3 shows Athenian women working making clothes in the Loom Room. Women's work was usually done in the home. Extremely high urban mortality, and the caring responsibilities expected from females, meant that many young women spent much of their time tending the sick and dying.

How Did the Greeks Successfully Resist Persian Domination?

By the beginning of the fifth century, a confrontation between Greeks and the expanding **Achaemenid** empire of Persia was probably inevitable. Almost everyone – including the prestigious Greek Delphic oracle – expected the Persians to win. Crucial to inspiring Greek morale was the Battle of **Marathon** (490 BCE). Faced with a much larger Persian army and delayed Spartan reinforcements, the Athenians and their allies confronted the Persians on the plain of Marathon. There, hoplite tactics defeated the larger but less disciplined Persian hosts. Fully as important as their military victory was the Greeks' symbolic representation of their achievement. Marathon came to stand not only for a heroic victory but as an objective lesson of the virtues of Hellenic (Greek) civilization.

Figure 6.3 Lekythos (oil flask) with women making woolen cloth. Greek, Attic, c. 550–530 BCE. Terracotta, h. 6 3/4 in. (17.15 cm). Fletcher Fund, 1931 (31.11.10). © The Metropolitan Museum of Art. Image source: Art Resource, NY. Athenian women worked at home to satisfy household needs. Family members and slaves worked together. Pitchers like this vase required more skilled labor and were often made by men. The pitcher shown here was inscribed by the individual artisan who made it, "Amasis made me." It was made by a man skilled in pottery whose labor was valued; it contrasts with the more anonymous work of women in the household shown on the vase.

This heightened self-confidence and sense of cultural independence contributed to the remarkable accomplishments of the **Classical Age** (490–323 BCE). In this period Athens, by far the largest city in Greece with 300,000–400,000 inhabitants, was a home to some of the greatest thinkers and artists in Western history. A dozen of the world's greatest thinkers and artists living together in a city the size of Fresno, California!

In any case, the victory at Marathon was the prelude to further heroism in which most of mainland Greece shared. Meanwhile victory at Marathon had given Athenians time to build a major fleet, financed with newly discovered silver mines. At Salamis

(479 BCE) the Persian navy was destroyed by lighter, more maneuverable Greek warships. The rowers who maneuvered these ships represented a new social group that made a military contribution to the city-state. By enabling adult men without military training to serve their city-state as rowers, Athens's naval power facilitated the extension of citizenship to poorer male Athenians. By spring 479 BCE Persian military and naval power was in ruins in the eastern Mediterranean.

Athens versus Sparta

Persian defeat cleared the way for confrontation between Athens and Sparta. Between 461 and 404 BCE Greek city-states exhausted their strength in a series of wars, declared and undeclared, interrupted by hostile truces. Athens turned the anti-Persian naval alliance it led, the Delian League, into the nucleus of an Athenian-dominated empire; once a voluntary association, the league was eventually required to contribute to Athenian naval supremacy. A successful Athenian revolt against aristocratic rulers and eventually the domination of Athenian politics by the democratic faction led by Pericles (d. 429 BCE) heightened Sparta's fear that a democratic spirit might spread to other Greek states.

The Athenian democracy that Spartan oligarchs so feared always had a personal and ethnic character that was a source of limitation as well as strength. At the very moment when Athenian institutions became most democratic, new restrictions were imposed on citizenship. Despite the existence of a larger Greek cultural identity, citizenship remained narrowly confined to the borders of the city-state, closing itself off from the migrants then flocking to the city. The face-to-face character of Athenian democracy – its reliance on family reputation and a shared civic culture – helps explain the narrowness of city-state democracy. As participation became ever more central to political life, Athenians excluded those who lacked an established family reputation and were tainted by their association with alien cultures. In fact, Greek victories over larger Persian armies sometimes changed self-confidence into overweening pride. The Greek term **barbaros**, originally a non-pejorative term for all non-Greeks, including such cultured peoples as the Egyptians, more and more came to describe peoples on the periphery of Greek society and to suggest their inferiority. Barbaros is the origin of our word "barbarian."

Initially, Athens defended itself successfully against Spartan hostility but the great plague of 430–429 BCE was a turning point; it killed roughly one third of the population, among them Pericles, democratic Athens's most talented leader. Defeating Athens, Sparta was unprepared to lead Greece. In 371 BCE a Theban army utterly destroyed the Spartans at Leuctra, a defeat from which the Spartans never recovered. Athenian defeat had opened an era of endless conflict and the rise and fall of individual city-states produced mercenaries whose own city-states could no longer support them. War destroyed the independence of the city-states but produced a level of military sophistication that promoted the growth of empires.

Greek Division Provides Macedonian Opportunity

While the Greek city-states fought among themselves, the powerful leader of the Macedonian state to the north, Philip II, was constructing a formidable military machine. Drawing on the new military innovations and recruiting Greek mercenaries, Philip ruled a land with a larger population than the biggest city-state and conquered lands with rich deposits of gold and silver. Philip's diplomacy played off the various Greek states against one another until he was ready to strike. At Chaeronea in 338 BCE a Macedonian army defeated the army of a resurgent Athens and made Macedonia the dominant power in Greece.

The powerful kingdom molded by Philip was intended for greater purposes than the mastery of Greece. Marathon had revealed the weak military foundations of Persian power and Philip accumulated the resources and hoplite army to invade Persia. Philip's projected invasion was stopped by his assassination (336 BCE). He left his military machine to his son Alexander. Using the army and the treasury that his father had accumulated, Alexander went on to become one of history's great military men. Conquering Persia between 334 and 331 BCE, Alexander went on to invade North India. Although sparking a brief but extremely interesting cultural exchange between Greeks and Indians, Alexander's eastern conquests proved ephemeral. But the administrative techniques and imperial institutions that Alexander found in place in the Persian empire were retained and even extended to the territories in the eastern Mediterranean governed by Alexander's squabbling generals and their successors. In the long run, Alexander's great achievement was to increase and widen the millennial-long interaction between East and West in the eastern Mediterranean and to open the region to Persian ideas, from their methods of imperial rule to their ideas about divinity.

6.3 THE ACHAEMENID EMPIRE OF PERSIA

The Persian War marked an intensification and acceleration of an interaction between the eastern Mediterranean and the eastern hinterlands that had already been going on for at least five centuries. The Persian Achaemenids dominated the Near East and the eastern Mediterranean for over two hundred years, ruling a huge empire that encompassed many of the most advanced civilizations in the world, including Mesopotamia, Egypt, greater Syria, Asia Minor, and the Indus Valley. Greek philosophy, Egyptian mathematics and architecture, Babylonian astrology, and Indian sciences all advanced under their rule. They bequeathed the region great landmarks of religion, culture, administration, and architecture. Later Hellenistic Greeks who ruled territories that had once belonged to the Achaemenids built on Iranian administrative techniques and institutions, and Persian methods of rule importantly influenced all later Mediterranean empire builders.

Greek critiques of the Achaemenids have been enormously influential, but they can often be shown to be incorrect when compared to the archaeological record. Few Greeks knew Old Persian, Aramaic, or Elamite – the languages of the empire – and Greeks tended to report palace gossip and hearsay, often from great distances in time and space. The great Greek historian Herodotus even maintained that the Persians rode giant ants into battle, probably a reference to elephants, but such assertions do not reassure the reader about his credibility in Iranian affairs.

Iranian Origins

As discussed in earlier chapters, beginning about 8,000 years ago, peoples speaking Indo-European languages spread gradually into Europe from Asia Minor, and brought farming with them, although farming also spread independently of the Indo-Europeans. About 4,000 years ago some speakers of Indo-European languages started making their way into the Near East, especially Syria and northern Iran. A few of these tribes ultimately went all the way to India, where they introduced Sanskrit civilization. Others, speaking Old Persian, settled in west central Iran around the 800s BCE. Old Persian is closely related to Sanskrit and more distantly to Greek and Latin. These newcomers, who called themselves Aryans, were mentioned by the Assyrian scribes in their histories in the ninth century BCE. The word "Iran," the invaders' name for the land they settled, is derived from the word "Aryan."

These Aryans or Iranians believed in a pantheon of gods and carried myths that were similar to those of the ancient Hindus in India. They worshipped Mithra, a god of light and of social order, to whom people swore when they made a contract. Anahita was the goddess of the waters and of fertility. She was also a war goddess and especially looked after women. Sometimes she was thought of as the consort of Mithra. The ancient Iranians revered a fierce god of victory and of fire. Haoma, a divine plant no longer known, was used to prepare an intoxicating drink used in rituals and also before going into battle. They believed, as well, in a divine world-lake, in the middle of which grew the Tree of Life, which threw off the seeds of all living things. At some point Iranians turned to a high god, Ahura Mazda, and either made him supreme over the other gods or demoted the other deities to mere angels and demons.

One of these ancient Iranian tribes, the Medes, proved troublesome to the Semitic-speaking Assyrians, who ruled a powerful empire in what is now northern Iraq, Syria, and western Iran in the 700s and 600s. At first the Assyrians defeated the Medes and kept them down. But in 612 BCE the Medes were able to make an alliance with the Babylonians. Led by the Median chieftain Cyaxares (or Hvakhshathra) (r. 625–585 BCE), they marched on the Assyrian capital of Nineveh and razed it to the ground. The Medes briefly became a sort of empire in their own right, conquering portions of Anatolia and dominating the Iranian plateau. The Medes, however, were apparently little more than chieftains who put together vague coalitions from their capital in Ecbatana (modern Hamadan).

The Persians: Cyrus, Darius, and Xerxes

The Medes were the most powerful of the Iranian peoples initially, but there were other formidable chiefdoms. Cyrus II led a people who had settled in Anshan, which they called Parsa and, because of this place name, became known as Persians. Babylonian sources report that Astyages, the Median chieftain, marched against Cyrus "the king of Anshan," but faced a mutiny among his own troops. With a much smaller force, Cyrus captured him and his treasure. Having tasted victory, Cyrus then launched extensive campaigns of military conquest. In the 540s he conquered most of Asia Minor, bringing many Greek-speaking cities under his rule. He went on to subdue eastern Iran, Syria, Palestine, and Babylonia, creating a massive new empire.

Cyrus established a general policy of tolerance toward the varied religions and peoples of his empire. When he took Babylon, he freed the Jews from captivity. The Book of Isaiah said of him in gratitude, "Thus says the Lord to his anointed, to Cyrus, whose right hand I have grasped, to subdue nations before him and ungird the loins of kings, to open doors before him that gates may not be closed" (45.1). Under the Iranian kings the Jews were allowed to rebuild their temple in Jerusalem. It must be admitted that despite his general tolerance, Cyrus did also sometimes destroy temples and crush cities that he conquered. He died fighting in Central Asia, having earned the name "Cyrus the Great."

A general, Darius (r. 522–486), was quickly put on the throne by the Persian aristocracy and stilled a revolt begun against his predecessor. Although probably from a different line from his predecessors, he claimed descent from Haxamanish, called by the Greeks Achaemenes, and succeeded in getting the entire dynasty known as the Achaemenids. He richly rewarded his supporters, and successfully crushed a number of uprisings that questioned his legitimacy. He bribed other challengers by bestowing on them noble status. Darius reformed the army, organized the administration of the empire, and expanded its borders into North India and to the west into all of Asia Minor. One of his inscriptions reveals his ideals, saying that he was supported by Ahura Mazda and the other gods "because I was not disloyal, and was no traitor, was no wrongdoer, neither I nor my family, but adhered to righteousness and did no wrong to the weak nor to the powerful."

Darius campaigned in Europe and established toeholds in Macedonia and Thrace, near Greece. Indeed, many of the famous ancient Greeks, such as the philosopher Thales, were actually Persian subjects. Supported by Athens, the Ionian Greeks under Persian rule rebelled in 500. Darius no doubt considered what the Greeks labeled "The Persian War" as a minor affair at the far western fringes of his mammoth empire. Even though the Persian invasion of Greece proper in 490 ended in failure, the Ionian Greeks were successfully brought back under Persian rule.

Xerxes (r. 486–465 BCE), Darius' successor, again subdued Egypt after a revolt there. The great size of the armies he commanded, and his success in putting down rebellions, as in Babylon, suggest that his reign was anything but decadent. He pursued great building works in Persepolis. Greek sources depict the last hundred years of Achaemenid rule as marked by harsh rule, weak kings, intrigues, and uprisings. By 403 BCE the Achaemenids had practically lost Egypt, but the empire retained vast territories in the Near East, Asia Minor, Central Asia, and India.

Around 518 BCE, Darius began constructing the magnificent capital of Persepolis, near to today's Shiraz. This impressive city took a century to complete, and involved carving into the stone of the mountains in which it nestled so that buildings could be erected there. In the huge royal treasury were stored the tribute and wealth that flowed in from the provinces. The buildings are decorated with reliefs that show all the major peoples of the world, with their distinctive dress and hairstyles, bringing tribute to the universal king. Unlike Assyrian art, the Persian carvings do not depict warfare. Rather, they show the way the Achaemenid empire incorporated various civilizations. Surviving clay tablets tell how the city was built by skilled workers from all over the empire, with goldsmiths coming from Asia Minor, stone sculptors from Egypt, and workers skilled in ornamentation from the old Elamite capital of Susa in southwestern Iran.

Administration of the Empire

The Persians initially consisted of martial clans who took over the bureaucratic institutions of the peoples they conquered. Thus, Elamite scribes were employed to keep records of taxation and administration in Iran in their own language. In Mesopotamia and the rest of the Near East, Aramaic scribes were generally used – Aramaic is a Semitic language related to Hebrew. Sometimes local languages were used for official purposes, as with Greek and Hebrew.

The empire was divided into provinces called satrapies, over which the Persian monarch appointed governors or satraps. The satraps were Iranian nobles and could stay in office a very long time, overseeing the payment of tribute, the collection of taxes, and sometimes waging war. The monarch often sent out spies to investigate the performance of the satraps. In the second century of Achaemenid rule, the satraps' autonomy increased. In accordance with the tolerant policies of the Achaemenids, these governors were expected to worship local gods. All the peoples of the empire were free to follow their own culture, customs, and religion, but they were expected to obey the laws issued by the ruler, and only the Persians were exempt from paying tribute to the king of kings. Darius I took over from King Croesus of Lydia in Asia Minor the practice of minting gold and silver coins. This new practice allowed some state salaries to be paid in cash, a very important administrative innovation.

The empire was the most centralized of its day. A number of factors held it together, and these would be used by subsequent empire builders. One was the codified law established by the Achaemenids. Another was the loyalty felt by provincial elites toward the king, whom they considered a provider of law and order. The Egyptians proved an exception here, often disliking Persian rule as alien and distant. The use of Aramaic documents written on clay tablets or papyrus throughout the Near East was an important unifying factor. Papyrus, fashioned from a plant first found along the Nile, was used by the Egyptians as a lightweight writing material. Papyrus reached Greece in 650 BCE just before the beginning of the Achaemenid period, and it quickly became one of the main media for producing documents and books, in the form of scrolls.

A superb system of highways linked the provinces. The Achaemenids invented a kind of pony express, consisting of mounted courier relays, who could get a message even to the most distant province in as little as two weeks. Darius I paid attention to water navigation, having the first Suez Canal built and sending explorers to find the mouth of the Indus River, which empties into the Arabian Sea.

A strong economy promoted unity. The carefully patrolled highway system and the inns built alongside it had the side effect of encouraging trade and commerce, which appear to have expanded substantially in the Achaemenid period. Farmers were the mainstay of the economy, and the Persian monarchs invested heavily in their success. In arid Iran they built underground irrigation canals to deliver spring water to crops, and they spread this impressive engineering feat to other parts of the empire.

Persian society was divided into "castes" of warriors, priests, and farmers. Among the warriors there were ranks of nobility; these depended in part on the pleasure of the monarch and on the size of the estates he bestowed on them. The kings allowed into their service non-Persians, some becoming quite powerful.

The kings were not considered divine and were not even the only kings in the empire. Rather the Achaemenid ruler was the "king of kings," the one who ordered and ruled them all, and he was believed to possess a special halo of divine favor. The backbone of the army in the first century of Achaemenid rule was the Persians and the Medes, acknowledged great warriors. Some formed part of the royal guard, some 10,000 strong. Others were garrisoned throughout the empire. Troops from each of the provinces also served in the Achaemenid army, armed and outfitted according to their local customs. Late in the empire the kings increasingly employed Greek mercenaries of doubtful loyalty, to their regret.

Female nobles had great property, including numerous palaces and estates. They disposed as they desired of the crops produced on their estates. They traveled through the land, receiving food and drink from the subjects for themselves and their courtiers. They gave their own orders to officials signed with their own seals, and employed their own bureaucrats. Noble women were depicted in art, though little survives, and were not secluded when outside the palace. They sometimes accompanied their husbands on the hunt and on official missions. The king of kings set limits on the power of these women, and punished them if they overstepped their bounds, but they nevertheless did get a hearing. The Greek writers felt that such prominence for women made men effeminate, and they depicted the women as universally manipulative and treacherous. These attitudes probably tell us more about the Greek males who wrote these tales than about Persian women. Royal women were married off only to Persian nobles. One noblewoman, Irdabama Abbamush, repeatedly shows up in the Elamite tablets as receiving large payments from the court to employ teams of working-women, presumably as weavers and in other craft occupations, with better-paid women serving as overseers.

No one can be sure exactly when it happened, but the polytheistic, Hindu-like religion of the ancient Iranians was reformed over time. Perhaps the recognition of Ahura Mazda as a high God above the other deities was the first stage of this reform. The Achaemenid monarchs gave credit for their successes to Ahura Mazda, but they were not monotheists or believers in a single God though they seemed to be moving in the direction of giving one god primacy.

Zoroastrianism

Iran produced the only major prophetic tradition of monotheism in the ancient Near East apart from Judaism. The prophet, whose dates are given by various scholars as anywhere between 1200 and 600 BCE, was named Zarathustra. The Greeks called him Zoroaster, and for this reason his religion is known as **Zoroastrianism**. He may have arisen in eastern or northwestern Iran. Zarathustra taught that Ahura Mazda was the supreme God, and demoted the deities of the old Indo-European tradition either to angels or to demons.

Zarathustra envisaged this world as an arena where good and evil, truth and the lie, were battling it out. Ahura Mazda was the God of good and truth, who created the world, but he was opposed by an evil supernatural force, Ahriman. Every time human beings lie, break a contract, or act unethically, Zarathustra believed, they defect to join the army of the evil one, Ahriman. By living a life of good thoughts, good speech, and good deeds, human beings can join in the struggle on Ahura Mazda's side to defeat evil and suffering in the world. This system has been called dualism, as opposed to pure monotheism. It is not, however, really dualist, because Zarathustra was certain that in time Ahura Mazda would destroy Ahriman. Zoroastrian rituals came to revolve around fire ceremonies, though they do not worship fire as a god, and see it rather as a symbol of divinity. Zoroastrianism was one of the first religions to give deep thought to the future. It predicted that at the end of time a savior, Saoshyant, will arise who will defeat the demons and usher in a time of world renewal. After that, the world will "never grow old and never die, never decay and never perish," and "the dead will rise."

The Achaemenid empire was the greatest empire of its day, probably the greatest erected to that date. Its traditions of relative tolerance, and its impressive techniques of rule for such a vast territory, left a lasting legacy to the Hellenistic world that succeeded it. Its halting moves toward a more monotheistic vision proved prophetic for the region in the long run.

6.4 THE RISE OF ROME

The intensified interaction that began in the eastern Mediterranean spread throughout the entire basin, promoting the development of commerce and cultural innovation and spurring political and military competition throughout the whole region.

By 219 BCE Rome had established its hegemony in the western Mediterranean and by 150 BCE dominated the entire Mediterranean. While Roman elites gradually embraced the cultural heritage of the eastern Mediterranean and struggled with its complexity, Rome slowly developed its own inclusive conception of political commitment. Rome's unification of the Mediterranean world opened the way for an era of enormous commercial prosperity and a period of unrivaled cultural and intellectual interaction throughout the urban Mediterranean.

Rome's victory arose on the mutual exhaustion of the rival empires that constituted themselves after the death of Alexander. Alexander's sudden death (323 BCE) left his empire in disarray. For several centuries afterward, Greek-speaking military men, Hellenes – men of Greek culture, if not of Greek ethnicity – disputed his succession. When the first generation of Alexander's generals died away, their legacy included a reconstituted Macedonian kingdom that exerted great influence over mainland Greece, a Ptolemaic kingdom of Egypt, a Seleucid kingdom in Mesopotamia and Syria, and a breakaway kingdom of Bactrian Greeks who briefly extended Alexander's Indian conquests. In the process all these states continued to rely on recruiting troops from Greece and Macedonia, often establishing them in colonies at strategic points in Southwest Asia.

Meanwhile in the central and eastern Mediterranean, Greek traders established their own districts in leading port cities where they linked native peoples to the Mediterranean economy. Describing these urban colonies, the Roman orator Cicero jested: "The shores of Greece are like hems stitched on to the lands of barbarian people." Without predominating anywhere outside of mainland Greece and its islands, Greek became the lingua franca of the cities of the eastern Mediterranean. Jewish communities also spread to many of these same areas.

Deep-seated political rivalries consumed the attention of major political actors in the eastern Mediterranean and made them relatively oblivious to the rise of new powers in the western Mediterranean and to the realities of Roman military ascendance.

Why Was Rome Able to Unify the Mediterranean?

Like the armies of the Greek city-states, the Roman army was based on a concatenation of taxpaying and military service that defined citizenship. But Rome succeeded in developing a more comprehensive concept of citizenship. It created a sense of shared citizenship based not on ethnic identity but on political rights that extended to include those who never crossed the **pomerium**, the sacred borders of the city of Rome.

Roman citizenship was hierarchical, with an elite involved in public service at the top, wealthy citizens who participated in the cavalry next in importance, and poorer taxpayers below. War was disproportionately funded by the wealthier groups in society and the Roman republic sometimes has the appearance of a military joint-stock corporation; if wars proved profitable, the contributions that taxpayers made were rewarded with war booty. Young aristocrats saw war as an opportunity to demonstrate their abilities and become wealthy. Warfare also benefited the ordinary citizen-soldier. As long as Rome fought for hegemony over its close neighbors, Roman victories led to confiscation of the land of defeated rivals and its distribution to Roman citizens; thus warfare protected debtors and prevented their falling into the ranks of the unfree. After their victory over Perseus of Macedon and the seizure of his treasury in 167 BCE, the Roman state commuted direct taxes on citizens and this commutation remained in effect for 124 years.

In part the difference between the Greek polis and the Latin civitas and their attitude toward neighbors corresponds to their environment. Rome grew up at the confluence of key roads and a navigable river, the Tiber. Rome was surrounded by a host of other small Latin states, based on micro-regions, that shared a common language and culture. But unlike Greece, mountainous Italian micro-regions were often connected by river valleys. "Latio" means "on the plain" and the Latin region lacked protective mountain walls that could provide defense against invasion. It was a natural invasion route. To protect themselves, the Latin peoples were forced to co-operate and work together by forming religious leagues and military federations. Militarily, Rome dominated the Latin League of city-states downstream the Tiber.

Ethnic diversity was also important. The Italian peninsula in which Rome emerged was a hothouse of diverse peoples and cultures. Celtic chiefdoms predominated in northern Italy and Greek city-states in southern Italy. Central Italy was occupied by the Etruscans, a people whose origins are much debated but who show Phoenician influences and in turn influenced the early Roman state and society. Rome adopted many practices from its neighbors and slowly developed the military and political institutions that would give it Mediterranean dominance.

Why Did Rome Become the Dominant Power in Italy?

By the end of the fourth century BCE Rome emerged as the dominant power in Italy (see Map 6.2). In 390 BCE, a Celtic invasion sacked Rome and threatened Rome's standing within the Latin League. As so often in the future, the Roman fall before the Celts was only a prelude to another rise. Rome responded by reorganizing its hoplite military. Breaking up the old solid phalanx into smaller units of maniples and centuries made Roman armies more maneuverable, and the adoption of throwing

Map 6.2 Ancient Italy and the city of Rome

javelins and shorter, cut-and-thrust swords increased their striking power. Departing from tradition, the Romans began to pay their soldiers, making it easier for poorer Romans to enter the ranks and enlarging the numbers of soldiers.

Roman innovations soon restored its power within the Latin League but Rome also benefited from declining Etruscan power and alliance with the aggressive Samnites inhabiting the mountainous regions of southern Italy. When the Latins revolted in 340 BCE, the Romans defeated them in battle, but instead of confiscating their property and enslaving their population, the Romans offered them various degrees of citizenship (338 BCE). A few Latin cities were made full citizens of Rome while others were given partial citizenship – the right to make contracts enforceable in Roman courts and to marry Roman citizens but no obligation to pay Roman taxes or serve in the army. At the same time, Rome began a policy of extending partial citizenship to Roman colonies established in strategic places, first in Italy and then in the central Mediterranean. By extending citizenship or partial citizenship, Rome acquired 100,000 new citizens and increased its territory by almost a third. Outside Rome newly made citizens were not forced to renounce their prior customs and their small-town identities; they could be both citizens of Rome and of Gabii. The extension of Roman citizenship was an important precedent. With their integration of the Latin League into the Roman state, the enlarged state next turned and defeated their former Samnite allies. In later centuries, Rome would continue to extend citizenship.

6.5 THE ROMAN REPUBLIC

Despite its sophisticated concept of citizenship, Rome's basic institutions were fashioned to govern a city-state composed of small farmers more or less dominated by an elite of large land-owners. The aristocratic factions that overthrew Rome's ancient kings divided power to prevent the return of dictatorship, and two annually elected consuls occupied the summit of the Roman state. The Senate comprised the military, political, and administrative elite and provided a place for elites to discuss and debate. The office of tribune was a product of the conflict between aristocratic (patrician) and popular (plebeian) factions. Elected by popular assemblies, the tribunes were designed to protect poorer citizens. They had the power to veto senatorial legislation, to suspend magistrates' judgments, and to enact legislation at plebeian assemblies. Acting on their own in a determined manner, ordinary Roman citizens could exert real influence at meetings by proposing laws in the Forum, responding to speeches, and voting.

The elite-dominated Senate's authority increased during the Punic Wars with Carthage, Rome's great rival for control of the western Mediterranean. The Second Punic War (218–202 BCE), a titanic struggle between Rome and the brilliant Carthaginian general Hannibal, occupied a symbolic status similar to that of the Persian War among Greeks. Except in its closing stages, the war was not marked by talented Roman generalship or Roman military innovation but rather by grim determination to keep on fighting when faced with a series of overwhelming defeats. The psychological turning point was the Senate's response to the terrible defeat at Cannae (216 BCE). Despite the loss of fathers, sons, and brothers, the Senate refused to negotiate or even redeem captured prisoners. In the end, unable to negotiate with Rome, to recruit allies in central Italy, or to win control over a port city to supply his troops, Hannibal had to return home to be defeated by Roman armies invading his homeland.

The prestige of the Senate reached its acme in the decades after the Punic Wars. In 221 BCE a Roman aristocrat eulogizing his father, Lucius Caecillus, summed up the aspirations of this Roman elite: "He wished to be the first of warriors, the best of orators, and the most valiant of commanders; to be in charge of the greatest affairs and held in the highest honor; to possess supreme wisdom and to be regarded as supreme within the senate; to come to great wealth by honorable means; to leave many children; and to be the most distinguished person in the state."[1] The male heroic ideal had grown considerably more complicated since the days of Achilles and Peleus as described in Homer and mentioned earlier.

Why Couldn't the Roman Republic Respond to the Problems of Growth?

Rome's triumph in the Second Punic War renewed Roman confidence in the superiority of its traditional institutions – just at the moment when these were failing and most in need of revival. The long war with Hannibal had involved nearly continuous campaigning. Deprived of the chance to work their farms, many small citizen-soldiers had lost their land. Italian cities far from the southern Tiber Valley felt that their loyalty to Rome deserved grants of citizenship, and many wealthy Romans resented senators' accumulation of conquered land and the bribes they received from foreign powers. Divisions within the Senate allowed two aristocratic brothers, Tiberius and Gaius Gracchus, to mobilize outside groups for reform. A new popular politics emerged as Tiberius Gracchus rallied the rural population to demand a fairer distribution of land confiscated from Rome's defeated rivals.

Popular reform enraged senators who were forced to disgorge public land they had seized and who resented Tiberius' appeals to the people. Although conceding some of his important demands, his senatorial opponents incited a crowd to kill Tiberius (133 BCE). Twelve years later, Tiberius' brother Gaius attempted to mobilize a broader coalition for reform including some wealthy Romans disgusted by senatorial greed. This was a threat to rich senators who produced grain and speculated on the grain market. It was one of the reasons why the army was called in to kill Gaius and his supporters (121 BCE). While the murder of Tiberius and Gaius Gracchus temporarily ended their call for reforms, in the long run senatorial aristocrats had the most to lose from the introduction of violence into political life. In striking down Gaius, Roman elites had called upon the army and broken an ancient taboo; armed soldiers had never before entered the pomerium, the sacred boundary of the city. And important Gracchian reforms survived; political commitment to public subsidy of grain prices in the city of Rome waned for a brief time after the death of the Gracchi but it became one of the bedrocks of Roman politics.

While displaced Roman small farmers, discontented Roman allies, and non-senatorial elites all found representatives for their causes among aristocratic reformers, rebellious slaves did not. Three great slave rebellions swept Sicily and southern Italy between 140 and 70 BCE. The root cause of these rebellions was the deteriorating condition of slavery in Sicily and southern Italy partly due to Roman military successes that increased the number of slaves and decreased their price. Enslaved soldiers and gladiators played a prominent role in these rebellions; the most famous slave rebel was the gladiator Spartacus. These rebellions, especially that led by Spartacus, challenged Roman military power, but the elite was united in its determination to make no compromise with rebellious slaves. Their voices find no record in Roman politics.

In the years between the death of the Gracchi and the rise of Augustus, as Rome conquered the Mediterranean world, Roman politics became increasingly dominated by problems that the Senate had refused to acknowledge. Slowly Roman citizen farmers were transformed into professional soldiers who felt more loyalty to their legion than to Rome. Landless citizens swelled the population of Rome where they looked for casual labor and claimed the cheap bread and later bread rations that were their due as Roman citizens.

Why Did the Republic Fall?

While Rome succeeded in instilling Roman identity into elites throughout the empire, a haphazard collection of political customs and traditions that had accumulated over centuries and occupied a venerated status among Romans could not provide a framework for Mediterranean-wide government. Inadequate institutions were an easy prey to corruption. The enormous wealth that poured into Rome from every corner of the Mediterranean bought senatorial loyalties and financed ambitious senators who funded gangs of toughs to intimidate voters. Since the Senate used violence against reformers, reformers sought violent men to implement reform.

Ambitious generals played an ever more central role in Roman politics. In 107 BCE, to put down a dangerous guerrilla warfare in Numidia, the popular consul Marius abolished the property qualification for military service and took another step in the construction of a permanent standing army. Later, in alliance with an ambitious tribune, Marius mobilized military force and obtained land grants for veterans from the legislative assembly. Marius died suddenly and his short rule was followed by a conservative reaction. Still, his combination of popular leader and successful general who channeled dissatisfaction against oligarchical rule provided a model for ambitious aristocrats, most notably Marius' nephew, Gaius Julius Caesar.

Julius Caesar and the End of the Republic

Contenders for popular favor organized public games and distributed money to the impoverished Roman citizenry who – in theory – ruled the Mediterranean world. The vast growth in gladiatorial games occurred at a time when growing violence cheapened human life in the political arena and when no Roman political figure, however powerful, could be sure of dying peacefully. Competition increased the cost of building a popular constituency greatly. Even wealthy aristocrats who

sought popularity, men like Gaius Julius Caesar and Gnaeus Pompeius Magnus, sought to replenish their finances to stay competitive.

As violence trumped all in Roman politics, the most important political rivals sought to acquire military renown – and the allegiance of troops. Pompey first demonstrated his military talents with victories in the east but soon his exploits were equaled by Caesar's Gallic campaigns. Caesar's conquests were the first great Roman advances into the European heartland, the first to incorporate large numbers of non-state peoples into the Roman commonwealth, peoples who were mainly familiar with tribal or clan organizations. Caesar's terse narrative of his conquests – I came, I saw, I conquered – was propaganda intended for a Roman audience.

In the end, Julius Caesar forged a popular base in Rome that secured his control over armies, and then the loyal support of his Gallic veterans determined his final victory. Caesar's triumphs effectively ended the Roman republic. Alone at the summit, Caesar sought to adapt the Roman world to its new position, reforming everything from the calendar to the taxation system. Caesar inaugurated the Julian calendar, naming a month after himself, and instituted direct taxation to replace oppressive tax farmers.

Caesar recognized that the old republican institutions were inadequate for the capital of a Mediterranean empire but his efforts to have himself crowned king proved unpopular. Attempts to assert his own divine origins may have had some resonance in parts of the Mediterranean where rulers were traditionally viewed as divine but such claims only hardened the resolve of his assassins (March 15, 44 BCE).

6.6 THE ROMAN EMPIRE

Octavian Becomes Augustus

Caesar's assassination set off a prolonged civil war in which Caesar's loyal general Mark Antony and adopted son Octavian defeated his assassins' armies. Victorious, Octavian and Mark Antony soon became rivals. Octavian used Antony's marriage to the Egyptian queen Cleopatra to discredit him in the eyes of Roman opinion, always suspicious of eastern influences. Octavian's generals defeated Antony on both land and sea.

Sole ruler of the Roman world (see Map 6.3), Octavian took the name "Augustus" and in his long regime (27 BCE – 14 CE) sought to resolve the problems that had eluded his predecessors. Remembering Caesar's fate, Augustus abandoned Caesar's efforts at political reform and carefully preserved the forms of republican rule while consolidating all power in his hands.

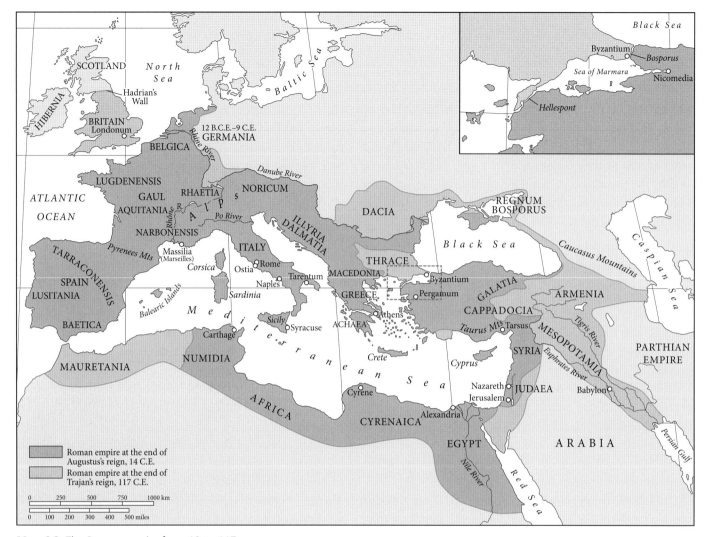

Map 6.3 The Roman empire from 12 to 117

To express his position of supreme power, Augustus used the term *imperator*, a traditional accolade given by victorious troops to their commander. Augustus portrayed himself as the "restorer of the world," launching a massive propaganda machine proclaiming his goal of restoration on public buildings, coinage, and in statuary. To rival Homer, Augustus subsidized the great Virgil who wrote a national epic the *Aeneid* that proclaimed victory to be "hostage of Rome."

Augustus' efforts to return to an imagined traditional morality may have won respect in the provinces where his own dissolute past was unknown but met with ribald responses from Roman aristocrats, its intended targets. This destroyer of traditional political life promoted a return to a traditional family life. Traditional law, however, was open to interpretation. Roman law provided for several types of family and all involved female subordination but divorce was easily available. With luck an astute woman might be able to manipulate Roman laws to retain some independent wealth – if family members were supportive.

The great wealth that poured into Rome sometimes fell under the control of women, and some wealthy divorced women such as Augustus' daughter Julia pursued an independent life. But as both Julia and Ovid discovered, it did not pay to challenge Augustus' moral revolution too directly. Both were sent into a desolate exile.

Julia's position as the daughter of a ruler and scion of a noble family was hardly typical. Within the Roman family mothers were often recognized as powerful figures but Roman women were excluded from public life. The epitaph for a beloved wife in the second century BCE in Box 6.1 shows what was demanded of a Roman wife and mother. We know that many Roman women were powerful figures within the household who commanded their sons and daughters with near dictatorial authority but a mother's influence remained within the family. The virtues required from her were very different from those expected of Achilles or Lucius Caecillus. Still, over time, although Roman women were trained primarily in domestic skills, many

Box 6.1 The Ideal Wife

What follows is the epitaph of a Roman matron from the second century BCE.

Stranger, I have only a few words to say. Stop and read them. – This is the unlovely tomb of a lovely woman. Her parents named her Claudia. She loved her husband with all her heart. She bore two sons; one of these she leaves here on earth, the other she has already placed under the earth. She was charming in speech, yet pleasant and proper in manner. She managed the household. She spun the wool. – I have spoken, go your way.

What can this epitaph tell us about Claudia's roles? Who is speaking? Who wrote the epitaph? Suppose that Claudia had written her own epitaph, what might it say?

middle-class girls were educated and able to enter the world of male concerns and even to study science.

Whether in families or outside them, Augustus used the rhetoric of restoration of tradition to stabilize his own rule but, while scrupulously respecting senatorial conventions, he did not restore its former power. Republican forms concealed dictatorship. But Augustus' hypocrisy in preserving old republican forms did not allow him to address the all-important issue of imperial succession. When the succession was in doubt who would select the emperor? The Senate – an elite composed of the empire's most prominent men? Or the army – a military body with an increasingly independent corporate identity? Augustus temporarily solved the problem by adopting a tough general, Tiberius, as his heir, as he himself had been adopted by Caesar.

The Mediterranean Connected to the Indian Ocean and to China

Augustus' long and relatively peaceful reign was a golden age for the commercial cities of the Mediterranean. Land and poll taxes, the major sources of imperial income, gave Rome enormous buying power. The wealth of Rome and the enormous task of feeding its growing population encouraged long-distance commerce protected by Roman power. As the city of Rome grew, from 375,000 in 130 BCE to 1 million under Augustus, and as the unemployed or partially employed population of citizens grew disproportionately, the need for wheat and olive oil grew prodigiously. The trade was in the hands of private merchants from all over the Mediterranean, from southern Italy and Sicily to North Africa and Egypt. These merchants contracted to supply millions of bushels of grain annually – thus the name for this trade and their ships, the **annona**. While the state enforced its deadlines harshly, it also rewarded these merchants with subsidies for the construction of ships and for their carrying cost. The trade in wheat and olive oil was an enormous force propelling trade throughout the entire Mediterranean.

The subsidy of shipping and the encouragement of maritime trade helped increase the flow of other commodities in their wake, as did the relative peace and security that Roman power gave to commerce. Through the eastern Mediterranean Rome supplied itself with goods from all over Asia and from Africa. Spices and silks were the great objects of Roman trade; spices here are broadly defined to included medicines, preservatives, perfumes, cosmetics, and incense, as well as condiments. Map 6.4 gives some idea of the enormous division of labor that developed within the Mediterranean world during the height of its power. Through Arabia, Mediterranean merchants were in touch with merchants who sailed down the African coast for balsam, frankincense, and myrrh, across the ocean to India for ginger, pepper, and sandalwood, and to Southeast Asia for cloves, cinnamon, and nutmeg. Caravans across the Sahara brought gold, ivory, and aloe to East African ports. In the Persian Gulf traders were able to connect with the Silk Road from China, another branch of which went through Petra in Jordan. The trade was so extensive that Roman emperors worried about the drainage of currency to the east. The age of Augustus was a great age of cities and the linkages established during this period would survive, on a smaller scale, for the remainder of the empire.

Mediterranean Citizenship

Although the republic was no more, citizenship was extended widely in the western Mediterranean, less widely in the eastern Mediterranean (see Figure 6.4). Even under the empire, citizenship mattered, as shown by the treatment of an accused political dissident in a distant Roman province. Arrested for sedition and routinely beaten, the Christian apostle Paul addressed the presiding official. "Is it legal for you to scourge a Roman and that without trial?" Immediately, according to the Christian scriptures, those preparing to torture Paul desisted and "the tribune himself was alarmed to find that Paul was a Roman citizen, and that he had bound him."

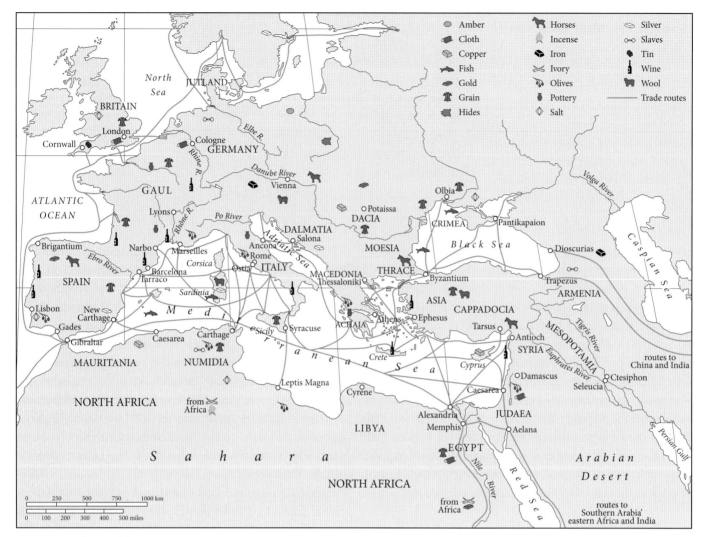

Map 6.4 Products of the Roman empire, *c.* 200 CE

508 BCE	130,000:
393–392	152,573
204	214,000
115	393,336
70–69	910,000
14CE	4,937,000

Figure 6.4 Adult male citizenship in the Roman empire, 518 BCE – 14 CE

The Margins and the Marginal of the Empire

While barbarians roamed the northern and southern margins of the empire, slaves were a marginalized group in the center of the empire. The condition of slaves varied greatly. Slaves working in the mines or in the fields led hard and short lives. Slaves working as domestic servants shared the fate of the households in which they worked although subject to the narrow supervision that close physical proximity made possible. A lot depended on the personal character of the master or mistress (see Box 6.2). Slaves who possessed skills, such as accountants, barbers, chefs, and craftsmen, might be rented out or allowed to set up their own shops. Under these conditions slaves might be allowed to save their own money and purchase their freedom. The hope of freedom and the presence of savings were expected to act as a stimulus to make the slave work hard and to keep him honest when close control was not possible. Slaves were often used in business matters because they could be tortured if the master felt that they were concealing something. In Mediterranean societies where family honor was so important, the sexual availability of slaves tainted the respectability of even the freedman. In respect to his own slaves, the usually gentle, humanistic poet Horace declared "I like sex to be there and easy to get." In Roman

Box 6.2 Recent Research on Slavery in Rome

We know much about Roman society in years of the late republic and the early empire but we know little about the attitudes of slaves who figure so prominently as background figures in Roman literature.

In general, slavery was much less harsh for slaves who lived in Rome than for those who labored in the countryside. Many Roman slaves, particularly those who possessed skills or were in close contact with their masters or their masters' families, were freed in their adult years. Such freed slaves were expected to continue to honor their masters and to retain ties of dependence with the master's family. When the master was a powerful Roman, such relations often made sense given the slave's continued need for work and for protection in a society where powerful men were expected to use their influence to favor dependents both free and unfree. Freed male slaves became Roman citizens upon their manumission. Though some freed slaves were successful in becoming wealthy and powerful in their own right, even the most successful could never expect to wholly escape the legacy of slavery. No slave could legally possess a father, and taunts about a freedman's legitimacy were common among envious Roman citizens.

Epitaphs provide some clues about the attitudes of less well-to-do slaves and freedmen in ancient Rome. The following epitaph comes from a tomb that a group of freedmen had purchased for their ex-master and for themselves:

For Publius Avillius Menander, the freedman of Publius, patron after his death his freedmen made (this) and for themselves who are named below: Avillia Philusa, the freedwoman of Publius (dead), Publius Avillius Hilarus, the freedman of Publius, Publius Avillius Anteros, the freedman of Publius, Publius Avillius Frelix, the freedman of Publius; tailors on the smaller Cermalus.

This epitaph suggests that Publius Avillius Menander required the aid of his freedman for his funeral commemoration. The freedmen and freedwomen show their own dignity by keeping faith with expectations of post-manumission loyalty to their patron. But they also assert their free identity and also assert a new identity for themselves, as tailors.

---

theater, no matter how clever or talented he might be the slave was usually a comic figure.

Weak Roman Institutions and Strong Enemies

The accession of Marcus Aurelius (r. 161–180 CE) witnessed a period of renewed military threat; this earnest, philosophical emperor spent most of his reign repelling foreign invasions. The murder of his mad son and successor, Commodus, began a series of succession crises that grew ever more serious and threatened the empire's existence. In the almost fifty years between the murder of Severus Alexander by his troops in 235 CE and the accession of Diocletian in 284 there were twenty-two emperors and countless more contenders; only one died naturally. Imperial reliance on the soldiery, so carefully concealed by Augustus' insistence on republican forms, became obvious. On his deathbed, Emperor Septimius Severus (211 CE) told his sons, "Stick together, pay the soldiers, and despise the rest." Unfortunately for them, they obeyed the last two injunctions but not the first. Almost continuous civil wars weakened the military forces protecting the empire's boundaries and opened the way for foreign invasions.

On Rome's northern borders German tribes descended upon unwalled Gallic towns, and in the east the Sasanid dynasty, replacing the Parthians, threatened to reassemble the Persian empire. In the end, Rome survived but at a steep price. Increasingly, generalship became the criterion for emperor, the emperor spent much of his time with his troops, and new – and very expensive – investments in fortresses and troops reinforced weakened borders. The soldiers' personal loyalty to their leader usually extended to his son and family, and military pressure worked in favor of hereditary succession. Increasingly emperors earned their right to rule as military leaders and the center of rule shifted from Rome to wherever the emperor had his camp. The great Diocletian was absent from Rome for the better part of twenty years and Nicomedia in Turkey was his real imperial capital.

6.7 MEDITERRANEAN DISUNITY

The triumph of Diocletian in 284 CE marked a fundamentally new phase in the history of the Roman empire. Ruling for twenty-two years, Diocletian labored mightily to restore imperial vigor. He began a process of reform that extended the life of the Mediterranean-wide empire – at the cost of crippling the urban commercial economy. Diocletian vastly increased the number of soldiers and inaugurated a policy of fortifying the border regions in depth. Such expenses placed an enormous burden on an economy long wracked by civil war. Diocletian introduced measures for more efficiently levying taxes but he also increased tax burdens, which made tax collecting an onerous task. Diocletian's intensified efforts to make urban officials responsible for levying taxes gave urban administration a reputation for bankrupting men and made them violently unpopular. The lust for urban prestige that had led wealthy citizens to build stadia and churches in their communities was cut off at its roots. Ever higher taxes demanded by Diocletian's successors encouraged elites to leave cities for the countryside where they could less easily be saddled with onerous and impoverishing governmental responsibilities. Armies increasingly requisitioned needed goods and commerce was raided by troops assigned to protect it.

Diocletian and the Problems of Imperial Reform

To confront threats on all sides, Diocletian divided the empire into East and West, each half run by a senior emperor, assisted by a junior emperor, the so-called **tetrarchy**, and then retired. Diocletian's personal authority made the system work but it did not survive his retirement. Nonetheless, Diocletian's division of the empire acknowledged that, faced with powerful and diverse enemies, the empire was just too large and varied for a single centralized ruler. Within a century and a half, an East–West division of the empire had become permanent, a division more or less corresponding with the division between areas where Greek or Latin was the administrative language.

The faltering pulse of urban life and commercial activity caused most concern in the West where commercialization was always weakest. The western Mediterranean was poorer and more seriously threatened.

Roman extension of citizenship and an astute imperial foreign policy had proven far more successful in incorporating existing states into the empire than it had in dealing with tribal societies in France and Spain or in Germany. Following imperial precedents as old as the Achaemenids, the imperial conquest of Macedonia and Egypt had simply integrated existing administrative units into the empire. In Gaul and Spain only an embryonic state existed and no established administrative system. Imperial conquest of Spain and Gaul depended on Celtic noblemen and Roman conquerors working together to create an administrative apparatus. The Celtic elites, co-opted by the Romans, proved remarkably quick in adopting Latin and in creating Roman-style cities but they did so with wealth extracted from the great estates they consolidated at the expense of the rural population. The poverty of the Gallic countryside and the corruption of the landholding bureaucracy kept these regions poorer than the traditional peasantries of Egypt and the Near East and less able to support armies.

Why Did the Barbarians Pose Such a Threat?

Neither was Rome able to adopt a successful strategy for dealing with the non-state tribes across the Rhine. These were not necessarily more formidable than the Persian armies in the East but they were much less stable and more capable of sudden action. Unlike Rome's frequent treaties with the Parthians and Sasanids, it was impossible to come to long-term agreements with the Germans.

Paradoxically, in seeking to weaken the Germans, the Romans provoked the creation of great federations from the small chiefdoms flourishing in the German forests. The Roman system of fortifications and armies stationed across the border transformed the German tribes on the other side. Roman barracks towns, including Belgrade, Budapest, Coblenz, Cologne, Mainz, Trier, and Vienna, were enriched by the payment of soldiers. Over time, the security found in areas with Roman troops, the freely flowing cash from soldiers' wages, and the military's personal tax exemptions led the garrison areas to grow at a time when the empire's population declined.

Roman commerce also attracted Germans. Roman troops used large quantities of leather in their uniforms and often purchased cattle from the Germans across the Rhine. Paying Germans in gold created customers for Roman goods, and Roman merchants followed the gold across the Rhine. Well beyond the Rhine, Mediterranean statues, pottery, jewelry, and ornamented weaponry were exchanged as presents among German elites. Roman administrators were aware of the importance of trade to Germanic rulers and used the threat of trade bans to influence the behavior of Germanic chieftains.

The simultaneous lure of Roman gold and the menace of Roman manipulation provoked the formation of German confederations on the Rhine borders. The great Germanic tribes, actually confederations, that appeared out of nowhere to threaten Roman Gaul were typically not long-existing tribes careening into the empire from distant regions, but alliances of nearby chiefdoms formed in response to the Roman presence on the Rhine. Threatening groups of Germans that the Romans identified as "Marcomanni" simply meant "frontiersmen" while the "Allemanni" were a confederation open to "all men."

Barbarian invasion, such as the seizure of North Africa, the Roman breadbasket, by the Vandals, and the successive attacks on Rome that led people to flee the city, also began to weaken an empire that found it increasingly difficult to collect taxes. The gradual decay and final disappearance of the Roman annona, the grain trade supplying the city, in the fourth and fifth centuries was only partially compensated by the growth of imperial grain subsidies for Constantinople. As Roman power weakened,

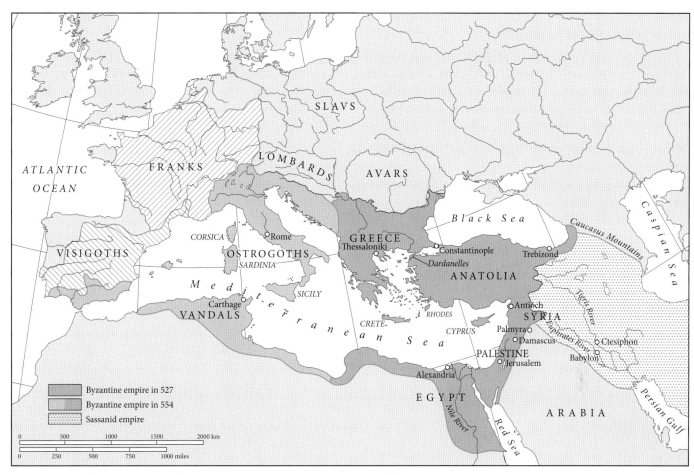

Map 6.5 Map of the eastern Mediterranean, *c.* 450 CE, showing territory of the Byzantine empire

pirates began to take a greater toll of the decreased shipping in the western Mediterranean.

Constantine's New Grand Strategy of Imperial Defense

Like Diocletian, Constantine the Great (r. 312–37 CE) struggled to devise a grand strategy for the empire. Recognizing its dangerous exposure, Constantine abandoned Rome for a more fortifiable and strategically located Byzantium which he renamed "Constantinople" (Map 6.5). Crucial to this new consolidation were his military reforms. Constantine reorganized the Roman military to create a mobile strategic reserve. His assumption was that either the borders could not be held or that Diocletian's deep border defenses were too costly. Constantine instituted a mobile reserve located in the imperial centers that would track down and defeat invaders slowed down at the frontiers. The problem with this strategy was that it consigned the border armies to secondary status; they were no longer expected to stop invaders. Quickly enough, the morale and quality of the border troops declined, a decline accelerated by the incorporation of German mercenaries into the border troops. Again, Constantine's strategy entailed the greatest tribulations for the western empire, which was most exposed to northern invasion.

Battling to keep together an empire torn by internal discord, Constantine adopted Christianity, a religion offering a new framework for imperial unity. No single factor can explain Christianity's rise as a world religion. A comprehensive explanation must include a series of factors specific to different historical eras, but Constantine's allegiance to Christianity was certainly of enormous importance.

6.8 CHRISTIANITY AND THE ROMAN EMPIRE

Rome searched for an imperial religion because its own state religion would not serve. Its priests set dates for religious observances, maintained the divine fire, and predicted the future but lacked the authority to adapt doctrine to new cultural or political needs. In the interior of their homes, Romans worshipped household gods and the spirits of their ancestors. While a foreigner might offer sacrifice to Rome's main gods, it was practically impossible to fully observe Roman rites without being admitted into an existing Roman household.

The very success of Roman arms and the rise of Rome as a world capital brought Romans into contact with new peoples and ideas. For Romans as for most of the peoples of the ancient Mediterranean, polytheism, the belief in many gods, seemed both plausible and open-minded. Civilized Romans and Greeks assumed that while peoples might have their own unique gods, they also might worship the same gods in a variety of ways and under different names. Ignoring the great Celtic earth mother and the many local war gods, Caesar explained Celtic religion to Romans by noting that "The god they worship most is Mercury. After Mercury they worship Apollo, Mars, Jupiter, and Minerva."

Still, spiritually oriented Romans could not help but wonder whether the Phrygian's Cybele or the Egyptian's Isis and Serapis had not imparted some bit of knowledge to their devotees that the Romans' gods had neglected. Although Roman authorities sought to limit the entry of foreign religions, Roman gold attracted an influx of holy men and women from all over the Mediterranean. A host of astrologers and magicians descended on the city, while Greeks brought new philosophies such as Stoicism and Epicureanism, which contained codes of morality dictating behavior.

The Temple in Jerusalem and the Development of Christianity and Judaism

In the eastern Mediterranean an era of religious ferment had begun early with the Hellenistic wave of empire-building. The eastern Mediterranean's long-established religions, competing priestly hierarchies, and extensive temple centers made religious debate particularly intense. Nowhere was the ferment more productive than in the **Hasmonean** Jewish kingdom and its successor states incorporated into the Roman empire by Pompey. The Hasmonean kingdom originated in a revolt against a Hellenistic ruler's desecration of the Temple. The center of this religious ferment was Jerusalem and its Temple. A client of the Romans, Herod the Great, rebuilt the Temple, making the so-called "Second Temple" into what was probably the largest religious structure in the Roman world and attracting the attention and devotion of many non-Jews. While many Jews sought to reconcile their monotheism with the Hellenistic heritage, others denounced all efforts at accommodation. Collections of documents from this era discovered in the twentieth century, including the celebrated Dead Sea Scrolls, reveal the existence of extremely diverse currents among various Jewish communities. In passages scattered throughout these religious manuscripts glimmer many of the basic ideas of both Christianity and rabbinic Judaism. This was the Jewish religious environment in which new religious figures appeared such as John the Baptist and Jesus of Nazareth.

The spread of the Jesus movement was profoundly influenced by its historical context. Jewish revolt and the destruction of Jerusalem and of the Temple by Rome during the revolt's suppression (66–73 CE) produced a religious crisis of the first magnitude among Jews and those non-Jews who also worshipped at the Temple. Both Christianity and rabbinical Judaism developed by providing responses to the destruction of Jerusalem, its priesthood, and their Temple. Both replaced a Temple-based religion with a re-emphasis on scriptural authority and with new types of religious hierarchy.

The religious vacuum occasioned by the Temple's destruction encouraged the spread of Christian beliefs throughout the Jewish diaspora. Like the Judaism of the Second Temple priesthood, Christianity demanded exclusive loyalty from its followers; one could not be a priest of Isis or a Mithraic initiate and a Christian deacon at the same time. Like Judaism, it fiercely asserted that there was only one God and only one set of practices for worshipping him. Key in forging a Christianity capable of attracting a wide audience throughout the Mediterranean world was Paul (5 BCE – 64/67 CE). Under Paul's leadership Christianity evolved from a more traditionally oriented variety of Judaism into a conversionary religion, open to anyone willing to make an act of faith and minimizing the connection between religious practices and ethnic identity. Christianity's universalism distinguished it from cults like Mithraism or philosophical schools such as Stoicism that emphasized their elite character.

Religious Persecution and Christian Martyrs

Unlike many of the newer religions, Christianity did not promise success in this world for those who practiced its rites. Indeed, Christianity's cult of the martyrs, so important in the early church, pointed in a very different direction; the Christian's life was organized toward winning rewards in another world. Still, Christianity did offer real and tangible rewards in this world. First and foremost it provided membership in a close-knit religious community. Christianity did not condemn slavery but demanded the masters treat their slaves justly. Rich Christians were encouraged to contribute to the poor, particularly the poorer members of the Christian community. While males dominated the early Christian movements, Roman observers were shocked that Christian observances generally included women as well as men. Imperial persecutions created opportunities for female leadership. In the early third century CE the Carthaginian matron Perpetua converted to Christianity, despite her father's wrenching pleas. During her time in prison she became a model for and leader of the North African Christian community (see Box 6.3). Her writings reveal an independent woman undaunted

Box 6.3 Women and Christianity

Although many Romans males were surprised by Christians' insistence that women possessed souls and should participate in Christian rites, early Christianity was dominated by male figures. The periods of persecution to which Christianity was subject, however, gave opportunities for women to assume new roles. In 203 CE, during the persecution launched by Emperor Septimius Severus, 21-year-old Perpetua, the daughter of an important Carthaginian family and a convert to Christianity, was arrested. The four Christians arrested with her also included Felicity, a young slave woman. Both the slave Felicity, and the Carthaginian lady Perpetua, refused to renounce Christianity and were sentenced to death by exposure to wild animals. In the weeks before their execution and in the centuries that followed, Perpetua and Felicity became powerful symbols to Carthaginian Christians.

In Perpetua's case, loyalty to her religion meant breaking with her family and rejecting the appeals of a father that Roman law made all-powerful. Perpetua's diary depicted wrenching paternal appeals: "Daughter . . . have pity on my grey head . . . have pity on your father . . . If I have favored you above all your brothers, if I have raised you to reach the prime of your life. Do not abandon me to be the reproach of men. Think of your brothers, think of your mother and your aunt, think of your child who will not be able to live once you are gone." In response, Perpetua sought to comfort him: "It will all happen in the prisoners' dock as God wills; for you may be sure that we are not left to ourselves but are all in his power." Both Perpetua and Felicity went to death bravely on March 7, 203 CE.

---

by appeals to family and society. She died bravely, exposed to wild animals in the arena at Carthage in 203 CE.

Though relatively tolerant of religious diversity, Roman emperors initially saw Christianity as a threat. State-promoted empire worship expressed imperial loyalty in the same mysterious way as flag-waving demonstrates patriotism; the rapid spread of a religion that refused to participate was seen as a political challenge. In the wake of the Jewish millenarian revolt of Bar Kochba in 132–35 CE, the Christian belief in an approaching last judgment was viewed suspiciously. A half dozen attempts were made to uproot Christianity. The martyrs' bravery won the admiration of crowds and imperial persecution was too sporadic and incomplete to seriously threaten the new religion.

While Christian martyrs and clergymen rejected Roman gods and imperial cults, and sometimes perished for doing so, in its long struggle with the empire the church developed some institutions similar to its enemy's. Just as Rome was the center of the imperial world so Rome, the See of St. Peter, assumed a special place in the Christian hierarchy, along with other important imperial cities such as Antioch and, later, Constantinople. To co-ordinate its Mediterranean-wide organization, the church developed a hierarchy modeled on that of Rome with dioceses, vicars, and curates, all Roman administrative terms. Even the basic design of the Christian church, the basilica, was adopted from the Roman meeting house.

Why Did Constantine Choose Christianity?

The sudden decision of the Roman emperor Constantine to tolerate (313 CE) and later to encourage Christianity had momentous consequences. There is no reason to deny the authenticity (or the incompleteness) of Constantine's conversion, yet since Julius Caesar the desire to deepen the connection between religion and the Roman ruler had been a recurrent theme of empire builders. Martyrs' enthusiasm, freshly demonstrated in the Diocletian persecutions, the last and largest of the murderous waves, demonstrated the powerful sentiments that Christianity had harnessed. Its universal aspirations and its conversionary character were desirable qualities in an imperial religion. Its spread beyond the boundaries of the Roman empire into the Sasanid empire might yield benefits to a Christian Roman empire. The religion's new hierarchical structure must have increased its attraction to an emperor used to top-down administrations.

Constantine's support was welcomed joyously by the church. Christian writers such as Eusebius responded enthusiastically: "One faith, one empire, one emperor." What Constantine did not bargain for, however, was internal religious division, the inevitable product of the close collaboration between religious faith and world empire. Even though his understanding of Christian theology was foggy, Constantine involved himself unhesitatingly in defining and enforcing Christian orthodoxy. He convened and presided over the crucial Council of Nicaea (325 CE) that drafted the Nicene Creed as the standard of Christian orthodoxy while condemning the Arian view that Christ had two absolutely separate natures, human and divine. The experience of persecution had not made the Christian church tolerant. The ease with which a truly great mind like that of Augustine (354–430 CE) turned to persecution, at a time when memories of imperial persecution were vivid, is still startling.

The difficulties of imperial intervention in clerical affairs were also revealed by the Council of Nicaea. Constantine's condemnation and the church council's disapproval did not finish Arianism. An Arian missionary carried it to German tribes and soon western Christian clergymen were dealing not only with invading barbarians but even worse with heretical, invading barbarians. In the eyes of the zealous, religious difference cropped up everywhere, Nestorian heretics in Egypt and Monophysites in Ethiopia, while Manichaean heresy spread both east and west. To maintain the unity of the faith emperors found themselves forced to define religious orthodoxy. Imperial efforts to enforce orthodoxy and unite the empire produced regional hostility and secessionist movements among those condemned as heretics.

Had the western Roman empire endured, its leaders would surely have come in conflict with western Christianity's leading spokesman, the bishop of Rome. As it was, conflict between the eastern emperor and the papacy was postponed by mutual adversity and by the eruption of powerful new tribes who threatened the eastern empire and destroyed the western empire. Barbarian invaders were warded off from the eastern empire by a combination of eastern military strength and bribery. In 443 CE, the eastern emperor Theodosius II paid the Huns 6,000 pounds of gold to leave his empire alone, financing the Huns' move westward. In the end German westward movements ended the western Roman empire (476 CE), but this occurred long after Rome had ceased to count as a significant power even in the Western world.

Conclusion Under the auspices of Greece and Rome and Persia, new kinds of connection arose among the peoples who lived along the Mediterranean's shores and its hinterland. Greco-Roman ideas of citizenship, eastern religious ideas, and Persian administrative practices were all absorbed into a polity tied together by Roman arms and integrated into a Mediterranean-wide economy.

This chapter has particularly focused on two great changes. The first change was the spread of citizenship – an idea of shared entitlements including the right to vote and debate state policy and many other privileges. By the end of the republic it was extended not only to Roman freemen but to the sons of freedmen (the male ex-slaves of Roman freemen) and to regional elites when present in the city. Other categories of citizenship with lesser rights also existed, such as those that pertained to Roman women. Citizenship promoted identity; the ordinary freeman in the Roman street and elites scattered throughout the empire felt that they were Romans whether they spoke Latin or Greek, lived in Hadrianopolis (Adrianople) or Gades (Cádiz), worshipped Isis or Zeus.

As we have seen, the concept of citizenship originated with the military revolution that began in the Greek city-states; this revolution linked military participation to political inclusion. The end product was the citizen-soldier based upon small cultivators who had the time and resources to equip and train. The success of these units allowed these soldiers to demand greater participation in political decision-making. The genius of Rome lay partly in the superior military organization and tactics of its citizen-soldiers but most importantly in its willingness to transcend the narrow loyalties of the polis and enlarge citizenship to include neighboring cities and even military allies. Ultimately, though, military success undermined the rural economy on which the citizen-soldier was based; while away conquering the world, the soldiers lost the farms that had secured their independence. The army was transformed from a host of small producers to a force of penniless warriors, a professional military, who depended on military victory for their livelihood. Unsurprisingly soldiers looked to generals for leadership.

The second great change was the rise of Christianity. Initially the empire followed a policy of lackadaisical repression that sometimes concluded with publicly staged executions. The Christians gave as good as they got. Many Christians, including the author of the biblical Book of Revelation, saw the empire as a monstrous beast whose death would signify the imminent apocalypse. Yet within three centuries Romans were required to be Christians. Part of the reason for Christianity's amazing turnabout was its ability to appeal to so many different elements of the Mediterranean world. It drew on the fierce monotheism of Judaism, Persian theology, the universalist appeals of the new eastern religions, and the hierarchical structure of the empire itself. In its origin Christianity was an urban religion, a product of the enormous eastern Mediterranean cities where all variety of religious beliefs confronted one another. Christianity's efforts to appeal to women, to slaves and slave masters, to intellectuals and the common man made it a formidable competitor among urban religions, although the Emperor Constantine's conversion was probably key.

Why did the Roman empire fall? Historians are frequently asked this question. The easiest answer is surely the worst. Rome did not collapse because of the increased moral failings of individual Romans as so many contemporaries alleged. Those Roman historians who actually witnessed the events, to a man (and they were all men) were members or friends of a senatorial aristocracy, envious of imperial power, who loved to pass on gossip about the colorful goings-on of emperors. The vast amount of wealth from all over the Mediterranean that poured into Rome certainly encouraged corruption. But corruption and excess were not imperial inventions and some of the most honest and capable emperors, such as Marcus Aurelius, were faced with the worst catastrophes. Perhaps the question is wrongly posed?

One might better ask how the empire went on so long? It outlasted successors, from the Holy Roman Empire to Hitler's so-called Thousand Year Reich. It may well surpass in longevity the consolidated states that dominated Europe and North America in the nineteenth and twentieth centuries as well as the European Union.

More than anything though, the question is misleading if it makes us think of political institutions as possessing life on the model of organic structures that are born and die. Between its foundation and the deposition of the last emperor, Rome rose and fell many times. Rome could have disappeared in the era of civil wars that began with Caesar and Pompey or during the crisis of the third century. Instead it was reformed by talented leaders like Constantine and Diocletian. Whether the survival of the Roman empire in the third century was a benefit for Mediterranean society remains an open question. It might have been better for Mediterranean society if the economy had survived at the expense of an increasingly onerous political unity.

Still, genuine opportunities were squandered that might have made Roman rule last longer with more beneficial effects. Serious opportunities for reformation were lost by political generations who could have taken advantage of them the most easily. Many of the worst problems of the later empire, chiefly those of creating empire-wide institutions and of finding a formal solution for the succession problem, might have been reached early on with much saving of human life and imperial resources. At the time when Caesar and Augustus ruled the world, a rich and powerful empire had the resources and ample political leeway to reorganize and reform. The years after the Second Punic War when the Gracchi sought to address Roman decay were even more promising. Yet reform is often most difficult to those who can most easily afford it; the very success that creates opportunities, encourages the overconfidence that denies the need for change.

Study Questions
(1) Discuss the forces that promoted Mediterranean unity and the forces that encouraged disunity. What drew the Mediterranean together between 600 BCE and 200 CE? What drew it apart thereafter?

(2) Why did Germanic and Slavic tribes pose such a threat to the Roman empire?

(3) Why did the Roman empire survive in the East while it collapsed in the West?

(4) Discuss the rise of Christianity. Why did Roman emperors such as Diocletian and Septimius Severus persecute it? Why did Constantine favor it?

Suggested Reading
CHARLES FREEMAN, *A New History of Early Christianity* (New Haven, CT: Yale University Press, 2009). Freeman explores the processes by which competing Christianities became one religion.

CLAUDE NICOLET, *The World of the Citizen in Republican Rome* (Berkeley: University of California Press, 1980). Nicolet studies the actual practices of citizenship and how they changed over the course of the republic.

SARAH B. POMEROY, *Families in Classical and Hellenistic Greece: Representations and Realities* (Oxford: Clarendon Press, 1997). This is a pioneering work on the study of the family in the classical period.

KURT RAAFLAUB AND NATHAN ROSENSTEIN (eds.), *War and Society in the Ancient and Medieval Worlds: Asia, The Mediterranean, Europe, and Mesoamerica* (Cambridge, MA: Harvard University Press, 1999). Important historians offer strongly comparative overviews of war and society.

SETH SCHWARTZ, *Imperialism and Jewish Society, 200 BCE to 640 CE* (Princeton University Press, 2001). Schwartz deals with interaction between Jewish and Christian beliefs in the first century.

RONALD SYME, *The Roman Revolution* (Oxford University Press, 1939). This is a classic study of the Augustinian revolution in Roman government.

PAUL VEYNE (ed.), *A History of Private Life,* vol. I: *From Pagan Rome to Byzantium* (Cambridge, MA: Belknap Press, 1992). This collection is a masterly study of everyday life in Greece, Rome, and the early Middle Ages.

MATT WATERS, *Ancient Persia: A Concise History of the Achaemenid Empire, 550–330 BCE* (Cambridge University Press, 2014). Waters provides the best general introduction to the Achaemenid empire.

CHRIS WICKHAM, *The Inheritance of Rome: Illuminating the Dark Ages, 400–1000* (New York: Penguin, 2009). Wickham defends the notion that the Dark Ages are not as dark as they are claimed to be.

GREG WOOLF, *Becoming Roman: The Origins of Provincial Civilization in Gaul* (Cambridge University Press, 1998). This study describes how Celtic elites assimilated to the empire and became Roman.

Glossary

Achaemenid: The Persian dynasty (525–404 BCE) that produced Cyrus the Great, Darius, and Xerxes. At its greatest extent it reached from Libya to North India. It developed many of the basic tools of imperial rule that were to be used by all the Mediterranean and Iranian empires that succeeded it.

annona: "Yearly," the Roman term for the movement across the sea of bushels of wheat to supply Rome. The trade was in the hands of private merchants under contractual obligation to the Roman state and subject to serious penalties if they failed to deliver. In turn the Roman government subsidized the costs of transportation.

Archaic Age: A period (800–510 BCE) in which Greek and Aegean society began to recover from the trauma of the Greek Dark Ages. In this period key institutions such as the citizenship, the polis, the hoplite army began to form.

barbaros: Originally a term for anyone who was not Greek. It might include civilized people, such as the Egyptians, but from the fifth century on it was generally used to describe people who were considred inferior to the Greeks. The word "barbarian" comes from barbaros.

citizenship: Among the Greeks citizenship was defined as "having a share in the public life of the polis." Note that Greek citizenship did not mean that all citizens had equal rights. In many city-states, poor non-noble citizens had only limited rights and women citizens hardly had any at all.

Classical Age: The golden age of Athens and the Greek city-state (490–323 BCE). It was an age of philosophers such as Aristotle, Plato, and Socrates, Greek tragedians such as Aeschylus, Euripides, and Sophocles, and the historians Herodotus and Thucydides.

Hasmonean: A dynasty of ancient Judea, descendants of the Maccabees. The last Hasmonean, Antigonus, was deposed and executed by Mark Antony.

hoplite: Greek infantryman equipped with large round shield and long thrusting spear. In battle they marched together in tight formation, moving together in unison.

Marathon: Athenian defeat of a Persian invasion force on the Plain of Marathon, northeastern Attica, in 490 BCE. Although the battle itself was only the first in a series of engagements, the Athenian victory surprised and encouraged all of Greece. In subsequent years, Marathon became a symbol of how Greek discipline and initiative overcame larger numbers and arbitrary imperial judgments.

Mycenaean Age: Term for the advanced civilizations of the Aegean from 1400–1200 BCE. The name comes from the city of Mycenae in the northeast Peloponnesus, the richest and earliest of the sites discovered and excavated by archaeologists.

phalanx: The basic unit of a hoplite army, consisting of heavy infantry usually eight deep.

polis: Originally meant city or town, but in the eighth century BCE it increasingly came to mean a town surrounded by an agricultural countryside joined together by participation in a political community.

pomerium: An open space in ancient Rome bounded by the fours hills, Esquiline, the Palatine, the Quirinal, and the Capitoline. Originally intended to give defenders of the city space in which to manuever, it became a sacred space. April 21, the date on which the pomerium was demarcated, was celebrated as the foundation of Rome. Under the republic, military units in arms were forbidden to cross the pomerium.

tetrarchy: Literally, "rule of four," the term denotes the Emperor Diocletian's effort to make a coherent system from what had been a series of improvisations. A fellow commander Maximian was awarded the title "Augustus" and became joint emperor. Seven years later two younger commanders, Constantius and Galerius, were added as junior members or "Caesars." At the same time the division of labor among the emperors was supported by marriage alliances among their families. Although the tetrarchy indicated Diocletian's view that the empire had become too big for any one man to rule, it fell apart after his retirement as the three imperial candidates fought among themselves.

Zoroastrianism: The religion founded by the prophet Zarathustra, known by the Greeks as Zoroaster, whose dates are given by various scholars as anywhere between 1200 and 600 BCE. Zarathustra had a vision of this world as an arena where good and evil, truth and the lie, were battling it out. This system has been called dualism, as opposed to pure monotheism. It is not, however, really dualist, because Zarathustra was certain that in time the good principle, Ahura Mazda would destroy the evil principle, Ahriman. Its ultimate monotheism would have a profound influence on the Hellenistic world.

Note   1 Charles Freeman, *Egypt, Greece and Rome: Civilizations of the Ancient Mediterranean* (Oxford University Press, 1996), pp. 332–33.

World map, c. 700 CE

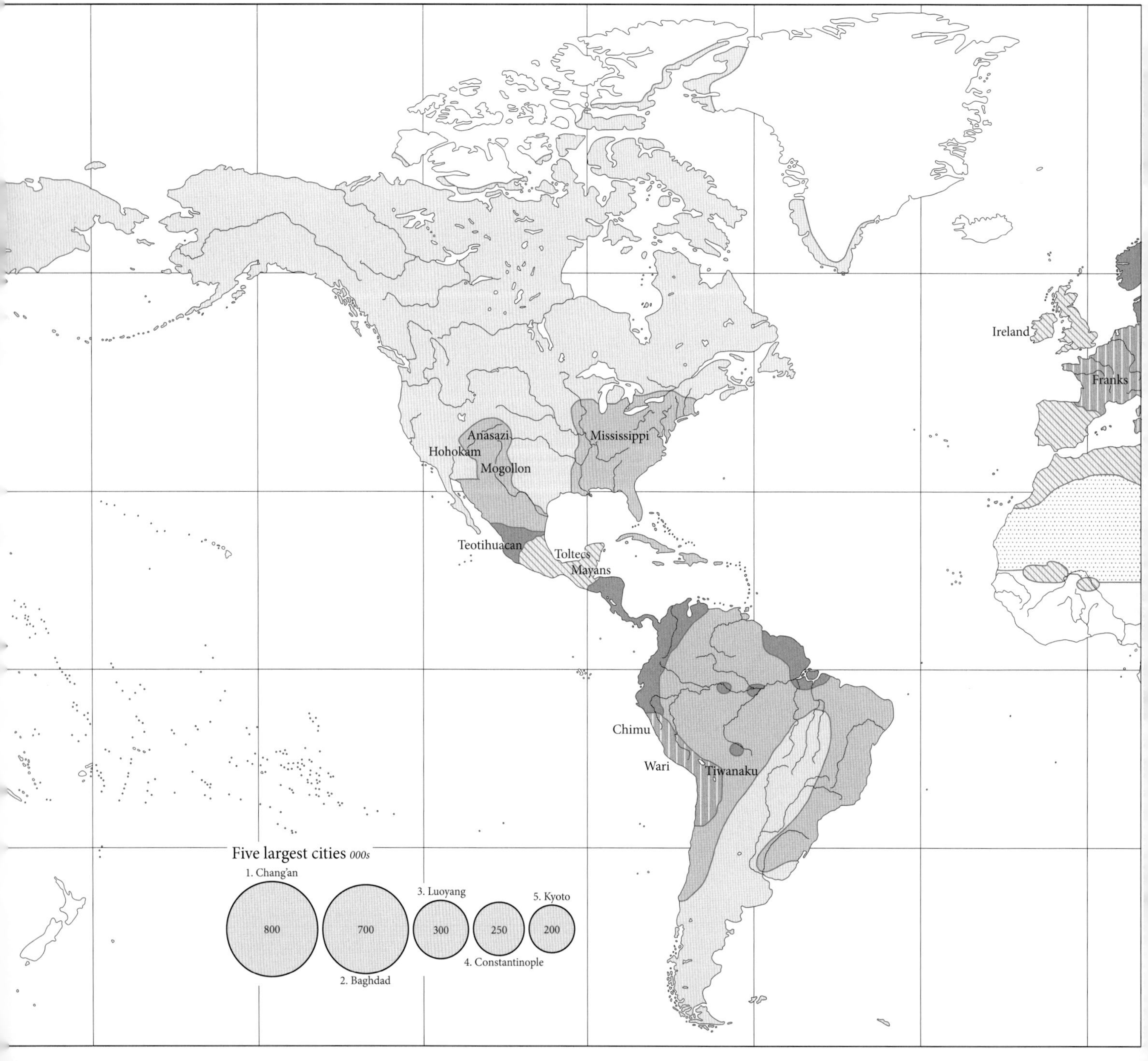

Ireland

Franks

Anasazi

Hohokam

Mogollon

Mississippi

Teotihuacan

Toltecs

Mayans

Chimu

Wari

Tiwanaku

Five largest cities *000s*

1. Chang'an

3. Luoyang

5. Kyoto

800

700

300

250

200

2. Baghdad

4. Constantinople

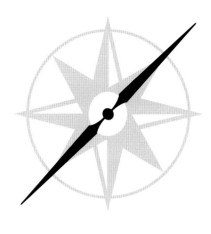

PART III

600–900 CE: States, empires, and religions

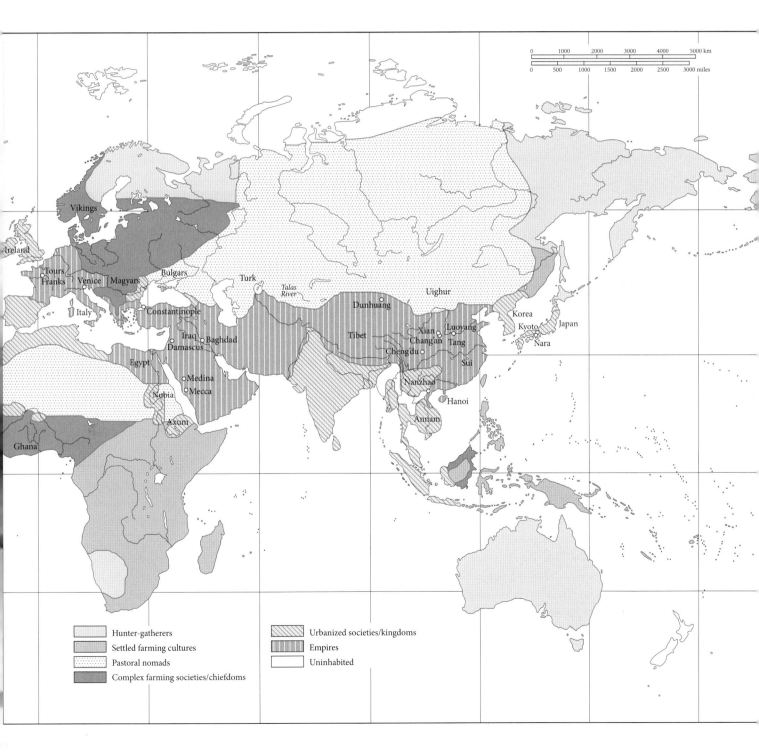

Hunter-gatherers	Urbanized societies/kingdoms
Settled farming cultures	Empires
Pastoral nomads	Uninhabited
Complex farming societies/chiefdoms	

Vikings
Ireland
Tours
Franks · Venice · Magyars
Italy
Constantinople
Egypt
Nubia
Axum
Ghana
Bulgars
Turk
Talas River
Iraq · Baghdad
Damascus
Medina
Mecca
Dunhuang
Tibet
Uighur
Xian · Luoyang
Chang'an · Tang
Chengdu · Sui
Nanzhao
Hanoi
Annam
Korea
Kyoto · Japan
Nara

Africa	
600–900	East African trading towns, Sofala and Kilwa, flourish.
600–800	Decline of kingdom of Axum (Ethiopia).
800–1076	Powerful kingdom of Ghana.

Americas	
400–900	Wari empire.
699–900	Rise and fall of Mayan city-states in Mesoamerica.
900–1168	Toltec empire in Central Mexico.

East Asia	
552–620	First Turk empire in Eurasia.
581–617	Sui dynasty reunifies China.
618–907	Tang dynasty in China.
626–49	Rule of Taizong – high point of Tang dynasty.
634–804	Tibetan empire.
683–734	Second Turk empire.
710–84	Nara period in Japan.
755–63	Rebellion of An Lushan.

Western Europe and the Byzantine Empire	
673–80	Great siege of Constantinople.
716–54	Mission of Wynfrith/Boniface to reorganize the German church.
771–814	Reign of Charles the Great.
800	Coronation of Charles the Great by the pope as emperor.

Middle East, North Africa, and Spain	
610	Beginning of Muhammad's public mission.
622	Hijra – the emigration of Muhammad and his followers from Mecca to Medina.
630	Meccans capitulate to Muhammad.
632–750	Period of Arab conquests.
639–42	Arab conquest of Egypt.
642–44	Arab conquest of western Iran.
661–750	Umayyad caliphate.
711–15	Muslim conquest of Spain.
750–1070	Abbasid caliphate.

The periods examined in these chapters, the three centuries between 600 and 900 CE in Eurasia and the six centuries between 600 and 1200 in Africa and the Americas, were glorious, tumultuous, or catastrophic, depending on the region of the world in which a person lived and his or her status in that society. For the Islamic Umayyad conquerors of Spain, the southern Mediterranean, and Persia, and for the Tang dynasty rulers, who subdued large portions of Central Eurasia, this was a period of unparalleled glory. In the Middle East and China, rulers and elites created basic institutions of society and government that would endure for centuries. Chinese and Middle Eastern historians would look back nostalgically on these years as "golden ages" of territorial conquest, political innovation, and cultural accomplishment. Even

so, by the end of our period, the once mighty Tang emperor confronted rebellion on every front, and the Abbasid caliph had become a figurehead. In both empires, after an age of heroic victories, rulers had to confront populations alienated by the high cost of continued military preparedness and military men angered when their counsels were ignored.

For Japan these years, particularly those when Nara was the Japanese capital, marked a very significant transformation although not quite a golden age. This period, marked by a large-scale importation of Chinese institutions and culture, forged a unified Japan. Wrestling with the Chinese heritage and reshaping it to fit Japanese needs was a task left for the succeeding generations. Silla Korea faced similar problems.

In other regions, empires took shape and dissolved, leaving less tangible legacies. On the steppes of Eurasia, evanescent empires of the Turks and Tibetans rose and fell; Turkish and Tibetan rulers exacted tribute from the Chinese empire and came under its proverbial spell, sending young men to study their institutions and adopting Chinese religious and cultural practices. But Sinicized sons found it difficult to call upon the same loyalty from tough military commanders as their fathers, and Sinicized rulers spurred local rivals who scorned their distance from tribal culture. In West Africa the Senegalese kingdom of Ghana rose to great power, only to collapse before Berber attacks. The monarch's monopoly of the gold trade increased his power and his standing within the international political order but gold attracted military adventurers, and the economy on which Ghanaian power rested proved fragile.

In Western Europe and in Central America, political collapse and economic slowdown were also the order of the day. Even here the news was not totally bad. Although this era has been labeled the European "Dark Ages," the figure of Charles the Great (Charlemagne) acquired legendary status among succeeding European generations. Still, in terms of political chaos and economic stagnation, the year around 750 CE, the middle of our period, marks a low point for a newly forming European society that included Celtic, Germanic, and Slavic peoples. For Central America (considered here between 600 and 1200) the later period was one of imperial decline. The collapse of the Mayan civilization in Mesoamerica and of the Toltec empire in Central Mexico as well as the abandonment of the Tiwanaku and Wari empires in the Andes allowed the jungle to reclaim great stone cities. Still, the Toltec and Wari empires left a rich legacy to subsequent empire builders and their influence persisted in their Inka and Aztec successors.

Climatic changes probably played a role in the rise and fall of empires. A colder, drier climate may have pushed nomadic raiders from Northern Europe and Central Eurasia toward Mediterranean Europe. Climatic change probably contributed powerfully to the destruction of Andean, Mayan, and central Mexican societies. Since the sophisticated agricultural technology of these societies required large quantities of water, they were unprepared for the long period of colder, drier weather. The collapse of the Ghanaian kingdom may also have been thus strongly influenced. Here as in Mesoamerica, the water supply was fragile and overgrazing may have already made the land susceptible to climatic change. While climatic change played an important role in this period, it is not an all-encompassing explanation. Not all nomadic intrusions into imperial societies can be explained by climatic change, nor can it explain the brilliance of society in Baghdad, Damascus, or Chang'an.

The era also witnessed a great expansion of trade throughout Eurasia and Africa, which deeply influenced the rise and fall of empires. Strong governments in both the eastern Mediterranean and in China created large and secure markets at both ends of the road and, as in the days of the Romans and the Han, generated strong incentives for intercontinental exchange. In this era, trade routes linked the Mediterranean to Africa, India, and China on a scale and intensity exceeding that of earlier eras. Trade enriched urban life in such disparate settings as the port city of Kilwa in East Africa and the caravan center of Dunhuang in northwest China, filling both cities with merchants speaking many languages. Both cities were stations on trade routes that reknit the bonds that tied the Middle East to East Africa, India, Southeast Asia, and China. Unfortunately, American states and economies emerged in relative isolation and lacked the rich intercontinental interactions available to Eurasians and Africans. Central American ways did begin to spread to North America where they stimulated the growth of vigorous new societies. Still, Toltecs, Maya, and Wari did not confront societies as vastly different from themselves as Abbasid Baghdad was different from Tang Chang'an. What if the American empires had been able to share their calendars, agricultural technologies, and domestic crops with those of Eurasia/Africa in the years between 600 and 1200? What if American empires had received in turn the culture and technologies of the Eurasian/African world? Clearly, both New and Old Worlds would have been very different.

Religious transformations in Eurasia and Africa illustrate the great forces of cultural interaction. Ideas accompanying the baggage trains of conquerors and following the trade routes reshaped cultural and intellectual attitudes, establishing new connections between peoples while sundering old ones.

This era was one of the greatest moments, perhaps the greatest, in the history of religious expansion. The Arab armies conquered states from Spain to Persia, but Islamic policies of toleration and accommodation impressed more people than the force of arms. These policies rallied non-Muslim populations to Islamic rule and inclined them over time to conversion. Muslim beliefs also spread south to portions of East Africa. Religious controversies within the Islamic world produced the divisions between Sunnis and Shi`ites that still persist. The Tang empire's embrace of Buddhism, although it was sometimes a troubled relationship, marked the high point of the spread of Buddhism in China. But new religions spread everywhere along these new, more secure imperial roads and across empire-linking trade routes. Islam followed the commercial paths of the Silk Road connecting the eastern Mediterranean to China, a path already trod by Buddhism. Buddhism declined in its home country of

India but acquired solid roots in China, Japan, Korea, Sri Lanka, and Southeast Asia. For Buddhists, too, persisting divisions between Hinayana and Mahayana traditions emerged in this period. More transitory in its influence, Nestorian Christianity also joined Islam and Buddhism along the Silk Road. Entrepreneurial Sogdian merchants, many of whom were Manichaeans, supplied different armies and acted as intermediaries between different religious cultures while they disseminated their beliefs along the same route. The eastward spread of Nestorian Christianity proved temporary but the spread of Roman and Orthodox Christianity to the Celtic, Germanic, and Slavic peoples proved lasting.

7 The Middle East and Europe

786–809	Reign of Harun al-Rashid.
800	Coronation of Charles the Great as emperor by the pope on Christmas day.
820	In a treaty Charles the Great and the Byzantine Emperor Nicopherous recognize Venice as a Byzantine territory and recognize her mainland trading rights. This is a major step in the growth of Venetian economic power in the Mediterranean.
863–65	Missionary activities of Cyril and Methodius among the Slavic peoples of Moravia and Bohemia. Beginning of the Christianization of the Slavs.

The name and legend of Charlemagne dominated the early Middle Ages. With reason. His rule marked the end of a long period of Western economic and political decline.

Charles the Great was a remarkable man, tall and well-built and of regal bearing. His numerous military campaigns against Saxons, Lombards, and Catalans over his forty-seven year reign demonstrate his imperial ambitions. His close alliance with the papacy demonstrates his faith as well as the importance of the already long-established alliance between the papacy and the Franks. This alliance resulted in the pope crowning him emperor on Christmas day 800 in Rome, an event with profound significance for European history. The continent of Europe now had an emperor but the ability of the pope, a religious leader, to make emperors was also not without consequence.

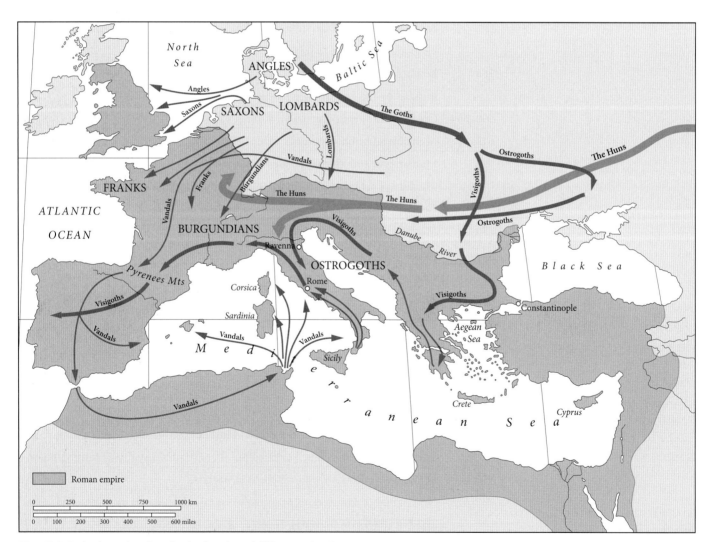

Map 7.1 Barbarian migrations in the fourth and fifth centuries CE

Charles's accomplishments are all the more remarkable because they were made in a period when conceptions of civic obligation and state competency had reached their nadir in the West. Military bearing was necessary to a Frankish king because personal prestige more than state obligation brought together warriors to assist in his summer campaigns. A few spectacular victories such as his defeat of the Avars and confiscation of the horde of wealth they had accumulated from conquering other peoples brought rich rewards to those who accompanied him and rallied followers for the next campaign. Fortune also played a role. The Frankish kings regarded their territory as personal property and divided the kingdom among their male children. Charles's own father Pepin had divided his empire between Charles and Carloman but Carloman died young, leaving his brother an undivided kingdom.

Charles was the first of the Franks to have a fixed political capital, **Aachen**, today on the German side of the German–Belgian border. The growing prosperity of the Carolingian economy enabled Charles to build a palace and a royal chapel but Aachen remained a modest city. Among its most famous sites was a technologically advanced water clock and an elephant, both gifts of the **caliph** (the successor to the Prophet) Harun al-Rashid.

Charles sought to make his capital a center of learning and searched Western Europe for celebrated scholars. The great emperor himself sought to share in this learning. During his meals he had religious works and histories read to him. Besides Frankish, he spoke Latin fluently and had limited ability in Greek. Sadly, the great emperor was never able to add literacy to his accomplishments. In his later years, just before he went to bed, the emperor tried hard to master writing. He had a copy book in which he practiced making his letters but even his adoring biographer noted that, due to his age, he made little progress.

Charlemagne's younger contemporary, the Abbasid Caliph al-Ma`mun (786–833), was in contrast a great scholar in his own right. On the death of his famous father, the Caliph Harun al-Rashid, in 809, al-Ma`mun came to power in the eastern territories of the empire, whereas his brother al-Amin ruled in Baghdad to the west. The two brothers had very different interests and personalities. Al-Amin, whose mother had been a free Arab, was devoted to Islamic traditionalism. Al-Ma`mun's mother was an Iranian slave-girl, and he gained the support of Iranian generals and politicians in the east. He proved more cosmopolitan and interested in various kinds of culture.

The two caliphs soon fell to fighting. Al-Amin attempted to invade Iran, but his armies were defeated near Rayy in 811. By 813 al-Ma`mun's riposting armies had taken Baghdad and killed al-Amin, reportedly against his brother's wishes. Al-Ma`mun had a reputation for being a hands-on ruler, who declined to have a **vizier**, or first minister (after deposing al-Fadl ibn Sahl in 817), and who closely monitored his provincial governors. He even attempted to resolve the Sunni–Shi`ite conflict by giving the eighth Shi`ite Imam, Ali Rida, his daughter in marriage and making him his successor as caliph. This plan was derailed when hard-line Sunnis mounted a revolt in Baghdad in 819. Al-Ma`mun set out for that city with his vizier and Ali Rida, both of whom died during the journey. Some blamed al-Ma`mun for their deaths, though he denied it. Al-Ma`mun had tried to rule from Marv in the east, but after this revolt he accepted the necessity of taking up residence in Baghdad. Although he reunited the empire, afterwards it faced increasing decentralization.

Al-Ma`mun appointed the great philosopher al-Kindi as a scholar in the House of Wisdom, a philosophical institute where Greek philosophy was translated and studied. It is said that the caliph sent a special delegation to the Byzantine empire to bring back Greek manuscripts. An impressive staff of translators, including Arab Christians, brought Greek and Syriac works into Arabic. Al-Ma`mun debated Aristotle with his scholars. He also had an astronomical observatory installed in the House of Wisdom. There, Muslim astronomers made new observations that corrected those of the ancient Greek authority, Ptolemy. Some other wealthy families imitated the caliph's example, establishing similar research institutes themselves. The translation movement of the ninth century forever changed Islamic culture, allowing scholars access to Plato and Aristotle. Ultimately Greco-Islamic philosophy came to exercise a profound influence on Europe when these works were translated from Arabic into Latin some three hundred years later, influencing the first renaissance of the 1100s.

The splendor of Harun al-Rashid's Baghdad, contrasted with the poverty and reduced scale of Charlemagne's Aachen, illustrates the fate of Europe and the Middle East in the wake of the collapse of the Roman empire. This chapter explores the forces that shaped the rise and fall of empires in the former Mediterranean world:

- It shows how the Mediterranean world we studied in Chapter 6 fragmented, with its northern sections moving toward integration into the heart of the European continent and its southern and eastern sections reorienting themselves toward the Middle East, Iran, India, and Eurasia.
- It considers why age-old empires like that of the Sasanian and western Roman empires collapsed and why Arab rule established itself so quickly over the southern and eastern Mediterranean world, extending its power into Iran and even Eurasia.
- It examines not only the rapid expansion of Islamic rule but why the Islamic empire in the Middle East managed to

Map 7.2 Germanic states in Europe

establish institutions and a religious identity that endured while all traces of so many empires established by military conquest proved fleeting.

- It takes up again the Roman empire and why the western Roman empire dissolved while the eastern Roman empire laid new foundations that would help it to last another thousand years.

- It scrutinizes the changing world of the West, how it overcame the deadly and confining urbanism of the last days of the Roman empire, and the transformations of Western Christian and Byzantine culture.

7.1 THE DECLINE AND DISAPPEARANCE OF OLD EMPIRES; THE RISE OF NEW EMPIRES

In the period 600 to 900 CE, the old established empires of the greater Mediterranean fell to, or were besieged by, tribal and pastoral peoples from the fringes and new empires arose. The Germanic tribes in Western Europe conquered and gradually replaced the western Roman empire. Eventually some would seek to create a new Germanic empire in Western and Central Europe. The center of the Roman empire shifted east to the Greek-speaking areas around Constantinople, but even these were challenged by Slavic tribes who moved into the Balkans. The southern reaches of the old Roman empire across the Mediterranean, stretching from Syria to Spain, fell to the Arab Muslims, as did the Sasanian empire in Iran. Why the balance of power shifted so heavily toward tribalists and pastoralists in the period 400 to 700, and what allowed these peoples to create flourishing new empires in 700 through 900, has been much debated among historians. Many of the tribalists were pastoral peoples and, since a shift in favor of pastoralists occurred over such a large area of the earth, it seems likely that climate changes were involved, but their details are still controversial.

Much of the Roman period was apparently fairly warm, implying increased rainfall, flourishing agriculture, and population growth. The period from approximately 400 to 900 CE was marked by cooler average temperatures, which sometimes caused extended drought and also extremes of hot and cold. Such cold and drought could cause pastoral nomads to leave their usual grazing lands in search of pasture further afield, sometimes provoking mass migrations, as with the coming of the Huns, the Germans, and later the Slavs into Europe. Pastoralists were more nimble in dealing with unpredictable weather than settled farmers, since they could simply take their livestock to new locations where pasture was more abundant. Farmers had less flexibility, and the empires and traders that depended on their produce were weakened by extended bouts of bad weather. Recent scientific discoveries have confirmed another hypothesis, which was that the Roman empire might have been further undermined from the fourth century by the advent of malaria in Italy, which traveled up from Africa. A debilitating disease borne by mosquitoes that breed in swampy areas, malaria may have weakened the settled farming populations of the wetter areas in the south while not affecting the Germanic tribes in the north (see Map 7.2).

Taking into account changing cycles of weather and disease can help us understand the background against which large changes in history occurred, but they cannot explain much in themselves. We need to know how societies dealt with such changes, and what institutions they erected to continue to strive for order and prosperity. Thus, we must look elsewhere in explaining the ability of the Arab Muslim pastoralists who exploded out of the arid Arabian peninsula into the Levant, Iraq, North Africa, Iran, and Central Asia to establish a large and imposing new Islamic empire from the 600s forward. Their adoption of the religion of Islam, for instance, gave them a strong cultural identity and what we might now call an ideological unity. The vast extent of the new empire allowed the regional import of new crops from elsewhere, improving agricultural productivity. Likewise, the Germanic tribes showed an ability to adopt administrative techniques and even language

from the declining Roman empire, allowing them to erect a new imperial structure over much of Western Europe, though it was poor and backward compared with the glories of Baghdad.

7.2 THE BYZANTINE EMPIRE

In the 500s and early 600s, Arab tribes and townspeople dominated the Arabian peninsula and inhabited the edges of what are now Syria, Jordan, and Iraq. A small, marginal people, they were surrounded by the great empires of their day. The largest, the Roman empire, had shifted its main institutions to Constantinople and begun giving up Latin for some purposes in favor of Greek. We now refer to this eastern state as **Byzantium**, but its emperor and nobles continued to think of it as the Roman empire, and its emperor as the direct successor to Augustus.

The Byzantine empire was weak in the old strongholds of Western Europe, where Germanic tribes and rulers increasingly asserted authority, but it dominated the Balkans and much of what we now think of as the Middle East – Anatolia, Syria, Palestine, and Egypt. While the bureaucracy for the most part used Greek, subjects of the empire spoke many languages. Balkan peoples increasingly spoke Slavic languages; Egyptians spoke Coptic, an Afro-Semitic language descended from that of the pharaohs; Syrians and Palestinians spoke Aramaic, a Semitic language related to Hebrew and Arabic.

Most of the inhabitants of the empire were Christians of one sort or another. A religious dispute divided these Byzantine Christians, as theologians argued over the relationship of the human to the divine within Jesus Christ. What became the official orthodoxy upheld "two natures in one," asserting that Jesus had both a divine and a human nature, both coexisting within him. Most Egyptians and Syrians, however, insisted that Jesus had a single nature, a position called **Monophysitism** (mono = single, physis = nature). Since it was considered a heresy in Constantinople, imperial officials and churchmen attempted to suppress it. This religious struggle took on ethnic and political overtones, with the Greek-speaking upholders of two natures from the imperial center persecuting the Coptic- and Aramaic-speaking Monophysites of the Middle East. Over time, this religious difference with the center caused Egyptians, Palestinians, and Syrians to view the Byzantine rule as oppressive.

7.3 THE SASANIAN EMPIRE: BYZANTIUM'S EASTERN RIVAL

The other challenge in the Middle East for the Byzantines was the powerful Sasanian empire of Iran, with which they were

Map 7.3 The Middle East in the time of Muhammad

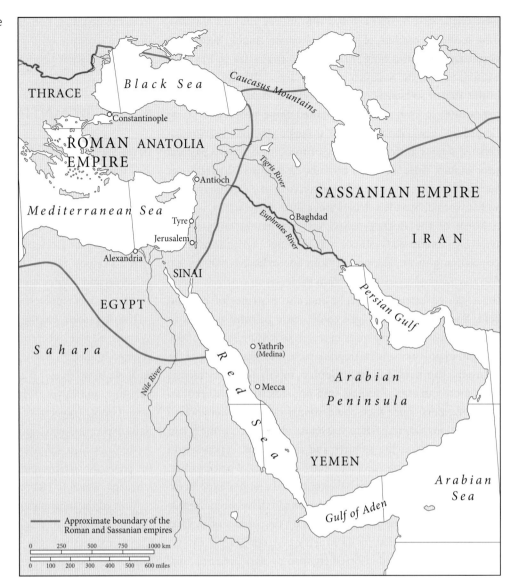

often at war in the 500s, and which sometimes bested them. During the 500s the balance of power between the settled, urban centers of the Byzantine empire and the pastoral nomads on its fringes shifted in favor of the nomads. Repeated outbreaks of plague significantly reduced the urban population, but did not affect nomadic peoples. The reduced tax base from lost population hurt the empire's finances. The Byzantines increasingly used tribal or peasant troops such as Goths, Armenians, and even Persians and Near Easterners. In the early 600s the empire was weakened by attacks in the Balkans and by a very successful push by the Sasanian empire of Iran into Syria, Palestine, and Egypt. The Sasanian empire had been founded in the 200s CE and had been Byzantium's most important rival in the east for some time. It not only ruled the Iranian plateau, but also Armenia and much of what is now Iraq and even Yemen. Its rulers became fierce supporters of the Zoroastrian religion, and often persecuted the minority Christians.

The Arabs who dwelt on the edges of these powerful empires were mostly organized by tribe or town. They had a few chieftains who might be thought of as provincial kings, especially at Hira in what is now south-central Iraq. Its Lakhmid rulers adopted Christianity and gave support to poets who developed a standard dialect of Arabic that came to be widely understood among the Arabs of the peninsula. They also developed a writing system for the language.

7.4 MUHAMMAD

Across the deserts of Arabia, near the Red Sea, two Arab city-states did without kings or a central state. These were the trading centers of Mecca and Medina. Mecca served as the center of a pagan religious cult that worshipped many deities, including star goddesses (among them an Athena-like goddess of war and a provincial version of Venus). Its religious festivals also served as local trading fairs. The most powerful tribe in this region, the **Quraysh**, dominated both politics and trade. Around 570 CE a woman of the Quraysh who had been recently widowed gave birth to a boy she called Muhammad, "the praised." She herself died when he was 6, and the orphaned boy became the ward of his grandfather and then his uncle. We know little of Muhammad's youth, but he had a weak position as an orphan. He certainly attended the trade fairs and saw the religious rites of his people. Like other Meccans, he could not escape hearing oral accounts of the major neighboring religions, of Christianity, Judaism, and Zoroastrianism, from traders who belonged to them, from Arabs who had encountered them, and possibly even from local members. Many Arabs appear to have been dissatisfied with their star goddesses and to have yearned for a new kind of religion, closer to the sophisticated forms of **monotheism**, belief in one God, that held sway in neighboring empires. Muhammad was among them.

Muhammad married Khadija, a wealthy widow somewhat older than he was. With her backing, he led trading caravans up to what is now Jordan and Syria. He saw cosmopolitan Byzantine-ruled cities such as Damascus just before they fell to Iran. He encountered Syrian Christianity, which insisted that Jesus had but one, divine, nature and which emphasized monasticism. He came to feel that both positions were extreme. Meccans who were interested in spirituality had a custom of withdrawing for a time every year from human society and journeying to nearby caves to meditate. Muhammad, thirsty for things of the spirit, engaged in such retreats when residing in Mecca. Then around 610, according to early Muslim chronicles, something unexpected happened. While out meditating, Muhammad heard what sounded to him like the tolling of a loud bell. When it ceased, early sources maintain, he found words in his mind that represented themselves as coming from the divine. The first said:

Recite, in the name of your Lord, who created –
Created human beings from a speck.
Recite, and your Lord is most generous,
Who taught with the pen –
Taught human beings what they did not know.
(K. 96.1–4)

According to the biographies written much later, Muhammad was at first confused and frightened by this experience. He rushed home to tell Khadija about it, and when he recited the verses for her, she concluded that he might be a prophet. She knew a Christian, and took Muhammad to him. On hearing what Muhammad recited, this man declared that it seemed to him very much like what was spoken to Moses.

What is the Koran?

Muhammad thereafter continued to go off to meditate, and more verses came to him. They represented themselves as being from God, the merciful, the compassionate. The **Koran**, as these collected verses are now known, calls God "Allah" or "the deity," as well as "the Compassionate." The Koran does not use Allah as a personal name, but rather identifies him as the God of the Bible and of all revealed religion, and the creator of the universe. The new verses were sometimes laden with danger for a man from his society. One said:

He is God, the one,
God, the absolute.
He does not give birth and was not born
And no one is at all like him.
(K. 12.1–4)

That is, the revelations Muhammad said he received instructed him to preach monotheism. He began gathering a few disciples, including his young cousin Ali, and sharing with them the new message. By about 613 it had become controversial in Mecca. Many powerful Meccans still revered their star goddesses, and they were proud of their parents and forebears, who worshipped them. To say that they did not exist and that their worshippers were infidels fit for hell fire, as Muhammad did, was not only an insult to living Meccan pagans, but a cutting slander of their ancestors. Further, it had the potential to damage the economic vitality of the fairs held in conjunction with pagan worship.

From 613 to 622, the followers of Muhammad in Mecca were subjected to sometimes severe persecution for adopting the new religion of Islam. The verses of the Koran (in Arabic "Qur'an" or "recital") continued to flow. They condemned the rich for callousness toward the poor. They began maintaining that the God who spoke to Muhammad was the same one who had sent earlier prophets, such as Abraham, Joseph, Moses, Solomon, David, John the Baptist, and Jesus. The Koran taught that all these prophets were human beings and not divine, and had come serially to remind God's peoples of the need to worship and have faith in him and to lead moral lives. It retold episodes from the lives of the prophets, often in the style of a sermon that draws a moral from the story. It forbade dishonesty, theft, and murder.

Mecca and Medina

Muhammad's followers at some point became known as **Muslims**, Arabic for those who surrender themselves, i.e. to God. Many were from the lower orders of society and so were particularly open to being harmed or humiliated by wealthy Meccans. The Meccans announced a social and economic boycott of the Muslims. At one point a significant number of Muslims had to take refuge in neighboring Christian Ethiopia, across the Red Sea. The Koran says of Muhammad during this period of persecution that he had no political authority and was only someone sent to warn, and he and his followers responded to the provocations non-violently.

In 622 the Meccans, having failed to wipe out the new religion, plotted to assassinate Muhammad. The Prophet heard of this conspiracy, and left Mecca with a loyal disciple for the nearby city of Medina. He had relatives there on his mother's side, and the city elders had tried to convince him to come and live there. Medina suffered from tension among its various tribes, some of which were Jewish, and its inhabitants believed that Muhammad could serve as a good-faith broker among them. Most of the Muslims in Mecca then emigrated as well. The year 622 marks the beginning of the Muslim calendar, which is now in its fourteenth century. Mecca and Medina fell into a sort of west Arabian civil war. Muhammad was convinced that the powerful Quraysh would continue to attempt to wipe out the new religious community, and that the best defense was a good offense. Mecca was too well fortified to attack it directly, so instead, the Muslims raided Meccan trade caravans to weaken their foes economically.

Tribal Allies

At the same time, the Muslims sought allies among the Arabian tribes, who were more eager for plunder than thirsty for a new spirituality. Many aligned themselves with Muhammad. The Koran says that most of the Arab tribesmen were merely persons who had accepted Islam, not really believers or persons who had fully made an internal commitment of faith to God (K. 49.14). Muhammad, as was the custom of Arabian chieftains, contracted a number of marriages as a way of cementing political alliances. The Arabs practiced child betrothal, and one of Muhammad's wives was a child when given to him, but he did not consummate the marriage until she was of age. Some of the women he married were widows of Muslims slain in battle, and this was a way of providing for them. Although the Koran, like the Hebrew Bible, recognizes polygamy (up to four wives are allowed), in many ways it improved the position of women. A man could only have more than one wife if he could provide equally for them. The Koran abolished the tribal practice of killing girl babies as a way of limiting population growth, and gave women inheritance and property rights, something they did not achieve on the same scale in Europe until the 1850s.

The Koran accepted that righteous Jews, Christians, Muslims, and other monotheists need have no fear in the afterlife, and noted that Muslims were "closest in love" to the Christians (2.62,

5.82). It urged Muslims to live in harmony with other believers, and to take advantage of the differences among human beings to learn from that about God's designs. Still, Muslims were to avoid adopting Christians and Jews as patrons. In ancient Arabia a special relationship existed between a patron or protector (*wali*) and his client, and poor Muslims could be forced by such social superiors to give up Islam. (In some modern renderings of the Koran, this verse is mistranslated so that it seems the Koran is forbidding Muslims to take Jews and Christians as their "friends," but this way of putting it is a mistake and contradicts many other verses of the Muslim scriptures.)

The Society of Medina

Within Medina, four groups jockeyed for position: the Muslim immigrants from Mecca, their Medinan helpers or allies, the Medinans with continued pagan sentiments who were only lukewarm about Muhammad, and the Jews. The Muslims were hampered in their struggle with Mecca by the neutrality adopted by the Jews and the lukewarm Medinans, and this led to conflicts in which some Jewish clans were expelled from the city. The Koran respects the religion of Judaism, and assures righteous Jews of salvation, and Muslims initially prayed toward Jerusalem just as Jews do. It does not condemn Jews in the abstract, but does criticize those who deserted the Muslims in their struggle against pagan Mecca. After his political difficulties with some Jewish tribes, Muhammad changed the point toward which believers prayed to Mecca, perhaps signaling the greater independence of his religion from its Jewish and Christian heritage.

Mecca and Medina fought many small skirmishes and three large pitched battles. The Muslims won the first, more or less lost the second, and won the third. They triumphed in the third, the Battle of the Trench, because Muhammad was open to borrowing Iranian military tactics, consisting of the digging of a protective trench that would trip up the Meccan cavalry. In 629 the Muslims took Mecca. Rather than the generalized massacre that might have been expected in a feuding, tribal society, Muhammad generously gave his conquered foes amnesty. He did insist, however, that the polytheistic cult they had practiced be given up and that the one God be recognized, as a prerequisite for their rehabilitation. This ruling out of pagan religion recalls the similar edicts promulgated by eastern Roman emperors such as Justinian (r. 527–65), who similarly outlawed paganism in Christendom.

Many clans that had bitterly opposed Islam now attained prominence and wealth in the new religion, somewhat to the dismay of the old-time Muslims and their helpers in Medina. Mecca emerged as the capital of a new sort of kingdom, in which Muhammad was both prophet and monarch. Islam spread throughout the Arabian peninsula, including to Yemen and over to the Persian Gulf. It is difficult to distinguish between the impulses of early Islam and the actions of the Arab tribes who had adopted it. The Koran is much like the Bible in the sense that it has war-like parts and other passages urging peace and conciliation. The major early wars fought by the Muslims were in a sense forced on them by the fierce hostility of the Meccans, who had tried to kill their Prophet and wipe them out. With regard to such bitter and determined foes that take to the battlefield against Muslims, the Koran urges, "Kill them wherever you find them" (4.89), a sentiment not different from many verses in the Book of Joshua and elsewhere in the Bible.

In contrast, the Prophet was willing to make a place for non-Muslim allies once he went to Medina, even though the alliance later fell apart. The Koran does not command Muslims to conquer other peoples or to fight wars of aggression. It says, "Fight against those who fight you, but do not commit aggression, for God does not love aggressors" (2.190). Indeed, it urges believers to negotiate peace offers in good faith: "If they withdraw, and do not fight you, and offer you peace, God offers you no avenue of attack against them" (4.90). This sort of counsel, however, made little sense to the lightly Islamized Arab tribes, who were used to raiding each other's livestock and feuding with one another as a way of life. The large numbers of tribesmen who had entered the religion determined subsequent policy more powerfully than did scripture verses.

Muhammad's Legacy

After Muhammad's death, the Muslim community split over who should succeed him. Some tribes in Medina wanted his vicar to be **Ali**, his young cousin and son-in-law. Since Muhammad did not have a son, Ali was the closest thing to one, and this faction appears to have favored descent as the criterion of leadership (as with monarchies). The majority of Muslims, especially the Meccans, in contrast wanted a respected elder of the Quraysh, Abu Bakr. These won out. After two years, during which he put down a rebellion of Arab tribes who briefly renounced Islam, Abu Bakr was succeeded by another Quraysh notable, Umar. He was followed by a very wealthy Meccan, Uthman. By this time, the Muslims who had early on supported Ali for the position were increasingly upset. Uthman was controversial for his further political and economic centralization of the empire. He made many enemies, especially in the southern Mesopotamian city of Kufa and in Egypt, among early Muslim conquerors who felt he was now robbing them of their hard-won wealth by his fiscal and tax policies. That his family, the Banu Umayya, had opposed Muhammad until they were conquered made him unpopular among the Medinans and their sympathizers. Uthman was finally assassinated.

Ali then became **caliph**, or successor to the Prophet, in 656, but only ruled for about five years before he, too, fell victim to an assassin. Several controversies led to this tragedy, including a clan feud between the Banu Umayya and Ali's supporters. One of Uthman's relatives, Mu`awiya, governed Syria, from which he challenged the new caliph. Ali was forced to move to Iraq to pick up support there. The Muslim Arabs of that region, however, were themselves divided between early Muslim soldiers of humble origins who had invaded and settled, and powerful tribal chieftains who reasserted themselves later on. When Ali agreed to the arbitration of his dispute with Mu`awiya, the pious settlers were dismayed. Some of them deserted Ali, insisting that he should have treated his authority as absolute and not agreed to mediation. These "secessionists" (**Kharijites**) for the first time started branding as infidels other Muslims whose practice was laxer than their own. The Kharijites established some small, militant, Bedouin communities in the Gulf from which they raided other Muslims. Their view remained a minority one in Islamic history, since most Muslims did not believe it was right to call other Muslims unbelievers, but extremists have had more influence than their numbers would predict. One of the Kharijites assassinated Ali. He and his three predecessors were canonized by later generations of the branch of Islam known as **Sunnis** ("followers of the tradition") as the "rightly guided" caliphs. In contrast, the partisans of Ali, later known as the **Shi`ites**, continued to feel that he should have been the leader or "Imam" all along, and that the position should have been passed to his lineal descendants, after the fashion of a monarchy.

What are the Essential Beliefs of Muslims?

Islam as a religion came to have five pillars or central practices, upon which all Muslims agree. These included first of all the declaration of faith, which consists of affirming that "There is no deity but God and Muhammad is his Prophet." Muslims were to pray five times a day, facing toward Mecca. They were to fast from food and water from sunrise to sunset one lunar month (Ramadan) every year. They were to donate money (zakat) to the poor. All able-bodied male Muslims were required to make a pilgrimage (hadj) to Mecca once in their lifetimes if they could afford to do so. Figure 7.1 shows an entrance portal to Mecca. Many tribal peoples in the first decades of the religion probably contented themselves with the first pillar, the declaration of faith. But gradually these five practices helped create a Muslim piety that was shared across the breadth of the old southern Roman empire and the Sasanian dominions, which had fallen to the Muslims. In addition, Muslims naturally wanted to be able to

Figure 7.1 Caravan of Muslim pilgrims to Mecca in Ramleh, c. 1237. Ramleh is today in central Israel. Pilgrimage was an important institution that brought together believers from all over the Muslim world and beyond. Pilgrims and merchants often traveled together for protection and in turn became acquainted and shared the news and rumors with their traveling fellows. From a manuscript of Maqamat of al-Hariri by Al-Wasiti, Yahya ibn Mahmud (active early thirteenth century).

recite the Koran (it was a largely oral culture) in Arabic. Because of the many dialects of Arabic, and the dangers posed by the practice of some early Arab converts translating the words into their dialect, the Caliph Uthman issued a standard edition of the Koran that was made the only acceptable text. The new Muslim state began constructing mosques where Muslims gathered for communal prayer, especially on Friday afternoon.

Why did Islam as a Religion Spread?

This process is now difficult to reconstruct, but some factors seem clear. It should be remembered that the Koran is an appealing and powerful text, which has touched the hearts of literally billions of human beings over the centuries with its lyrical praise of the one God, its celebration of human solidarity, its appeals for the poor, the orphan, and the widow, and its often striking retelling of the stories of the Bible (it devotes more space to Mary the mother of Jesus than do the Gospels). As the religion of a ruling elite that presided over a vast realm, it appealed even to those superficial status-seekers who would have otherwise remained immune to the charms of its spirituality. Muslims took over from the Sasanian empire the practice of taxing non-Muslims at a higher rate than they did Muslims (though they in return exempted non-Muslims from military service). Some of the wealthy traders in Damascus or Qom sought to become Muslims in order to escape this extra tax. Far from demanding such conversions, Muslim officials often refused to recognize them or insisted that the extra poll tax be paid anyway.

Muslim civilization was unusual in granting relative tolerance (though not equality) to Jews, Christians, and other religions considered sufficiently monotheistic. In contrast, medieval Christian leaders most often declined to tolerate other religions, and at some points even refused to allow Jews, much less Muslims, to live in much of Europe. Of course, in some times and places episodes of persecution of non-Muslims or of particular Muslim sects broke out under Muslim rule. But the Muslim record of religious tolerance is certainly superior from a modern point of view to that of medieval Christianity.

The older societies produced their own discontents that converts wished to redress. Zoroastrian Iran, for instance, and the Hindu areas of Afghanistan and the Indus Valley were caste societies. Those born into lower castes found it difficult, though not impossible, to move up in status. In contrast, Islam was an egalitarian religion if one could get into it, with ample opportunity for upward mobility. Likewise, some Christians were tired of the theological wrangling over Jesus' nature or over the Trinity, and the simplicity of Islam's monotheism may have appealed to them as an escape from such tired controversies. Those disagreements had after all produced much persecution and social turmoil in Christendom.

The spread of Arabic as a language may also have helped conversion. The Aramaic spoken in much of the Fertile Crescent was near enough to Arabic to allow local populations fairly quickly to learn the new imperial tongue for the purposes of communication with the rulers and soldiers. The history of the adoption of Arabic throughout the Near East and North Africa is now difficult to reconstruct, and it was certainly gradual. Not only did knowing Arabic perhaps make it easier to appreciate the Koran and to convert to Islam, but also converts to Islam had a strong motivation to learn Arabic. Out of an Aramaic- and Coptic-speaking population, over the next centuries Islam and Arabic helped create a new ethnicity, the Muslim Arab who was not from the Arabian peninsula. The populations of Iran and points east never adopted Arabic as their daily language. This may have in part been because they spoke Indo-European languages that are distant in grammar and vocabulary from Semitic languages like Arabic. They mixed Arabic words into their languages as they converted to Islam, but retained distinctive linguistic identities.

7.5 HOW DID THE ARABS CONQUER THE CIVILIZED WORLD?

Despite the jockeying for position and feuding in the center, the Muslim community achieved incredible triumphs between the death of the Prophet in 632 and the assassination of Ali in 661. Arab Muslim tribesmen raiding up into Syria discovered that the Byzantines, who had regained the area after a hard-fought war with Iran, were still militarily weak in this region. They raided further north, taking Damascus in 635, and the following year defeated the forces of the Byzantine Emperor Heraclius (r. 610–41) when he tried to counterattack. For the old, established eastern Roman empire, which was steeped in the traditions of Augustus Caesar and Constantine, this defeat at the hands of an upstart band of Arab tribesmen was bewildering. In 638 the Muslims entered Jerusalem, where they later built the important

shrine-mosque, the Dome of the Rock, atop the Temple Mount where the Jewish temple once stood. Although Jerusalem had ceased being the point toward which Muslims prayed even in the lifetime of the Prophet, it remained one of the three holiest cities for them. European Christians had difficulty accepting the loss of Jerusalem to the Muslims, whom they viewed as heretics. The Muslims then headed west to Egypt across the Sinai peninsula in 639, with a small force of 4,000 men, where they – amazingly enough – again defeated the Byzantine garrisons. Muslims repulsed a Byzantine naval attack on newly Muslim-ruled Egypt in 645. The low esteem in which Byzantium was by that time held by the Coptic Christians undoubtedly made the Muslims' conquest easier than it would have otherwise been. The Byzantines had also been exhausted by their decades of war with Sasanian Iran, which had after all dislodged them briefly from the Middle East.

Meanwhile, other Muslim tribesmen, foraging in the east in what is now Iraq, initially met a serious defeat in 634 at the hands of Iranian forces. The Muslims regrouped and mounted a concerted attack with several thousand troops in 637. This time they succeeded in scattering the Iranian armies at Qadisiyya and then taking Mesopotamia (what is now Iraq). The Sasanian king had his court at Ctesiphon, and had to flee back to Iran as it fell to the Arabs. They, however, then invaded Iran, and tracked down and killed the Iranian monarch in 651. The Arab Muslims went as far as Afghanistan, but in the first decades had difficulty firmly establishing their rule so far east, in a largely Buddhist and Hindu area. In a short period of time the Muslims conquered a large portion of the civilized world (see Map 7.4).

The vast scale of the Muslim conquests remains something of a mystery. They do not appear to have possessed any military technology superior to that of their imperial foes. Their own equipment and weaponry, including armor, mail, horse armor, straight Indian swords, iron-tipped spears, and an archer infantry, appear to have been state of the art for the period. In the 600s they probably adopted cord and wooden stirrups, which made them somewhat better able to fight from horseback than previously.

The Muslim Arab armies had several advantages. As pastoral nomads their troops were used to using what we would now call guerrilla tactics, including surprise lightning-fast assaults and nimble retreats. This unusual mobility allows pastoral nomads to throw up large empires quickly. Since their new religious ideology, Islam, was universalistic, they were open to welcoming into their ranks defecting troops or other local allies when it seemed advantageous. As pastoral nomads who tended to settle in separate garrisons, they were spared the disease pandemics that weakened the towns and cities of their enemies. Although they only appear to have used camels as pack animals, these

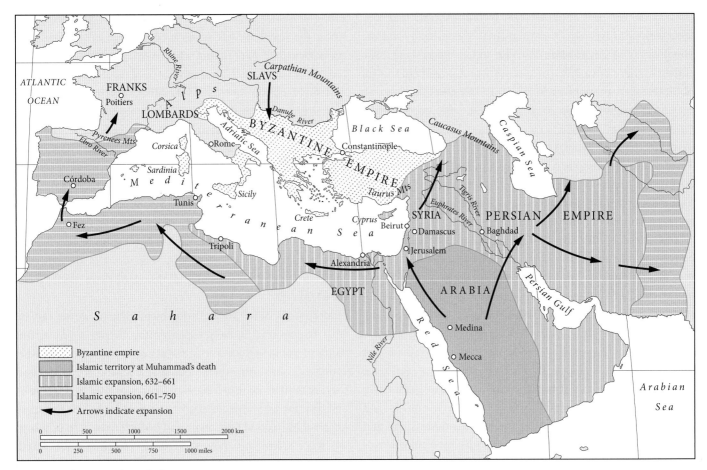

Map 7.4 The expansion of Islam

beasts may have given them a logistical advantage. Logistics involves the delivery of weaponry, food, and equipment to a battlefield army. Camels were ideal for moving such key supplies across deserts, in such a way that the Byzantines and Iranians could not easily cut them off or capture them.

The Arab Bedouin were aided in this empire-building by their recent adoption of Islam. The new religion gave them a sense of cohesion across tribes, prescribed personal status law, and threw up in the person of the caliph a central leader to whom most looked for guidance. The early caliphs had both a worldly and a religious role, and were respected in both spheres by the Muslims.

7.6 UMAYYADS

After Ali's death, Mu`awiya succeeded in becoming caliph in his capital of Damascus. He founded an empire that lasted almost a century and united a colorful assemblage of peoples from southern France to the borders of China. This new empire was dotted with important cities that served as trade entrepôts, and it connected by land the realms of Europe, Africa, India, and China. That is, the major overland trade networks linking the various civilizations of Eurasia and Africa now flowed through the Arab kingdom. Silk came from China into Muslim-dominated Central Asia along the Silk Road, and was then exported to Europe. Precious metals also circulated through Muslim lands from one region of the world to another. Crops from one region were adopted by others, and technological innovations spread. Thus, the Muslims were quick to adopt the Sanskrit number system, which is much more convenient than Roman numerals. The Europeans in turn adopted these notations from the Arabs, calling them "Arabic numerals."

Unlike his immediate predecessors, Mu`awiya was not chosen by a council of Quraysh elders, but rather emerged because of his political and military abilities. He paid Ali's son Hasan a stipend to renounce the caliphate for himself, and then passed the position to his own descendants. His dynasty was known as the **Umayyads**. Later Sunni Muslims made a distinction between the first four "rightly guided" caliphs, whom they saw as holy figures, and the rulers of the Umayyad dynasty, whom they viewed as more worldly, as little more than Arab kings. At the time, however, some early Muslims invested the Umayyad caliphs with a definite religious aura. Others criticized them either for neglecting to seek consultation with the elders of Quraysh in Mecca or for pushing aside the relatives of the Prophet Muhammad. Most Umayyad rulers were not particularly pious, as attested by the pleasure palaces they built in the desert, which survive and were decorated with nudes.

The population of the enormous Umayyad empire, which ruled much of the world from Damascus, may be divided into four basic groups. The first was the Muslim Arab soldiers who spread out into garrisons in the new territories, settling in barracks towns such as Kufa in southern Iraq, Fustat in the center of Egypt, and Merv in Central Eurasia. They and their descendants were paid stipends from the central treasury for their service according to an official register. They tended to put themselves forward as especially pious and puritan Muslims, and to be scornful of the hypocrisy of practical rulers like the Umayyads and their provincial governors.

The second was Arab tribal chieftains who already had a presence in the conquered areas before Islam (such as in southern Iraq), and on whom the new state depended for support. The Umayyads relied especially heavily on the Arab tribes of Syria, who proved a formidable military force. The tribes increasingly divided into two artificial factions, the northerners and southerners, referring to their supposed origins rather than their geographic location. The feud between the two began in Syria and gradually afflicted the rest of the empire. The tribal chieftains were often at odds with the pious soldier-settlers.

The third was the conquered population, comprising the vast majority of inhabitants. Mostly city- and town-dwellers and peasant farmers, they belonged to many different religious and linguistic ethnic groups. They included Greek-speaking Christians in Damascus, Christian Palestinian peasants in Palestine who spoke Aramaic, and Jewish townspeople in Iraq with their great rabbinical scholars. They included Persian-speaking Zoroastrians on the Iranian plateau and Buddhists in Afghanistan, Sindh, and Central Eurasia. They included Coptic Christians in Egypt, Nubians in Upper Egypt, and Berber tribespeople in North Africa. Although the Umayyads were an Islamic empire with regard to the upper echelons of state officials, they depended on the conquered populations for much local administration and for key sorts of knowledge. For instance, Hindu rajas at odds with the Buddhists who dominated Sindh appear to have made an alliance with the invading Arabs in the early 700s, helping them establish Umayyad rule there. The early Islamic empires were multicultural and many non-Muslims contributed to their civilizational success.

The fourth group was the converts to Islam. Islam was not initially a missionary religion. It was, rather, an exclusive club, open only to those considered highly desirable. To be an Arab Muslim in Iraq or Egypt was to be relatively rich and powerful, and few wished to dilute their status by admitting converts. Nor did governors wish to lose the tax revenue they received from extra taxes on non-Muslims. Although the early Muslim state was spread by the sword, Islam as a religion most definitely was not. The Iraqi Christian who wished to convert to Islam in the first decades had to first become a client or honorary member of an Arab tribe. Converts resented that they were not viewed as equals in the faith by their Arab rulers, and often the pious Arab soldier-settlers agreed with their grievances, especially where the two came to mix. Over time, substantial numbers of converts began to come into the religion, and it became a universal faith. But this process largely proceeded through the demand of the masses to be admitted to the club rather than an imposition of the religion on unwilling populations.

The Techniques of Umayyad Rule

The techniques of rule in the Umayyad empire changed dramatically in the late 600s. Initially the king in Damascus appointed Arab governors from "noble" tribes over whom he exercised relatively little oversight. These governors depended heavily not only on the Arab tribal chieftains but also on local notables and scribal bureaucrats from the previous empires. Records continued to be kept in Greek in Egypt until around 700. This loose structure proved inadequate to deal with various crises the new kingdom faced. The Umayyads faced three serious uprisings in the late 600s.

The soldiers of Islam, the conquering troops who invaded Iraq and had settled in Kufa in southern Iraq, grew increasingly unhappy with Umayyad policies. They resented having to pay land taxes to the central government, which it increasingly demanded, and they were bitter about the favoritism they felt Damascus showed to the tribal chieftains. They began favoring a descendant of Ali, the Prophet's son-in-law, for the caliphate. In 680 Ali's son Husayn was convinced to set out for Kufa from Mecca with a small party of relatives and supporters, in hopes of leading an uprising. The Umayyad governor cut him off and encircled his party, however, before he could head south. They killed him and his family and supporters and are said to have taken his head to Damascus. Many pious Muslims were outraged by this brutal treatment of a grandson of the Prophet. Some Muslims increasingly looked to Husayn's surviving son and his descendants as spiritual guides. A custom eventually grew of up annually mourning the martyrdom of Husayn. Eventually, these sectarians became known as the Shi`ites. Another, later, Kufa-backed revolt had messianic overtones. It was defeated, but the idea that a savior or **Mahdi** would arise from the family of the Prophet who would restore the world to justice became widespread in Muslim popular culture.

Another revolt centered on Mecca and was only put down after the Umayyad generals besieged and bombarded the Muslim holy city, provoking further criticism of their lack of piety. After this battle, called a civil war by most historians, a more centralized style of rule was imposed. Arabic was increasingly used for scribal record-keeping. Direct rule by appointed government officials was preferred over the previous dependence on tribal chieftains and local notables. Umayyad coins with Arabic inscriptions were issued. A postal system like the pony express, which had earlier been used in the area by the Achaemenids, was set up for swift communication with the provinces of the far-flung empire. The couriers doubled as spies for the court.

Why did the Umayyad Empire Collapse?

The Umayyad empire probably grew beyond the ability of Damascus to control it politically. Continual Umayyad attempts to defeat the Byzantines and take Constantinople by land or by sea were defeated, though sometimes only barely. The idea of holy war or **jihad** as formulated in later Islamic history may have been born on the Umayyad–Byzantine frontier. In the West, in 732 Arab Muslim tribesmen wandering up into France were stopped by Charles Martel at Tours. This was more a chance encounter than an epic battle, and Arabs continued to hold territory in southern France. They had come up from Spain, which they invaded from Morocco in 711. Still, Spain was,

practically speaking, the furthest the Arabs could hope to go and administer territory effectively in the west. In the east, the Umayyads took Sindh in North India in 711–13, but could only lightly rule it in alliance with local non-Muslim elites. In Central Eurasia, the Umayyads defeated Turkic tribespeople who had invaded these areas, sometimes with Chinese backing. Despite their victory over a Chinese army at Talas in 751, however, the Arab Muslims were not able to extend their rule toward China. Map 7.5 shows the breadth of early Muslim conquest.

By the 740s the over-extended empire faced several severe rebellions, including that of the Berbers in North Africa and revolts in Syria and northern Iraq. The most serious and ultimately fatal challenge to Damascus, however, came from the area called Khurasan, stretching from what is now eastern Iran into Central Eurasia. This area had among the heaviest Arab settlements on the Iranian plateau, and also was the site of extensive early conversion to Islam among the local population of Zoroastrians and Buddhists. Those of Arab descent and the converts appear to have mixed unusually freely on this agriculturally rich eastern frontier, such that they were sympathetic to each other's grievances. A movement began in Khurasan that aimed at replacing the Umayyad kingdom with a pious Muslim caliphate headed by a relative of the Prophet. A true popular social movement, it was led by Arabs, but gained substantial support also from converts. Supporters argued that all Muslims, Arab or not, should be equal. The rebels raised a black flag and

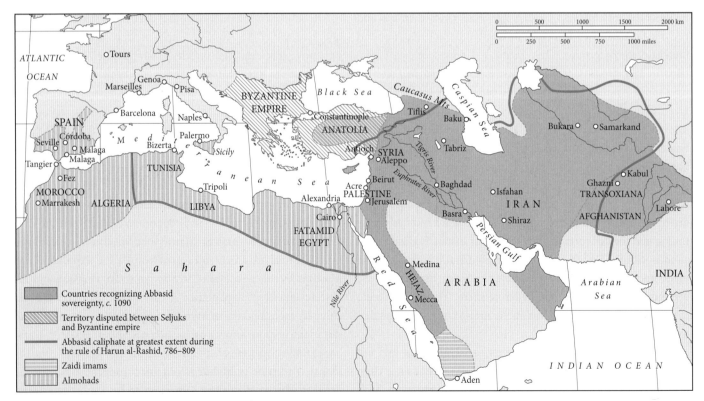

Map 7.5 The Abbasid caliphate at the height of its power

swept west, defeating the formerly invincible Syrian armies and overthrowing the Umayyads between 749 and 750. They gained the support of the Shi`ites who favored a descendant of Ali, but in fact the new dynasty that became caliphs claimed descent from an uncle of the Prophet Muhammad, Abbas.

7.7 ABBASIDS

Rulers of a vast new realm, the **Abbasid** dynasty built its own capital, Baghdad, in Iraq beginning in 762 (see Map 7.5). Since its support had mainly come from Iran, the caliphs often drew on that population for high officials and scribes. In a sense, the Abbasid empire became a successor to the Sasanians, being heavily influenced by Iranian traditions of bureaucratic administration. It lost Spain, as a branch of the Umayyads established itself there, and was weak in North Africa, which it eventually lost. The formerly unified Muslim realm broke up now into a number of small dynasties. The Abbasids were initially both temporal and spiritual rulers. As minor monarchs peeled off from the empire, they often denied the Abbasids any practical power in their realms but recognized them as spiritual leaders of Islam.

The Abbasids appointed family members and supporters from Khurasan to high government posts and as provincial governors. They attempted to centralize rule even more than had the later Umayyads, and to more systematically tax their provinces. The tightening of their grip, however, provoked many disputes and even revolts. Nevertheless, some periods of Abbasid rule were undeniably prosperous and glorious.

Harun al-Rashid

The Caliph Harun al-Rashid (r. 786–809) ruled a Baghdad that was among the more advanced and populous cities of the world in that era. His mother, originally a slave-girl from Yemen, had been freed by his father and enjoyed great influence at the Abbasid court. This woman, al-Khayzuran, also influenced her son's policies once he came to the throne. Harun al-Rashid fought bravely as a youth against the Byzantines, raiding as far west as the Bosporus. He served as governor of a number of provinces, including Egypt and Azerbaijan. He was disliked by his predecessor and almost renounced his claims to succeed. When the previous caliph died in a court plot, he found himself on the throne in his early twenties. He was an enthusiastic supporter of war against Byzantium, and sometimes forced the emperors to make embarrassing concessions. He also revived Muslim naval power in the eastern Mediterranean. He had a keen sense of curiosity and an interest in philosophy, and he

sponsored one of the most important translation movements of the medieval period. His translators rendered the major works of the Greeks into Arabic. Some minor treatises of Aristotle are preserved only in that language.

He employed powerful and able viziers of the Barmakid family, who had originally been Buddhist holy men in eastern Iran but had adopted Islam. These ministers, however, appear to have grown so powerful that they threatened the caliph, and eventually he deposed them. Thereafter he and his successors depended for administration on relatives or slaves who were completely dependent on the caliphs. Harun was strict with local Christians. He made those in Baghdad wear special clothing to distinguish themselves from Muslims, and destroyed some churches on the Byzantine frontier. He also kept the Shi`ites, who thought a descendant of Ali should rule instead, under strict surveillance. He lost direct control of North Africa and Egypt, though the Egyptian government of the Aghlabids, established in 800, did agree to pay him tribute as a vassal state. Charlemagne sent him two embassies with gifts, perhaps seeking privileges in Jerusalem, but these negotiations do not appear to have had any result. Harun al-Rashid became so celebrated in story and legend that he entered the Thousand and One Nights cycle (see Box 7.1) as a character. Some remembered him as pious and generous, others as a man who enjoyed fine wine and who lacked political wisdom. He decided, late in life, to divide his empire among his two sons, which provoked a long and destructive civil war after his death.

Abbasid Urban Life

The city from which Harun al-Rashid ruled, Baghdad, had been built on a site chosen carefully by the Abbasids (see Box 7.2). On the Tigris River, it was surrounded by a fertile plain, and was in the center of the caravan routes. It was in an area relatively free from mosquitoes and the diseases they carried. It and its hinterland were serviced by a network of canals for irrigation, which could also be used as moats to defend against cavalry charges. The city plan was round, so that each of the gates was the same distance from the center. A walled city, it had gates that could be locked. Each of the four gates faced a major road, and the city was at first divided into four quarters, each of which could be locked off from the others. The city quarters and their alleyways specialized in particular crafts and housed particular ethnic groups, and each had its own markets, in which the goods of the entire world were traded. City neighborhoods grew up around the mansions of great nobles, where craftsmen serviced them and their retinues. The soldiers were garrisoned outside the walls. It was replete with domed, marble palaces, and with mosques and beautiful gardens. A queen named Zubayda alone

Box 7.1 The Thousand and One Nights

The mixing of cultures and stories in the cosmopolitan Abbasid empire is witnessed by the story cycle of the Thousand and One Nights, which began orally. One of the first written versions was an Arabic translation of Hizar Afsanih (A Thousand Fables), done around 850 CE.

The frame story has to do with a cruel Sasanid king, Shahriyar, who kills his wife for committing adultery and then begins a rampage of executing virgins, whom he would marry for a day before dispatching them. The daughter of his first minister or vizier, Shahrizad (Scheherezade), volunteers to marry him and then entertain and divert him by regaling him with tales. She outwits him by telling him the first part of a story each day, with a cliff-hanger, which she refuses to finish until the following day, for 1,001 nights. In the end he gives up his bitterness and lets her live.

Many of the stories are clearly Indian or Iranian, or Iranian reworkings of Indian material, which then were put into Arabic. Much of the material was worked up in Baghdad, but several cities, including Cairo, provided stories as time went on. A book by the title of *A Thousand Nights* is mentioned by the traveler and historian Abu al-Husayn al-Mas`udi (d. 957 CE), who wrote: "The case with [these legendary stories] is similar to that of the books that have come to us from the Persian, Indian and the Greek and have been translated for us, and that originated in the way that we have described, such as for example the book *Hizar Afsanih*, which in Arabic means 'thousand tales' ... The people call this book 'Thousand Nights.' This is the story of the king and the vizier and his daughter and her servant-girl; these two are called Shirazad and Dinazad."

The stories, coming out of the folk process, are often bawdy or naughty, and have sometimes shocked later audiences or been censored. Even after the corpus was given a more extended written form, around 1000 CE, it continued to be performed by storytellers and to evolve at their hands. Typically in surviving manuscripts there is a Baghdad part and an Egyptian part. Some stories now associated with the book in the West were originally distinct. For instance, the tales of Sindbad the sailor formed a separate story cycle, but were added by the French translator to the first Western translation of A Thousand and One Nights. Likewise, the famous stories of Ali Baba and the forty thieves and Aladdin and the lamp do not appear in the older manuscripts but were included by Antoine Galland in his French translation from Syrian manuscripts.

Galland published the first Western translation in twelve volumes in 1704–12, which became a sensation. Sir Richard Burton's uncensored Victorian-era translation entertained and titillated nineteenth-century readers. The tales have exercised an enormous influence on modern literature both in the Middle East and in the West, attesting the continued impact of the cultural achievements of Abbasid Baghdad.

---

built two mosques and a palace. Its population is said to have grown to several hundred thousand, making it one of the great metropolises of the medieval world (at that time Paris and London were in comparison merely small towns).

Abbasid cities were fed by irrigation-based agriculture supported by extensive canal-building. Irrigation works are key to farming in the arid Middle East, but require substantial investments by the state in upkeep. Trade routes bulging with fine goods crisscrossed the realm, with heavier bulk goods shipped by sea and river. Gold and slaves came from Africa, silk from China, spices, perfumes, medicines, textiles, and steel from India, and arms, tin, wood, and slaves from Europe. The new gold and silver resources of the Muslim realms, traded to neighbors like Europe, helped to put money back into circulation and may have helped Europe begin recovering from a deflated and bullion-starved economy. Likewise, André Wink has argued that the coastal trade of India, mainly in the hands of Buddhist merchants, was reinvigorated by the bullion and other goods that came in from Islam. He has also argued that far from being in a Dark Age, India's Hindu rajas in the 700s through 800s benefited from renewed trade and access to gold and silver. He has suggested that both early medieval Europe and India were economically invigorated by the impact of Muslim trade.

Why was Social Conflict Endemic in the Abbasid Realm?

Despite the economic, cultural, and urban flowering of the period, social conflict was endemic to the Abbasid realm. Some conflict came because of rivalries among candidates for the throne. Harun al-Rashid's decision to apportion his realm between his two sons provoked a prolonged and bloody civil war from 809 to 833, resulting at last in a restoration of most of the eastern portion of the empire to unified rule. This period of severe military conflict badly damaged Baghdad. Social struggles also underlay a great many of the rebellions of the 800s. As usual after a conquest, there were lingering resentments. Local Iraqi elites resented the tax and other benefits enjoyed by the Khurasani troops who settled near the new capital. The supporters

Box 7.2 Geographical Encyclopedia

The city of Baghdad formed two vast semi-circles on the right and left banks of the Tigris, 12 miles in diameter. The numerous suburbs, covered with parks, gardens, villas, and beautiful promenades, and plentifully supplied with rich bazaars and finely built mosques and baths, stretched for a considerable distance on both sides of the river. In the days of its prosperity the population of Baghdad and its suburbs amounted to over 2 million! The palace of the caliph stood in the midst of a vast park several hours in circumference which, besides a menagerie and aviary, comprised an enclosure for wild animals reserved for the chase. The palace grounds were laid out with gardens, and adorned with exquisite taste with plants, flowers and trees, reservoirs and fountains, surrounded by sculpted figures. On this side of the river stood the palaces of the great nobles. Immense streets, none less than forty cubits wide, traversed the city from one end to the other, dividing it into blocks or quarters, each under the control of an overseer or supervisor, who looked after the cleanliness, sanitation, and comfort of the inhabitants.

The water exits both on the north and the south were like the city gates, guarded night and day by relays of soldiers stationed on the watch towers on both sides of the river. Every household was plentifully supplied with water at all seasons by the numerous aqueducts which intersected the town; and the streets, gardens, and parks were regularly swept and watered, and no refuse was allowed to remain within the walls. An immense square in front of the imperial palace was used for reviews, military inspections, tournaments, and races; at night the square and the streets were lit by lamps.

There was also a vast open space where the troops whose barracks lay on the left bank of the river were paraded daily. The long wide esplanades at the different gates of the city were used by the citizens for gossip and recreation or for watching the flow of travelers and country folk into the capital. The different nationalities in the capital had each a head officer to represent their interests with the government, and to whom the stranger could appeal for counsel or help.

Baghdad was a veritable City of Palaces, not made of stucco and mortar, but of marble. The buildings were usually of several stories. The palaces and mansions were lavishly gilded and decorated, and hung with beautiful tapestry and hangings of brocade or silk. The rooms were lightly and tastefully furnished with luxurious divans, costly tables, unique Chinese vases, and gold and silver ornaments.

Both sides of the river were for miles fronted by the palaces, kiosks, gardens, and parks of the grandees and nobles, marble steps led down to the water's edge, and the scene on the river was animated by thousands of gondolas, decked with little flags, dancing like sunbeams on the water, and carrying the pleasure-seeking Baghdad citizens from one part of the city to the other. Along the wide-stretching quays lay whole fleets at anchor, sea and river craft of all kinds, from the Chinese junk to the old Assyrian raft resting on inflated skins.

The mosques of the city were at once vast in size and remarkably beautiful. There were also in Baghdad numerous colleges of learning, hospitals, infirmaries for both sexes, and lunatic asylums.

---

who had put the Abbasids on their throne, in contrast, often felt aggrieved and inadequately rewarded for their sacrifices and loyalty.

Ethnic and social grievances became more complex than just conflicts between Persian-speakers and Arabic-speakers, or between the northern and southern coalitions of Arab tribes. Turkic peoples began moving west even before the Abbasid period, from grazing grounds near Mongolia in East Asia, across Central Eurasia, and into the Middle East. The Sasanids had begun the practice of employing them as troops. Turks had been shamanists or Buddhists originally, but gradually adopted Islam once it arose as the major force in the west. This Turkic migration gradually made available to the Abbasid state a new pool of soldiers, typically taken as slaves and sworn to loyalty to the caliphs. The distinctive Middle Eastern practice of employing slave-soldiers was intended to ensure the loyalty of the military

to the ruler, because slaves were cut off from their previous relatives and friends. Some historians define slavery as a form of "social death" because of this isolation from the social networks of their birth. By the 830s, there were 60,000 Turkish slave-soldiers in the Abbasid army. For a while, the caliphs moved their capital to the nearby city of Samarra in order to garrison the rowdy Turkish troops there. In 861–70, faction-fighting among the Turkish commanders produced chaos, as caliphs succeeded for short terms one after another, several of them assassinated.

Slaves were important to the Abbasid economy for economic as well as military reasons. By 850, it is estimated, 10,000 African slaves were sent by Arab traders every year across the Arabian Sea and Indian Ocean to West and South Asia. Many served as household slaves, but others worked in agriculture. A substantial population of African slave workers was settled in southern Iraq, known as the Zanj. They were tasked with draining the marshes east of the city of Basra. In 869 through 883 they staged a major slave revolt, harrying the caliph's forces and even taking the nearby Iranian city of Ahvaz, before the rebellion was finally put down. Slaves or their descendants could convert to Islam and at that point would most often be freed, and such freedmen had full rights under Islamic law and could freely intermarry with other Muslims. They therefore did not come to constitute a separate "race" in Muslim society, but rather tended to meld into Arab populations over time. Moreover, slavery was not associated with only one geographic origin, since fair-skinned slaves were taken from the Caucasus or Central Asia. Although in strict Islamic law it was forbidden for a Muslim to make a slave of another Muslim, in actual fact Muslim Arabs were sometimes enslaved as well.

Intellectual and Cultural Foundations

During the Abbasid period, many of the foundations of the Muslim intellectual and cultural tradition were laid down. The rate of conversion appears to have increased, so that some estimate that by 900 about 40 percent of Iranians were Muslim. Jewish converts to Islam in Iraq brought with them many ideas about religious law that became widely influential. Zoroastrian converts from Iran's scribal caste brought in new ideas about administration. From the time of Harun al-Rashid forward, many works of Greek and Hellenistic philosophy, medicine, and social thought were translated into Arabic, enabling the growth of a stratum of Muslim philosophers and physicians who made their own contributions to this tradition. Some two centuries after their ancestors had been conducting raids on one another's livestock in the desert, the descendants of pagan Arab tribesmen were debating the merits of Plato and Aristotle in the round metropolis of Baghdad. They produced historians who attempted to chronicle the history of the entire world, geographers who described places as far afield as Sri Lanka, and mathematicians who invented algebra and decimal places. The Thousand and One Nights cycle shows the sophisticated and frequently bawdy urban culture that developed among elites in this opulent and highly literate world.

Specifically Muslim sciences grew up. These included the study of the Koran and its history and variants. It also included the collection and study of **hadith**, or anecdotes about the sayings and doings of the Prophet Muhammad and his companions that were passed down orally. Contemporary academic historians consider these stories unreliable in the main, since many were collected two centuries after the Prophet's death and probably represented the workings of the folk process (whereby people elaborate and change narratives over time). They nevertheless became an important part of Islamic law and practice, and some Muslims began devoting themselves to their study in their spare time. There was little in the way of a professional clerical class in early Islam, and most such specialists were what we would now think of as hobbyists. Another Muslim science was the principles of jurisprudence. It asked the question of how you got from the abstract laws and principles in the Koran and hadith to a specific ruling in a specific case.

Four major schools of Islamic jurisprudence grew up in the majority Sunni tradition, the Shafi`i, Maliki, Hanafi and **Hanbali**. The Shafi`i was the most intellectual and broad-minded, and the Hanbali the most strict and literal. In medieval Islam sometimes adherents of one of these schools would clash with the others, causing rioting that disrupted whole cities. Muslims also developed an approach to theology. Again, disputes arose between the more literalist Hanbalis and the rationalists. The major rationalist school, which was influenced by Greek philosophy, was the **Mu`tazilites**. The Mu`tazilites believed that reason could tell human beings what was good and bad, that God had to be just, and that the Koran was a created text. Their opponents held that God was unconstrained and could act as he pleased, that human reason was inadequate to understanding why he considered some things bad and others good, and that the Koran had always existed. For a time at the Abbasid court the rationalist Mu`tazilites became extremely influential and even persecuted their literalist foes. In the long term, however, their sort of theological rationalism came to be a minority taste among Sunnis.

Shi`ites and Sunnis

It was in the Abbasid period, as well, that a strong sectarian division grew up between Shi`ites and Sunnis. Shi`ites developed an increasingly exclusive allegiance to leaders descended from the Prophet in spiritual matters, and many continued to hope that these could come to power as temporal rulers as well. (The Abbasids only claimed descent from the Prophet's uncle.) Imam Husayn's great-great grandson, Ali Rida, was almost put on the throne by a sympathetic Abbasid ruler, but that plan went awry. For the most part, the Shi`ite Imams were kept under strict surveillance or even house arrest. Their followers increasingly saw them as possessing divine, secret knowledge.

The rapid rise of the Muslim Arab empire is among the more remarkable events in world history. While nomadic conquest states, erected speedily, are not unusual, for them to survive very long is. The Muslim empire not only survived, but it created a new culture, with a distinctive set of languages and ideas, that deeply informed the development of Islam as a world religion. In contrast, most nomadic conquerors adopt the language and administration of the states they conquer. Rome fell to the Germans but did not come to speak German or worship Teutonic gods. Achaemenid Iran had fallen to Alexander but Iranians did not adopt Greek as their mother tongue or give up Zoroaster for Zeus.

The Muslim empire flourished by carefully balancing the development of a distinctive cultural identity with the incorporation of knowledge and techniques from the older civilizations over which it ruled. Greek philosophy and mathematics, Iranian medicine, and Indian astronomy all had a great impact in Baghdad. Yet so did the study of the Koran and Arabic literature.

7.8 EUROPE UNDER ASSAULT

As we have seen, partly as a result of the climate change discussed above, the years between 600 and 900 CE were a period of great upheaval throughout Eurasia. Nomadic peoples and tribal confederations brought long-established empires crashing to the ground. Nowhere were nomads and tribal invaders more successful than in Europe, where their invasions commenced a sustained period of warfare and civil violence. In the ninth-century Balkans, Khan Krum of the Bulgarians (r. *c*. 803–14) drank from a goblet made from the head of the Byzantine emperor he had defeated, and in tenth century Scandinavia a leading political figure and Norwegian king was named "Eirik Bloodax (*c*. 885–954)." Such men found it easier to conquer than to rule and their attempts to govern opened the way to recurrent civil wars, in turn encouraging further attacks from outside by new tribal or nomadic groups.

As violent conflict spread, trade diminished, urban commercial centers declined, and the weakened remnants of Roman administrative structures faded away. For a time efforts were made to preserve the rule of law by using Germanic law for Germans and Roman law for Romans. Box 7.3 shows an example of the heroic effort to integrate two codes of law which basically had very different conceptions of right and justice. The Frankish "Salic Code" was the law of the majority of the Franks. It applied only to people with families and it denied to women the right to inherit land. The waning of the commercial economy made it difficult to collect monetary taxes or to pay wages for services. The scarcity of silver and gold currency in turn forced political leaders to look for new methods to attach followers to their standards and for new ways to extract resources. The decentralized character of the resulting new institutions allowed more leeway for violence and local conflict than the preceding Roman administration.

During the period when Charles the Great had restored a semblance of unity, the emerging city of Venice began to link Northern Europe to the Near East, a linkage that persisted even after the breakup of Charles's empire. And even as old taxation systems collapsed, as methods of working the land changed, and as population fled the cities, the European population began to increase demographically. During this period, peasants began the long task of cultivating abandoned land and reclaiming land lost to forest. This slow but sustained population growth after 600 was the underpinning of European future development.

Box 7.3 The Law of the Salian Franks

This law was composed about 500 CE and illustrates the Germanic law codes that spread throughout Northern Europe with the German invasions. The fines mentioned, called wergeld, were to be paid by the offender or his family to the victim or his family. The amount and nature of the penalties provides insight into the values of Germanic societies.

If any free man steal, outside the house, something worth 2 denars, he shall be sentenced to 600 denars, which makes 15 shillings.

If any slave steal, outside the house, something worth 2 denars, he shall, besides paying the worth of the object and the fines for delay, be stretched out and receive 120 blows.

If any one shall have assaulted and plundered a free man and it be proved against him, he shall be sentenced to 2,500 denars, which makes 63 shillings.

If a Roman has plundered a Salian Frank, the above law shall be observed.

But if a Frank have plundered a Roman, he shall be sentenced to 35 shillings.

[For a fist blow] so that the blood does not flow, for each blow up to three blows [penalty 3 shillings].

If any one shall have called a woman a "wanton" and shall not be able to prove it, he shall be sentenced to 1,800 denars, or 45 shillings.

For calling another "fox" [penalty 3 shillings].

For calling another "hare" [penalty 3 shillings].

If any man shall have charged another with having thrown away his shield, and shall not be able to prove it, he shall be sentenced to 120 denars or 3 shillings.

The years between 600 and 900 also mark the beginning of a sense of Europe as a shared cultural and political destiny. Interior continental forces exerted an increasing pull over the old Mediterranean world as Italians waited upon the words of German emperors and Libyans and Syrians were ruled from Baghdad. Large areas of continental Europe, including Germany, Poland, Hungary, and western Russia, which had been ruled by tribal chieftains were being organized into states, while tribal and clan leaders were turning themselves into hereditary monarchs. Central and Eastern European lands were converted to Christianity and began to play a leading role in European affairs. Increasingly relations between the eastern empire and Western Europe began to diverge as both Catholic and Orthodox Christianity took on distinctive forms.

A look at the most important European regions shows the progress of political decentralization, market contraction, and the expansion of the countryside at the expense of cities. Although they did not operate with the same strength in every region, important trends can be seen working throughout Europe, operating with particular strength in Northern and Eastern Europe but also at work in Southern Europe and the eastern Roman empire. To summarize:

- Money revenues from taxation declined or disappeared and in their stead states were financed by income from royal estates and war booty.
- Centralized government by civilian bureaucrats was replaced by decentralized government by religious and military leaders.
- Written law enforced by state authorities gave way to or was challenged by customary law enforced by kinsmen; immunities from state power were formally conceded to powerful figures.
- Old markets shrank and, for most of the period, currency became scarce or disappeared – military services formerly paid for by money or in kind were secured by giving control over land and its cultivators. Markets for commodities, for wage laborers, and for slaves diminished, to be replaced by personal bonds and new forms of unfree labor.
- The population of cities generally declined and in many areas their number also diminished.
- Urban cultural lifestyles embodied in a lay elite of senators, government administrators, and city councilors were replaced by monasteries and great landlord-warriors.
- Under the empire of Charles the Great, European traders, led by the Venetians, began slowly to reach out again to the Mediterranean but in a new fashion. Instead of mediating ties through Byzantium, European traders established direct links with the Islamic Near East, selling slaves and raw materials for the silks and spices on offer in the Islamic east.

7.9 THE EASTERN ROMAN EMPIRE

Despite the ferocity of the tribal and nomad attacks, not all established empires collapsed. While the western Roman empire ended in 476 CE, the eastern Roman empire fended off Germans and Slavs to its north and west and Arabs and Turks to its south and east and survived another thousand years. The eastern Roman empire saw itself as the legitimate inheritor of the western Roman empire and several times launched massive invasions of western lands to enforce its claims. The most notable effort at reconquest came just prior to the opening of our period. In 534 the eastern Emperor Justinian I (485–565) sent his great general Belisarius on a successful effort to reconquer the Vandal kingdom of North Africa and then in 535 made an effort to restore imperial authority in Italy.

Threats to the Eastern Roman Empire

Justinian's efforts to dramatically expand his power disturbed the old Persian enemy and the ensuing conflict between Persia and the eastern empire exhausted both of them. Inter-imperial conflict created new opportunities for nomadic peoples in Arabia and Palestine where both the eastern empire and the Persians had employed nomadic proxies to carry out their quarrels. In the desert areas, the nomadic allies of both empires had accumulated lists of grievances during the preceding era of peace. From their discontent sprang the great Arab uprising and Islamic revolt.

Meanwhile, in the northern regions of the empire a new threat emerged as Slavic tribes entered the Balkans, joining with the Turkic Avar nomads to raid the eastern empire. Between 581 and 584, a massive Slavic raid occurred in which many invaders occupied the land. This raid marked the beginning of Slavic settlement of the Balkans. While the Emperor Maurice (539?–602) was able to use a peace with Persia to defeat and turn back the Avars, many of the Slav settlers remained. Before Maurice could address the problem of the settlers, he was overthrown and assassinated by a rival. Maurice's assassination rekindled the war with Persia, and while the eastern empire dealt with Persian threats, the Slavic invasions of the Balkans occurred on a more massive scale. Within two decades Slavic invaders had reached the tip of the Peloponnesus, although their hold on this area proved temporary.

Between 626 and 641 war transformed the balance of power in the Middle East. The year 626 began with a massive combined assault on Constantinople by Avars and Bulgarians from the north and Persians from the south. Abandoning his capital to local defenders, the Emperor Heraclius I struck unexpectedly and captured the Persian capital in 628. His military successes led to Persian retreat and a series of internal revolts that brought Persian collapse. Defeating the Persians, Heraclius was in turn defeated by Arab cavalry – Islamic warriors who carried the field between 633 and 641 until finally stopped before the walls of Constantinople itself.

Religious controversy also split the empire. Justinian I and his successors tried to reshape Orthodoxy to incorporate religious groups such as the Monophysites formerly condemned as heretics. Such compromises pleased neither Monophysites nor Orthodox and the compromise itself was denounced as a new heresy, **Monotheletism**. Further religious division was promoted by the Iconclast controversy within the Eastern church (726–843). Islamic victories led many eastern Christians to search for reasons why God seemed to have abandoned them. Time and again, sacred religious icons failed to protect eastern Christian cities from Islamic armies. Some eastern Christians, particularly in the precarious frontier areas and in the armies, perhaps influenced by the Islamic prohibition of sacred images, attacked the use of religious icons.

Why did the Byzantines Survive?

Despite menaces on every side the empire did not fall. The survival of the eastern Roman empire depended partly upon the strategic location of its capital. In 413 CE Theodosius II began the construction of the triple walls on the landward side of the Golden Horn that successfully defended Constantinople for so many centuries. As long as the city held, the empire survived, although on occasion the entire empire was constricted to little more than the city and its environs.

The survival of the eastern Roman empire also depended on its ability to preserve key Mediterranean institutions that collapsed in the West. Although much reduced, urban commerce remained a vital element of the eastern Roman empire. Its survival represented the triumph of the richer and more populous portion of the Roman empire, an area less exposed to invasion by non-state peoples. Commercial activity diminished but continued to flow and to provide a source of monetary tax revenue. The population of great Eastern cities like Ephesus, Miletus, Pergamum, and Sardis contracted. Some essentially became small fortresses. But the great city of Constantinople, heart of the empire, continued to be one of the world's great cities, a never-ending source of marvel to Western European visitors. Eastern peasants continued to bring their grain to market and this provided the basis for a land tax that was paid, at least in part, in gold. With hard cash, the imperial court was able to maintain its centralization of power and thus to keep essential decision-making in Constantinople.

Recruiting and training its own soldiers, the eastern empire of the early Middle Ages maintained a continuous military tradition that benefited from the age-old experience of Roman arms. Elaborate manuals of arms, Roman texts updated to include innovations, were still studied in the East. Foremost of these innovations was the much-feared "Greek fire" that appeared sometime in the seventh century. It was a chemical concoction sprayed on enemy ships that burst into fire on contact and was said to be inextinguishable, even burning on the water.

Eastern Roman armies were trained in established Roman tactics, and the careers of generals, who were appointed from Constantinople, depended on their standing in the capital city. Faced with heavy new military challenges and declining resources, Heraclius' grandson Constans II reorganized the administration in the same direction but not to the same degree as Western rulers. The old imperial provinces were divided into districts or "themes" in which military men assumed judicial and administrative functions. These themes served as the basis for recruiting peasant militias, while ordinary soldiers were exempted from taxes and installed on land in the frontier.

Also a new Byzantine identity powerfully mobilized Orthodox Christians to defend the empire. In the end the conquest of Monophysite and Iconoclastic centers by Islamic armies helped to bring religious consensus to the empire. The fall of the great patriarchates of Eastern Christianity, Alexandria, Antioch, and Jerusalem, to Islamic armies allowed Orthodox churchmen to focus on the remnant populations and to articulate religious doctrines that resonated with them. The reaffirmation of their heartfelt convictions inspired Orthodox Christians to resist, even though it ended all hope of gathering together Syrian and Egyptian Christians. This new unity of religion and people constituted the Byzantine synthesis.

7.10 WHAT HAPPENED TO THE OLD WESTERN ROMAN EMPIRE?

In the old territories of the western Roman empire, even more than in the east, the years between 600 and 900 CE witnessed an almost unending wave of invasion. From the Germanic north, Goths were followed by Visigoths, Vandals, Alans, Sueves, and Burgundians. From the plains of Central Asia came nomads, Huns followed by Avars and Magyars. From the south, Arabs. In 793 just as Europe was totally absorbed in civil wars, Vikings sacked the monastery of Lindisfarne in northern England, announcing the beginning of two and a half centuries of Nordic incursions. The long, narrow, lightweight longboat could navigate in waters three or four feet deep, making them easy to beach in many environments. It was the perfect vessel for raiders (see Figure 7.2).

Figure 7.2 Viking longboat. The Viking longboat was an important element in their success as raiders. A long, narrow boat, built for speed, the longboat's shallow draft allowed navigation in waters three or four feet deep and facilitated beach landings; its light weight enabled it to be carried over portages. Longboats were also double-ended, the symmetrical bow and stern making it possible to reverse direction quickly without having to turn around; this trait proved particularly useful in northern latitudes with ice floes. Longboats were speedy, and fitted with oars along almost the entire length of the boat.

In this atmosphere of warfare and political chaos, trade within the Mediterranean world contracted in two great waves, the first in the fourth century as Germanic and Hunic invaders swept into the western Roman empire. The second wave occurred at the very beginning of the seventh century as Islamic armies conquered many eastern trading centers and as endemic civil war engulfed warrior kingdoms whose Germanic rulers looked on their lands as more a private inheritance than a civic responsibility. The Frankish practice of dividing kingdoms, like property, among the monarch's eligible sons was a sure recipe for civil war.

Decline of the Money Economy until 750–800 CE

The money economy slowed down during the **Merovingian** period. The Merovingian period refers to the roughly three hundred years (457–752) when kings descended from a common ancestor ruled most of France and large portions of modern Germany. Demonetization undermined the ability of Roman-influenced leaders to form mercenary armies. Merovingian power depended upon tribal loyalties. The first great Merovingian leader, Clovis I (481–511), influenced by his wife Clotilde,

converted to Christianity and brought his followers with him. Clovis forged an alliance between the Catholic Franks and the Latin papacy that was to make the Franks pre-eminent in Europe and the papacy the foremost ecclesiastical power of the age. In the eighth century Frankish power continued to grow but Merovingian leadership declined. Eventually Pope Zachary deposed the incompetent Merovingians and appointed in their place a new dynasty that would go far, the Carolingians. The immediate effects of this deposition changed little, but the idea that a pope could depose a monarch would not be forgotten.

The European economy did not begin to revive until Charles the Great fashioned a state that connected northern Germany to Italy (see Map 7.6). Finding it difficult to collect monetary taxes, the Merovingians and the early Carolingians depended more on their personal estates and their own vast Crown lands for revenues. Even Charles the Great, often referred to as Charlemagne (742–814 CE) – the powerful ruler discussed earlier – who dominated the history of the age in Europe, found it too cumbersome to generously provision his capital on a year-round basis. The center of Charles's government, Aachen, remained a small town devoid of the magnificent churches and palaces of Rome or Constantinople or even Ravenna, home of the

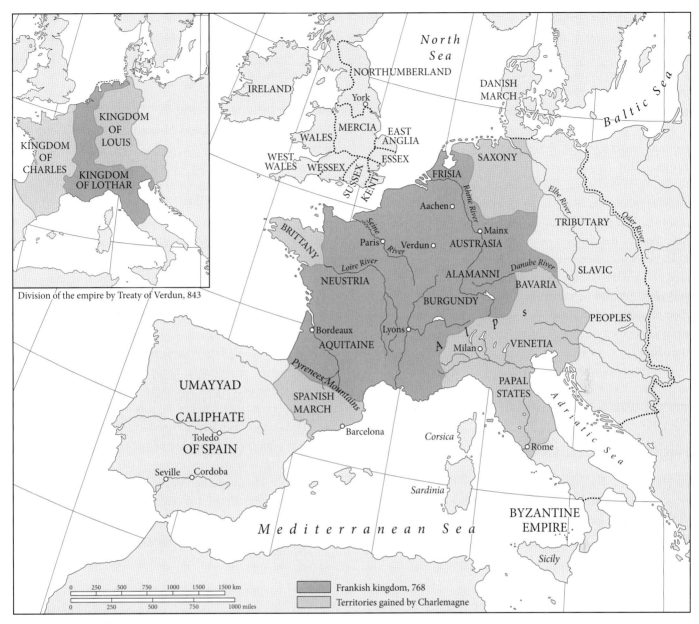

Map 7.6 The Carolingian empire

Byzantine governor in Italy, the exarch. Aachen served as a nodal point for Charlemagne's traveling court which circulated from one royal estate or great monastery to another in search of provision and hospitality.

Military Prowess

The real power of the Frankish monarchy was not expressed at Aachen but in the spring assembly of armed free men. These assemblies were the great decision-making bodies of the monarchy. An assembly well attended by commoners and powerful nobles was an affirmation of support for the monarchy. At the assembly, court cases were settled, religious decrees proclaimed, and diplomatic decisions taken. Assemblies often coincided with the mustering of troops, and decisions for war might be followed by immediate action. Poor freemen who worked their small farms assembled along with powerful nobles who controlled independent warrior bands supported by their great landed estates. This assembly of armed men represented a non-monetary alternative to the old imperial Roman army of paid professionals.

The problem of course was that a sustained period of peace produced poorly attended assemblies and military defeat deprived the monarch of the booty and conquered land that induced many to follow his lead. Outside the assembly government administration was weak. Unable to recruit or fund a real bureaucracy, the Carolingians depended on powerful noble families, bound to rulers by ties of personal allegiance, to enforce its laws. As the military power of the Carolingians was dissipated by civil war, the loyalty of powerful noble families was retained by parceling out Crown lands to them and then by offering them political and economic immunities. Offering exemptions from the law to those charged with enforcing it only further contributed to the dissolution of government.

Military prowess became the indispensable prerequisite for political leadership and Germanic and Celtic bards sang the praises of the valiant warrior as, twelve hundred years before, Greek bards had sung the virtues of Achilles (see Box 7.4). Achilles would certainly have understood the motivation of Beowulf, the hero of one of the earliest works of English literature. Few of the warriors who listened to the tale of Beowulf would have been familiar with Homer but the tough code generated in a warrior society had some basic similarities across time and place. Interest in literature or history on the part of wealthy men or women was a sure sign of a religious vocation. While many clergymen mastered church Latin, knowledge of Greek by the educated – and access to the Greek classics – was dying out. Books were pillaged for their rich coverings. Important works by such classical masters as Aristotle, Livy, and Virgil were irretrievably lost. What learning there was retreated to the monasteries.

Population Trends and Society

As hungry armed groups roamed the highways, foreign merchants who specialized in costly products were an easy target but even local merchants who exported food or cloth were subject to ruinous requisitions. As commerce declined along the old commercial routes, the population of the great European cities that had been the centers of commerce and political bureaucracy shrank dramatically. Rome, whose population had been over a million, fell to half a million by 400 CE and to under 50,000 by 600. In northern France, in Britain, and along the Rhine, cities almost disappeared.

Change in the countryside had been occurring for a long time and was accelerated by political chaos. The great Roman landed estates with their gangs of slave workers and their large herds of cattle were replaced by cultivators who worked small patches of land and kept chickens. Distinctions between rents and taxes merged into in-kind obligations to powerful local men. Slavery lost its meaning with the decline of the monetary economy and freemen often had good reason to work on great nobles' estates and so put themselves under obligation to local military men who could offer them protection. Roads and bridges were maintained by corvées of forced labor from the surrounding countryside.

On the land, the big fact of the period escaped most observers; while population in Western Europe had been declining for centuries, it began to pick up slowly between 600 and 900. Evidence of population change is pieced together from documents from widely separated regions of Europe and includes large blanks but the evidence seems consistent.[1] That the rural population began to grow in an age of personal violence when governmental administration was weak speaks volumes about earlier Roman agriculture. No evidence of technical progress is evident but European cultivators may have benefited by being thrown back on their own resources. The weakening of the

Box 7.4 *Beowulf*: The Ideal of the Male Warrior

Composed sometime between 650 and 1000 CE, *Beowulf* is one of the foremost poems in the Anglo-Saxon or Old English language. Written in England, it describes Beowulf the man as a great warrior and, in later life, king of the Geats, a Germanic people of southern Sweden. *Beowulf* was written in an Anglo-Saxon world that was Christianizing and the text pays homage to Christianity. Yet again and again the attitudes of a warrior society where force rules and fatalism predominates come to the fore when important decisions have to be made.

In the passage following, the hero Beowulf, come to aid the Danish king, Hrothgar, is preparing to fight the vengeful mother of Grendel, the monster that he has earlier slain. A fearful King Hrothgar seeks to inspire Beowulf with promises of gold but Beowulf responds with a classic statement of the warrior ethic.

Beowulf, son of Ecgtheow, spoke:
"Wise sir, do not grieve. It is always better to avenge dear ones than to indulge in mourning.
For every one of us, living in this world
means waiting for our end. Let whoever can
win glory before death. When a warrior is gone,
that will be his best and only bulwark."

How would a Christian regard Beowulf's professed ideals? Compare Beowulf's ideals with those of Achilles and with that of the Roman senator, Lucius Caecilius, discussed in Chapter 6. How do you explain these differences and similarities? What does the comparison tell you about Western Europe between 600 and 900?

monetary economy made it more difficult to calculate and compare the value of different products and small farmers may have taken advantage of such difficulties to increase their own consumption. Climate change may also have influenced the decision to abandon the concentration on a wheat monoculture that made agriculturalists over-dependent on a single crop. In northern France and Germany the move away from more marketable wheat to hardier rye and barley, more suited to colder climates, probably benefited local men and women.

Bursting with armed men and lacking civil administrators, the societies founded by the Germanic conquerors were not peaceful. Except for the Franks and Anglo-Saxons, most of the Germanic tribes were relatively small and unprepared to undertake the duties of Roman administration. Great Germanic leaders like the Ostrogothic king of Italy, Theoderic I (r. 493–526) recognized that stable government required German arms and Roman administration. Theoderic himself was the embodiment of this ideal: the son of an Ostrogoth chief, he had grown up in Constantinople. His mother was a Byzantine princess.

Unfortunately, Germanic intransigence and Roman loyalty to the eastern empire hindered efforts at reconciliation and doomed Theoderic's Ostrogothic kingdom. It fell apart shortly after his death as Italo-Roman aristocrats and the papacy rallied to Justinian's efforts to restore Italy to the empire. While Justinian's efforts were initially successful, Ostrogothic collapse eventually provoked the entry of the less Romanized and more brutal Lombards to replace them. The renewed wars between Lombards and Justinian's troops lasted over twenty years and took a terrible toll of Italian lives. In the end the Lombards controlled much of Italy while the empire retained a weakened hold on the south and the Adriatic shores from its exarchate in Ravenna.

If Germans were to rule the complex societies they had conquered, they needed the co-operation of existing elites, but religious differences between Germans and Romans were a serious obstacle to inter-elite co-operation. The first generation of Germanic invaders, the Goths, the Visigoths, and the Vandals, had been converted to Arian Christianity at a time when that brand of Christianity was being rejected by the great majority of Christians east and west.

Also, the very different character of Roman and Germanic legal codes made administrative co-operation difficult. Roman law resembled modern European law; indeed it formed the basis for many modern legal codes. In contrast, Germanic legal codes consisted of lists of crimes and fines that differed according to the social status, age, and gender of the victim. Enforcement was left to the victim's kinsmen who could take their vengeance on any kinsmen of the offender – unless these kinsmen paid the required fines or reached some common understanding. The basic idea was to make a man's kin responsible for his behavior;

in fact, the system just as often produced vendettas among whole families that lasted for generations.

Beset by violence, many Western Europeans looked to the eastern empire for protection. The single most important political authority in the West, the papacy, long acknowledged the authority of the eastern emperor and appealed for his protection. The association between the Christian religion and the Roman empire was deeply rooted. The early church fathers had often conflated the Roman empire and Christendom and this association had worked to the advantage of the Christian church.

7.11 VENICE: EMERGING INTERMEDIARY BETWEEN EAST AND WEST

Other Westerners also looked east. Growing up in the lagoons and protected by the sea, the newly emerging city of Venice recognized imperial Byzantine authority. Originally formed by peasants from the lands between Aquileia and Concordia and townsmen from Oderzo, Padua, and Treviso fleeing the Lombard invasion, the citizens of Venice first established commercial links with the eastern Mediterranean through Constantinople but quickly began to look beyond. Formally loyal to the Byzantine empire, the city was distant enough from Constantinople to pursue its own goal of linking the North Sea and Rhine Valley with an Arabic East that offered reliable access to greatly desired luxury goods, silk and spices. It used the labor shortage produced by the bubonic plague of c. 748 in the Abbasid empire to establish a trade in Western slaves, often Slavic peoples (thus the word slaves). Over the years, Venice became a key link in the exchange of European slaves and fur for Eastern silk and spices. Venice also proved a key intermediary because it tied the sea routes to the east with new land routes that brought Westerners into more direct contact with the Arab world, abandoning old Byzantine routes. Venice's role between a highly commercialized East and a poorly commercialized West had important similarities with the trading position of sub-Saharan African cities discussed in Chapter 9. One difference that later proved important was that the Venetian trade to the East was largely in the hands of Western merchants while Arab merchants played a more important role in the African trade.

In other regions of Italy in the south and on its Adriatic coast, where eastern Roman rule remained the longest, urban populations survived better than elsewhere and no large cities disappeared. Incorporation into the eastern Roman empire kept these areas in touch with its trade and commerce. But incorporation into the empire also subjected the rural population to heavy imperial taxation, which became even heavier as the war in Italy dragged on; in imperial Italy, the countryside exhibited the same decline that had characterized the western Roman empire of the late imperial era. Unable to renew its rural population, imperial rule in the West had little future.

7.12 WHY DID ROME RE-EMERGE AS A CENTER OF WESTERN POWER?

Torn between Lombards and imperial soldiers, Rome emerged as an independent force that would lead Europe in creating a new political order. Among Western Europeans, long accustomed to think of Rome as the center of the world, Rome was regarded as a uniquely holy city. Rome boasted of being the burial ground of the apostles Peter and Paul, and the Roman bishopric claimed to have been founded by the apostle Peter. Rome was the only one of the five great patriarchates – elevated positions within the Christian religious hierarchy of the time – located in the western Mediterranean. Tension had always existed between the Romans' assumption of superiority in all things and Easterners' pride in being the original center of Christianity. As the Eastern patriarchates fell to Islam, as imperial power faltered, and as the burden of defending Rome and adjacent territories fell on the bishop of Rome, the papacy's sense of its unique religious responsibilities grew.

While popes had consistently acknowledged their allegiance to the empire, relations were frequently difficult. Several popes had been arrested and imprisoned in Constantinople and popes had denounced Monophysite and Iconoclastic emperors. Only the great distance between Rome and Constantinople and the feeble and erratic imperial military hold on Rome prevented more serious confrontations.

As the power of the eastern empire faded, a series of vigorous popes, exemplified by Gregory I (540–604), acted independently from the Byzantine exarchate at Ravenna and undertook to defend Rome on their own authority. Gregory I appointed a military commander to defend the city from Lombard invaders, negotiated the terms of a treaty that saved the city from being captured by the Lombards, and drew on church lands to feed migrants to Rome fleeing the war. Staking out his independence, the bishop of Rome began to involve himself in broad issues of vital concern to Christianity. Gregory encouraged the conversion of the English and also helped to convert the Lombards from Arianism to Catholicism.

Gradually the papacy abandoned its eastern focus and began to look north.

Missionaries

The long effort of Christianity to convert and to remake the Roman world had made it largely oblivious to the northern peoples outside the sway of Rome. Patrick's missionary work in Ireland provided an important model but the greatest of the missionaries was Wynfrith (685?–755) from Wessex who received a commission from Gregory II to evangelize the heathen. From the pope, he also received a new name, Boniface. Boniface played an important role in reviving German Christianity and implanting a solid church hierarchy in the German lands. From Boniface's mission followed that of Cyril (827–69) and Methodius (826–85), two young Greek brothers who evangelized the Slavic Moravians. Alive to the political consequences of whether Rome or Constantinople would integrate new converts into their faith, Roman and Orthodox church hierarchies competed to convert Slavic peoples to Christianity. The Roman church was the first in the field but the Orthodox willingness to allow the use of Slavic languages in church rituals gave them important advantages.

In the case of the Germans, the early conversion of one important tribe, the Franks, to Roman Christianity had momentous consequences. Legend has it that Clovis was converted in 496 by his wife Clotilde, an ardent Christian. Clovis and his descendants, the Merovingians, established the beginnings of the alliance between Franks and papacy. At this time, rulers who converted to Christianity expected to bring along their people. In general the Germanic conversions were not the product of missionaries winning the loyalty of the masses. This came later. The Germanic conversions originated in the conversion of powerful rulers. If subjects refused to convert, they revolted, and a few cases of premature conversion to Christianity lost rulers their kingdoms and their lives.

Why did the Germans Adopt Christianity?

Christianization generally succeeded because it offered rulers powerful advantages. Clovis's conversion had the effect of helping consolidate his kingdom. The Franks' adoption of Catholicism united German elites with the solidly Catholic Gallo-Roman nobility. Roman Catholic bishops mobilized to support Catholic kings. The church bureaucracy alone survived to link together the disparate elements of kingdoms and to provide rulers with a corps of literate officials.

The direct ties with Rome increased the prestige of Germanic leaders, who were deeply impressed with Roman culture and tradition, and encouraged international intermarriage with Roman elites. Religious coronation gave a new legitimacy to rule and helped support principles of hereditary succession that were only beginning to take root among the Germanic and Slavic peoples.

Among the most difficult prospects for missionary activity were the Scandinavians. Partly this was because Christian religious institutions were becoming the natural prey of Viking warriors. In the ninth and tenth centuries, booty from British, Irish, and French churches and great estates were added to the goods – mainly slaves and raw materials such as wool and hides – that were already circulating along a great trade route that led from Scandinavia, through the Russian lands, to the Abbasid caliphate. This trade route was entirely non-Roman and stimulated economies in European regions largely outside the Mediterranean-based trade routes of the old Roman world. The route led from the emporia of Dorestad in modern-day Holland to Staraja Ladoga at the mouth of the Volga, and down the Volga to the Caspian Sea. The early ninth century witnessed a temporary high point in trade activity, which may have provided an economic stimulus to Charlemagne's empire, although it declined temporarily as the Abbasid empire was shaken by civil war between 809 and 833. In time, as power centralized in societies that alternated between agriculture and piracy/trading, the strongest leaders aspired to become religiously sanctified kings like their Germanic counterparts and Scandinavia joined the ranks of Christianity.

7.13 WHY DID THE FRANKS SUCCEED IN GOVERNING AND BUILDING AN EMPIRE?

The transformation of kingship into a sacred office and the role of religion in kingmaking were products of the Merovingian and Carolingian Ages. Early on, the papacy played a key role in altering the Frankish succession. As the power of the Merovingians declined, the powerful mayors of the palace such as Charles Martel gathered effective power into their hands. In 733 at Poitiers Charles Martel turned back Islamic armies in a battle that turned out to be a decisive check to Islamic advance. Frankish power combined with their Catholicism led to a close relationship between Frankish leaders and the papacy. The pope recognized the powers of the mayors of the palace and approved when mayor of the palace Pepin the Short deposed the ineffective Merovingian Childeric III. In 754, Pope Zacarias anointed Pepin as king of the Franks, formally ratifying the decision he had taken in 751. The role of the papacy in legitimizing this transition was an important precedent and it raised unsettling questions not directly addressed at the time. It raised the key question whether, if popes could make emperors, they might also unmake them.

The partnership between Franks and the papacy essentially created an axis of power in Western and Central Europe. When the Lombards threatened Rome and the lands that the popes protected, the popes called on their Frankish allies for help. Eventually the Franks recognized papal claims to the territory around Rome which the popes had sought to defend. This republic of Saint Peter was the origin of the papal states that were to make the popes important secular rulers.

The climax of papal and Frankish collaboration came with the coronation of Charlemagne in Rome on Christmas day, 800 CE. Charlemagne was the greatest of the Frankish conquerors. He united the divisive Frankish kingdoms into a single empire, destroyed the Avar nomadic kingdom on the Hungarian plains, and fought one long bitter battle after another to conquer and to forcibly Christianize the Saxons. His coronation by the pope was fateful. The future of both Germany and Italy would be strongly shaped by the efforts of German rulers to assert imperial claims over Italian territory. German resources would pour into Italy and imperial claims would pre-empt the growth of national monarchies in both Germany and Italy during the medieval period. Above all, the vision of a Europe united by a common emperor and a common faith ignited the imagination of Europeans and would do so for centuries. Despite religious schisms and the ebb and flow of imperial power, the creation of the idea of Western Christendom would be one of the most important legacies of the age.

Conclusion

The years between 600 and 900 CE witnessed the birth of Islam, one of the great world religions, and a vast expansion of Islamic power in the southern and eastern portions of the ancient Mediterranean and points east. Culture and intellectual innovation flourished in large and well-maintained cities such as Damascus and Baghdad. In this period Arabic began to become the common language of the Near East and Islam began to convert not only elites but masses to the new religion. Strong Islamic states provided security for merchants that enabled them to reopen roads to the east that had declined in the previous centuries. Faced with Islamic expansion, the Byzantine empire defensively reshaped itself around its Orthodox Christian core. Basing itself on its Roman heritage of military tactics and administration, the Byzantines prepared themselves for the long contest with their dynamic Eastern Islamic rival. In contrast, Western Europe fell into a period of political chaos and economic decline. By the end of this period commercial decline had begun to end but the age when the eastern Mediterranean sent its grain and oil in tribute to Rome was gone. The trade relationship had changed dramatically. Western and Central Europeans were mainly suppliers of raw materials, including a substantial trade in slaves, to the Islamic world. An independent commentator apprised of the facts might have guessed that Europe's fate would be reintegration into the Mediterranean commercial world as a peripheral, dependent trading partner of Islamic empires who controlled access to the luxury goods of China and India.

Study Questions

(1) Discuss the reasons for the spread of Islam after the death of Muhammad.

(2) Summarize the major tenets of the Islamic faith and compare them with those of Christianity.

(3) Compare and contrast the empire of Charles the Great with the empire of Harun al-Rashid. Discuss the political and economic organization of the two empires.

(4) What place did trade have in the early medieval empires and urban life? How did the politics of the day affect trade?

Suggested Reading

RICHARD FLETCHER, *The Barbarian Conversion: From Paganism to Christianity* (New York: Henry Holt, 1997). Fletcher describes the Christianization of Europe in the first millennium CE as a broad cultural process including literacy, beliefs, and tastes in food, drink, and dress.

PATRICK J. GEARY, *Before France and Germany: The Creation and Transformation of the Merovingian World* (Oxford University Press, 1988). The foundations of the modern state are located in the Merovingian world.

JUDITH HERRIN, *The Formation of Christianity* (Princeton University Press, 1987). Herrin looks at the Roman contribution to Christianity and Islam and stresses the influence of Byzantium.

RICHARD HODGES AND DAVID WHITEHOUSE, *MOHAMMED, CHARLEMAGNE AND THE ORIGINS OF EUROPE* (ITHACA: CORNELL UNIVERSITY PRESS, 1983). A review of one of the oldest professional debates in history, it still inspires.

GWYN JONES, *A History of the Vikings* (Oxford University Press, 1968). This important and highly readable overview of the Vikings by a leading scholar looks at many aspects of their life.

THOMAS V.X. NOBLE, *The Republic of St Peter: The Birth of the Papal State, 680–825* (Philadelphia: University of Pennsylvania Press, 1984). Noble argues that papal states were less a creation of Charlemagne than a response to an aggressive Byzantine empire.

PIERRE RICHÉ, *The Carolingians: A Family Who Forged Europe* (Philadelphia: University of Pennsylvania Press, 1993). Riché traces the move toward European unity to the Carolingians, showing the familiy solidarity that led to their rise and the murderous internal quarrels that destroyed them.

WARREN TREADGOLD, *The Byzantine Revival, 780–842* (Stanford University Press, 1988). This study looks at a key period when the empire survived despite almost overwhelming odds.

SUZANNE FONAY WEMPLE, *Women in Frankish Society: Marriage and the Cloister, 500 to 900* (Philadelphia: University of Pennsylvania Press, 1981). Wemple looks particularly at the role of women in religion and changing property laws, and why Frankish women had more power than Roman women.

CHRIS WICKHAM, *The Inheritance of Rome: Illuminating the Dark Ages* (New York: Praeger, 2011). Wickham is part of a massive reappraisal of the so-called "Dark Ages": They weren't so dark and were a vast improvement over the late Roman empire.

Glossary

Aachen: The political capital of Charles the Great, today on the German side of the German–Belgian border.

Abbasid: An imperial dynasty of caliphs claiming descent from Abbas, the uncle of the Prophet Muhammad. The empire was established after a revolution against the Umayyad caliphate in the late 740s, and the line of the caliphs lasted until the Mongol invasion of 1258.

Ali: The young cousin and son-in-law of Muhammad. Many Muslims believed that he should have inherited the religious mantle of Muhammad. Others wanted a respected elder, Abu Bakr, to take the leadership and these won out. Ali did become caliph in 656 but for only five years before his assassination. Dispute over the rights of Ali to succession became a major area of controversy and still divides Muslims.

Byzantium: Term for the Greek-speaking, Christian eastern Roman empire after 600 CE. Byzantium was the original name for the city which Constantine in 330 CE refounded as Constantinople.

caliph: Muslim ruler, successor to the Prophet Muhammad.

hadith: Anecdotes about the sayings and doings of the Prophet Muhammad.

Hanbalis: Followers of a legal school of early Islam that was particularly puritanical and strict in its approach.

jihad: Originally a term that referred to any struggle for the sake of Islam, it developed into a term of art on the Muslim–Byzantine frontier for Muslim warfare against enemies of the Muslim state.

Kharijites: Literally, "those who go out, withdraw"; a sect in early Islam that broke with Ali, the fourth caliph, over his willingness to submit to arbitration. A Kharijite assassin killed Ali in 661. The group became a strict sect that excommunicated believers whose behavior was not spotless. In mainstream Islam, one can be a Muslim despite occasional moral lapses, but Kharijites considered such persons non-Muslims.

Koran: The holy book of Islam, believed by Muslims to be the word of God revealed to the Prophet Muhammad. Contains praises of God, stories of Arabian, Jewish, and Christian prophets, and moral advice. Relatively little of the book concerns law.

Mahdi: In Islam, the promised one, a descendant of the Prophet Muhammad, who would arise at the end of time to restore the world to justice after it had been filled with wickedness.

Merovingians: Descendants of King Clovis, the Frankish leader who converted to Roman Christianity. In 751, with the approval of the pope, the Merovingian Childeric III was deposed by Pepin the Short, the son of Charles Martel. In 754 Pope Stephen anointed Pepin "king of the Franks" thus beginning the Carolingian dynasty.

Monophysitism: The belief that in the person of Christ there was only one single divine nature. It represented an effort to elaborate the Christian doctrine of the triune nature of the deity. Monophysite beliefs can be traced to early churchmen of the fourth, fifth, and sixth centuries and won many supporters in Armenia, Egypt, and Syria. Imperial persecution of Monophysite believers undermined loyalty to the Byzantine empire in the century before the Muslim conquests.

monotheism: The doctrine or belief that there is only one God.

Monotheletism: A seventh-century belief that Christ only had one will, which attempted to elaborate the doctrine of the triune nature of the deity. It originated in the efforts of Emperor Heraclius to win back the Monophysites of Egypt and Syria by a religious compromise. The compromise, Monotheletism, failed and only added to the religious divisions within the empire.

Muslims: Arabic term for "those who surrender themselves to God." It became a term for the followers of Muhammad.

Mu`tazilites: Believers in rationality and the validity of Greek logical and philosophical tools within Islam. They held that God is invariably just and his justice can be understood, but that he is beyond all knowable attributes or characteristics. They also believed that the Koran is created in time, rather than being eternal. They became extremely powerful at the Abbasid court and persecuted more literalist or "fundamentalist" Muslims for a time, but eventually lost favor in the Muslim world.

Quraysh: The noble tribe of Mecca into which the Prophet Muhammad was born.

Shi`ites: Partisans of the close family of the Prophet. They believed that the first caliph leader of the Muslim community after Muhammad should have been his cousin and son-in-law Ali, who had married the Prophet's daughter Fatimah, and that subsequent leaders should have been descendants of Ali and Fatimah.

Sunnis: The majority branch of Islam, which accepted the four orthodox caliphs (Abu Bakr, Umar, Uthman, and Ali) and believed that the community could be headed by persons unrelated to the Prophet Muhammad. They stressed loyalty to the sayings and doings of Muhammad and his early companions.

Umayyad: The dynasty that immediately succeeded the four orthodox caliphs. It ruled from 661–749 and presided over expansion of Muslim-ruled lands from Spain to Afghanistan.

vizier: First minister, who advised the king or caliph and often gained great executive power in his own right in the early Muslim empires.

Note 1 Jean-Pierre Devroey, "The Economy," in Rosamond McKitterick (ed.), *The Early Middle Ages* (Oxford University Press, 2000), pp. 97–129 (104–05).

8 The heyday of the Silk Road

China	
581–617	Sui dynasty reunites China.
587	First examinations introduced.
602	Sui armies conquer Hanoi.
604–18	Sui Yangdi.
618–907	Tang dynasty.
618–26	Reign of Tang Gaozu.
626–49	Reign of Tang Taizong.
c. 629–45	Xuanzang leaves China for India and returns.
690–705	Wu Zhao rules as Empress Wu Zetian.
712–56	Reign of Tang Xuanzong.
755	An Lushan rebellion.
781	Nestorian Christian stele erected in Chang'an.
c. 820	Han Yu attacks worship of Buddha.
841–45	Emperor attacks Buddhist temples.
854	Emperor confiscates wealth of Buddhists and forces many into lay life.

Japan and Northeast Asia	
552	Arrival of Buddhism in Japan.
593–622	Reign of Shotoku Taishi
604	Seventeen Injunctions of Shotoku Taishi.
632	Arrival of Chinese mission to Japan.
646	Japanese emperor's reform movement transforms Japan.
663	Japanese lose battle with Chinese troops in Korea.
668	Goguryo state eliminated.
702	Emperor Temmu declares comprehensive reforms.
710–94	Nara Japan.

752	Buddha of Todaiji temple cast.
894	Japan stops embassies to China.
Central Eurasia	
550–840	Turk and Uighur empires.
552	Bumin Qaghan creates Turk state.
634–50	Reign of Songtsen Gampo, founder of Tibetan empire.
656	Islamic armies reach Oxus River.
659	End of western Turk empire.
683	Second Turk empire.
716–34	Reign of Bilge Qaghan.
734	Uighurs destroy Turk empire.
751	Arab armies defeat Chinese at Talas River.
	Nanzhao defeats Tang invasion.
763	Tibetans invade Chang'an.
781	Tibetans seize Dunhuang.
790	Nanzhao allies with Tang against Tibet.
821	Chinese make peace with Tibetans.
829	Nanzhao sacks Chengdu.
840	Kirghiz destroy Uighur empire.
850	Chinese recover Dunhuang.
858	Rebellion of Annam put down by Tang.
911	Uighurs capture Dunhuang.

In the early seventh century CE, a Chinese monk named Xuan-zang (600–64) developed an intense passion to study Buddhism at its source in India. Officials rejected his application to go to India in 629, but he left in secret anyway. He spent fifteen years in India studying with eminent masters. On his return, he wrote to the emperor to apologize for breaking the law. The emperor did not punish him, but invited him to tell about the foreign lands he had seen, and even asked him to leave the religious world to become his political advisor. Xuanzang, like a true academic, rejected the political world but made good use of his powerful patron. He only asked for funding to set up his own research institute to translate Indian texts, and the emperor granted his wish. Xuanzang translated over seventy-six Indian Buddhist texts, but his doctrines did not last as long as his personal example. Inspired by his tremendous dedication in braving so many perils to reach India, legends about him spread through China. They reached their most popular form in the sixteenth-century novel *Journey to the West*, which gives Xuanzang animal companions with supernatural powers, including the famous monkey Sun Wukong, a figure taken from Indian mythology. This story, known to everyone in China in the form of novels, comic books, films, and TV shows, comes from the extraordinary adventures of one Buddhist monk in a time when China and India were close to each other in culture, though far away in geography.

During these three centuries, in Eastern and Central Eurasia, great empires, trade routes, and religions flourished:

- China reunited itself once again into a great empire.
- The Silk Roads attained the peak of their activity.
- Two great religions, Buddhism and Islam, spread their influence far across Eurasia.
- The **Turks** formed a large nomadic empire in Central Eurasia which constantly fought and negotiated with China, while Tibet and Japan also created powerful states.

China's unity was relatively brief, but the military and bureaucratic power of the Sui and Tang empires drastically changed not only China itself, but all of its neighbors. Commerce on the Silk Roads tied all these states together in the midst of war. Buddhism rose from a small sect in India to become the dominant religious influence in China and neighboring states, while Islam gained permanent roots across the continent. Expansive power, flourishing trade, and dynamic religious activity marked this period. So did wars and rebellions. It was a time of newly intensified interactions across the Eurasian continent. China in particular was a more cosmopolitan society than it ever had been, and more open than it would be again until the Mongol conquest.

8.1 THE REUNIFICATION OF CHINA

For nearly four hundred years, China had been divided into two or more states. No single ruler had been able to put an empire back together since the fall of the Han. In the north, conquerors from the steppe established a state, the Northern Wei (386–534 CE), which lasted for over a century until it split apart. In the south, as many as sixteen kingdoms competed with each other until the lower Yangtze Valley achieved nominal unification under weak emperors centered in Nanjing. At the local level, elite families increased their landholdings, establishing large estates that provided the base for independent power. "Feudalism," in the sense of fragmented sovereignty, had returned with a vengeance, as in the days of the Warring States.

Yet in a very short time, **Sui Wendi** (r. 581–604), a leader of a noble family in North China, conquered all his rivals to create a single empire. As always, his political power grew out of the strings of his crossbows and the blades of his swords, but he established radically new civil institutions that laid the basis for long-lasting unity. The Sui dynasty fell quickly, in 617, but the Tang built on its legacy.

Sui Wendi and his successor **Sui Yangdi** (r. 604–18) set up the basic governmental institutions that made it possible for the empire to last for nearly three hundred years. He created a highly centralized bureaucracy, run by the autocratic emperor at the top with a small group of tough, northern, military men. They made sure that the officials under them were loyal to the center, as they set out to break the hereditary control of entrenched local families by recruiting men by merit, not by birth. The Sui introduced China's first regular examination systems to select and rank local officials, in 587. These exams were not the main route to office yet, but they were a start on the road to a meritocratic bureaucracy. The taxation system took over the "equal field" land allocation method of the Northern Wei dynasty, which gave each married couple 120 *mou* (20 acres) of land to support themselves and the state. They paid three kinds of tax on this land: grain, bolts of silk, and labor services (corvée). By equalizing landholdings and tax burdens, the Sui and Tang rulers ensured steady income for the state and basic subsistence for

the people they ruled. When the registration worked efficiently, at least 8 million households were on the books. Powerful officials, local magnates, and Buddhist monasteries, among others, still grabbed more than their share of land, but initially, at least, the Sui and Tang rulers made a powerful move toward equality.

Military organization depended on the land and tax system, as local forces drew their men and support from the taxpayers of the community. As in the Qin dynasty, community groups (**bao**) watched over each other to make sure that everyone performed his required service. Finally, a comprehensive law code, designed in the Sui and refined in the Tang, stripped away complicated legal technicalities, creating a rationalized system of procedures and punishments which every official in the empire had to learn. The Tang law code lasted with little change until the collapse of China's last dynasty in 1911, and it had great impact on the legal systems of Vietnam, Korea, and Japan. Legal contracts preserved in the distant oasis of Turfan, described in Box 8.1, show that the Tang law code did regulate local transactions throughout the empire.

The two Sui emperors made their largest economic impact by building the Grand Canal linking the north and the south. This great civil engineering project, extending from the fertile, well-watered lowlands of Hangzhou to the northern capitals at Chang'an (modern Xi'an) and Luoyang, with an extension toward Beijing, made it possible to move food, clothing, armed men, and imperial wealth by boat through the core of the empire. Thrifty Confucian historians described with awe and horror the extravagance of imperial processions on the Canal: "Boatmen hired from all the waterways . . . pulled the vessels by ropes of green silk on the imperial progress to Yangzhou . . . The boats followed one another poop to prow for more than 65 miles."[1] They disapproved of the lavish spending which unfairly burdened the local people; they failed to see the long-term effects of the Canal in binding the empire together.

After taking power in the ancient core of China, the Yellow River valley and the North China Plain, the Sui emperors launched military campaigns in all directions, determined at least to recover the huge expanse controlled by the Han and even go beyond it. They crushed the southern rulers in the Yangtze, sacking the refined capital at Nanjing and wrecking thousands of monasteries, but they soon rebuilt a new capital at Yangzhou and patronized Buddhist establishments to win over the southern population. Sui Yangdi, whose devout, cultured wife came from the south, learned the southern Chinese dialect and ingratiated himself with the locals. The Sui armies marched further south into northern Vietnam, taking Hanoi in 602, but they failed to conquer the rich state of Champa in southern Vietnam, seen as an El Dorado of riches. Their largest challenge came from the powerful Turkic qaghanates of the

Box 8.1 A Contract from the Desert

Tombs in Turfan, an oasis in the desert in Chinese Xinjiang, contain documents that show how ordinary people conducted their business. Mr. Zuo, a soldier and merchant, had fifteen contracts buried with him in his tomb in 673. One of them reads:

On the twenty-sixth day of the fourth month of the first year of [666] Zheng Haishi of Chonghua district borrowed 10 silver coins from Zuo Chongxi. In addition, he will pay interest of 1.5 silver coins every month. The day when Zuo wants the money back, Zheng will *promptly return it. If Zheng keeps Zuo's money for a prolonged period, then Zuo is authorized to take over Zheng's family assets and various possessions, and his personal share land and his gardens, to make up the original amount. The family can make no excuses preventing him from taking their goods ... If Zheng absconds, his wife and children will pay first, and then his guarantors will make up the debt for him. Officials have government law, and common people follow private contracts. The two sides agree to make* *this contract, and they draw their finger joints as a sign of good faith.*

Mr. Zuo followed customary practice, charging 15 percent interest per month, using guarantors, and demanding confiscation of the borrower's goods if he could not pay. All the provisions of the contract match those of the official Tang law code. Thus even in faraway Turfan, Tang legal codes and customs protected private commercial transactions, spreading China's market culture into Central Eurasia.

---

northwest and the Goguryo state of Manchuria. Sui Yangdi kept himself well informed about this region through intelligence-gathering and personal tours of the northwest. Without conducting major military expeditions, he won over some of the **qaghans** (supreme leaders of Turks) and exploited internal divisions among the Turks, so that they never united against him. He set the stage for the great Tang invasions fifty years later.

Despite its achievements, the Sui dynasty fell under the combined impact of fiscal strain, military failure, and internal revolt. Failed expeditions against the Goguryo state pushed the military to the breaking point, while over two hundred rebel groups rose up in the interior. Sui Yangdi fled to the south, where he was murdered by the son of his most trusted general.

Yet almost immediately thereafter, Li Yuan, one of the most powerful Sui generals, reconquered the capital and founded the new dynasty of the Tang, calling himself emperor **Tang Gaozu** (r. 618–26). Map 8.1 shows the maximum extent of Tang expansion. In name at least, the Tang endures as China's most glorious empire, famed for its territorial conquests, its cosmopolitan culture, its great poets and glittering metropolis, Chang'an, and its international influence. Map 8.2 of Chang'an demonstrates the vast size of this imperial city. In fact, the real power of the Tang empire was fairly brief: it reached its peak under the second emperor, Taizong, and by 755 the An Lushan rebellion had shattered any genuine central control. But its mythical glory endured long beyond the painful declining years.

Tang Gaozu rebuilt the central government on the Sui model, ruling with a small group of military nobles at the top of an extensive civil bureaucracy. He restored the essential institutions of taxation and militia, and pushed further toward standardization by imposing a uniform coinage on the empire. His successor, **Tang Taizong** (r. 626–49), gained the greatest renown, however, for expanding the empire in all directions and leading it to new heights of prosperity. At first, he too lost battles with the Turks, but he soon demonstrated such strength that a group of Turks asked him to take the title of qaghan. In an impressive ceremony, the Tang ruler took on the symbolic role of combining legitimate rule over both settled Chinese and nomadic horsemen. Many tribes swore loyalty to the Tang emperor, but others lamented that the Turks had now become "slaves" of the Chinese. The defeat of the eastern Turks by Tang armies, and the collapse of the western Turk empire, allowed the empire to project its power far into Central Eurasia, including the major oases of the Tarim Basin. Now the Tang had gone far beyond the achievements of the Han. They only stopped when the newly united Tibetan empire held them off in the west, and when military expeditions against the Goguryo state of Korea ended in disaster.

Tang Taizong has gone down in history as the ideal ruler, joining military and civilian power to bring his people unprecedented territorial control and economic prosperity. From the Sui through his reign, China benefited from a lucky succession of vigorous leaders who mobilized the empire's coercive and commercial resources with great effectiveness. Later rulers could not measure up to these models.

The ineffectual, sick emperor Gaozong, infatuated with his beautiful concubine **Wu Zhao**, elevated her to supreme power. By 655, she completely dominated the court and the hapless emperor, and she took ruthless revenge on all those who opposed her. In 690 she took power in her own name, establishing a new

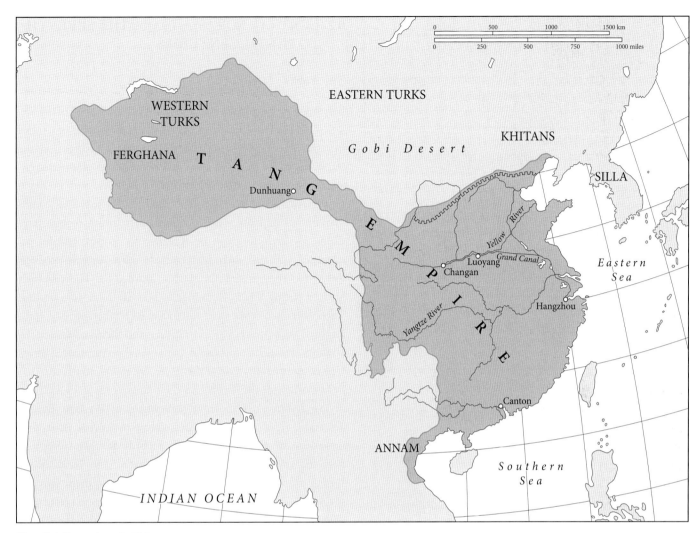

Map 8.1 Tang dynasty China

dynasty that lasted until 705, when the Tang was restored. Empress Wu was in fact a highly capable, politically astute woman, and except for purges at the top level of power, most of her subjects prospered under her rule. Confucian patriarchal historians, however, violently condemned her, reinforcing the prejudice that women always inflict calamity on an empire.

Under **Tang Xuanzong** (712–56), especially, a craze for "Western" music swept the court. Highly educated courtesans sang songs like "The Three Platforms of the Turks," "Songs of South India," "The Music of Kucha," and "Watching the Moon in Brahma Land," accompanied by Persian and Turkestani orchestras, for the entertainment of the emperor and his nobles. Xuanzong, in the moralistic accounts of orthodox historians, lost his empire because of his passion for a woman, the voluptuous concubine **Yang Guifei**. Because of his blind devotion, Guifei was able to install her vicious cousin, Yang Guozhong, in the post of prime minister, where he repressed all opposition. Meanwhile, non-Chinese military men took charge of the frontier

garrisons, for good strategic reasons: they knew how to fight the Turks. As the Romans knew well, "barbarians" made the best soldiers; Chinese officials called them the "claws and teeth" of the empire. But the claws and teeth, if not controlled, could tear apart the soft underbelly, the rich provinces of the interior.

While General **An Lushan**, of mixed Sogdian and Turkic descent, entrenched himself in the north and northeast, Yang Guozhong alienated the people of the interior with excessive taxation and administrative neglect. In 755, An Lushan proclaimed a rebellion to oust the "bandit" Yang Guozhong; the emperor fled with his court from Chang'an, and along the way his troops mutinied, demanding the death of Yang Guifei and her hated cousin. Sobbing, the distraught emperor allowed her to be strangled. Only then did the troops rally to his side and hold off An Lushan's effort to take over the entire empire.

The story of Tang Xuanzong and Yang Guifei has been celebrated in poetry, drama, and popular history ever since. Like all dramatic stories, it is too good to be true. Tang Xuanzong was an

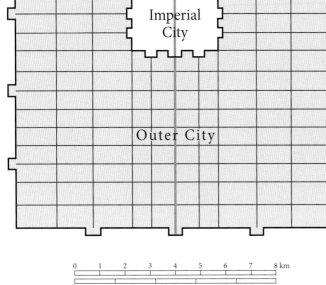

Forbidden Park

Palace City

Imperial City

Outer City

| 0 | 1 | 2 | 3 | 4 | 5 | 6 | 7 | 8 km |
| 0 | | 1 | | 2 | | 3 | | 4 | | 5 miles |

Map 8.2 Chang'an

immensely capable ruler; his passion for Yang Guifei was not the main cause of the rebellion; frontier defenses were weak and underfinanced in any case. The Tang faced new rising powers which strained its resources to the breaking point. For the next century and a half, the Tang was an empire in name only. Regional frontier governors, with autonomous military forces, outweighed the power of the court in Chang'an until the dynasty fell in 907.

To understand the decline of the Tang, after its early spectacular successes, we need to examine the powers that surrounded it. The Tang empire, at its height, ruled up to 60 million people. It was a mighty powerhouse of economic production and military expansion. The regions around its edges had much fewer people, including about 3–5 million Turks and other nomads, 500,000 Tibetans, 1 million Vietnamese, 1 million Koreans, and 3 million Japanese. To keep themselves from submitting to the Tang juggernaut, they had to mobilize all available resources of manpower, food, horses, money, and diplomatic skill. But they also learned valuable techniques from their powerful neighbor, borrowing what they found useful. At the same time, Central Eurasian cultural influences poured into China. Chinese and Central Eurasian cultures mingled far beyond the reach of even the most adventurous armies.

8.2 CENTRAL EURASIA FROM THE SEVENTH TO NINTH CENTURIES

The Turks

Beginning in the mid sixth century, just before the rise of the Sui, a new people known as Turks created a large empire in Central Eurasia. The Turks were pastoral nomads who drew on the traditions of the Xiongnu and other nomadic peoples to dominate the steppes. As Box 8.2 indicates, the horse was the most prestigious animal for pastoral nomads, the key to military domination and mobility. They obtained their wealth mainly from China, by extracting silk in exchange for horses, and by co-operating with Silk Road merchants to move Chinese products westward. The Sui and Tang, who regarded the Turks as their greatest enemy, were determined to prevent them from uniting. The Turks often broke apart and fought each other, but over three hundred years, from 550 to 840, they and their successors, the **Uighurs**, remained a powerful military and political force across Central Eurasia. Because of them, the silk routes flourished.

The origin of the Turks and their language is unclear. Their myths describe a clan from somewhere in Western Eurasia descended from a young boy brought up by wolves. Later, they moved to the Altai Mountains to subordinate themselves to a nomadic confederation called the **Rouran**. The Turks had a special affinity with metallurgy, and many of them lived in caves. In 552, they threw off their Rouran masters to create their own state under their qaghan, **Bumin**. Bumin ruled the eastern half of the empire, which raided the Chinese border, while his brother **Ishtemi** ruled in the west. Bumin used his military forces to put pressure on the northern Chinese dynasties to give him large quantities of silk in exchange for horses. He co-operated with the **Sogdians**, the chief mercantile group of the Silk Road, to sell these products for gold and silver. Meanwhile, Ishtemi in the west tried to negotiate access to the markets of Sasanian Persia, allying with the Persians to take control of Turkestan. When he was shut out of Persian markets, he turned to the Byzantine empire, which had a high demand for silk. Box 8.3 describes the importance of silk as a luxury cloth worn by Chinese for which there was a high demand among Central Asian traders.

With the rise of the Sui dynasty, the western Turks no longer faced a weak state, but a powerful ruler, skilled in the use of war and diplomacy. The Sui and early Tang emperors used China's wealth to lure several of the Turk tribes to their side. Up to 10,000 Turks settled in Chang'an itself, and many of the warriors submitted to China in order to gain secure grazing lands within Chinese borders. By 630 the eastern Turks had disintegrated into civil war, and by 659 Tang Taizong had marched into Central Eurasia to destroy the western Turk empire.

Box 8.2 The Horse: The Prestige Animal

Horses were as crucial for Central Eurasian warfare as tanks and airplanes are today, and only certain people could master them. Most of China's territory could not support horses, because it was either mountainous, too hot, or occupied by peasant fields. Peasant farmers in China, unlike Europe, had little experience with horses: They used oxen to till their fields. Only the wide open spaces of the steppe could support large numbers of horses, and only the steppe nomads had the skills to ride them. The Xiongnu, Turks, Mongols, and many other peoples built their society around the mounted horseman. Nomadic economies in fact depended more on large herds of sheep and goats than on horses, but horseriders held the prestige. Young boys learned to ride and take care of horses from their fathers, and grew up with the ambition to become a heroic warrior.

The Sui and Tang conquerors of China came from the same background as the horseriding warriors of the steppe, so they knew of its importance in both warfare and culture. The vivid ceramic figurines of horses are some of the most striking works of Tang dynasty art. Tang nobles also introduced the game of polo to China from Persia. Because the rulers needed so many horses for their military expeditions, they had to find allies among the nomadic tribes, and show themselves to be just as heroic. Tang emperors and officials actively endorsed the military arts of archery and horsemanship. The Confucians who wrote poetry and examination essays did not control the elite culture as they would later.

All the cultures around China also relied heavily on horsemanship. The first Japanese states were probably founded by horseriding invaders who crossed over from Korea. The Tibetans built their large empire on a very different kind of warfare, depending on large slow horses and heavy chain mail. When mounted Arab armies met Chinese armies in 751 CE, both sides embraced the cult of horses, even though they had diametrically opposed religious convictions. The cult of the horse demonstrated the deep penetration of Central Eurasian traditions into the heart of settled agrarian societies.

Box 8.3 Silk and Camels

Silk comes from the saliva secreted by the larvae of the moth *Bombyx mori*, or silkworm, which feeds on mulberry leaves to produce its cocoon. The Chinese discovered very early that boiling the cocoons yielded a single thread, which could be wound into a strong fiber. Egyptian tombs contain silk cocoons dating from as early as 1000 BCE. For two millennia, China held the monopoly of this technology, and its fabrics fascinated all of Eurasia. Our word "silk" comes from the Latin and Greek name for the Chinese, the *Seres*. Chinese exports of silk generated a trading network that spanned the Eurasian continent. Because silk was so valuable in relation to its weight, traders profited from it despite the extremely high costs of overland transportation. Still, the trade could only flourish under special political conditions. The seventh to ninth centuries were the peak period of the Silk Road, when the great empires met and provided security guarantees for the caravans crossing the steppes.

Silk trade depended on the endurance of an animal much less handsome, or tractable, than the horse: the Bactrian (two-humped) camel. These camels moved slowly and steadily across the vast expanse of steppe and desert, stopping at oases to refuel with grain and water. Unlike Arabian (single-humped) camels, they were useless in warfare, but they could withstand cold, and travel further without water. The men who trained these beasts were highly skilled specialists, essential elements of every caravan. While the dashing horsemen provided the military arm to extend the empires' reach, the cantankerous camel was the essential lubricant that kept goods flowing through the trade arteries. Without the money from the silk trade, none of the great empires could have supported their armies, and without protection from the horsemen, none of the merchants could have made their profits, or the religious missionaries found their believers.

A second empire arose in 683, under **Bilge Qaghan** (r. 716–34), who set up his base around the Orkhon River in Mongolia. Bilge hired Chinese artisans to carve two large inscriptions in a runic script, derived from the Sogdian alphabet. These are the first genuine writings produced by a steppe empire. They describe the divine power of Heaven that determined the founding of the first empire, under Bumin, and celebrated his victories:

"When high above the blue sky and down below the brown earth had been created, betwixt the two were created the sons of men. And above the sons of men stood my ancestors, the qaghans Bumin and Ishtemi. Having become the masters of the Turk people, they installed and ruled its empire and fixed the law of the country. Many were their enemies in the four corners of the world, but, leading campaigns against them, they subjugated and pacified many nations in the four corners of the world. They caused them to bow their heads and to bend their knees."[2]

But they lamented the decline of the Turks, seduced into slavery by Chinese luxuries: "The sons of the Turkish nobles became slaves to the Chinese people, and their innocent daughters were reduced to serfdom. The nobles, discarding their Turkish titles, accepted those of China ... to the Chinese qaghan they surrendered their empire and their institutions." The writers recognized the insidious skills of the Chinese in inducing the Turks to fight each other: "because the Chinese created conflicts between younger and older brothers and armed the people and rulers against each other, the Turk people fell into disarray."[3]

Bilge Qaghan learned from his ancestors' experience and from his advisors that the only way to preserve the Turk empire was to stay away from China. He said, "The Chinese gave us gold, silver, and silk in abundance. The words of the Chinese people have always been sweet and the materials of the Chinese people have always been soft. Deceiving by means of their sweet words and soft materials the Chinese are said to cause remote peoples to come close ... Having been taken in by their sweet words and soft materials, you Turkish people were killed in great numbers."[4] He refused to build a city, and tried to keep his men far away in the outer frontier. But others could not resist the fatal attraction of Chinese goods. In 734 another nomadic warrior federation, the Uighurs, destroyed the divided Turks.

The Turk empire at its peak stretched from Manchuria to the Volga River. Although much bigger than the Tang in size, it had far fewer people in it, and most of them were not Turks. The top-level elite was a military aristocracy, headed by the divinely appointed qaghan and a small retinue of loyal chieftains. At this level, it was not so different from the Tang. But administration below the top was tribal; there was no equivalent to the elaborate Chinese bureaucracy. The Turks knew that they needed a literate class of clerks, so they relied on the expert Sogdian merchants to provide them with a writing system and administrators. In this respect they went beyond the Xiongnu, but their written output was nowhere near the Tang literary corpus, and it was fragmented into many languages and cultures. Turk qaghans, who lived from trade and war, could amass impressive heaps of gold

and large amounts of silk, jade, and wine, to impress Byzantine and Chinese envoys alike. They usually had military superiority over their neighbors, because like all nomads, they lived by horsemanship. But their fatal weakness was internal disunity: China could use its wealth to turn them inward and weaken their fighting spirit. In the end, however, the Sogdian–Turk alliance, in the person of An Lushan (Rokshan), infiltrated the Tang and brought down its centralized power. This intimate interplay between the steppe and the settled zones directly shaped the fates of Chinese and nomads alike.

The Uighurs were a multicultural nomadic military confederation like the Turks, but they moved further toward settling down. Their qaghan built a new city near the Orkhon River, called **Ordu Baliq**. Its walls encompassed a vast area, 4.5 by 1.5 miles, but much of the space inside was taken up by tents, not buildings. Most of the Uighurs still lived as nomads within city walls. The qaghan, however, was anxious to obtain Chinese goods, so he offered to put the Tang emperor back on his throne in exchange for marriage alliances and tens of thousands of bolts of silk. Uighur troops took Chang'an with the emperor in tow, then looted the second capital of Luoyang until they were paid off. Their close connection to China made the Uighurs richer than any previous steppe empire, but it drew part of them away from their steppe roots. After staying in Luoyang, the Uighur qaghan adopted the Persian religion of Manichaeanism, the most popular religion of the Sogdian merchants. Others in the Uighur elite resented this accommodation to settled urban religious life, especially when the Manichaean priests banned the consumption of meat and fermented milk. They assassinated the Manichaean qaghan, tearing the empire apart between those pulled toward settled, urban life, and those who longed for the austerity of the steppe. In 840, the next group of tough nomads, the **Kirghiz**, destroyed the Uighur state. Many of the remaining Uighur people moved to the oases of Turfan and the Tarim Basin, where they became vital links in the trade routes. The modern Turkic populations of Xinjiang, China, who call themselves Uighurs, have only a very distant relationship with these nomadic ancestors who settled down in the oases over a thousand years ago.

The Tibetan Empire

Next to the Turks, the Tibetans mounted the most threatening challenges to Tang imperial aims. Living on the roof of the world, the Tibetans were a sparse population spread over a vast plateau covering 1.5 million square miles, whose terrain included harsh deserts, snowy mountains, river valleys, pastures, and woodlands. Many were herdsmen, grazing yaks, goats, and Mongolian ponies, but other Tibetans were farmers and forest people, cultivating barley, grapes, and honey. Huge mountain ranges and uninhabited terrain divided them, making unification nearly impossible. But their great king **Songtsen Gampo** (r. 634–50) achieved this nearly impossible feat, making the Tibetans one of the strongest empires in Eurasia for two hundred years. Tibetans were great horsemen, who wore strong iron coats of mail. Under a strong leader, no one could beat them. Songtsen Gampo first marched into Kokonor, demanding a Chinese princess as the price of peace: after a stinging defeat, the Chinese realized they had to give in. The king got his princess, but he also began turning to China for books and advice. He sent young Tibetans to China to obtain classical texts, while at the same time, through his Nepalese princess, he developed links to India. In the 660s he took control of the Tarim Basin kingdoms from China and created the Tibetan alphabet, based on Indian models. At its peak, Tibet drew on both Indian and Chinese cultural traditions. Tibetan armies continued to raid the Chinese frontier, interrupting their attacks to sign peace treaties, which both sides soon violated. The An Lushan rebellion weakened the Tang so much that Tibetans could invade Chang'an in 763, looting and burning for days until they withdrew. The main Tibetan interest was, like the Turks, not to conquer China, but to use it as their cash cow. China's only hope was to turn to the Uighurs for defense, so they could finally defeat Tibetan forces and make peace in 821. Meanwhile, the Tibetan king made the decisive move of converting his people to Buddhism. After hearing debates between Indian and Chinese monks, he eventually chose the Indian school. With his death in 804, however, Tibetan glory rapidly faded. Struggles between noble families and Buddhist monastic interests weakened the country, until the Turks and Uighurs destroyed the kingdom in the middle of the ninth century.

Thus, like the Turks, the Tibetans mounted a serious, long-lasting challenge to Chinese imperial power, at the same time as they used Chinese literary and bureaucratic techniques to strengthen their state. Tibet, however, had alternatives in the Indian direction not open to the Turks. As if the high altitude and rough weather were not enough, Tibet's fateful orientation toward Indian Buddhism made it an utterly alien place for most Chinese.

8.3 THE NANZHAO STATE AND ANNAM, 650–900

On a plateau 7,000 feet high in western Yunnan, bordered by the deep Erhai lake, a small plain provides fertile soil and abundant rainfall to support agriculture. The Tibeto-Burman peoples here joined in a confederation that created a powerful kingdom, called **Nanzhao**, which challenged Tang control of the southwest. Nanzhao rulers built a fortified capital at Dali, taking Chinese

titles for their administration, and first submitted as vassals to the Tang. But in 751, after disputes over border districts, Tang armies attempted to conquer the kingdom. They suffered a disastrous defeat, and Nanzhao allied itself with the Tibetans, threatening Tang rule of Sichuan. In 790 Nanzhao returned to the Chinese side, helping the Tang to attack Tibet, but it also expanded southward against Burma and Tang administration in the kingdom of **Annam** (northern Vietnam). By 829, Nanzhao armies, again hostile to China, sacked the capital city of Sichuan, Chengdu. The Annamese, who resented Tang domination, called on Nanzhao to help them when they rebelled in 858. Tang armies put down this revolt and removed the Nanzhao threat, but at a very high cost. The heavy fiscal burdens of supplying armies in the south touched off the major rebellions that brought down the dynasty.

8.4 KOREA AND THE NORTHEAST

In Northeast Eurasia, the Tang model was the strongest, and its cultural influence created the states most able to resist Chinese domination. Three states emerged on the Korean peninsula and southern Manchuria: **Goguryo**, **Baekje**, and **Silla**, during the fourth century CE. The most powerful of these, the Goguryo kingdom in the north, held off repeated Sui and Tang attacks for nearly three hundred years. Sui Yangdi had brought down his dynasty because his obsession with conquering Goguryo bled his troops and people dry. In the early Tang, Goguryo negotiated peaceful relations, in order to bolster its defenses and expand southward against Silla. But Tang Taizong, dreaming of restoring Han glories, launched a personal expedition, against the advice of his ministers, in 644. Goguryo repulsed a series of sieges, forcing the Tang armies to withdraw. In the words of a Korean historian, Goguryo's stubborn resistance "occup[ies] a special place in the annals of the resistance of the Korean people to foreign aggression."[5]

But the Korean rulers were divided. Silla, a vassal of the Tang, appealed to the great empire for aid with a plan for a joint expedition against Goguryo. First the armies took Baekje in the east, to provide a maritime base for the invasion of the north. Japan sent armies to rescue Baekje, and fought a naval battle with the Tang, to no avail. Tang and Silla then turned north against an enfeebled Goguryo state, finally eliminating it in 668. But the Tang could not hold Korea. Silla, which copied Tang institutions very carefully, drove out the Chinese armies, thus preserving the independence of the Korean peninsula. Further north in Manchuria, another powerful state, **Balhae**, also copied Tang institutions and obtained recognition as a tributary state from the Tang. By the mid eighth century, both Silla and Balhae had established peaceful relations with the Tang and maintained their autonomy. They both imported books, monks, and art works from China to develop their own distinctive cultures. The kings learned from the Tang how to assert authoritarian power over their aristocracies, and how to use Confucian classics to justify centralized control.

8.5 NARA JAPAN, 710–84

In the eighth century the Japanese, hundreds of miles across the sea from China, also fused their own cultural elements with imported Tang innovations to create a unified state. Human beings have lived on the Japanese islands for 100,000 years. Paleolithic cultures developed there in 10,000 BCE, and Japan contains some of the most ancient and elegant pottery in the world, dating to *c.* 7000 BCE. The Neolithic Age, including agriculture, bronze, and iron, arrived around 300 BCE. Japan had cultural contacts through Korea with Han China, but no state formed on the islands until the seventh century CE. Before this time, clans controlled separated farming units. Large keyhole-shaped tombs indicate that some major kings of the chieftain culture had emerged by the third century CE. Some of these tombs, concentrated in the **Yamato** Plain at the eastern end of the Inland Sea, are larger than the pyramids of Egypt. They contain large burial chambers with symbols of wealth, swords, and armor. Outside them lie ceramic figurines, called **haniwa**, wearing the quilted jackets and trousers of the horse-riding peoples of Northeast Asia. Japanese legends also tell of "horseriding invaders" who crossed over from the Korean peninsula in the sixth century CE. Horses had definitely arrived in Japan early from China and Korea, but they were small and unarmored until the sixth century. Japanese warriors fitted them out with bridles and military gear, and began to learn the skills of mounted archery.

Powerful warrior clans, called **uji**, had begun to consolidate their control by the fourth century, but the country remained highly fragmented. Chinese records called Japan the land of "one hundred [i.e. many] kingdoms." Slowly, after a great deal of negotiation, the Yamato clan made itself superior to the others, claiming descent from the sun goddess and holding the three sacred jewels of the Japanese monarchy: the sword, the mirror, and the jewel. By the fifth century, Japan had adopted the Chinese script, and in 552 Buddhism arrived from Korea.

The unification of China under the Sui and Tang dazzled the rising Japanese clan leaders. Japan's first political hero, **Shotoku Taishi** (r. 593–622), decided to transform his entire state on the Chinese model. By combining the Tang bureaucracy with the glorification of rulers by Buddhist monks, he aimed to maximize his power. He introduced a system of court ranks modeled on the Tang, and in two of his famous Seventeen Injunctions of 604 he urged his people to "sincerely revere the three treasures of Buddhism (Buddha, the Law, and the Priesthood)." Thus he linked obedience to Buddhism to his claim to supreme power. The other injunctions instructed officials on how to act justly, select able persons for office, and not oppress the people.[6] These Confucian maxims, like the claim that "the emperor is Heaven," supported the ruler and his bureaucracy against rival claims by powerful clans.

At his death, factional conflict broke out, but the victors carried on contact with China via Korea. A Chinese mission arrived from the Tang in 632. Japan's warriors suffered mostly from a shortage of iron to make weapons. This need led them to intervene in the Korean peninsula, where they faced threats from the expanding Tang dynasty and its Korean allies. In 646 the winning faction, advised by Chinese specialists, launched a drastic reform movement. The emperor claimed his right to rule all his territory under his state, instead of yielding power to clan leaders. The civil and military reform provided for units of border guards to defend the country against foreign attack. In the 660s, Tang troops invaded Goguryo in northern Korea, crushed the Baekje state, Japan's ally, and forced Silla to ally with China. Japanese soldiers and sailors fought a fierce battle with the Chinese at the Paekch'on River in 663, which led to a military disaster for Japan: the loss of 400 ships, 10,000 men, and 1,000 horses. This catastrophe caused civil war in Japan, which only ended when the Emperor **Temmu** took power in 672, determined to reinforce the military power of his state.

In 702 Temmu declared comprehensive measures modeled on the Tang system to reinforce his power, including a uniform law code and taxation system, a census, and the minting of copper coins. Like it or not, every peasant household had to provide soldiers to serve the emperor. In Japan's earliest poetry collection, the **Manyoshu** (eighth century), a border guard laments, "The dread imperial command / I have received; from tomorrow / I will sleep with the grass / No wife being by me."[7] The emperor now had his own military force to undercut the power of provincial leaders and expand his realm.

These reforms, driven by military necessity, also brought with them substantial Chinese cultural influence. Japan now became a literate society at its elite level. The Chinese classical language became the language of administration, and the Japanese took over Buddhist scriptures wholesale in Chinese. The first historical chronicles written in Japan used the Chinese language. Since Japanese words have many syllables, however, while most Chinese words have only one syllable, adapting the Chinese script to the Japanese language was awkward. Japan's great poetry collection, the Manyoshu, recorded moving folk songs and lyrical ballads by using one character for each syllable. Later, Japanese women writers developed a more efficient method, by reducing the Chinese forms to a syllabic alphabet.

These reforms culminated in the building of the capital of Nara in 710. Nara was a carbon copy in miniature of Tang Chang'an. It united the straight avenues, officially controlled districts, and heavy investment in Buddhist architecture. The great Buddha of **Todaiji** temple, 52 feet high, completed in 752, required over 3 million pounds of copper, tin, and lead, and 15,000 pounds of gold. Its purpose was to inspire awe of the mighty Buddha and the state that supported it. But unlike China, these resources came from a very poor economy where money was still quite scarce. The emperor and the Buddhists had succeeded in extracting enormous amounts to support their regime.

Japan now had international recognition in East Asia, accepting envoys from Korea, intervening in battles with China, and sending tribute missions to the Tang. The **Shoso-in**, an imperial storehouse in Nara, contains valuable trade goods from all over the Eurasian world. It includes the oldest example in the world of the **biwa** (Chinese: pipa), a lute with Persian origins, along with zithers, harps, flutes, and drums modeled on Tang styles which in turn reflect the strong connections of China with Central Eurasia. These instruments formed the orchestra for Japanese court music, known as **gagaku**. Gagaku is still performed today, and it has definite links with the music of the dancers of Central Eurasia transmitted through China and Korea.

But the Chinese model did not fit Japan well, and soon turned into something very different in practice. The court ranks did not become bureaucratic positions, determined by competition for imperial favor; instead they became hereditary, the basis of a new aristocracy. The top leaders moved to the capital, as new wealth flowed in from the provinces. Soon the pressure from the nobles and the Buddhists threatened the emperor's control. He moved the capital away from Nara to Heian, modern Kyoto, in 794 to escape them. Outside the capital, when there were no further censuses or redistribution of land, local landowners held back their tax revenues and established local estates. The emperors had used their peasant conscripts to conduct campaigns against the "barbarian" peoples of northeastern Honshu, but these ended in failure, only exhausting the state's resources. They had to abandon the costly centralized regiments and allow local strongmen to take control once again of military forces. These strongmen, skilled horsemen using sharp curved swords, who controlled their own pastures, created hereditary military houses that centuries later became the warriors known as samurai.

Gradually Japan turned away from China and developed its own distinctive style. Unlike the continental empires, it never

had to fear an invasion. In 894 Japan decided not to send an embassy to China: it had lost interest in the continental model. Over this period, Japan had turned sharply toward China to create a powerful new state and social structures that built up its coercive, commercial, and spiritual resources, and then it turned away. The first of many pendulum swings outward and inward had begun.

8.6 SILK ROAD TRADE

The "Silk Road" got its name only after it had disappeared. The name is really a creation of nineteenth-century geographers looking back on vanished Central Eurasian routes. The name "Silk Road" is evocative, but inaccurate: Silk was not the only product, and there was not just one road. Yet it captures a reality: a network of trade routes crossing vast distances linking vastly different civilizations together. We may think of these routes like volleyball nets: the poles were the densely populated cores of China, India, Persia, and Byzantium; the strings were the trains of camels and their drivers; the knots were the oases where the caravans stopped to shift their goods and restock supplies. Then think of placing these nets into a great ocean: the grassland sea, containing roaming pirates (nomads) who preyed on the caravans like floating treasure. Protection costs for this trade were high: only a powerful military regime could drive back the nomadic raiders or negotiate with them. Yet all the participants had strong interests in keeping the trade going: No one wanted to kill the golden goose. Most of the time, Chinese officials allowed the nomads to exchange poor horses for large quantities of valuable silk. The Chinese called this "paying tribute" to the emperor; the nomads called it good business. They in turn relied on skilled Central Eurasian merchants to organize the caravans, distribute the goods, and collect the gold and silver from the peoples to the west. The final key participant in the trade was the Bactrian two-humped camel, the ship of the desert. He was slower, heavier, and perhaps nastier than his cousin, the single-humped dromedary of the Arabian Desert, but he could withstand the cold better and travel further. Slowly but steadily, he carried large loads, up to 500 pounds, across thousands of miles of inhospitable terrain, at a rate of about 15 miles per day.

The central areas of silk production were in the lower Yangtze Valley. From there, the cloth made its way to Chang'an, the imperial capital and the jumping-off point for caravans heading west. They followed the long Gansu corridor, a string of towns lying between the desert to the north and the high mountains to the south, to Anxi and Dunhuang, where the road divided in two branches, north and south of the Taklamakan Desert. On the northern route, the more common one, the travelers passed

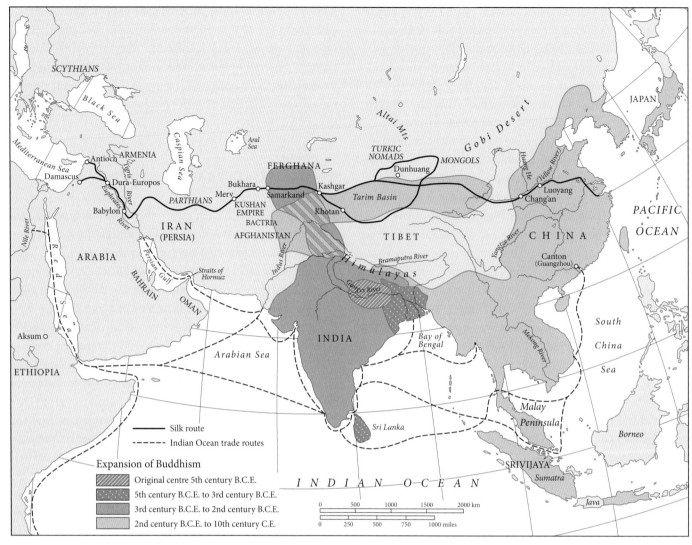

Map 8.3 Asian trade and commercial routes

through the oases of Hami, Turfan, Korla, Kucha, Aksu, and Kashgar; to the south, through Charkhlik, Cherchen, Khotan, and Yarkand, meeting the northern route at Kashgar. Kashgar, in the foothills of the Pamir Mountains, was the key western crossroads. From here, one could head south to India through the Karakorum Mountains, northwest to the heart of Central Asia at Kokand, Samarkand, and Bukhara, or west through Persia and Afghanistan. South of the Caspian Sea, the routes joined again, passing through Baghdad and Damascus to end at the shores of the Mediterranean at Antioch and Byzantium. Map 8.3 shows these routes.

Second only to the subject peasantry, the silk trade was the vital element that kept the empires afloat, so securing access to silk routes was as strong a motivation for war as oil is today. The Tang, the Turks, the Tibetans, and the Uighurs sent their armies far away not to control poor soils and grasslands, but to keep a foothold in the oases that linked the silk routes. Alongside the armies marched the camels, the merchants, and their goods, and

the monks, missionaries, and spies. Let us briefly examine a few of the key places and peoples along these roads.

Dunhuang: The Great Port

Over 500 miles west of Xi'an lies the town of Dunhuang. It was the key point of access to China for nomads, as it protected the throat of the western empire, the Gansu corridor. It was likewise China's western outpost for the penetration of Central Eurasia. The name Dunhuang itself may come from an Iranian word for "fortress." Chinese rulers made intensive efforts to defend this spot, erecting watchtowers and defensive fortifications there. Fifty miles further west, at the Jade Gate, the Great Wall ended, looking out on boundless steppe.

The people of Dunhuang had many ups and downs. Chinese garrisons first fortified Dunhuang in 121 BCE, and by the second century CE its population exceeded 76,000. The Tang dynasty protected and promoted trade and religion in the town when they established their administration there. The Tibetans seized Dunhuang from the Tang in 781 CE, but a Chinese warlord took it back in 850. It fell to the Uighurs in 911, then the Tibetan Xi Xia kingdom, and then the Mongols.

Dunhuang was, however, much more than a military camp. It was a major cultural and economic crossroads, through which people of almost every imaginable culture and religion passed. It was the essential stop for Chinese monks heading to India and back, so Buddhists collected here in large communities. The Sogdian merchants, following the Manichaean religion, had a significant presence. Turks, Uighurs, and Tibetans, when they were not at war with China, made it a prosperous trading post. The oasis flourished by resupplying caravans heading east and west; the local inhabitants collected money from everyone who passed through. They spent their money in bustling market-places on food from the irrigated fields, clothing of silk and cotton, storytellers, dancers, and brothels. As many as seventy-five different languages might be spoken there.

Outside the town, Buddhist monks lived in grottoes carved out of the soft sandstone mountains. They had begun carving their caves in the mid fourth century, and by the ninth century they had created nearly one thousand of them. Inside the caves, they lined the walls with dried mud and straw attached to bamboo scaffolding, and on these surfaces they painted some of the most spectacular religious art in the world. Over 500 caves, with 45,000 murals and 2,000 stucco figures which still retain their bright colors, survive today. The murals portray stories from the life of the Buddha, rich merchant patrons of the monastic community, Silk Road caravans, warriors, cities, flying angels, and elegant bodhisattvas in a tremendous range of artistic styles. Indian models of the Buddha, influenced by Greco-Roman art as they passed through Central Asia, then responded to cultures of the steppe and the refined, orderly perspectives of Chinese sculpture and painting. The Dunhuang paintings are a true hybrid of multiple cultures, brilliantly successful at merging many religions in one visual spectacle.

Besides the paintings, Dunhuang contained another precious room: a library which stored thousands of scrolls and manuscripts in many languages, on history, religious scriptures, medicine, mathematics, and daily life. Most precious for the social historian are the scraps of paper which were saved because they were written on the back of Buddhist scriptures: these reveal daily life in the oasis under Chinese rule, showing that people wrote legal contracts, shopping lists, letters, just as they do today.

Dunhuang, the town and the caves, continued their activity after the fall of the Tang, but in 1006 Islamic forces took its neighbor, Khotan, and the monks sealed up the documents and fled. The painters created new work under the Mongols, but by the fourteenth century Chinese and Central Asians alike had forgotten them. Then, over five hundred years later, the British-Hungarian explorer **Aurel Stein** set out from India into the Taklamakan Desert to search for traces of vanished civilizations buried in the sands. The Swedish explorer **Sven Hedin** had found several cities in the desert, and German expeditions had discovered ancient manuscripts in Turfan, and cave murals nearby. In 1900 a Daoist monk, Wang Yuanlu, who had settled near the caves to take care of them, discovered the hidden cache of manuscripts. Stein was determined to get them. In 1907 he reached the caves and saw the murals on the walls. After he praised Xuanzang, the heroic seventh-century Chinese Buddhist who had gone to India and back to retrieve precious scriptures, Wang brought him the actual Chinese manuscripts translated by Xuanzang himself. Stein then got to see the huge mass of documents, and purchased 7,000 manuscripts and 6,000 fragments for a total cost of 130 British pounds. Next year, the French linguist and explorer **Paul Pelliot** came to grab the cream of the crop for France. Unlike Stein, he knew many of the languages of the documents, so he took only the best, thousands of them, back to Paris. Japanese and Russians got into the act, and even an American, art historian Langdon Warner, who had twelve sections of the wall paintings carved away to take back to the Fogg museum at Harvard. Then the Chinese slammed the door shut on the pillaging imperialists. In the early twentieth century, China was indeed a victim of Western greed for ancient treasures. But if foreigners had not taken them away, would they have survived China's wars and revolutions?

Dunhuang's vibrant culture made it look like a great seaport, even though it was in the midst of sand, not water. The coming and going of all sorts of goods, peoples, religions, and wars made its life tumultuous and endlessly inventive. Its great remoteness from the core agrarian civilizations preserved its art from war and persecution, as the arid climate kept it free from rot. Western empires, preying on China's collapse, opened it up again and spread its marvels around the globe. Dunhuang is a microcosm of our times.

The Sogdians

The Sogdians had some of the most profound effects on Eurasia in this period, yet they are among its least-known peoples. They powered the economic engine that kept the Silk Road trade going for centuries. They spoke an Iranian language, and their homeland was in Bactria, the oasis cities of Bukhara and Samarkand, but they moved across the entire continent. A seventh-century gravestone of a Sogdian merchant states that he had been to both Byzantium and China. Sogdians penetrated North India, in Kashmir and Ladakh; they controlled trade routes through Persia, and they dominated the caravans passing through Turk and Chinese territory. The Sogdians never ruled an empire, but as crucial intermediaries they supported the armies and diplomats. They could do business with anybody. The Turks contracted with them for supplies, and so did the Chinese. They had few military forces of their own, but they contracted with Turks and Chinese forces to defend their home cities. Arab armies, however, conquered their oases in the mid eighth century and suppressed them when they rebelled.

They carried not only goods but information along the trade routes: whatever Chinese knew of the Byzantine empire they learned from the Sogdians. Beautiful Sogdian women from Samarkand, dressed in crimson robes, brocaded sleeves, and red deerskin boots, entertained the caravans with the fascinating "Sogdian whirling" dance: later, Islamic whirling dervishes and Christian mystics took up this dizzying practice for religious inspiration. Everyone used the Sogdian language to conduct trade. The Sogdians used the Syriac alphabet of the Middle East and transmitted it eastward, where it was taken up by the Mongols, and later the Manchus. The canny Sogdians knew how to bribe the right officials, how to find the finest wool, silk, jewelry, and drugs, how to cheat the unwary buyers, and how to arrange credit for the professionals. They braved sand storms, death from thirst, and bandit attacks to carry goods over thousands of miles. In the midst of constant warfare and uncertainty, they kept the trade going that made economic and cultural contact possible.

8.7 RELIGIONS OF EAST ASIA AND THE SILK ROAD

Before the expansion of the great empires and the knitting together of the trade routes, most of the great religious traditions, except for Buddhism, remained separate from each other. One stream of Buddhism originated in India, passed into China through Afghanistan in the late Han dynasty, and traveled from there into Japan, Korea, and Vietnam. The two huge Buddhist rock sculptures at Bamiyan in Afghanistan, one of which is shown in Figure 8.1, were destroyed by the Taliban in 2001. They testify to Buddhism's position linking South Asia, the Middle East, and China. The other stream of Buddhism moved south from India into Ceylon and Southeast Asia.

Aside from Buddhism, one or two major creeds dominated each civilization: Christianity in the West, Daoism and Confucianism in China, Hindu beliefs in India, Zoroastrianism in Persia. The nomads in between mainly paid respect to shamans who could put them in touch with supernatural forces. Then came the explosion of Islam eastward, the drive of the Chinese westward, and the mixing of faiths among the caravan traders.

Figure 8.1 In northern Afganistan, in the sixth century, Buddhist sculptors carved two enormous statues out of the mountain rock, standing 115 and 174 feet tall. They followed the Gandharan art style of Bactria, and they were the largest standing Buddhist figures in the world. Other Muslim rulers had tried to destroy them in the past, but the Taliban blew them up in 2001. Many Islamic states condemned the Taliban action as a cultural crime. They still have not been reconstructed.

All the missionaries, pilgrims, monks, and texts who traveled these great distances jostled up against each other.

Manichaeanism

The Sogdian traders, the most mobile of all these peoples, picked up all these religious influences. Some Sogdians converted to Islam, but most of them became either **Manichaeans** or Nestorian Christians. Manichaeans were followers of the prophet Mani, who had preached his doctrine in Iran and northwest

Box 8.4 Telling Stories with Pictures

Among the precious documents brought back from Dunhuang by Paul Pelliot is a scroll showing a disciple of Buddha, Sariputra, debating doctrine with heretics. At one time, large scrolls like this rolled up on sticks were presented to popular audiences as a backdrop for storytellers. The performers told tales of miraculous feats performed by the Buddha and his disciples, illustrated by the scrolls. They used the vernacular language, translating the esoteric doctrines of Indian Buddhism into versions easily understandable by large audiences. They were not real monks, but entertainers who made their living by preaching Buddhism in the streets. A hostile Chinese poet described one of them: "They call him 'foul face' and he styles himself a Buddhist. But who ever heard of a master going door to door asking whether people want to make vows on the sutras, and spending the whole night long without sleep? ... When he finishes proclaiming the Precious Scroll on the Diamond Sutra, it's inevitable that he'll ask for some vegetarian food. But he's only interested in getting something to eat; he's not after money."

This type of picture-telling performance probably originated in India as early as Buddhism itself, but from there it spread to China and the rest of Asia, and eventually Europe. Other religious traditions, like Daoists in China, picked up the same technique. The famous Indonesian *wayang* performances of Hindu epics, with storytellers or shadow puppets in front of a painted background, came from India too.

More than the esoteric disputations of monks, these popular performances spread Buddhism throughout East Asian populations and deeply embedded it in the culture. Stories, not theories, changed how common people placed their own lives in deep spiritual time.

India in the third century CE. He drew his ideas from many sources, especially Buddhist doctrines of the transmigration of souls and ancient Iranian doctrines of the division of the world into forces of light and dark. Mani saw himself as the culmination of a prophetic tradition established by Zoroaster, Buddha, and Jesus. He originally intended his doctrine for an elite who would abstain from sex and alcohol in order to concentrate light particles in their bodies, so as to liberate themselves from all contamination. The Sogdians in Samarkand made Manichaeanism into the living religion of a large community, and they transmitted it far and wide. Chinese, Christian, and Islamic rulers all looked on them with suspicion, but they established churches across the Eurasian continent, from Baghdad to Chang'an. They fled persecution from oasis to oasis, but kept contacts with each other to support their priests and protect their scriptures. The Dunhuang caves contain portraits of Manichaean priests, showing that they were a regular feature of the town.

Buddhism in China

In China, the Tang dynasty was the golden age of Buddhism, the period when it held a dominant position among the state officials and the general populace alike. State sponsorship of monastic building projects, the generation of new sects suited to Chinese beliefs, and the strong role of Buddhists in the economy embedded Buddhist teachings and activities deeply within Chinese society. The Buddhists' rivals, especially Daoists and Confucians, held their ground, but had still not recovered from the collapse of the Han dynasty and the wilder excesses of popular Daoism during the period of division. The monumental scale of Buddhist statues and temples, and the great impact of East Asian Buddhism in Japan and Korea, also express this spirit of self-confident expansiveness. For the common people, however, exotic stories from the Indian Buddhist tradition, told by puppeteers and oral narrators, had more influence than metaphysical texts and giant statues. Box 8.4 discusses the role of stories and pictures in disseminating Buddhism.

Buddhist monks had come to China from India in the later Han dynasty. By the second century CE, officials helped them to build monasteries, and Chinese scholars launched translation projects to make the Indian writings accessible to the literate elite. By the end of the third century, they had translated hundreds of works, and over 37,000 clergy lived in the capital cities of North China. With the collapse of the Han, the destruction of major cities by nomadic invaders, and the flight of many people south, Buddhism attracted disillusioned Confucian officials who saw no hope of restoring a just imperial order based on classical texts. Some of them withdrew from the political world to become monks. They could also draw on the Daoist Zhuangzi's teachings about the unreality of the material world to make Buddhist doctrine more plausible in Chinese terms.

Buddhists, for their part, soon accommodated themselves to state power. Although the historical Buddha had rejected wealth and power in order to pursue an ascetic ideal, many Buddhist preachers found no problem in accepting large gifts from aristocrats and emperors. Just like the Christian church, the

Buddhist faith evolved from a small group of believers determined to leave the world into a large, wealthy establishment supported by the powers that were. There was no Buddhist pope, however, to lay down a uniform doctrine, so many different sects proliferated with varying interpretations of the sacred texts. Since the Buddhist canon of scripture is huge, and less clearly defined than the Judeo-Christian one – the corpus of Chinese canonical texts alone is seventy-four times as large as the Bible – there was plenty of room for interpretation.

The reunification of China under Sui and Tang gave the Buddhists even more access to patrons. The Sui emperors invested heavily in monasteries, although they also supported Daoist temples and Confucian ritual. Imperial support came with a price, however: closer control over monastic activities by the state. The monks had to enforce their rules closely, control disorderly behavior, and suppress heretical doctrines. Tang Taizong's ambivalence toward Buddhist influence indicates the hazards of depending on the state. The second Tang emperor came from a prominent military family with a Turkic background in North China, where Buddhism had already penetrated widely. It may seem paradoxical that military warriors endorsed Buddhism's pacifist ideals, but we should not isolate elements of Buddhist doctrine from their context. Buddhists did believe in compassion and non-violence, but they lived in a society full of treachery, insecurity, and threats. Monks had to hire warriors to defend their monasteries, and many monks themselves went into battle. Tang Taizong relied on these warrior-monks to help him take over the empire. When in power, he ordained thousands of new monks, listened to their advice, and built an especially lavish temple in honor of his mother. He had long discussions with the great traveling monk Xuanzang, who returned from India with fabulous stories and new sources of religious inspiration. Yet in the middle of his reign, the emperor turned against the Buddhists, claiming that they were corrupt, and only Daoists represented the truly Chinese faith. He even traced his own family's roots back to Laozi. The heroic monk **Zhishi** showed that some Buddhists would stand up for their beliefs: when he rejected imperial edicts to shut down temples, he was flogged, and died in exile. The capricious autocrat vacillated between attacks on "false Buddhists" and support of their activities. In the end, the emperor did believe that Buddhists could help the welfare of the people, but only if they were kept under close watch.

Imperial and noble patronage, however, gave the Buddhists large amounts of capital, which they could invest in profitable economic enterprises. Buddhist monasteries had the advantage of being long-lasting, collective, disciplined communities, in a time still filled with uncertainty. Before reunification, they seemed more likely to last than state authority, so they attracted charitable donations. Buddhists were also clever managers of their collective property. They established the first pawnshops, allowing poor farmers and workers to hand in their winter clothing, for example, in exchange for money or food. Unlike Muslims or Christians, Buddhists held no firm prejudices against charging interest. They spread philanthropic activity widely through Chinese society, helping to unite the concerns for social justice of local elites with the need for relief of the poor.

Under the Tang, monks, translators, and preachers made Buddhism truly Chinese. Even in the fifth and sixth centuries, despite receiving gifts from wealthy patrons, the Buddhists' teachings were too Indian to appeal to Chinese laymen. The Indian texts held that achieving enlightenment was an arduous process, which could require many eons of reincarnations before the believer escaped into **nirvana**. Only a small elite of dedicated, ascetic monks could ever reach this goal. Chinese Buddhists were more practical. They modified Indian scriptures in translation to find in them an inspiring "hidden message" that anyone could achieve enlightenment, possibly in a very short time. The supreme Buddhist goal now became available to everyone. Disagreements on this and other doctrinal issues had divided the world of Buddhism into two great camps: the Theravada, or **Hinayana**, "Lesser Vehicle," and the **Mahayana**, or "Greater Vehicle." The Theravada, closer to the original Indian version, died out in India, but survived in Southeast Asia and Sri Lanka, while the Mahayana sects became the predominant version in East Asia (see Chapter 5).

Buddhist teachers in China developed new schools of thought, in both philosophical and popular forms. The most influential philosophical school, **Tiantai** (named after the mountains where the sect flourished), laid the basis for all East Asian teachings. Its founder, Zhiyi, asserted that all sentient beings, not just humans, could be enlightened, that religious practice mattered more than nuances of doctrine, that Chinese patriarchs served as models of perfect behavior, and that it was even possible to achieve enlightenment in this life. Zhiyi found all these teachings in one relatively obscure Indian text, the **Lotus Sutra**. How then to explain all the contradictory teachings in other writings? Zhiyi ranked the other writings and schools on a scale, according to how closely they approached his ideal of perfection. Only the *Lotus Sutra* was perfect, but others came close. He could thus bring together conflicting doctrines and claim them to be ultimately part of the same mission. Zhiyi's syncretic approach mixed elements from divergent teachings together in the interest of unity. He did for religious unification what the Sui and Tang emperors did for political unity.

Other Buddhist schools spread among the common people for much simpler reasons. Each of them had a special feature and a special niche. The **Pure Land** school argued that to achieve enlightenment, one only had to chant the name of **Amitabha**

Buddha (in Chinese, Emituofo) over and over again, millions of times. The Esoteric school stressed the use of secret handshakes, mystical signs, and powerful magic. The Three Stages school said that the entire world would go through cataclysmic transformations that would overturn all existing social institutions and bring a new world of universal peace and justice. The Tang suppressed this clearly subversive school, but it reappeared over and over again in later centuries. The **Chan** (in Japanese, **Zen**) school is probably the one best known in the West today. Its proponents focused on intense meditative activity leading to inexplicable mystical insight, unattainable solely by studying texts, virtuous behavior, or philosophical reflection. One could only look to earlier Chan masters for examples: their cryptic conversations ("What is the sound of one hand clapping?"), or even beatings, might lead their disciples to enlightenment. The Chan teachers themselves divided on the question of whether enlightenment could be sudden or gradual. Each of these teachings developed strong groups of believers during the Tang, and many of them had even more powerful influence in Japan.

By the end of the ninth century, despite their success, Buddhists suffered from increasing hostility. Their rivals, Daoists and Confucians, attacked them for being foreign, or for rejecting the crucial ties between parents and children. Officials resented all the tax-free wealth tied up in Buddhist foundations; they indicted many monks as dissolute drunks or lascivious rapists. In 854 the emperor confiscated much of their wealth and forced many Buddhists to return to lay life. After this period, Buddhism's rivals gained greater state and popular support. Thus the story of this period in China is not a smooth one of increasing Buddhist power: the monks and their supporters had to struggle against persecution, and they suffered many ups and downs. Still, in general, the Buddhist story shows that a foreign religion, based on many principles quite alien to the basic assumptions of Chinese polity and society, could establish strong roots in China. Their pragmatically enlightened monks adapted the classic teachings to fit China more closely, and the Chinese kept an open mind toward new cultures.

Buddhism in Japan

In Japan, Buddhism had an even more powerful impact than in China, because it faced no organized rivals and offered many advantages to the newly centralizing state. The Japanese did, however, have their own religious beliefs, which coexisted with the foreign religion. These native beliefs found expression in thousands of widely scattered small shrines, and they supported each of the clan communities. In order to centralize his rule, the emperor and his Buddhist supporters had to dominate or incorporate these local traditions.

Japanese believed strongly in **kami**, or local spiritual powers, which protected their villages and communities. They venerated the kami of mountains and fields and the guardians of roads, and in prehistoric times they produced figurines representing the power of fertility goddesses. When rice agriculture arrived in Japan, the great shrine at **Ise** included worship of the food goddess alongside the sun goddess, considered to be the founder of the Japanese people. Clans adopted different kami as their chief deities, and often worshipped them as their ancestors. As the Yamato clan built up its authority in the sixth and seventh centuries, it promoted the central creation myth that justified imperial rule: Izanami had mated with Izanagi to produce the Japanese islands, and she gave birth to the sun goddess **Amaterasu**, the mother of the unbroken Japanese imperial line. By subordinating other local myths to this one, and insisting on the link between the gods and the emperor, the Yamato rulers established an official state cult, known later as **Shinto**, the indigenous religion of Japan.

Buddhism in Japan was a foreign import, as it was in China. It challenged Shinto by claiming greater magical powers and greater sophistication. The Buddhists, backed by the prestige of China, also brought the Chinese writing system to Japan. Their huge scriptural archive, their intricate philosophical debates, and their massive statues seemed to give them all the advantages over the dispersed, oral, simple beliefs in local kami. Yet Shinto survived, as many Buddhist believers did not give up the kami, but simply added them in. Each had its own function: the kami linking the Japanese people to their natural surroundings, Buddhists forming the basis for a state and an organized church. Kami were sentient beings who needed salvation from Buddha, but they were also protectors of the Buddhist law. Just as in China, native Japanese beliefs merged with Buddhist beliefs and transformed the religion in the process.

Japanese Buddhists produced far more impressive art than philosophy. The scale of this art ranges from the huge Buddha of Todaiji, intended to inspire awe at the Buddha's power and the emperor who protects him, to the much more artistically impressive **Miroku Bosatsu** of Nara, modeled on a Korean original, one of the oldest, and most beautiful, Buddhist statues in the world. This small, feminine-looking wooden figure, with his contemplative smile, sums up the essence of Buddhist teaching: achieving personal tranquility and detachment while never forgetting the suffering of others.

Islam

In a very short time after Muhammad's revelations, Arab armies burst out of the Arabian peninsula, carrying his teachings huge distances both east and west. By the 640s they reached Iran, and by 656 they reached the Oxus River in the heart of Central Asia. During the next century, Islamic forces made much less rapid progress eastward. They took Bukhara, but failed to hold Ferghana in the teeth of Chinese and Sogdian resistance. In 751, when Arab armies defeated Chinese armies at the Talas River, the way might have opened for the conquest of China itself, but it did not happen. Islam spread no further by military means thereafter. Carried by merchants, however, Islam continued to diffuse more gently along the silk routes. Gradually, Persian replaced Sogdian as the lingua franca of Central Asia, bringing many Arabic elements along with it. Muslim preachers, Sufi mystics, and merchants carried the Islamic message in peaceful form into nomadic encampments, impressing the warriors with powerful magic spells. By the ninth century, Islam had made substantial inroads among nomadic confederations, although no Islamic state had formed there. Arab traders also brought Islam to China by two routes, overland and maritime. The southern coastal ports of Guangzhou, **Quanzhou**, Minzhou, and Hangzhou attracted Indians, Persians, and Arabs who lived in their own communities under their own laws. Some of them took Chinese wives, remained in China for generations, and over time became the first Chinese-speaking Muslims. In Chang'an likewise, and other northwestern trading towns, Muslims from abroad began to put down roots in China. Although they regarded them as foreigners, Tang officials did not persecute them. They formed part of the great mix of religions and cultures coming into the empire.

Nestorian Christians

Few people know that Christians came to Asia long before Western European missionaries arrived in the sixteenth century CE. One thousand years earlier, controversies within the Christian church produced a great eastward migration of those condemned as heretics. This migration brought Christians to Asia along the caravan routes, where they settled as far east as Chang'an. Christians, including Europeans, were just another one of the mobile peoples of the Silk Road.

Bishop **Nestorius** (d. 451?), patriarch of Constantinople, took a position in a fine point of theology that sharply divided the Christian church. He held, contrary to orthodox doctrine, that Jesus had two separate natures, divine and human, not one. Mary was his human mother, but she was not the mother of God. Denounced as a heretic, he and his followers were expelled from the Byzantine empire. They spread out to Egypt, Syria, Iraq, and Persia, where they still have communities today. When the Persians persecuted them, they moved further into Central Asia, attracting support from the Sogdian merchants. Some of them won over Turkic tribes when they showed their magical powers

by using crosses to stop thunderstorms. Nestorian priests could act as shamans to spread their message, just as the Jesuits later would pose as arms specialists. They left writings across Asia expounding their doctrine. The oasis of Turfan contains Nestorian texts, and a great stele erected in 781 CE in Chang'an in Chinese clearly expounds the Christian message. But the Nestorians had absorbed many Persian elements in their doctrine, and their belief in the dual nature of Christ sounded too much like Manichaeanism. When the Tang persecuted Buddhists in the mid ninth century, the Nestorians suffered near-extinction in China. But when the Jesuits arrived in China 700 years later, they were astounded and delighted to discover that the Nestorians had already introduced the Christian message, because they could argue that Christianity was not a foreign religion to the Chinese.

On Native Ground: Confucians and Daoists

Islam and Buddhism were the two most dynamic, expanding religions of this period. All the other traditions, however, held their ground, and even revived in support, in competition with these two rivals. In China, Confucians and Daoists actively contested the entry of the Buddhists, often getting support from factions among the official class. Under a newly centralized empire, Confucians revived their role as masters of bureaucratic procedure and defenders of cosmic unity, as they exalted the emperor as the Son of Heaven. Buddhists, for their part, praised him as the **Chakravartin Raja**, the wheel-turning king who controls the entire universe.

The Sui and Tang rulers saw themselves as heirs to the united Han dynasty, and they knew that the long life of the Han had depended on enforcing orthodox Confucian ideology. They commissioned scholars to correct and comment on new editions of classical texts, and they set up a hierarchy of schools reaching from the capital to the villages, where teachers drilled Confucian maxims into bored students. The examination system became an increasingly important route to office, although family background counted for much more, and many of the exams only required regurgitating stereotyped answers. **Han Yu** (768–824), a passionate proponent of a Confucian revival, denounced the system, saying that Mencius himself would have refused to take these exams. Yet their pervasive familiarity with these classical texts gave the elite a common language, and a common moral reference point, while the unified empire seemed to provide once again opportunities for literate men to influence policy. The emperors themselves conducted elaborate, formal rituals following the rules of classical texts, including every year a ceremony in which the emperor symbolically began the agricultural year by plowing the first furrow in the ground outside the capital. Confucian thought was not intellectually creative during this period, but it regained its stature as the key underpinning for a unified state.

By the late Tang, when anti-foreign sentiment was rising, Confucianism regained strength as the elite turned inward. When the emperor accepted a gift said to be a bone of the Buddha, and had it reverently moved to a temple, the incisive writer Han Yu wrote an impassioned essay denouncing worship of such a "disgusting object." "Buddhism is nothing but a cult of the barbarians!" he protested. It arrived late in China and caused the Han dynasty to collapse. He scolded the emperor for trying to curry favor with the people by supporting their "delusive mummery": "Buddha was a barbarian. His language was not the language of China; his clothes were of an alien cut. He did not utter the maxims of our ancient rulers, nor conform to the customs which they have handed down. He did not appreciate the bond between prince and minister, the tie between father and son." He demanded that the emperor destroy the bone, so as to "exterminate this great evil for all time." Although banished, Han Yu expressed the hidden sentiments of his class.[8]

Daoism as an organized religion also gained strength under the Tang, with support from the imperial family. The wild popular movements that led to rebellions in the period of division had been tamed. Daoist priests offered their believers a wide pantheon of deities, mystical rituals, and magical techniques, just like the Buddhists. The Daoists had thousands of registered monasteries across the country, sixteen in Chang'an alone, although the Buddhists outnumbered them by about five to one. The Tang rulers claimed to be descendants of Laozi, and Tang exams even included questions on the *Zhuangzi* and the *Daodejing*, Daoism's two classic texts. This would never happen again. Daoists participated in regular debates with Buddhists and Confucians at the imperial court. Their main advantage over the Buddhists was their claim to be native to China. When one emperor went on a rampage in 841–45, destroying over 45,000 Buddhist temples, forcing over 400,000 clergy into lay life, and attacking Manichaeans, Nestorians, and Zoroastrians, he defended Daoism and Confucianism as the only true Chinese faiths. Tang openness, which allowed so many different beliefs to coexist, was ending by the mid ninth century.

8.8 TANG POETRY

These competing doctrines inspired poetic genius. This was the golden age of Chinese poetry, never since surpassed in the brilliance of its achievements. The main anthology of Tang poetry has 900 volumes by over 2,000 poets who wrote nearly 50,000 poems, of very high quality. The poets were officials as well as writers, sometimes in office and sometimes in retirement. In their poetry they paid little attention to doctrinal disputes; they combined Buddhist, Confucian, and Daoist themes to fit the mood they wanted. They wrote about public and private events; they discussed everything from wars to willow trees. Using the greatest virtues of the classical language – its conciseness, its balanced forms, and its allusive power – they compressed into very small spaces large themes of human feelings, natural change, and the fate of their country.

Wang Wei (699–761), for example, the most explicitly Buddhist of the great poets, earned high praise as a man of letters from Emperor Taizong, but he renounced public office to return home, saying:

Now, late in life, I love only stillness;
The affairs of the world touch not my heart.
I look within, there find no great plans,
Know nothing more than return to the forests of home.

He wrote about journeys through broad landscapes that indicated a world beyond them:

Adrift by boat upon the Great River
Massed waters touching the sky's very edge
Sky and waves suddenly split apart
The million houses of a district capital . . .
I look back toward my homeland –
Vast floods stretching to the clouds.

His most famous poem, "Seeing a Friend Off," simple but extremely evocative, joins the themes of renunciation, friendship, parting, and death:

Dismount and drink this wine.
Where to? I ask
At odds with the world:
Return to rest by the South Hill
Go. Go. Do not ask again.
Endless, the white clouds.

The nineteenth-century Austrian composer Gustav Mahler ended his great symphony set to Chinese verse, *The Song of the Earth*, with this poem. Somehow, these themes have carried their emotional power for over a thousand years, across vast cultural distances.[9]

Li Bo (701–62), the apostle of freedom, expressed his drive for liberation from social constraints by writing songs in praise of drink. The story goes that he died drunk, trying to embrace the reflection of the moon in the Yellow River. He also wrote ballads in the style of folk songs that gained him instant popularity. He suffered, too, like his friend Du Fu, from the An Lushan rebellion, and spent most of his life wandering, but the tone of his verse is sunny, visionary, and fantastic. In "Bring on the Wine," he exclaimed:

O don't you see the waters of the Yellow River pouring from the sky
Rushing downward to the sea never to return
O don't you see the mirrors in the mansions where they grieve for graying hair
Black silk floss at dawning that by dusk has turned to snow?
When you have some little triumph, you must fully taste the joy
And never let a golden cup go to waste beneath the moon.

But Li Bo was serious in his play. In the "Song of the Heavenly Horse," he summarized his career, or the life of anyone whose fondest hopes had been crushed:

From the Scythian cave came the heavenly horse,
With tiger-stripe back and dragon-wing bones,
Neighing to clouds in the blue. Shaking a mane of green
Orchid, strong jaw sinew, speed tokened cheeks,
He vanished when he ran . . .

But the powerful horse, "a spirit apart, proud and assured," who could "leap and rear to tumble the passing clouds," ended up locked in his stall:

In my youth they used my strength, they cast me off in age. . .
In the stall I furrow my brow, the bit of injustice in my teeth.
I beg that you will redeem, me, send me off to Emperor Mu,
That I may yet play with my shadow
And dance by the Jasper Pool.[10]

Du Fu (712–70), whom many consider the greatest Chinese poet of all time, drew together all the stylistic resources of the language and crafted them into an amazing variety of tones, influencing all those who came after him. He wrote poems of social protest, comic poems, praise to the emperor, simple descriptions of daily life, and mystical visions. Confucian commentators made him into a great sage. They praised his love of country, his compassion for the common people, his integrity, and his loyalty to his friends. He gained an official post in 755, just when the An Lushan rebellion broke out. He tried to flee, but was captured by the rebels and held in Chang'an, where he witnessed the horrible destruction of the world's most civilized city. Afterwards, he left office and wandered around the country until his death. His sense of duty inspired him to serve the dynasty, but his integrity prevented him from tolerating corruption and oppression. In only eight lines, he epitomized the despair and anxiety he felt in the burning capital:

The state is ruined; the mountains and rivers remain;
Spring in the city; the grass and trees are thick

Moved by despair, the flowers shed tears
Anguished by separation, the birds seem startled
Beacon fires have continued for three months
A letter from home would be worth a fortune
I scratch my thinning white hair
Soon I'll have nothing left to hold my hatpin![11]

No two people react the same way to misfortune. Li Bo and Du Fu express diametrically opposite sensibilities, but with equal skill. We might simplistically classify Wang Wei as the Buddhist, Du Fu as the Confucian, and Li Bo as the Daoist, but poetic genius transcends pigeonholes. Far more than the emperors' edicts, the stiff moralists, and the dull exam questions, Tang poetry provides intimate glimpses of personal sensibilities in this time of grandeur and disaster.

8.9 WOMEN, THE FAMILY, AND THE STATE

We have far more information about the lives of women, at least at the elite level, in China in this period than for earlier times. In the Tang court, women gained significant influence on policy as the wives or mothers of the emperors. The Confucians who wrote the histories hated them for going beyond their proper roles, but we can still tell that they had power. Other documents of ordinary life also show women engaged actively in the marketplace and in Buddhist associations. Beyond China, women seem to have had even higher status. The Central Asian influences on the Tang brought with them clothing fashions and styles of behavior that freed up some women from the strict bonds of the patriarchal family.

Here are a few examples of female influence at court. The founder of the Sui dynasty married a woman with a nomadic background, who refused to allow him to take concubines. Only she could bear him children. Her son, the second emperor, married a woman from the south, who brought refinement to his rough military court. She actively supported Buddhism, urging her husband to have scriptures recopied and new Buddhist libraries built. The most powerful woman in Chinese history was Wu Zhao, the wife of Tang Gaozong (r. 649–83) and the real power behind the throne held by her husband and, later, her son. In 690, she declared herself empress and founded a new dynasty. She disposed of her rivals cruelly, but she had considerable support from factions at the court. Empress Wu brought patronage of Buddhism to its peak, giving large donations to support the carving of Buddhist sculpture at the Longmen Grottoes outside Luoyang. These giant statues, shown in Figure 8.2, still impress visitors today. The empress saw herself as a Buddhist goddess, brought to earth to transform the empire

Figure 8.2 These giant Buddhist guardians carved into caves in North China, at the Longmen Grottoes, show the monumental power of Buddhist deities, who could protect the ruling empress. The Empress Wu was a devout patroness of Buddhism, but she alienated supporters at court and lost her power in a coup in 705 BCE. Her monuments still survive, testifying to the dominant influence of Buddhism in the Tang dynasty.

into a paradise. At the same time, wild rumors of her insatiable sexual desires spread among her enemies. In 705 a palace coup threw her out and restored the Tang. Orthodox historians have castigated the empress for usurpation, for excessive Buddhist patronage, and for ruling as a woman, but modern scholars must give her credit for administrative reforms and an expansionist foreign policy.

As noted above, Confucian accounts blame the collapse of the Tang on the emperor's infatuation with his concubine, the beauteous Yang Guifei, but surely other factors played a part. Yang Guifei, whatever her political influence, also changed Chinese ideals of beauty. Until the mid eighth century, the ideal woman, as represented in figurines, was slim and often wore tight-fitting clothing derived from Central Asian jackets. Tang women rode on horseback, played the Persian game of polo, and wore trousers like their Turk sisters. The craze for the voluptuous Yang Guifei caused painters to show beautiful women as plump in face and body, covering their curves with loose gowns. By the Song dynasty, Chinese feminine ideals had shifted back to the willowy type, but the Japanese picked up this ideal of large women and maintained it through the twelfth century.

Stories and routine documents give us some glimpses of more ordinary women. They had to hear lectures, telling them to serve their husband as they served their father. "[A woman's] voice should not be heard / Nor her body or shadow seen." But land contracts recovered from tombs in the desert show that women could bring suit in court to defend their property rights. Some of the most popular stories of the time tell the tale of a scholar who falls in love with a prostitute with a heart of gold, bankrupting his family by his passion. At the end, after many adventures, he recovers his wealth, buys the girl's freedom from her madam, marries her, and has male heirs: the perfect happy ending.

Did these events ever happen? At least a few beautiful women probably did use their charms to rise out of poverty, but this was rare enough to be remarkable. Women had greater collective power as members of lay associations of Buddhists. Dunhuang documents show that they gathered at major feasts, donated offerings to temples, and worked to support the monks and nuns. Local farmers could send their daughters to a nunnery to avoid paying dowries to have them married. They could hear lectures about the filial son, **Mulian**, who traveled to hell in order to rescue his mother. He found her having her bones crushed, but he finally brought her back as a living person. A story like this, with graphic descriptions of tortures for disloyal Buddhists, certainly helped the monastery's fund-raising campaign, but it also asserted the great devotion sons owed to their mothers. It must have made the elderly women in these lay associations feel better.

Conclusion

In sum, these three centuries drastically changed the face of Eurasia, tying its parts together more closely than ever before. The coercive power of imperial conquest, and the more peaceful processes of commercial exchange and religious community-building, acted together for a time to promote unprecedented mobility and mixing of cultures, peoples, and goods. The Turks came first, in the mid sixth century bursting out of Mongolia in both directions. They patronized trade at both ends, allowing the Sogdians and other merchants to build their far-flung networks. China then unified, adding a huge agrarian population's production to the supplies of the Silk Road. The Arabs moved east in the seventh century, meeting with the Chinese and Turks in the center of the continent, just as the Tibetans reached the peak of their power in the mid eighth century. After the 750s, major cataclysms shook all these empires, but they survived in reshaped forms for another century.

These east–west connections furthered common trends across the continent, including Europe. Literacy spread out from established cores in Arabia or China, or in the form of newly invented scripts for the Turks, Sogdians, and Tibetans of Central Eurasia. Cities grew, as did local industry and trade. Silver and gold coinage financed long-distance trading links. The Sogdians, Norsemen, and Jews established huge overlapping spheres of mercantile networks pushing goods in all directions. Western Europe also flourished in the Carolingian Age, likewise increasing its stores of coins, literate culture, architecture, and trade. Many religious traditions organized their believers and gathered new converts. This was hardly a Dark Age.

By the mid ninth century, all these empires faced troubled times. Tang China only barely held together, helped by Uighur nomads. The Abbasids withdrew from Central Eurasia, and the Tibetan empire collapsed, as did Charlemagne's. Even isolated Japan slowly disintegrated. Western Europe's failure to rebuild the Roman empire was not, after all, so exceptional. It was difficult for any empire to hold together for long, and along with the decline of central political power went a decline in trade and a rise of intolerance. The Eastern empires encompassed far greater spaces for longer periods primarily because of their close connection with steppe nomads, who generated powerful military and tribal solidarities capable of explosive expansion. The compound of nomadic military power, Chinese wealth, gentility, civil administration, and Buddhist organization held solid for quite a while. The Abbasids and Byzantines also kept their control of most of the Middle East. Europe lacked comparable resources of wealth or large military formations, so its centralization was briefer, and smaller. This cycle of integration and disintegration left an indelible legacy, however, on which future generations would build.

Study Questions

(1) Why did Tang China, the Turk empire, Tibetans, and Japanese all create empires at roughly the same time? How did they use trade, military power, and religion to reinforce their rule? How did each empire's state-building effort influence the others?

(2) What basic economic needs drove the merchants on the silk routes to travel such long, hazardous distances in pursuit of profit? Explain how transportation, security, currency, religion, and environmental change affected trade across Eurasia?

(3) How did the great religions of this time spread their teachings beyond monks and scholars to convert large populations? Did Buddhism, Islam, Confucianism, and Hinduism use different techniques and appeal to different kinds of people, or was their message essentially the same for all?

Suggested Reading

China VALERIE HANSEN, *The Open Empire: A History of China to 1600* (New York: W.W. Norton, 2000). This is an excellent overview of the Tang dynasty and the steppe empires.

VALERIE HANSEN *Negotiating Daily Life in Traditional China: How Ordinary People Used Contracts, 600–1400* (New Haven, CT: Yale University Press, 1995). Hansen uses Dunhuang and Turfan documents to reveal the role of contracts in daily life.

VICTOR H. MAIR, *Painting and Performance: Chinese Picture Recitation and its Indian Genesis* (Honolulu: University of Hawaii Press, 1996). This is a brilliant study of the extensive cross-cultural contacts between China and Eurasia during the Tang and later.

ARTHUR F. WRIGHT, *The Sui Dynasty* (New York: Knopf, 1978). This is the classic study of this key period.

Central Eurasia THOMAS J. BARFIELD, *The Perilous Frontier: Nomadic Empires and China* (Oxford: Basil Blackwell, 1989). Barfield summarizes the Turks' and Uighurs' relations with China.

PETER B. GOLDEN, *Central Asia in World History* (New York: Oxford University Press, 2011). This is an excellent short survey.

The Silk Road VALERIE HANSEN, *The Silk Road: A New History* (Oxford University Press, 2012). Hansen's study is the most up-to-date synthesis, based on a broad array of local documents in many languages.

SUSAN WHITFIELD, *Life Along the Silk Road* (Berkeley: University of California Press, 1999). Whitfield gives composite biographies of Silk Road characters based extensively on Dunhuang documents.

Japan and Korea WAYNE WILLIAM FARRIS, *Population, Disease, and Land in Early Japan, 645–900* (Cambridge, MA: Harvard University Press, 1985). This is an outstanding study linking ecology, population, and military power.

KI-BAIK YI, *A New History of Korea* (Cambridge, MA: Harvard University Press, 1984). This is the best modern survey.

Glossary

Amaterasu: Sun goddess, mother of the Japanese imperial line.

Amitabha: A manifestation of Buddha, the central focus of the Pure Land sect. (Chinese: Emituofo; Japanese: Amida.)

An Lushan: Frontier general who began rebellion against Tang dynasty in 755.

Annam: Kingdom in northern Vietnam, under rule of the Tang dynasty.

Aurel Stein: British-Hungarian explorer who rediscovered the Dunhuang caves in northwest China in the twentieth century.

Baekje (or Paekche): Kingdom in eastern and central Korea.

Balhae (or Parhae): State in Manchuria and northern Korea in the eighth century.

bao: Chinese community groups which monitored the members' performance of required military service.

Bilge Qaghan: Founder of the second Turk empire (r. 716–34).

biwa (Chinese: pipa): Japanese (and Chinese) lute with Persian origins.

Bumin: The first qaghan of the Turks.

Chakravartin Raja: Indian Buddhist term for the wheel-turning king who controls the universe.

Chan (Japanese: Zen): Chinese Buddhist sect focused on intense meditation leading to mystical insight.

Du Fu: Chinese poet (712–70) of the Tang dynasty, admired for his brilliant style, moral sense, and compassion.

gagaku: Japanese court music of the eighth century, with Central Eurasian influences.

Goguryo: Kingdom in Manchuria and northern Korea in the seventh to ninth centuries.

Han Yu: Chinese Confucian writer (768–824) who denounced Buddhist and Daoist doctrines.

haniwa: Ceramic figurines found in early Japanese tombs.

Hinayana: Term for form of Buddhism most prevalent in Southeast Asia and Sri Lanka.

Ise: Shrine in Japan, centered on worship of the sun goddess.

Ishtemi: Brother of Bumin and ruler of the western Turks.

kami: Japanese local spiritual powers.

Kirghiz: Steppe nomads who defeated the Uighurs in the mid ninth century.

Li Bo: Chinese poet (701–62) known for his praise of drinking and moonlight.

***Lotus Sutra*:** Indian Buddhist text which became the central teaching of the Tiantai sect in China.

Mahayana: Term for form of Buddhism most prevalent in East Asia.

Manichaeans: Followers of the Manichaean religion originating in Persia which spread into Central Eurasia in the eighth century.

Manyoshu: Large eighth-century collection of Japanese poetry.

Miroku Bosatsu: Japanese term for Buddha of the Future, a sculpture in Nara.

Mulian: Chinese filial son, in legend believed to have traveled to hell to rescue his mother.

Nanzhao: Kingdom in southwest China which fought off Chinese Tang rule in the eighth century.

Nestorius: Christian bishop (d. 451?) in Constantinople, founder of Nestorian sect of Christianity.

nirvana: In Buddhist belief, a state of enlightenment, when all desire and suffering cease. Later interpreted as entry into paradise.

Ordu Baliq: Capital of Uighur empire, near Orkhon River.

Pelliot, Paul: Brilliant French linguist who obtained large quantities of scrolls from Dunhuang in northwest China in the twentieth century.

Pure Land: Buddhist sect stressing repetition of the name of Amitabha Buddha as the means to enlightenment.

qaghan: Name for supreme leader of Turks.

Rouran: A nomadic confederation, originally ruling over Turks, then overthrown by them.

Shinto: Indigenous Japanese religion and an official state cult.

Shoso-in: Imperial storehouse in Nara, Japan, containing trade goods from all over Eurasia.

Shotoku Taishi: Early ruler of Japan (r. 593–622) who adopted Chinese institutions.

Silla: State in southern Korea.

Sogdians: Trading groups along the Silk Road whose homeland was Bactria.

Songtsen Gampo: King and unifier of Tibetan empire (r. 634–50).

Sui Wendi: Aristocratic warrior who reunited China (r. 581–604).

Sui Yangdi: Second ruler of Sui dynasty (r. 604–18), builder of Grand Canal of China.

Sven Hedin: Swedish explorer who discovered buried cities in the deserts of Chinese Turkestan in the twentieth century.

Tang Gaozu: Imperial name of Li Yuan (r. 618–26), reunifier of China after fall of the Sui dynasty.

Tang Taizong: Chinese emperor (r. 626–49) during peak of prosperity of the Tang dynasty.

Tang Xuanzong: Emperor of China (r. 712–56), known for his infatuation with concubine Yang Guifei.

Temmu: Emperor of Japan (r. 672–86) who reinforced his state with Tang Chinese institutions.

Tiantai (Japanese: Tendai): Chinese Buddhist sect asserting that all sentient beings can achieve salvation through specific practices.

Todaiji: Temple in Nara, Japan, site of the Great Buddha bronze sculpture built in the eighth century.

Turks: Pastoral nomads dominating Central Eurasia from the sixth to ninth centuries.

Uighurs: Nomadic warriors, conquerors of Turk empire in the eighth century.

uji: Warrior clans of ancient Japan.

Wang Wei: Chinese Buddhist poet (699–761) of the Tang dynasty.

Wu Zhao (Wu Zetian): Concubine of Emperor Tang Gaozong who made herself ruler of China in 690.

Yamato: Fertile plain on Honshu island in Japan, origin of Japanese state.

Yang Guifei: Concubine of Emperor Tang Xuanzong who used her power to install her brother as prime minister.

Zen: See Chan.

Zhishi: Chinese Buddhist monk who resisted Tang imperial efforts to shut down temples.

Notes

1 Arthur F. Wright, "The Sui Dynasty (581–617)," in Denis Twitchett and John K. Fairbank (eds.), *The Cambridge History of China*, vol. III: *Sui and T'ang China, 589–906, Part I*, (Cambridge University Press, 1979), p. 137.

2 David Christian, *A History of Russia, Central Asia and Mongolia* (Oxford: Blackwell, 1998) p. 252.

3 Christian, *History of Russia*, p. 259.

4 Christian, *History of Russia*, p. 262.

5 Lee Ki-baik, *A New History of Korea*, trans. Edward Wagner (Cambridge, MA: Harvard University Press, 1984), p. 48.

6 Delmer M. Brown (ed.), *The Cambridge History of Japan*, vol. I: *Ancient Japan* (Cambridge University Press, 1993), pp. 382, 387.

7 William Wayne Farris, *Heavenly Warriors: The Evolution of Japan's Military, 500–1300* (Cambridge, MA: Council on East Asian Studies, Harvard University, 1992), p. 66.

8 John Minford and Joseph S.M. Lau (eds.), *Classical Chinese Literature: An Anthology of Translations* (New York: Columbia University Press; Hong Kong: Chinese University Press, 2000).

9 Stephen Owen, *The Great Age of Chinese Poetry: The High T'ang* (New Haven, CT: Yale University Press, 1981), pp. 27, 31.

10 Minford and Lau, *Classical Chinese Literature*.

11 Minford and Lau, *Classical Chinese Literature*.

9 The rise and fall of states in the Americas and Africa, 600–1200

Timeline	
c. 600 BCE – 950 CE	Kingdom of Axum (Ethiopia); King Ezana (r. 320–50) converts to Christianity; decline begins in 600s.
100 BCE	Camels boost trans-Saharan trade between Mediterranean coast and sub-Saharan Africa.
150–550 CE	Teotihuacán, city in the Valley of Mexico, builds first large empire in Mesoamerica.
200–1000 CE	Tiwanaku, city on Lake Titicaca, builds large tributary empire in southern Andes.
200–900 CE	Mayan city-states flourish in Mesoamerica; collapse coincides with era of droughts, 800–1000.
400–1000 CE	Wari, city-based empire in the northern Andes, is first to manage reciprocity and trade for state-building.
400s–1100s	Ghana kingdom; decline begins late eleventh century; capital Kumbi Saleh sacked by Berbers in 1076.
600–900	Maize cultivation reaches southwestern USA.
500–1400	Hohokam, Mogollon, and Anasazi cultures in southwestern USA.
500 – *c.* 800	Nubian kingdoms of Nobatia, Maqurrah, and Alwah; ruling dynasties convert to Christianity between 543 and 580.
800–1000	Mississippi chiefdoms arise; maize cultivation reaches the central USA.
831	Arab treaty (bakt) with Beja.
900–1470	Chimú state on Pacific coast of Peru.
900–1168	Toltec empire in Central Mexico.
c. 1000	Maize cultivation reaches Amazon, Orinoco river areas; first large chiefdoms are created (e.g., Santarém in the Amazon region).
1100s	Muslim influence comes to predominate in East African coastal cities.
1171	Nubian invasion of Egypt.

Yax Pac, last known ruler of the Mayan city-state of Copán, tried desperately to save his city from starvation. He failed. He could not create more land for his 20,000 subjects, nor bring back the abundant rainfall his ancestors knew. Pushing his malnourished people to appease the gods and demonstrate his power by rebuilding two of the city's largest temple-pyramids (see Figure 9.1) did no good. Not long after his death in 820 CE, the surviving inhabitants of Copán abandoned their city forever. Copán's fate is not unusual in human history, but even cities that avoided environmental disaster faced many other serious threats to their inhabitants.

Figure 9.1 The Copán hieroglyphic staircase of Temple 26 was completed in 755 CE. Every block is carved with hieroglyphic inscriptions – 2,200 glyphs in all, the longest known Maya text – that relate the history of Copán's rulers. The staircase was the last major construction undertaken by the rulers of Copán. The city may have boasted a population of 20,000 or more. It became a major regional power in the fifth century, but was abandoned by the end of the ninth century.

For most of human history, cities have been death-traps so dirty and disease-ridden that they could not grow by natural increase (i.e., more births than deaths). Cities as diverse as ancient Chang'an and Rome, medieval Delhi and Genoa, industrial Manchester and Mexico City, grew in population only by luring or forcing people to move in from elsewhere. Urban death rates until the twentieth century were so high that urban life could not have existed without immigration from outside. Life expectancy in imperial Rome was only 25 years. The average age at death in 1840s Manchester was 17 years. Cities were especially dangerous places for children; in most cities before 1900 one third to one half of all children born alive died before they reached their first birthday. Tropical cities in hot damp climates were deadlier than most, but cities everywhere were extremely unhealthy. Cities were not only vulnerable to food shortages, they were downright deadly even in times of abundant food.

Nonetheless, it is true that city-states and empires built on the resources mobilized and controlled by urban elites have dominated the history of most world regions. Some lasted for centuries and proved remarkably stable, but all succumbed sooner or later to natural or human-caused disasters. Sub-Saharan African cities and states faced especially difficult climatic and physical challenges. In **Mesoamerica** (Mexico and Central America) and the Andes, favorable conditions fostered urban development and state formation, but when cooler and drier trends set in between 800 and 1000, even the most powerful succumbed.

In this chapter, we will see that:

- The separate histories of Africa and the Americas moved in nearly opposite directions between 600 and 1200 CE. As trade and cultural contacts between sub-Saharan Africa and the rest of the world grew, trading towns grew up south of the Sahara and along the coast of East Africa. Trade helped to stimulate the growth of coastal trading posts into city-states and the rise of the first large territorial states in West Africa. In the Americas, after a period of major advances, major cities were abandoned and great empires collapsed between 800 and 1000.
- Arab invasions spread Islam, displaced the predominantly Christian elites of Egypt and Nubia, and then transformed all of North Africa; Muslim merchants became key players in the growth of East African trading posts, which developed into city-states as far south as modern Mozambique; Christian Ethiopia turned inward and lost trade and other contacts with the rest of the world.
- Rising agricultural productivity, iron weapons, and the intensification of the trans-Saharan trading networks were the key ingredients in the development of the kingdom or empire of Ghana south of the Sahara in West Africa.

- In the Americas, the Mayan city-states in Mesoamerica (Southern Mexico and northern Central America) and the empires of Tiwanaku and Wari in the Andes flourished until the ninth century when prolonged drought, ecological disasters, warfare, and instability produced a stunning sequence of collapse and abandonment between 800 and 1000. A new Toltec empire arose in Central Mexico after 900, but it too succumbed to a combination of drought, rebellion, and invasion by 1168.
- As the highly stratified highland societies of the Americas dissolved and reformed, complex chiefdoms or early states arose in the lowlands of the Amazon and Mississippi basins and the southwestern United States, linked to the spread of maize agriculture after about 800 from drought-stricken Mesoamerica; in some cases, this led to the development of large towns and cities that appear to have been more egalitarian in social and political structure than elsewhere.

9.1 AFRICA, 600–1200

The history of Africa in the medieval period was profoundly affected by the continuing migrations of the Bantu-speaking peoples into the central, southern, and eastern regions of the continent, and their transition to iron tools and weapons (see Chapter 4).

Long-distance trade played an increasingly key role in this era. African exports included Ghanaian gold and salt, Nubian gold and emeralds, and East African leopard skins and ivory. The trans-Saharan trade was made possible by the importation of the camel from the Middle East beginning in the first century BCE. The gold-trading networks founded then were expanded in our period. Although a steady stream of African captives found their way across the Sahara to slave markets in the Islamic world, slavery did not develop extensively within Africa and the slave trade does not appear to have been an important feature of the economy at this time except in Berber North Africa. African trading networks reached deep into the Middle East and the Persian Gulf, and spanned the Indian Ocean to Indonesia and China.

Africa also underwent many changes consequent on the rise of Islam in the north of the continent, and the relations with Muslims that developed in the east and the west. Large-scale immigration into East Africa from the Middle East and South Asia took place. Iranians and Indonesians settled in Mogadishu and Madagascar respectively. Arab tribes invaded the north and ultimately wandered into West Africa. African slaves were taken as far away as southern Iraq to work on Arab plantations.

Islam made major gains among the Copts and Berbers of the Roman and then Byzantine empire.

The development of trade and the spread of Islam were often linked. Merchants and traders labored in a world of risks. Ships sank in bad weather or were lost to pirates. Greedy rulers confiscated cargoes or taxed away profits. Loans were not repaid, contracts to deliver goods were broken, laws and customs varied from place to place, courts barely functioned if they existed at all and had no jurisdiction beyond each city's walls. Islamic "law" and custom worked to overcome some of these difficulties. Muslim traders were expected to follow an evolving set of norms and rules wherever they went. Muslims who cheated were ostracized; reputations crossed boundaries where courts could not. Islam helped to build business confidence in a world full of dangers. Most other religions of Africa developed locally and made no effort to win converts, so they could not project codes of conduct across great distances. Christianity, which did seek converts, became a religion of monks and farmers with a strong anti-commercial bias from Egypt south to Ethiopia.

Important non-Muslim sub-Saharan polities thrived in these centuries. The introduction of iron weaponry and the increasing use of horse cavalry often underpinned the power of these states. They included Christian Nubia and Ethiopia in the Nile Valley as well as new states in West Africa and what are now Kenya, Tanzania, and Mozambique. These latter practiced African religions centered on worship of a sky god or creator god, on ancestor worship, and on spirit possession and avoidance of human malevolence.

Nubia (The Sudan)

What is now the Sudan has been the site of Middle Nile kingdoms, cities, and civilization since pharaonic times. The Egyptians referred to much of the region as Nubia, since it was a major source of gold ("nub" means gold in the old Egyptian language). When the Romans ruled Egypt, they occasionally attempted to assert their authority in the south, but often failed. After the collapse of Meroë in the fourth century CE, three major independent kingdoms arose in the 500s to dominate the Middle Nile: Nobatia, Maqurrah, and Alwah (see Map 9.1). The dynasties of each adopted Christianity between 543 and 580.

Islam and Christianity Compete Missionaries brought Christianity to Nubia from Egypt. The first missionary was Julian, a priest from Alexandria. He reported that it was so hot in this area that he could only spread his message in the late afternoon and evening, since from "nine o'clock until four in the afternoon he was obliged to take refuge in caverns, full of water, where he sat undressed and girt only in a linen garment, such as the people

Map 9.1 Africa, 600–1200

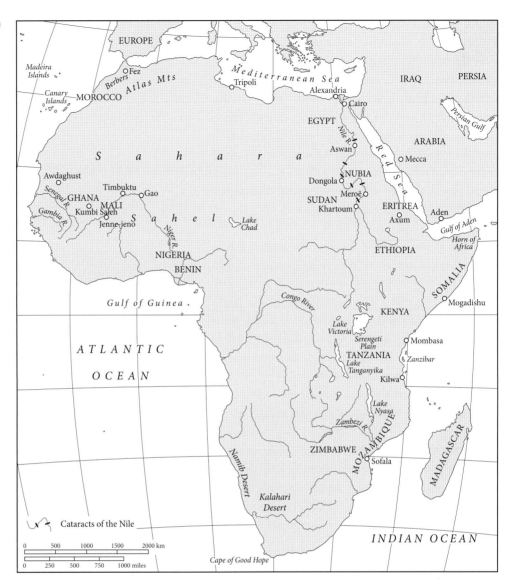

of the country wear." Julian believed in the Monophysite branch of Christianity, which held that Christ had just one nature, which was divine but could express itself in human terms. Orthodox Christianity held that Christ united in himself two natures, one human and one divine. Although Orthodox missionaries appear to have had some early successes, the Monophysite brand of Christianity, whose monasteries and peasant tenants were exempted from taxation by Christian Rome, ultimately won out all along the Nile Valley. The new Christians began remodeling old temples to the pharaonic gods as places of monotheistic worship, and built the region's first churches. Eventually, the church divided Nubia into three provinces with seventeen bishops. Christianity probably spread only slowly from the courts and cities to the villagers and nomads, but it ultimately gained great popularity, and dominated the region for a thousand years.

In the middle of the 600s, Maqurrah was invaded by a Muslim Arab force from Egypt, which had fallen to the armies of Islam.

This action was more an incursion than a conquest, however, and the Arabs withdrew after concluding a treaty, the **bakt**, with the Maqurrah sovereign in his capital of Dongola. The treaty pledged both sides to peace with one another, and gave free passage to merchants and travelers in the lands of each. It required that 400 Nubian slaves be sent to Egypt each year, to be paid for by a large shipment of wheat, wine, and cloth sent to Dongola from Egypt. The treaty was viewed by the Arab Muslims as a reduction of the Maqurrah kings to vassals, but since they paid for the slaves, this offering was not really a tribute. Some have argued that the bakt was an unusual medieval "non-aggression pact."

King Merkurios (r. 697–c. 722) is said to have united Nobatia and Maqurrah into a single Nubian realm. Nubian civilization was marked by its own distinctive language. Increasingly Christian, the Nubian kingdom established excellent trade and cultural relations with the Byzantines. Byzantine art and architecture exercised deep influence in the Middle Nile. A majority of Egyptians remained Christians for centuries even under Arab Muslim rule, and the Nubians maintained strong relations with their Coptic coreligionists. In 745, when the Muslims imprisoned the patriarch (chief Christian official) of Alexandria, a Nubian military force marched north to Cairo and sent an emissary to request that he be released. The governor of Egypt, not eager for a major war in the tropical south, agreed. The arid plains south of Aswan are hard to cross and discouraged military campaigns for most of this period, in the absence of strong motivations for conquest.

Gold Trade and Wars for Gold Gold in the Red Sea hills eventually supplied the motive for numerous incursions. Arab prospectors and freebooters flooded into the region in the early 800s, coming into conflict with the local Beja people. The Arabs concluded a separate treaty with the Beja in 831, allowing them to enter Egypt freely but forcing them to pay tribute as vassals to the Muslims. Peace did not last, and the Beja had to pledge in 851 not to interfere with the Arab gold traders. One Muslim Arab prospector established a virtual state in the region for a short period, and mosques were built as the gold traders settled in for a permanent presence. In the 820s and 830s, Nubia and Abbasid Egypt fought a long conflict, probably at least in part over incursions into Beja territory and wrangles over the gold trade. That war appears to have been settled when the Nubian king sent his son as an envoy to Baghdad and renewed with the **caliph** (Muslim ruler) the bakt, or non-aggression treaty, between their two states.

Over a century later, the decline of Abbasid control in Egypt in the 900s led to political chaos in that country, and gave an opening for a Christian Nubian invasion of Upper Egypt in 962. Dongola appears to have dominated this region for some decades, and found support in the local Coptic Christian population. This part of Egypt remained majority Christian far longer than the delta. The later Fatimid period in Egypt (969–1171) was marked by relative peace between Nubia and Egypt. An Arab traveler in the early 1000s described the Nubian capital of Dongola as impressive and prosperous: "Here is the throne of the King. It is a large city on the banks of the blessed Nile, and contains many churches and large houses and wide streets. The King's house is lofty with several domes built of red-brick and resembles the buildings in Iraq."

When the Fatimids fell in 1171, Nubia invaded, took Aswan, and marched into Upper Egypt yet again. They were expelled, however, by the Kurdish conqueror Saladin (Salah al-Din al-Ayyubi), who established a new dynasty in Egypt. His brother attacked Nubia from Yemen. He turned at least one church into a mosque, captured the bishop, enslaved some locals, and left a garrison for a while. The northern part of Nubia was occupied. Thereafter the Nubian kingdom went into a gradual political decline, and over the succeeding centuries it was penetrated by Egyptian Muslims. Ultimately the Middle Nile largely adopted Islam, and the Arabic language came to predominate in the region from Aswan to what is now Khartoum.

The Decline of Axum (Ethiopia) and Rise of Islam

In the century before the beginning of Islam, Axum (site of the **stele**, or inscribed column, in Figure 9.2) was one of the world's

Figure 9.2 The obelisk shown here – properly termed a "stele" (plural: stelae) – is found along with many other stelae in the city of Axum in modern-day Ethiopia. The stelae were probably carved and erected during the fourth century CE by subjects of the kingdom of Axum. Their function is thought to be that of "markers" for underground burial chambers. The largest of the grave markers were for royal burial chambers and were decorated with multi-story false windows and false doors.

great empires and trading entrepôts, attracting a cloud of merchants bearing iron, cattle, and salt to exchange for gold dust and nuggets in its bustling markets (see Chapter 4). Although sited high on a plateau, it had several important ports on the Red Sea below, which it controlled militarily. Axum even occasionally asserted its military power across the sea in Arabia. It was allied with the Byzantines, and stayed in close touch with the patriarch of Alexandria.

The trading routes and imperial alliances that contributed to Axum's greatness changed decisively in the 600s, leading to centuries of political decline and obscurity. The Sasanian empire of Iran increasingly challenged the Byzantines in Yemen and the Red Sea in the 500s. The rise of Islam cut Axum off from effective Byzantine help and trade, and weakened ties with Egypt. The Negus or king of Axum, ironically, played a helpful role in early Islamic history. The pagan Meccans persecuted and boycotted the early Muslims, and in 615 a group of Muslims took refuge in Axum. The king showed the members of this new sister religion to Christianity great kindness and toleration. As a result, Muslims ever after retained a positive view of the Christians of what is now Ethiopia. Some Muslim jurists considered the Muslim empire to have established a relationship of friendly non-aggression with them.

In the 700s large numbers of Beja people from what is now northern Sudan migrated into Axum and elsewhere in Ethiopia. At the same time, Arab Muslims took control of the low-lying coastal areas, leaving the Axumites stranded on their plateau. The Muslims increasingly controlled the Red Sea and, now lacking a port of their own, the Axum people could not maintain their trading links to Byzantium. The Axum empire declined into a small, inward-looking kingdom, with new Beja rivals in the heartland and Muslim Arab ones along the coast. After 950, Axum was sacked by the queen of a nearby people. She appears to have been hostile to Christianity, having many churches burned and killing the local head of the church. The Axum king appealed for help to the ruler of Christian Nubia, and to the Christian church authorities in Alexandria. The queen is said to have ruled Axum for some years after the death of its defeated king. From the 1000s, the Axum rulers relocated to the center of the Ethiopian plateau, with a new dynasty, the Zague, arising. The most famous Zague king was Lalibela. The displaced Axum kingdom continued to profess Christianity and to spread the religion among African tribespeople and peasants.

Along the Red Sea lowlands of the Horn of Africa, people gradually converted to Islam. Likewise, Islam was adopted by some of the pastoral nomads in the interior, and in the 1100s and 1200s it spread in the south of what is now Ethiopia, as well as Somalia. One of the ways Islam spread was along trading routes, including the slave trade. Cities such as Mogadishu (now in Somalia) had important slave markets, and these linked the largely Muslim traders with the interior. This lucrative trade threw up extensive organizational links among port cities, trading "firms," raiding expeditions, and interior tribes. In some instances these networks underpinned the rise of Muslim states or sultanates. Since Muslims were forbidden by Islamic law from enslaving other Muslims, moreover, some tribes of the interior may have converted so as to exempt themselves from the slave trade.

East African City-States

In the period before 600 CE, Bantu migrants settled throughout the eastern part of Africa from the Lake area of the interior south to the Serengeti Plain, especially in wooded areas with good rainfall where they could grow yams. They organized themselves into small clan-based villages with a chief, and grew some grain, especially sorghum. In some areas they planted banana trees introduced to the region from Indonesia. They had already given up stone tools in favor of iron by the first centuries of the Common Era, which increased the productivity of their farms and encouraged population growth.

Between 600 and 900, trade expanded between the predominantly Bantu coastal villages and a growing number of itinerant Arab, Indian, and other South Asian traders. The peoples of what are now Kenya, Tanzania, Zanzibar, and Mozambique were referred to by Arab geographers as **Zanj**. They reported that the Zanj worshipped local gods and believed in spirit possession. Villages became ports of call with trading posts and markets where products from the interior were exchanged for goods from throughout the Indian Ocean and the Red Sea region. The better located trading ports developed into independent city-states with resident colonies of foreign, usually Muslim traders.

The evolution of a distinct Swahili language and culture took place in this era. **Swahili** is a Bantu-based language with many Arab, Persian, and other non-Bantu words and concepts. The language was first written down in Arabic script, but not until much later. The elite of the Swahili trading towns intermarried with foreign merchants and eventually converted to Islam. The transformation of the East African coast in this era shaped the history of the region until today.

East Coast Trading Towns Since the Bantu migrants did not have a strong history of raising cattle, they could move easily into these coastal regions, where the **tse-tse fly** (an insect that spreads trypanosomiasis (commonly called **sleeping sickness**), deadly to hoofed animals, made it difficult to keep livestock. There they founded trading posts that evolved into bustling port cities open to all of Asia across the Indian Ocean. Bantu iron was exported to India, where it was worked into swords and re-exported to

Damascus. Although Muslim traders settled along the coast, there is little evidence of conversion to Islam of significant numbers of Africans in this area before about 1000.

After about 1000, there is archaeological evidence both for increased trade and urbanization and conversion to Islam (i.e. there are more Muslim burial sites, alongside non-Muslim ones). These developments may have been linked to a greater demand for gold in the thriving Middle Eastern Muslim empires of the Fatimids and Buyids. Until the 1100s, few sources speak explicitly of Muslim rulers, and it seems clear that the coastal city-states were ruled by a Bantu majority alongside a Muslim, mainly immigrant, or mixed-population minority. The ports were the places that the Bantu culture of the interior met the polyglot world of the Indian Ocean, with its Persian, Arab, Indian, and Indonesian sailors and merchants. There, Africans and their neighbors mixed the two streams into a new and distinctive civilization.

Sofala (Mozambique) The development of trade was not entirely new, since East Africa has long been integrated into world trading networks. It was mentioned by Greek and Roman sources, and there is evidence of extensive trade with Sasanian Iran. With the rise of an Islamic world economy in the medieval period, the Zanj and related peoples of this region began trading with Arab and Iranian Muslim merchants, with Hindu mercantile clans from India, and with what we would now call Indonesians. The southern (or Sofala) Zanj supplied gold, ivory, amber, and mangrove poles to merchants from all over the Indian

Ocean, and their ports were the last stop to the west in such trading journeys. Sailors feared passing into the turbulent and uncharted Atlantic beyond what was later termed the Cape of Good Hope, though they were aware that a "Western ocean" or "Ocean of Darkness" lay beyond Africa. Although slaves were abducted from the coast, Arab geographers and historians do not mention a systematic slave trade at this time. It is likely that the African slaves working plantations in southern Iraq in the 800s, although called "Zanj," were actually purchased elsewhere, especially in North Africa. Descendants of this medieval slave population, modern-day African-Iraqis, still preserve elements of their African cultural heritage.

Sofala, in what is now Mozambique, was dominated by Bantu-speakers in the 800s when we first have Arabic textual reports of it. Al-Bakri (916 CE) reported that the Zanj king had a great capital at the city of Sofala, and employed 300,000 soldiers (an exaggeration, obviously, but an indication of power). He wrote that they used oxen both as beasts of burden and, outfitted with leopard-skin leather saddles, as war steeds for cavalry. He also reported that they had their own sophisticated language and men who preached in it to crowds, exhorting them to obey the deity. Preachers warned of the punishments visited on the disobedient, and held up as examples the ancestors and kings of former times. He added, "Each person worships whatever he pleases, whether plants, animals, or minerals." He noted that the Sofalans had no codified religious law, and that the kings ruled in accordance with custom and practical necessity. More

Box 9.1 Islam and African Religions

The following passage, by the Arab geographer al-Bakri, shows how Islam and native African religions flourished side by side in the state of Ghana during the eleventh century.

The king's residence comprises a palace and conical huts, the whole surrounded by a fence like a wall. Around the royal town are huts and groves of thorn trees where live the magicians who control their religious rites. These groves, where they keep their idols and bury their kings, are protected by guards who permit no one to enter or find out what goes on in them.

None of those who belong to the imperial religion may wear tailored garments except the king himself and the heir-presumptive, his sister's son. The rest of the people wear wrappers of cotton, silk or brocade according to their means. Most of the men shave their beards and the women their heads. The king adorns himself with female ornaments around the neck and arms. On his head he wears gold-embroidered caps covered with turbans of finest cotton. He gives audience to the people for the redressing of grievances in a hut around which are placed 10 horses covered in golden cloth. Behind him stand 10 slaves carrying shields and swords mounted with gold. On his right *are the sons of vassal kings, their heads plaited with gold and wearing costly garments. On the ground around him are seated his ministers, whilst the governor of the city sits before him. On guard at the door are dogs of fine pedigree, wearing collars adorned with gold and silver. The royal audience is announced by the beating of a drum, called daba, made out of a long piece of hollowed-out wood. When the people have gathered, his coreligionists draw near upon their knees sprinkling dust upon their heads as a sign of respect, whilst the Muslims clap hands as their form of greeting.*

of al-Bakri's report can be found in Box 9.1. Other Muslim historians report that Sofalans worshipped pagan gods and wore leopard skins. Al-Mas`udi may have witnessed sermons on obedience to "God" in Sofala because southern Bantu (on later evidence) believed in a high creator-god, who stood above lesser gods and spirits. Gold-digging was the major industry, and Sofala was a major source of gold nuggets. The area also produced iron and ivory. The Chinese chronicles for 1071 and 1083 report major trading missions from a Zanj king, perhaps that of Sofala, which brought gold, silver, and copper.

Madagascar The island of Madagascar, off what is now the Mozambique coast, was settled in the first millennium of the Common Era by Indonesian immigrants as well as by Africans from the mainland, who intermarried with one another. The Malagasy language is 90 percent Austronesian (a language group that includes Malay as well as the Polynesian languages). It also has some Bantu, Arabic, and Sanskrit influences. From the 500s Hinduism began spreading in the Indonesian islands from India, so the Sanskrit words may have been brought by early Southeast Asian Hindus, though they did not succeed in introducing the religion to Africa on a permanent basis. Traditional Madagascar religion focuses on ancestor worship. Madagascar conducted substantial trade with Indonesia throughout this period. Indonesian merchant colonies there raided for slaves and learned local languages. As in Zanzibar, the southeast monsoon winds in spring favor trade with Southeast Asia, whereas the northwest monsoon of winter favors trade with the Middle East. Thus, Madagascar also traded with the Persian Gulf and Yemen. Over time, the trade of the Indian Ocean came to be dominated by Muslim sailors. Even though Islam gained little purchase on Madagascar, local merchants trading amber and wax often depended on Muslim ships for their exports and imports after 1100.

Somalia In the north, by the 900s people in what is now Somalia were actively trading with southern Arabia and with the Persian Gulf. Iranian merchants immigrated to the coastal towns of East Africa and settled, becoming known at first as **Banadir**, or "port people." They intermarried with local Bantu-speaking families, and the resulting new ethnic group became known as **Shirazi**. Shiraz was a major southwestern city in Iran, and many of the immigrant merchant families were from that area. Later on, "Shirazi" became the common term applied to Muslim groups along the East African coast with mixed Middle Eastern and Bantu-speaking heritage, regardless of whether they had any strong Iranian influences. The coastal cities in which they settled were not "Arab colonies," but rather mixed-population sites with strong African influences, despite the occasional adoption of Islam. In the period 650–1100, only a small minority of coastal

populations was likely to have been Muslim. Among the first big cities in which the Shirazi played a major role was Mogadishu, in what is now Somalia, which by the end of our period (1200s) had become one of the more important ports on the East African coast. Some Shirazi populations migrated south, settling in what is now Kenya. The language produced by this interaction of Bantu-speakers, Iranians, and Arabs became known as Swahili (literally "of the Coast"). It gradually spread all along the East African coast.

Kenya and the Island Trades Likewise, the ports of Malindi and Mombasa in what is now Kenya came to be inhabited by a mixture of Shirazi and Bantu-speakers, especially during the 1100s. The Arab geographer al-Idrisi reports around 1150 that Mombasa was a small town and that its inhabitants had a source of iron and hunted leopards. Bananas, lemons, and oranges were also grown. The inhabitants by this time included many Muslims, who worshipped in wooden mosques. Al-Idrisi also says that the king of the Zanj had a palace there. In contrast to Mombasa, which got high marks from Arab writers for the piety of its minority Muslim inhabitants, they considered the port of Malindi a center of "witchcraft," indicating the predominance there of African religious practices such as spirit possession. Similar social and commercial developments took place on the islands of Zanzibar and Manda by the 900s. There are reports of substantial Muslim trading settlements on the island of Zanzibar by the 800s. Large mosques that served these communities have been excavated, dating back to the 700s or 800s. Down the coast in what is now Tanzania lay the wealthy port of Kilwa. On an island, it served as the port for the southern Sofala region, and was one of the greatest commercial centers in East Africa.

Growth of Islam in East Africa The East African city-states, lacking an overarching political unit, often feuded with one another and with peoples of the interior. Although the Arab sources often speak of a "king of the Zanj," there was no such unified monarchy, but rather feuding city-states. Muslim sources tend to focus on Muslim populations such as the Shirazi, but these were probably small minorities for most of this period, living under the rule of Bantu-speakers. Only from the 1100s were there powerful Shirazi or Muslim ruling clans, their economic power bolstered by their dominance of the trade in cloth. Even where there were Muslims and mosques, the evidence is that the port cities were not consistently pious places.

After 1100, archaeologists find increasing numbers of mosques on the East African coast, made of cut coral and coral plaster. By the 1300s, travelers such as Ibn Batuta found that the Muslim communities in the ports had formal officials such as court judges (**qadis**) and were organized for the practice of Sunni

Islam. As East Africans entered the international world of Indian Ocean trade, their local gods had to compete with the universalizing, rationalist, monotheistic religion of Islam. Muslims were taught that God had sent many prophetic religions into the world and this message may have appealed to these cosmopolitan Africans. Islam's appeal included the attraction of connecting to a community of believers stretching across the known world, a community that recognized and sought to practice honesty and fair dealing in commercial relations. Although Arabic was used as a liturgical language by Muslims, there is little evidence of a tradition of writing in it in these areas in the medieval period, in contrast to West African centers such as Timbuktu. The everyday language of Muslims in the East African port cities was Swahili.

The Sahel and West Africa

As in East Africa, the adoption of iron-smelting technology in West Africa contributed to the rise of larger and more centralized states. Iron hoes allowed greater agricultural productivity, and iron weaponry made for more effective militaries, especially against enemies that lacked iron. Ironsmiths gained a special position in West African society in this period. The increasing use of the horse helped to strengthen military forces, while the camel contributed to increasing long-distance trade. With mobile horse warriors, tax revenues collected from merchants, and imported horses, weapons, and prestige goods, more powerful states emerged from the ethnic chiefdoms of the West African **savanna** (grassland).

Origins of West African States Two key river valleys, the Niger and the Senegal, gave birth to the first centralized states in West Africa in this period. Both rivers have their headwaters in what is now Guinea, in the middle mountain range of Fouta Djalon. Coming after only the Nile and the Congo in length, the Niger is 2,600 miles long. It starts in what is now Guinea and flows northeast into Mali, then across western Niger. The other major body of water, the Senegal River, also begins in what is now Guinea. It, however, flows north to form the border between present-day Senegal and Mali, in tributaries. These tributaries join together to become the Senegal River at the border point between Mauritania and Senegal, which flows north and northeast to trace the border between Senegal and Mauritania.

The river valleys, with their fertility-enhancing inundations and easy transport, were the most important geographic foundation for the new West African states. The agricultural transformation and the introduction of iron tools and weapons encouraged the aggregation of bands into settled communities headed by chiefs from a founding or dominant lineage. The transformation

of small chiefdoms into city-states, and the rise of dominant cities controlling extensive empires, seem to have required two further changes: the growth of the trans-Saharan trade and the introduction of horse and camel cavalry, especially in the dry areas of the northern Sahel where the tse-tse fly posed less of a threat to the horses.

It became possible to cross the Sahara itself only from about the first centuries of the first millennium CE, when Berber clans began using camels imported from the Middle East for this purpose. Other, easier routes went through the **Sahel**, the region just south of the Sahara. The Mediterranean world, like sub-Saharan Africa, already imported salt from the Sahara. Beginning in the 900s, the demand for gold rose inexorably. West African gold ore, tinged with copper and sometimes silver, came out of the mines so pure it did not need to be processed, and so was much sought after for Egyptian Muslim mints. Since West Africa had little need for the major products of the Mediterranean, and since gold was highly valued, it almost certainly ran a balance-of-trade surplus with the Middle East. One import that West African rulers with access to gold could now afford had far-reaching consequences: military technology.

Recent archaeological findings show that the northern Niger basin had several urban centers and a complex social hierarchy from the late centuries BCE and into the first millennium CE. The early city of Jenne-jeno (see Chapter 4) grew to its greatest extent around 850 CE, and people moved from constructing buildings of puddle mud (*tauf*) to cylindrical bricks. A brick city wall was erected around that period, for instance. In 800–1200, ironsmiths and coppersmiths in the city were forging iron into tools and weapons and forming copper and bronze into decorative objects. By this time, there were over sixty major settlement sites in the region, though few as large Jenne-jeno (27,000). The Niger Delta supported rice-growing and the river facilitated trade networks despite frequent rapids and falls.

Ghana Among the important West African states of this period was the Senegalese kingdom of Ghana, which also came to encompass southern Mauritania. (The ancient Ghanaian kingdom or empire is not related to the present country of Ghana.) It was founded late in the first millennium by a distinct ethnic group of farming people speaking **Soninke**, a Niger–Congo language like Bantu but descended from the Mande languages that arose further west. Until about 900, excavations in the middle Senegal Valley basin find no evidence of complex societies, with little variation in basic pottery or building techniques.

Since Ghana did not develop a written language, in contrast to the Nubian kingdoms further east, historians have to rely for detailed knowledge of its development on Muslim travelers whose reports have survived. The Spanish Muslim geographer al-Mas'udi, for example, describes the kingdom of Ghana in 1068 as very prosperous. For more of al-Mas'udi's account, see Box 9.2. Situated south of the Sahara between the Senegal and Niger rivers, it possessed, he said, great reservoirs of gold, which was the basis of its economy. The capital, Kumbi Saleh, was located just south of the Sahara at the northern fringe of viable agriculture. At its peak in the eleventh century, the city had a population of 15,000–20,000 people. The wealth of its rulers came from the trans-Saharan trade, exporting gold, kola nuts, and slaves acquired in trade with the forest peoples to the south or in raids into neighboring regions. In exchange, Ghana traders imported salt (for the salt-scarce savanna and forest areas of the Sahel), as well as cloth, glass beads, and other Berber goods, including horses and camels. The capital was composed of two separate compounds with residential structures between them. One was for Arab and Berber merchants, and the other, 6 miles away, housed the king and his court.

The king, named Tunka Manin, maintained a powerful army that could field, al-Bakri said, 200,000 troops and 40,000 archers (these numbers are probably exaggerated). The king also acquired horses in exchange for gold from Berber traders, but even in areas north of the tse-tse fly frontier, other endemic diseases and parasites made it difficult to breed new stock. Horses had to be continually imported from North Africa.

The Ghanaian king was considered divine by the Soninke, and wore special ritual clothing. Al-Bakri wrote:

The King adorns himself like a woman wearing necklaces round his neck and bracelets on his forearms and he puts on a high cap decorated with gold and wrapped in a turban of fine cotton. He holds an audience in a domed pavilion around which stand ten horses covered with gold-embroidered materials ... and on his right, are the sons of the vassal kings of his country, wearing splendid garments and their hair plaited with gold.

The subjects bowed down when he came near and poured earth over their heads. This African king was himself clearly enormously wealthy, and kept close control over taxation policy, charging a local tax for bringing goods in and out of the capital. He kept all gold nuggets mined in his treasury, releasing them gradually so as to avoid causing a drop in their value. "Around the king's town are domed buildings and groves and thickets where the sorcerers of these people, men in charge of the religious cult, live. In them too are their idols and the tombs of their kings." These holy men presided over the ritual practices of the polytheistic Soninke religion, which included adoration of the king as a symbol of the divine. Some legends suggest that every year they sacrificed a virgin to ward off the anger of the gods. The kings were buried in tombs in sacred groves, along with their servants.

The king appointed literate Muslims as ministers and as treasurer. He maintained a corps of Muslim translators to interpret Arabic and Berber into Soninke. The Muslim quarter near

Box 9.2 The Zanj of East Africa

The following is a description of the people along the coast of East Africa, written by the Arab traveler al-Mas'udi, who visited the "land of Zanj" in 916.

The land of Zanj produces wild leopard skins. The people wear them as clothes, or export them to Muslim countries. They are the largest leopard skins and the most beautiful for making saddles ... They also export tortoise shell for making combs, for which ivory is likewise used ... The Zanj are settled in that area, which stretches as far as Sofala, which is the furthest limit of the land and the end of the voyages made from Oman and Siraf on the sea of Zanj ... The Zanj use the ox as a beast of burden,

for they have no horses, mules or camels in their land ... There are many wild elephants in this land but no tame ones. The Zanj do not use them for war or anything else, but only hunt and kill them for their ivory. It is from this country that come tusks weighing fifty pounds and more. They usually go to Oman, and from there are sent to China and India. This is the chief trade route ...

The Zanj have an elegant language and men who preach in it. One of their holy men will often gather a crowd and exhort his hearers to please God in their lives and to be obedient to him. He explains the punishments that follow upon disobedience, and reminds them

of their ancestors and kings of old. These people have no religious law: their kings rule by custom and by political expediency.

The Zanj eat bananas, which are as common among them as they are in India; but their staple food is millet and a plant called kalari which is pulled out of the earth like truffles. They also eat honey and meat. They have many islands where the coconut grows: its nuts are used as fruit by all the Zanj peoples. One of these islands, which is one or two days' sail from the coast, has a Muslim population and a royal family. This is the island of Kanbulu [thought to be modern Pemba].

the royal compound of Kumbi Saleh had mosques and other Muslim institutions, to make the traveling merchants feel at home. The quarter "is inhabited by Muslims, is large and possesses twelve mosques in one of which they assemble for the Friday prayer. There are salaried imams and muezzins [prayer leaders and callers to prayer], as well as jurists and scholars." Although the Soninke practiced West African religion and saw their king as divine, they bestowed religious toleration on Muslims.

Outside the capital there were other large cities, including the Berber-dominated commercial center, Awdaghust, which the Ghanaian ruler conquered and incorporated into his realm late in the 900s. He appointed a Soninke governor over it. Berbers, a people of North Africa who often lived as pastoral nomads, were early adopters of Islam in Africa. They had settled in this oasis town and eventually owned plantations on which black African peasants or slaves worked to raise wheat, dates, cucumbers, and henna. The Soninke workers used hoes to break the soil and brought buckets of water out from wells to water the crops. Awdaghust itself had one cathedral mosque and many smaller ones, and it hosted, along with local Berbers, many traders from what is now Tunisia. In the middle of the eleventh century, al-Bakri said, "The market there is at all times full of people." He also remarked on the large number of slaves, saying that each inhabitant of the town could have a thousand servants. Local Soninke artisans worked cotton, jewelry, ceramics, copper, and brass. They were also renowned for their production of the large leather shields favored by Berber horsemen, made from the skin of gazelles found in the vicinity of the city. Archaeologists have shown that the city began to acquire mud brick buildings and walls in this era, and even became so prosperous that some stone structures were built, before it declined.

The kingdom of Ghana declined in the second half of the eleventh century for many reasons. The most important appears to have been a series of dry spells that devastated the local agricultural economy. Some parts of the kingdom, such as Awdaghust, may have grown populations too large for the fragile water supply to support, even in wetter times. The growth of the livestock population, including cattle, sheep, and goats, may also have put pressure on the pasturage in this area near the desert. Sheep are notorious for eating the grass too close to its roots, which weakens it, especially during dry spells or when there are plant disease outbreaks. Archaeologists find evidence that the variety of livestock supported in parts of the Ghanaian kingdom declined, with tougher strains of goat surviving. In addition, Ghana suffered incursions by nomadic Berbers caught up in a particularly zealous and intolerant movement of North African Islam, the Almoravids (al-Murabitun). Although the Almoravids did sack Awdaghust in 1055, and Kumbi Saleh itself in 1076,

their attacks alone cannot explain the decline of the Ghanaian kingdom, and Berber immigration into the area in this period was probably gradual. On the middle Senegal River, a state ruled by a Muslim king, Takrur, actually spread and consolidated its power in the 1100s, after the decline of Ghana.

Other West African States The political decline of Ghana led to a century of decentralization in the north, with each town or village managing its own affairs without interference, or protection, from any larger state or empire. The wealth of the West African gold mines and the continuously expanding trade across the Sahara gave birth to further African states. The Susu kingdom succeeded Ghana, ruled by the Kante dynasty, in the 1100s. By the early 1200s they had been defeated and incorporated into the new kingdom of Mali (see Chapter 12). In 1100, the city of Timbuktu was founded by Berber traders on the Niger River, and over time it grew into an extremely important commercial and cultural center. Another important trading center and kingdom in twelfth-century West Africa, Gao, arose under the Dia dynasty and used the Niger River for its commerce.

The Berbers

The Arab Muslim conquerors who flowed into formerly Byzantine North Africa in the seventh and eighth centuries CE garnered extensive booty from the subject population. As historian Elizabeth Savage has shown, among their loot were slaves held by Berbers, and Berbers made into slaves themselves. Indeed, some early sources give the search for lucrative slaves as among the motives for the Arab conquest of areas like Morocco. Berbers were the leading ethnic group in North Africa, speaking an Afro-Semitic language. Many practiced pastoral nomadism, though there were important Berber cities. Many Berbers proved willing to join Arab armies in search of loot and conquest. Still, the caliph's authority did not run far in rugged North Africa, which often witnessed the rise of Berber Muslim kingdoms like Tahart (761–908) in what is now Algeria. Much North African history after the advent of Islam consisted of clan feuds among Berber converts, who sometimes managed to found small chiefdoms or even states that lasted for various periods of time.

Gradually the Berbers themselves adopted Islam, though in the first centuries they favored the strict Ibadi branch of it and were considered heretics by the caliphs in the heartlands of Islam. They objected to religious authority being in the hands of the caliphs instead of being the preserve of learned men, and stressed the equality of all believers. Although, technically speaking, Islamic law came to forbid the enslavement of Muslims, Berbers continued to be taken as slaves long after they converted.

Ironically, in time the Berbers themselves organized a system of slave trading, and probably from the middle of the 700s the Ibadi slave merchants dominated the market. The Berber traders bought slaves from the African kings in the south, who were said to "sell their people without any pretext or war." By the 800s, the trading city of Tahart had grown extremely wealthy, and the Berbers remained a symbol of opulence for later writers.

Despite the wealth generated by the gold and slave trade, the Berber areas remained politically fragmented for most of the first three centuries of Islamic history there. These areas were united in the early 1000s by the Berber Almoravid movement. Founded by a strict, orthodox preacher, this movement insisted on carrying Islam to black Africa. It appealed to Berbers in what is now Morocco and West Africa. It not only conquered Morocco but also united the Muslims of southern Spain against the northern Christians by the late 1000s. Over time their rulers ceased being zealous Muslims, indulging instead in decadent pursuits, and they increasingly hired Christian mercenaries for their military in Spain. They therefore faced a revolt in 1147 by a new puritan movement, the Almohads (literally al-Muwahhidun or the monotheists). The Almohad kingdom overthrew the Almoravids, and grew to be an even larger empire. Its rulers remained somewhat fanatical in their approach to Islam. This dynasty also declined in its political strength during the subsequent century. The Berber tribespeople living in rugged North Africa were extremely difficult to unite for long periods of time, and most political units broke up eventually through clan feuds.

9.2 THE AMERICAS, 600–1200

In the Americas, this era begins at the high point of the wealth and power of the Mayan city-states and the empires of Wari and Tiwanaku in the Andes. In Central Mexico, however, the fall of the empire centered in the city of Teotihuacán in about 550 CE led to a decentralization of power as warring city-states emerged to vie for dominance. Elsewhere in the Americas, population growth, incipient urbanization, the development of larger and more complex chiefdoms, and the transition to city-states were also occurring.

As elsewhere in the world, the cities and states of the Americas developed complex administrative structures to organize agricultural production, collect taxes, build large cities and manage their daily life, and construct civic and religious monuments. Their cultural and intellectual achievements were equally impressive. Mayan astronomers and mathematicians produced a more accurate calendar than the European calendar of the time, a great advance that made it possible to predict the seasons more accurately and thus ensure more successful planting and harvesting of crops. City managers and architects in the larger cities of Mesoamerica and the Andes laid out entire neighborhoods, organized water and food supplies, and supervised the construction of massive temples and civic spaces for public rituals and ceremonies. Large empires facilitated trade by providing safety and predictability for traders. Monarchs and the leading lineages employed priests, scribes, orators, sculptors, and courtiers of all kinds to convey earthly praise and the approval of the gods. Priestly specialists developed popular religious ideas and symbols into complex cosmologies requiring expert interpretation and impressive artistic representation in temples, statues, murals, pottery, and elaborate rituals.

Unlike Africa, however, the people of the Americas were unable to share their achievements with other continents or to import technology, religions, and flora and fauna. Raised-field agriculture and food crops such as corn, potatoes, and manioc, developed by millennia of selective breeding, did not reach the rest of the world until after the Spanish conquest that followed Columbus' first voyage in 1492. Ironmaking, which helped Africans produce food crops in difficult environments, was unknown in the Americas. The Americas also lacked beasts of burden to transport food and merchandise. Though llamas were used as pack animals in the Andean highlands, they could not survive in the hot lowlands and were unknown elsewhere. The American deserts had no camels. Horses, donkeys, and mules invaded with the Europeans much later. Trade made use of inland rivers, like the Usumacinta in the Maya heartland, but most of the other great cities and states were based in highland regions far from navigable rivers or seacoasts.

Lack of communication with other world regions made the complex societies of the Americas vulnerable, despite natural environments that in many regions were far more favorable than in most of sub-Saharan Africa. The development and survival of urban societies in the Americas depended on intensively exploiting the ecological resources of relatively small areas. Food is bulky. Human porters could not carry corn or potatoes more than two or three days without eating most of their cargo. Llamas carried heavier loads, but ate even more. Transporting food by river or across lakes made it possible for fewer people to move bigger loads. So where rivers or lakes could be used for transportation, cities were more common and could grow much larger. Even the best located cities, however, could not long survive changes in climate or the effects of ecological damage. When environmental conditions suddenly changed, temperatures fell, rains failed, lakes and streams dried up, soils became exhausted or turned to dust, these societies were unable to import new methods or to develop them quickly enough to avert catastrophe. As crops failed and hunger spread, people lost faith in their rulers and religions. Elites became rapacious, grabbing dwindling food supplies for themselves. Farmers fled tax collectors, urban artisans rebelled, and governments disintegrated. Old and new enemies looking to solve their own problems with new conquests invaded, looting stored food, desecrating temples, humiliating proud monarchs, and sacrificing them to alien gods.

Mesoamerica

Disaster struck first in **Mesoamerica**. In the Mayan regions, a catastrophic dry spell lasting two centuries caused a demographic disaster, the collapse of city-states, and the abandonment of urban life everywhere, beginning in 800 (see Map 9.2). In Central Mexico, the Toltec empire (established *c.* 900), a successor state to Teotihuacán with its capital at Tula further north, also fell to drought and invasion in about 1168. While something of the culture and politics of the Toltecs survived after their fall, the Mayan collapse was virtually total.

Collapse of the Mayan Cities Sometime between 800 and 900, the Mayan cities collapsed, suddenly and almost simultaneously. The Maya population (between 2 and 14 million in 800) fell to only 1 million in the 900s. Dozens of Mayan cities now suffered fates similar to Teotihuacán in Central Mexico: revolt or invasion and abandonment.

The main cause of the Mayan collapse was a long dry spell that lasted from approximately 800 to 1000, the driest two centuries in 7,000 years. Most Mayan cities had fewer than 50,000 inhabitants and controlled less than 770 square miles of territory. Urban settlement patterns were dispersed, with gardens and fields often separating clusters of homes, more like tropical Jenne-jeno in West Africa than Teotihuacán, where people lived in densely populated residential compounds without much intervening space. The Mayan cities depended on rainfall to fill the rivers that fed their irrigation systems and to replenish the wetlands and swamps where they constructed highly productive **raised fields**, a farming technique that involved constructing earthen platforms above the level of the surrounding countryside. The region had already experienced a long dry period from 536 to 590, which caused widespread famine and depopulation, but nothing prepared the Maya or their rulers for a dry spell that lasted for more than two centuries.

The last known construction date on a newly built Mayan building was carved in 790. Hieroglyphic inscriptions on older buildings and stelae cease sometime in the 820s. Stone inscriptions in the late eighth and early ninth centuries give evidence of intense warfare between city-states, though such conflicts had taken place earlier. As conditions worsened, the authority of kings declined; monuments began to depict groups of nobles

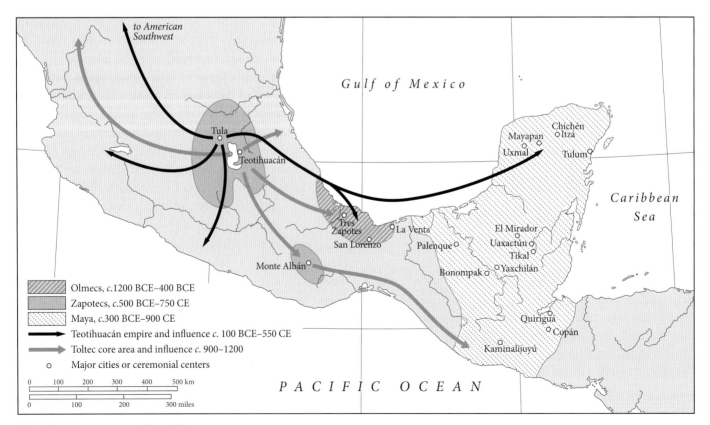

Map 9.2 Mesoamerica, 600–1200

rather than all-powerful monarchs. Skeletal remains from this period show evidence of periodic famine and malnutrition as well as a sharper decline in the stature of commoners than of nobles. Trade goods, especially luxury and ritual items like green obsidian figures and spear points from Central Mexico as well as fancy pottery and figures carved from jade, bone, and shell, all disappear. After an initial period of population decline, when crude fortifications were constructed in a number of sites, the cities were all abandoned.

When the Spaniards arrived half a millennium later, they found not city-states but local chiefdoms centered in small towns with a dispersed agricultural population that depended on **slash-and-burn** (**swidden**) agriculture. The climate conditions that had made Mayan agriculture so productive had slowly returned after 1000 CE, but the Mayan knowledge base had disappeared. The writing system had died with the last scribes, the calendar lost with them. Something remained of Mayan irrigation and raised fields, but only on a small scale. Some of the chiefly lineages claimed glorious ancestors. Oral traditions embodied in elaborate epics and folk tales contained glimpses of the past. Mayan religious beliefs came to focus on local deities that required less effort to appease.

Rise and Fall of the Toltecs After the fall of Teotihuacán in 550 (see Chapter 4), political power in the Valley of Mexico gradually devolved to a number of city-states in which urban centers established control over small hinterlands of villages and trading centers and occasionally warred or allied among themselves. Some of the towns and cities that arose after 550 may have been founded or taken over by warriors or nobles from defeated Teotihuacán. It was not until more than two centuries later that another attempt was made to create a large territorial state, this time to the north of the Valley of Mexico, at a site referred to in legends as Tollan or Tula. The city was founded in approximately 800–900, possibly by descendants of the Teotihuacán aristocracy, but more likely by others who later incorporated elements of Teotihuacán religion and politics. The city grew to a maximum population of 40,000–50,000, smaller than Teotihuacán but large enough to deploy a big military force and exact tribute from a large area of Central Mexico. Toltec-like architecture and religious imagery has been found throughout the Valley of Mexico and adjacent areas and as far south as the Maya region, especially at Chichén-Itzá in Yucatan.

Eventually, the Toltec state fell victim to prolonged drought and invasion in 1168. Figure 9.3 shows the huge statues that survived the collapse and abandonment of Tula, the Toltec capital. The invaders may have been an alliance of rival cities, as a later chronicle suggested, or nomadic invaders from the north. The last Toltec monarch, Huemac ("Big Hand"), seems to have been captured and executed, though another account claimed that he fled to the Chapultepec area (now a park in Mexico City) where he committed suicide. The inhabitants of Tula fled and never returned. Box 9.3 cites a later account of Tula's collapse in which Huemac's legendary father, Topiltzin, is the victim.

Yet Toltec influence persisted. Many communities in the Valley of Mexico proudly traced their ancestry to Tula centuries later. Noble lineages claiming Toltec origins dominated Central Mexico until the arrival of the Spaniards in 1519. Toltec gods, many similar to those at Teotihuacán, became part of the religious heritage of the entire region. The most important were later called Tlaloc, the god of rain and storm represented with a square headdress, and the plumed serpent Quetzalcoatl, the god of creation and knowledge.

Figure 9.3 Once the capital of a great state in Central Mexico, Tula was abandoned in 1168 CE amid evidence of prolonged drought, rebellion, and invaders from the north. The appearance of the warrior statues has been compared to space suits of modern astronauts.

Box 9.3 The Toltec Dispersal

The Toltec dispersal under King Topiltzin, as recounted by Fernando de Alva
Ixtlilxóchitl, great grandson of the last
ruler of Texcoco, written about 1600,
but referring to the fall of Tula in the
twelfth century:

*In the tenth year of his reign, the famine
and barrenness of the land began. Most
of the people were dying and the weevils
ate the supplies stored in the granaries.
Many other persecutions and calamities
came from heaven, which seemed to*
*rain fire, and the drought [which lasted
twenty-six years] was so great that the
rivers and springs dried up. In the
twenty-third year of his reign, they were
so lacking in strength and sustenance
that the three kings mentioned came
with a powerful army and easily took
the city of Tula, the capital of the
empire. Even though King Topiltzin fled
the city, a few days later they caught up
with him and killed his people ... and
the few Toltecs that were left escaped*
*into the mountains of the lake at Cul-
huacán. This was the end of the Toltec
empire, which lasted 572 years; and the
kings who had come to subjugate it,
seeing it so ruined, returned to their
provinces. Although they were victorious, even they were very damaged and
had lost most of their armies, most of
whom had died from the famine. The
same calamity befell their lands,
because the land was everywhere dry
and barren ...*

Empires in the Andes

Empires based at Wari in the north and Tiwanaku in the south divided the highland regions of the Andes from Ecuador to Bolivia beginning in the seventh century until sometime in the tenth (see Chapter 4). The two empires differed in organization and impact. When Tiwanaku collapsed, its culture and technology disappeared with it, like the Mayan cities in Meso-america. The empire of the Wari, on the other hand, left a powerful model for state-building that influenced all of the successor states in the Andes, including the Inkas, the Spanish colonial rulers, and even the modern states of Bolivia and Peru (see Map 9.3).

Legacies of the Tiwanaku and Wari The ancient city of Tiwanaku on the southern shore of Lake Titicaca arose in a difficult environment and was based on exceptionally productive agriculture, which depended on irrigation canals that brought water from Lake Titicaca to raised fields (see Chapter 4). Unfortunately, an era of much drier weather began sometime in the tenth century. Each year, Lake Titicaca shrank a little further during the dry season and did not recover when the rainy seasons brought less and less rain. Desperate efforts to extend the canals failed and they began to dry up. Eventually, the raised fields had to be abandoned. The city itself collapsed and its population dispersed to other places well before 1000. When Inka armies conquered the Titicaca basin in the fifteenth century, nothing remained of the ancient city but huge abandoned stone buildings. The Inkas found a sparse population of llama herders, who supplemented their diet with crops planted using digging sticks along the lake shore.

Archaeologists excavating the temples and palaces at the center of Tiwanaku paid no attention to the outlying bumps on the landscape until late in the twentieth century. Once redis-covered, in a period of moderate to abundant rainfall and with Lake Titicaca back to its Tiwanaku-era dimensions, the archae-ologists persuaded some of the local farmers to restore the raised fields and canals. The results were spectacular, with yields run-ning many times higher than the farmers were used to extracting even with modern tools, pesticides, and fertilizers.

The Wari state of the northern Andes also collapsed in the long era of dry weather that began in the tenth century. Unlike Tiwanaku, however, the Wari did not depend on the resources mobilized in their principal city to sustain their empire. The Wari used elaborate public rituals of reciprocity plus corvée labor for designated fields and centralized control of stored food surpluses to maintain control. The drier weather undermined this strategy by making food so scarce that conquered regions balked at trading it for Wari craft goods. Food shortages pro-voked resistance to labor from peasants worried about their own fields. Wari food warehouses were emptied to feed populations facing repeated harvest failures. Wari state-building strategies survived the collapse of the Wari state to be incorporated by the Inkas four centuries later.

Survival of the Chimú State on the Pacific Coast As the Tiwanaku and Wari states dissolved, a powerful new state called the Chimú (or Chimor) empire arose to dominate the desert coast of Peru from the modern border between Ecuador and Peru in the north to just north of the modern city of Lima, 600 miles to the south. The origin myth of the Chimú rulers claimed that the legendary founder of the dynasty, Taycanamu,

Map 9.3 Andean empires

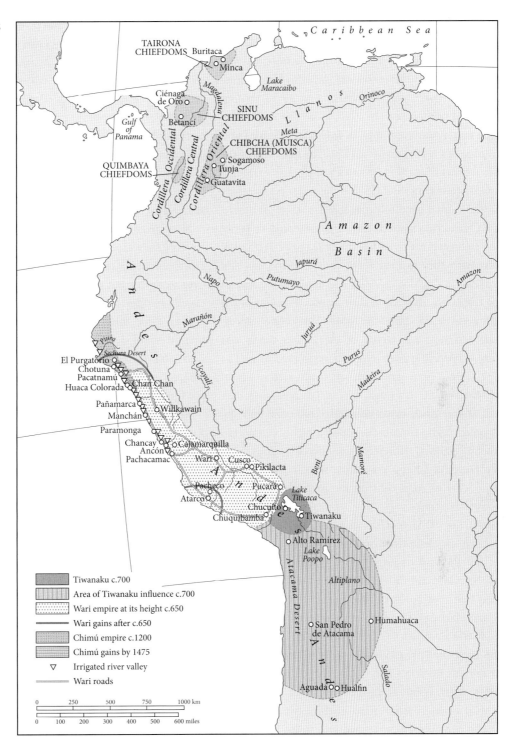

arrived in the Moche River valley after a long sea voyage on a balsa raft; his children were credited with taking over the entire valley and beginning the conquests of adjacent valleys.

More than fifty rivers flow down from the Andes. Each must pass through the narrow strip of desert coast to reach the Pacific Ocean. The desert is seldom more than 30 miles wide, except in the north. The rivers create what archaeologists have called "linear oases," separated from each other by long stretches of uninhabitable arid terrain. By the time of the Moche cultures (c. 375–650), people, trade goods, and ideas moved easily from one oasis city to another, particularly in the north where the distances between the river oases was shorter than elsewhere. However, most of the villages, towns, and cities that evolved on the coast looked toward the mountains where they could trade their fish, maize, cotton, craft and luxury goods, and other lowland products for food and craft products not easily produced on the coast, such as tropical fruit and the wool, fat, and meat of llamas. The Chimú state was not only the first to unite the entire northern coast, but also the first to do so without acquiring highland territories.

The Chimú empire survived until an Inka army invaded and seized the capital of Chan Chan in *c.* 1470. The longevity of the Chimú state, like that of many early states and empires, stemmed from its capacity to manage and develop the water resources on which all of the coastal peoples depended. Unlike most others, however, the Chimú rulers honed their organizational skills not by managing a single great river, like the Nile or the Euphrates, but by taking what they learned about canal construction and irrigation systems in the Moche Valley and applying the lessons to each new river oasis that fell to their armies. Portions of the Chimú water systems are still in use today. Many were impressive in scope and size. The largest of the Chimú canals was 52 miles long, though it appears not to have worked as well as planned. The Chimú even built canals between rivers, one of which united five streams in a single system. To accomplish such feats, as well as the urban expansion and ceremonial building that accompanied it, the Chimú developed a highly centralized and hierarchical political structure. Conquered regions were governed by powerful Chimú governors, who mobilized local populations to work on huge construction projects. Rulers were officially revered as godlike.

Unfortunately for archaeologists, stone was not available for the construction of Chan Chan and the other Chimú cities. They were built instead of dried adobe bricks of such high quality that they were still in use in the late twentieth century (and so good that they sold at prices higher than new bricks of modern manufacture). Chan Chan grew to a population of more than 30,000 by 1000 CE and may have been twice as large by the time the Inkas captured it. Most of the Moche Valley's inhabitants lived in Chan Chan, with only a few thousand in scattered settlements along the river. As in Teotihuacán in Central Mexico, many if not most of the city's inhabitants must have been agriculturalists, pushed into town to allow the rulers better control. Despite (or perhaps because of) their high level of centralized state organization, Chimú artistic expression did not match that of previous cultures, which were more loosely organized and less successful at controlling water and people.

Complex Chiefdoms: Egalitarian Alternatives to Empire?

In recent years archaeologists, anthropologists, and historians have begun to examine and debate evidence that may point to an unusually egalitarian path of human social evolution that eventually died out, but may nevertheless have left its mark on some later societies. In the standard histories, city-states – and the large empires that sometimes grew out of them – are associated with the emergence of social stratification and elite rule. As societies became more complex, they became more and more unequal. In many societies, for example, elite men and women commonly averaged 2 to 4 inches taller in height (due to better nutrition) than the rest of the population until well into the twentieth century. Did alternative paths to urbanization and state formation exist in the premodern world?

In some parts of the Americas, complex chiefdoms appear to have evolved around 1000 CE in ways that made it possible to create urban centers and establish political and cultural unity over extensive territories without sacrificing the egalitarianism usually associated with less complex societies. The most compelling case for this suggestion is associated with work on the mound-building cultures of the Amazon region of modern Brazil, but similar questions could be raised about the relatively complex societies that developed in the US Southwest as well as the Mississippi Valley.

Amazonia Human migrants moved into the flood plains of the Amazon and Orinoco rivers about the same time that others were arriving in the Andean mountain valleys (*c.* 9000–7000 BCE). Beginning in about 500 CE, there is evidence of larger and more complex settlements, but the absence of stone construction or metal objects means that the remains of these societies are more difficult to locate, uncover, and analyze. The tropical climate facilitates decay, so human remains, wood buildings, clothing, and most cultural objects disintegrated in the distant past. The earliest pottery-producing cultures subsisted largely on fish and shellfish. The transition to sedentary agriculture is especially difficult to date. Maize did not become a staple food until about 1000 CE, when it appears to be associated with a widespread transition from small bands to larger and more complex chiefdoms.

The most interesting and impressive of the Amazonian sites explored to date is undoubtedly Santarém, located on a flood plain adjacent to a region of mixed forest and savanna where the Tapajós River empties into the Amazon. The site derives its name from that of the modern city built over it. The Tapajós chiefdom included an area of some 10,000 square miles. The ancient city of Santarém itself covered as much as 2 square miles and may have had a population as large as Teotihuacán (over 100,000). Other cities with relatively dense populations have been tentatively identified at other sites in the Amazon and Orinoco regions.

So far as archaeologists can determine, these Amazonian societies did recognize and privilege certain lineages or clans, but never allowed them to accumulate the wealth and power that kings and nobles managed to seize for themselves in most other premodern societies. Instead of a single highly stratified social order, the Amazonian societies described by the earliest European travelers were organized as small chiefdoms united under a single paramount chief, whose authority was widely recognized and enforced by loyal warriors. The paramount chief did not rule directly, but through subordinate chiefs who paid tribute and supported religious observance by extracting goods from the farmers and craftspeople over whom they ruled. There were few, if any, governors, priests, tax collectors, or bureaucrats to do the bidding of the paramount chief.

In the larger towns, urban populations lived in communal residences each with its own chief. It was not uncommon for women to head such extended households. Inheritance, including hereditary rule, could be matrilineal. Elite families may have had access to a more varied diet, performed high-status roles in religious observances, and reserved for themselves certain roles, like leadership in making war. Slavery existed, but was uncommon. There is no evidence to suggest anything like the levels of social inequality that are so marked in the city-states and

Map 9.4 Southwest and Mississippi chiefdoms

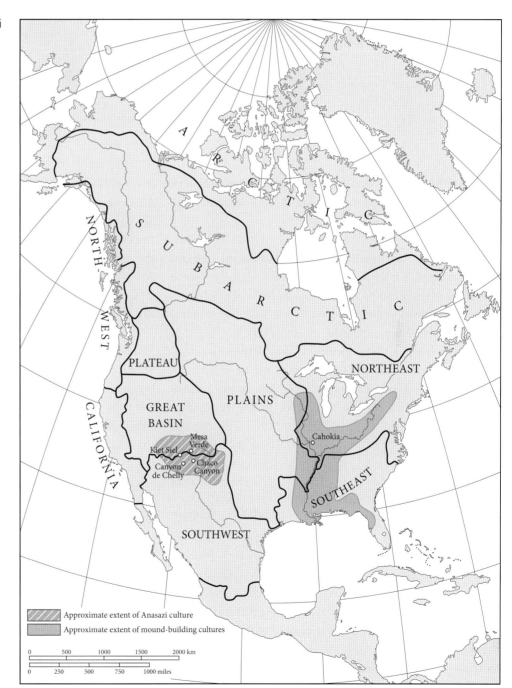

Figure 9.4 The cliff dwellings of Mesa Verde are among the most notable and best preserved in North America. In the late 1190s, after living on the mesa top for 600 years, many Ancestral Puebloans built pueblos beneath the overhanging cliffs, ranging from one-room storage units to villages of more than 150 rooms. While still farming the mesa tops, they continued to live in the alcoves.

empires of Mesoamerica and the Andes, but archaeological work is much less developed in the Amazon so firm conclusions are still difficult to draw.

North America: Southwestern USA and Mississippi Cultures

The agricultural transition, based on maize cultivation mixed with other crops, occurred in the southwestern region of today's United States between 600 and 900 CE. It is likely that migrants from Central Mexico facilitated the transition, because it is associated in some areas with unmistakable Mesoamerican cultural practices, including religious symbols and the building of central plazas, mounds, and ball courts. Three major cultural traditions are associated with the chiefdoms that emerged in this area.

The most complex of the three, known as the Hohokam culture (after a major site), developed in southern Arizona in the Tonto basin and the valleys of the Gila and Salt rivers after about 500 and flourished between 975 and 1150 (see Map 9.4). Like the river basin cities in the desert along the Peruvian coast, the Hohokam towns depended on irrigation. Unlike the Chimú state and its predecessors, however, there is no evidence of the emergence of a centralized state to organize and coerce the labor force required to build and maintain the irrigation systems. The Mogollon, which flourished to the east and south of the Hohokam, covered a larger territory, showed fewer Mesoamerican influences, settled in somewhat smaller communities, and made less use of extensive irrigation. The Anasazi culture to the north extended over the largest

territory and resembled the Mogollon in farming techniques. All three of these cultures suffered during a prolonged era of dry weather that began late in the twelfth century and stretched into the next century. By 1400, only ruins remained, the most impressive of which are the stone buildings of the Anasazi (the Mesa Verde complex is shown in Figure 9.4), though the size and complexity of the Hohokam sites is generally greater.

The agricultural transition also spread eastward to the vast Mississippi basin and northward to the Great Lakes. The Mississippi chiefdoms emerged with maize cultivation sometime between 800 and 1000 CE. As in the Amazon and the US Southwest, the Mississippi societies brought together lineages and clans, each with its own chiefs, in a decentralized governing structure that inhibited the growth of the kind of social inequalities evident in other premodern societies.

The Mississippi basin culture, like that of the Amazon, built flat-topped platforms or "mounds" raised above the surface of the surrounding terrain. In the Amazon, entire villages and towns were built on the raised surface of the mounds; towns of several thousand inhabitants consisted of a large number of adjacent mounds. In the Mississippi culture, the population centers were built inside palisade fences. In the center of the settlements were large plazas. Residential housing surrounded the plazas. The houses of notables were built atop mounds, as were religious structures or lodges corresponding to corporate or clan groups. The larger mounds had multiple structures atop them, perhaps houses and lodges for all the members of an elite clan. The largest mound (Monks Mound at the Cahokia site in southern Illinois) measures 6.5 hectares in area and rose 100 feet above the plaza level.

As in the Amazon and the US Southwest, the archaeological record does not provide abundant evidence on social and cultural practices. The evidence is consistent with later observations that tended to depict indigenous societies as hierarchical and resistant to change. Rulers exerted a dominant authority, high-status families and clans guarded their privileges, and social mobility was severely constrained. Nonetheless, in material terms (if not in terms of political authority), the gap separating commoner from noble or monarch was small in comparison to Mesoamerica or the Andes.

Conclusion   Africa in 600–1200 developed agrarian and trade-based states that dominated extensive territories for the first time outside the Nile Valley and North Africa. A number of new developments created conditions favorable to the erection of such states. These included the rise of a corps of expert African ironsmiths in many parts of the continent, who produced large numbers of weapons and agricultural implements. Merchants imported horses for cavalry. Also important was tighter integration into world trading networks that increased surplus wealth for elites. The adoption of the camel for trans-Saharan trade had already begun before this period, but the commercial links between North Africa and the areas south of the Sahara intensified with the rise and spread of Islam. New monarchs, such as the kings of Ghana, arose in this area, clothed in leopard skin and gold, and worshipping a sky god. The city-states that arose along the East African coast were also linked to sub-Saharan Africa's unprecedented opening to the rest of the world. African trading squadrons ventured as far as China, and African goods such as gold and furs crisscrossed the Indian Ocean. Berber merchants of North Africa intensified a slave trade that ultimately created an African diaspora throughout the Middle East.

Increasingly complex states and societies also evolved in the Americas between 600 and 1200. Building on earlier developments, great empires arose in Central Mexico, the Andean highlands, and the desert coast of Peru. City-states dominated the Mayan regions from Southern Mexico south into Central America. Like the Ghanaian state in West Africa, virtually all of these complex societies proved vulnerable to climate change, particularly to long periods of cooler and drier conditions. The collapse of Teotihuacán (550) and the Toltec state (1168) in Central Mexico, the abandonment of all Mayan cities (800–900), and the disintegration of the Tiwanaku and Wari empires in the Andes (900–1000) were all related to changing weather that made old systems of irrigated or raised-field cultivation impossible to sustain. Human factors, including overpopulation, overuse of fragile soils, social and political strife, and foreign invaders made things even worse.

In Africa as well as the Americas, the collapse of great states and cities brought down not only monarchs and their powerful lineages but with them the entire edifice of high culture, official religion, and state-sponsored science and technology that had taken centuries to create and nurture. In the Americas, only Chimú on the Peruvian coast survived beyond our period to be conquered by the Inkas in the fifteenth century. In Africa, some of the coastal city-states managed a shaky continuity, but did so by accommodating themselves to changes in language, religion, and society produced by outside influences, including trade and immigration.

Looking through modern eyes, we tend to see the collapse of empires and the abandonment of great cities as the termination of important eras in human society. They were catastrophes that caused huge losses of human knowledge, like writing and literacy, astronomy, agricultural techniques, metalworking, and other craft and industrial skills. Great artistic traditions and the religions that inspired them also disappeared, while insecurity and lawless-ness invariably increased. Most of the people who lived through these eras, however, may not have experienced an abrupt break with the past as a painful ending at all. To suffering populations, overthrowing elites, abandoning cities, and recovering local community control may have looked less like disasters and more like solutions to the overcrowding, chronic disease, and increasing malnutrition afflicting city-dwellers as well as the oppressive labor drafts for building temples and tombs that diverted energy from agriculture and the burden-some taxes and sumptuary rules that channeled food supplies to arrogant elites.

Though apparently more egalitarian, the complex chiefdoms of the Amazon and later US Southwest and Mississippi also disappeared amid evidence of both environmental and human-caused difficulties. The same was true in various regions in sub-Saharan Africa. Throughout vast areas of both Africa and the Americas, most people continued to live in small bands and chiefdoms, vulnerable to many dangers but with a flexibility and mobility that others did not have.

Study Questions

(1) What makes cities and states rise and fall?

(2) Describe and explain the spread of Islam along the trade routes and in trading cities of sub-Saharan Africa.

(3) Describe the economic, social, and cultural life of the flourishing East African city-states in this era. How was life in these cities different from life in the vast interior of the continent?

(4) Compare and contrast the Mayan city-states to the city-states of the East African coast.

(5) Compare and contrast the African kingdom of Ghana with the territorial states and empires of the Americas, such as the Teotihuacán and Toltec states in Mesoamerica and the Chimú, Tiwanaku, and Wari states of the Andes.

(6) Could the relatively egalitarian chiefdoms of the Amazon and North America have represented a historical alternative to cities and empires?

Suggested Reading

MICHAEL D. COE, *Breaking the Maya Code* (New York: Thames & Hudson, 2012). This is a fascinating account of the academic debates and struggles over the organization of Mayan society, and the breakthroughs in decoding the Mayan hieroglyphs that revolutionized our knowledge of their culture and politics.

GRAHAM CONNAH, *African Civilizations: An Archaeological Perspective* (Cambridge University Press, 2001). Connah surveys African cultures and states from earliest times, based on archaeological evidence of settlement patterns, agricultural activities, and cultural changes.

WILLIAM L. FASH, *Scribes, Warriors, and Kings: The City of Copán and the Ancient Maya* (New York: Thames & Hudson, 1991). This book is a copiously illustrated account of a major Mayan city by the Harvard archaeologist who led the work of uncovering and understanding it.

RICHARDSON BENEDICT GILL, *The Great Maya Droughts: Water, Life, and Death* (Albuquerque: University of New Mexico Press, 2000). Gill's work provides an environmental history of the Mayan collapse.

JOHN WAYNE JANUSEK, *Ancient Tiwanaku* (Cambridge University Press, 2008). This study is a major survey of the pre-Inka Tiwanaku empire and the archaeological discoveries of recent years.

FRIEDRICH KATZ, *The Ancient American Civilizations* (London: Weidenfeld & Nicolson, 1969). This classic work was the first to systematically compare Aztec, Inka, and Mayan civilizations.

JOHN READER, *Africa: A Biography of the Continent* (New York: Knopf, 1999). This overview is a lively account by a leading historian and scholar of Africa.

KEVIN SHILLINGTON, *History of Africa* (London: Macmillan, 1995). Shillington's classic work is a highly readable survey.

JOHN H. TAYLOR, *Egypt and Nubia* (Cambridge, MA: Harvard University Press, 1991). This is a richly illustrated short survey of the Nubian cities and kingdoms of the upper (southern) Nile.

Glossary

bakt: Treaty of peace between Muslim and non-Muslim states, authorizing trade and the free passage of travelers and merchants.

Banadir: "Port people," the name given to Iranian merchants who immigrated to the coastal towns of East Africa in the tenth century.

caliph: Muslim ruler, successor to the Prophet.

Mesoamerica: Also called Middle America, this is the region in North America where agriculture and urbanization developed after 2000 BCE; it extends from Central Mexico to northern Central America.

qadis: Muslim judges who settled disputes in many East African trading towns.

raised fields: Farming technique that involves creating earthen platforms above the level of the surrounding countryside for growing crops.

Sahel: Arid steppe (flat plain) 120 to 250 miles in width, stretching 4,000 miles in length from the Atlantic Ocean to the Red Sea.

savanna: Extensive area of grassland with occasional bushes and trees.

Shirazi: Name first applied to Iranian merchants (Banadir) who settled in the East African port towns and intermarried with local Bantu-speaking families. Shiraz was a major southwestern city in Iran, served by the medieval Gulf port of Siraf. Later this term was applied to any Muslim groups along the East African coast with mixed Middle Eastern and Bantu-speaking heritage, regardless of whether they had any strong Iranian influences.

slash-and-burn: See swidden.

sleeping sickness: Common name for trypanosomiasis, also known as nagana; carried by African tse-tse fly; causes death in hoofed animals like horses and cattle and serious illness in humans.

Soninke: West African ethnic group and core population of the Ghanaian state.

stele: Stone pillar or column covered with inscriptions.

Swahili: Bantu-based language with many Arabic and Persian words that developed in the East African port cities.

swidden: Agricultural technique used in forest areas where soils are thin; also known as slash-and-burn agriculture. Farmers cut down trees and undergrowth ("slash"), burn off the remaining plants, sow crops for a year or two, then leave the land fallow for up to ten years.

tse-tse fly: The African tse-tse fly, which thrives in areas of high annual rainfall (at least 20–28 inches) and mixed vegetation of trees, bushes, and grasslands, spreads trypanosomiasis (sleeping sickness).

Zanj: Bantu-speaking ethnic group in the East African interior near the port city of Sofala; also the name given to any African slave in Iraq in the 800s (though most of the Iraqi slaves came from Nubia or Ethiopia).

Global map, 900–1200 CE

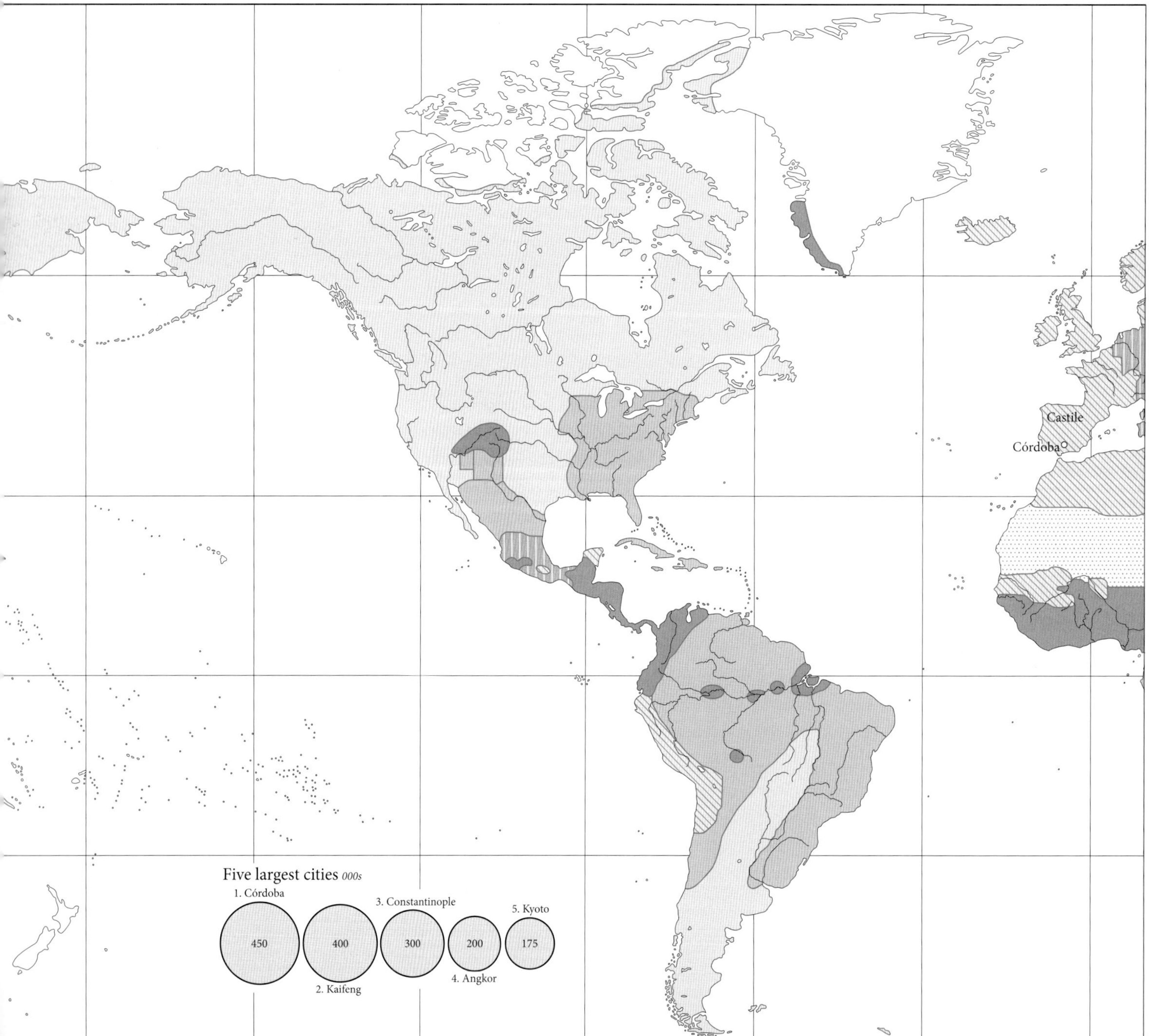

Castile

Córdoba

Five largest cities *000s*

1. Córdoba
3. Constantinople
5. Kyoto

| 450 | 400 | 300 | 200 | 175 |

2. Kaifeng
4. Angkor

PART IV

900–1200 CE: Fragmentation, feudalism, and urbanization

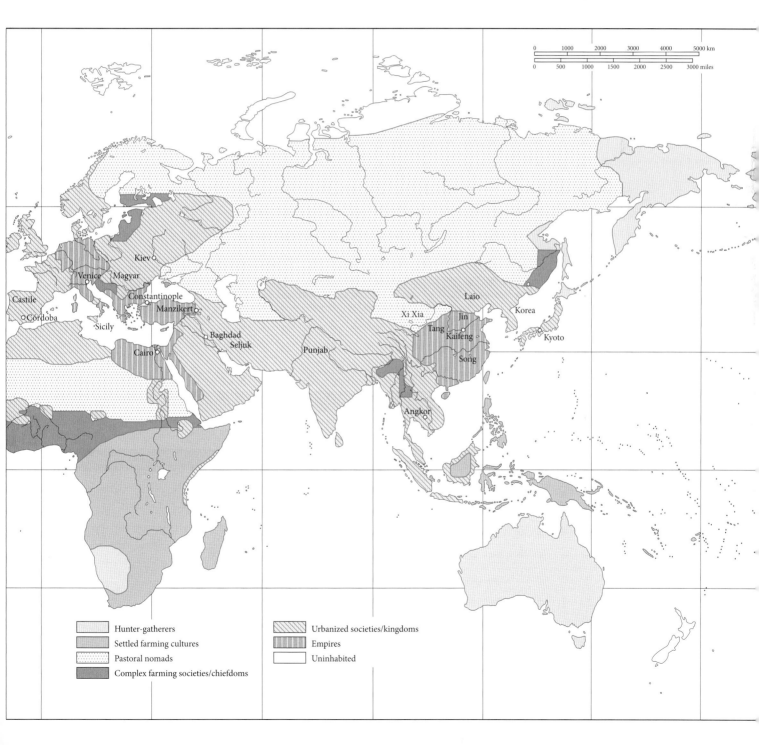

Hunter-gatherers

Settled farming cultures

Pastoral nomads

Complex farming societies/chiefdoms

Urbanized societies/kingdoms

Empires

Uninhabited

Europe	
c. 895	Settlement of Magyar invaders (ancestors of Hungarians) on the Danube.
936–73	Reign of Otto I, consolidating German ruler, who checks Magyar expansion (955) and receives the crown of the Holy Roman Empire (962).
1001–35	Reign of Sancho the Great of Navarre, who creates union of Castile with Navarre and begins conquest of Léon from Muslim rulers.
1054	Definitive break between Byzantine and Roman churches.
1066	Norman conquest of England.
1072	Normans conquer Sicily.
1095	At Council of Clermont, Pope Urban II issues call to conquer the Holy Land for Christianity.
1096–97	First attempt of Christian forces to retake the Holy Land.
1147	Almohads invade Spain.

Middle East	
929	Abd ar-Rahman III, Umayyad caliph of Spain, establishes capital in Córdoba.
945	Buyid dynasty in Baghdad, from northern Iran, favors Twelver Shi`ism. Rules until 1055.
963–1025	Basil II "the Bulgar slayer" expands Byzantine empire to the northeast.
969	Fatimids take Egypt and found Cairo. Rule until 1171.
1055	Baghdad falls to Turkic Seljuk dynasty, which favors Sunni Islam.
1071	Seljuk Turks defeat Byzantines at Manzikert.
1171	Ayyubid dynasty takes Egypt.
1187	Muslim forces under Salah al-Din expel Latin Christian rulers from Jerusalem.
1202–04	Venice diverts Fourth Crusade into conquest of Constantinople.

Russia	
907	Russians under Prince Oleg receive right to trade in Constantinople.
980–1263	Kievan period.
980	Vladimir said to have brought Norsemen from Scandinavia to establish capital of Rus at Kiev.
988	Vladimir converts to Christianity; has new Russian alphabet designed.

India	
997	Beginning of invasions of Panjab (India) by Ghaznavid Muslim forces from Central Eurasia.

China	
904	Discovery of gunpowder by Chinese.
907	End of Tang dynasty.
907–1125	Liao dynasty.
960–1126	Northern Song dynasty.
1004	Wang Dan signs peace treaty with Liao.
1038–1227	Xi Xia kingdom.
1068	Debate over Song fiscal crisis initiates major reforms led by Wang Anshi.
1125–1234	Jin dynasty.
1127–1276	Southern Song dynasty.
1141	Song peace treaty with Jin.
1280	Gunpowder used in bronze mortars by Chinese.

Japan and Korea	
784	Construction of capital city of Kyoto begun.
794–1185	Heian period.
794–864	Ennin, Japanese Buddhist priest, who travels to China (838–47).
894	Japanese send last tribute mission to China.
918–1392	Goryeo (Koryo) kingdom of Korea
1185	Minamoto Yoritomo defeats and annihilates Taira clan.
1185–1333	Kamakura period.

During these three centuries, most of Eurasia was fragmented. The great unifying empires of Tang China and the Islamic lands broke into pieces, while Europe splintered into hundreds of small domains of feuding lords. Only the Byzantine empire held on to most of its territory, but it too suffered heavy blows from invading Turks. Heian Japan kept its emperor and court, but provincial military lords ate away at Kyoto's power. The major states of this period found themselves divided into rival powers with alien traditions. North China, ruled by steppe warriors, began a different path from the commercialized society to the south. In the Islamic world, Sunnis and Shi`ites purified their traditions, consolidating their political and doctrinal hostility. The Christian churches of Europe split definitively between Eastern Orthodox and Western Catholics, in spite of efforts to bring all Christian powers together to recover the Holy Land.

Four new empires did flourish for a time, although their survival was precarious. The founders of Kievan Rus, the most long-lasting of these states, forged a new unity out of the steppe lands and forests of Western Eurasia. Beginning as Viking river and maritime pirates, they put together a trading network that linked the Baltic to the Caspian, centered on the large trading city of Kiev. They relied heavily on resources from the Byzantine empire and other cities of the East, and they took their religion from Constantinople. Kiev laid the basis for Russian culture, even after it was destroyed by the Mongol invasions.

The Seljuk Turks made a strong incursion into Anatolia, fatally weakening the Byzantine empire and laying the basis for the later rise of the Ottoman Turks. They, like their nomadic predecessors, relied mainly on cavalry mounts, using rapid attacks to extract resources from wealthy Middle Eastern cities. The Khazars, the third empire of western Central Eurasia, had fewer mercantile resources, but their more remote position ensured them some security. Further east, the Uighurs showed that nomadic conquerors could adopt urban culture and settle down in cities with new economies, religions, and identities. They persisted as city-states replacing a lost empire.

In general, centralizing emperors and military conquerors could not dominate local powers, because they did not have overwhelming superiority in military force. They found it more profitable to leave the local elites alone, delegating authority to them in exchange for at least nominal loyalty. The "feudalism" of this period, named after the European form of these land grants, found similar expression across the Eurasian continent. Some of the lords, as in Japan and Europe, created concentrated landed domains, where they lived in their manor houses and forced peasants to labor for them. In the Middle East and China, for the most part, local lords did not live on the estates, and their landholdings were closer to rental properties than unified manors. Still, throughout Eurasia, local elites seized greater authority from their superiors. Many of them fought wars against each other incessantly to expand their domains.

And yet, unlike the earlier collapses of the Han and Roman empires, which led to centuries of upheaval and decline, this period saw dynamic growth. The global climate turned warmer, encouraging the spread of agricultural cultivation and the growth of population. But what mainly rescued these societies from endless turmoil was trade, especially maritime trade. Rulers and lords alike discovered that they could get large revenues by taxing the merchants shuttling across the Mediterranean, from the Mediterranean to the Indian coast, and from Southeast Asia to the South China coast. Trade supported larger cities with great merchant establishments. New "victorious cities" like Cairo sprang up; in South China, Hangzhou became the biggest city in the world; Constantinople/Byzantium continued to flourish astride the Bosporus. Mobile, aggressive trader-warriors like the Vikings and Rus took advantage of the wealthy Islamic and Byzantine trade routes, first to plunder the merchants, and later to establish settled kingdoms. This southward shift in the focus of trade, wealth, and culture made the land silk routes of northern Eurasia relatively less important, although they continued to be active.

The expanding trade networks also helped new religions to spread. The preachers of these new faiths did not radically overthrow the existing cultural traditions, but they modified them so as to gather in larger numbers of believers, including many from the merchant class. Religious competition set in. The Neo-Confucianists of China attacked the predominant Buddhists as superstitious, and remolded Confucian beliefs with a stronger dose of metaphysics and rational inquiry. Japanese Buddhists, rivals of Shinto sects, created larger mass religions, whipping up popular enthusiasm. Mystics in Europe and Sufi devotees of Islam promoted passionate devotion to one god, producing inspiring poetry and dedicated schools of disciples to spread their message. Hindu Brahmin revivalists succeeded in driving out Buddhism from its home in India.

Popular religion and commercial networks also reached into the heart of Eurasia. Although Turkic pastoral nomads continued to break out of the steppes and conquer significant parts of China and the Middle East, some of them, like the Uighurs, soon built their own cities, while adopting religions like Manichaeanism from Persia. The Khazars even embraced Judaism as their faith. The traders of the Silk Road, the Sogdians, also spread mass religions along their time-honored routes.

Although few people could boast of living under grand central empires, their standard of living was usually higher than in the imperial ages of the past. They produced more goods, had more money, and more of them lived in cities, wore valuable clothing like silk, and enjoyed urban entertainments. They had new religious opportunities too. Women probably had more mixed experiences. In China, many gained from the new opportunities offered by urban culture, but they also suffered increasing pressure to bind their feet to attract prosperous husbands. The freest women were those of the steppe, who tended herds outdoors and exerted power on their husbands and sons behind the scenes. This period demonstrates that centralized military rule had its limits: in these centuries the urban civilian found his home.

10 Europe and the Muslim world

Timeline	
c. 895	Settlement of Magyar invaders (ancestors of Hungarians) on the Danube.
907	Russians under Prince Oleg receive right to trade in Constantinople.
929	Abd ar-Rahman III, Umayyad caliph of Spain, establishes capital in Córdoba.
936–73	Otto I, consolidating German ruler, checks Magyar expansion (955) and receives the crown of the Holy Roman Empire (962).
945	Buyid dynasty in Baghdad, from northern Iran, favors Twelver Shi`ism. Rules until 1055.
969	Fatimids take Egypt and found Cairo. Rule until 1171.
1001–35	Reign of Sancho the Great of Navarre, who creates union of Castile with Navarre and begins conquest of Léon from Muslim rulers.
1020	Death of the great Persian epic poet, Firdawsi.
1037	Death of the Muslim philosopher Avicenna.
1054	Definitive break between Byzantine and Roman churches.
1055	Baghdad falls to Turkic Seljuk dynasty, which favors Sunni Islam.
1066	Norman conquest of England.
1071	Seljuk Turks defeat Byzantines at Manzikert.
1072	Normans conquer Sicily.
1084	Consecration of San Marco, Venice.
1095	At Council of Clermont, Pope Urban II issues call to conquer the Holy Land for Christianity.
1096–97	First attempt of Christian forces to retake the Holy Land.
1111	The great Muslim mystic and scholar Abu Hamid al-Ghazali dies.
1122–1204	Lifetime of Eleanor of Aquitaine, successively queen of France and England.
1126	Death of the Persian poet Omar Khayyam.
1142	Death of French philosopher and theologian Peter Abelard.
1146	Saint Bernard preaches Second Crusade for recapture of the Holy Land.
1147	Almohads invade Spain.

1171	Ayyubid dynasty takes Egypt.
1187	Muslim forces under Salah al-Din expel Latin Christian rulers from Jerusalem.
1198	Death of the Aristotelian Muslim philosopher Averroes.
1202–04	Venice diverts Fourth Crusade into conquest of Constantinople.

In Navarre, northern Spain, the small city of Tudela commands a crossing of the River Ebro not far south of Pamplona. Founded by a Muslim monarch in 802 when most of Iberia lay under Muslim rule, Tudela fell to the Christian rulers of Navarre during Muslim–Christian wars of the later tenth century. Over the following two centuries, Muslim forces retreated south, battling all the way and repeatedly taking back lost territory; as of 1150, Muslim kingdoms still occupied about half of the Iberian peninsula. Spaniards commonly call the long struggle against Muslim rulers "la **Reconquista**" – the Reconquest. Communities of Muslims and Jews, however, continued to live in many "reconquered" places until much later.

In 1159 rabbi Benjamin, of Tudela's Jewish community, undertook one of the great journeys of his time. For fourteen years he traveled through France, Italy, the Balkans, and much of the Middle East, returning through Egypt and North Africa. He inserted descriptions of Iran, Afghanistan, Central Asia, and Tibet into the splendid memoir he wrote on his return, although how far he actually traveled into Asia remains uncertain. He described Mongols of Central Asia fantastically, for example, as people

who worship the wind and live in the wilderness, and who do not eat bread, nor drink wine, but live on raw uncooked meat. They have no noses, and in lieu thereof they have two small holes, through which they breathe. They eat animals both clean and unclean, and they are very friendly toward the Israelites. Fifteen years ago they overran the country of Persia with a large army and took the city of Rayy; they smote it with the edge of the sword, took all the spoil thereof, and returned by way of the wilderness.

Despite hearsay and exaggeration, the rabbi's account makes three related facts vividly clear. First, rabbi Benjamin found communities of Jewish merchants, artisans, and scholars almost everywhere he went, and could therefore use a colloquial version of Hebrew as a traveler's language for much of his voyage. Second, most of the time he was journeying through predominantly Muslim lands; in the later twelfth century, the Mediterranean around which rabbi Benjamin journeyed remained mainly Muslim territory. Third, European knights maintained precarious control of some territories along the southeastern Mediterranean and nearby sections of the Middle East, where Crusades of the previous centuries had established Christian enclaves; in those regions, however, Europeans and Christians were losing ground to Muslim forces in repeated small-scale wars. Muslim strength, in short, was receding in Iberia as it rose in Southeastern Europe, in Africa, and in Asia. Yet in their zones of overlap, Muslim, Christian, and Jewish cultures intertwined.

They intertwined, but they did not merge. In a time of fragmented power, religious affinities offered reliable connections that political authorities rarely supplied. Religions maintained common languages: Arabic for most Muslims, Hebrew and Hebrew-inflected dialects for Jews, Latin for the world of Roman Catholicism, Greek for Orthodox Christians. They also provided personal connections and institutions for the protection of traders and travelers; even where they wielded little local political power, religious leaders often figured significantly as guarantors of risky transactions. Over the period from 900 to 1200, Europe and the Muslim world interacted triply: in a series of political struggles that realigned the boundary between territories controlled chiefly by Muslims and mainly by Christians; in expansion of trade between Europe and Asia that stimulated a remarkable revival of Europe's economy; and in intensified exchanges of ideas and technologies between the Muslim and Judeo-Christian worlds. In the course of these three processes, Europe moved from being a dull backwater of the great Eurasian commercial system to being an attractive target for Asian invaders.

A few centuries later, European commentators began calling the period between the collapse of the Roman empire and the rise of centralized states the Middle Ages or the medieval period. Still later, historians began using the name Dark Ages for the centuries from the Roman empire's collapse to the revival of trade, art, and politics in the northwest after 1200 – chaos before, coherence afterward. The rise of Islam after 600, ran the argument, had shattered European unity, and only a mighty effort begun after 1000 and fully under way by 1200 restored that unity. According to this chronology, the later Middle Ages produced a rebirth of commerce, a flowering of religiously tinged arts, a revival of the Catholic church, and a laying of the groundwork for subsequent political centralization. From the perspective of London or Paris, the chronology makes some sense.

For the whole space of Europe, North Africa, and the Middle East, however, the idea of a Dark Age obscures more than it reveals. The three centuries from 900 to 1200, as we shall see, actually sparkled with the energy of innovation and cultural contact. We now know that in Europe these centuries were also marked by unusually warm temperatures, called by climatologists "the medieval warming period" (a misnomer since it was not a global phenomenon, but mainly a European one) and caused by warm winds coming off the Atlantic. A warmer Europe may have enabled martial groups such as Normans and Vikings, giving them a stronger local economy and a thriving base from which to launch their conquests, thus contributing to political decentralization.

The dynamism of these three centuries is clear if we consider the shift in the world's ten largest cities between 900 and 1200:

900   Baghdad, Chang'an, Constantinople, Kyoto, Hangzhou, Alexandria, Córdoba, Manyakheta, Luoyang, Fostat.
1200   Hangzhou, Fez, Cairo, Constantinople, Canton, Pagan, Nanking, Kamakura, Angkor, Palermo.

Never take such lists too seriously, since they always depend on shaky estimates and controversial definitions of city limits. Still, comparison of the two lists provides a general idea of shifts over the three centuries covered by this chapter.

In 900, Muslim centers Baghdad, Alexandria, Córdoba, and Fostat (predecessor of Cairo) neighbored with the Byzantine capital Constantinople, Indian metropolis Manyakheta, and East Asian cities Chang'an, Kyoto, Hangzhou, and Luoyang, were the world's largest cities. By 1200, Fez and Cairo had probably become the largest Muslim cities, Constantinople had held its own despite fierce attacks on the crumbling Byzantine empire, as South and East Asia continued to flourish. The fragmentation and recession of Muslim power in Iberia had knocked Córdoba from the ranks of the world's largest cities. Palermo's Sicily, long under Muslim rule, had become a property of the expanding Holy Roman Empire after Normans conquered it battle by battle, then brought it to the empire through marriage alliances. Of the other two biggest European cities, Venice prospered through its exchanges with Byzantium and nearby Muslim territories, while only Paris lay in a region whose economy, politics, and culture operated in relative independence of the Muslim world. Over the three centuries from 900 to 1200, in fact, the Mediterranean became an even more crucial connector between non-Muslim Europe and the Muslim world.

Although the Catholic church involved itself increasingly in the affairs of Northern Europe after 900, Europe's major religious centers – Constantinople, Rome, and Córdoba – remained within the Mediterranean zone. As Chapter 11 shows, the conversion of Russia to Christianity during the tenth century operated through the connection of Kiev with Byzantium rather than under the influence of Western Europe. Although Scandinavians ventured far in the Baltic, the North Sea, and the Atlantic Ocean, they maintained major commercial relations with the Black Sea and the Mediterranean along rivers that led south through Russia. Large hoards of silver from the Muslim Middle East accumulated in Scandinavia, gained from sales of northern hides, honey, and slaves. A rule of thumb follows: over the period from 900 to 1200, the more closely a European region connected with the eastern Mediterranean, the more prosperous, cosmopolitan, and extensive was its public life. Only toward the end of the period do we see distinctive new forms of culture and commerce beginning to flourish in Northwestern Europe. Even those innovations depended significantly on the acceleration of trade via the Mediterranean.

For the sake of clarity, this chapter takes up the Judeo-Christian European world and the Muslim world separately, only shifting now and then to focus on their interaction. If we were making a film of the story, however, we would do better to keep three screens running at once: the first showing interplay within the vast, changing territory dominated by different groups of Muslims, the second concentrating on internal developments within the smaller European space that operated outside of day-to-day Muslim influence, the third aiming especially at the Mediterranean, where Muslim–European confrontation and collaboration took center stage. Map 10.1 shows a contemporary map of these lands by the Arab geographer al-Idrisi.

Chapter 8 has already told part of the story, showing how changing relations with Asia and the Muslim world shattered a once brilliant Byzantine empire. It has also established that Asian economies were becoming more active and connected between 900 and 1200. This chapter stresses the following points:

- Despite repeated attempts at conquest and consolidation, throughout the period from 900 to 1200 Europe and the Muslim world remained politically fragmented.
- Religious connections and institutions therefore played exceptional parts as connectors and stabilizers of social life.
- Trade between Asia and Europe intensified dramatically, increasing interactions of European merchants with the Muslim merchants who predominated in Western Asia, Southeastern Europe, and North Africa, while stimulating commercial activity within Europe as well.
- Partly as a result of that economic expansion, the Abbasid caliphate of Baghdad lost its dominant position within Islam, as Umayyads based in Córdoba, Spain, established their own caliphate (929) and Fatimids founded a separate regime in Cairo (969).

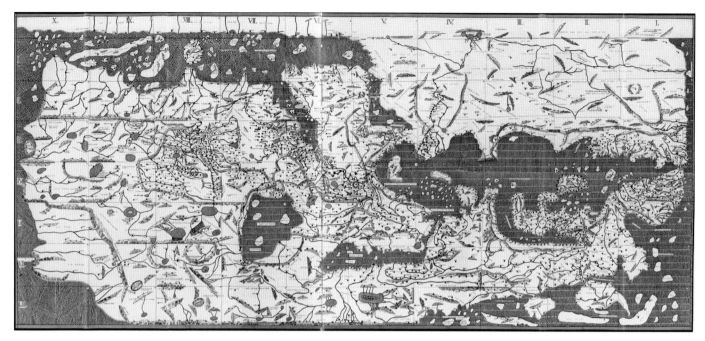

Map 10.1 Al-Idrisi map of Mediterranean and Middle East. Moroccan geographer Abu al-Idrisi served at the court of Roger II, Norman king of Sicily from 1130 to 1154, preparing a huge, detailed map to accompany his Book of Roger

- Despite rising economic interdependence, Muslim and non-Muslim political leaders continued to fight each other, redrawing the boundaries between Muslim-ruled and Christian-ruled regions of Europe.
- Some of the fiercest conflicts, however, pitted different Muslim states and sects against each other.
- Although the Crusades loomed large in European politics and reinforced connections of Northwestern Europe with the Middle East, from Asian and Muslim perspectives they had little long-term impact.
- Toward 1200, new concentrations of political and commercial power were becoming visible at multiple points in Europe and the Muslim world.

10.1 FRAGMENTED EUROPE

The sort of political map we use today – neatly bounded jurisdictions, each with its own capital – would make no sense for Europe of the tenth century. As of 900, non-Muslim Europe fragmented into hundreds of overlapping political units, some of them nominally subject to others, but even those typically bound more by multiple ties among ruling families than by any sort of governmental hierarchy. The Italian peninsula, for example, hosted a dozen more or less independent dukes and kings plus dozens more city-states despite (from 901) being nominally subject to the Holy Roman Emperor. Even England of the time fragmented into zones dominated by Danes, Norwegians, Anglo-Saxons, and hundreds of local warlords.

Throughout Europe, furthermore, these sorts of ruler fought each other incessantly, claimed jurisdiction in each other's territories, and preyed on each other's trade. Five factors favored Europe's extensive political splintering:

(1) Relatively inexpensive military technology (bows, lances, swords, horses, boats) meant that rulers could not monopolize military force, and ruthless local warlords who had access to steady revenues and/or loyal followers could easily expand their operating ranges.

(2) The residues of larger political and commercial units such as Charlemagne's empire meant that enterprising rulers could nevertheless build on existing institutions, connections, and military means (e.g. forts, walled towns, roads, trade routes, and courts) as means of control at a regional level.

(3) A royal and noble strategy of building dynasties through marriage of children into families of rival or neighboring families created ties of alliance that simultaneously established claims on military support and promoted struggles over succession.

(4) Mobile warriors (e.g. Magyars and Vikings) continued to invade Europe's flanks by land and sea, repeatedly breaking up whatever stable relations had developed between agricultural populations and regional rulers.

(5) Until well past 900, the Roman Catholic church, by far the largest single connected organization in Europe, worked mainly to establish its own secular power, and often made leveraged alliances with one party or another in regional struggles.

Map 10.2 Europe in the high Middle Ages

Map 10.2 displays the extremely fragmented power structure of Europe during the high Middle Ages.

Some combination of these factors defeated every effort to build up centralized political power in Europe during the tenth century. German rulers, for example, began consolidating power again after mid-century, with Otto I establishing military dominance in much of Central Europe, defeating Hungarian forces (955), and receiving the crown of the Holy Roman Empire from the pope (962). Yet by 1000, successor emperors Otto II and Otto III had lost a significant share of the power Otto I had accumulated.

In much of Central and Western Europe, would-be rulers faced well-organized resistance to centralization from within their own realms. After the Roman empire's collapse, many landlords consolidated their local power by organizing manors: they maintained their own armed forces, built forts, seized control of agricultural land, held the peasantry in place, extracted income from peasant production, sold off a surplus, and established autonomous political control within their territories. When not at war, they lived on their estates, making sure that their stewards worked the manor's peasants and artisans hard. The system became "feudal" when such landlords recognized overlords who received tribute and intermittent military assistance in return for providing protection against marauders and outside armies. Rulers fostered the idea that in the mists of time their predecessors had owned all the land, but had granted segments of it to faithful followers as "fiefs" for which the followers owed obeisance, tribute, and military service. Indeed, rulers even enacted the feudal system when they conquered new territory and parceled it out to their clients. When Normandy's William the Conqueror took hold of England in 1066 and thereafter, for example, he turned over significant patches of English land to his lieutenants, who became regional rulers on his behalf. Nevertheless, such a system produced powerful pressures for decentralization: regional and local lords who could secure their own protection could also survive very nicely without fulfilling their obligations to higher authorities, or by fulfilling those obligations in ways that enhanced their own power and profit.

After 900, furthermore, Central and Western Europeans were converting large blocks of previously uncultivated land to intensive agriculture. Very likely a combination of population growth and rising demand for agricultural products spurred their extensive conversion of forests, fields, and marshes to pasture and grain production. More so than their Mediterranean neighbors, farmers of Central and Western Europe had long invested in a combination of dairy and grain agriculture in which field-grown fodder sustained animals through the cold season. During our period, farmers were adopting deep-digging horse-drawn plows, and thus increasing the old system's productivity. Some of the clearance occurred under the auspices of great lords and monasteries, who established manors or their equivalent where they could, and in any case drew new revenues from the cleared or drained land. But at the edges of noble and monastic power individual peasants and peasant communities also joined the agricultural expansion. In either case, the new agriculture gave those who controlled the land means of resistance to higher authorities.

Still, the tide was turning. For centuries, Scandinavia's Vikings had split their efforts among three strategies: taking over and extending existing trade routes; exploration and conquest by sea (they reached Iceland in 860, Greenland in 982, and North America around 1000); and creating beachheads in other lands along both the Atlantic and Mediterranean coasts from which they could use military force to extract tribute. In 896, however, well-armed Danish Vikings set themselves down at the mouth of France's Seine, already an important site of trade with the British Isles and the Atlantic coast. By 911 the Seine Vikings were compacting with the French king, Charles the Simple (r. 898–923), to defend the region on the king's behalf; the king named their leader Rollo duke of Normandy (= Land of the Norse). Rollo's successors became major European rulers, with William I conquering England in 1066.

Although the major obstacles to extensive political centralization stayed in place for several centuries more, the tide turned for two other related reasons. First, the expansion of Mediterranean commercial activity itself strengthened connections with Asia and the Middle East by land and sea. That expansion provided outlets for the timber, iron, honey, weapons, slaves, and other products of Northern Europe. North European wares complemented the olive oil, grain, slaves, and wood products that were already flowing to Islamic ports from Southern Europe. Second, the same powers that spearheaded attacks on Muslim forces also benefited from their connections with Muslim commercial and intellectual activity. Thus toward 1000, Venice, Amalfi, and Christian Spain were simultaneously facilitating expeditions to attack Muslim powers and extending their commercial outposts within Muslim territory. Box 10.1 shows how Venice stocked its great cathedral of San Marco with plunder from the Muslim world. Barcelona became as much a Mediterranean as a Spanish commercial center. Meanwhile, the city-states of Pisa and Genoa were also shifting from being recurrent victims of raids by Muslim forces to raiding and trading the length and breadth of the Mediterranean. If we add Byzantium and Viking-origin Kiev from Chapter 11, we see Europe's proliferating connections to the Mediterranean and thence to further east as a crucial basis of commercial and political expansion.

The combination of dynastic strategy and political expansion had some surprising by-products. Noble and royal successions

Box 10.1 San Marco and the Muslim World

Venice's dramatic cathedral of San Marco illustrates the close connections between Southern Europe and the Muslim world. Two Venetian merchants stole the supposed remains of St. Mark (San Marco in Italian) from a tomb in Muslim-held Alexandria (Egypt) in 829, and soon began building the first church to house those relics. Venetians burned down the first San Marco during a rebellion of the 970s, but the doge (Italian for duke) quickly had it rebuilt. Under a later doge, Venice tore down the old church and built most of the present structure between 1063 and 1073. Although the cathedral's floor plan is Byzantine – it forms a Greek cross – many of the decorations adopt Islamic art forms and display scenes from Egypt. As thirteenth-century artists covered San Marco's bare interior walls with mosaics, they often inserted images from Alexandria, such as the city's famous lighthouse. From commerce to politics to religion and art, life in eleventh-century Venice showed the influence of continuous contact with Alexandria, Cairo, and many other Muslim cities.

became worth fighting for. Disputed successions including inheritance of crowns by infants or incompetents regularly started major power struggles, including open wars and deliberate assassinations among the claimants. Correspondingly, monarchs who lived long lives and married their children well enjoyed great advantages over their shorter-lived or childless competitors. Under exceptional circumstances, furthermore, noble women could wield great power. Since they made the marriages and produced the heirs that continued a dynasty, they sometimes exercised great political leverage.

In this period, Eleanor of Aquitaine probably topped all her competitors. Eleanor inherited claims to extensive lands in southern and western France – the lands of Aquitaine. At age 15, in 1137, she married Prince Louis, heir to the French throne; he became king, as Louis VII, only a month later. At the time, the French kingdom consisted only of contested territories around Paris plus a number of scattered claims elsewhere. But it was a kingdom on the make. Louis's ambitious father, Louis VI (r. 1108–37) had been conducting wars with England, battling rival lords in northern France, and establishing an independent royal administration. His advisors included Suger, abbot of St. Denis, who started building a new abbey church – the first **Gothic** building – in the Parisian suburb of St. Denis shortly before Louis VI's death and Louis VII's accession to the crown. Thus Eleanor married into a rising royal family. In fact, Louis VII was soon fighting with the pope over the right to nominate his own bishops.

Partly as a settlement of that dispute, King Louis joined the Second Crusade (more on the Crusades later) which the famous monk Bernard of Clairvaux began preaching in 1146. By then the mother of two daughters, Eleanor began the voyage with Louis in 1147, but dropped out of the group in Antioch. Eleanor renounced her marriage, but Louis refused to accept her rebellion, and forced her to accompany him back to France. (The Crusade itself failed calamitously to liberate any of the Holy Lands, but allowed Roger, Norman ruler of Sicily, to seize a number of Greek islands and attack the Greek mainland.) In 1152, Eleanor and Louis had their marriage annulled by mutual consent, despite the two daughters, most likely because Eleanor had not produced a male heir. Eleanor immediately married the French king's enemy, Henry duke of Normandy. Henry became king of England in 1154. Eleanor and Henry thus ruled England, Normandy, and much of France. During their long marriage, they added Brittany, Wales, Ireland, and Scotland to their portfolio. They also had five children who lived to adulthood, including future English kings Richard the Lionheart (r. 1189–1199) and John Lackland (r. 1199–1216).

Eleanor supported her sons in their 1173 rebellion against their father Henry; as a result, she spent a dozen years in confinement. But Henry died in 1189. Eleanor's political influence rose again as first Richard, then John, became king. Richard spent much of his reign warring and crusading on the continent, thus leaving Eleanor great political scope within England. John, who survived his mother's death in 1204, continued his father's claims to royal prerogative. Those claims eventually resulted in rebellion by his English and Norman barons, with support from France. John capitulated by signing **Magna Carta** (the "Great Charter") in 1215. This document confirmed political rights of the barons as against the king's arbitrary power; when later regimes reissued the charter, courts and magnates began to interpret it as extending rights such as trial by jury to all free men. Although subsequent English monarchs greatly increased the Crown's power, Magna Carta established grounds for representation of major lords and their regions that never quite disappeared, and eventually provided a basis for parliamentary power. Through marriages, parenthood, and statecraft, Eleanor of Aquitaine thus significantly affected the interacting fates of France and England.

Eleanor's career also underscores two other important features of twelfth-century history in Northern Europe: the expansion of monarchies and the significance of understandings with the Catholic church. Despite John Lackland's momentous setback, kings were beginning to win their battles with rival lords more frequently, and thus to create larger, more centralized political units. Not all kings gained, by any means, but those who could find stable sources of revenue in the continent's expanding economy had a greater chance to increase their scope. To put it crudely, rulers in zones of expanding trade began making deals with the merchants who ran major cities within their realms; they traded protection of commercial transactions for taxes. The bargaining remained delicate, for the merchants preferred protection without much intervention, but war-making kings always needed more money, and therefore intervened whenever they could. Still, expansion of royal power depended not only on military and matchmaking skills but also on the ability to draw merchants and their money into collaboration with royal programs.

10.2 CHURCH AND STATE

The Catholic church presented a different problem. As the largest, richest, and most centralized European organization, it constituted a major secular power in its own right. From 1000 onward, the church was extending its reach by authorizing the creation of many new religious orders, both monastic and military – for example, the Vallombrosians (1036), the Carthusians (1084), and the Teutonic Knights (1190). Box 10.2, which

Box 10.2 Heloise and Abelard

The story of the philosopher Peter Abelard, who fell in love with his student Heloise, is one of the best-loved stories of medieval Europe, revealed in intimate detail by Abelard himself. It indicates deep personal tensions that lay beneath the outward mask of religious discipline in Europe's monastic scholarly communities.

After a few days, I returned to Paris, and there for several years I peacefully directed the school ... At the very outset of my work there, I set about completing the glosses on Ezekiel which I had begun at Laon. These proved so satisfactory to all who read them that they came to believe me no less adept in lecturing on theology than I had proved myself to be in the field of philosophy ... But prosperity always puffs up the foolish and worldly comfort enervates the soul, rendering it an easy prey to carnal temptations ...

Now there dwelt in that same city of Paris a certain young girl named Heloise, the niece of a canon who was called Fulbert. Her uncle's love for her was equaled only by his desire that she should have the best education which he could possibly procure for her. Of no mean beauty, she stood out above all by reason of her abundant knowledge of letters. Now this virtue is rare among women, and for that very reason it doubly graced the maiden, and made her the most worthy of renown in the entire kingdom ... Thus, utterly aflame with my passion for this maiden, I sought to discover means whereby I might have daily and familiar speech with her, thereby the more easily to win her consent. For this purpose I persuaded the girl's uncle, with the aid of some of his friends, to take me into his household – for he dwelt hard by my school – in return for the payment of a small sum ...

Why should I say more? We were united first in the dwelling that sheltered our love, and then in the hearts that burned with it. Under the pretext of study we spent our hours in the happiness of love, and learning held out to us the secret opportunities that our passion craved. Our speech was more of love than of the books which lay open before us; our kisses far outnumbered our reasoned words. Our hands sought less the book than each other's bosoms – love drew our eyes together far more than the lesson drew them to the pages of our text ... What followed? No degree in love's progress was left untried by our passion, and if love itself could imagine any wonder as yet unknown, we discovered it. And our inexperience of such delights made us all the more ardent in our pursuit of them, so that our thirst for one another was still unquenched.

In measure as this passionate rapture absorbed me more and more, I devoted ever less time to philosophy and to the work of the school. Indeed it became loathsome to me to go to the school or to linger there; the labor, moreover, was very burdensome, since my nights were vigils of love and my days of study. My lecturing became utterly careless and lukewarm; I did nothing because of inspiration, but everything merely as a matter of habit ...

It was not long after this that Heloise found that she was pregnant, and of this she wrote to me in the utmost exultation, at the same time asking me to consider what had best be done. Accordingly, on a night when her uncle was absent, we carried out the plan we had determined on, and I stole her secretly away from her uncle's house, sending her without delay to my own country. She remained there with my sister until she gave birth to a son, whom she named Astrolabe.

Meanwhile her uncle after his return, was almost mad with grief; only one who had then seen him could rightly guess the burning agony of his sorrow and the bitterness of his shame ...

[Heloise] reminded me of the hardships of married life, to the avoidance of which the Apostle exhorts us, saying: "Art thou loosed from a wife? seek not a wife. But and if thou marry, thou hast not sinned; and if a virgin marry she hath not sinned. Nevertheless such shall have trouble in the flesh: but I spare you" (1 Corinthians 7.27–28). And again: "But I would have you to be free from cares" (1 Corinthians 7.32). But if I would heed neither the counsel of the Apostle nor the exhortations of the saints regarding this heavy yoke of matrimony, she bade me at least consider the advice of the philosophers, and weigh carefully what had been written on this subject either by them or concerning their lives. Even the saints themselves have often and earnestly spoken on this subject for the purpose of warning us ...

[But] after our little son was born, we left him in my sister's care, and secretly returned to Paris. A few days later, in the early morning, having kept our nocturnal vigil of prayer unknown to all in a certain church, we were united there in the benediction of wedlock, her uncle and a few friends of his and mine being present. We departed forthwith stealthily and by separate ways, nor thereafter did we see each other save rarely and in private, thus striving our utmost to conceal what we had done. But her uncle and those of his household, seeking solace for their disgrace, began to divulge the story of our marriage, and thereby to violate the pledge they had given me on this point. Heloise, on the contrary, denounced her own kin and swore that

Box 10.2 (*cont.*)

they were speaking the most absolute lies. Her uncle, aroused to fury thereby, visited her repeatedly with punishments. No sooner had I learned this than I sent her to a convent of nuns at Argenteuil, not far from Paris, where she herself had been brought up and educated as a young girl. I had them make ready for her all the garments of a nun, suitable

for the life of a convent, excepting only the veil, and these I bade her put on.

When her uncle and his kinsmen heard of this, they were convinced that now I had completely played them false and had rid myself forever of Heloise by forcing her to become a nun. Violently incensed, they laid a plot against me, and one night while I all unsuspecting

was asleep in a secret room in my lodgings, they broke in with the help of one of my servants whom they had bribed. There they had vengeance on me with a most cruel and most shameful punishment, such as astounded the whole world; for they cut off those parts of my body with which I had done that which was the cause of their sorrow.

tells the story of Heloise and Abelard, describes the tensions created by the conflict between the demands of monastic discipline in these orders and passionate love. Typically, rich merchants or landlords endowed the orders with rents and lands, thus linking the church's expansion to the widespread revival of the European economy. A definitive break between the Byzantine and Roman churches (1054), known as the Great Schism, increased the orientation of the Roman church to Northwestern Europe, and accentuated its tendency to support aggressive conversion and conquest of the non-Christians on European frontiers.

With a near-monopoly on literacy, the Catholic church supplied record-keepers, authors, correspondents, and diplomats to most royal administrations. Its convents provided shelter and education for women as well. (Figure 10.1 shows a group of nuns.) It also offered legitimation for royal power. Christian kings fared badly without church support. But revenues and properties in church hands escaped royal control. Where civil authorities had great independent sources of strength (as for example in Venice), they dealt with the church as equals, and resisted church pressure. Where civil authorities lacked power (as for example in Poland), they collaborated with church officials and settled for some voice in ecclesiastical appointments. But wherever civil authorities – especially ambitious kings – were expanding their scope, they inevitably struggled with the church. They struggled to exert influence over church policy, church property, and church personnel. When existing ecclesiastical authorities opposed their interests, civil powers even supported schisms within the church.

One of the most momentous cases in point pitted the Holy Roman Emperor against the pope. In 1056 the 6-year-old Henry IV inherited the imperial crown. His mother Agnes served as regent for nine years, a period in which both ecclesiastical and lay officials grabbed whatever pieces of royal property and power they could. In 1062 two archbishops kidnapped the

Figure 10.1 St. Jerome reading the scriptures to nuns. Convents of the Catholic church in Europe were nearly the only place where women could achieve literacy, and they also provided shelter for abused women, orphans, and the poor.

king (now 12 years old), governed in his name, and divided German monasteries (major sources of royal revenue) between them. A rebellion of clergy and nobles against the archbishops liberated the king, and started the king's attempt to reimpose royal control over secular and ecclesiastical domains alike. Henry switched sides repeatedly, sometimes aligning himself with the pope against German clerics and nobles, sometimes drawing strength from German towns in the face of papal opposition. But he pursued control over German ecclesiastical appointments relentlessly.

Pope Gregory VII excommunicated Henry in 1080, only to have a conclave of German and Italian bishops elect an **antipope**, a bishop elected in opposition to the seated pope, who was friendlier to Henry. Henry invaded Rome, had himself crowned emperor by the antipope, then suffered expulsion from Rome by Norman forces allied with Gregory. In their turn, the Norman forces sacked Rome, which drove Gregory from the city as well. After Gregory's death (1085), his successor popes supported revolts against Henry by his sons Conrad and Henry. Germany spent much of Henry's remaining reign beset by civil war. But his rebel son, become Henry V (r. 1106–25), actually continued the father's consolidation of power against papal resistance.

10.3 CONQUERORS AND CRUSADERS

While Normans were throwing their weight around Italy and the Mediterranean, other European forces were struggling to take back territory from Muslim rulers. Iberia typified the peculiar combination of struggle and coexistence that recurred along much of the Muslim–Christian boundary. Within Iberia (especially the remaining Muslim-controlled sectors), Muslims, Jews, and Christians lived in collaboration and mutual comprehension most of the time, even if rulers marked their own legitimacy with ostentatious religious observances. Recurrently, however, ambitious leaders led their military forces against enemy territory, doubling the usual justifications for conquest with calls for defense of the true religion – whichever religion they favored. In the northern, Christian-dominated half of Iberia, mobilizing warlords often recruited urban militias and freebooting soldiers with promises of booty, land grants, and chartered privileges if they vanquished their Muslim enemies. They attracted many an adventurer, and sometimes even deployed Muslim mercenary bands. Box 10.3 tells the story of the Spanish conqueror known by the Arabic name of "El Cid," who became a famous figure in drama and legend.

The Crusades followed a similar pattern, and overlapped in some regards with the Iberian Reconquista. Map 10.3 displays the Crusader states which temporarily occupied parts of the Holy Land. In 1095 a Roman Catholic Council met at Clermont (today's Clermont-Ferrand) in France's Auvergne. There Pope Urban II preached the need for military action against the infidels who had blocked Christian access to the Holy Land. Christians, like Muslims, had long practiced pilgrimage to sacred sites in the Holy Land and elsewhere. Clermont itself served as a major provisioning point on the popular Christian pilgrimage to northwestern Spain's Santiago de Compostela. After the Muslim general al-Mansur sacked Santiago in 997, Spaniards rebuilt the city (which housed the reputed relics of the apostle James, known in Spanish as Santiago), and made it a major destination for pilgrims. Travelers to Santiago could thus display their piety and their hostility to Muslim rule in Iberia at the same time. In 1075 leaders of Santiago began a great new cathedral as a monument to the Christian presence in Iberia. Toward the end of the eleventh century, pilgrims to Santiago began hearing about the Norman seizure of Sicily from Muslim control, which had begun in 1061 when one of the local Muslim competitors for power invited Normans in to help him. By the 1090s, Normans based in Sicily were making forays against Muslim territory in the eastern Mediterranean. That word percolated back to Clermont.

Pilgrimage to Christian religious sites in Palestine had earlier offered an especially powerful form of penance for sins. Like their Muslim counterparts who journeyed to Mecca and Medina, pilgrims to the Holy Land (a voyage that commonly went via Rome) usually had the resources to support travel for long periods. Enterprising authors had written widely read guidebooks for the journey. In 1095 the indignant pope complained that Muslim military force had closed free access of pilgrims to those sites for nearly 400 years. (In fact, Muslims tolerated Christians inhabiting the Holy Land in a way few Christians tolerated Muslims anywhere in their realms.) What was needed, Urban declared, was a united effort by Christians to regain control of those places in Palestine that currently lay under Muslim control.

In his speech, the pope did not use the word "Crusade," which only came into use much later. But he did call for European knights to join Byzantium's defense against the advancing Seljuk Turks. His call received an unexpected response: At first, lightly armed crowds of poor people and adventurers led by charismatic preachers heeded the call. In 1096–97, they rushed to Constantinople and then into Anatolia, massacring Jews along the way. When the ragtag pilgrims entered territory controlled by the Turks, Seljuk forces slaughtered them in their turn. This response to the pope's appeal produced nothing but disaster.

The pope also recruited a number of noble military specialists. They included the marquis of Provence, the duke of Normandy (brother of England's king), the duke of Lower Lorraine, and the

Map 10.3 The Crusader states and the empire of Salah al-Din

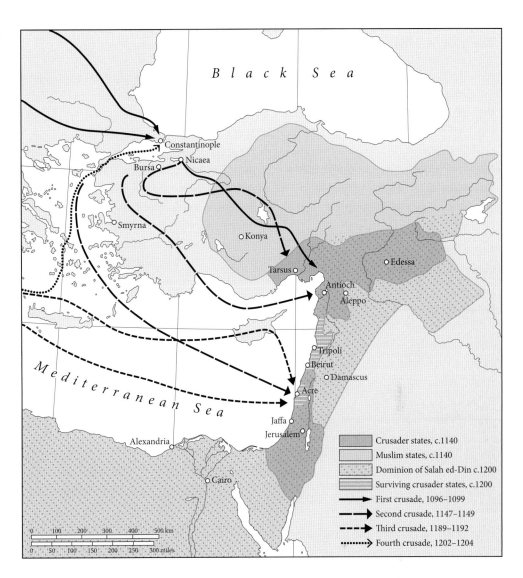

Crusader states, c.1140
Muslim states, c.1140
Dominion of Salah ed-Din c.1200
Surviving crusader states, c.1200
First crusade, 1096–1099
Second crusade, 1147–1149
Third crusade, 1189–1192
Fourth crusade, 1202–1204

Box 10.3 El Cid in the Reconquest

In the eleventh century, struggle against the Muslims provided European men at arms with opportunities to make their fames and fortunes. The legendary El Cid is a figure representative of the adventurers who took part in the Christian campaigns to take back Iberia from Muslim kingdoms, but who actually dealt with both sides. Rodrigo Díaz de Bivar became famous as El Cid Campeador, meaning the Lord (said in Arabic) Who Leads the Field. El Cid helped King Alfonso VI (r. 1072–1109) reunite Castile and León,

then strike out against Iberian Muslims. But in 1081 Alfonso banished the Cid for his misdeeds, including failure to respect Alfonso's guarantees to the enemy. The Cid then signed up to fight for the Muslim lord of Saragossa, who was battling not only the Muslim lord of Lerida, but also Lerida's allies King Sancho of Aragon and the Count of Barcelona. Heading his own army, the Cid besieged Muslim-held Valencia for twenty months of 1093 and 1094. He finally beat down Valencia's defenses. With Alfonso again

on his side, the Cid then ruled Valencia until he died in 1099. (After the Cid's death, Muslim forces retook the city, and did not lose it definitively to Christian forces until 1238.) Meanwhile, Alfonso married his two daughters to noble northerners who had crossed the Pyrenees to join the anti-Muslim wars and make their fortunes. Alfonso made one of them, Henry of Burgundy, Count of the portion of Castile that eventually became the nucleus of Portugal.

Box 10.4 A Muslim Gentleman Joins an Attack on Crusaders

In 1131 CE, a Muslim army set out to retake the Crusader fortress of Kafartab, southwest of Aleppo in today's Syria. Usama Ibn-Munqidh was a son of a general in the attacking force. At that point, the two sides fought with bows, arrows, swords, lances, stones, and fire, but knew nothing of gunpowder. Here is how the battle began:

The [Muslim] troops from Khurasan entered the trench and began to dig an underground tunnel. Convinced that they were on the point of perdition, the Franks set the castle on fire. The roofs were burned and fell upon the horses, beasts of burden, sheep, pigs and captives – all of whom were burned up. The Franks remained clinging to the walls at the top of the castle ...

After resting until noontime, there set out all of a sudden a footman from our ranks, singlehanded and carrying his sword and shield. He marched to the wall of the tower which had fallen, and the sides of which had become like the steps of a ladder, and climbed on it until he got as far as its highest point. As soon as the other men of the army saw him, about ten of them followed him hastily, in full armor, and climbed one after the other until they got to the tower, while the Franks were not conscious of their movements. We in turn put on our armor in our tents and advanced. Many climbed the tower before all our army had wholly arrived.

The Franks now turned upon our men and shot their arrows at them. They wounded the man who was first to climb. So he descended. But the other men continued to climb in succession until they stood facing the Franks on one of the tower walls between two bastions. Right in front of them stood a tower the door of which was guarded by a cavalier in full armor carrying his shield and lance, preventing entrance to the tower. On top of that tower were a band of Franks, attacking our men with arrows and stones. One of the Turks climbed, under our very eyes, and started walking towards the tower, in a face of death, until he approached the tower and hurled a bottle of naphtha on those who were on top of it. The naphtha flashed like a meteor falling upon those hard stones, while the men who were there threw themselves on the ground for fear of being burnt. The Turk then came back to us.*

The battle continued, but eventually the Muslim force, after heavy losses of its own, overwhelmed the Franks, who surrendered the castle.

Count of Flanders. They and their knightly followers took their horses, arms, and retainers overland through Anatolia and Syria, since a sea voyage would have required braving Muslim forces most of the way. They took Jerusalem in July 1099, massacred or expelled all the Jews and Muslims they found there, and installed the ailing duke of Lower Lorraine as governor. Christian forces likewise conquered three other nearby territories. Box 10.4 gives a description by the Muslim gentleman Usama Ibn-Munqidh of one of these "Frankish" attacks in 1131.

Latin Christians ruled Jerusalem until Muslim forces under Salah al-Din (known in Europe as Saladin) retook the city in 1187. For those eighty-eight years the Christian kingdom of Jerusalem and its counterparts depended heavily on the Italian merchants who mediated trade with Asia in such coastal cities as Beirut, Acre, Haifa, and Jaffa. Hostility often broke out, in fact, between zealous anti-Muslim newcomers from Europe (known generically as **Franks**, whether or not they came from France) and the old Middle Eastern hands, who learned local languages, adopted local styles of life, and worked out easy collaborations with their Muslim commercial allies. In any case, the Frankish states of the Middle East only lasted as long as Fatimid Egypt, the dominant regional power, tolerated them.

Despite the mutual adaptation of Franks, Italians, and the Middle East's Muslim majority, popes continued to promote or authorize Crusades for recovery of the Holy Land. Seven more official Crusades departed between 1147 and 1270. They produced no durable losses of territory by Muslim rulers, but frequent struggles over Mediterranean properties among Christian belligerents. Venice helped divert the Fourth Crusade (1202–04) into seizure of Constantinople from what remained of Byzantium. A bizarre episode arrived with the unauthorized Children's Crusade of 1212, during which one contingent of children passing through Marseilles ended up sold into slavery and the other contingent turned back far short of the Holy Land. From the Muslim perspective, in any case, Christian attempts to retake Palestine amounted to no more than minor interruptions of overall Muslim expansion in the east.

10.4 WHO WERE THE MUSLIMS?

At the time, Islam had nothing like political, cultural, doctrinal, or even linguistic unity. In the period 900–1200 the Muslim world fragmented into large numbers of political units. Egypt-Syria and Iraq-Iran emerged as rival centers of imperial power, but even their considerable might and territorial sweep left many smaller independent Muslim states, in Iberia, North Africa, and West Africa in the west, and in Anatolia, Central Eurasia, and India to the east. As in Christendom, substantial disputes existed between the religious authorities and state officials. Whereas the Baghdad-based Abbasid caliph had at one time united temporal and spiritual authority in his person, by the middle of the tenth century the Abbasids had lost most political power to the Buyid kings who swept into Baghdad from Iran. Worse yet, the Buyids favored Twelver Shi`ism, putting the Sunni caliphs on the defensive. Map 10.4 shows the Abbasid caliphate at the peak of its power around 800 and its reduced influence by 1090.

The Abbasids suffered the further indignity of seeing the rise in Egypt of a new dynasty of **Ismaili** Shi`ite leaders, the Fatimids, who offered not only a political but also a spiritual challenge by calling themselves caliphs. (The Ismaili were the followers of Muslim leaders descended from the Imam Ismail.) What later generations called "Sunni" Islam developed during this period in response to challenges from an increasingly well-defined and powerful set of Shi`ite movements, as well as in reaction to the Christian Crusades. The struggles over the relationship of religious institutions to civil power ultimately led to a new status quo in Sunnism that prevailed in most of the Muslim world until the twentieth century.

Institutional, social, and environmental changes deeply affected the fortunes of the Abbasid caliphate. The prosperity of Baghdad as a city came in part from its position as imperial capital, a place to which vast tax revenues collected from the peasantry were sent. It particularly benefited from levies on the rich farmlands of southern Iraq, called the **Sawad**. It is not entirely clear why, but this key source of revenue declined dramatically in the late 800s and throughout the 900s, much weakening the Abbasids. In part, this drastic drop in agricultural productivity and revenues may have come about because of the rise of a distinctive Middle Eastern version of feudalism. Formerly, the Abbasid state collected taxes through a sophisticated bureaucracy manned by salaried accountants and revenue agents. Increasingly in the late 800s, however, the caliphs resorted to giving big grants of land to courtiers and generals. These individuals were responsible for collecting taxes on these estates, part of which they forwarded to the caliph, but much of which they kept for themselves.

Unlike Europe's manorial feudalism, the lords did not reside on these large estates, called **iqta`**. There was no manor or sense of belonging to the area among these courtiers, who continued to reside in the capital. The river valleys of the Tigris and Euphrates are key to Iraq's agricultural economy. Unlike the much gentler Nile, these fast-flowing rivers often flooded violently. Managing irrigation networks in their hinterlands was delicate and

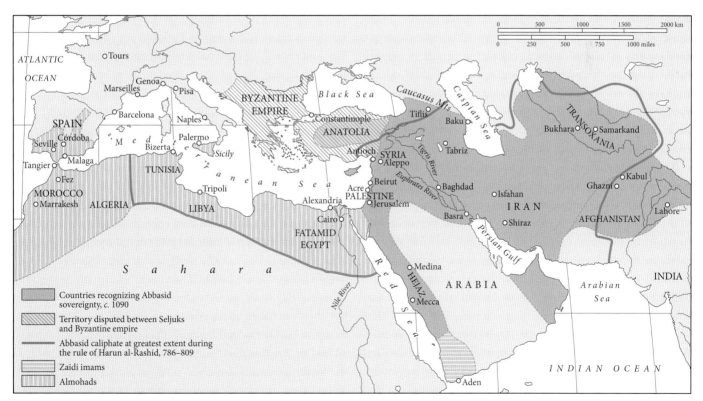

Map 10.4 The Abbasid empire

time-consuming work that required substantial investment in administration and manpower. The new feudal lords of the hacienda-like iqta` appear to have been more interested in taking a quick profit from their estates than in carefully tending the fragile irrigation networks, and so contributed to declining agricultural productivity. It seems likely, however, that other changes contributed to the problems in southern Iraq, including perhaps soil exhaustion or climate shifts.

With one of their prime tax bases in drastic decline, the Abbasid caliphs in Baghdad grew increasingly weak and unable to raise large armies or guarantee security. They faced several different sorts of military threat. One was the Bedouins, the Arabic-speaking tribes that constituted a significant proportion of the population of Syria, Iraq, and Arabia, and who were sometimes capable of uniting in an attack on the caliph's forces. Bedouin could sometimes throw up a natural cavalry of significant military strength. Small breakaway states based on Bedouin cavalry were set up in this period in southern Iraq and in city-states like Aleppo. These Bedouin challenges to the caliphs further sapped their strength, since raising armies to fight them was expensive, and the imperial treasury was emptying.

The peasant clans of Iran's Caspian Sea region launched another challenge. Although most of Iran was arid and did not support dense swathes of settlement, the southern shores of the Caspian Sea were green and agriculturally fertile because of lake-effect rains. There, peasant villages could grow and could crowd one another, allowing the clans to network politically. Most of the peasant revolts in Iranian history have centered on the Caspian region. In the 900s, clans from the Daylam region of the Caspian, employing armies of peasant infantry as their shock troops, began having a great deal of military success in subduing large parts of Iran. These clans spoke a new sort of Persian that mixed Persian grammar and basic words with an Islamic Arabic higher vocabulary. They favored the Shi`ite branch of Islam.

The leading clan among them became known as the Buyids (945–1055), because they were initially led by three brothers whose father was named Buyah. One of them, Ali, established himself and his forces in the then fertile and populous Fars province in the southwest of Abbasid Iran, with its regional capital at Shiraz. The two other brothers came to control other provinces of Iran. The weak Abbasid ruler recognized Ali in Shiraz as his governor, even though Ali had come to power by conquest rather than imperial appointment. The Buyids then joined Baghdad's power struggles. In 945 one of the brothers, Ahmad, entered the capital and established a new temporal dynasty. They ruled many of the old eastern provinces of the Abbasid empire, but lost Egypt and North Africa in the west, and never conquered Central Eurasia in the east.

The Buyids were new converts to the Twelver branch of Shi`ism, and it flourished under their more than a century of rule. The Shi`ite canon emerged at this time; some of its first great textual scholars, jurists, and scholastic theologians were active under Buyid rule. The Buyids reduced the resentful Sunni caliphs to mere spiritual figureheads, denying them real political power and even limiting their religious authority. The caliphs remained responsible for the religious and legal affairs of the Sunni Muslim community, especially the designation of religious court judges (**qadis**) who served the Sunni community. The caliphs received a generous stipend from the new rulers rather than being in charge of the budget themselves, as in the past. The Buyids did not, however, depose the caliphs. Instead, they claimed their own authority stemmed from the caliph's appointment of them to rule. They revived the old Iranian title of "king of kings" for themselves. The first minister or vizier to the caliph now began reporting instead to the monarch. A certain separation of religious and state authority stemmed from this arrangement, which was fairly new and distinctive for Muslim culture.

The Buyids aggressively extended the practice of tax farming, called the iqta` system. They benefited from not having to maintain an extensive tax-collecting bureaucracy themselves. But they thereby lost financial control of much of their empire, creating powerful barons who collected local taxes on the Buyids' behalf and forwarded to the center some portion of the revenues. The lands that were thus granted often went to pay the salaries of generals and powerful courtiers. They were not really a fief in the European sense, just a sort of backstop for the official's salary. The soldiers still got their pay from the central treasury out of tax receipts. Under the Buyids, a new military landed aristocracy grew up that dominated the old Baghdad merchant class.

Historians think of the Buyids as able administrators, even though their resort to tax farming further weakened central authority and even though Iraq continued its economic decline under their rule. It was in the tenth century, during their reign, that the Muslim proportion of the Iranian population rose to about 70 percent (in 900 it was probably still only 40 percent). Members of the old Zoroastrian religion labored under disadvantages, having to pay a special poll tax not levied on Muslims. Zoroastrianism had a caste system that discriminated against persons in the lower castes. They could escape this low status by converting to Islam. Other factors may have been important, but the attractions of an egalitarian religion like Islam and a desire to escape the poll tax and other disabilities are probably among the reasons most Iranians adopted the new faith, though the attractions of Islam as a religion played a part as well. This change, along with the prosperity of Fars and other eastern provinces in the face of declining Iraqi agricultural yields, may have been among the factors that allowed a Muslim Iran-based dynasty to come to the fore in what remained of the empire.

Twelver Shi`ites came to believe in this period that the last (twelfth) Imam had disappeared from the earthly realm but would come back one day from the supernatural realm to restore justice to the world. In his absence, Twelver Shi`ites were free to be politically loyal and subject to other sorts of leader, including the caliphs and the Buyids. Some have seen these doctrines as products of the Buyid period that were especially convenient for Twelver Shi`ites given the political situation then. The Buyids came to depend on the support of wealthy Shi`ite families who claimed descent from the Prophet Muhammad through his cousin and son-in-law, Ali ibn Abi Talib. They gave their support to new Shi`ite forms of public ritual, such as annual public mourning processions at the beginning of each Islamic year to commemorate the martyrdom of the Imam Husayn, the Prophet's grandson. Shi`ite seminaries opened. The Twelver Shi`ites, still a numerical minority, did not persecute Sunnis in this period. But periodic urban street clashes did break out between the two communities from this time forward. The Buyids faced continued challenges in the west from Bedouins and from mini-states with a Turkish slave-soldier cavalry in Iraq and Syria.

For much of the 900s the most important such state was that of the Carmathians (Qaramita), based in eastern Arabia. They adhered to the Ismaili branch of Shi`ite Islam but were often willing to ally with the Abbasid caliphs and later the Twelver Shi`ite Buyids. The movement was made up of Ismaili townspeople in eastern Arabia and southern Iraq, as well as great merchants who profited from the Persian Gulf trade and Bedouin allies in Arabia, Iraq, and Syria. Their income depended on tolls extracted from caravans and pilgrims to Mecca, as well as on trade through the Gulf and land taxes. The Carmathians gained a reputation for having a relatively egalitarian and prosperous society, which seemed less based on social distinctions than was the case in the increasingly feudal regimes around them. It should be remembered, however, that they did own slaves, and had great merchants and tribal chieftains among them who were far wealthier than the average town-dweller.

They suffered ill repute among strict Sunni Muslims because of the exaggerated claims they made for their religious leaders, to some of whom they attributed an aura of divinity. When Carmathian forces sacked Mecca and stole the black stone that is central to Muslim pilgrimage ritual, they struck a blow at conventional orthodoxy but increased their reputation for extremism and blasphemy in the eyes of many Sunnis. The rise of the Fatimid Ismaili state in Tunisia and Egypt, which claimed Syria, posed a severe challenge to the Carmathians. They refused to recognize the Fatimid leader as the rightful head of the Ismaili

branch of Islam, and went to war with his forces over Syria. The Carmathians lost this battle and thereafter were confined to eastern Arabia. They ultimately did acknowledge the Fatimids, but they lost their political primacy in Arabia in 988 so that they became irrelevant.

The Ismaili Fatimids in Egypt

The Carmathians were an example of secretive Ismaili Shi`ism, organized in cells. It operated primarily in the eastern Muslim world in the late 800s and early 900s. Ismaili leaders kept their position secret from all but close lieutenants so as to be able to hide their activities from the Abbasid police and intelligence agents. The Ismailis had substantial numbers of adherents and good organization in parts of Iran, eastern Arabia, Yemen, and Syria. They even attempted to spread their version of the faith in Spain, southern Italy, and Byzantine Constantinople, though without much success in these places. Because of the secrecy and the dependence on cell-like organization, however, the movement lacked unity.

Carmathian leaders, for instance, were often at odds with the other branches. Ismailis were looking for leadership from descendants of Ali ibn Abi Talib and the Prophet's daughter Fatimah, through Isma`il ibn Ja`far al-Sadiq, whom they considered the seventh "Imam" or divinely guided leader. By 900 there were a number of possible claimants from this house. One of them, who styled himself al-Mahdi, had a career in Iran and Syria as secret Ismaili missionary and great merchant. The Abbasid police discovered him in Syria, however, forcing him to flee first to Egypt and then to the Berber regions of North Africa. There, beyond the weakening grasp of the Abbasid state, he was able to make many converts among Berber tribes. Berbers became the backbone of his growing military. Berbers were the indigenous inhabitants of North Africa, speaking an Afro-Semitic language distantly related both to ancient Egyptian and to Arabic. Many of them were pastoral nomads, though some also dwelled in towns. They had adopted Islam, but from all accounts were less versed in that faith and less orthodox than the Arab Muslim immigrants who flooded into the area after the Muslim conquest of it.

Supporters of al-Mahdi, including Berber tribespeople, were able by the early 900s to take most of what is now Tunisia for him and to put him on the throne as an infallible Imam or theocratic ruler claiming descent from Fatimah, daughter of the Prophet Muhammad. The dynasty thus became known as the Fatimids. He and his successors strove to extend their sway in the east, to Libya and ultimately Egypt, which was then only formally under Abbasid rule, having in fact fallen into the hands of a local ruling group. In 969 the Fatimids took Egypt, and founded a new city as a symbol of their victory; they laid out magnificent Cairo adjacent to the old metropolis of Fustat. The new city allowed them to garrison their Ismaili Berber tribal armies away from the local Sunni and Christian population, to reduce the chance of popular disturbances. There they constructed a major Ismaili mosque and seminary, al-Azhar, as well as many smaller ones, which aimed at producing Muslim intellectuals steeped in the theology and law of this branch of Islam, who could support the bureaucracy of the new state and help spread Ismaili ideas.

By this time, the majority of Egyptians were probably Sunni Muslim, though perhaps as late as 1000 a third or more of the population likely remained Coptic Christian. Although they ruled Egypt until 1171, the Fatimids did not succeed in converting any large number of Egyptians to their branch of the faith, though they did make missionary efforts among them. As we have seen, the Fatimids were not even able to attract the loyalty of the Ismaili Carmathians, and had to fight them in Syria. Had these two Ismaili states combined forces, they might well have fulfilled their dream of taking Baghdad and altogether displacing their enemy, the Abbasid caliph. Their inability to unite gave Sunni and Twelver Shi`ite leaders in Iraq and Iran the respite needed to regroup and begin fighting back against Ismailism's increasingly powerful claims to dominance over the Muslim world.

The Fatimid state initially depended on its loyal Berber tribal cavalry for its military success. It also used African and Slav slaves for foot-soldiers. Over time, it came to incorporate Turkish slave-soldiers into its military, as was common in the Muslim east. The theory was that slave-soldiers, alienated from ties of family, native region, and tribe, would have no local interests of their own and so remain fiercely loyal to the caliph. This theory was not always correct, since the Turkish soldiers over time became wealthy and powerful in their own right and did develop interests that sometimes interfered with their loyalty to the ruler. A chronic rivalry also developed between the Berber tribal troops, the African slave-soldier infantry, and the Turkish slave-soldier cavalry, which required strong leadership on the part of the Ismaili caliphs and their ministers to manage. The Ismailis were displaced in the mid to late 1100s by the Ayyubids. These Kurdish warriors began as viziers or first ministers of the weakened Fatimids and had been based in Syria. Saladin (Salah al-Din al-Ayyubi, d. 1193) established a new, Sunni state in Egypt and Syria. As we have seen, Saladin defeated the Latin kingdom of Jerusalem in 1187 and restored that holy city to Muslim rule.

India

Muslim India also comes under the heading of Fatimid history in this period. Late in the Abbasid period the Indus Valley region that had been conquered by the Muslims early in their imperial expansion gradually came under the control of a number of locally based Arab "barons," who became much more powerful than the Abbasid governor. Two of the more important such local magnate families were based in the towns of Mansura and Multan. Subsisting on the frontier with Hindu India and its rajas, they mentioned the Abbasids in their Friday prayers, a sign that they saw themselves as vassals of the caliph. From 879 the Arab chieftains of Sind became heads of virtually independent principalities, benefiting from the Persian Gulf trade. The rise of the Fatimids in Egypt threatened them economically, however, since the Ismaili rulers attempted to throttle the Persian Gulf trade and to reroute trade from India to the Red Sea, bringing it through Cairo on its way to Alexandria and then, via the Mediterranean, to Europe. Recognizing the new power of the Fatimid empire, the Arab chieftains of Sind adopted the Ismaili branch of Islam and announced themselves vassals of the Fatimid ruler.

Because of the weakness of Abbasid rule in North India, Sind had become a haven for all sorts of persons with unusual or officially disapproved beliefs, according to the chronicles. It had many freethinkers and "atheists." Its position on the borderlands between the Muslim and Hindu civilizations also probably prompted local thinkers to be less orthodox than in the heartland. Among the groups viewed as heretical in Baghdad that were able to organize in Sind was the Ismailis. Ismailism was especially open to non-Muslim philosophical ideas, perhaps because of its emphasis on the importance of esoteric (hidden) knowledge, which resembles that of the ancient Greek Gnostics. Thus, in the Middle East Ismailis took in many ideas from the old Hellenistic culture, and from Neoplatonism and Neo-Pythagoreanism (a revival of the notions of Pythagoras about numerical symbolism underlying the universe).

In Sind, Ismailis were especially open to Sanskrit philosophy and Hindu religious ideas. The **da`i**, or chief Ismaili missionary in Sind, established a mini-state by the 960s or 970s, based at a fortress, where Friday prayers were said in the name of the Fatimid caliph. This da`i was known for being especially tolerant of converts to Ismailism retaining many of their old Hindu or Buddhist customs. In 983–84 the Fatimid ruler al-`Aziz dispatched a military force to Sind under Julam ibn Shayban. Julam conquered the area up to and including the major city of Multan, an entrepôt river port in the middle of the Indus Valley. There, he had the old Sunni mosque from Umayyad times bolted up. He also destroyed a major Hindu or Buddhist idol, dispersing the monks who had promoted its cult. The historian al-Muqaddisi, who visited Sind in 985, wrote, "In Multan the Khutba is read in the name of the Fatimid (caliph) and all decisions are taken according to his commands. Envoys and presents go regularly from Multan to Egypt. Its ruler is powerful and just."

Egypt's power in India was underwritten by the resurgence of trade between the Indus Valley and the Red Sea. Egypt had conquered Yemen and the coast of East Africa, and its navies and key port garrisons allowed the flourishing of an Arabian Sea–Indian Ocean trade on a new and larger scale, tying the Sindis to Cairo commercially as well as politically. At the same time, the rival Buyids, vassals of the Sunni caliph in Baghdad, had depended on the Persian Gulf trade for part of their prosperity, and the Fatimids had managed to at least partially block it and cut Iraq off from the lucrative India trade. Buyid rule was also increasingly threatened by Turkic invasions, as we will see. By the middle of the 1000s, the Ismaili mission had also become highly influential along the Gujarati coast to the south of Sind, with its bustling seaports.

Fatimid Sind and the rest of India faced increasing incursions by Sunni Turkic tribes led by the Ghaznavids, based in what is now eastern Afghanistan, and its rulers attempted to fight these off by allying with the neighboring Hindu Shahi kingdom. From 997, Mahmud of Ghazni began his invasions of the fertile Panjab region, invading every winter. His Muslim troops smashed Hindu idols, and the Turkic tribespeople looted the cities of jewels, gold, and silver, and female and male slaves. The raids on India contributed to the wealth and splendor of the Ghaznavid court.

In 1025 the Hindu inhabitants of Somnath in southwestern Gujarat are said to have waited quietly as Ghaznavid cavalrymen approached, confident that they would be protected from harm by their huge temple to the god Siva, which housed an iron phallic symbol of the god that was suspended by magnets in such a way as to seem supernatural to the Hindus of the time. In fact, Mahmud's troops savagely subdued the city, wreaking a massacre of its inhabitants. Mahmud broke the iron lingam or symbol of Siva's fertility with his sword, spilling the jewelry treasured within it, and taking off an estimated 2 million dinars worth of gold and other valuables from this Hindu stronghold. The Turkic invasions were probably as motivated by search for loot as by a zeal for Islam or against idolatry, and they did not differ materially from the sort of tribal raid launched from Central Asia on North India well before the rise of Islam. But they left a legacy of bitterness among Hindus in the subcontinent.

Nor were Hindus Mahmud's only object of conquest. In 1010 the Ghaznavids had taken Multan, on the grounds in part that it was a nest of heretics. He had many Ismailis killed or persecuted and reopened the Sunni mosque for Friday prayers, whereas the Ismaili mosque was now abandoned. The Ghaznavids only lightly and temporarily established their rule in Sind, however. Ismailis remained active in the province and were able to stage a comeback from the middle of the eleventh century, urged on by coreligionists in the Middle East and fortified by powerful new Hindu converts from among the local rajas.

The second Ismaili period was brought to a close in Sind in 1175 by Muhammad Ghuri, a Turkic general based in what is now Afghanistan. The Ghurids, supported by Turkic tribal cavalry and slave-soldiers, first defeated the Ghaznavids in Central Eurasia. Then they followed the same strategy, of invading India. They had more success, however, being interested in actually ruling the subcontinent rather than just plundering it. They invaded India for the first time in 1175. By 1186 they had captured the important Panjabi city of Lahore, and by 1193 they had taken Delhi. The Ghurid state began a long period of Sunni Muslim rule of North India by Turkic dynasties. Ismailis were again persecuted in Sind. They therefore took refuge in Sufi orders, where they pretended to be Sunnis, or they converted to the more acceptable Twelver Shi`ite branch of Islam.

As for Hindu India in the period 900–1200, controversy rages about its character. An influential school of Indian historiography has seen it as mired in a Dark Age, characterized by feuding among petty rival rajas and economic stagnation caused by the development of a form of Hindu "feudalism" and by marauding Muslim invasions. Historian Andre Wink has argued that, on the contrary, the Indian economy expanded in this period. He maintains it was helped by the incorporation of India into the prosperous Muslim trading networks of the Middle East, which allowed Indian merchants to market their goods to the Mediterranean world more generally. He sees evidence that some of the inland rajas ruled principalities such as Kashmir that were extremely prosperous, their treasuries full of gold.

In fact, both integrative and disintegrative forces were at work in India in this period. Fatimid Sind, whatever disruptions its wars with neighbors might have produced, probably did draw the Indus Valley into the Muslim-dominated Indian Ocean trade in a way that benefited the Indian economy. On the other hand, the marauding raids from Central Eurasia, from places like Ghazni, must have been bad for the Indian economy. Wink in any case does seem to have established that the picture was more mixed than some historians have allowed. The wealthy Hindu rajas and merchants supported a brahminical revival.

Brahmins, the priestly caste of the Hindus, strove to reconvert the populace to Hinduism from Buddhism, and to displace the powerful Buddhist monasteries with Hindu equivalents. In all this, they succeeded in India. The period 900–1200 therefore can be seen as roiled by two great religious struggles. In the Muslim world, Ismaili Shi`ism battled Sunni Islam for domination, whereas in the Indian subcontinent south of Sind, Hinduism and Buddhism confronted one another. Each of the four contenders had a radically different vision of civilization, and the contests were epic ones. When the smoke of battle cleared by 1200, the Sunnis had largely won out in the Middle East and Sind, and the Hindus had won out in India.

A Buddhist India and a Shi`ite Egypt were relics of the past, not waves of the future.

10.5 THE SELJUKS

During the tenth and eleventh centuries, a resurgent Sunnism challenged the ascendancy of Shi`ite Islam. Rising dynasties stemmed from pastoral nomadic clans who favored the Sunni form of Islam. From 1040 the Turkic Seljuk dynasty established itself in eastern Iran (Khurasan). Turkic tribes had been migrating into the Transoxania region of Central Asia from points east for some time. They had gradually converted from shamanism and Buddhism to Sunni Islam. Having defeated or displaced eastern Muslim Persian-speaking dynasties such as the Samanids, the Seljuks turned their eyes on western Iran and Iraq, taking on the Buyids. In 1055 the Seljuks took Baghdad, bringing it once again under Sunni rule, and soon thereafter all of Iran and Iraq was united by the new monarchs. Like the Buyids, they claimed temporal rule as agents of the caliph, who continued to be denied much real political power, being reduced to a spiritual leader.

The Seljuks took over the Persian bureaucracy and its practices from their predecessors. They soon forsook their tribal armies for a standing force of some 15,000, mainly slave-soldiers

of Turkic ethnicity. The Turkic tribal cavalries remained a source of instability. Constrained by the power of the Seljuks and their standing army in Iran, the tribesmen increasingly headed northwest into Anatolia, then under Byzantine rule. The Byzantines viewed their invasion of this region as a hostile act even though it occurred without the permission of the Seljuks, and it provoked a war between the Byzantines and the Seljuks that the Turks won in 1071 at Manzikert. (Remember that Anatolia's Turks slaughtered the ragtag European Crusaders of 1096–97.) Map 10.5 shows the extent of the Byzantine empire in 1025.

Turkic tribes continued to pour into Anatolia, gradually transforming it from a Greek-speaking to a Turkish-speaking region, detaching it from Byzantium and encouraging the conversion of the population to Sunni Islam. Most of the population in Anatolia remained descendants of Greeks, since the tribal invaders were relatively few in number, but they gradually adopted Turkish as their primary language and Islam as their religion. They did so in part to ally with powerful Turkic tribes, and in part because of the attractions of the mystical Sufi form of Islam that the tribesmen often brought with them, which stressed singing, dancing, attaining trance-like states, and yearning for union with the divine beloved.

A separate Seljuk state took hold in Anatolia. After that, the Byzantine empire was based mainly in the west of Asia Minor,

Map 10.5 The Byzantine empire, 1025

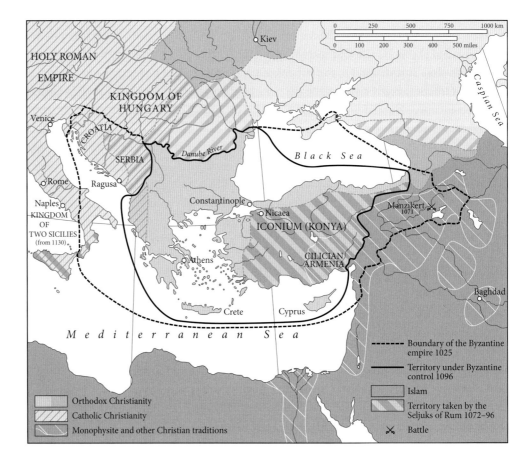

ruling over a much smaller region than before, and it continued to shrink over the next centuries. The Seljuks in Iran and Iraq were powerful only until the end of the eleventh century. During that time they and their ministers established Sunni seminaries and one effect of their rule was the revival of Sunni Islam. In the middle of the twelfth century, they had grown so weak that the caliphate revived as a political institution with real power, at least around Baghdad. In the east they were overthrown by Persian-speaking dynasties. Political power was somewhat fragmented in the east, laying the region open to the Mongol invasions of the 1200s.

10.6 MIDDLE EASTERN SOCIAL ORGANIZATION AND MATERIAL LIFE

The arid zone of the Middle East produced three major ways of life that interacted heavily with one another. Land along the coastlines of the Mediterranean or in Anatolia and western Iran that received at least 10 inches of rainfall per year could be employed for rainfall agriculture and support a peasantry. Peasant villages also clustered near river valleys such as the Nile or the Tigris and Euphrates, the waters of which could be used to irrigate the land beyond the banks. More arid lands sometimes were dotted with pasture, but it was often short-lived and often not reliable, and certainly could not support regular farming by peasants. The pastoral nomads (Berbers, Bedouin, and Turkoman or other Turkic clans) specialized in making good use of this marginal land, herding sheep, goats, horses, and camels in search of pasturage.

In areas with snow-tipped peaks in the winter, such as northwestern Iran, they could be assured of spring pasturage at the foothills, but migrated elsewhere when that withered in the summer. Many pastoralists thus migrated twice a year within a fairly regular circuit. At other times, as with the Turks and Mongols from eastern Central Eurasia, pastoralists could undertake lengthy journeys of migration across steppes and marches. Throughout the period 900–1200, large numbers of Turkic tribespeople made their way into the Middle East from Inner Asia, though they had a bigger impact on Iran and Anatolia than on Egypt. They were often taken as slaves in battles with existing states, and sometimes these slaves were converted to Islam and used as soldiers to garrison particular towns and cities.

Pastoralists, as we have seen, often benefited from serving states as a sort of natural cavalry in wars of conquest, being rewarded with booty or immunity from taxes. Pastoralists produced meat and dairy products, but seldom grain, and so traded with peasants, who had grain in abundance but less meat and milk. Peasants made up the majority of the population throughout the Middle East, though in arid Iraq and Iran the pastoralists may have at some points been a third to a half of the population. Cities probably seldom exceeded 10 percent of the population in most of the medieval Middle East. They were extremely important, however, as centers of trade and of production and consumption of economic goods beyond subsistence. Towns and cities in Egypt and south-central Iran appear to have flourished in our period, whereas Baghdad seems to have declined economically.

Medieval Muslim cities served as centers of bureaucracy, religious law, mysticism and commerce, as well as being heavily garrisoned by troops. Among the better documented cities in this period was Buyid and Seljuk Shiraz. The Iranian city of Shiraz was reported by geographers to be a large and flourishing town in the late 900s; it still had a substantial Zoroastrian population that supported two fire temples. The Buyids favored it, constructing mosques and palaces, promoting its bazaar, and establishing caravanserais to encourage long-distance trade. The Buyids put a garrison for their troops in a cantonment near Shiraz, to which merchants and artisans flocked with their wares. Shiraz and the garrison accounted for some 15 percent of all the revenues of Fars province in the late 900s. By the middle of the next century the military cantonment had disappeared and the city had fallen into substantial disorder. A late Buyid ruler built a wall around the city, with about eight gates.

Shiraz was looted early in the Seljuk period, but after a long period of instability, some later Seljuk governors returned it to fair prosperity. Sunni seminaries and libraries were established. It is reported that a wife of one of the Turkic governors, Zahidah Khatun, more or less ruled the city herself for twenty years in the mid-1100s while her husband was away on campaigns and then after his death. In contrast to the often flourishing state of Shiraz in this period, Baghdad and Basra suffered long stretches of economic malaise.

One of Egypt's major cities in this period was Qus, in largely Christian Upper Egypt. It lay on the major route that Indian Ocean merchants took to get their goods from the Red Sea up to Alexandria and then to the Mediterranean. When the Crusaders took Palestine, many pilgrims from the east began going by sea to Alexandria and then up the Nile to Qus before going on to Mecca and Medina. Qus became an administrative center for this part of Egypt, and acquired a majority Muslim population with the typical complex of mosque, law court, and bazaar. Some of the governors of Qus became extremely powerful because of the city's strong economic position. The advent of stronger government administration in this area led to more conversions to Islam in the Christian countryside. Cities in general formed important nodes for the transmission of urban Islamic culture to members of older religions who tended to be rural.

At the other end of Egypt, on the Mediterranean, lay Alexandria, a city with strong links to North Africa. It had a large North African immigrant population that included long-distance merchants, clergymen, and some Jews. In the medieval period it still had a big Christian population, and the Christians had their own harbor, distinct from the Muslim one. It was the headquarters of the Coptic church. With regard to the Muslims, because of the North African influence its legal and educational culture had more of a Sunni tinge than did that of Cairo, even at the height of the Ismaili Fatimid period. It was a major transit point for the trade in spices, slaves, silk, and Alexandrian-made cloth. Neither Qus nor Alexandria could begin to compare to the capital of Egypt, Cairo, which included the major borough of Fustat. Fustat was more cosmopolitan and was the commercial center of Egypt, with many Christians, Jews, foreigners, long-distance merchants, and moneylenders. Merchants from all over the Mediterranean and Indian Ocean trading areas would come there to trade and find goods in its bustling, well-stocked bazaars. Cairo proper was dominated by the Ismaili administration of the Fatimids, and was the center of administration, law, and bureaucracy. It was the site of such Ismaili institutions as the seminary and cathedral mosque, al-Azhar.

In the tenth through twelfth centuries, Fatimid Egypt was by all accounts quite prosperous. One traveler from Iran in the 1000s was astonished at how much wealthier and better off Egypt was than Iraq and Iran in the same period. Egypt's prosperity depended a great deal on the Nile. It was fed by headwaters in sub-Saharan Africa, and was swollen every year with rains in Ethiopia and Uganda that formed part of the same storm system as the Indian monsoons. As a result of this late summer rainy season upriver, the Nile annually overflowed its banks and deposited a rich layer of silt on the surrounding lands. This automatic replenishment of the topsoil, akin to the application of fertilizer today, made the Nile Valley excellent farmland and helped guard against soil exhaustion at a time before the need for systematic crop rotation was understood. Wealth in the medieval period derived mainly from agriculture, though trade in luxury goods was also lucrative.

Egypt had both sectors in abundance. The main staple crop was wheat, from which bread was made, and barley was raised as feed for livestock. Flax was also grown in great quantities, and was used to make linen cloth. In some years the rains came less abundantly, so that there was a "low Nile" that did not flood nearly as much. The crop yields in those years declined badly. For twenty years (1060s–1080s) one caliph's rule suffered such a succession of low Niles that he appealed to the Byzantines for grain to avert starvation. Prosperity was more common, and this long period of poor Niles was unusual; it was an occurrence against which governments had to plan, however. For this reason, stable government in Egypt usually required control over another source of foodstuffs, typically Syria.

Although the Fatimids faced many difficulties in subduing and controlling Syria, from the early 1000s Damascus and points west usually were under their rule. Turkish slave-soldiers played an especially important role in garrisoning that province. The Fatimids were hampered in expanding their territory in the east by the opposition of the Byzantine Christians, who controlled nearby Anatolia. They compensated for their long supply lines and weakness on land that far east by developing their navy and giving better security to Syrian coastal towns along the Mediterranean. This tactic caused Syrian port cities to grow and flourish in the 1000s before the arrival of the Christian Crusaders from Europe.

Aside from agriculture, the other pillar of prosperity was commerce. The Fatimids promoted trade, and were themselves major investors in it. One traveler in the early 1000s maintained that the caliphs owned most of the shops in Cairo, amounting to thousands of establishments. From these, as well as from caravanserais (inns and stables for long-distance caravan merchants), bathhouses, and other establishments, the caliphs extracted regular rent. The government promoted the making of flax into fiber, and this was Egypt's biggest manufacturing sector. The by-product of this industry, linseed oil, was abundant and used for lighting lamps. Much trade was carried on with North Africa and (before the Crusaders) Syria, but also in the 1100s increasingly with Europe and India. The Fatimids benefited from the gold mines in Upper Egypt and Nubia further up the Nile Valley, and in Ghana. The Egyptians also dug some gold out of pharaonic tombs.

Gold from these sources accumulated in Cairo, allowing the Fatimids to mint highly valued gold coins that strengthened their commerce. (By the end of our period, around 1200, the main sources of gold had dried up.) The economic difficulties faced in the same era by Baghdad appear to have reduced the importance of the Persian Gulf route for the long-distance trade from India and points east. More trade appears to have come through the Red Sea, controlled by the Fatimids, instead, making its way from coastal ports overland to the Nile, then up through Cairo and Alexandria to the Mediterranean. Even the rise of the Crusader states on the coast of Palestine and Lebanon did not interfere with this Red Sea trade. In fact, it may have helped Egypt by ensuring that Muslim and Indian merchants preferred to transport their textiles, pepper, and spices through the more stable Egyptian territories to the Mediterranean, avoiding the unpredictable Crusaders.

That Europe could afford these imports points to its growing economic importance in this period, and Italian and other merchants began settling in Egypt. In Egypt and throughout the greater Mediterranean, trade was relatively free, and despite the squabbles among governments and occasional instability, merchants appear to have been able to move their goods without much interference. At most, a state might insist that it had first rights on buying their goods. Merchants often made good faith oral contracts with their partners, but sometimes entered into more formal arrangements under the aegis of Islamic law, which recognized some limited types of business partnership.

10.7 ISLAMIC RELIGIOUS ORGANIZATION

Unlike Christianity in this period, Islam increasingly lacked unity or a strict hierarchy. During these centuries the Abbasid caliphate went into steep decline, losing its temporal authority altogether and facing many challenges to its religious authority. The Ismaili attempt to mount a counter-caliphate proved successful for a time, but ultimately it was overthrown by the Ayyubids. Increasingly, Muslim lands were ruled by de facto kings, and religious affairs were managed by a corps of seminary-trained Muslim learned men or **ulama** who were loyal to particular kings. The kings and their courtiers often set up pious endowments to support mosques that they built. They dedicated the profits of certain estates to paying the salary of the leader of the Friday prayers and other officials employed at the mosque.

More secular, administrative law became increasingly distinct from the **shariah** or Muslim religious law. The latter, governing personal status, inheritance, some forms of commerce, and some areas of crime and punishment, was administered and interpreted by Muslim learned men. The state appointed some of them qadis or court judges in the cities and larger towns, where they came to enjoy enormous respect. Although the learned as a social class had once been a mixture of hobbyists and appointed officials, the rise of the formal seminary, as with al-Azhar in Cairo or the Nizamiyyah seminary in Baghdad, led to the development of a greater separation between the formally trained Muslim jurists and the laity. Some historians believe that these mosque-seminary complexes proved influential on the later rise of the university in Europe. Great schools of law were founded and developed. These included the Hanafi, Maliki, Shafi`i and Hanbali among Sunnis, and the Ja`fari among Shi`ites. The schools of law differed relatively little from one another on major positions, but sometimes those differences seemed very great at the time, and eastern Iran was racked by riots between competing legal rites at some points.

Among Sunnis, it was increasingly considered illegitimate for a Muslim jurist to adopt a position on a major issue that differed from that of the founder of his school. Jurists in the **Shafi`i**
tradition retained more flexibility and more emphasis on the right of a well-trained legal mind to engage in independent legal reasoning. Although Twelver Shi`ites began by insisting on a strict and close adherence to whatever the Imam said, after the disappearance of the Twelfth Imam a corps of Shi`ite learned men grew up with great authority in the community. These divided into two schools, the **Akhbari** and the **Usuli**. Akhbaris were literalists, and they forbade independent legal reasoning. Usulis were more like Shafi`is in their rationalism and their authorization of Shi`ite jurists to use the Koran, the sayings of the Prophet and the Imams, consensus, and simple syllogisms to derive the law in a particular case. Usuli Shi`ites demanded that laypersons, that is, those who lacked a rigorous and formal seminary education, follow without question the rulings of the learned men on issues of religious law.

Most ulama were mainly interested in the study of Islamic law and its bases, mainly oral reports attributed by previous generations to the Prophet Muhammad and those close to him. Some few developed an interest in theology, which tended to use the tools of Greek dialectical thinking (thesis, antithesis, synthesis). The Muslim theologians borrowed some ideas from Greek philosophy, but tended to reject many Greek notions, such as the eternality of the world and impersonal causality.

Another group of religious specialists was the Sufis. These began as especially pious persons who practiced self-denial and left behind sayings or poetry. The origins of **Sufism** are complex and debated. Some see an influence of Buddhism, which had been dominant in eastern Iran, Afghanistan, and Central Eurasia before Islam. Others point to currents coming from Syrian Christianity, which had an emphasis on saints who went off to the wilderness to worship. Still others insist that the Koran itself gives a warrant for a moderate sort of mysticism, that is, cultivating feelings of love and ecstasy in the worship of God as a divine beloved. Toward the end of our period persons of a Sufi or mystical turn of mind had begun meeting regularly at mosques to chant prayers, and gradually they organized themselves into orders or brotherhoods. These bear some resemblance to Catholic orders such as the Franciscans and Dominicans, but since Islam did not have monks, they were more like lay organizations, whose members married, had families, and held jobs. Indeed over time the Sufi orders developed links to urban guilds and to gangs of young men in urban quarters dedicated to chivalric ideals.

Among individual Sufis, perhaps the most important figure was Abu Hamid al-Ghazali (d. 1111), who began as a seminary teacher concentrating on law and theology. Ultimately he had something like a nervous breakdown, and his problems were only solved when he turned to Sufism. Rather than abandoning law and theology, however, he integrated them with Sufism, helping to create a more orthodox version of it that proved acceptable to more and more members of the literate classes.

The Sufi poet Rumi (1207–73) lived at the end of this period. Born in Balkh, Afghanistan, he moved at a young age to Qonya, then under the Seljuk Empire, where he wrote large collections of verses in Persian. Inspired by spiritual fervor, he called for all men to destroy their worldly attachments in order to submerge themselves in a mystical divine unity. Rumi is now one of the world's best-selling poets in English translation.

10.8 ISLAMIC CULTURE

In the area of culture, some have referred to the tenth and eleventh centuries as an Islamic "Renaissance." In Baghdad, Arabic literature flourished and a great anthology of early Arabic verse, the Book of Songs, was compiled by Abu al-Faraj al-Isfahani. Arabic poets were active who have been much treasured in the subsequent millennium, such as al-Mutanabbi (who turned to a more successful career as a poet after an early turn as a self-proclaimed "prophet") and al-Ma`arri, whose blindness did not interfere with his insight. In the east, a new form of Persian emerged, mixing the old Zoroastrian language with Arabic words, called "New Persian." It proved a flexible and beautiful vehicle for secular and mystical poetry and for verse epics such as the Shahnameh of Firdawsi (d. 1020). The Shahnameh collected the old pre-Islamic legends of the Iranians, which have many parallels to stories in the ancient Hindu sources. Ibn Nadim (d. 995) compiled a vast bibliography of the great works written by Muslims up to that point, called the Fihrist (Index). Arabic calligraphy developed into an outstanding form of aesthetic expression, as shown in Figure 10.2

Philosophy flourished, with greater knowledge of Greek thought having been made available through the earlier translation movement. Al-Farabi (d. 950), based largely in Aleppo, attempted to reconcile Plato and Aristotle. Avicenna (Ibn Sina, d. 1037), a true genius, wrote on every subject treated in classical Aristotelian philosophy, and his work on medicine, the Canon (al-Qanun), became a standard textbook in the Muslim world and Europe in the medieval and early modern periods (it was taught at Leipzig in Germany as late as the early 1700s). Avicenna began his education in Bukhara under the patronage of the Samanid dynasty of Central Eurasia, which had Iranian ethnic roots, but he was displaced west by the rise of the Turkic Ghaznavids. He then made his living as a physician in a number of Buyid cities, writing and teaching philosophy on the side. Another great mind of this period, Biruni (973–1048), flourished at the Ghaznavid court and accompanied Mahmud on some of his raids into India. Biruni, a philosopher, historian, astronomer,

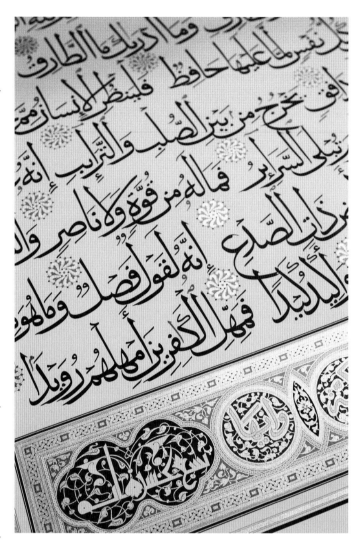

Figure 10.2 Calligraphy in Arabic, usually based on quotations from the Koran, became a sophisticated and elaborate form of artistic expression. Since Arabic interpretations of Islam banned the use of portraiture, calligraphy and landscape were the primary forms of visual expression for artists.

and mathematician, learned Sanskrit and wrote a massive Arabic Description of India that attempted sympathetically to understand Indian Hindu learning and give a dispassionate overview of Indian culture. It is among the great premodern works of comparative religion.

Platonism revived, in the face of a dominant emphasis on Aristotle or subordination of Plato's ideas to an Aristotelian framework, in the work of Suhrawardi (1154–91), who founded the school of philosophy and mysticism known as Illuminationism, which proved especially influential in Iran and South Asia. In the far west of the Muslim world, Averroes (Ibn Rushd, 1126–98), in contrast, strove for an almost pure Aristotelianism in Muslim Spain. He responded to al-Ghazali's attack on the

Greek-influenced Muslim philosophers and attempted to reconcile philosophy with revealed religion.

Science and mathematics made great strides in the Muslim world in these centuries, far beyond what occurred in Europe and on a scale comparable to that of the most advanced scientific civilization of the time, China. The Muslims adopted the Sanskrit number system, then added a zero to it, arriving at an extremely easy to use and supple system of mathematical notation that still serves us today: we call our numerals "Arabic." Algebra, invented by al-Khawarizmi around 850, continued to be refined and extended by his Muslim successors, in continued dialogue with Greek sources. Although these Muslim figures are often referred to as "Arab," many were in fact Iranians. Al-Khawarizmi's treatise on algebra was twice translated into Latin in the 1100s. Such translations of Muslim scientific works helped pave the way for Europe's "little Renaissance" of the 1200s.

The astronomy carried out by Muslims, though influenced by Iranian and Indian Hindu observations, generally remained within the framework of Ptolemy, which put the Earth at the center of the universe. Muslims not only translated from Greek, Sanskrit, and Middle Persian, but also carried out new observations. Their attempt to reconcile Ptolemy's system with Aristotle's assertion that heavenly bodies travel in a circular orbit led to the establishment of an observatory at Maraghih in western Iran in the thirteenth century. There, some work was done on planetary orbits that proved influential on European astronomy. Muslim astronomers also calculated the procession of the equinoxes, as well as the circumference of the Earth. They made key contributions to other sciences, such as chemistry, medicine, and mechanics. Their work led to the discovery of potash, alcohol, and sulfuric acid. They established the institution of the hospital, and developed new knowledge of herbal medicines. They also made advances in surgery, and one Muslim physician who saw Europeans amputate a Crusader's leg with an axe described their medicine as barbaric. Because they had to deal with a relatively arid environment, Muslims devoted great attention to water management, irrigation, underground canals, water wheels, and other such engineering problems. They made important contributions to the science of navigation.

Conclusion Historians of the Greater Mediterranean often neglect the period from 900 to 1200, seemingly dwarfed in significance by the political developments before and after it. Before, we saw the Umayyads and early Abbasids in the Muslim world and Charlemagne in Europe – all rulers of large, "universal" empires. After 1200 come the later Middle Ages and their build-up to the European Renaissance and the great Muslim land empires. In 900–1200, both Europe and the Muslim world underwent significant political decentralization, with the old massive empires of the Abbasids and Carolingians breaking up into much smaller political units. Although a Holy Roman Empire that traced itself back to Charlemagne survived in Germany and Italy, it was only one of the European kingdoms, and was not necessarily the most militarily important of them at any one time.

Because historians tend to tie their narratives to strong governments, times of political decentralization are difficult to treat coherently. This chapter has neglected small Muslim states such as Aleppo and the smaller kingdoms of North Africa and Spain because including them would have complicated the narrative too much. History, however, is not just the history of governments, and for ordinary people smaller states may have had advantages. They may have set tax rates lower than empires with large armies and bureaucracies. And they were more accessible to the people. During these years very different types of feudalism became entrenched in Europe and the Middle East. In Europe the manor became important as a site of the lord's power and interaction with his peasants. In the Middle East, the iqta` "fief" as a way of paying military leaders allowed them to be absentee landlords, mere farmers of taxes, and so ensured that they had less connection to peasants ceded them by the monarch.

This period witnessed struggles over the boundaries of the great world civilizations and the bold marking off of religious identities. The Roman Catholicism of Western Europe broke decisively with the Greek Orthodoxy of Byzantium. Ismaili Shi`ism, Twelver Shi`ism, and Sunnism contended with one another in the Middle East, with the Shi`ites for a time gaining great political power and the opportunity to gain large numbers of converts. Some historians believe about half of the population of greater Syria became Shi`ite in this period. In the end, the rise of the Sunni Seljuks in Iran and of the Ayyubids in Egypt swept away the Shi`ite supremacy. Ismailism was reduced to a small sect that had to take refuge in rugged areas such as Yemen or in distant ones such as Gujarat in India.

Twelver Shi`ism developed a more bookish culture under the Buyids, with a strong corps of seminary-trained jurists who could provide leadership to ordinary Shi`ites even when the state had become Sunni and turned against them. In subsequent centuries most Syrians returned to Sunnism, except in the mountains of the north or in the south of what is now Lebanon. Shi`ism remained popular in some areas of Iran, however. Sunnism itself had been radically changed by the decline of the Abbasids, whose caliphate was finally abolished by the Mongols after they took Baghdad in 1258. Sunnism became more like Twelver Shi`ism in the sense of being a community of believers led by a corps of trained clergymen rather than by a centralized caliphate. In India, the Ismailis were able to convert many Hindus in the Sind region by finding similarities between Islam and Hinduism, between Muhammad and Krishna. Elsewhere in the subcontinent, feudal rajas allied with Brahmins to foster a Hindu revival that finally ended the popular appeal of Buddhism in India.

Despite the "Dark Ages" tag, these centuries witnessed significant scientific and technological advances, many of them the result of civilizational interaction and borrowings. Muslims engaged in wide-ranging translations from Greek, Syriac, Middle Persian, and Sanskrit, attempting to garner the collective wisdom of the pre-Islamic peoples. They not only transmitted this older knowledge but also added their own experiences, observations, and analysis. They contributed significantly to the development of science in this period, creating algebra, and making advances in astronomy, metallurgy, chemistry, medicine, optics, and many other fields. Europeans added the crucial zero to their number system in emulation of Muslim mathematicians. Major Muslim thinkers such as Ibn Sina (Avicenna to Europeans) and Ibn Rushd (Averroes) exerted great influence on Western intellectuals.

From the 1100s Europeans began making Latin translations of some of the more important of the Muslim works in these fields, which they encountered in Spain or the Holy Land, the two major points at which Muslim and Western European civilization intersected. These translations provoked the beginnings of a major intellectual revival in Western Europe. With regard to technology, the iron plow, the windmill, the canal lock, and the second lateen sail (adopted from the Arabs) all contributed to a slowly improving economy. The start of Gothic cathedral-building in Northwestern Europe demonstrated a new mastery of construction techniques, to say nothing of expanding financial resources. By 1200, the manifest superiority of Muslim civilization in science, technology, and the economy was drawing to a close.

Study Questions

(1) What major shifts in Muslim control of European territory occurred between 900 and 1200? Why did they occur?

(2) How did Europeans try to displace Muslims from control of the Holy Land between 900 and 1200? How successful were they?

(3) How did contacts with Asia affect European economic and political life?

(4) How accurate is the name "Dark Ages" for European history between the fall of the Roman empire and 1000 CE?

(5) What social and economic factors contributed to the prosperity of Fatimid Egypt?

(6) What was the social base of the Carmathian, Buyid, and Seljuk movements in the Islamic East? How did they differ from one another?

(7) Compare the bases of prosperity of Fatimid Egypt and Western Europe. Who had stronger armies, bigger cities, wealthier merchants, and a more dynamic culture? Who were the biggest threats to each of these societies?

Suggested Reading

ROBERT BARTLETT, *The Making of Europe: Conquest, Colonization and Cultural Change, 950–1350* (Princeton University Press, 1993). Bartlett's sweeping history accents both internal colonization and interactions between Europe and the worlds to its south and east.

JONATHAN P. BERKEY, *The Formation of Islam: Religion and Society in the Near East, 600–1800* (Cambridge University Press, 2002). This well-regarded survey of the history of the peoples of the Middle East from approximately 600 to 1800 has a focus on religion and synthesizes a wide range of information.

HUGH KENNEDY, *The Prophet and the Age of the Caliphates: The Islamic Near East from the Sixth to the Eleventh Century*, 2nd edn. (London: Longman, 2004). This is a new and revised edition of an accessible survey of the formative period of early Islamic society, including the life of the Prophet Muhammad, the early caliphates, and the expansion of Islamic empire from Spain to China. The author uses Arabic primary sources as well as engaging with more recent historiographical controversies.

ADAM J. KOSTO, *Making Agreements in Medieval Catalonia: Power, Order, and the Written Word, 1000–1200* (Cambridge University Press, 2007). Enumerations of regional lords' powers reveal a process of feudal political consolidation.

DAVID LEVINE, *At the Dawn of Modernity: Biology, Culture, and Material Life in Europe after the Year 1000* (Berkeley: University of California Press, 2001). European expansion is seen here as changes in population, technology, and social life.

MICHAEL MCCORMICK, *Origins of the European Economy: Communications and Commerce, AD 300–900* (Cambridge University Press, 2002). This work explores the multiple connections with Asia and within Europe that formed the context for change between 900 and 1200.

DAVID MORGAN, *Medieval Persia* (London: Longman, 1988). Morgan's book is a clear, short overview of the history of Iran or Persia from the time of the Turkic Seljuk dynasty to the eve of modernity in the late eighteenth century. He shows the continuities of administrative and institutional structures in this period despite the religious break in the middle of it, with the rise of the Shi`ite Safavids from 1501.

CARL F. PETRY (ed.), *The Cambridge History of Egypt*, vol. I: *Islamic Egypt, 640–1517* (Cambridge University Press, 1999). This now-standard work collects important chapters presenting and summarizing the findings of specialists on Egyptian history from the rise of Islam through 1500. It attends to social and economic as well as political history.

ANDRE WINK, *Al-Hind: The Making of the Indo-Islamic World*, 2nd edn., 2 vols., (Leiden: E.J. Brill, 2004). The first two volumes of this massive five-volume work cover the advent of Islam in India and the rise of Muslim polities and conversion through the thirteenth century. Volume I argues that the incorporation of India into the Muslim economic sphere caused an efflorescence, not a dark age. Volume II argues that from the twelfth century Central Asian frontier ways of life and technologies were fused by the Delhi sultanates with South Asian village folkways.

Glossary

Akhbari: Literalist school of Twelver Shi`ism that held that the sayings of the Prophet and the Imams (Ali and his eleven descendants), taken at face value, could solve all legal problems.

antipope: Bishop elected pope in opposition to a seated pope.

da`i: An Ismaili term for a secret missionary dedicated to spreading the movement. The term could also mean "leader."

Franks: Common Middle Eastern name for European invaders.

Gothic: Name later applied to new form of church architecture originating in northern France during the early twelfth century.

iqta`: A grant of land to a high state official or military officer, the taxes from which were used to back-stop his salary from the state.

Ismaili: Followers of Muslim leaders descended from Isma`il, the son of the sixth Shi`ite Imam, who in turn was descended from the Prophet Muhammad. An esoteric branch of Shi`ite Islam.

Magna Carta: The "Great Charter": guarantee of rights granted to English and Norman barons by King John in 1215.

qadis: Muslim court judges who rule in accordance with Islamic law.

Reconquista: Spanish for "Reconquest": drive by Iberia's northern Christian kingdoms to drive Muslim kingdoms from southern Iberia.

Sawad: Fertile region south of Baghdad in what is now Iraq.

Shafi`i: School of Sunni Muslim law, generally viewed as rationalist in orientation.

shariah: Muslim religious law.

Sufism: Mystical form of Islam that emphasizes pious emotions, mild self-denial, mystical experiences, and learning from a great mystic master.

ulama: Seminary-trained Muslim learned men.

Usuli: Rationalist school of Twelver Shi`ite law. Requires laity to obey the religious rulings of the clerics.

11 Paradoxes of plenty: Central and Eastern Eurasia

China	
755	An Lushan rebellion nearly destroys Tang empire.
868	Publication of Buddhist sutra, world's oldest extant printed book.
904	Discovery of gunpowder by Chinese.
907–1125	Liao dynasty.
907	End of Tang dynasty.
960	Zhao Kuangyin founds Song dynasty.
960–1126	Northern Song dynasty.
1004	Wang Dan signs peace treaty with Liao.
1038–1227	Xi Xia kingdom.
1068	Debate over Song fiscal crisis initiates major reforms led by Wang Anshi.
1125–1234	Jin dynasty.
1127–1276	Southern Song dynasty.
1141	Song peace treaty with Jin.
1280	Gunpowder used in bronze mortars by Chinese.

Japan and Korea	
784	Construction begins of capital city of Kyoto.
794–1185	Heian period.
794–864	Ennin, a Japanese Buddhist priest, travels to China (838–47).
894	Japanese send last tribute mission to China.
918–1392	Goryeo (Koryo) kingdom of Korea.
1002	*The Pillow Book*, by Sei Shonagon.
c. 1020	*The Tale of Genji*, by Lady Murasaki Shikibu.
1180	Full-scale Battles of Taira and Minamoto.
1185–1333	Kamakura period.
1185	Minamoto Yoritomo defeats and annihilates Taira clan.

Central Eurasia and the Middle East	
867–86	Emperor Basil I rebuilds Byzantine armies and expands empire.
963–1025	Basil II "the Bulgar slayer" expands Byzantine empire to northeast.
1071	Seljuk Turks defeat Byzantines at Battle of Manzikert.
1204	Normans plunder Constantinople.
Russia	
980–1263	Kievan period.
980	Vladimir said to have brought Norsemen from Scandinavia to establish capital of Rus at Kiev.
988	Vladimir converts to Christianity; has new Russian alphabet designed.

We like to say, "You can't take it with you," but Master Zhao, a wealthy Chinese merchant and landowner who died in 1099 CE, disagreed. He had a lavish tomb built for his wife and himself near the Yellow River, which was a close imitation of his own house. It had two sitting rooms, two halls, and a main dining room, built with elaborate wooden roof beams, imitation windows and drapes, and portraits of Master Zhao and his wife with four servants waiting on them.

Like so many wealthy merchant-landlords, Master Zhao liked to travel in style. Even when he moved from this world to the next, he brought his possessions with him. To survive in the afterlife, the Zhaos brought with them pictures of money, wine, grain, and musicians, and just to be sure, contracts proving their title to the tomb's plot. It cost 99,999 strings of copper cash. The Zhaos knew that, even after death, spirits acted like officials: they respected documents and money.

One detail reveals an important fact about the Zhaos: they could not read very well. The characters on the Chinese painting on the wall are only scribbled gibberish; the writing in the tomb that we can read is a label on a bag of grain, with Master Zhao's name. He cared little for literary arts, but he was a good businessman. The highly educated officials of the Song dynasty regarded people like him as "leeches" who corrupted society with bribery and luxury. On the other hand, without upstarts like Master Zhao, the Song rulers would have had no revenue to support their state.

For Central and Eastern Eurasia, this period is full of paradoxes. China failed to restore the grand imperial dreams of the Tang dynasty, though not for lack of trying. For nearly half a millennium, from the great rebellions of 755 to the Mongol conquests of the 1200s, multiple regimes contended for power in China, and none dominated the entire region. From the orthodox Chinese point of view, it was a time of military failure and frustration. Yet China flourished as a commercial and cultural center as never before. The core values of Confucian orthodoxy re-established themselves, new agricultural technology supported a much larger population, cities grew dynamically along with trade, and Chinese moved south, on land and across the seas. Peace proved more profitable than military conquest.

In Central Eurasia, likewise, no single empire rivaled the power of Turks and Tibetans, but many nomadic empires founded cities, and even shifted from horseriding to settled urban life. They adopted new religions like Judaism and Manichaeanism to mark themselves off from their settled neighbors. They, too, were militarily more modest, but commercially and culturally innovative.

The old doctrines of Confucianism, Islam, and Buddhism penetrated their societies more deeply, and Orthodox Christianity expanded from the Byzantine empire northward into Russia. There was less mingling, jostling, and mixing, and more efforts to "purify" the old traditions to resist their rivals.

Two new states entered the arena. The Viking **Rus** created a trading warrior state along the rivers of Russia, centered in Kiev, and the Seljuk Turks penetrated the Middle East, decisively defeating the Byzantine empire. They set the stage for the rise of the Ottomans, who would dominate the Middle East from 1300 to 1914.

China's innovations in agricultural, commercial, and military technology made it the richest society in the world, but these advances diffused across the empire's borders, allowing neighboring states to grow as well. Korea, Japan, Manchuria, and Southeast Asia all benefited from China's new wealth. The old Silk Road had more difficulty in continued operations during times of warfare between the regional states, and it was challenged by new maritime routes, created by the great Chinese, Indian, and Arab expansion into the southern seas. Many powers reoriented themselves toward the south, where they found new land, new products, new neighbors, and new trading partners.

In sum, new balances of commercial and coercive power characterized this period: instead of huge imperial conquests, medium-sized states interacted with each other, and extensive maritime and monetized commerce and urban production complemented agrarian production and nomadic tribute trade.

Master Zhao's life and death illustrate the important developments of these three centuries in Central and Eastern Eurasia:

- Merchants gained a great deal of money and bought themselves cultural status, while officials and scholars resented them.
- Military conquerors from less commercialized Northeast Asia took over much of China, drastically separating the societies of north and south. In Western Eurasia, two new warrior bands, the Viking Rus and the Seljuk Turks, linked old commercial centers in fragile states.
- Cities grew everywhere, even in nomadic regions.
- Along with urban life, religious doctrines spread further into social life, attracting large masses of believers.
- China's powerful commercial networks shifted south, making an impact throughout the coastal regions and Southeast Asia.

11.1 THE LATE TANG AND SONG DYNASTIES

Although it still had one nominal emperor, China had in fact been divided since the An Lushan rebellion of 755. Provincial governors turned themselves into powerful military clans that controlled large regions. The end of the last Tang emperor's reign in 907 produced a short interlude of fighting among these military clans, until the most powerful general, **Zhao Kuangyin**, defeated his rivals and established the Song dynasty, with its capital at his home base in **Kaifeng** in North China.

Unlike the Tang, the rulers of the Northern Song (960–1126) and Southern Song (1127–1276) never penetrated Manchuria, Mongolia, northwest China, or Turkestan, and never even drove out their rivals from North China. Although orthodox historians considered only the Song to be a legitimate dynasty, several equally powerful states had parceled out Chinese territory. The Song had the largest, most expensive, and most

technologically advanced military forces in the world, but they could not defeat the nomads of the north. Even though 83 percent of the government budget of the richest state in the world went to the military, the much poorer states of Manchuria and Mongolia held their own in major battles. In 1004, after several costly defeats in trying to recapture Beijing, the Song prime minister Wang Dan signed the first of several peace treaties with the enemy Liao state in Manchuria, agreeing to pay the Liao rulers 100,000 ounces of silver and 200,000 bolts of cloth per year. Map 11.1 shows the border between the Song and Liao empires.

Why did the Song Fail to Drive out the Liao?

Was the peace treaty a costly delusion? These questions provoked intense debates at the time, and they still do now. The relative weakness of the Song military against its foes is an instructive example of the limits of wealth and technology. The Song army was a bureaucracy, in which officers received salaries and ranks according to merit, but merit often meant good administration, not victory in battle. The nomad armies had much looser organizations, but more intense loyalties among their fighting men, and devoted their entire society to warfare. The well-paid Song soldiers served for money, not for life and death.

We should not, however, blame military defeat on the army alone. The Song army was a professional one, where officers stuck to their jobs as military men, and did not intervene in politics. As Song China prospered commercially, and civil officials came to dominate over generals, the role of the military shrank. Recovering some lost territory seemed to many officials less important than reducing the loss of life and money in endless battles. The emperors, too, no longer made war their essential mission.

Zhao Kuangyin distrusted his rivals, so he gave them generous pensions and excluded them from power. He invited the leading generals to a banquet, and told them: "Why don't all of you relinquish your military authority, leave the court, and serve as prominent military governors. You could select a convenient and good piece of land and a mansion ... and establish a permanent inalienable estate. You could get many singers and dancing girls, drink daily, and enjoy their company to the end of your natural life." He promised them marriages into the imperial family, as long as they stayed out of politics. Later emperors gained more fame as painters and calligraphers than as military leaders.

Finally, technology transfer explains Song failures. Even though the Chinese army developed the military arts to a high degree, creating the first effective gunpowder weaponry, and

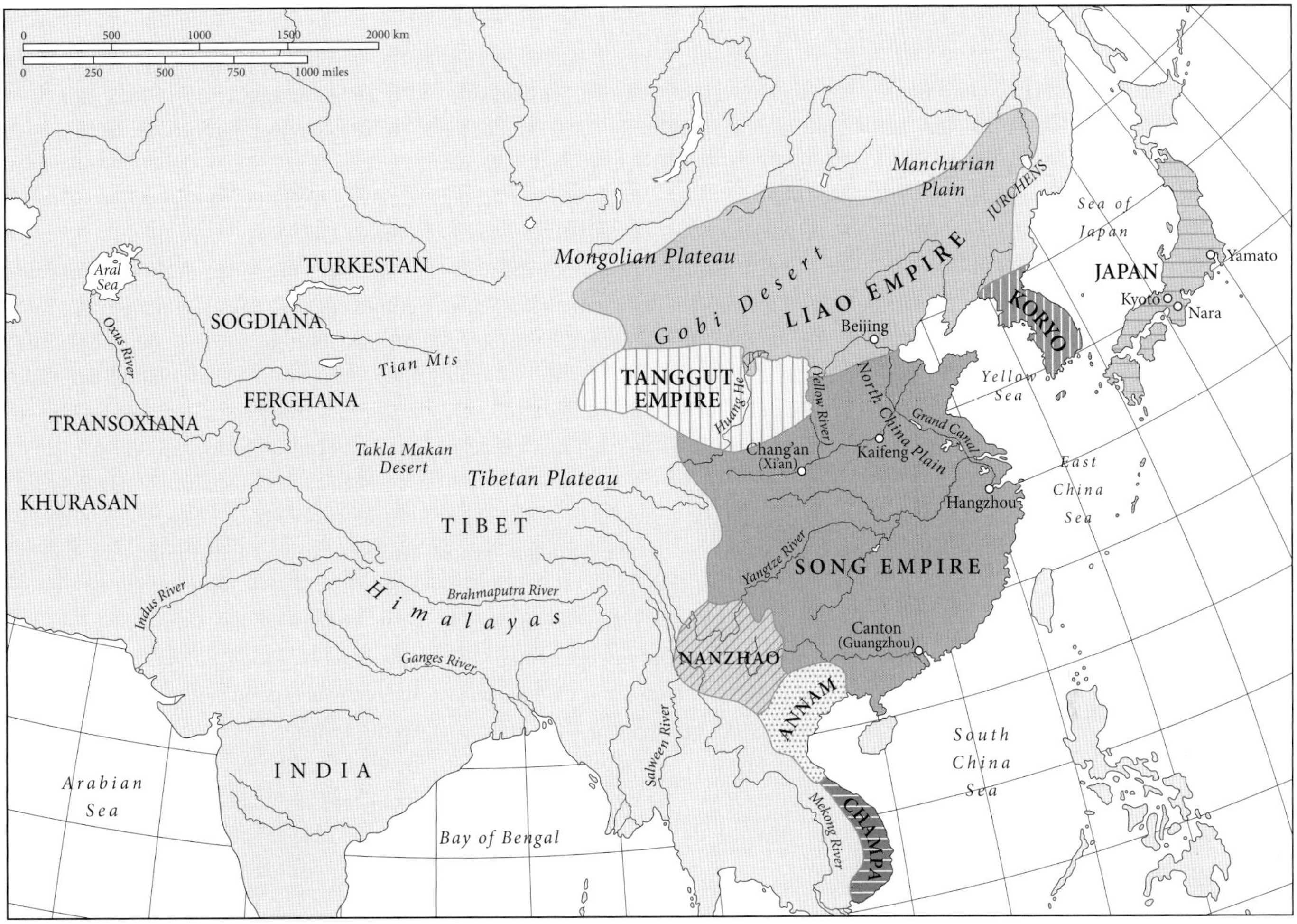

Map 11.1 Liao and Song empires

separate divisions specializing in flame throwers, sapping, catapults, and incendiaries, their rivals quickly learned from them. (Box 11.1 describes the Chinese discoveries of gunpowder technology.) The Liao picked up gunpowder technology from the Song and passed it to their successors the Jin, who in turn could not prevent it from leaking to the Mongols.

In sum, civilian arts and technological transfer limited the superiority of the wealthy Song military over its foes. But ultimately, silver payments were a low price to pay for peace, or so many thought. At the cost of the tax revenues of a single prefecture, or only 1 to 2 percent of the total annual revenue, the Song could avoid the much higher price of a major war. The peace party had good arguments in its favor.

Later historians unfairly accused Song officials of making humiliating bargains with barbarians for corrupt motives, comparing the Song military record with the glories of the Han and Tang. They neglected the fact that the Song's neighbors were much stronger than the earlier nomads, mainly because they had strengthened their military and government institutions with Chinese techniques.

How to Pay for the War? Wang Anshi's Answer

The foreign policy issues, however, had domestic implications. In order to provide the monetary payments demanded by the peace treaty, the Song state had to raise its tax revenue, which meant standardizing the currency. Chinese in different regions used many types of coin, made of copper, iron, lead, and even cowrie shells. The Song created a standard round copper coin with a square hole and a unit called a "string of cash," defined as one thousand coins held together by a string. It multiplied the minting of coins to 6 million strings per year, and reduced the copper content in each new coin. The state thought it had discovered a money machine. But consumers of coin had their defenses. They melted down the old valuable coins for their metal, while the new ones lost value. As always happens, bad money drove out the good, and inflation set in. The later invention of paper currency made things even worse. So creative financial engineering by the government in the end only weakened its economic position.

By 1068, two camps of officials lined up in a great debate over how to solve the fiscal crisis. They faced the same problems, with

Box 11.1 Gunpowder, or Why Secrets are Hard to Keep

The Chinese discovered gunpowder, mankind's deadliest weapon before the atom bomb, while searching for the secret of eternal life. The key element in gunpowder is saltpeter, or potassium nitrate. A manual for Daoist alchemists published in the ninth century CE warned them not to mix charcoal, saltpeter, and sulfur, because it would blow up in their face. By 1000 CE, military chemists had learned how to make simple bombs and grenades with this "fire medicine." The fierce wars of the eleventh century stimulated further advances. Raising the proportion of nitrate increased explosive power, allowing attackers to knock down city walls. But stronger explosives needed stronger containers. Chinese found their model in nature, in the hollow bamboo stalk. Bamboo tubes provided the first flame throwers, rocket launchers, and portable guns in the world. Chinese skilled in bronze and iron casting made the first metal gun barrels, which probably appeared around 1280 CE. The Mongols on horseback at first had no use for such heavy weapons, but when they besieged Chinese cities, they soon discovered the value of gunpowder artillery. Chinese military manuals have many pictures of "bombards," a rounded vase with a narrow neck used to launch projectiles. The English bombard of 1327, the first gunpowder weapon in a Western source, follows the Chinese model.

Who brought the idea of gunpowder to Europe? Was it the Mongols, who bombarded Hungary in 1240, or did it come earlier? Could it have been one of the Franciscan friars who visited the khan's court? The idea is attractive, considering that the Jesuits later reintroduced European gunpowder technology to China. Or was it a companion of Rabban Sauma, the Chinese traveler to Europe, who met with the pope in Rome? Although it took a long time for China to develop gunpowder technology into a serious military threat – nearly five centuries – their secret got out soon, with destructive results everywhere.

Still, let's not forget the positive uses of gunpowder. Chinese launched the first rockets, although they could not ride them into space. They blasted rock for irrigation canals and mines, and they made beautiful fireworks. Finally, note the very different effects of gunpowder on the two ends of Eurasia. Gunpowder weapons knocked the European knight out of his ruling position; China, however, which did not want horsemen to rule, simply added gunpowder units to its huge bureaucratic army. By the seventeenth century, the Chinese had fallen far beyond the Europeans, and the Japanese had given up the gun entirely. New technologies have vast consequences, but they do not dictate simple results.

the same ideas, as during the Salt and Iron debates of the Han dynasty (see Chapter 5). The leaders of the two factions were **Sima Guang** (1019–86), a renowned historian and proponent of gradual reform, and **Wang Anshi** (1021–86), the prime minister whose radical new proposals dominated discussion until his death. Wang's arguments joined philosophical and political ideals into a powerful project. Wang claimed that China had degenerated from the ideals of the classical age of Confucius, which had created a coherent order uniting moral and political goals. Now, only drastic changes could save the government from military defeat and moral decay. Although he called for a return to the past, he knew a great deal about the opportunities offered by the booming commercial economy, and wanted the government to extract its revenue from trade rather than the traditional source of income, the land. Wang put all bureaucrats on cash salaries, established a new branch of government, the Tea and Horse Agency, run by merchants, to make profits on selling Chinese tea for Tibetan horses, and initiated the Green Sprouts program to give loans to poor peasants, as well as evernormal granaries to buy and sell grain on the market to maintain level prices. His new officials were bureaucratic entrepreneurs, given the mission to expand government power and wealth by intervening actively in the economy. On the local level, Wang enforced the **baojia** system of collective responsibility for crimes and military service by households organized in groups of tens and hundreds. This way, he hoped to unite peasant and soldier, and put everyone on an equal level. Wang thought that the government could stimulate economic growth, reduce the disparity between rich and poor, and generate revenue for frontier defense, all at the same time, and he found justification for his program in the Confucian classics, as interpreted by him. He purged anyone who objected that such Utopian visions would only cause disruption, and he set up a large network of local schools to make sure that students learned only his interpretation of the classic texts.

Sima Guang Points out Wang Anshi's Faults

Reality, unfortunately, did not conform to Wang's and his followers' expectations. Officials used the Green Sprout loans to charge the peasants high interest, leaving them no better off than when they depended on usury from private moneylenders. They fell even further into debt. The Tea and Horse Agency did not generate profits, as the canny nomads and Central Asian traders outsmarted Chinese officials who did not know their horseflesh. The burdens of the baojia system only forced farmers to flee the land and military service. Sima Guang, Wang's greatest critic, rightly charged that peasants had too few coins to pay back loans; he preferred an unmonetized, stable agrarian economy to a risky commercial one. Sima Guang did not see a need for radical changes: he approved of the existing order, believed that hierarchy was natural, and thought that rich people could usefully serve the state. At the same time, in his great universal history, the *Comprehensive Mirror*, he criticized irresponsible rulers of the past who ignored the sage advice of their ministers. Sima Guang opposed arbitrary, autocratic power, but he defended the political role of the literati, or **shi** class, as historically informed guides to practical, gradual change.

At Wang's death, the emperor, helped by Sima Guang, abolished his policies, but in 1101 the next emperor started them up again. These policy zigzags only exacerbated factional conflict, which grew increasingly vicious until the Northern Song fell in 1126. Wang and his followers received the blame for causing the upheavals that brought down the dynasty, but did they deserve it? They had tried to alter state policy from the top down to respond to urgent imperatives of national security and take advantage of commercial growth: were these simply good ideas too soon and too fast? Their opponents called for slower change, but they worshipped a backward-looking agrarian ideal, just as out of touch with the times. No dynasty ever tried such a drastic reform program again, until the mid nineteenth century, but the dilemma of choosing between ambitious, large-scale programs and small-scale, slower reforms has constantly recurred throughout imperial and modern Chinese history.

11.2 THE NON-CHINESE REGIMES: LIAO, JIN, AND XI XIA

Peace, however, also depended on the reactions of the Song's enemies, the highly militarized states of the north. The Khitan tribes of Mongolia and Manchuria were horseriding nomads, like their predecessors the Xiongnu and the Turks. Just as the Tang dynasty fell, **Abaoji** (r. 907–26) united them in a single state, which took the name Liao, from the Manchurian river in their homeland. Over the next two centuries, the Liao expanded their territory over all of modern Manchuria and most of Mongolia, and they took sixteen prefectures in North China. The Liao had five capitals, moving their court from one to another, and Beijing was one of them. (Although the name "Beijing" means "northern capital" to the Chinese, it began as the southernmost capital of the Liao nomadic state.)

The Liao, much more successfully than the Turks, combined Chinese and nomadic techniques to ensure stable rule. By the terms of the 1004 peace treaty, they obtained large payments of cloth and silver, and the right to address the Song emperors as brothers on equal terms. The Song had, in effect, accepted that China was only one among other equal powers in a multi-state system, a recognition that no Chinese ruler had made since the end of the Warring States period in 221 BCE. The Liao used Chinese for diplomatic correspondence, but created their own written language, with distinct Chinese characters, for internal administration. Most of these characters are indecipherable today, so we know much less about the Liao than about Song society. But we know that the Liao created a dual administration to join the nomadic and settled elements of their state. In the north, officials gained posts through family connections and spoke only Khitan. While in the south, they often had to pass exams and learn Chinese. Taxes in the north came from nomad herds and war booty; in the south from the same fiscal system used by the Tang. The capital cities followed Chinese models, but each did not have a separate palace, and they included Buddhist, Daoist, Shamanic, and Confucian temples whose ceremonial rituals had equal rank. Women, especially empresses and mothers of emperors, had much higher status in the Liao than they did in the Song, and they even conducted military campaigns.

Song–Liao relations remained stable until the rise of another nomadic power, the Xi Xia kingdom of the Tangut people, created by another powerful military ruler in 1038. He, too, asserted equal status with the Song emperor, created his own script, and tried to extort money with a peace treaty from the Song. But the Khitans invaded Xi Xia, initiating a complex three-way competitive state system. In southern Manchuria, on the Liaoning peninsula, in the twelfth century, the Jurchen leader **Aguda** (r. 1113–23) created a fourth state. The Jurchens, however, were forest people: hunters, fishers, and farmers, not nomads. They rejected Liao domination, fought off Liao armies, and declared a new dynasty, the Jin, in 1115. Soon they took the Liao heartland, forcing the Liao to flee to Central Asia, but they took over the Liao dual administration, the Khitan script, and the Chinese officials serving the Khitan. Map 11.2 shows the expanded territory of the Jin dynasty.

The Jin moved even further into Chinese territory, and further toward using Chinese practices for their own benefit. Their armies drove the Song out of Kaifeng and south of the Yellow River, took the emperor and his son prisoner, and extracted higher indemnities for peace: 300,000 ounces of silver, one million strings of copper coins, and 300,000 bolts of silk per year, plus a one-time payment of 180 times the annual rate. The Jin rightly claimed superiority, not equality with the Song: the Jurchen rulers were now uncles and the Song only

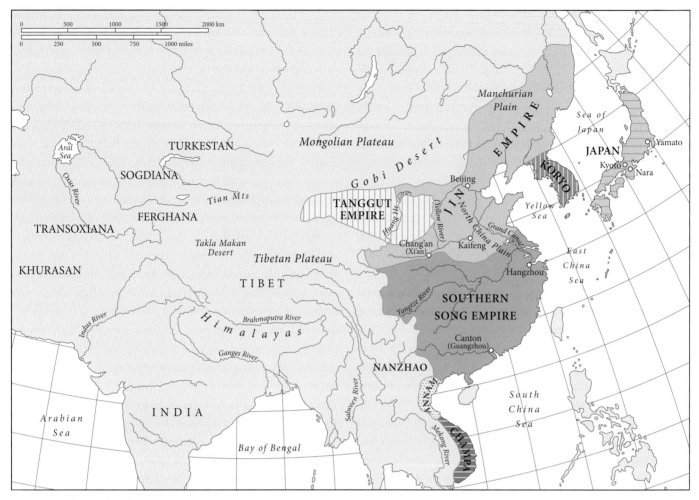

Map 11.2 Jin and Southern Song

nephews. This peace treaty of 1141 meant true humiliation. Now the Song peace policy did not look like such a good idea, but the Chinese had little choice.

The Jin ruled North China from 1141 until the Mongols destroyed them in 1234. After the brutal conquest, however, many of the Jurchens settled down, learned Chinese, drank tea, and promoted scholarship. Others attacked these acculturated Jurchens for blindly copying Chinese ways and betraying steppe traditions. Unlike the Liao, the Jurchens, immersed in a vast Chinese multitude, had difficulty keeping their dual administration balanced. The emperors themselves were ambivalent. They forbade their people from wearing Chinese clothing or taking Chinese names, but they themselves studied the classics, and could not stop the Jurchen language from dying out. Nearly all books written in the Jurchen language, using the Khitan script, were translations from Chinese. The Chinese civil exams expanded their recruitment in the north just as in the south, and the emperors sponsored readings of texts supporting filial piety.

The northern dynasties successfully conquered and maintained legitimate rule over their territories for many centuries. Therefore, we should not view them as alien barbarians ruling over disgruntled Han Chinese. Few Chinese even saw much of their northern rulers, and almost none of them rose up against them. The northern dynasties did cause destruction by their many wars, and they made a number of Chinese into slaves, but in peacetime, they left the basic elements of Chinese society alone. At the top level of government, they certainly reduced the power of the Confucian scholar-official elite, leaving them without policy roles, but many of these literati redirected their passions toward cultural activities, continuing to produce scholarship, poetry, and art. In fact, as mentioned earlier, the northern emperors employed them by launching projects to translate the Chinese classic works into Tangut, Khitan, and Jurchen.

North and South China diverged radically during this period of division. Each region developed related cultural elements in different directions. In some ways, northern political traditions were less autocratic than those inherited from the Qin and Han. The emperors had to consult with the important nobles on major policies, and they met in councils with them where votes were taken. Local administration was quite flexible, not to say chaotic, giving a great deal of autonomy to provincial officials. There is no basis for saying, as many Chinese do, that the northern barbarians destroyed "natural" Chinese tendencies toward peace, prosperity, and democracy. As we shall see, under the Song in the south, the Chinese were wealthy, but they had their own problems.

11.3 THE SOUTHERN SONG, 1127–1276: PRESERVING CULTURE

Let us now turn to the densely populated south, which generated the elements that formed the core of later Chinese civilization. While Central Asian nomads and warriors took over the north, the Han Chinese dynasties of Northern and Southern Song retreated and transformed their government and society. The primary social trend was the rise of a new class of educated, literate men, who called themselves *shi*, or literati. They had studied intensively the Confucian classics, and now most of them gained recognition in official service by passing a series of difficult examinations, which gave them degrees recognizing their abilities in literary study. This was not a really meritocratic system: in the eleventh century, they all came from a small group of about one hundred families, who had carried on official and scholarly service since the late Tang. The **yin**, or shadow privilege, allowed them to pass on their achievements to their sons, who could then skip several stages in the exam system.

These bureaucratic elites defined themselves as guardians of **wen**, a comprehensive term meaning "culture," "civilization," "literature," and especially, civilian as opposed to military (**wu**) achievement. They praised the poets, the scholars, the bureaucrats, and the peasants who supported them, but not the warriors, the merchants, or their rival Buddhist or Daoist monks. Note that although *wen* did mean "civilization," it did not also mean, as it does in Western languages, "urban," "city," or "citizen." Many of the elite were rural landlords, collecting rents from large estates to support themselves, and they glorified the simple peasant life, although they did not live it. Even if they lived in cities, there was no sharp barrier between city and country. These elites often moved back to their estates to mourn the death of relatives, or to retire from official life. Because they formed an elite class in the countryside who assisted local officials with government, we often call them "gentry," referring to somewhat similar roles of nobles in early modern England. Like the English gentry, they could influence legal cases, provide charitable aid, and keep order by supervising local police forces. Unlike the English, they did not hunt foxes, build large country estates, or serve in Parliament.

The victory of this civilian class over the rough warriors who had dominated the government from the Tang through the tenth century strikingly illustrates the power of ideas, when backed by elite interests in political influence, over brute force. Zhao Kuangyin, the Song founder, had his own reasons for pensioning off his generals and keeping them out of power. He also wanted to portray himself as a patron of culture, so he promoted "civil" (*wen*) methods of rule over the "military" (*wu*) culture. Later emperors also sponsored vast compilation projects to promote civil rule. For example, they published a huge collection, in 1,000 chapters, of the fiscal and administrative precedents of the previous dynasties. The elite, who saw themselves as preserving "this culture of ours," happily joined this endeavor to unify the empire under joint imperial and bureaucratic rule.

11.4 THE LITERATI DEBATE THE MEANING OF CULTURE (*WEN*)

The honeymoon, however, did not last long. By the eleventh century, different groups broke into factions, arguing, as academics always do, over fine points of textual interpretation and major questions of morality and philosophy. Could you become a "superior man" (**junzi**), Confucius' ideal person, only by reading philosophy, or did you need government experience? In examinations, should elegant poetic writing be the real test of merit, or should it be the ability to discuss contemporary political issues? If the government was corrupt, should the moral person engage in dirty politics to reform it, or withdraw into a private sphere? Did the government need radical change, or only gradual reform? Should officials respond to the commercial economy and profit from it, or restore the ideal agrarian society of the classics? As we have seen, these debates came to a head in the intense politicking surrounding Wang Anshi's new policies, and ended with the Song loss of North China to the Jin.

After the loss of the north, intense debate continued over whether to increase military spending to recover the lost territory, or buy peace from the Jin. Just as in the Northern Song, the prime minister, Qin Gui, decided for peace, signing a treaty with the Jin in 1141. One recalcitrant general, **Yue Fei**, argued strongly for an aggressive military campaign, but he was purged and executed. Later historians castigated the pragmatic Qin Gui for treason, and exalted Yue Fei for "loyalty" to the lost cause. But the treaty did preserve the Song dynasty for nearly one hundred years in the face of overwhelming military superiority.

Zhu Xi Promotes Personal Moral Cultivation

Once the dynasty moved to the south, most of the *shi* reoriented themselves toward local affairs. Now it seemed that engagement in national politics had only produced chaos, division, and defeat.

They still wanted to change the world, but perhaps they could make more of a difference in their communities, as teachers and scholars, than at court. **Zhu Xi** (1130–1200), the greatest of the Southern Song philosophers, provided a synthesis of classical traditions that justified and inspired the *shi* with this new mission. Calling his philosophy **daoxue**, the "study of the Way," he raised private funds to set up his own academy to teach his doctrines. He argued that the true Way of Confucius had been lost for centuries, mired in political controversy and polluted by the insidious doctrines of Daoists and Buddhists, but he and his followers had recovered the basic teachings of Chinese civilization by reinterpreting the old texts. In Zhu Xi's view, Confucius' primary teaching had been the moral education of the individual, not the effort to get into office by passing exams. This moral education did not mean just soul searching and meditation, but intensive study of history, ritual, philosophy, and the natural world (the "investigation of things"). His goal was to discover **li**, the basic, universal principles that organized all the **qi**, or material stuff of the world. Once a person truly understood the proper moral Way, he could extend his influence to change first his family, then his community, then the state, and finally, bring peace to the entire world.

Zhu Xi based his vision on four texts: the Confucian *Analects*, Mencius, the *Doctrine of the Mean*, and the *Great Learning*. These four books became the primary texts tested in the examination system after Zhu Xi's death. Zhu Xi had stripped Confucian doctrines down to essentials, absorbing the appealing focus on individual self-cultivation promoted by Buddhists and Daoists, but without the need to withdraw from the human world. As a supreme synthesizer, he did for Confucian teaching what Thomas Aquinas (d. 1274) did for Christianity. While serving as a local official, Zhu Xi also aimed to improve the common people's lives with schemes, such as the charitable granaries, set up by local elite families to give loans to poor farmers who suffered from famine. A follower of Zhu Xi could do good for his community, study books for a living, and keep his respected local position, while hoping to avoid the nasty vicissitudes of political life. Zhu Xi was not a major figure during his own lifetime, and he even had many enemies, but his school of thought, called Neo-Confucianism, embedded in examination system, became the dominant intellectual force under all the dynasties after the Song. Neo-Confucian teachings became the vehicle by which the *shi* carried on the *wen* which they saw as the essence of Chinese civilization.

11.5 CHINA'S ECONOMIC REVOLUTION

"[Even if] the state is destroyed, the mountains and rivers endure." So the poet Du Fu summed up China's desperate state after the rebellions of the mid eighth century. He saw that the basic productive resources of China – her fields, rivers, mountains, and forests – held tremendous potential regardless of military victory or defeat. Over the long run, during the centuries from about 900 to 1300, China grew to become the world's largest and most dynamic economic power. Even though this happened slowly, the changes are dramatic enough to be called an economic revolution. Map 11.3 shows the major economic centers of Song China.

Why Did Population Grow?

Let's begin with the people, the ultimate productive power. The limited output of dry-field agriculture in the north had held China's population stable at about 50 million for one millennium until the Song breakthrough. China's population then grew to at least 100 million in the Song. Nearly all of this population growth took place in South China, which more than doubled in size, and especially in the lower Yangtze Delta (Jiangnan) and southeast coast, which multiplied by a factor of six. Migration of refugees fleeing the northern wars started the growth, but it needed an agricultural revolution to sustain it. The greater labor supply meant that peasants could be put to work draining marshes, leveling hills, and planting rice in paddies, under the sponsorship of landlords, monasteries, and officials. Centuries of backbreaking labor by peasant farmers built the beautiful green rice fields we now see. The lower Yangtze Delta and Chinese coast used to be nothing but malaria-infested marshes, but when turned into paddy fields they became the most productive agricultural lands in the world.

The agricultural revolution depended on foreign trade, and supported urbanization. To exploit fully the potential of these fields, Chinese peasants needed new seeds, which they obtained from the Hindu state of **Champa**, in southern Vietnam. Imported on the maritime trade routes, the Champa rice seedlings sprouted early, allowing farmers to plant a second rice crop, thus nearly doubling annual yields. Emperors and officials helped distribute information about new crops by giving tax incentives and publishing manuals of agricultural instruction. The northern Song capital of Kaifeng, which was closer to the south than Tang Chang'an, relied on rice shipments from the south to support its large population. Other crops like silk, hemp, and tea also spread through the deltas, stimulating trade and agricultural processing industries. The large cities of Hangzhou, Wenzhou, Fuzhou, and Quanzhou grew because they were supported both by the rich agricultural hinterland and maritime trade. A map of economic activity in the Song, with its large concentrations of wealth along the coast, looks remarkably similar to the geographic distribution of wealth in China today.

Map 11.3 Economic centers of Song China

Why Chinese Cities Grew So Large

The urban revolution in turn depended on a revolution in transportation and merchant practice. In the Tang, urban people lived in closed wards within the city walls, which were locked at night to prevent theft. In the Song, the cities never slept. Urbanites either tore down the walls or spilled outside the old walls, creating lively, bustling quarters of incessant activity. Merchants formed their own commercial associations to regulate trade, and craftsmen set up guilds to initiate apprentices and worship their own gods. Boats of all shapes and sizes moved up and down the Yangtze River and its tributaries, and sailed down along the coast and into Southeast Asia. Even in the late seventh century one writer had exclaimed: "Great ships in thousands and tens of thousands carry goods back and forth. If they lay unused for a single moment, ten thousand merchants would be bankrupted."

Box 11.2 Big Cities, Little Cities: The Development of Urban Systems

Hangzhou, in South China, was the largest city in the world. It drew crowds of people to it to trade in its markets, and it sent products out in all directions. Constantinople, the largest city in the West, also drew in merchants, pilgrims, and warriors who wanted its riches. But the world had seen large cities before. The great cities of the past, however, had been primarily imperial cities, centered on military and bureaucratic demands. Hangzhou and Constantinople had plenty of soldiers and officials, but in addition a much bigger urban society grew up around them. Even more important, these cities linked with a series of other cities around them, forming urban systems tied by active trading networks.

Each of the regional cities had its own specialties, determined by its location and skills. For example, Quanzhou (Zayton),

on China's southeastern coast, drew in the seafarers of Southeast Asia and the Indian Ocean. Kiev performed a similar function for Constantinople: It provided the route by which the riches of the south could percolate northward along the Russian rivers, and it brought down furs, honey, and wax from the forests. Nomads from the East also brought horses, furs, and sheep into the great markets. Even further north, Novgorod offered the main gateway to the far north, the source of the most valuable furs. Here, too, traders of many lands gathered to collect the forest products and ship them south.

Russia's infant urban network, tied together by the princes of Rus, spanned huge distances and many cultural traditions. The Kievan "state" was mostly a network of traders who connected small

princely kingdoms together. It built the backbone of Russia's urban structure, spreading from the wealth of Byzantium in the south to the Baltic fish and Siberian furs in the north.

Unlike Russia, North and South China were sharply divided by the wars between the Song and the Liao and Jin rulers. China already had large cities in the north, which the nomadic conquerors took over; now South China developed the great urban concentrations that made it the wealthiest part of the empire. Great cities do not grow by themselves. They need other cities to provide the resources of money, people, and goods that make them dominate. Intricate urban networks developed in both Western and Eastern Eurasia in this period that defined new economic regions with long-lasting effects.

By the tenth century, another writer stated: "Most of the empire's profits from trade depend on the use of boats." Business partnerships allowed investors to pool their capital and share risks; brokers took care of the distribution and sale of goods, managed inventory, and delivered orders. The Italian and Middle Eastern traders of the high Middle Ages in **Constantinople**, the capital of the Byzantine empire, would have felt perfectly at home in Hangzhou. Marco Polo was very impressed by the city, but he was only one of many visitors. (Box 11.2 describes the major urban systems of the world at this time.)

Hangzhou indeed grew to be the largest and richest city in the world, with a population of over one million, when no city in Europe except Constantinople had more than a few tens of thousands. The emperor and his officials at first invested little in the place when they fled there for protection. They hoped to reconquer the north quickly after staying only a short time in this "temporary capital." But the commercial population, attracted by government and private demand, soon flooded the capital, spilling beyond the city walls in all directions. Even the officials and scholars appreciated the cooling waters of Hangzhou's great artificial lake and its green mountain scenery. A great imperial thoroughfare, sixty yards wide and three miles long, cut through the city from north to south. Chinese sources, filled with detail on daily life, confirm Marco Polo's vivid account. Ten great markets

supplied the insatiable demand for rice, pork, fish, and regional delicacies; teahouses, wine shops, and brothels served every conceivable taste. Water provided cheap transportation for large and small boats on hundreds of canals, and sanitation channels. The "honey bucket" brigades carried human manure out of the city to use as fertilizer in the rice paddies.

Let us not, however, praise urban culture at the cost of forgetting the poor. Not everyone was rich in Hangzhou: it also attracted beggars, prostitutes, refugees, and criminals. Hangzhou showed the world that urban settlements, in all their glory and squalor, could reach incredibly large sizes when founded on commercialized agriculture and cheap water transportation.

Why China Dominated the Seas

In foreign trade, China dominated the ocean from the eleventh century to the early fifteenth. Following the monsoon winds, huge junks moved into the southern seas. Great innovations in naval technology, like watertight compartments, the sternpost rudder, the maritime compass, and progress in cartography all came from these maritime traders. In the late twelfth century they appeared in Europe, transmitted from China by the Arabs. Arab traders also came to Chinese ports, where they established their own urban districts, ruled by their own laws. They

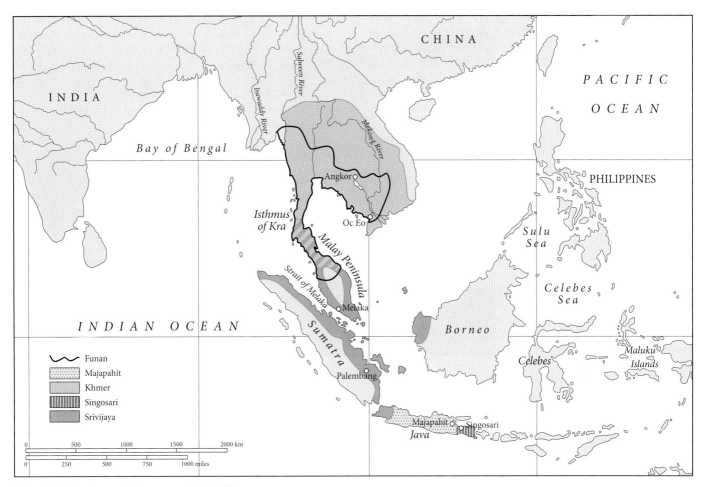

Map 11.4 Southeast Asian states, 500–1200

brought rich Chinese brocades to the prospering cities of the Mediterranean. Zayton (Arabic for Quanzhou) gave its name to the most popular silk yarn, *zaytuni*. Jewish traders with networks reaching from Tunis to India also brought Chinese silks to Islamic and Christian lands. The sea routes came to carry more goods than the old overland routes, but they were silk routes just the same.

Chinese ships moved into Southeast Asia in greater numbers than before, seeking rare products to buy and markets for their goods. Chinese commercial demand stimulated the formation of strong mercantile kingdoms throughout the islands. The **Srivijaya** maritime empire, centered around the Malacca Strait, had thrived since the seventh century on the trade that moved from China to India, delivering goods like fragrant woods and rhinoceros horn (used as a male sexual tonic) to the South China ports. Envoys sent golden bowls filled with pearls as gifts to the Song emperor to display their wealth.

Other Southeast Asian kingdoms also thrived on the China market. Chinese thought that the incense of the Malay peninsula was "something belonging to the immortal. Light one stick and the whole house is filled with a fragrant mist which is still there after

three days." The Vietnamese coast was especially rich. The **Dai Viet** state had succeeded in freeing itself from Tang domination in the ninth century, and held off Chinese threats of invasion by calling themselves "vassals" of the emperor, while remaining autonomous. Vietnam kept itself independent and profited greatly from the tribute trade missions with China. Meanwhile, the Cham state in southern Vietnam made its living by legal trade, smuggling, and preying on the merchant vessels which had to pass its coasts. Despite protests, China could not stop this piracy, but the trade still offered enough profit to be worthwhile. In the south as in the north, military weakness did not mean the end of commerce. Map 11.4 shows the relationship between China and Southeast Asian states, and Figure 11.1 shows the vast extent of the great temple city of Borobudur in Java, whose construction began in the ninth century under the influence of the Srivijayan empire.

Despite warfare, trade continued across the northern borders as well. The indemnities paid by treaty to the nomad states in silk supplied them with products to sell further west. Special plantations in West China provided just the kind of tea the nomads wanted, pressed into large bricks and exchanged for horses. Chinese also bought exotic goods as they had in the

Figure 11.1 The great temple complex at Borobudur in Java was begun in the ninth century CE, during a time of influence from the Indian Srivijaya empire. It mixed Hindu and Buddhist elements, but it includes over five hundred Buddhist statues. Its central dome, covering a stupa, contains seventy-two Buddhist statues. It is the largest Buddhist temple in the world.

Tang: carpets, swords, perfumes, ivory, and rare medicines. The relative weight of trade routes began to shift south to the maritime routes, but the overland routes remained active.

Where Did the Money Come From?

Finally, commercial growth demanded more money. Eager Confucians melted down Buddhist statues to supply copper. As we noted, the early Song minted large amounts of copper coin, but still could not meet demand. More taxes were collected in money, and everyone from peasant traders to wholesale merchants and urban consumers needed cash. But silver and gold were scarce, and copper supplies limited. Even so, copper coins flowed out of China to stimulate commerce in Japan and Southeast Asia. The only solution was a brilliant, and ominous, invention: paper money. The Tang had created "flying cash," allowing merchants to receive receipts for payments to one local government treasury and draw money from an office in another town. Soon, private deposit shops also stored money and honored checks presented on their customers' accounts. Then Song finance officials discovered that they could just print paper with the emperor's seal and make it worth the same value as strings of cash. This was true 'fiat money,' worth only what people believed it to be worth.

The magic money machine appealed to everyone. The state could increase its tax income at will, merchants could issue paper money to cover their debts, and everyone merrily wheeled and dealed – until the crash. Overissuing paper currency inevitably caused severe inflation and devaluation of the notes, until the state stepped in to control it. Song merchants learned by painful experience what any stock investor can find out for himself today.

New Inventions: Gunpowder and Printing

Industry also grew in the Song, stimulated by state demand. In the Northern Song, entrepreneurs managed thousands of men who excavated ore and built furnaces to supply arrowheads and uniforms to the army. This iron industry reached the stage of mass production, enough to supply a standing army of 1.25 million men. Gunpowder, first discovered in 904, used as a propellant in 1132, in catapult grenades in 1161, and in bronze mortars in 1280, became a widespread weapon during the Song wars, stimulating chemical industries and metal casting. Thirteenth-century Buddhist cave paintings contain the world's first portrait of a gun, in the hands of a demon. There is no truth to the myth that the Chinese only used gunpowder for fireworks; they developed all of its military potential, but their enemies learned it equally fast. Europeans called saltpeter, the essential chemical in gunpowder, "Chinese snow."

Printing also became a mass production industry under the Song. World historians still have to struggle to convince many Westerners that Gutenberg's Bible was not the world's first printed book: printing with woodblocks had begun in the Tang dynasty and reached large urban markets in the Song. The world's oldest extant printed book is a Buddhist sutra dating to 868 CE. A printed calendar from 877 advised farmers about the right dates to plant seeds, and when to get married. Printed books met the needs of scholars who cribbed for exams, doctors collecting information about herbs and drugs, officials looking for practical advice and legal precedents, and general readers who wanted good stories and fresh news. Storytellers had set up booths on city street corners to attract audiences with tales of heroic warriors, lovers, and virtuous officials. They printed prompt-books with abbreviated scripts to advertise their skills and stimulate new versions. These pamphlets were the origin of Chinese literature written in the vernacular language, which mirrored the culture of the streets.

11.6 SOCIAL LIFE IN THE SONG

The sources for the Song, written and pictorial, give us a richer picture of social life than for any previous period. One of the most paradoxical aspects of the Song is the change in the position of women. On one hand, the growth of markets and the spread of money gave women more opportunities to move around and to earn an income from spinning and weaving. On the other hand, the diffusion of footbinding and the reinforcement of patriarchal family values tied them down and

sealed them up within the walls of their family compounds. How could both happen at the same time?

Were Women Strong or Crippled?

Women did participate in public economic life during the Song. Widows ran their own inns, midwives delivered babies, nuns traveled to preach to female audiences, and courtesans and dancers entertained city teahouse patrons. In the countryside, daughters of farmers practiced weaving, while literati families taught some of their daughters to write poetry. China's most famous female poet, **Li Qingzhao**, impressed even the most refined male connoisseurs. Box 11.3 gives the story of her life with her husband as book collectors and poets.

But economic change also made women a commodity on the marriage market, just as elite males learned to desire a new female body. Instead of the portly, voluptuous women of the Tang modeled on the emperor's mistress, Yang Guifei, male tastes shifted to slim, willowy, delicate figures. Footbinding probably began among court dancers in the tenth or eleventh century, but the fashion spread to elite families by the twelfth century. Footbinding meant wrapping a bandage around a

---

Box 11.3 Li Qingzhao and her Husband, Bibliophiles

Li Qingzhao, the great woman poet of the Song dynasty, wrote a moving account of how she and her husband shared an obsession with collecting books and inscriptions:

In 1101 ... I came as a bride to the Zhao household ... My husband was then twenty-one and a student in the Imperial Academy. In those days our two families, the Zhaos and the Lis, were not well-to-do and we were always frugal. On the first and fifteenth day of every month, my husband would get a short vacation from the Academy; he would "pawn some clothes" for five hundred cash and go to the market at Xiang-guo Temple, where he would buy fruit and rubbings of inscriptions. When he brought these home, we would sit facing one another, rolling them out before us, examining and munching ... Pointing

to the heaps of books and histories, we would guess on which line of which page in which chapter of which book a certain passage could be found. Success in guessing determined who got to drink his or her tea first. Whenever I got it right, I would raise the teacup, laughing so hard that the tea would spill in my lap, and I would get up, not having been able to drink any of it at all. I would have been glad to grow old in such a world.

When the Jin armies invaded North China, they had to leave most of their precious collection behind. Jin forces sacked the city and burnt their house down. They fled south with only(!) fifteen cartloads of books. Her husband was summoned to an audience with the emperor, but died of malaria and sunstroke on the way.

After her husband's death, she wrote a poem looking back on their days of happiness:

Fifteen years ago, beneath moonlight and flowers,
I walked with you
We composed flower-viewing poems together.
Tonight the moonlight and flowers are just the same
But how can I ever hold in my arms the same love.

Li had to flee south again, while Jin troops again sacked the city and burnt most of the collection. Thieves took most of the rest. Looking at the few remaining, she thought, "When I have a chance to look over these books, it's like meeting old friends ... It is so sad – today the ink of his writing seems fresh, but the trees on his grave have grown to an armspan in girth."

Figure 11.2 Footbinding meant crushing the bones of a young woman's foot with tightly wound cloths in order to create a tiny sole which forced the woman to assume a mincing gait. Song dynasty men found these feet erotic, and Confucian moralists accepted the practice because, by limiting the mobility of women, it kept them safely within the household.

young girl's feet before they grew, forcing the toes to bend inward toward the sole. The smallest feet were only three to five inches long. Special embroidered shoes adorned these stunted feet. Needless to say, this practice made walking very painful, but men liked the dainty step, and crippling women this way made it impossible for them to walk far without help. Men brought in concubines to live in their household, and confined their women in secluded quarters, much like a Middle Eastern harem. Soon, all families who wanted their daughters to marry rich men realized that their daughters must bind their feet. Mothers even forced their own daughters to do it. Women then bound their feet to compete with other women for men's attention. Figure 11.2 shows the crushing effect of footbinding on women's mobility. In this way, as a fashion statement, footbinding spread by the same process as nineteenth-century corsets and twentieth-century breast implants. Confucian scholars did not disapprove: they wanted women to stay within the household in order to reinforce the cohesion of local families. Likewise, they thought that allowing widows to remarry was even worse than having them starve to death. Philosophy, fashion, and commerce all worked together to keep women down, even while the economy boomed.

In North China, by contrast, the non-Han regimes gave women a much higher position: they took care of the vital herds of sheep while the men pranced on their horses in battle, and the mothers and wives of tribal rulers had great influence behind the scenes. Empress **Chunqin**, for example, the widow of Abaoji, the founder of the Liao dynasty, declined the customary offer to kill herself and be buried with her husband. Instead, she cut off her hand, placed it in his coffin, and kept power for many years, ruling through her sons. She even commanded her own army and led it into battle. The northern nomads lacked high "culture," but they gave women more political influence than the southern literati did.

Legacy of the Song

The Song left a rich and complex legacy to its successors. They could not boast of military victories, but instead they established *wen*, or civil, literary culture, as the essence of the Chinese way. In the Neo-Confucian synthesis, they revived classical ideas in such a powerful form that they lasted until the end of China's last dynasty in 1911, and affected the societies around them. China's economy dominated East Asia and had an impact on the rest of Eurasia, but social life driven by economic change moved in contradictory directions: great wealth for some, grinding poverty for others; high culture and entertainment for the privileged, crippling subordination and exploitation for the unlucky and weak. Chinese writers knew about these paradoxes and described them in detail; that is why the Song looks so "modern" to us.

11.7 HEIAN JAPAN, 794–1185: A CLOSED SOCIETY?

With the collapse of the Tang and the division of China, Japan turned in on itself. The Japanese sent their last tribute mission to China in 894. After that, they no longer saw China as the fount of knowledge and culture. Japan escaped nomadic invasion and the dramatic economic and intellectual changes of the continent; instead, it developed a very distinctive culture of its own, centered on a tiny court elite in the capital city of Kyoto. Some of the greatest works of Japanese literature and art come from this period, including the world's first genuine novel, *The Tale of Genji*. Buddhism, which pervaded Japanese society, developed new forms that drew mass support. Heian Japan eventually collapsed under military conflict, but it was more than a fragile flower: its culture lasted for three hundred years.

The Imperial Capital is Built

In 784 the Emperor Kammu ordered the construction of a new capital for his court, on the site of modern Kyoto. The Kyoto basin, surrounded by mountains on three sides, was a good place to establish a defensible stronghold, and roads and rivers to the south connected it easily with the Inland Sea. In 794 he named it **Heian**, or "Peace," beginning a new era which lasted for 400 years. He left the old capital of Nara in order to escape the power of rival political forces and the influence of Buddhist monasteries. Heian was an inland city, rainy and humid, and surrounded by marshes, with hot, muggy summers and freezing winters. Intensive forced labor, however, drained the marshes and made it one of the great cities of the world. The builders of Heian followed Chinese models. It measured 3.3 miles north to south and 2.8 miles across, one third the size of Tang China's Chang'an, and its population reached at most 100,000 to 150,000 people. Twenty-four large, straight avenues divided the city into a clear grid pattern, and as in China, the imperial palace in the north looked south over the emperor's realm. Unlike China's capital, Heian had no walls, but it did have two official market areas surrounded by walls and gates.

Heian was urban in its size and culture, but it was not very commercial. Japan did mint some of its own coins, but iron supplies were too scarce to support a monetized economy; most of its coins came from China. Over half the population were nobles, officials, and their families in government service. No other settlement in Japan even came close to being a city at this time. Although smaller than China's capital, Heian dominated its country much more, standing out like a huge monument in a land of villages. The great annual Kamo festival, the ancestor of modern Kyoto's Gion festival, featured a lavish procession to honor the founding gods and seek their protection. Masses of the city population crowded around, as tourists do today, to watch the decorated carriages, priests, officials, and troops leading the way to the central shrine. Box 11.4 describes the lives of the great Heian families.

The city consisted primarily of consumers, drawing in resources from the rest of the country to support a refined ruling class. They controlled their small society with strict regulations, defining exactly how one could dress, eat, speak, and travel in terms of one's court rank. Some of these rules came from China; others followed Buddhist prohibitions on moving in certain directions, or going out on certain days. Unlike the Chinese emperor, the emperor of Japan was a literal deity; no mortal could view or touch his sacred body without ritual cleansing. By contrast, he did little or no administrative work. Noble families ran the government behind the scenes. The basic support for the state came from manorial estates, or **shoen**, where peasant farmers labored in near serfdom to provide grain and labor services to estate managers, who sent the surplus to the nobles. In order to avoid supporting the court, local lords could present their land to monasteries, giving increasing power to Buddhist monks. Japan did not face the threat of foreign invasion, but it still had internal military rivalries. Even the monks hired their own soldiers to protect themselves, and sometimes raided the capital for gain. Without dramatic battles, gradually over three centuries more and more power slipped away from the court into the hands of regional lords and their military servants.

The elaborate Tang bureaucracy, designed for a continental empire, did not adapt well to the much smaller Japanese islands, and like most bureaucracies, it generated as much paperwork as action. Instead of drastic budget cuts or passionate debates over reform, Japan added new layers on top of old ones. The Fujiwara family took real power behind the throne by arranging for one emperor to retire young, marrying their daughters to the royal family, and acting as regents for the young heir. The most basic idea imported from China had nearly disappeared: the idea that the state had an existence independent from family and clan. While China developed an ideology of state service for its elite, Japan nearly returned to the clan government of the **uji** (warrior clans of ancient Japan) period, masked by the emperor as a unifying symbol. Even more than in China, peasant cultivators

Box 11.4 Japanese Noble Families in the Heian Period

From the voluminous literature written by court women in Heian Japan, we can learn the principles governing a very unusual society. Among this tiny aristocratic elite, women were highly educated and cultivated, and they had an extraordinary degree of sexual and economic freedom. They lived in simple but expansive mansions in the city of Kyoto, and they inherited their houses from their parents when they grew up. Their husbands and lovers visited them, but they stayed at home for most of their lives. These women owned a substantial amount of property, including their houses, agricultural lands, and, most importantly, expensive robes. This pattern differed dramatically from most other societies, like that of China, where women left their natal homes upon marriage to become part of their husband's family, bringing a small dowry chest with them.

Heian women and their servants ran their own households, and derived power from their relationships with the powerful men at court. Like women around the world, they could be given away in political marriages at a very young age to men they did not love, but unlike most other women, they engaged in frequent love affairs, and discussed them openly. In Lady Murasaki's *Tale of Genji*, the shining prince Genji has many affairs with beautiful, talented women, but he knows that he has many rivals. Sei Shonagon, the author of the *Pillow Book*, chronicled her own love affairs in great detail. The foremost concerns of these women were not so much sexual as emotional and artistic expression. Lovers must follow correct rituals to be acceptable: They must write elegant poems, behave like highly talented seducers, and they must say farewell to their women in the morning in an appropriately tender and nostalgic way.

Men had relationships with many women. They could have one principal wife, to provide an heir, and a number of concubines, each with her separate house. Although women had their own lovers, their husbands' infidelity caused them constant pangs of jealousy. Divorce for both men and women was easy and informal. Yet women were still insecure without a faithful man to protect them from the uncertainties of court politics. Genji is the star of Murasaki's novel because all his women think that in him they have finally found a handsome, wealthy, and faithful lover who will stay true to his vows of affection. They all end up being disappointed.

The literature of Heian Japan gives us a rare view of the private sentiments of a class of women who enjoyed an unusual amount of control over their lives. When the warriors took over in the Kamakura period, they lost most of their autonomy to male rulers and husbands. Like cherry blossoms, the fragile Heian society has left impressive evidence of intense personal emotion expressed in moving aesthetic form.

---

had no sense of being ruled by a state; they simply did their duty as demanded by local lords.

The Classic Women Writers and their Concerns

We see almost no evidence of the wider social world in the documents of this period. They focus almost exclusively on the aesthetic activities of the court elite. In striking contrast to patriarchal China, the most revealing literature was written by women. Japanese men, who still admired Chinese learning, wrote mainly derivative tracts on philosophy and history in classical Chinese. The great women writers, like Murasaki Shikibu, author of *The Tale of Genji* (c. 1020), and Sei Shonagon, author of *The Pillow Book* (1002), expressed finely tuned sensibilities responding to the subtlest details of human reactions to the natural world, and were remarkably explicit about sexual and romantic relations. They wrote in a syllabic alphabet created from Chinese characters which fitted the sounds of the Japanese language perfectly, and was easy for women to learn without classical Chinese training. Figure 11.3 displays one of the beautiful paintings that illustrated *The Tale of Genji*.

In Murasaki's novel, Genji, the "shining prince," grows up in court circles admired as a beautiful young man destined for greatness. He has many affairs with women, from whom he learns the secrets of love, and he exchanges his feelings with them in sophisticated wordplay through poetry. Genji and his friends are characters whom we know intimately, and they grow over time; they are not mere stereotypes carrying ideological arguments. Underlying Genji's quest for a role in the world, however, is a Buddhist sense of impermanence, a subtle melancholy implying that all human affairs are ultimately vain. After ups and down in love and in politics, Genji marries the commoner Murasaki, but she dies young, and Genji dies soon after. Despite overtones of sorrow and spiritual longing, the novel is not a religious tract. Murasaki captures the individuality of a single human life with great insight into social constraints, passion, and the value of artistic and religious commitment. Box 11.5 provides more details on Genji and the society in which he lived.

Box 11.5 *The Tale of Genji*: Complications of Love

The shining prince Genji has a child by his official wife, with whom he does not get along, but his real passion is for the young girl Murasaki. He is torn between so many women that he cannot choose a single one: "Among his ladies there was none who could be dismissed as completely beneath consideration and none to whom he could give his whole love." Each of them is jealous of the other. They communicate their feelings indirectly by writing elegant poems to Genji. One woman, whom Genji neglects, writes to him, "I go down the way of love and dampen my sleeves, and go yet further, into the muddy fields. A pity the well is so shallow." Despite the lateness of the hour, Genji answers, "You only wet your sleeves – what can this mean? That your feeling are not of the deepest, I should think: You only dip into the shallow waters, and I quite disappear into the slough?" Having brushed her off, he devotes himself to his beloved Murasaki, stroking her lustrous long hair: "May it grow to a thousand fathoms," said Genji. "Mine it shall be, rich as the grasses beneath the fathomless sea, the thousand-fathomed sea." Murasaki takes out brush and paper and sets down her answer: "It may indeed be a thousand fathoms deep. How can I know, when it restlessly comes and goes?" Murasaki is a very young girl, but she knows how to compose a witty answer. She, too, suspects that Genji's passion will not last.

Figure 11.3 Murasaki Shikibu, a court woman of Heian Japan, wrote *The Tale of Genji* in the tenth century, describing the shining Prince Genji and his relationships with many women. By the twelfth century, beautifully illuminated scrolls like this one depicted the Heian women in their households accompanied by quotations from the famous novel.

Sei Shonagon's *Pillow Book* collects poetry, anecdotes, stories of romantic relations, and gossip to provide intimate reactions of one woman to her daily life. Noble women were close observers of political life, and often had significant influence at court. They recorded the frank inside stories that the moralistic male accounts covered up. They also had a much higher position in their families than Confucian Chinese women. After marriage, men moved into their wives' households, just the opposite of China's patrilocal system. This meant that women owned property, lived their lives surrounded by their close relatives, and even had rights of divorce. They had affairs with other men, and often got away with little punishment. At least the small class of women in this civilian, urban society enjoyed great opportunities to develop their artistic and personal talents, and gain respect from the men who ruled. When the warriors took over Japan, they lost stature quickly.

Buddhism Spreads while Warriors Rise

We know much less of the world beyond Heian, but we do know that Buddhism spread widely, reaching wider audiences than in the Nara period. The emperors, suspicious of the power of Buddhist monks, kept their temples out of Heian itself, but the monks fortified themselves in strongholds on the hills around the city. Several intrepid monks left for China, bringing back new Buddhist teachings with them. Ennin (794–864), the most famous, spent ten years in China studying with the leading masters of esoteric Buddhism, which relied on magical spells and secret initiation rituals to lead its disciples to enlightenment. His knowledge attracted support from the imperial family itself, which sponsored the expansion of his temple Enryakuji on Mount Hiei, northeast of the city. As it expanded to become a huge monastic complex, Enryakuji abbots bent the Buddhist rules on non-violence a bit, collecting thousands of armed monks in their precincts. By the eleventh century, they regularly raided the city below for wealth, and fought pitched battles with rival sects in the streets of Heian.

Heian Japan's rule by a peaceful urban elite did not end with a bang; it eroded gradually, as rougher types rose to power in the east. As local estates grew in number outside the control of the court, the landlords needed strongmen to protect themselves, collect their rents, and expand their holdings. Military men began to group themselves on the estates and form connected clans. The court itself needed military protection, as armed monks raided the city, bandits preyed on the wealthy, and threats arose on the eastern frontier of Honshu. The **Minamoto** clan obtained imperial support as the defenders of the center, while the **Taira** left for the provinces. These professional warriors, or **bushi**, saw themselves as austere fighters who lived by the sword. They were servants, or **samurai**, who dedicated their lives to their lord. Both sides claimed to be the true defenders of the emperor, but in reality the emperors had retired from power, and the Fujiwara clan behind the throne had little force. The first major military revolt in the east against Heian in 935 failed because of rebel disorganization, but by the eleventh century Japan fell into full-scale civil war. After 1180, The Taira and Minamoto clans confronted each other in battles all over the island of Honshu, ending with Minamoto Yoritomo's victory in 1185. Keeping the emperor in Heian, he ruled as the **shogun**, or chief general, from his headquarters in Kamakura. The Heian age of the urban courtier had ended, and the rule of the warriors had begun.

11.8 GORYEO (KORYO) KOREA: BETWEEN CHINA AND JAPAN

As China fell into chaos from the mid eighth century, Korea also lost its unity under Silla, and split into three kingdoms. Silla and Baekje held the south, while a garrison commander in the north founded the new kingdom of **Goryeo**, with its capital at his local base of Gaeseong, about 40 miles north of modern Seoul. By the early tenth century, Goryeo kings had reunified the country, and they also absorbed elite families fleeing the attacks of the Khitans on the Parhae state in Manchuria. Goryeo held itself together for three hundred years, creating a new, distinctive culture on the Korean peninsula.

Aristocratic clans ruled Korea under the authority of the Korean king, but they maintained a centralized bureaucratic order that was strong enough to prevent disintegration and keep out foreign attacks. Unlike China, Korean society was strongly stratified into hereditary groups: the military order, the civilian official order, the priests, the peasants, and the slaves. Yet Goryeo greatly admired Song China, and introduced the civil examination system, Chinese learning, and a national university on the Song model. As in the Song, the noble lineages gave themselves privileges in the exams, excluding mobility from below. The Korean kings, although they claimed to have a heavenly mandate to rule, never pretended to have the sacred power of a Chinese or Japanese emperor. Military commanders defended the country ably, even building a series of long walls from the mouth of the Yalu River across to the east coast, over 180 miles long, to keep out Khitan attacks. Yet clever diplomacy kept Korea out of the continental conflicts: although Goryeo admired the Song, it refused to ally itself with Song China against the Jin, and instead bought peace.

Korea's Great Technologies: Printing and Ceramics

Korea, however, had other distinctive cultural features that made it more than a miniature copy of China. Buddhist temples were far more important and pervasive than Confucian rituals; the kings supported woodblock printing of the great Buddhist canon, the Tripitaka, one of the greatest early printing projects in the world. They carved wood blocks based on a Chinese copy, and supplemented it with additional works. This vast compilation contained over 1,600 different works in over 5,000 volumes. Goryeo was the first society in the world to use movable metal type in printing, and most of its printed books were Buddhist sutras and ritual texts.

Goryeo also perfected Song Chinese porcelain craftsmanship, creating the finest celadon ware ever made. Celadon is a type of porcelain with a partly translucent jade-colored glaze, often incised with floral patterns. Ranging from large jars to small plates and vases, Korean celadon ware has an unrivaled delicate beauty, reflecting the spiritual values influenced by the Buddhist and Daoist ideal of quiescence and transcendence of the material world. Figure 11.4 shows one of these elegant vases.

Despite its cultural advances, Korea remained an overwhelmingly agrarian society, where peasants and slaves living in poverty paid heavy rents and labor dues to the court and military elite. By the twelfth century, military revolts threatened central control, and rebellions by oppressed peasants and bandits spread through the country. The Mongols attacked in 1231, and then invaded six more times, while the court fled to safety on Kanghwa Island across the sea. Military rulers finally gave up the struggle. Goryeo became part of the Mongol Yuan dynasty in 1270, but the royal line continued until 1392. Koreans can tell a story of a continuous struggle to maintain their cultural identity, combining Chinese

Figure 11.4 Korean craftsmen of the Goryeo dynasty perfected the Song dynasty art of celadon porcelain glaze, producing highly sophisticated, delicate wares that are still the prize exhibits of many art museums today.

techniques with native cultural roots, during these three difficult centuries.

11.9 CENTRAL EURASIA: THE TURKS MOVE OUT

Central Eurasia, too, lost its coherence with the collapse of the Turkish qaghanates in the mid ninth century. A confusing swirl of nomadic groups appears in sources written by outsiders, who tried to decipher fragmentary signs of change. There are too many new names and invasions by mysterious peoples to describe here. We can concentrate only on some general features and two groups that had a major impact outside Central Eurasia: the Khazars and the **Seljuks**.

The most important new development was the joining of Turkic nomads with Islamic urban culture to create expansive Turko-Islamic states. Islam had spread eastward in the eighth century, first with Arab armies, but more enduring impact came from the merchants, Sufi mystics, and Iranian clerics who moved into Transoxania. Rulers of wealthy cities on the Silk Road found it profitable to buy Turkic slaves and make them into armies that served them personally. These slave-soldiers, or **ghulam**, helped the rulers, in turn, raid the steppes to find new recruits.

Meanwhile, in the steppes, the Turkic tribes on the one hand raided the oasis cities for goods, and on the other picked up Islam from their victims. The tenth century was the critical turning point, when Turkic soldiers fused with the Iranian and Islamic urban civilization, giving it new expansive power. The Qarakhanid qaghanate, with two centers, one near the old Uighur capital in Mongolia, and one in Samarkand, held the region together in the eleventh century until it fell.

The Turkic state of the **Seljuks** emerged from this incessant tribal competition as a nomadic dynasty grafted onto a Middle Eastern state. The powerful army of slave-soldiers moved out of Mongolia westward, across Iran, into Azerbaijan and eastern Anatolia, and defeated the weakening Byzantine empire at the Battle of Manzikert in 1071. It reached the peak of its power in the late eleventh century, and then fell apart, but left behind smaller statelets across the region. Chapter 10 describes the Middle East in this period as a phase of highly fragmented states, with competition between different sects of Islam, but the gradual process of Islamicizing nomads in contact with sedentary societies runs beneath the chaos. The ultimate outcome would be the founding of the Ottoman empire in Anatolia in the thirteenth century.

Further north, another nomadic confederation briefly encompassed vast expanses of steppe before it too collapsed, leaving traces behind. The Khazar qaghanate had emerged from a noble Turkish clan around the lower Volga River in the mid seventh century. At its peak, it controlled the region from Kiev through the Volga River to the borders of Byzantium and Iran, as far east as modern Uzbekistan. The **Khazars** embraced a huge variety of peoples, but they succeeded in extracting resources from settled populations by hiring tax collectors. Most interesting, the Khazars chose an unusual religion for their ruling core: They chose Judaism, to set themselves off from the Christian Byzantines and Islamic Iranians around them, and wrote many of their texts in Hebrew script. Yet they tolerated many creeds, and relied heavily on Muslim as well as Jewish merchants to serve them. The rising Rus state finally destroyed the Khazars in the late tenth century. The Khazars represent the culmination of cultural mixing in the wide open spaces of the steppe: they probably joined more religions, more peoples, more different territories and economies under their rule than anyone before the Mongol conquest.

11.10 THE BYZANTINE EMPIRE

In 285 CE Emperor Diocletian split the Roman empire into two parts, eastern and western. After the fall of the western empire in 476 CE, the eastern half endured for one thousand more years until its final conquest by the Ottoman Turks in 1453. Emperor Constantine in 330 had dedicated the small town of Byzantium in his own name as Constantinople, making it into a huge urban conglomeration, dominated by his military and civil bureaucracies. We now call his empire the Byzantine empire; later the Turks renamed Constantinople as Istanbul, its modern name. Located on a perfect strategic site overlooking the Bosporus, the waterway connecting the Black Sea to the Mediterranean, protected by huge walls and mountainous terrain, Constantinople/Istanbul became and remains today one of the great world cities. The hinterland of Anatolia, with its prosperous farmers along the seacoast, provided the grain supplies to support its enormous population, which reached 200,000 people by the fifth century, far larger than Rome, Antioch, or Alexandria.

The empire centered on Constantinople suffered many ups and downs, but proved to be remarkably resilient. In the mid sixth century, a severe bubonic plague devastated the empire and the capital, cutting its population in half, and the rise of the Arabs challenged its authority repeatedly, but from the eighth to eleventh centuries the Byzantine empire once again expanded and reached new heights of prosperity, territorial expansion, and cultural achievement. Emperor Basil I (r. 867–86), from Macedonia, founded a new dynasty that began rebuilding the army, navy, and legal system, and started expanding eastward. General Nicephorus II drove back the Arabs in 963, taking Aleppo and Antioch, and Basil II "the Bulgar slayer" (r. 963–1025) pushed successfully to the northeast against the nomadic Bulgar state. By 1025 the empire had recovered all the core territories of Greek culture, plus southern Italy, Armenia, and Mesopotamia.

Byzantium was a completely Christian empire, with an autocratic emperor claiming divinely justified rule, centered on a Greek-speaking church which supported lavish monasteries and the production of gilded religious images called icons, painted on wood or embedded in mosaics. The high clerics formed their own wealthy aristocracy, who had little respect for the nominal religious authority of the pope of the Roman church. Despite centuries of efforts at reconciliation, the final split with Rome occurred in 1054. Greek scholars carried on the philosophical speculation begun by Plato, and wrote their own military epics. **Hagia Sophia**, the huge Byzantine church in Constantinople, was filled with mosaics and icons in praise of emperors and saints. (It is now a mosque, stripped of its icons, but several beautiful mosaics remain.) It is no wonder that Slavic rulers, dazzled by the empire's gold, power, and spiritual supremacy, begged for missionaries to convert their peoples from paganism. As the Russian lands joined the Byzantine empire's cultural sphere, its Greek heritage, including the writing system which was the basis of Russia's Cyrillic alphabet, expanded into vast new realms.

Constantinople: Premier Trading City

Constantinople steadily grew to be the dominant city of the Mediterranean. By the thirteenth century, it had reached a population of 400,000, recovering or surpassing its level before the sixth-century plague. At less than half the size of the great Chinese capitals of Kaifeng or Hangzhou, but over twice the size of Japan's Heian, it was a key node in world trade. Byzantine traders controlled the silk trade from China via Trebizond, the spice trade from India via Antioch, the fur trade from Russia via the Crimea, and amber from the Baltic forests. They left Western European trade to the energetic Venetians, who had special privileges granted by the emperor to bring arms, slaves, wood, and coarse cloth. When the Byzantines revoked these privileges, the Venetians reclaimed them by force. Regular customs duties of 10 percent on all trade provided a steady flow of revenue into the imperial treasury, giving it the wealth to fund soldiers, administrators, churchmen, and scholars. The city also became a center of industrial production: ever since two monks had smuggled in cocoons from China in their walking staffs, the Byzantines had learned the secret of silk production. The imperial factories in Constantinople produced high quality brocades for markets across Europe and Russia, and all the profits went to the state. Goldsmith products, enamel, ivory, and other luxury goods, all under strict state controls, also brought in revenue.

The Empire Loses its Grip

At the same time, disastrous political and military mismanagement caused the empire to lose over half its territory from the eleventh to twelfth centuries. In 1071, after losing a battle with the Seljuk Turks at the Armenian border town of Manzikert, the generals could not stop Turkic raiders from penetrating the center of the Anatolian plateau. Incompetent officials squandered the state's great wealth, wrecking the gold and silver coinage, and losing land, trade, and cities to much poorer and more unorganized raiders from the east and the west. Of all the causes of Byzantine decline, debasement of the gold coinage for short-term fiscal profit was the chief factor sapping the basis of state power. In addition, Italians learned the secret of silk production, cutting into the Byzantine monopoly. Autocratic regulation of luxury trades could not compete against the unruly, but autonomous, commercial city-states of the western Mediterranean.

The Normans, equally savage raiders from France, took Sicily, an important source of grain. Then the Crusaders arrived on the Levantine coast, demanding large payoffs for their armies while they fought for the Christian God against Islam. In 1204, dissatisfied with the Byzantine offers, they conquered and sacked

Constantinople, even though they were astonished by its size and prosperity.

The Byzantine emperors recovered the city, and pieces of the shrunken empire, even without its Anatolian base, still hung on for two and a half more centuries. Greek language and culture survived in Greece, the Aegean, and the coast of Anatolia, while the Byzantine church found a new base in Slavic lands to the north. The Greek scholars who left Constantinople in turn inspired the revival of classical learning in Italy known as the Renaissance. As one of the longest-lived empires in recorded history, the Byzantine empire left an impressive heritage of art, religious culture, and scholarly learning. Despite its often feckless rulers and chaotic politics, it provided a continuous link from the ancient Mediterranean world to the early modern age of gunpowder empires.

11.11 KIEVAN RUS: MARITIME TRADERS AND RAIDERS

Kievan **Rus**, the ancestor of modern Russia, created its state deeply enmeshed in relations with a tumultuous Central Eurasia and the dazzling Byzantine empire. The debate over the origins of the Rus state has generated a huge amount of scholarly ink, because Russians see this question as closely connected to the place of Russia in the world. Romantic nationalists want to find the roots of Russia deep in the Russian soil, in native folk democratic traditions corrupted by later Western impact; Westernizers, by contrast, stress the origins of Russia in the culturally advanced regions of Western Europe. This polarity runs through all of Russian history. But both sides tend to neglect Russia's deep connections to the East, and the rise of Rus brings all these tangled questions together. (Map 11.5 shows the extent of Kievan Rus.)

An immense, fertile plain extends across northern Eurasia, nearly unbroken from northern Germany to eastern Siberia. No major mountain ranges stop the course of frozen northern winds; the Ural Mountains, less than 5,000 feet at their highest, do not create any climatic or cultural barrier. Great rivers slowly carry waters north and south, emptying into either the Baltic, Arctic Ocean, or Black and Caspian Seas. Rivers like the Dnieper, Don, and Volga provide excellent transportation routes to the warmer lands in the south. But the Russian lands are landlocked, and they suffer from a northern, continental climate, with extremes of heat in the summer, and cold in the winter. Eight months out of the year, the soil in the north freezes, making winter a better time for land transportation, over snow and ice, than spring, when all roads dissolve into mud. Further north lies the arctic tundra, then the *taiga* south of it

(a coniferous forest), another mixed forest belt, and then the steppe grasslands. Agricultural land is very scarce, only one eighth of this vast area, and the growing season short. Only the black soil region of the south has fertile conditions, and it often suffers from drought. Long after the core regions of Asia and the Middle East built their dense populations, and Western Europe, favored by the Gulf Stream, created productive agriculture and modest cities, Russia remained underpopulated and unurbanized. Neolithic cultures appeared in the fourth millennium BCE in the river valleys, but no major civilization centered in the north. Ever since the Scythians of the sixth century BCE, steppe nomads moved through the grasslands, but the forests and fields of the north remained mainly a land of forest hunters and scattered farmers.

Vikings Found the Rus State

From the east, the Khazars brought towns, commerce, laws, and international connections to the lower Volga in the eighth century. Meanwhile, from the Carpathians in the west, speakers of Slavic languages gradually settled the plain, mixing with Finns, Lapps, and other forest people. By the ninth century, agriculture had developed along with fishing, hunting, beekeeping, weaving, pottery, and other crafts, enough to support small river towns, like Kiev, Novgorod, and Smolensk. According to much later Russian chronicles, in 862 the Slavic tribes called in rulers from the Varangian Rus to the north. Rurik took charge of Novgorod, and in 980 his descendant Vladimir brought his Norsemen from Scandinavia to establish his capital in Kiev. The Rus state then ruled the entire expanse from Novgorod to the Dnieper River down to Kiev. Despite all the controversy, most historians agree that the ruling elite of this state clearly had Scandinavian roots, in a small group of roving merchant pirate kings, the eastern branch of the Vikings. Kiev was a good location for their capital, offering the chance to export the forest products of the north to the rich consumers of Byzantium across the Black Sea. Vladimir converted his people to Christianity in 988 to reinforce the connection, and married into the Byzantine ruling house. He brought in Greek clergy, who created a new alphabet for the Church Slavonic language. It was the origin of the modern Russian alphabet. Box 11.6 gives a description of early Rus society by an Arab visitor.

Although the Vikings began as raiders, they, like the nomads on the Chinese frontier, settled down to extract regular tribute from the Slavic peasants, taking their beeswax, honey, and furs to Byzantium in exchange for silver. Kiev rose to a population of 35,000–50,000 people, nearly the size of Paris or London. Kiev also sent caravans eastward, along the silk routes north of the

Map 11.5 Kievan Rus

Caspian Sea. At first the Rus traded peacefully with the Khazars, until the warrior prince Sviatoslav launched an eastern campaign to smash the Khazar state and plunder its capital. Kiev now briefly controlled the Volga, but it had only opened itself to attacks from fiercer nomads further east. The Pechenegs killed Sviatoslav, making a drinking cup out of his skull. Pechenegs

and, later, Polovetsians fought constantly with the Kiev rulers over the next three centuries.

The Kievan rulers had to fight on all sides: they had no "natural" borders to protect them. They expanded mainly to the northeast, following the riches of the fur trade. To the south, they could not penetrate the steppe against nomad

Box 11.6 A Muslim Envoy Observes the Rus

Ibn Fadlan, an Arab diplomat sent from Baghdad to the Volga in the tenth century, commented on the habits of the Rus rulers there. His description shows that the Rus were Scandinavian traders who had adopted some customs from the Slavic peasantry:

I saw the Rus when they arrived on their trading mission and anchored at the River Atul [Volga]. Never had I seen people of more perfect physique: they are tall as date-palms, and reddish in color. They wear neither coat nor mantle, but each man carries a cape which covers one-half of his body, leaving one hand free. Their swords are Frankish in pattern, broad, flat, and fluted. Each man has [tattooed upon him] trees, figures, and the like from the fingernails to the neck. Each woman carries on her bosom a container made of iron, silver, copper, or gold – its size and substance depending on her man's wealth . . .

They are the filthiest of God's creatures. They do not wash after discharging their natural functions, neither do they wash their hands after meals. They are as stray donkeys. They arrive from their distant lands and lay their ships alongside the banks of the Atul, which is a great river, and there they build big wooden houses . . .

If one of the Rus falls sick they put him in a tent by himself and leave bread and water for him. They do not visit him, however, or speak to him, especially if he is a serf. Should he recover he joins the others; if he dies they burn him.

resistance; to the west, they stopped at the Carpathian Mountains, and the borderlands with Poles, Prussians, and Lithuanians. Over huge distances, with poor communications, in the face of constant pressure from nomad warriors, the princes held their sprawling federation together with personal ties and trade goods. The state finally fell to the Mongol empire after a prolonged period of weakness created by the steppe wars and the shift of trade routes away from the Dnieper and toward the Mediterranean.

Kievan Rus: Trading and Raiding

Although the Kievan prince had only loose control over the provinces, and the princes constantly fought with their brothers over succession to the throne, Kievan Rus endured as a coherent state, centered on Orthodox Christian culture and the Byzantine–forest products trade. Only 7 to 8 million people were under Kievan control, most of them peasant farmers. They were mainly free peasants, not the bonded serfs of later Russian times; but below them were slaves. The clergy had a special position, as the only literate members of society and the link between God and man. The church, which lived off large landholdings, not only ran monasteries, but also hospitals, charities, and schools. The prince ran the state in consultation with a council of **boyars**, or nobles, while many of the towns had their own assemblies. The boyar council, or **Duma**, and the town assemblies indicate that certain democratic elements balanced the decision-making powers of the prince.

Novgorod was the state's second great trading node, linking Rus to the north and west. It exported furs and wax to Germany and Scandinavia, joining a network of trading cities around the Baltic Sea. German merchants also brought in silver, monetizing the economy and providing cash revenue to the princes who tapped the profits from trade.

The Kievan period created the central elements of Russian culture: its language, its core territory, and its religion. By translating the Greek liturgy into Slavonic, the Russian monks ensured that ordinary people could understand the basic rituals. Much of the written culture followed Greek religious patterns, but there was also a separate Russian literature of folk tales and epic sagas, celebrating the mighty warriors who founded the state. Most spectacular are the wooden churches, which translated Greek stone forms into remarkably innovative architectural shapes using the abundant supplies of the forest. Growing wealth allowed towns to rebuild in stone and brick. The masonry cathedral of St. Sophia in Novgorod, which replaced a wooden one that had burned down, displayed the wealth of the town and expressed a distinctive local style. Icon painting, the other great Russian art, also modified the Byzantine patterns into a distinctive Russian style.

Knowing the violence and oppression of later Russian history, it is easy to feel nostalgic for the spiritual and aesthetic beauties of Kiev. Yet this state, too, was a warrior state, plagued with factionalism and battles, built on a poor peasant base. Still, by blending the influences of the Baltic, Byzantium, and Central Eurasia, Kievan Rus planted itself in a strategic location and created a new, enduring cultural formation.

Conclusion

In this chapter, we have discussed empires, cities, and religious communities across Eurasia, showing how the interplay of warfare, trade, and pilgrimage created new cultural formations centered on regional states. In contrast to the great expansion of Islam and the Tang empire in the previous centuries, the states and religions of this period could not boast of permanent military conquests of new territories. On the other hand, they gained more by commerce than by military conquest. Those states that did best took advantage of their positions on the crossroads of continental and maritime trade routes. Song China, above all, consolidated its special position as the richest and most populous society on the continent by joining paddy rice agriculture with extensive maritime and riverine trade. Even though it did not control North China, it prospered greatly with its center in the huge southern capital of Hangzhou. Kievan Rus, with a much sparser agrarian base, still held itself together by adroitly seizing profits from trade running from the forests to the Mediterranean. This sprawling network of river traders and forest settlers established the cultural basis for Russian civilization. The Byzantine empire, even while it lost battles, still developed its economic links in all directions. In north and northwest China, the mixed nomadic and military conquerors held large portions of both steppe lands and agricultural regions. And the Turkic peoples of the steppes, with their newly consolidated alliance with urban Islamic settlements, likewise promoted commercial and cultural expansion.

The great religious traditions of Confucianism, Buddhism, Islam, and Christianity expanded their reach and deepened their penetration of these societies, supported by government and commercial patrons who built their churches and paid their monks, but also by mass audiences of believers who embraced new teachings. Cultural integration spread both horizontally across large territories and vertically into lower classes of the population. Zhu Xi's new version of Confucianism, in particular, created a powerful alternative to Buddhism that would come to dominate the Chinese elite cultural realm for the next eight centuries.

This world seemed to be permanently divided. Nothing indicated that new steppe nomads would soon conquer all of Eurasia and put it under one vast empire, the largest the world would ever see.

Study Questions

(1) If the Song dynasty of China was so wealthy, why was it unable to defend its territory against the Manchurian states of the northeast? Discuss fiscal policy, military administration, and currency circulation in the Song and its rival states. Compare Song China's experience with the ability of the Byzantine empire to resist the Seljuk Turks.

(2) What was the relative importance of land and sea routes across Eurasia in this period? Discuss the major goods that moved along each route, the traders who carried them, and the states that profited by taxing the long-distance trade.

(3) How did the spread of religions like Orthodox Christianity and Neo-Confucianism affect family lives? What allowed some women to gain political power in both steppe nomadic and settled regimes? Why was Heian Japan able to maintain such a distinctive structure of relations between men and women for so long?

Suggested Reading

China PETER BOL, *This Culture of Ours: Intellectual Transitions in T'ang and Sung China* (Stanford University Press, 1992). This study provides the broader cultural and intellectual context for political debates.

RUTH W. DUNNELL, *The Great State of White and High: Buddhism and State Formation in Eleventh-Century Xia* (Honolulu: University of Hawaii Press,1996). This is a basic study of the border dynasties.

Patricia Ebrey, *The Inner Quarters: Marriage and the Lives of Chinese Women in the Sung Period* (Berkeley: University of California Press, 1993). This is one of the best recent studies of women and Chinese families.

Robert P. Hymes, *Statesmen and Gentlemen: The Elite of Fu-chou, Chiang-Hsi, in Northern and Southern Sung* (Cambridge University Press, 1986). This is a classic study of the growing power of local elites.

Hoyt C. Tillman and Stephen H. West, *China under Jurchen Rule: Essays on Chin Intellectual and Cultural History* (Albany: State University of New York Press, 1995). This work, like Dunnell above, is a basic study of the border dynasties.

Japan and Korea   Ivan Morris, *The World of the Shining Prince: Court Life in Ancient Japan* (New York: Knopf, 1964). This is a brilliant evocation of Heian society, but also consult the following critique by:

William H. McCullough, "Japanese Marriage Institutions in the Heian Period," *Harvard Journal of Asiatic Studies*, 27 (1967), 103–67.

Russia   Janet Martin, *Medieval Russia, 980–1584* (Cambridge University Press, 1995). This is the best recent scholarly survey.

Omeljan Pritsak, *The Origin of Rus,* vol. I: *Old Scandinavian Sources* (Cambridge, MA: Harvard Ukrainian Research Institute, 1981). The introduction presents an exhaustive argument stressing Central Eurasian connections.

Central Eurasia   Richard C. Foltz, *Religions of the Silk Road* (Basingstoke: Macmillan, 1999). Foltz briefly covers Buddhism, Manichaeanism, Christianity, and Islam in Central Asia.

Glossary

Abaoji: Founder of Liao state in Manchuria (r. 907–26).

Aguda: Founder of Jin state in Manchuria (r. 1113–23).

baojia: Chinese system of collective responsibility for crimes.

boyars: Russian noble class.

bushi: Japanese professional warriors

Champa: Hindu state in southern Vietnam.

Chunqin: Empress and widow of Abaoji, ruler of Liao dynasty.

Constantinople: Capital of Byzantine empire, renamed Istanbul after Ottoman conquest in 1453.

Dai Viet: Independent Vietnamese kingdom in the tenth century.

daoxue: "The study of the Way": Chinese term for Neo-Confucian teachings of Zhu Xi in the twelfth century.

Duma: Boyar council of Russian states in Kievan period.

ghulam: Turkic slave-soldiers, fighting for Islamic rulers.

Goryeo (Koryo): Korean kingdom which reunified Korea in the tenth century.

Hagia Sophia: Great Byzantine church in Constantinople, now a mosque.

Hangzhou: Capital of Southern Song China, and the largest city in world in the thirteenth century.

Heian: Modern Kyoto, and the capital of Japan during the Heian period.

junzi: Confucian Chinese term for superior man or ideal moral person.

Kaifeng: Capital of Northern Song dynasty, in the North China Plain.

Khazars: Central Eurasian warriors who established a large state in the mid seventh century, and converted to Judaism.

li: "Principle": Chinese Neo-Confucian term for basic principles that organize the material and spiritual world.

Li Qingzhao: Chinese poetess (1084–1141) of the Song dynasty.

Minamoto: Japanese warrior clan defending Heian in the twelfth century.

qi: Chinese Neo-Confucian term for the material elements of the world.

Quanzhou: Called in Arabic "Zayton," a major trading city on the southeast coast of China.

Rus: Mainly Scandinavian traders and warriors who established a state at Kiev in the tenth century.

samurai: Japanese warrior class, servants of feudal lords.

Seljuks: Turks who established kingdoms in the Middle East and attacked the Byzantine empire in the eleventh century.

shi: Literati class of China, holding degrees in the examination system.

shoen: Manorial estates in Japan.

shogun: Chief general of Japan, protector of the emperor, and de facto ruler.

Sima Guang: Chinese historian and official (1019–86), an opponent of Wang Anshi in reform debates.

Srivijaya: An empire controlling the Malacca Strait.

Taira: Japanese warrior clan, rivals of Minamoto in the twelfth century.

uji: Warrior clans of ancient Japan.

Wang Anshi: Chinese official (1021–86) in the Song dynasty who promoted radical reforms.

wen: Chinese term for culture, civilization, and literature.

wu: Chinese term for military power.

yin: Privilege of Chinese official elite in Song dynasty, allowing them to pass on titles to their sons.

Yue Fei: Southern Song general who promoted reconquest of North China.

Zhao Kuangyin: Chinese general (927–76), founder of the Song dynasty.

Zhu Xi: Greatest of the Song philosophers (1130–1200), creator of a new synthesis of religious and cultural traditions called Neo-Confucianism, or *daoxue*.

Global map, 1200–1500 CE

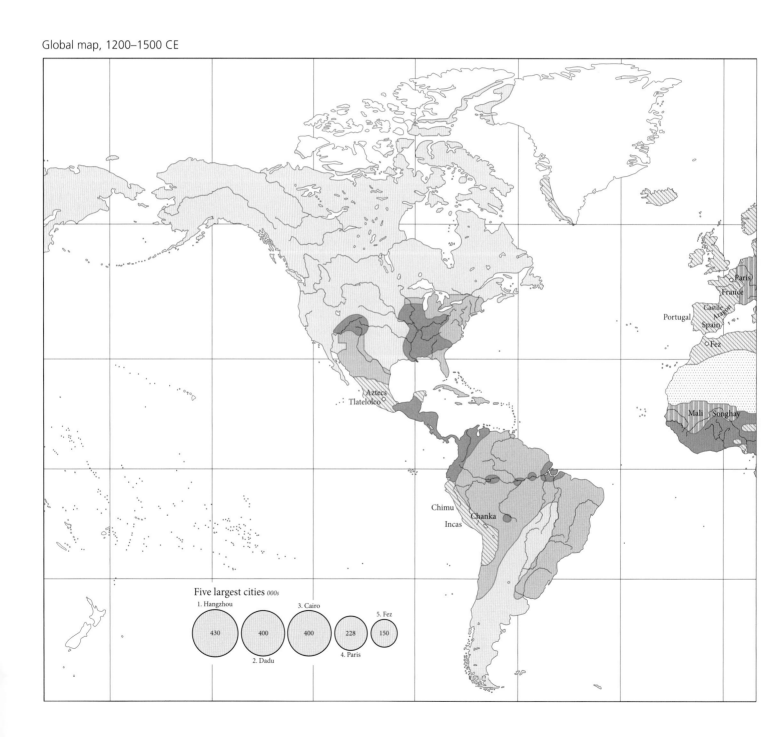

Aztecs
Tlatelolco

Chimu
Incas   Chanka

Paris
France

Portugal Castile Aragon
          Spain
          Fez

Mali Songhay

Five largest cities *000s*

1. Hangzhou		3. Cairo		5. Fez
430	400	400	228	150
	2. Dadu		4. Paris	

PART V

1200–1500 CE: Conquest and commerce

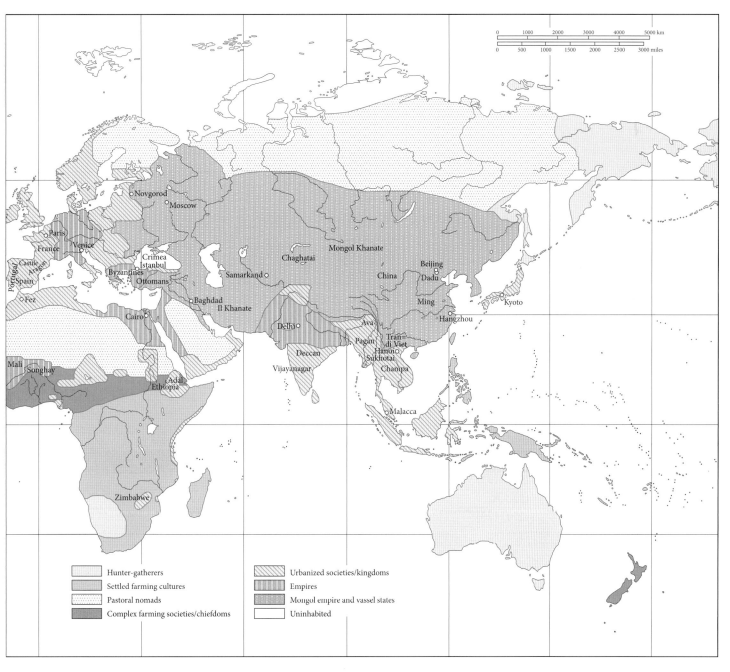

Map: Global map 1200–1500 CE

Africa

1200–1450	Great Zimbabwe empire.
1235–1433	Empire of Mali.
1405–33	Zheng He voyages visit Africa.
1441	Portuguese land on West African coast.
1468–1551	Songhay empire.
1502	Portuguese attack East African coast.

Americas

1248	Aztecs settle in Valley of Mexico.
1427–1521	Empire of Triple Alliance under Aztecs.
1438–70	Beginning of Inka conquests.
1521	Aztec capital of Tenochtitlán taken by Spanish and indigenous soldiers.
1572	Inka resistance to Spaniards ends.

Eurasia

c. 1162–1227	Lifetime of Chinggis Khan.
1190s – 1526	Delhi sultanates in India.
1206	Khuriltai confirms leadership of Chinggis Khan.
1220	Chinggis conquers Samarkand.
1224	Mongols raid Novgorod.
1247–1318	Rashid al-Din, chronicler of the Mongol empire.
1256–1335	Hülegü and the Il-Khans of Persia.
1260–94	Reign of Khubilai Khan.
1274, 1281	Japanese repel Mongol invasions.
1279–1368	Yuan dynasty of China.
1300	Metropolitan of Orthodox church moves to Moscow.
1328	Ivan Kalita named first Russian Grand Prince.
1331–48	First outbreaks of plague epidemics in Eurasia.
1335–1565	Vijayanagar empire.
1336–1405	Lifetime of Timur.
1368	Founding of Ming dynasty.
1380	Muscovites defeat Mongols at Kulikovo.
1405–33	Exploration fleets led by Zheng He.
1462–1505	Reign of Ivan III (the Great) of Moscow.
1480	Muscovites cut tribute ties with Mongol khanate.
1483–1530	Lifetime of Babur, Turkic conqueror of India.
1526	Battle of Panipat.
1547	Ivan IV takes title of tsar.

Japan

1185–1333	Kamakura period.
1222–82	Nichiren, a reforming Buddhist monk.
1274, 1281	Mongol invasions repulsed.
1331–92	War of Two Emperors.
1392 – 1573	Muromachi period.
1394	Building of Golden Pavilion.
1467–77	Onin War.

Middle East

1301	Ottomans defeat Byzantine army in Bithynia.
1332–1406	Lifetime of Ibn Khaldun, Muslim social analyst.

| 1389–1402 | Reign of Bayezid I, captured by Timur. |
| 1453 | Siege of Constantinople ends in Ottoman victory. |

Southeast Asia	
1100s	Construction of Angkor Wat.
1200s	Sukhotai kingdom of Thailand.
	Rise of Ayutthaya.
1222–1451	Majapahit kingdom in Java.
1225–1400	Tran dynasty of Vietnam.
1400	Founding of Malacca.
1407	Chinese army invades Vietnam.
1428	Le dynasty.
1511	Portuguese take Malacca.
1527	Sacking of Ava, capital of Pagan.

Europe	
1202–04	Fourth Crusade, ending in Venetian conquest of Constantinople.
1208–29	French kings crusade against Albigensian heretics in southern France.
1337–1453	Hundred Years War between English and French.
1415	Portuguese expansion along African Atlantic coast begins.
1431	Death of Joan of Arc.
1492–1500	Expulsion of Jews from Iberia.
	Reconquista military drive captures Granada.
1492	Christopher Columbus reaches the Caribbean.
1498	Vasco da Gama sails around Africa to India.

Map: Global map, 1200–1500 CE, from John Haywood, *The New Atlas of World History: Global Events at a Glance* (Princeton University Press, 2012)

The Mongol conquests are the primary political event of thirteenth-century Eurasia. Bursting out of their pastoral homeland, Chinggis Khan's warriors conquered a vast territory including China, Central Eurasia, the Middle East, Russia, and Eastern Europe. They tried and failed to conquer Japan, Southeast Asia, and Egypt. Although the empire soon split up, it left major disruption in its wake and facilitated the formation of regional states. We might even see this period as a time of abrupt globalization under the Mongol empire, followed by extended deglobalization and fragmentation. The Mongols fostered extensive contacts by land and sea when they unified the continent, but much of the world remained divided into small political units after the great empires fell, and trade linkages declined, leaving many areas isolated, including much of Africa and Japan. Northern Europe was still a backward outpost of the continent, while the great cities and cultures concentrated in the Mediterranean. It is no accident that the first famous European traveler to claim to travel to China, Marco Polo, came from Venice, a city on the eastern coast of Italy, linking both the Asian and the Mediterranean trades.

During these three centuries, the world population did not change much. It grew from about 360 million to 425 million, an overall increase of 19 percent. Europe grew the most rapidly, by 40 percent, reaching about 80 million people, but Asians still dominated the world population. China suffered the most, only just recovering its population of 1200 by the year 1500, while South Asia and Japan gained much more. In much of Eurasia, gains in the thirteenth century from a warmer climate were wiped out in the fourteenth and fifteenth centuries by the Mongol conquests, the plague known as the Black Death, and the onset of the period of cooler climate known as the Little Ice Age. We have no demographic data from the Americas or Africa, but there must have been significant increases in some regions to support the new empires. Still, these areas formed only a small part of the total world population.

In Africa and the Americas, agricultural cultivation intensified with warmer climates, allowing the construction of several large empires based on collection of tribute from subordinate peoples. The Americas were still isolated from Eurasia, but this region produced two great empires, the Inkas and Aztecs, who tied together peoples over vast distances and extremely rugged terrain. The Aztec and Inka empires relied primarily on tribute collection, as did the interior African empire of Great Zimbabwe, while the African empires of Mali, Songhay, and Ethiopia combined resources from tribute, trade, and slavery. Other trading towns flourished on the East African coast and in the Sahel. All of them, however faced increasing difficulties in the fifteenth century, and they collapsed in a weakened state just before or just after European conquest.

The overwhelming majority of the world's peoples were still agriculturalists, and nomadic warriors remained the dominant military force in Eurasia. In the Americas too, the men on horseback supported major empires. Yet the strong geographic continuities from 1200 to 1500 mask significant changes in the location of economic activity, the vitality of empires and states, and the flourishing of cultures.

In Europe, the economic center shifted gradually from southeast to northwest, within the central band of cities stretching across the core of the region from London and Paris to Constantinople. Amsterdam, dug out of the marshes, began its rise as a central trading point on the northern coast, laying the base for later imperial expansion. The Hanseatic League of northern German cities linked the Baltic Sea with the Eastern European hinterland, drawing in Scandinavia to the north. England and France were still fractured among multiple warring baronies, but the core rulers in London and Paris had begun to focus their efforts on building their domains, in some ways like their counterparts, the dukes of Muscovy to the east. In these peripheral regions, exports like wool, furs, and forest products supplied important extra resources beyond those available from poorly productive agriculture.

Under the Song and Yuan dynasties, China maintained its status as the pre-eminent urbanized civilization, with a heavy concentration of people in the south. Song China, even though it did not control the north, created large cities under bureaucratic rule, relying heavily on commerce for its tax revenues. Merchants prospered in the dense lower Yangtze Valley and southeast coast, and penetrated Southeast Asian maritime regions with large ships. China suffered tremendous destruction, however, from the initial Mongol conquests, political unrest, and economic turmoil, and its population dropped nearly as much as Europe under the Black Death. Under Khubilai Khan, though, the empire recovered much of its glory, expanding trade networks both across Central Eurasia and into the southern seas. The brief Yuan dynasty created the largest territorial space seen in all of Eurasia, and the resulting peace offered new opportunities for trade, religious pilgrimage, and cultural interaction.

After several bold expeditions into the southern seas that followed on Mongol expansion, the Ming rulers enforced a return to an agrarian economy. As Europeans entered the peak of the Renaissance and the Portuguese prepared for their voyages around Africa, the Chinese withdrew from the maritime frontiers and redirected their attention toward the menacing Mongols of the northwest. It was not an irrational decision at the time, since mounted nomadic warriors were still the major danger to settled empires. Only in retrospect does the Ming retreat from the seas look like an epochal turning point.

The great religious cultures lost ground in some regions, compensated by gains in others. Christians lost control of the Byzantine empire, although the Ottomans still allowed them to practice their faith, but gained new influence in the expanding state of Muscovy to the north. Buddhists driven out of India and under attack in China found new dynamism in Japan and held on in Sri Lanka and Southeast Asia. Jews suffered pogroms and expulsion from Spain. Islam was still the most dynamically expanding religion in the world. It spread along with traders and frontier settlers to West Africa, Bengal, and Southeast Asia. Turkic soldiers who saw themselves as holy warriors had conquered Central Eurasia and the Middle East repeatedly, and the last of these founded the longest-lasting empire of the Middle East, the Ottomans. During its great expansive period, it took over the Turkish heartland, surrounded the Byzantine empire, penetrated the Balkans, and topped off its achievements with the capture of Constantinople in 1453. Hapless Europeans launching Crusades to recover the Holy Land could do little against the disciplined and hardened Turkic warriors. Over three hundred years, they could only gradually achieve the expulsion of Moors, along with Jews, from southern Spain. Yet despite hardening religious lines, Christians and Muslims continued to trade and make diplomatic deals with each other around the Mediterranean.

By the late fifteenth century, Europeans, Russians, and Ottomans were pursuing rapid expansion projects, one by sea and two by land, while China pulled back under the Ming. The Portuguese ships sailing down along the coast of Africa and across to Brazil, and the Genoese sailor Christopher Columbus with Spanish support, created the first connections linking the two great land masses of the globe.

12 Indigenous states and empires: Africa and the Americas

Timeline	
c. 1100–1500	Drier weather hits West Africa; Sahara grows, and the tse-tse fly frontier recedes with the forest.
1200–1450	Great Zimbabwe territorial state in East Africa.
1235–1433	Empire of Mali.
1248	Aztecs arrive in the Valley of Mexico.
1324	Aztecs settle on island in Lake Texcoco, and begin building capital called Tenochtitlán.
1405–33	Voyages of Chinese admiral Zheng He.
1427–1521	Aztec empire, known as the empire of the Triple Alliance until 1516.
1438	Inkas defeat Chanka; first Inka conquest beyond Valley of Cusco; beginning of empire.
1441	First West Africans ever kidnapped and taken away by sea to slavery by Portuguese captain Antam Gonçalvez. (Note that slave exports from East African ports to Arabia and Egypt via the Red Sea, to the Persian Gulf region including Iran, and to India and East Asia via the Indian Ocean began many centuries earlier.)
1468–1551	Songhay empire in West Africa.
1470	Inkas capture Chan Chan, capital of Chimú state on Pacific coast.
1472	Aztecs take over neighboring allied town of Tlatelolco to better control the trading activities of the pochteca (long-distance merchants).
1492	Columbus' first voyage.
1500–1630	Trend of increased rainfall (and more productive agriculture) in West Africa ends just as European demand for slaves takes off.
1502	Portuguese begin marauding along East African coast, seizing port towns to control trade.
1521	Aztecs defeated by Spaniards and their indigenous allies.
1543	Portuguese aid helps Christian Ethiopia defeat Muslim invaders from Adal.
1572	Inka resistance to Spaniards ends.

In the first half of the fifteenth century, two great naval powers dispatched ships to explore the African coast: the great empire of China and the tiny kingdom of Portugal.

The Chinese moved first. The emperor ordered towns along the eastern coast to construct seaworthy ships for a series of naval expeditions into the Indian Ocean under the command of a trusted eunuch, Zheng He. The first expedition in 1405 consisted of more than 300 vessels and carried a complement of 26,000 soldiers plus officers, ships' crews, court officials, servants, and many others. This first fleet visited the Indian coast. Subsequent expeditions reached Arabia and the Red Sea and eventually the east coast of Africa.

On the sixth of Zheng He's voyages, in 1421–24, the fleet visited the East African ports of Malindi, Mogadishu, Mombasa, Zanzibar, Dar es Salaam, and Kilwa. In 1431, the fleet returned to East Africa. Though Zheng He did not venture further south than Kilwa, subsequent research has shown that Chinese maps of this era contain accurate drawings of the southern coast and rough though accurate sketches of the West African coast as well.

The Chinese treated the rulers of the kingdoms and city-states they visited with courtesy, exchanged gifts with their rulers, traded to the extent possible, and returned peacefully to China. Zheng He died in India on his seventh voyage. Shortly thereafter, a new emperor, with more domestic interests, ordered an end to the voyages. The Chinese never came back.

For the Portuguese, on the other hand, Africa became the first step toward the creation of a global empire. The Portuguese king began sending ships into the South Atlantic along the coast of Africa in the 1320s. Some went in fleets, though not as large as those of Zheng He, to seize Muslim ports in Morocco. Many Portuguese expeditions involved just one or two ships exploring for opportunities.

In 1441, ten years after Zheng He's last voyage, a Portuguese ship captain named Antam Gonçalvez landed on the West African coast at a place named Rio d'Ouro ("River of Gold") by an earlier Portuguese explorer. Captain Gonçalvez and nine armed crewmen seized a man and a woman, nameless victims who became the first Africans taken by sea from the West African coast for a life of servitude. After capturing ten more Africans some days later, Gonçalvez returned to Portugal where he was knighted by the king. A new era had begun.

This chapter is about Africa and the Americas from 1200 to 1500, the last three centuries before the European conquest and colonization of the Americas and before the onset of the Atlantic slave trade. (The conquest of the Americas, and the enslavement of Africans, will be taken up in Volume 2, Chapter 3.) The key developments in this era are as follows:

- Two powerful new empires, the Aztecs in Mexico and the Inkas in Peru, erupted in the Americas during the fifteenth century and expanded rapidly until the arrival of the Europeans in the 1500s.
- The tribute-based states in the Americas extracted resources indirectly by forcing local chiefdoms and clans to produce tribute goods for the imperial state. In the Aztec empire, this system was sustained principally by Aztec military forces recruited from the rich, densely populated Valley of Mexico. In the Andes, the Inka state did not have a central population and resource base, but succeeded by mobilizing other peoples and resources to serve them.
- New states arose in sub-Saharan West Africa linked to the trans-Saharan trade, including the Mali and Songhay empires as well as a number of smaller territorial states.
- In East Africa, Ethiopia survived as an agrarian-based Christian state, ceding its trading links to Muslim control; elsewhere in the vast hinterlands behind the East African ports, smaller states, like Great Zimbabwe, arose along several trade routes, but proved unable to consolidate long-lasting control over people or territory.
- Trade and other contacts between sub-Saharan Africa and other regions provided Africans with access to modern military technology; traders also carried diseases, but over many centuries, this exposure helped many Africans to develop at least partial immunity to many pathogens.
- Europeans, faced with well-armed and relatively healthy foes, soon abandoned efforts to invade Africa; instead, they purchased African kidnap victims and carried them off to the Americas where organized indigenous resistance collapsed soon after contact.

12.1 COMPARING AFRICA AND THE AMERICAS

The rise and fall of great cities and vast empires suggests that historical change does not always move in a straight line from "lower" to "higher" levels of culture, complexity, or civilization. It may be true that our ancestors passed from hunting and gathering through herding or farming to industrial and service occupations, and from living in small bands to chiefdoms to city-states and empires, and finally to urban living in modern nation-states. Until the Industrial Revolution, however, none of these changes proved irreversible. Failed harvests turned farmers into desperate foragers. Cities were abandoned as their inhabitants fled subsistence crises, recombined into villages, and found new chiefs. Empires arose, but also collapsed into warring city-states grabbing for trade and territory. In many regions of the world, agriculture proved impossible, disease destroyed incipient cities, and great states and empires never developed at all.

Environmental challenges in Africa and the Americas made agriculture more difficult than in most of Europe and Asia, especially in hot lowland deserts and rain forests near the equator. Much of Africa was populated by subsistence farmers or foragers until the twentieth century. The same was true for the Americas, but unlike sub-Saharan Africa, the Americas also possessed highland areas of richer soil and more temperate climate. By the dawn of the Common Era, a large part of the Native American population had migrated to the higher elevations found in Mesoamerica and the Andes.

The Americas' environmental advantage was balanced by Africa's contacts with other world regions. Until 1500, human societies in much of Africa and all of the Americas evolved and changed in relative isolation from each other and the rest of the world. Native Americans had no sustained contact with other world regions until the European conquest and colonization (see Volume 2, Chapter 3). While some long-distance trade occurred within the Americas, it was limited by geographic barriers and the absence of pack animals (except in the Andes).

Sub-Saharan Africans, by contrast, did maintain continuous contact with Europe and Asia. Altogether, Africa's trade and communication links to the rest of the world were not extensive and were often interrupted. They directly touched only a few areas and a small part of the population, but their impact echoed across the continent. By 1200, many Africans lived in regions that traded continuously with the outside world. Trade across the Sahara linked sub-Saharan Africa to the North African coast and from there to the Islamic states on the Iberian peninsula and the Mediterranean trading system. The **Sudan**, a vast area that stretches from the Sahel and savanna regions of West Africa eastward to the middle portion of the Nile Valley, exported gold and slaves in exchange for horses and other goods. The hinterlands behind the trading towns of the East African coast exchanged ivory, gold, and slaves for luxury goods from the Indian Ocean. The East African ports with their polyglot mixture of populations traded with Egypt and the Persian Gulf and participated in the Indian Ocean commercial system that linked them to India, South Asia, and even China. Small and fragile as they were, sub-Saharan Africa's contacts with the outside world had huge consequences for the history of the continent.

Trade played a key role in the development of African city-states and territorial empires. This was not so true in the Americas, where the growth of cities and empires depended less on taxing traders and more on taxes (commonly called **tribute**) extracted from sedentary producers like farmers and artisans. In the Americas, large territorial empires that lasted for many centuries arose from dominant city-states in the Valley of Mexico and from locally powerful city-states along the Peruvian coast and in the Andean highlands. Except for the Mali empire, African states tended to be smaller in territory, less populous, more fragile and short-lived, with the monarch's authority beyond his own city often in question.

Just after the end of our period, in the early 1500s, powerful European states sent military expeditions to plunder and conquer in both Africa and the Americas. The powerful Aztec and Inka empires collapsed in the face of the European invasions. In contrast, the weaker, smaller, and less stable sub-Saharan African polities successfully resisted European conquest for another three centuries. Most of sub-Saharan Africa did not fall to European colonial rule until after 1850.

Two sets of questions are suggested by these contrasts. The first has to do with the role of trade and tribute in the formation, consolidation, and survival of states. Why were most of Africa's trade-based states weaker, smaller, and shorter in life span than the tribute-based empires of the Americas? Why was it that the African states of this era proved less effective in extracting tribute from subject peoples and more dependent on the resources they drew from taxing trade? How did the Native Americans manage to build powerful states capable of extracting tribute goods and labor from every village and hamlet in addition to taxing trade? These questions are addressed in this chapter.

A second set of questions is suggested by the success of European colonial expansion into the Americas after 1500, and the contrasting failure to conquer Africa for another three centuries. The conquest of the Americas is taken up in Volume 2, Chapter 3. Africa's successful resistance is discussed later in this chapter.

12.2 MESOAMERICAN STATES AND SOCIETIES, 1200–1500

The region known as **Mesoamerica** to anthropologists and historians stretches from Central Mexico to Central America. In this region, indigenous societies made their own agricultural transformation and went on to achieve impressive economic, cultural, and political breakthroughs (see Chapters 4 and 9). In the Andes and along the Pacific coast other indigenous societies reached comparable levels of productivity, urbanization, and cultural complexity before the European conquest and colonization.

By 1200, Mesoamerican farmers commonly used irrigation, terracing, **raised fields** (a farming technique that involves creating earthen platforms above the level of the surrounding countryside), and a variety of wooden tools to produce food surpluses big enough to support themselves as well as large urban populations. Craftsmen produced vast quantities of clothing, pottery, and many luxuries, including jewelry and religious objects made of copper, silver, and gold. City planners, architects, and builders laid out great city plazas, built huge temples and palaces, and engineered the construction of aqueducts to bring in fresh water. The largest Mesoamerican city before the Aztecs built their capital was undoubtedly Teotihuacán in the Valley of Mexico. Its population grew to as much as 200,000 by 450–500 CE. Mayan cities in the south, like Copán in northern Honduras, grew as large as 40,000 to 60,000. The total population of Mesoamerica in 1519 will never be known precisely, but scholarly estimates range from 12 million to 30 million, with more than half living within the Aztec empire.

Three times in the millennium before the Spanish conquest in 1521, great tributary empires arose when large city-states in the Valley of Mexico united to conquer other peoples: the empire of Teotihuacán (150–550 CE), the Toltec empire (c. 900–1168), and the empire of the Triple Alliance eventually dominated by the Aztecs of Tenochtitlán (1427–1521) (see Map 12.1). These empires were built without modern weapons. Most indigenous warriors used weapons made of stone. The Aztecs also used bows and arrows, a recent innovation, with sharp obsidian arrowheads, but the arrows often failed to penetrate the padded cotton armor and shields of their enemies. Aztec spears had obsidian points, good mainly for superficial slashing of exposed limbs. Since it was difficult to kill opponents in war, harsh treatment of prisoners was used to punish opponents, deter rebellion, and induce quick surrenders in exchange for leniency.

Mesoamericans spoke many languages, worshipped many gods, and valued diverse cultural traditions. Migrations of new peoples into the region from the north occurred repeatedly. Distinct ethnic groups often lived in close proximity, occasionally warring and intermarrying according to circumstance. Several major deities appear in the religions of many otherwise different groups, such as the rain god Tlaloc and the plumed serpent Quetzalcoatl, the god of learning and fire. Most family groups and communities also worshipped local gods, sometimes linked to legendary ancestors and past migrations.

Mesoamericans also shared a common technology that made urban life possible, but did not include ironmaking or steel. They had no domestic pack animals nor had they discovered a practical use for wheels, which they installed on toys for their children. Overland trade relied on human porters. Commerce on the lakes in the Valley of Mexico and along the seacoasts relied on canoes; sails were unknown. Unable to trade or communicate with regions beyond the Americas, Mesoamericans could not learn of African, Asian, or European advances. Until it was too late.

Map 12.1 The Aztec empire

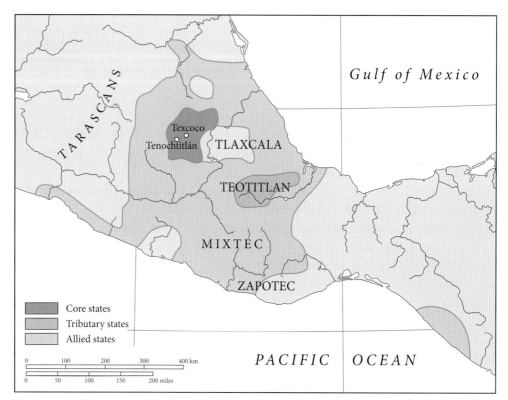

Aztec Origins and History

The tribe known to history as the Aztecs settled in the Valley of Mexico in the year 1248 CE. They were known as the Mexica, to distinguish them from other Nahuatl speakers. Their language originated in the arid grasslands and deserts of the far north of Mexico. The nomadic hunters and gatherers of that region migrated south during periods when game was scarce, invading the agricultural settlements of Central Mexico and contributing to the downfall of city-states and even empires. Civilized town folk called such people "Chichimecas" (literally "people descended from dogs," that is, barbarians). The Aztecs' own account (which they rewrote, suppressing earlier versions) claimed that they had migrated to the valley from a once bountiful, but civilized land north of the valley known as Atzlan, which they associated with the prestigious Toltec state that had collapsed in the twelfth century.

The Aztecs were not the first Nahuatl-speaking ethnic group to arrive in the Valley of Mexico (called Anáhuac by its inhabitants). At first, they settled on Chapultepec (Grasshopper) Hill, a park in today's Mexico City, but the rulers of powerful local city-states forced them to move repeatedly, each time to less desirable lands. They were tolerated because of their military skills, surviving as mercenaries in the petty wars between shifting confederations of city-states that erupted continuously in the thirteenth and fourteenth centuries.

The Aztecs finally settled in 1324 on a snake-infested island surrounded by swamps near the western shore of Lake Texcoco. According to legend, the fierce Aztec tribal god Huitzilopochtli told the Aztec leaders "Go thither where the cactus Tenochtli grows, on which an eagle sits happily . . . there we shall stop, there we shall wait, there we shall meet a number of tribes and with our arrows or our shield we shall conquer them. There will our city Mexico Tenochtitlán be, there where the eagle, its wings outspread, calls and eats." Figure 12.1 shows a colonial-era representation of the founding of this great city. In the center of the national flag of modern Mexico, this foundational legend is represented by an eagle atop a cactus grasping a snake in its claws.

The Aztecs thrived on their island. They drained the swamps and built a new town. Like many others in the valley at this time, they constructed **chinampas**, raised fields created by shoveling swamp mud high above the surrounding terrain. The raised fields were planted with maize (corn), beans (frijol), and other crops and proved to be highly productive. The Aztecs also dug canals to channel the water and reduce flooding. They built easily defended causeways to the mainland. Their new city grew rapidly and with it the wealth and power of its rulers.

The Aztecs' success was mirrored elsewhere in the Central Mexican basin as the long era of recurrent droughts that had

Figure 12.1 The Codex Mendoza is an Aztec codex (manuscript book), created about twenty years after the Spanish conquest of Mexico and named after the Spanish viceroy Antonio de Mendoza. It recounts the history of the Aztecs and their rulers. This page depicts the Aztec legend of the founding of Tenochtitlán. The codex was given to Oxford University's Bodleian Library in 1659.

contributed to the collapse of the Toltec empire gave way to more favorable conditions. The population of the Valley of Mexico, which had fallen to near 100,000 after the Toltec collapse, grew to more than 250,000 by the early 1400s and to over a million a century later. Many of the migrants moving into the valley were the descendants of ethnic groups that had lived under the Toltecs and survived the droughts, some by migrating temporarily out of the highlands altogether. Others came from more recent Chichimec origins, mixing with settled populations as they migrated. The population increase was accompanied by an intensification of agriculture, a rise in craft production, and the growth of local and regional markets. Long-distance trade also revived, linked to Aztec protection and the resale of tribute commodities.

The rise of new city-states made the politics of the valley unstable. The Aztecs' military prowess helped them to take advantage of the constant warfare. As Tenochtitlán grew, they gradually changed from despised mercenaries to respected allies. The early fifteenth century found them allied with the Tepanecas, descendants of earlier migrants to the Valley of Mexico, against an alliance of towns led by their neighbors and former employers, the Colhuas. In 1418 the Tepaneca alliance, led by the city-state of Azcapotzalco, defeated the Colhuas led by Texcoco. The Aztecs gained tribute from conquered towns, which included timber for construction as well as food, cloth, and other goods. They built an aqueduct to bring water to Tenochtitlán from springs on Chapultepec Hill. As Tenochtitlán grew in population and wealth, Aztec power grew apace.

The Aztec Empire

By the first decades of the fifteenth century, the Aztec city-state of Tenochtitlán had become one of the half dozen major powers in the Valley of Mexico, though still a junior partner in the confederation led by Azcapotzalco. This federation subdued competing towns in the valley and embarked on the conquest of several adjacent areas to the south and northeast of the valley. The Aztecs, however, did not receive as much in tribute or lands as did Azcapotzalco, so when Azcapotzalco's long-lived ruler Tzozomoc died in 1427, the Aztecs moved quickly and violently to take control. They crushed their former allies with help from Azcapotzalco's traditional enemies and formed a "Triple Alliance" with the cities of Texcoco and Tlacopan.

In 1428, with the lesson of Azcapotzalco still fresh, the Aztecs introduced a major innovation that protected their state from the instability that often followed the death of rulers. In that year, Tenochtitlán's elite agreed to deny the throne to the ruler's hereditary next in line. Instead they chose a leading noble to serve as "Chief Spokesman," henceforth called the **huey tlatoani**, based on the candidate's qualifications. This new procedure helped the Aztecs avoid civil strife between rival hereditary claimants to the throne. It also eliminated the risks associated with the elevation of inexperienced or incompetent rulers.

The Triple Alliance forced the fractious city-states of the Valley of Mexico to stop fighting each other in exchange for a junior share in the spoils of conquering others. They had to pay tribute to the alliance, but they could recoup their losses by contributing troops to conquer other cities and regions. This helped the Aztecs raise huge armies. Neither the Aztecs nor their allies made any effort to alter the structure of the societies they conquered. They exacted pledges of allegiance and imposed tribute obligations, but chose to rule indirectly through local rulers. Once or twice a year, tribute collectors from Texcoco or Tenochtitlán, or an allied city-state, visited the conquered areas to collect specified quantities of agricultural products, artisan goods like cloth and pottery, and hunted commodities like feathers and animal skins. The Aztecs also demanded respect and tribute for their principal deities. Nahuatl became a kind of lingua franca, but no effort was made to destroy local gods or impose the conquerors' language.

Indirect rule allowed the Triple Alliance to profit handsomely from its conquests without actually governing the conquered territories. This kept government spending down, but it also left in place the defeated rulers who searched constantly for opportunities to rebel and regain their independence. To solve the problem of potential defection, the Aztecs cultivated a reputation for ferocity. Local lords who failed to pay the full tribute or who were reported to be contemplating revolt or conspiring with enemies received the full fury of Aztec vengeance, including the mass execution of inhabitants and the razing of entire towns.

Texcoco and Tenochtitlán also benefited from particularly capable leadership. Under the poet king Netzahualcoyotl (1431–72), whose poetry survived the Spanish conquest (see Box 12.1), Texcoco became a center of learning and artistic expression. Texcoco also took the lead in building causeways, dikes, and canals that increased agricultural production in the valley, helped prevent floods, and facilitated canoe traffic across the lakes. Tenochtitlán also engaged in similar large-scale public works, including a huge new temple complex where thousands of prisoners of war were sacrificed each year.

The empire of the Triple Alliance did not become the "Aztec" empire until Tenochtitlán turned on Texcoco and forced its leaders to accept an Aztec lord in 1516. By this time, Tenochtitlán had a population of over 100,000 and the Aztecs' empire, with a diverse population estimated at between 6 and 15 million, stretched across Central Mexico from the Atlantic to the Pacific and included an important southern extension into the land of the Maya.

Aztec Society

Aztec social organization drew on traditions that shaped indigenous societies throughout Mesoamerica. Most Aztecs lived and worked in extended families that included several generations. Related families and kin groups belonged to calpultin (singular **calpulli**), whose leaders supervised production, saw to the collection of taxes and tribute, helped to mobilize soldiers, and managed religious festivities. In Tenochtitlán and other large cities and towns, the calpultin occupied and administered distinct neighborhoods.

Box 12.1 The Poet-King

King (tlatoani) Netzahualcoyotl (Hungry Coyote) ruled the city-state of Texcoco from 1431–72 during its alliance with the Aztecs of Tenochtitlán. Texcoco was renowned for its cultural and civic achievements. Some of his poetry survived in oral traditions to be written down by Spanish friars after the conquest. These fragments reveal a pessimism and pre-occupation with death, echoes of which can still be found in the popular culture of modern Mexico.

All the earth is a grave and nothing escapes it;

nothing is so perfect that it does not descend to its tomb.
Rivers, rivulets, fountains, and waters flow, but never return to their joyful beginnings; anxiously they hasten on to the vast realms of the rain god.
As they widen their banks, they also fashion the sad urn of their burial.
Filled are the bowels of the earth with pestilential dust
once flesh and bone, once animate bodies of men
who sat upon thrones, decided cases, presided in council,

commanded armies, conquered provinces, possessed treasure,
destroyed temples, exulted in their pride, majesty, fortune, praise, and power.
Vanished are these glories, just as the fearful smoke vanishes
that belches forth from the infernal fires of Popocatepetl.
Nothing recalls them but the written page.

Popocateptl (warrior) is the name of the tallest and most active of the three volcanoes located just to the south of the Valley of Mexico.

The basic unit of government in the Nahuatl-speaking communities of Central Mexico was called the **altepetl** (community or city-state). Each altepetl was composed of various calpultin and led by a hereditary lord, called the **tlatoani**, from the most prestigious lineage in the dominant calpulli (usually the calpulli that could claim to have descended most directly from the legendary founders of the altepetl). The origin myths of many altepetl in the Valley of Mexico included tales of migrations from the north. As an altepetl evolved from a small community to large city, new calpultin were sometimes formed to incorporate immigrants. Some cities expanded so rapidly that they incorporated several older altepetls, just as modern cities gobble up suburbs.

Aztec society was stratified and hierarchical, like all the other city-states of Central Mexico. Peasant commoners known as **macehuales** made up the vast majority of the population. A tiny minority in the leading calpultin in each city belonged to a distinct caste of nobles. Private property in the contemporary sense was not common among ordinary Aztecs. Farmland belonged to the calpulli and was reassigned by calpulli leaders according to status and need. Noble families, however, owned private lands farmed by a class of serf-like tenants, called **mayeques**, who may have made up as much as 5 percent of the population. Occasionally, war captives not needed for sacrifices to the gods also served these aristocrats as household slaves. As the empire expanded, noble families and leading warriors acquired additional lands and laborers in conquered territories. The ruler also rewarded especially brave and skillful warriors with lands and tribute.

In the cities of the Valley of Mexico and in important towns elsewhere, a minority of the population worked in more specialized occupations. Each altepetl and some of the wealthier calpultin employed priests and other specialists to interpret the will of the gods, perform public rituals, enforce a strict moral code, announce the seasons, and cure the sick. Aztec religious institutions in Tenochtitlán acquired great power. The Aztec rulers assigned lands and sources of tribute to support the temples of the major deities. The execution of large numbers of war prisoners to appease Huitzilopochtli and other Aztec deities served imperial aims by terrifying would-be enemies and discouraging rebellion.

As Tenochtitlán grew, it attracted craftsmen and merchants of all kinds. Artisans and their families moved in from other towns and cities. They produced weapons, vast quantities of pottery, and luxury goods like ceremonial dress and ornaments made from imported feathers, jade, gold, and silver. Traders flocked to Tenochtitlán's markets (see Box 12.2). Long-distance trade, however, was mainly in the hands of long-distance merchants (**pochteca**) of the adjacent city of Tlatelolco. Lacking land and other resources, Tlatelolco grew wealthy by bringing in luxury goods from the two coasts and as far away as the Mayan regions far to the south. In 1472, Tenochtitlán deposed the ruler of Tlatelolco and subjected the pochteca to regulation and control. The Aztecs did provide protection for pochteca traveling in distant lands, but in exchange demanded higher taxes and intelligence reports on the areas through which they traveled. The growth of long-distance trade fostered the use of rudimentary forms of money, usually cacao beans imported from the far south.

Tensions within Aztec society increased over time. Food production could not keep up with the growing population. Serious droughts caused widespread famine in 1450–54 and again in 1505.

Box 12.2 Markets and Merchandise in Aztec Mexico

One of our most valuable descriptions of Aztec civilization is *The Conquest of New Spain*, written by Bernal Díaz, a Spaniard who accompanied Hernán Cortés on his expedition to Mexico in 1519. In the following passage, Díaz describes the great market at Tenochtitlán:

Let us begin with the dealers in gold, silver, and precious stones, feathers, cloaks, and embroidered goods, and male and female slaves who are also sold there. They bring us many slaves to be sold in that market as the Portuguese bring Negroes from Guinea. Some are brought there attached to long poles by means of collars round their necks to prevent them from escaping, but others are left loose. Next there were those who sold coarser cloth, and cotton goods and fabrics made of twisted thread, and there were chocolate merchants with their chocolate. In this way you could see every kind of merchandise to be found anywhere in New Spain, laid out in the same way as goods are laid out in my own district of Medina del Campo, a center for fairs, where each line of stalls has its own particular sort. So it was in this great market. There were those who sold sisal cloth and ropes and the sandals they wear on their feet, which are made from the same plant. All these were kept in one part of the market, in the place assigned to them, and in another part were skins of tigers and lions, otters, jackals, and deer, badgers, mountain cats, and other wild animals, some tanned and some untanned, and other classes of merchandise.

There were sellers of kidney beans and sage and other vegetables and herbs in another place, and in yet another they were selling fowls, and birds with great dewlaps, also rabbits, hares, deer, young ducks, little dogs, and other such creatures. Then there were the fruiterers; and the women who sold cooked food, flour and honey cake, and tripe, had part of the market. Then came pottery of all kinds, from big water jars to little jugs, displayed in its own place, also honey, honey paste, and other sweets like nougat. Elsewhere they sold timber too, boards, cradles, beams, blocks, and benches, all in a quarter of their own.

Then there were the sellers of pitch pine for torches, and other things of that kind, and I must also mention, with all apologies, that they sold many canoe loads of human excrement, which they kept in the creeks near the market. This was for the manufacture of salt and the curing of skins, which they say cannot be done without it. I know that many gentlemen will laugh at this, but I assure them it is true. I may add that on all the roads they have shelters made of reeds or straw or grass so that they can retire when they wish to do so, and purge their bowels unseen by passersby, and also in order that their excrement shall not be lost.

Bad harvests pushed starving macehuales to sell themselves into servitude. With a dense population and a fragile food supply, the Aztecs could not put prisoners of war to productive use; even more were sacrificed to their gods. When the rate of new conquests slowed after 1500, noble families objected to further distributions of rewards and posts to talented commoners and resented the increasing concentration of power in the hands of the huey tlatoani. The pochteca of Tlatelolco grew wealthy buying up tribute goods and reselling them at higher prices, but they resisted Aztec taxation and control. These problems were heightened by the arrival of Spanish adventurers led by Hernán Cortés in 1519, but unlike the Inka empire, tensions within Aztec society were not decisive in the Aztecs' defeat.

Other Mesoamerican States

Powerful as they were, the Aztecs never managed to subdue rival states controlling extensive territories in Central and Southern Mexico. Their most bitter rivals were two independent states located within striking distance of Tenochtitlán: the confederation of city and tributary states led by Tlaxcala to the east, and the powerful Tarascan empire with its various allies to the north. Tlaxcala supplied most of the soldiers for the army that Cortés raised to defeat the Aztecs in 1521. The Tarascans resisted the Spaniards as they had the Aztecs and received especially brutal treatment after their defeat. To the south, the Aztecs conquered all the way to the Pacific coast but failed to subdue a powerful Mixtec state based in the Valley of Oaxaca until late in the empire.

12.3 THE ANDEAN EMPIRE OF THE INKAS

The Inkas called their empire Tawantinsuyu, which roughly meant the place that covers or unites all four directions. And so it did, stretching along the Andean Mountains from north of Quito in modern Ecuador south through the highlands of Colombia, Peru, and Bolivia to northern Chile. From east to

Map 12.2 Inka empire

ATLANTIC

OCEAN

Quito

Tumbes

Amazon River

Cajamarca

Lima

Cusco

Titicaca Valley

PACIFIC

OCEAN

ATLANTIC

OCEAN

The Inka empire 1463–1532

| 0 | 500 | 1000 | 1500 | 2000 km |

| 0 | 250 | 500 | 750 | 1000 miles |

west, the empire ran from the Pacific coast up to the highlands and down the eastern slopes of the Andes to the edge of the Amazon region. The Inka empire was the largest ever created in the Americas (see Map 12.2).

Andean Society

The indigenous population of the Andean region shared a number of important economic, political, and cultural practices with the indigenous societies of Mesoamerica. Agricultural techniques were similar, though terracing was more common in the Andean mountain valleys than in Central Mexico and large-scale irrigation works developed earlier along the rivers than traversed the Peruvian coastal desert. The use of llamas as pack animals as well as for wool and food had no parallel in Mesoamerica. However, llamas did not adapt well outside the cool mountain plateaus and long-distance trade in the Andes faced physical obstacles far more formidable than in Mesoamerica.

Cultural and social diversity was as great in the Andes as in Mesoamerica. By the time the Inkas began their conquests in the fifteenth century, however, Quechua had already come to be spoken as a first or second language by most of the 6 to 13 million people in what became the Inka empire. The Inka dialect of this language spread throughout the Andes. Family and kinship groups clustered in **ayllus**, similar to the calpultin of Central Mexico. The most important lineages of the dominant ayllus constituted hereditary nobility that supplied local rulers, called **kurakas**. In the larger city-states and empires, entire ayllus claimed noble status, with each member sharing in the benefits of conquest.

Markets functioned on the basis of barter, because no money or standard unit of accounting (like cacao beans among the Aztecs) existed in the Andean world. Andean traders and consumers had to commit to memory a complex set of equivalencies between different commodities. Instead of markets in the modern sense, Andean exchanges tended to involve elaborate gestures and rituals of mutual gift-giving according to the principle of reciprocity.

Andean communities and their ayllus could not rely on long-distance traders to transport bulky products over difficult terrain through contested territories. To secure reliable supplies of products they could not produce themselves, they often established colonies of relatives in different ecological zones. Some settled in the warmer lower elevations to grow fruit, vegetables, cotton, and maize that could be exchanged for dried fish from relatives on the coast. Others moved to higher altitudes in colder regions to herd the community's llamas and sow root crops like potatoes. Relatives then traveled between these sites exchanging products on the basis of familial reciprocity, with exchange ratios between different commodities based on custom. This practice created fragmented communities united by kinship over long distances. The historian John Murra once suggested that in contrast to the unitary communities of Mesoamerica, the villages of the Andes looked like **archipelagos** with islands of diverse production scattered across the landscape at different elevations.

Andean religious beliefs and practices, which may have seemed (and often were literally) written in stone, evolved in ways that accommodated the rise and fall of powerful states whose patron deities required deference from communities who nonetheless preferred to worship sites associated with their own mythical ancestors. The Inkas' chief deity was the sun, from whom the Inka ruler, the Çapa (or Sapa) Inka claimed to be descended. The Çapa Inka had to be treated as a living deity. Unlike the evangelizing Spaniards, however, the Inkas not only respected local shrines and idols, but also adopted them as their own.

Inka Conquests

Unlike Mesoamerica, where the large empires always arose from a base in the Valley of Mexico, the Andes contained no single region with such a natural geographic advantage. The Inka base in the Valley of Cusco boasted nothing like the population and resources of Tenochtitlán or its predecessors. The Inkas could not have succeeded without finding ways to mobilize other people and resources.

Inka legend claims that they began their conquests in a series of wars against the Chanka, a troublesome neighbor to the north, whom they defeated in 1438. An early Inka ruler, Yupanqui, used Chanka booty to secure pledges of loyalty from the kurakas (chiefs) of nearby valleys and then secured Chanka support by adopting the local shrine and endowing it with lands and sponsorship. With their basic strategy in place, the Inkas set out to extend their sway in all four directions.

One part of their strategy resembled that of the Triple Alliance. The Inkas left intact the political hierarchies of the regions they dominated and shared the fruits of their conquests with the communities and ethnic groups that fought with them and supplied their armies. Unlike the Triple Alliance, which limited its alliances to the Nahuatl-speaking city-states of the Valley of Mexico, the Inkas sought to incorporate and form alliances with diverse ethnic communities from one end of the Andes to the other. This strategy had three main components that together distinguished the Inka empire from that of the Triple Alliance and the Aztecs.

First, the Inkas turned Andean traditions of reciprocity to their advantage. Their first approach to an independent ruler was to shower him and his community with gifts, including food and drink (usually maize beer), richly decorated cloth, ornaments of gold and silver, and offers of Inka women as wives. In exchange, the Inkas expected the newly subject communities to set aside a portion of their lands to produce food supplies for Inka armies and officials, provide troops for conquests and laborers for public works, and accept many other obligations as Inka subjects. The Inkas were usually willing to bargain, but took refusal to reciprocate as an act of war subject to fierce punishment.

Second, the Inkas used the resources of the regions they conquered or incorporated peacefully for immense public works programs. They constructed 15,000 miles of roads paved with stone through mountain passes and across high plateaus running the length of the empire, with crossroads running east and west linking the highlands to the Pacific coast and to the hot lowlands of the Amazon region. They constructed food storage warehouses along the highways to provide supplies for Inka armies, but also relief to local populations in case of crop failure.

Nothing like this was ever undertaken by conquering states in Mesoamerica outside the Valley of Mexico.

Third, the Inkas appointed numerous officials to administer the territories they conquered and incorporated. Elaborate ceremonies of reciprocity accompanied tribute collections; Inka officials always gave something in return. Corvée labor obligations (the **mit'a**) forced local people to work on Inka public works, but many of the projects (roads, warehouses, terraces and irrigation canals for crops) also benefited local populations.

The Inkas conquered their vast and mountainous territory in less than a century. Throughout the Andes, the Inkas' roads, bridges, terraces, fortresses, warehouses, and irrigation works are still visible on the landscape.

Imperial Organization

In the Quechua of Cusco, the word Inka means lord. To distinguish the ruler of the empire from all other lords, he was known as the Çapa Inka or unique lord. As the empire grew in territory, the Çapa Inka acquired the status of a deity; when he died, his residences became shrines tended by hordes of servants. Beneath the Çapa Inka, the Inka state grew in size, capacity, and sophistication. The empire was divided into four main territories, each subdivided into provinces and districts. Inka officials governed at each level.

Inka governors did not content themselves with collecting tribute once or twice a year. They intervened in communities large and small to ensure that peasants worked the lands set aside for the Inka state and religious institutions and sent their quotas of draftees to the army and mit'a laborers to construction projects. The Inkas seized local idols and sent them to Cusco, but left Inka gods in exchange. They required the sons of some local lords to be educated at Cusco, but appointed them to lucrative positions in the Inka bureaucracy. As the empire expanded, the Inkas brought colonists to settle conquered lands and moved entire villages of conquered people (called **mitimaq**) onto lands close to the center of the empire. These and other integrative measures, overlaid with pan-Andean traditions of reciprocity, help to explain the generally benevolent reputation the Inkas enjoyed for centuries after the collapse of the Inka state. No comparable myth of Aztec benevolence existed in Mexico.

To keep track of their possessions, armies, and vast stores of food and commodities, the Inkas used **khipus**, which were sets of knotted strings invented earlier (perhaps by the Wari state), but now developed as a tool for communicating as well as storing information. Figure 12.2 shows one of the best

preserved and most elaborate of the khipus that survived the conquest. Relays of fast runners covered up to 150 miles a day carrying khipus and verbal messages; orders from Cusco could be delivered to Quito in a week.

Similarities in patterns of religious belief and observance as well as family, social, and economic organization also helped the Inkas establish their dominance over subject peoples. Inka organization was so effective that the bulk of its conquering armies eventually consisted of soldiers recruited from conquered regions serving under Inka officers and commanders. Because the empire was so short-lived, however, the Inkas had not yet managed to achieve as high a degree of cultural and political integration as they might have accomplished had the Spanish invasion come decades or centuries later.

The Inka rulers and the empire they built so rapidly faced two major structural problems. The first had to do with the growing costs of reciprocity. Unlike the Aztecs who simply ordered subject communities outside the Valley of Mexico to pay tribute or face the consequences, the Inka state legitimized its rule by providing gifts in exchange for its exactions. The system worked best, though not without stress, when new conquests of relatively rich areas yielded stockpiles of valuables to distribute. The richest of the Inka conquests took place in about 1470, when an Inka army finally seized Chan Chan, capital of the Chimú state that had controlled the river valleys of the Peruvian north coast for nearly 500 years.

By the late fifteenth century, however, imperial expansion had reached the point of diminishing returns. New territories were further from the core areas of the empire, armies were harder to supply, resistance grew stiffer, and the fruits of conquest less bountiful. As the costs of expanding and administering the empire grew, the balance between the Inkas' gifts and what they demanded in return may have shifted somewhat. The Inkas benefited, however, from the lack of highly developed markets and money. The illusion of reciprocity is easier to keep up when nothing has a price known to all. Perhaps to compensate for lack of booty, the Inkas set up entire factories to produce the specialized pottery, decorative textiles, and maize beer, which they distributed in exchange for harvested crops and labor drafts. Unlike the Aztecs, where resentments among subject people constituted a major source of vulnerability, the Inkas succeeded in keeping such tensions within limits.

The second structural weakness of the Inka state, its Achilles' heel, was the succession problem. The Çapa Inka ruled for life. As in most indigenous societies, only men could aspire to become the ruler. Since the Inka nobility, including the Çapa Inka himself, usually had more than one wife in addition to various concubines, they produced many sons. To avoid conflict among them, Inka rules of succession became more and more

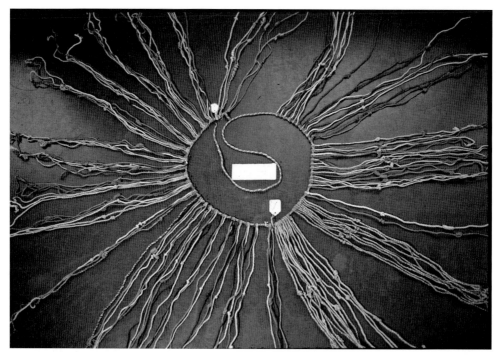

Figure 12.2 A khipu – which means "knot" in the native Inka language – in the collection of the Museum für Völkerkunde, Berlin. Khipus (also called "quipu" in Spanish) were recording devices used for record-keeping during the Inka empire. Khipus were generally made from colored thread that had been spun and plied. The thread came from llama or alpaca hair or cotton cords and had numeric and other values encoded by knots in a base 10 positional system. They could consist of just a few strands or up to 2,000. The full purpose of khipus has yet to be understood, but anthropologists believe they were used to record the information most important to the state, including accounting and data related to censuses, finance and taxes, and the military.

strict. The Inka ruler had to marry one of his sisters, who became his principal wife or **coya**. When the ruler died, the new ruler had to be a son of the coya. But ambiguities and exceptions created uncertainty. The Çapa Inka could designate which of these sons he preferred and his wishes had to be respected. But what if the ruler preferred a son by a different wife?

Even when the succession went smoothly, each new ruler faced a huge problem. At the time of the succession, the family of the deceased ruler (including his many wives and children and their relatives) took possession of all his lands and other sources of income. Each new Çapa Inka had to build his own personal and family fortune through new conquests. In time, as new lands far from Cusco proved more costly and difficult to conquer, the Inkas' rules of succession became more of a burden than an incentive. The last Inka ruler before the arrival of the Spaniards, Huayna Capac (r. 1493–1525), set out to change the rules, but it was too late to make a difference. He could not inherit the lands, laborers, and other wealth of his predecessor and thus was compelled to conquer new territory, even when attention to consolidating past gains would have worked better. This compulsion to conquer led him to undertake the conquest of Ecuador. Because Quito is so far from

Cusco, he established a permanent residence and court rivaling that in distant Cusco. Thus, to the intrigues and factionalism accompanying previous successions, geography added a new complication. Huayna Capac's death precipitated a civil war between rival claimants to the throne, one based in recently conquered Quito in the north and the other in the empire's historic capital of Cusco, on the eve of the arrival of the Spanish conquistadors.

12.4 WHAT IF THE EUROPEANS HAD NOT CONQUERED?

The Aztec capital Tenochtitlán fell to an army of Spanish adventurers and their indigenous allies in 1521. Two decades later, but with greater difficulty, Spaniards replaced the Inka state with a new colonial regime. But suppose that Columbus and his three ships had been lost at sea in 1492, that Europeans had taken decades or centuries longer to "discover" the Americas. What then?

Of course, we will never know how these societies might have evolved had they been left alone longer. Some historians would argue that such speculation is pointless and even anti-historical. Nonetheless, the similarities and differences between early modern Europe or Asia and the complex societies of the Americas have fascinated many scholars. French writer Louis Boudin, for example, argued that the Inkas had established an early form of socialism, a welfare state without markets or private property. More plausibly, historian Friedrich Katz compared Aztec society to that of Western Europe and the Inka state to the great empires of China and Southwest Asia. In the Aztec empire, the growing importance of private landholding, the wealth of the pochteca and other merchants, the development of local and long-distance trade, and the intense militarism of the Aztec state resembled somewhat the emergence of capitalism in an era of constant warfare in Western Europe after 1500. The Inkas' powerful state, with its tendency to centralize power and control economic life, Katz suggested, makes the Inkas look much more like the ancient empires of the Mediterranean or Asia than the increasingly competitive and market-oriented Western European societies of the early modern era.

Even if more time had allowed the governments and peoples of the Americas to overcome some of the technological and institutional disadvantages that hindered their defensive efforts, they could not have prepared themselves for the effects of European diseases. Soon they were threatened as never before.

12.5 WEST AFRICAN EMPIRES

Before modern times, most territorial states or empires arose either from the military conquests of armies mobilized by powerful cities or the marauding of mounted pastoralists. In most of sub-Saharan Africa, however, cities were too small and pastoralism too limited to provide a secure basis for the development of large states or empires.

In sub-Saharan Africa, environmental conditions precluded the development of big cities fed by large numbers of nearby peasant farmers. Dense urban populations like those of Mesoamerica and the Andes could not have survived in the tropical heat. The rural population lived in small clusters scattered across an unyielding landscape unable to produce a sufficient surplus to support a large non-agricultural population. The few cities that did develop were small (below 25,000 in population) with their inhabitants distributed over a large area rather than in densely packed neighborhoods.

Pastoralism could only develop north of the **tse-tse fly** frontier. Tse-tse flies carry **trypanosomiasis**, commonly called **sleeping sickness** or nagana, which kills horses, cattle, and other livestock. In the desert and the dry areas of the **Sahel** just south of the Sahara, the tse-tse fly cannot survive, but once rainfall

rises above 20–28 inches per year, livestock-raising is impossible (see Chapter 4).

Thus, the empires of sub-Saharan Africa differed from those of Mesoamerica and the Andes as well as the Asian steppes. Since Africa's farmers could not produce enough in a small area to feed great cities and pastoralists could not reach greener pastures without encountering tse-tse flies, states could not develop without finding other sources of revenue. So nearly all of sub-Saharan Africa's city-states and empires developed along trade routes that linked the interior of the continent to external trading networks. In West Africa, state formation concentrated in regions north of the tse-tse fly frontier where gold, slaves, and other commodities were sold to the Sahara caravans in exchange for imported salt, horses, luxury goods, and weapons (see Map 12.3). West African states used the revenues from taxing traders to develop specialized horse cavalries that compelled deference and a meager tribute from conquered communities and ethnic groups, but specialized in controlling and taxing market towns and trade routes.

West African Society

In most of West Africa, people lived in small, rural, relatively autonomous communities outside the direct control of territorial states. Most such communities were governed by elders who had worked their way up an age-based hierarchy that tended to leave major decisions in the hands of the oldest and usually most conservative and risk-averse members of the community. Rules were embodied in customs and practices transmitted orally across generations. In environments where small mistakes could bring disaster, this decision-making structure made sense.

Despite this tendency to conservatism (or perhaps because of the protection it afforded), West Africans were highly mobile people. North of the tse-tse fly frontier, nomadic pastoralists moved their herds frequently, in search of water and fodder. South of the tse-tse frontier, apparently sedentary farmers also moved periodically, pushed to new lands by soil exhaustion and the opportunity to acquire more fertile lands and produce charcoal for iron furnaces by clearing the forest. As people moved, they encountered other groups, some smaller and weaker, others more powerful. As migrating groups merged or pulled apart, dominant clans or lineages emerged. Over time hereditary chiefdoms based on these lineages became common in this area.

States emerged, historians believe, when the leaders and leading lineages of West African chiefdoms became connected to trade. While local trading in West African societies was based mainly on bartering complementary products between neighboring communities, long-distance trading introduced new

Map 12.3 Africa, 600–1200

possibilities for accumulating wealth in the form of gold, slaves, imported luxury goods, permanent residences in trading towns, and paid employees, both military and bureaucratic. Usually, successful chiefs looked first to recruit followers from other communities of their own ethnic group, that is, people who spoke the same language and worshipped the same gods. As wealth, power, and bureaucracy developed, chiefdoms became states.

Because of the crucial role of trade in the development and maintenance of West African states, the influence of Islam spread rapidly. Muslim traders provided the key connections to the outside world. Their literacy also made them useful as employees. At first, West African rulers merely appointed literate Muslims to manage their accounts. Eventually, most rulers and elite lineages converted to Islam. These Muslim rulers did not usually devote much effort to proselytizing the populations in their kingdoms. The ruler's family and court, chief administrators and judges, and key military personnel were usually Muslim, as were the caravan merchants and occasional invaders from across the Sahara. The rest of the West African population continued to worship local deities linked to their homes and ancestors.

In Africa as in the Americas, the transition from chiefdoms to states involved an increase in inequality. But in most of Africa, rulers could not enrich themselves much by extracting resources from peasant agriculturalists, because most peasants had little surplus to part with. Thus, states were generally less exploitative of peasants, but also more distant from the rural majority of the population.

On the other hand, state formation in West Africa was linked to the spread of slavery. As in the Andes, private property in land was uncommon in sub-Saharan Africa. In much of Africa, the land was so unproductive and weather so changeable that it was uneconomical for individuals to own it. African legal trad-itions recognized that the lands used by a community belonged to the community. Farm plots and work tasks were assigned by community leaders. Though landed wealth could not be accumulated, slaves could be. Rulers acquired slaves, gold, and trade goods through taxation and purchase. In the West African states of this era, slaves came to be used not only as servants and producers, activities in which women predominated, but also as civil administrators and warriors.

It is impossible to know from existing records just how many slaves there were in West African societies before the onset of the Atlantic slave trade. Some historians have suggested that slaves could have made up as much as 30 to 60 percent of the population. On the other hand, African slavery differed sub-stantially from the commercial plantation slavery that developed later on in the Americas. When female slaves became the wives and concubines of rulers and nobles, their children went free. Male slaves occupied positions of trust and responsibility in civil and military affairs. The stigma and low status associated with slavery in the New World was muted or absent in African slavery.

The Empire of Mali (1235–1433)

The first states in West Africa arose, like Ghana (*c.* 900–1076), during an unusual spell of wet weather that made it easier to cross the Sahara. The Ghanaian state collected tribute from the gold producers in the Bambuk region along the upper Senegal River and extracted taxes from merchants in exchange for access to markets and protection. Drier weather set in after 1100 and continued to about 1500. This encouraged pastoralism and pro-moted the development of mounted cavalry, which increased the military and thus the taxing capacities of states. The dry weather that killed the tse-tse flies, however, also killed crops so that

peasant farmers had even less to contribute in tribute than in earlier eras.

The Mali state was uniquely successful, in part, because it developed near the midpoint of this dry era. Trade across the Sahara had not yet begun to shrink, peasant farmers had not yet given up on the rain, but the dry weather had advanced enough to give horse warriors more territory to operate in.

The Mali empire was the largest territorial state ever created in Africa in its time (see Map 12.3). At its greatest extent, it stretched from **Senegambia** on the Atlantic coast (the region south of the Sahara along the bulge closest to the Americas) westward beyond the great bend in the Niger River, a distance of nearly 1,200 miles. The empire's northern border ran along the southern edge of the Sahara Desert, incorporating the key trading towns of Awdaghust, Walata, and Timbuktu. Box 12.3 quotes a mostly admiring tenth-century visitor to Awdaghust. The empire also included the gold-producing region of Bambuk and Akan and controlled the approaches to a new goldfield on the upper Niger River at Bure. The southern border of the empire reached the edge of the forest zone, a distance of up to 370 miles. Virtually all the gold produced in West Africa had to cross Mali to reach the trans-Saharan caravans.

In the core areas of Malinke settlement in the **savanna** and the Niger flood plain, the state governed indirectly through local rulers who paid a tribute, but who may also have benefited from participating in the conquests. The rest of the empire was governed less densely, with Mali cavalry deployed mainly to protect trade routes and the main trading towns. The towns were home to craftsmen organized into endogamous occupa-tional groups like smiths, leatherworkers, and other artisans. Malian conquests also yielded numerous slaves, many of whom were sold to traders for export across the Sahara.

The wet era that ended in the twelfth century benefited the Malinke agricultural villages, whose populations had increased

Box 12.3 Awdaghust in the Tenth Century

The Muslim geographer al-Bakri's description of Awdaghust in the tenth century, before the wells ran dry and the town had to be abandoned:

Awdaghust possesses wells with sweet water. Cattle and sheep are so numer-ous that for a mithqal [4.25 grams of gold] one may buy ten rams or more. Honey, too, is abundant, brought from

the land of the Sudan. The people of Awdaghust enjoy extensive benefits and huge wealth. The market there is at all times full of people, so that owing to the great crowd and the noise of voices it is almost impossible for a man to hear the words of one sitting beside him. Their transactions are in gold and they have no silver. There are handsome

buildings and fine houses. It is a country where citizens have yellow complexions because they suffer from fevers and splenitis. There is hardly one who does not complain of one or the other. Wheat, dates, and rice are imported to Awdaghust from the domains of Islam despite the great distance ... There are also pretty slave girls.

with abundant harvests. New lands had been settled and made productive. As the climate became drier, however, the Malinke suffered. Part of the push to unite to take control of trade routes and conquer new territory may have come from the need to find new sources of livelihood.

The Mali ruler, called the **mansa**, built a capital city and organized a splendid court at Niani on the upper Niger near the Bure goldfields. Though respected as religious figures among the Malinke, the mansas became Muslims, established mosques and schools, and made pilgrimages to Mecca. The pilgrimage of Mansa Musa (r. 1312–37) was especially impressive; the ruler arrived in Cairo on his way to Mecca with a hundred camel-loads of gold, which he spent lavishly. Figure 12.3 shows the impressive mosque constructed during Mansa Musi's reign.

By the late fourteenth century, however, the drier climate had pushed the Sahara's borders relentlessly toward the south. Awdaghust had to be abandoned by the end of the century for lack of water. Peasant farmers migrated south to find rain. As the forest receded, ironmakers also moved south in search of wood for charcoal. Livestock herders invaded as the tse-tse fly retreated. Discontent fed succession disputes and distant provinces rebelled. Berber (Tuareg) horsemen invaded from the Sahara, seizing Timbuktu in 1433. The empire disintegrated as competing states took over Mali's main sources of wealth. A much reduced Mali state persisted in the Malinke regions for many years, but without imperial aspirations.

Songhay Empire (1468–1551)

After the Mali state collapsed, new states developed across the Sahel region from Songhay in the west to the Hausa states and the Kanem-Borno sultanate to the east. As the tse-tse fly frontier receded to the south, horses, cattle, and states moved south as well. Even more than Mali, but in sharp contrast to the Native American empires, the new African states focused mainly on controlling trade routes and entrepôts. They ruled most of their territories indirectly by forcing independent chiefdoms and towns to pay some tribute, but they made few efforts to govern directly, collect taxes, or mobilize labor for public works in the rural areas they nominally controlled.

Figure 12.3 Mansa (ruler) Musa led the Mali empire from 1312–37. A devout Muslim, he built mosques, libraries, and universities, imported Muslim scholars, poets, architects, and skilled craftsmen from north of the Sahara, and made a famous pilgrimage to Mecca in 1324.

The gradual disintegration of the Mali empire coincided with a wave of competitive state-making in the former Mali territories. State-making also advanced to the south of the empire's frontiers as the forest retreated. Most states attempted to extract tribute from peasant communities in favored locations, but concentrated mainly on controlling the trade routes that took exports of gold, slaves, pepper, **kola nuts**, iron, and other products north to the Sahara in exchange for horses, salt, cloth, and luxury goods.

The largest of the successor states was the Songhay empire, based in the middle Niger River in the important trading town of Gao. The Songhay cavalry successfully asserted the region's independence from Mali in the fifteenth century and then forced other states in the Sudan to accept Songhay dominance and pay tribute. The expansion began when Songhay horsemen led by ruler Sonni Ali the Great (r. 1464–92) captured Timbuktu from the Tuareg in 1468. Later rulers embraced Islam, attempted to centralize tribute collection, and established slave estates in the Niger Bend.

The Songhay rulers did not succeed in conquering the recently developed Hausa states to the southeast, never extended their sway to the Atlantic coast, and faced continuous challenges to their control from within and without. Each new drought reduced tribute income, while Berber incursions threatened from the north. Finally, the sultan of Morocco, Ahmad al-Mansur, mounted a full-scale invasion across the Sahara to secure control of the main trade routes. Early successes, using firearms, allowed the Moroccans to seize Timbuktu and Jenne-jeno, but resistance from Songhay troops, the Tuareg, and many others proved costly. The Moroccans succeeded in fracturing the Songhay empire, but failed to make themselves masters of the Sudan.

Other States in West and Central Africa

The drier climate made it feasible for other ambitious chiefs to use cavalry to expand their territory. In the more fertile regions along the Niger Valley, and in smaller regions elsewhere, local chiefdoms and city-states hired horse warriors and fought their neighbors. Further south, state-making swept across the forest regions and extended into the savannas of Central Africa.

The Muslim-led states of the Sahel and northern savanna also prospered despite the drier weather. These included the state of Kanem, established by nomad clans from the Sahara during the eleventh century in the area around Lake Chad astride a major trade route that took gold and slaves north in exchange for salt from the mines at Bilma. By the thirteenth century, Kanem had incorporated the neighboring territory of Borno and gained direct access to trade with the Hausa city-states and the Akan goldfields beyond. Eventually, the nomad clans intermarried with the farming and fishing population around Lake Chad. Though peasant agriculture in the lake regions probably did better than elsewhere, the Kanem–Borno sultanate faced peasant revolts when it attempted to raise taxes and tribute.

The Hausa city-states took shape from a similar mix of nomads and agriculturalists, who came to specialize in producing cotton cloth, leather goods, and eventually slave captives for the caravan trade. Among the Yoruba of modern Nigeria, the forest kingdoms of Ife and Benin also developed, as long-distance traders based in the Mali empire penetrated southward in search of gold and other products. The development of these new states was soon to be influenced by growing trade with the Portuguese, beginning in the first half of the fifteenth century.

12.6 EAST AFRICA

Christian Ethiopia and the Muslim-ruled city-states of the East African coast did not change dramatically during the three centuries before the arrival of the Portuguese in the Indian Ocean (see Map 12.3). The Christian state that dominated the Ethiopian highlands was poor in resources, but denser on the ground than in most other areas due to the region's fragile but productive agriculture. Unlike the Sudan, where only traders and rulers had converted to Islam, Ethiopia's Christian rulers and peasants practiced the same religion. The close ties between the Ethiopian church and state strengthened both.

Along the East African coast, city-states with Muslim rulers speaking **Swahili** (a Bantu-based language with many Arabic and Persian words), stretching along the East African coast from Mogadishu in the north to Sofala in the south, had already developed as entrepôts where ivory, slaves, and gold from the interior were exchanged for luxury goods from the Indian Ocean trading system (see Chapter 9). The vast, sparsely populated hinterlands behind the ports were organized mainly into chiefdoms whose people kept the ports supplied with export commodities. Several territorial states of modest size, like Great Zimbabwe, developed along key trade routes to the coast.

Ethiopia

In Ethiopia, successive dynasties attempted to expand the empire's boundaries by moving south toward the sources of the gold, ivory, furs, and slaves that passed through the kingdom on the way to Ethiopia's Red Sea port of Massawa and the adjacent Dahlek Islands. After the center of the Islamic world moved from Cairo to Baghdad in the eighth century, the Persian Gulf supplanted the Red Sea as the main destination of African exports. This brought Muslim merchants and soldiers to the lowlands east of the Ethiopian plateau, where they established a new port at Zeila in *c*. 900. Moving inland, they set up a series of small city-states, which began encroaching on Ethiopian lands in the thirteenth century. The Ethiopian government, its resources diminished by the diversion of trade, still managed to resist these attacks and even expand further to the south until the Muslim states united to create the kingdom of Adal. In 1529, Adal mustered a large army, equipped it with new firearms, and defeated the much larger Ethiopian army at the Battle of Shimbra-Kure.

As the Ethiopians staggered in the face of these attacks, they appealed for help from European Christians with whom they had already re-established contact. The Portuguese had been seeking the kingdom of "**Prester John**," a legendary figure said to be the leader of a "lost" Christian kingdom in the African interior about which they had heard and read stories for more than a century. The Portuguese began attacking the city-states along the East African coast in 1502. They hoped to find a strong ally to aid them in their wars against Muslim states from Morocco to Mogadishu, but what they found in Ethiopia was not a powerful new ally but a crumbling kingdom with few resources. Despite their disappointment, however, they came to Ethiopia's aid. In 1543, the Ethiopians defeated Adal and went on to recover much of their lost territory in the ensuing decades. Without Portugal's help, Ethiopia would have been overrun.

East African Coastal City-States

Africa maintained commercial and cultural links to Egypt, Persia, India, and the rest of Asia through more than forty ports on the East African coast. By 1200, the major ports had already developed into city-states ruled by Muslim sultans and an elite of educated administrators and magistrates. Many of the foreign merchants resident in these port towns were Muslims from the Red Sea and Persian Gulf, who intermarried with the local Swahili-speaking elite. Beneath this upper class of rulers and merchants lived a free population of traders and artisans from the interior of Africa, many of whom were involved in supplying the ports with trade goods from their home areas or in carrying imported goods into the hinterland. Most were not Muslim, but many of those who took up permanent residence tended to convert. At the bottom of the social ladder were large slave populations that did the work of the ports and served in the households of the more prosperous families.

The impact of the trade links that passed through the East African coastal cities influenced the development of the East African interior behind the ports. The interior hinterland included both nearby agricultural and pastoral villages that supplied food to the port towns as well as more distant areas that produced and refined gold, hunted for ivory and furs, or raided to capture slaves. As in West Africa, state formation in the interior tended to concentrate along the trade routes that linked these export-producing areas to the coast. Unlike West Africa, however, no large empires arose to incorporate both the producing regions and the trading cities.

Great Zimbabwe

The interior savannas of east and south Central Africa with their sparse populations of farmers, pastoralists, and foragers were even less suited to surplus production and state formation than the Sahel and savannas of West Africa. Most of the region supported clan- or lineage-based and relatively egalitarian chiefdoms, but could not produce enough to provide for more elaborate political structures. Several territorial states did develop, however, during the fifteenth and sixteenth centuries, notably including the Kongo kingdom in Angola, the Luba and Lunda states based in the Lake Kisale region, and the Shona state Great Zimbabwe (*c*. 1200–1450).

Great Zimbabwe, a town of perhaps 10,000 inhabitants at its height, was built on the Zimbabwe plateau astride the trade routes that ran from the goldfields to the west and north to the port of Sofala on the east coast. The Shona people of the area prospered by raising cattle. In about 1200, they began building an impressive fortified town on a hill, using dry stone construction techniques common at the time (see Figure 12.4). Whatever threats had motivated the initial building soon disappeared, but construction continued and moved to the valley in the fourteenth century. The rulers of Great Zimbabwe extended their dominion to include a wide territory that covered perhaps 120 to 190 miles in every direction. They derived tribute from the Shona chiefdoms and taxed the trade goods that had to pass through their realm. This gave the city effective control of the growing trade to Sofala. The city's wealth attracted artisans, especially metalworkers, and merchants.

Great Zimbabwe declined in the fifteenth century and was abandoned by 1450. The causes of the decline are not known with certainty, but probably included overuse of the ecological resources of the surrounding countryside. In modern times, when the British colony of Southern Rhodesia, named for the famous British adventurer and mine owner Cecil Rhodes, gained its independence in 1980, the new country adopted Zimbabwe as its new name to emphasize its connection to its precolonial roots.

Figure 12.4 Great Zimbabwe is the largest ancient stone construction south of the Sahara. Built by cattle-raising Shona people astride the trade route that brought gold from the interior to the port of Sofala on the east coast of Africa, the city covered almost 1,800 acres and had a population at its apex in the late fourteenth century of between 10,000 and 20,000 inhabitants.

12.7 AFRICA CONFRONTS EUROPE

In 1500, the West African state system looked like that of Europe at the time of the Islamic and Asian invasions between 600 and 1200: a patchwork of hundreds of small, often warring chiefdoms, city-states, and loosely controlled empires that recognized no central authority. New and more powerful European states emerged partly in response to invasions. In Africa, the external challenge did not come as invaders grabbing territory, proclaiming false gods and looting towns and villages, but as traders on the coast offering cloth, tools, and firearms in exchange for traditional African trade goods, including slaves. African governments responded by taxing the increased trade passing through their towns. They used their new revenues to buy arms and horses to reinforce and extend their authority.

If the Europeans had not faced what appeared to be increasingly well-armed and well-organized West African governments, they might have invaded, enslaved the local inhabitants, and avoided the cost and trouble of setting up plantations on the other side of the Atlantic and transporting African slaves to work there. Unlike the Native Americans, Africans had iron weapons nearly as efficient as the Europeans' steel swords and soon began buying steel weapons and guns from European traders. Moreover, Africans had the same resistance as the Europeans to smallpox and the other pathogens that decimated New World populations and were better prepared than the Europeans to cope with tropical diseases and parasites.

The Portuguese and others intervened several times in the sixteenth century, probing the political and military defenses of various African governments, but each of these efforts met stiff resistance. It was not until the late nineteenth century that the Europeans succeeded in invading and creating a new set of plantation colonies, beginning with the Portuguese in Angola. As it turned out, however, sugar did not grow as well in as many places in Africa as in the Americas because of unfavorable soil conditions and rainfall patterns.

Since most of Africa retained its political independence until the late nineteenth century, the supply of slaves for the Atlantic slave trade always depended on African suppliers and on African economic and political conditions that either fostered or discouraged slave exports. In the century and a half after the Portuguese first arrived on the West African coast, they traded mainly for gold. Slaves did not come to dominate West Africa's trade with Europeans until well into the seventeenth century.

Tragically, European demand for slaves began rising after 1630, just as the West African climate entered another long dry period that lasted until 1860. As the rains failed year after year, the trans-Saharan trades declined and famine spread through many farming regions. With commercial competitors in retreat and many thousands of farming and herding people suddenly more vulnerable, slaves became easier to capture in the interior and cheaper to buy along the Atlantic coast. In addition, Africans often preferred female slaves, incorporating them as wives and producers, whose children eventually became full and free members of the community. Europeans preferred male slaves, whom they thought more suitable for plantation work, not realizing that in much of Africa it was the women who labored in the fields. European demand complemented the African internal demand.

The Atlantic slave trade also depended on African political conditions. This is illustrated by the persistently low level of slave exports from Senegambia. From the beginning of the Atlantic slave trade in the early 1500s until well after 1700, Europeans had trouble acquiring slaves in Senegambia. Instead, slave traders had to travel hundreds of miles further south and east into the Bight of Benin and south to Congo and Angola to acquire their human cargoes. This costly inconvenience came from two main causes. First, the Senegambia savanna lies above the tse-tse fly frontier, so its population could raise cattle and other livestock. With a diet much richer in protein than in regions further south, Senegambians grew taller and stronger. Reports reaching the coast suggested they were harder to capture. In the Americas, Senegambians acquired a reputation for rebelliousness that made them less desirable commodities in the slave trade. Slaves taken from areas further south like Angola were smaller in stature and widely described as more "docile."

In addition, European traders complained for more than two centuries that European goods did not sell as well in Senegambia as elsewhere. Senegambians liked their own cloth better, found European tools (except guns) no more serviceable than their own, and often preferred the salt and luxury items that continued to arrive by camel. Thus, slave exports from the Bight of Biafra lagged behind other supply areas due to local conditions over which the Europeans had no control.

Along the East African coast, Europeans encountered quite different conditions. The Portuguese sent naval vessels into the Indian Ocean in the sixteenth century. Their goal was to seize control of the Indian Ocean trade routes, force traders to pay them taxes, and monopolize the supply of goods, especially spices and gold, for which they could obtain high prices in Europe. By the end of the century, they had seized Mombasa, Kilwa, Mozambique Island, and Sofala, turning them into naval bases for Portuguese warships.

After their initial success, the Portuguese followed the pattern set by the Muslim rulers they replaced. They made little effort to conquer and colonize the interior of Africa until much later. Like their predecessors, they were interested primarily in profiting from trade. The export of slaves from East Africa never matched the West African experience in numbers or impact. The greater distance to the sugar plantations in Portuguese Brazil made it more costly to ship slaves from East Africa, while the longer voyages raised mortality among the victims.

An eyewitness described the Portuguese occupation of Kilwa after the defeat of the defenders: "Then the Vicar-General and some Franciscan fathers came ashore carrying two crosses in procession and singing the Te Deum. They went to the palace, and there the cross was put down and the Grand-Captain prayed. Then everyone started to plunder the town of all its merchandise and provisions." Quite a contrast to the visit of the much larger, and more diplomatic, Chinese fleet a century and a half earlier.

Conclusion   Agriculture and pastoralism developed later in Africa and the Americas than in Asia and Europe. Once underway, the agricultural transformation spread slowly, but farming became productive enough to support urban development and state formation only in limited areas. In the Americas, this included the Mesoamerican and Andean highlands and the Pacific coast of Peru. In sub-Saharan Africa, even where agriculture benefited from the spread of iron tools and enjoyed favorable climate and soil conditions, large-scale urban development could not take place because disease spread so quickly in the tropical heat. Empires were not based on mobilizing great armies of city-dwellers, but on harnessing horse warriors to tap into the wealth accumulated along trade routes.

The contrast between Native American and African state formation should not be exaggerated, of course. Though states in the Americas relied mainly on mobilizing laborers and warriors, at least some of the great wealth displayed by elites in Mesoamerica and the Andes came from taxing trade. This was particularly true of the Aztecs, who not only taxed the pochteca (long-distance traders), but also used them to market tribute goods and to serve as spies. Similarly, while most African states relied on taxing trade to acquire needed revenues, and used imported arms and horses for their military establishments, they all made efforts to extract tribute and labor from the agricultural producers and pastoralists in their territories. This was particularly true of the states that arose in the more productive Niger River bend country of West Africa, the Lake country further east and south, and the Ethiopian highlands.

To one degree or another, trade and tribute both served as catalysts for the evolution of trading towns into powerful city-states and even large territorial states or empires. In Africa, trading towns developed into city-states along the East African coast and in the Sahel south of the Sahara. Up to about 1200, however, territorial empires developed in only two areas, the Niger Valley in the Sahel and the Ethiopian highlands. In the Americas, where tribute was more important than trade, city-states developed mainly in Mesoamerica and the Andean region. Great territorial empires arose from dominant city-states in the Valley of Mexico and from locally powerful city-states along the Peruvian coast and in the Andean highlands.

The new territorial states that arose between 1200 and 1500 were more powerful and extensive than any of the earlier empires in Africa and the Americas. Studying them provides a window on how these two regions might have evolved and developed if they had not been so profoundly affected by the Atlantic slave trade and the European conquest of the Americas, both of which had barely begun by the end of fifteenth century.

Speculation about what might have been in the Americas always runs up against the catastrophic decline of Native American populations after exposure to European diseases (see Volume 2, Chapter 3). Perhaps, with more time, indigenous medical knowledge would have developed enough to make a difference, but this seems unlikely given how long it took to produce effective remedies, other than through acquired immunities, elsewhere in the world. In the case of Africa, the increase in external trade with Europeans in gold and pepper up to the 1630s and in slaves thereafter appears to have had the predictable effect of stimulating the development of territorial states and empires as rulers used revenues from slave sales to strengthen and consolidate their control of territory. Without the integration of Africa into the Atlantic trading system, however, West African states would have been weaker and conquest by aggressive Europeans might have occurred far sooner.

Study Questions   (1) Compare and contrast the development of the Aztec and Inka societies and empires.

(2) Why did the death of the ruler cause few problems for the Aztecs, but precipitate crises among the Inkas?

(3) Why do you suppose that legends and myths extolling Inka benevolence continue to circulate in the Andes, while the Aztecs are famous mainly for their ruthlessness?

(4) Why did African states rely more on taxing trade than on extracting tribute as in the Americas?

(5) How did climate and environment affect the rise and fall of African states like Mali, Songhay, and Great Zimbabwe?

(6) How do you explain the short-lived success of the Mali empire?

(7) Why did the East African city-states along the coast not seek to conquer territory in the interior of Africa?

(8) Why did resistance to European conquest and colonization prove to be so effective in Africa and collapse so quickly in the Americas? (You can look ahead to Volume 2, Chapter 3 to answer this question.)

Suggested Reading

DAVID CARRASCO AND EDUARDO MATOS MOCTEZUMA, *Moctezuma's Mexico: Visions of the Aztec World* (Boulder: University Press of Colorado, 2003). This book focuses on Aztec culture and religious life.

MICHAEL D. COE AND REX KOONTZ, *Mexico from the Olmecs to the Aztecs*, 5th edn. (New York: Thames & Hudson, 2002). This is an excellent survey of pre-Conquest societies and cultures in Mexico.

GRAHAM CONNAH, *African Civilizations: An Archaeological Perspective*, 2nd edn. (Cambridge University Press, 2001). This excellent study focuses on urbanism and state formation over the past 4,000 years in seven main areas of Africa: Nubia, Ethiopia, the West African savanna, the West African forest, the East African coast and islands, the Zimbabwe plateau, and parts of Central Africa.

JOHN HYSLOP, *The Inka Road System* (Orlando, FL: Academic Press, 1984). This is a detailed study of the Inkas' impressive public works and the extensive road network that linked the far-flung parts of their empire.

FRIEDRICH KATZ, *The Ancient American Civilizations* (London: Weidenfeld & Nicolson, 1969). Katz's classic work was the first to systematically compare Aztec, Inka, and Mayan civilizations.

JOHN V. MURRA, *The Economic Organization of the Inka State* (Greenwich, CT: JAI Press, 1980). This is a pioneering study by the historian and anthropologist who first discovered that Andean communities (ayllus) created colonies at different elevations and ecological zones that created opportunities for reciprocal exchange without markets or money.

MARIA ROSTWOROWSKI DE DIEZ CANSECO, *History of the Inca Realm* (Cambridge University Press, 1999). This is an important work by a leading Peruvian scholar.

KEVIN SHILLINGTON, *History of Africa* (London: Macmillan, 1995). Shillington provides a highly readable survey of the sweep of African history from earliest times.

Glossary

altepetl: Nahuatl (Aztec) word for community or city-state.

archipelago: Usually refers to a chain or cluster of islands. Historian John Murra used the term to describe the way Andean ayllus sent members to create colonies at various elevations to produce different products (e.g. fruit in hot lowlands, potatoes in the cold plateaus).

ayllu: Set of families and kin groups that formed the basic organizational unit of Andean society; similar to the calpulli in Aztec society.

calpulli (*pl.* calpultin): Set of families and kin groups that formed the basic organizational unit of Aztec society; similar to the ayllu in the Andes.

chinampa: Mexican version of raised fields.

coya: Full sister and wife of the Inka emperor or Çapa Inka; only sons of the coya were eligible to succeed to the throne.

huey tlatoani: "Chief Spokesman" (emperor) of the Aztecs.

khipus: Knotted strings attached at the top used for record-keeping by Andean governments, beginning with the Wari.

kola nuts: Major export from West African forests, valued by Muslim consumers as a stimulant and symbol of hospitality.

kuraka: Local Andean lord, similar to the tlatoani among the Aztecs.

macehual (*pl.* macehuales): Aztec common people, mostly farmers.

mansa: Name given the ruler or king of the Mali empire.

mayeques: Service tenants attached to lands owned by Aztec nobles.

Mesoamerica: Also called Middle America, this is the region in North America where agriculture and urbanization developed after 2000 BCE; extends from Central Mexico to northern Central America.

mit'a: Name given by Inkas to corvée (forced or obligated) labor on public works by peasants throughout the empire.

mitimaq: Peasant communities resettled by Inka colonists; Quechua-speaking loyal subjects from core areas of the empire were settled on the periphery, while communities of newly conquered people were resettled in the interior of the empire.

pochteca: Long-distance traders in the Aztec empire, based in the city of Tlatelolco adjacent to the Aztec capital of Tenochtitlán.

Prester John: Legendary figure said to be the leader of a "lost" Christian kingdom in the African interior.

raised fields: Farming technique that involves creating earthen platforms above the level of the surrounding countryside for growing crops.

Sahel: Arid steppe (flat plain) 120 to 250 miles in width, stretching 4,000 miles in length from the Atlantic Ocean to the Red Sea.

savanna: Extensive area of grassland with occasional bushes and trees.

Senegambia: West African region roughly bounded by the Senegal and Gambia rivers, from the Atlantic coast to the interior.

sleeping sickness: See tse-tse fly.

Sudan: Portion of sub-Saharan Africa known to Muslim geographers in medieval times; includes both the West African regions below the Sahara (the Sahel and savanna areas) and the middle portion of the Nile basin; in modern times, the eastern portion of this vast region forms most of the contemporary nation of Sudan.

Swahili: Bantu-based language with many Arabic and Persian words that developed in the East African port cities.

tlatoani: Nahuatl (Aztec) term for leader of a community (altepetl); the tlatoani of the larger towns and cities belonged to noble families; similar to kurakas in the Andes.

tribute: Agricultural products, artisan manufactures, and luxury products extracted from conquered populations by conquering states and empires; such taxes in kind were common in Mesoamerica and the Andes, but less common in Africa.

trypanosomiasis: See tse-tse fly.

tse-tse fly: The African tse-tse fly, which thrives in areas of high annual rainfall (at least 20–28 inches) and mixed vegetation of trees, bushes, and grasslands, spreads trypanosomiasis (sleeping sickness).

13 The Mongol conquests and their legacies

The Mongol Empire and Central Eurasia	
c. 1162	Birth of Chinggis Khan.
c. 1185–1242	Chaghatai is khan of Central Asia.
1186–1241	Őgődei khan of khans
1206	Chinggis declared khan of Mongols.
1209	Chinggis attacks Tanguts; signs peace treaty.
1215	Mongols seize Beijing from Jin dynasty.
1220	Chinggis takes Samarkand.
1227	Death of Chinggis Khan.
1259	Death of Great Khan Mőngke.
1260–94	Reign of Khubilai Khan.
1279–1368	Yuan dynasty of China.
1336–1405	Lifetime of Timur.

Middle East	
1256–1335	Il-Khans of Persia.
1295–1304	Reign of Il-Khan Ghazan.
1301	Ottomans besiege Iznik, and defeat Byzantines.
1325–54	Travels of Ibn Battuta.
1401	Timur sacks Baghdad.
1402	Timur captures Sultan Bayezid of Ottoman empire.
1405	Death of Timur.
1453	Ottomans capture Constantinople, renaming it Istanbul.

Russia	
1224	Mongols sack Novgorod.
1300	Metropolitan moves Orthodox church headquarters to Moscow.
1328	Ivan Kalita named first Grand Prince of Muscovy.
1336	Plague appears in Crimea.
1380	Dmitri Donskoi defeats Mongol army at Kulikovo.

1382	Moscow sacked by Tokhtamysh.
1462–1505	Reign of Ivan III (the Great) of Moscow.
1478	Ivan conquers Novgorod.
1480	Muscovy formally cuts tribute ties with the khan.
1547	Ivan IV assumes title of tsar.

China

1234	End of Jin dynasty.
1279–1368	Yuan dynasty.
1331	Plague appears in North China.
1368	Zhu Yuanzhang founds Ming dynasty.
1402–24	Reign of Yongle emperor.
1405–33	Zheng He leads seven maritime expeditions into Indian Ocean.
1449	Chinese emperor captured by Mongol khan.

South Asia

1206–1526	Delhi sultanates.
1325–51	Reign of Muhammad bin Tughluq.
1351–88	Reign of Firuz Shah.
1398	Timur sacks Delhi.
1469–1539	Nanak, founder of Sikhs.
1483–1530	Babur.
1510	King of Vijayanagar allows Portuguese to build a fort on Malabar coast.
1526	Battle of Panipat, in which Babur defeats the sultan and founds Mughal empire.
1565	In Battle of Talikota, sultans of the Deccan defeat the Hindu army of Vijayanagar.

Japan

1185	Battle of Dannoura, in which Minamoto crush Taira.
1185–1333	Kamakura period.
1274 and 1281	Mongol invasions driven back.
1331–92	Period of civil war.
1392–1573	Muromachi, or Ashikaga shogunate.
1394	Building of Golden Pavilion in Kyoto.
1401	Japan resumes official trade with China.
1467–77	Onin War.
1482	Building of Silver Pavilion in Kyoto.

Southeast Asia

1222–1451	Kingdom of Majapahit in Java.
1225–1400	Tran dynasty of Vietnam.
1238–1438	Sukhotai state of Thailand.
1257	Hanoi sacked by Mongols.

1280s	Vietnamese drive off Mongol invasions.
1287	Mongol invasions severely damage the Burmese kingdom of Pagan.
1293	Javanese kings drive out Mongol warships.
1350	Founding of Ayutthaya.
1400	Founding of Malacca.
1407	Chinese armies invade Vietnam.
1428	Le Lo'i defeats Chinese forces.
1471	Annam annexes Champa in southern Vietnam.
1511	Portuguese take Malacca.
1527	Shan highlanders sack Burmese capital of Ava.

In the 1160s, a young man named **Temujin** was born to an aristocratic nomadic family in the Central Eurasian steppe. His father was a warrior who spent his life fighting with other clans, living mostly in poverty and insecurity. When Temujin's father died, all his followers deserted him, leaving his family destitute, forced to live on berries, fish, and rats. Temujin was captured by another tribe and imprisoned for many years. He escaped and found a patron, whom he joined in battle against the Merkits to the north, his first major victory. His dream, however, was not to be a follower, but a khan, a leader of leaders elected by all his tribesmen at a **khuriltai**, or acclamation ceremony. It took him twenty years. He had to betray his closest blood brothers, spend a long time in exile in China, and defeat powerful rivals before gaining the recognition of all the Mongols at the khuriltai in 1206. Then he called himself "Great Oceanic (or Heavenly) Leader," that is, **Chinggis Khan** (or Genghis Khan). He took terrible vengeance on the tribe that had imprisoned him, massacring all their young men, but he was extremely generous to his friends. He never forgot a favor, or a grudge. His people, the Mongols, would soon be feared all across Eurasia. The Mongols created the largest empire the world ever saw before the British empire of the late nineteenth century.

The story of the Mongols is irresistibly dramatic, yet we know surprisingly little about them. Since the Mongols did not create their own written language until after Chinggis took power, nearly all our information about their early years comes from mostly hostile Persian and Chinese chronicles, and from one valuable but partly legendary source, *The Secret History of the Mongols*. We do not even know for certain the date of Chinggis's birth. We do know that in the mid twelfth century the Mongols were only a weak tribe in the steppes of Central Eurasia. To their east were powerful nomadic confederations. South of them were large empires founded by nomads who had conquered north and northwest China. The **Jurchens**, from Manchuria, established

the **Jin** empire in 1115; the Tibetan **Tanguts** held northwest China under the Xi Xia empire. South of the Yangtze River, the Song still held out against the Jin. Further west, the **Uighurs**, the **Karakhitai**, and the Tibetans each occupied huge expanses of desert, oasis, and steppe, and the **Khwarazm Shah** occupied the fabled cities of **Samarkand**, **Bukhara**, and much of Persia. By the end of his life, Chinggis Khan had overpowered all these empires, except for the Southern Song. He did it through incessant military campaigning and adroit diplomacy, but most of all by his stunning character.

The secret of success for a nomadic leader was to attract followers, and the way to attract followers was to win in war. Mongolian tribes competed desperately for grasslands and water. Young men attached themselves to the most promising leader. Oaths of blood brotherhood and marriage alliances also tied men intimately, solidified by comradeship in battle. The losers died, or became slaves. As Chinggis became well known among the nomads, he attracted the most aggressive young men to him. He appointed brave men from the lowest classes to top military ranks. He distributed the booty gained from victory widely, but controlled its allocation strictly. All his rivals were equally treacherous, and generous, but somehow Chinggis stood above them all. He also understood how to win over people peacefully. Strategic oaths of friendship, signed in blood, won over important defectors from other nomads and even from the powerful Jin. Tribes who resisted were plundered and enslaved; those who surrendered kept much of their property, but owed the khan men, horses, and taxes. Their leaders became governors under the growing empire.

The Mongols left a paradoxical legacy:

- They destroyed vibrant cities and civilizations ruthlessly, *but* they treated generously those who surrendered, and tolerated many religious faiths.

- They created a peaceful environment for trade, *but* they extracted revenue from merchants and brought down their states with fiscal mismanagement.
- In the long run, occupation by Inner Asian conquerors, beginning with the Mongols, set the Middle East, India, China, and Central Eurasia on a different course from more protected areas like Western Europe, Japan, or Southeast Asia. Russia falls somewhere in the middle.

13.1 THE MONGOL CONQUESTS

Chinggis Khan's Final Achievements

After the khuriltai of 1206, Chinggis planned to take on the wealthiest states around him: first the Jin, then the Xi Xia, and ultimately Song China, but to do this he needed a much tighter organization. He drastically reformed his military, creating a personal bodyguard unconditionally loyal to him, and ordering the rest into units of thousands and tens of thousands that crossed tribal lines. Men and their families were totally under the control of their military commander: this was literally a nation in arms. Finally, the illiterate Chinggis ordered all his princes to use the Uighur script to write the Mongolian language. Writing and the military were the two central technologies of Mongolian power, yet oddly, writing gave them more problems than warfare. The Uighur script did not fit the Mongolian language well, and other khans tried other systems, derived from Tibetan or Chinese, but in the end they used a vertical alphabetic script derived from the Central Asian trading language, **Sogdian**. From the historian's point of view, they chose well. The **Khitans**, Jurchens, and Tanguts used instead modified Chinese characters which are still mostly undeciphered. Even so, Mongolian documents are scarce.

The Tangut Xi Xia empire, Chinggis's next target, had fortified cities, which the Mongols had not yet learned how to besiege. Chinggis attacked them in 1209, but had to sign a peace treaty in return for rich gifts. Only at the end of his life could he destroy them utterly. The Uighurs submitted quickly, but the Jin in North China were the really tough opponents. Chinggis successfully besieged their capital, at present-day Beijing, but it was a tough struggle. Both Mongols and Jurchens suffered starvation and disease, and the city was destroyed. The Jin emperor, however, moved south to Kaifeng, and despite massive destruction inflicted on North China, held out there for the rest of Chinggis's life.

Chinggis's final Central Eurasian rival, **Sultan Mohammad**, the Khwarazm Shah, ruled a vast expanse from the Aral Sea to the Persian Gulf, and from the Pamirs to the Zagros Mountains in Iran. The sultan refused peace offers, declaring that Allah had decreed a holy war against the Mongol idolaters. But many lords, merchants, and peasants hated the shah's heavy exactions, and even the caliph of Baghdad urged Chinggis to attack him. Chinggis cleverly exploited divisions in the empire, and the sultan feared giving his commanders too much power, so the Mongols, even though inferior in numbers, picked off the pieces of his army one by one. In Bukhara they inflicted exemplary terror, burning down the city and plundering it ruthlessly. When Samarkand fell in 1220, the shah's empire fell soon after.

During the last years of his life, Chinggis shifted his attention from war to spiritual matters. He had always embraced religious diversity: when he plundered cities, he seldom desecrated temples or mosques. The Mongols' native religion was shamanism, led by priests who went into trances to gain special access to the spirits of the sky. Because the shamans could foretell the future, expel evil spirits, and call on storms to guarantee military victory, they had political influence. In his early years, Chinggis had the spine of a powerful shaman broken, but it was politics, not dogmatism, that motivated his religious policy. He proclaimed religious freedom to incite people to rebel against his enemies, and tolerated Christians, Buddhists, Muslims, and Daoists, without showing much interest in their teachings. The aging khan had heard, however, of the Daoist priest **Changchun**, said to be 300 years old, who seemed to know the secret of longevity. Chinggis summoned him to his camp, wrote him many letters, and gave him power over all the monks in his empire.

Chinggis was indeed one of the greatest military commanders of all time, but what did he leave behind? He had begun a rudimentary administration of his territories, based on the idea that all subject people belonged to his household, but his center did not hold. The empire broke apart into four separate khanates soon after his death. He created the Great Seal to legitimate his decrees, he established a rapid courier network, and he codified Mongolian customs. He certainly enriched the Mongols, as he impoverished others. Today, the Mongols celebrate him as a national hero, Russians attack him as nothing but a destroyer, while the Chinese focus on his positive role in linking east and west.

Khubilai Khan in China: The Yuan dynasty (1279–1368)

After Chinggis, the Mongol empire expanded east and west, but broke apart into warring khanates led by his sons. Nomadic empires had to either grow or die. Continual expansion brought more booty, more followers, and more prestige for the leader, while losses led to a vicious circle of defeat and desertion. The riches of settled societies tempted many Mongols to seek a more secure, non-nomadic way of life, but others held out for the austere, but more equal, life of the steppe. **Khubilai Khan,**

Figure 13.1 This Yuan dynasty ink painting on silk shows Khubilai Khan on horseback hunting with his comrades.

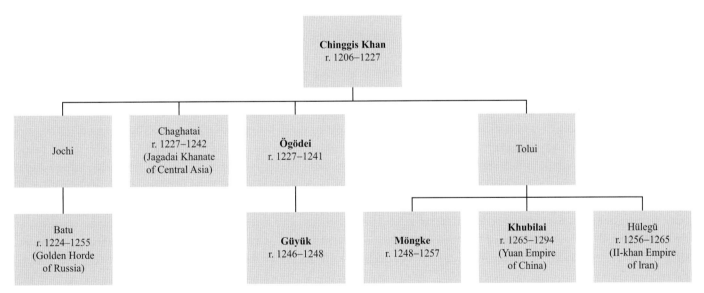

Figure 13.2 Chinggis Khan and his descendants. Bold indicates Great Khans.

grandson of Chinggis, completed the conquest of China and settled down there. His portrait appears in Figure 13.1. He created a legitimate Chinese dynasty, the **Yuan dynasty** (1279–1368). His brothers and their successors had more difficulty in balancing the steppe and the sown lands.

The Mongols had no definite rules about succession to the khanate. The khan's youngest son usually inherited his father's herds, but his elder brothers held rights of seniority. In principle, the "most worthy" brother was elected khan by a khuriltai that assembled all the major chieftains. This usually meant in practice continual warfare between rivals until one eliminated all the others. Then the khuriltai acclaimed him as the legitimate leader. Figure 13.2 shows the relationships between the members of the conquest family.

Women also played important indirect roles in selecting new Mongol leaders. Temujin's mother had decisive influence in bringing him to power. As regents, wives, and marriage kin, women of the ruling elite used personal connections to persuade their quarrelsome men to favor their sons and relatives. Women also kept the basic pastoral economy going by managing the herds while the men charged around on horseback. They did not live in seclusion like so many of the women of Russia, the Middle East, or China. When the Mongols expanded into settled territories like Persia and China, the official historians found it awkward to explain to their readers the powerful influence of women on the Mongol leaders.

Never before, however, had any nomads dealt out territory on such a vast scale. Compromise was necessary. Chinggis chose his third son Ögödei (1186–1241), a lovable drunk, to be his successor, the "khan of khans", or khaghan, but Ögödei's brothers temporarily divided the empire into four parts: Ögödei held the center, while Chinggis's grandson **Batu** became khan of the "**Golden Horde**," or **Kipchak khanate**, in the west, including most of Russia; his second son Chaghatai (c. 1185–1242) inherited most of Central Eurasia, and his youngest son Tolui (c. 1190–1231) received North China. Ögödei and Batu continued the expansion east and west. Ögödei crushed the Jin dynasty in 1234, taking all of North China. Then all four khans joined to subdue Russia, Poland, and Hungary. Only the death of Ögödei in 1241 spared the rest of Europe; at the gates of Vienna, the khans rushed back to Mongolia for the khuriltai to determine the next khaghan.

During his brief reign, Ögödei established the Mongols' first capital, at **Karakorum**, in the Orkhon Valley. It was a rudimentary city, and nothing survives of it today. The title of khaghan, however, was worth a bloody struggle, finally won by Tolui's son Khubilai (r. 1260–94). Khubilai definitively directed his followers' energies toward China, but his relatives in Mongolia attacked him for abandoning traditional Mongolian customs. The four huge sections of the empire took more definitive shape. Khubilai gave up Central Eurasia and moved south, descendants of Chaghatai kept Central Eurasia, Khubilai's brother Hülegü established a dynasty in Persia, and the Kipchak khans ruled Russia. Box 13.1 describes the variety of reactions to Mongol expansion across Eurasia.

The conquest of China was the richest prize for any Mongol leader. Khubilai's early victories against the Song entitled him to claim the khanship, but the taint of illegitimacy always hovered over his reign. Until he proved his valor with a definitive conquest, his Mongol rivals would not accept him. Khubilai did all he could to influence the Song to surrender peacefully. The **Southern Song**, however, was a wealthy, proud society. Its capital, **Hangzhou**, was the largest city in the world (see

Chapter 11). The Song rulers' primary goal was to recover North China from the despised barbarians. They had paid large sums of money to the hated Jin to prevent attacks across the Yangtze. Political factions divided intensely over the wisdom of defensive payments versus aggressive campaigns north. At one point, the Song had even helped the Mongols to attack the Jin. Now they defiantly faced the Mongols alone. But Song government was corrupt. Its emperors were weak, and its armies were decaying. Large landlords refused to pay taxes. The army looked large, but greedy commanders inflated its numbers. The state's fiscal crisis and factional politics seriously undercut its strength just when it needed unity.

Even so, invasion was a formidable challenge for the Mongols. Tropical heat, disease, waterways, and deep forests were alien terrain to both the Mongol warriors and their horses. What they needed were sailors, merchants, and naval warfare technology. One of the most amazing testimonials to the Mongols' flexibility is their ability to learn these new techniques, with the help of many willing Chinese. Khubilai enticed many defectors to his side with generous grants of aid, relying heavily on Chinese generals to lead his campaign. Long, exhausting blockades of major cities, aided by new artillery support, in the form of catapults, finally ground the Song down. After Hangzhou fell, Khubilai declared himself emperor of a new Chinese dynasty in 1279. He called it "Yuan," from the ancient Chinese classic *Book of Changes*, meaning "origin," the cosmic point from which the universe grew.

Before finishing the conquest of China, Khubilai decided to establish a new capital. He called it Shangdu ("upper capital," famed in Coleridge's poem as "Xanadu"), and located it 125 miles northwest of Beijing. It was built on a Chinese model, with some nomadic touches. It had the usual walls and a large palace, but also a hunting reserve, and indeed a "stately pleasure dome" in the middle of a park filled with protected animals. Later, he moved his primary capital to Beijing and kept Shangdu as a summer residence. Beijing followed classic Chinese architectural models even more closely than Shangdu. With its construction, Khubilai staked his claim to appeal to Han Chinese cultural tradition. The modern status of Beijing as an imperial city, with its peculiar position so far north, dates from Khubilai's time. For Mongols, Beijing is much too far south for comfort, but within China, Beijing is so far north that supplying its food demands was very difficult. Khubilai extended the Grand Canal north to reach nearly to Beijing, at huge expense, so as to ensure reliable grain shipments from the productive south.

From his youth, Khubilai oriented himself toward China. Chinese advisors helped him to conquer the Southern Song, teaching the Mongols new military tactics. In the watery lands of South China, the Mongols of the arid steppe learned to cross

Box 13.1 Reactions to the Mongols

These sources show diverse reactions to the Mongol conquest by chroniclers and visitors across the continent. Many were appalled by Mongol destruction, but those who met the khans often found a friendly welcome. Both the pope and the khan could invoke the will of God to justify their actions.

The Secret History of the Mongols tells the story of the rise of Chinggis Khan to power as a family history. To become Khan, he first had to defeat or win over his closest kinsmen and blood brothers. In this passage, he forgives his blood brother (*anda*), Jamugha, who had fought against him, but Jamugha insists on being executed in order to wipe out the shame of betrayal. Chinggis has him executed with full honors, not shedding his blood on the ground:

Chingis Khan said: "Tell Jamugha this. Now we two are together. Let's be allies. Once we moved together like the two shafts of a cart, but you thought about separating from me and you left. Now that we're together again in one place let's each be the one to remind the other of what he forgot; let's each be the one to awaken the other's judgment whenever it sleeps. Though you left me you were always my anda. On the day when we met on the battlefield the thought of trying to kill me brought pain to your heart."

Jamugha answered him, "Long ago when we were children in the Khorkhonagh Valley I declared myself to be your anda. Together we ate the food which is never digested and spoke words to each other which are never forgotten, and at night we shared one blanket to cover us both. Then it was as if people came between us with knives slashing our legs and stabbing our sides ... and my face was so red from the heat of my shame that I went far away from you ... Now my anda, you've pacified every nation; you've united every tribe in the world. The Great Khan's throne has given itself to you. Now that the world is ready for you what good would I be as your ally? ... My anda, if you want to favor me, then let me die quickly and you'll be at peace with your heart. When you have me killed, my anda, see that it's done without shedding my blood."

And Chingis Khan made a decree, saying: "Execute Jamugha without shedding his blood and bury his bones with all due honor." He had Jamugha killed and his bones properly buried.

The Franciscan William of Rubruck traveled from Constantinople to the camp of the Great Khan in order to convert the Mongols to Christianity. He found Nestorians, Manichaeans, Muslims, and others there already competing for the khan's attention. The khan ordered each of the clerics to argue the merits of his religion in front of him. He seems to have been impressed with William, because he summoned him to a private audience soon after, and expressed to him his own faith: "We Mongols ... believe that there is but one God, by whom we live and by whom we die and towards him we have an upright heart ... But just as God gave different fingers to the hand so has He given different ways to men. To you God has given the Scriptures and you Christians do not observe them." Although skeptical of most Christians' sincerity, the khan made an exception of William, and treated him well. He sent him home with a letter for the pope and welcomed him to return.

A Russian chronicler described the destruction of Ryazan: They "burned this holy city with all its beauty and wealth ... And churches of God were destroyed and much blood was spilled on the holy altars. And not one man remained alive in the city. All were dead ... And there was not even anyone to mourn the dead."

Pope Innocent IV wrote to the Mongol khan in 1245 to persuade him to stop his destruction of Christian lands and accept the Christian message: "Seeing that not only men but even irrational animals, nay, the very elements which go to make up the world machine, are united by a certain innate law after the manner of the celestial spirits, all of which God the Creator has divided into choirs in the enduring stability of peaceful order, it is not without cause that we are driven to express in strong terms our amazement that you, as we have heard, have invaded many countries belonging both to Christians and to others and are laying them waste in a horrible desolation, and with a fury still unabated you do not cease from stretching out your destroying hand to more distant lands ... [We] do admonish, beg and earnestly beseech all of you that for the future you desist entirely from assaults of this kind and especially from the persecution of Christians, and that after so many and such grievous offences you conciliate by a fitting penance the wrath of Divine Majesty, which without doubt you have seriously aroused by such provocation."

The khan replied that, on the contrary, he had not offended God, but that his victories came from Heaven's will: "The eternal God has slain and annihilated these lands and peoples, because they have neither adhered to Chinggis Khan, nor to the Khagan, nor to the command of God. Like your words, they also were impudent, they were proud and they slew our messenger-emissaries. How could anybody seize or kill by his own power contrary to the command of God? Although you likewise say that I should become a trembling Nestorian Christian, worship God and be an ascetic, how do you know whom God absolves, in truth to whom He shows mercy? ... From the rising of the sun to its setting, all the lands have been made subject to me. Who could do this contrary to the command of God?"

rivers and even build a fleet. But the Chinese also stressed the peaceful arts of administration and tried to protect their people from massacres. Khubilai was willing to accept their advice, but only if the towns surrendered without a fight. He avoided relying exclusively on Chinese Confucian officials, by balancing them with Buddhists, Uighurs, merchants, and all kinds of foreigners. Khubilai followed the scholar officials in many policies, such as building schools and restoring imperial rituals, but he rejected two important ones: He did not restore the examination system, and he did not have a history written of the Song (his successors did this later). (See Chapter 11 for more discussion of the Song examination system.)

More intellectual than his grandfather, Khubilai researched rival religions. He refereed a savage debate between the Daoists and Buddhists, but he preferred Tibetan Buddhism, which offered magical powers and politically experienced lamas. The close connection of the Mongols to the Tibetan church began in his reign and continues today. Khubilai also employed and debated with Muslims, Nestorian Christians, and Jesuits.

Khubilai restored peace and unity to a China that had been divided de facto for 500 years. He gave tax relief, supported the restoration of agriculture, stored grain to relieve famines, and protected the peasantry from nomadic harassment. The Khitan advisor Yelu Chucai is said to have convinced Ögödei that it would be more profitable to let the Chinese live and pay taxes than to slaughter them to make room for horses and sheep. Khubilai went much further in protecting the peasant base of the Chinese economy, but he also imposed heavy corvée burdens on them in order to knit the country together. The postal relay stations (**yam**), adapted from Khitan practice, were a decisive jump forward in communications density, equivalent in these times to the impact of the telegraph or the internet. Every 25 or 30 miles, local people had to support horses and supplies at postal stations, which could transmit messages as fast as 200 miles per day. Military demands clearly motivated the construction of this extraordinary network, which extended throughout the Mongols' domains, but worked best in China. All later Chinese dynasties, Russians, Persians, and Ottomans continued what the Mongols built.

Commerce was equally important. The Song had already developed paper currency for commercial transactions; Khubilai imposed its use by government fiat. At least in the early years, paper money greatly stimulated the exchange of goods. Chartered merchant corporations obtained government loans at special interest rates to finance trade caravans, and Central Eurasian Muslim merchants co-operated with the Yuan government.

Devastating as conquerors, the Mongols were not ruthless rulers. Khubilai's new law code adapted Mongol and Jin customs for Chinese use. It specified capital punishment much less often than the Song code, and few people were executed. Though hardly literate himself, he supported the publication of Chinese Confucian literature, and had his son tutored in the classics. His tutor used an interesting maxim that reflects the impact of printing on China: "Man's heart is like a printing block. If the block does not err, then even if one copies ten million papers, there will not be errors."[1]

Mongol administration was by Chinese standards rather ramshackle and unsystematic. Beneath the façade of a uniform bureaucracy, local governors had a great deal of autonomy. Foreigners at the top focused on extracting wealth from merchants. Perhaps the peasants were luckier to have a government that mostly left them alone. There was little sign of anti-Mongol mobilization or popular revolt in the early years. Most Chinese had to admit, grudgingly, that these barbarians deserved to inherit the Mandate of Heaven. Later historians wrote the Yuan history as if it were an ordinary Chinese dynasty, completely ignoring the Mongol empire's expanse.

Even so, Yuan rule deviated from Confucian ideals. Fearful of being absorbed into the large Chinese mass, the Mongols kept themselves apart. They classified the population in a way that no Chinese would do, separating the northern Chinese from the southern Chinese, and establishing privileged categories for the Mongols and "miscellaneous" foreigners. Only Mongols and Central Eurasians could occupy the top military and political posts. No examinations in the classics were held until the 1340s. What were the Confucian literati to do? Some became very influential advisors; others sulked in isolation as hermits. But many educated Chinese took creative advantage of their misfortune by turning to the popular classes. When Marco Polo visited Hangzhou, he found not a ruin but a bustling metropolis, continuing to grow since its days as the Song capital. Chinese technical arts like medicine, mathematics, and artisanry also thrived under patronage by the practical Yuan rulers. The Yuan dramas, written in colloquial style for large audiences, still inspire huge adulation in their modern forms as Beijing opera and film, as do the popular tales of bandit heroes told in the streets. Box 13.2 describes the origin of the Chinese vernacular novel from street-corner stories told in the Song and Yuan dynasties.

Khubilai saw himself, however, not just as a Chinese emperor, but as a sovereign who deserved to rule the entire world. Despite disastrous outcomes, he kept on fighting. Angered by Japanese arrogance, he forced the unlucky Koreans to build him a great invasion fleet. The fragmented Japanese warriors had a great deal of trouble uniting against the full force of the Mongol army, but in 1274 and 1281 they were saved by the defensive wall they built on Kyushu and by the providential typhoons, the **kamikaze**, that destroyed the Mongol fleet. His second great effort at maritime invasion, in Southeast Asia, also came to

Box 13.2 The Origins of the Chinese Novel

The first Chinese vernacular novels evolved under the Yuan from storytellers' booths on street corners. *Outlaws of the Marsh*, based on a rebellion against corrupt officials in thirteenth-century Shandong, describes a band of 108 brothers united to fight for righteousness on behalf of Heaven. The vivid characters include Li Kui, the savage rebel, who responds with great affection to true friendship; Wu Song, who can drink gallons of wine and still wrestle a tiger to death; and Song Jiang, the upright scholar-diplomat, learned in the classics but strangely devoted to this crude but honest gang. The subversive implication of the novel is that true justice is found among the outlaws, not among dull bureaucrats. No wonder the heretical Ming philosopher Li Zhi praised the novel highly! The story has a darker side, too: women portrayed as sexual temptresses, innkeepers who surreptitiously serve their guests human meat, and random sadism, including rape. In the Ming dynasty, the popular novel even inspired a set of 108 playing cards, but the Qing rulers banned it. In the twentieth century, communists praised it for expressing peasant consciousness, even though its basic values are by no means Marxist. The brothers do not aim to spark a revolt of the masses against the state, but only to protect each other. But the theme of

haohan (a few good men) who demonstrate mutual loyalty and unbelievable fighting skill has inspired hundreds of martial arts novels and Hong Kong films. Wu Song, meet Jackie Chan!

In this excerpt, fifteen of the brothers plot to rob porters who are carrying a large amount of gold and jewels sent by a provincial governor as a birthday present to his father-in-law, the chief minister: They pose as peddlers offering dates and wine to Yang Chih, the head of the convoy, but he is suspicious, until he sees them drink the wine themselves:

Yang Chih told himself: "I watched those fellows myself buying his wine and drinking it over there. And I saw one of them right here in front of me drink half a ladleful out of the other bucket, it must be all right. I might just as well let them buy a bowl of wine" ... But the vendor said, "I'm not selling, I'm not selling! This wine has a drug in it!" ...

The date peddlers tried to pacify him: You silly fellow, they've upset you again, you take things too seriously. We had to put up with a scolding from you too. It was nothing to do with these men, just let them have a drink and be done with it."

[All the porters drink the wine.] Yang Chih saw that the men had come to no harm, but he himself had not had a drink. Now for one thing the heat was

intense, and for another he was unbearably thirsty: he picked up a ladle and drank only half, and took a few dates to go with it ...

The seven peddlers of dates now ranged themselves at the edge of the pines and pointed at the fifteen porters. "Go on, fall down!" they cried.

And the fifteen men, heads heavy, feet light, gaped at each other and one after another crumpled to the ground.

The seven peddlers pushed out their seven Chiangchou wheelbarrows from within the pine copse, dumped their loads of dates out on the ground and filled up the barrows again with the eleven porters' loads of gold and jewels and precious things. They covered them up to conceal them, called out "Excuse Us!" and went trundling their barrows off down the ridge. Truly,

The gift was bought with the people's blood,
None cared whether they lived or died.
Now it is clear why thieves come forth,
This is the way that leads to crime.

All Yang Chih could do was moan aloud, for his limbs were too weak for him to rise to his feet. The fifteen of them with eyes wide watched the seven load up the precious bundles and make off with them, for they could neither stand nor struggle nor speak.

nothing. Although his army defied elephant charges to destroy the king of Burma, he failed to hold Vietnam, and Java, like Japan, brazenly defied him.

Khubilai's last years, and the last years of the Yuan, were a sad spectacle. Obese, drunk, and disappointed, the khan lost his beloved wife, who had been a valuable political advisor, failed in his military campaigns, faced rebellions in Tibet and Manchuria, and saw fiscal problems grow. None of his successors showed much ability. They spent their time in ruthless factional fights, neglecting the administration, while the Central Eurasian officials preyed on the helpless

peasantry. In 1280, the Yuan was glorious, and admired; by the 1350s, it was on the way to collapse. Perhaps Khubilai's greatest achievement was to make nomadic rule look normal to the Chinese.

Hülegü and the Il Khans of Persia (1256–1335)

Like the Yuan emperors, the Mongol rulers of Persia, known as **Il-Khans**, or viceroys, also faced alien settled populations, and struggled to establish civil administrations while still making war. The Il-Khans' rule was somewhat shorter than the Yuan, and they had no equivalent to Khubilai, yet their reigns also mixed religious and social influences.

Hŭlegŭ, younger brother of Khubilai, was given two assignments in the Middle East: to destroy the feared Ismailis and to crush the caliph of Baghdad. The Ismailis, or **Assassins**, a Shi`ite sect of Islam, had entrenched themselves in inaccessible mountain castles in northern Persia. From there they spread terror with their specialty of political murder by dagger. Hŭlegŭ captured their leader and wiped nearly all of them out after they surrendered. For this, the English historian Edward Gibbon credited the Mongols with a great "service to mankind."[2] The caliph of Baghdad, supreme representative of the Islamic community, arrogantly thought that Allah would defend him, but he lost his life when he was trampled to death in a carpet (so as not to shed his royal blood) and his city to a siege, after which the city was plundered and over 200,000 people killed. Thus ended 500 years of symbolic authority over the Sunni Muslim community.

Despite the destruction of the caliphate, most of the Il-Khans turned to Islam and reinforced its hold. Yet the Il-Khans, like Khubilai, encouraged religious pluralism. Hŭlegŭ's wife energetically supported the Nestorian Christians, and Hŭlegŭ, even though he personally was a Buddhist, went along. Buddhism held on for some time, even though the bulk of the population rejected it. Temples carved in the rocks in Azerbaijan, converted to mosques, still show traces of the furthest westward penetration of Buddhism until the arrival of the Kalmyk Mongols on the lower Volga in the seventeenth century.

Hŭlegŭ aimed to conquer the entire Middle East, but he faced strong resistance from the **Mamluks**, Turkish mercenary soldiers who had seized control of Egypt from the sultan. They were the strongest military force the Mongols had yet encountered. The providential death of Great Khan Mŏngke in 1259, forcing Hŭlegŭ to return to struggle for the succession, allowed the Mamluks to inflict the first major defeat a Mongol army had suffered. In fact, after 1260, except for Khubilai's personal conquest of China, the Mongols did not expand any further. Map 13.1 shows the extent of Khubilai's conquests.

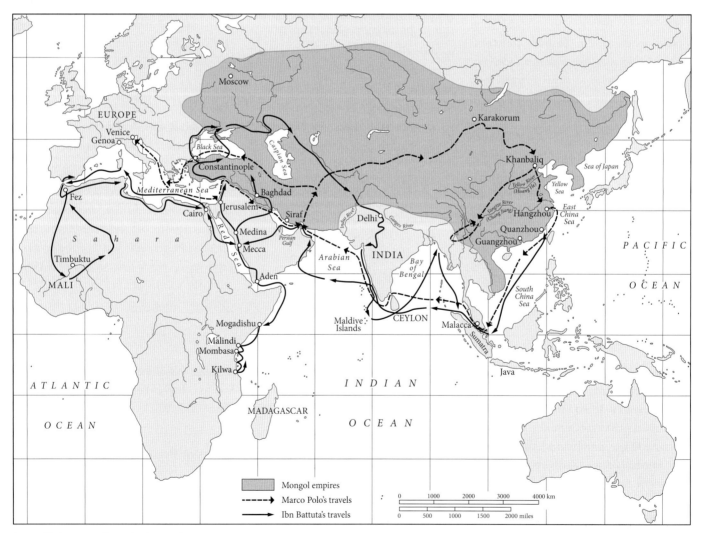

Map 13.1 Mongol empire in 1255

Box 13.3 Great Travelers

Although the famous Marco Polo claimed to have traveled from Genoa to China, we should not neglect the equally extraordinary odyssey of Rabban Sauma (c.1220–94), who traveled in the opposite direction at the same time. He was the first Chinaman to leave a detailed account of his experiences in the West. A Nestorian Christian monk of Turkic descent born near Beijing, he left with a disciple, Markos, on a pilgrimage to Jerusalem in 1275. Khubilai Khan himself supported their mission, in order to demonstrate his even-handed backing of all the major religions. They followed the caravan routes across the perilous deserts of Central Eurasia, staying with Nestorian communities along the way, until they arrived at the headquarters of the Il-Khan in Tabriz. There, Rabban Sauma was appointed the leading representative of the Nestorian church in East Asia, and Markos was made Catholicus, or leader of the entire Nestorian church. But Rabban Sauma was given an even more extraordinary mission, when the Il-Khan sent him to Europe to propose an alliance against the Mamluks. The Christian states of Europe, and especially the pope, had long dreamed of finding a Christian kingdom in Asia, the mythical "Prester John," that would ally with them against the hated Muslims.

Rabban Sauma went to Rome and Paris and met the pope and the kings of England and France. He impressed them with his amazing credentials, and they seriously considered joining with the Mongols to drive out the infidels from the Holy Land, but the Western powers were too preoccupied with their own internal disputes to make any positive response. Some Christian historians see this moment as a lost opportunity to obliterate Islam from the Middle East. Rabban Sauma nevertheless achieved his life's dream, touring the holy sites of Rome and Paris and returning to Persia, where he died in 1294. His biographer left a remarkable account of his journeys, less fantastic and colorful than Marco Polo's, but more reliable, and of greater political importance.

Ibn Battuta, however, traveled further and longer than anyone else. Born in Tangier, Morocco, in 1304, he made his pilgrimage to Mecca and toured Iraq and Persia on the way home. He took a sea voyage down the east coast of Africa, and then decided to seek employment from the sultan of Delhi. He arrived at the Indus River by way of Constantinople, crossing the Central Asian steppes, through Afghanistan. He made it to Guangzhou, China, after suffering a shipwreck, returned to Morocco, visited Granada in southern Spain, and crossed the Sahara Desert to Mali. Over thirty years, he visited the equivalent of forty-four modern countries and traveled about 73,000 miles. He left a large book of travels giving detailed information of all that he saw. Ibn Battuta's journeys spanned nearly the entire extent of the Islamic world when it was expanding rapidly. This was a familiar world to him, and everywhere he went in search of the mosques, the pious scholars, and the famous monuments of Islam. He also learned about the political and economic history of the cities where he stayed, and reported on events ranging from military marches to Sufi ecstatic exercises:

When the afternoon prayers had been said, drums and kettledrums were beaten and the brethren began to dance. After this they prayed the sunset prayer and brought in the repast, consisting of rice-bread, fish, milk, and dates. When all had eaten and prayed the first night prayer, they began to recite their dhikr ... They had prepared loads of firewood which they kindled into flame, and went into the midst of it dancing; some of them rolled in the fire, and others ate it in their mouths, until finally they extinguished it entirely ... Some of them will take a large snake and bite its head with their teeth until they bite it clean through.

Ibn Battuta, an educated urban scholar, looked with distaste on such passion, but he reported it accurately. His account gives vivid, invaluable information about the diversity of the Islamic world of his time.

During the 1260s, Berke, khan of the Golden Horde, allied with the Mamluks against the Il-Khans, the first time a Mongol ruler had broken away from his kinsmen. The Il-Khans spent much of their time fending off invasions from all sides. As their hold became increasingly precarious, fiscal crises increased. On the one hand, conversion to Islam drew them closer to their subjects, and commercial alliances with Western powers gave them wealth. Venetians in Tabriz established important trading colonies. Chinese junks moved up the Persian Gulf, bringing trade goods and Chinese princesses, escorted by Marco Polo (or so he claimed). (Box 13.3 tells about other travelers who visited the Mongol realm.)

But like the Yuan rulers, successive Il-Khans alienated the local population by imposing harsh fiscal exactions and bringing foreigners (like an oppressive Jewish fiscal minister) into government. Their most curious echo of China was the abortive effort to force paper money on the Persian marketplace. Invented in China in the tenth century, paper currency flourished under the Song, when there was an exploding demand for credit; but the later Yuan rulers succumbed to the irresistible temptation to overissue bills to pay their expenses. As one would expect, they prompted inflation that seriously weakened them. The Mongol rulers of Persia had even less success. They tried to force merchants to trade in all their gold and silver for paper, but when the merchants shut down the bazaars, touching off riots, the Mongols had to end the experiment within six months.

Ghazan (r. 1295–1304), an energetic, reforming leader, almost managed to save the dynasty. He made Islam the official religion, repressing Christians, Jews, and Buddhists, restored the agricultural economy, and constructed many fine buildings in Tabriz. He shifted the basis of law from Mongolian custom to Islamic **shariah**, derived from interpretation of the Koran. Under him, the brilliant administrator **Rashid al-Din** (1247–1318), wrote his great chronicle of the Mongol empire. It is the first world history of Eurasia, ranging from the Franks in the West to China in the East, providing by far the most reliable and detailed account of the entire empire.

After Ghazan, however, the reforms lapsed. Oljeitu moved the capital to Sultaniye, and built his mausoleum there, the one great monument that survives from the Mongol age. These Islamicized Mongols mingled with their close neighbors the Turks, so that when the Il-Khan regime collapsed, the Mongols themselves disappeared. They had assimilated more than the Mongols in China, who were expelled by the Ming but remained as independent tribes in their homeland.

Russia and the Kipchak Khanate ("Golden Horde")

In 1224 the chronicler of Novgorod did not know what had hit him. A strange, unknown army of people named "**Tatars**" (the general European word for nomads) had just smashed the Russians. They were the Mongols, of course, on their way back home after destroying the Khwarazm Shah. In the 1230s and 1240s they returned to attack Russia and Eastern Europe. They left Kiev, the center of Orthodox Christianity, in ruins, on their way to Hungary and Vienna. Russia in general was, however, only spottily damaged, but the princes ruling the vast steppes and forests all were forced to submit to the khan. The Kipchak Turks, who also submitted, gave their name to the khanate. The term "Golden Horde" is a later invention.

Batu, Chinggis's grandson, established his capital in the new city of **Sarai**, on the lower Volga. His successor, Berke, converted to Islam and oriented the khanate's foreign policies toward the south. In alliance with the Mamluks of Egypt, he aimed to seize rich pasturelands and caravan routes in Azerbaijan and to prevent his cousins Hülegü and the Il-Khans, whom he detested, from controlling the Middle East. In the khans' eyes, Russia itself was a distant, poor periphery, useful only in providing tax revenues and slaves to be shipped to Egypt to become Mamluk soldiers.

Only about 4,000 Mongols lived in the khanate, and most of their army was Turkish. Turkish soon became the dominant official language. As in Persia, the Mongols assimilated quickly with the Turks, but in contrast to China, they shut themselves off sharply from their Orthodox Christian subjects by becoming Muslims. Even so, they tolerated Christianity, allowing the Orthodox Metropolitan to control his church as long as he paid tribute. The Metropolitan shifted the center of Russian spiritual life to Moscow in 1300. He and the Muscovite princes increased their control by obeying the khans in Sarai. As in Yuan China, the princes beat their heads on the ground, or kowtowed, before the khans to obtain licenses to rule, and ensured good treatment by suppressing other princes and loyally delivering tribute. **Ivan Kalita** ("Moneybags"), who married a Tatar princess, was named the first Grand Prince in 1328. Sometimes Mongol armies had to slaughter rebellious Russian princes, but usually the Muscovites took care of this task for them.

Sarai flourished from commerce between Russia, the Middle East, and the Mediterranean. As Italian traders competed for privileges from the khans, the Genoese established dominance there and in the Crimea, driving out their rivals, the Venetians. Sarai also borrowed culture and technology from Egypt. The khans even built dams to provide hydraulic power for extensive ceramic factories. Until about 1350, Russia and the khanate flourished because of these contacts with the wealthy south. Soon after, however, internecine warfare disrupted trade at Sarai, and Russian princes began to break away. In 1371 the first Russian prince refused to pay tribute to Sarai, and in 1380, at Kulikovo on the Don, Dmitri Donskoi led the Muscovite army to their first major victory over the Mongols. The Horde seemed to be breaking apart until Eastern nomads injected new energy. Tokhtamysh, a follower of Timur, took over the Horde, sacked Moscow in 1382, and forced the Muscovites to resume tribute. Until the late fifteenth century, Russian princes remained firmly dependent on the Mongol khans.

Central Eurasia: Timur (1336–1405) Tries to Recreate the Mongol Empire

Of the four great divisions of the empire, the heartland, under Chaghatai, had the most tumultuous experience. This khanate included all the oases and steppes from Bukhara and Samarkand in the west to Turfan in the east. Its rulers, dependent on the khan in Karakorum, were embroiled with the succession struggles in Mongolia, and battled continually with the Il-Khans and the Golden Horde. Unlike the khans of Persia and China, the Chaghatai Mongols had no contact with the administrative traditions of an old, densely populated society. The hapless urban dwellers suffered constant military devastation. In the end, **Transoxania** (the region between the Oxus and Jaxartes rivers in Central Eurasia), like the other western regions, turned almost exclusively Turkish and Islamic, expelling most Persian, Mongol, and Buddhist elements. The cosmopolitan oases of the old Silk Road now deserved their modern name of **Turkestan**, as they created a cultural center quite distinct from the Mongolians and Tibetan Buddhists to their east.

Just as the pieces of Chinggis's empire seemed to be pulling apart, a new conqueror from the east aimed to put them back together. **Timur** emerged from the chaos of Transoxania with military abilities nearly equal to Chinggis, determined to repeat the world conqueror's feat. Because he was crippled in his youth, the Persians called him Timur-i Lang (the lame), and the Europeans called him Tamerlane. As a Turk born near Samarkand, he had no direct kinship link with Chinggis's Mongols, so he needed Mongol patrons to legitimate his victories. He linked himself through political marriage to the Chinggisid line, calling himself "son-in-law" of the Chinggisids. After first subordinating himself to the Chaghatai khan, he raised an army in Persia and drove the khan out of Transoxania in 1363. Like Chinggis, he knew when to use duplicitous diplomacy and when to use direct military assaults. But unlike Chinggis, he had no coherent strategy, and he left no new administrative structures behind him. Often he had to return to fight the same battles over again, even more ferociously.

As he marched through Persia, he left mounds of skulls and pillaged cities in his wake. He invaded the eastern Chaghatai territories, then headed back to Persia to sack **Herat** (a prosperous city in Central Eurasia) and **Khurasan** (a region of northeastern Persia). By destroying the irrigation works of the arid countryside, he turned precariously productive fields into desert. Marching through western Persia, Georgia, and Armenia, he proclaimed loudly his Islamic dedication, paying special attention to crushing the Christian communities. But though he claimed to love Persian poetry, he wreaked equal destruction on the centers of Islamic culture. Baghdad surrendered in 1394 without a fight, but he sacked the city anyway in 1401.

Meanwhile his disciple Tokhtamysh had reunified the Golden Horde, but then ambitiously attacked Timur in Azerbaijan. Timur defeated him twice in the 1390s, ravaged the steppe, burned Sarai, and wiped out the Christian trading colonies at the mouth of the Don River, ending Russia's trading connections with the Mediterranean. Moscow only narrowly escaped the sack. Next came India. The weakened sultans of Delhi, once powerful Turkic Islamic soldiers themselves, allowed Timur to pillage the capital. Timur drove his Indian elephants west to besiege Damascus and Aleppo, driving out the Mamluks, temporarily. Then he faced his most formidable foe, a Turk like himself, Sultan **Bayezid I** of the Ottoman empire. In a decisive battle northeast of Ankara, Timur crushed the sultan's army,

capturing the sultan and imprisoning him in an iron cage, hung on the city wall. This became a memorable scene in the English dramatist **Christopher Marlowe**'s great play, *Tamburlaine*, of 1590. He returned again to Samarkand, his beloved city, where he had built his own impressive mausoleum, to plan his last, glorious campaign: the conquest of China. Fortunately for the Chinese, Timur died in 1405, his wishes unfulfilled.

It is hard to find much positive in this dismal catalogue of battles and massacres. Historians can defend Chinggis and the Mongols, who did develop administration and commerce, despite their frightful destruction, but Timur left nothing lasting in his wake. Only Samarkand benefited from his booty. In this case, nearly all the European and Middle Eastern stereotypes about nomadic conquerors seem to be true. After the ferocious army passed through, local Persian bureaucrats carried on, and in some places people laboriously reconstructed shattered cities and fields. Other places never recovered.

Timur's successors, however, did create an Islamic renaissance in Herat and Samarkand. They built mosques, palaces, and gardens, and sponsored some of the greatest Persian literature and art. **Ulugh Beg** (1394–1449), ruler and outstanding mathematician and astronomer, established **madrasas** (Islamic schools) specializing in the sciences, and built a great observatory in Samarkand. Figure 13.3 shows the great mausoleum they built for Timur, following his plans. Their achievements rivaled or even surpassed those of Western Europe in science and the arts. The Timurid rulers created a lasting cultural legacy which inspires the Central Asian peoples today.

13.2 THE FIFTEENTH CENTURY AFTER THE MONGOLS: COLLAPSE AND RECOVERY

The Legacy of the Mongols

Chinggis Khan's empire expanded explosively and broke up slowly. The empire reached its maximal limits less than a century after Chinggis began his conquests. By 1300, khans held China, Central Eurasia, Russia, Iran, and much of the Middle East, but Japan, Southeast Asia, India, and Western Europe escaped, and the powerful Mamluk soldiers of Egypt beat them back. The divide between those regions that escaped Mongol conquest and those that suffered it strongly marks the subsequent history of all these countries. On the other hand, the Mongols often take too much of the blame. They destroyed many cities, but not those which surrendered, and they knit together regions that had never before been in such close contact. Overall, the Mongols tightened systematic linkages between the great cities of the world. From 1250–1350 the Pax Mongolica, a time of unprecedented security,

Figure 13.3 Timur, a Turkish warrior known to Europeans as Tamerlane, briefly conquered all of Central Asia and large parts of the Middle East, and planned the invasion of China before his sudden death. He left as his legacy the destruction of many prosperous cities, the wealthy city of Samarkand, and this large mausoleum built for him by his successors.

encouraged merchants and pilgrims to move by caravan and across the seas. The great urban markets of South China continued to send their giant junks into Southeast Asian seas, as they did under the Song, as Indian and Arab traders moved bulk commodities and luxuries in great quantities between ports around the Indian Ocean. With the breakup of the empire, these trading circuits broke up. On land, the new regimes looked inward toward their agrarian bases, instead of out to sea, but they all adapted many Mongol institutions to their own needs.

By the mid to late fourteenth century, the tight threads connecting Eurasia began to unravel. The collapse of the Il-Khanate in 1335, and Yuan China in 1368, ended the unity of Mongol rule in the settled civilizations. Timur's conquests only added to the destruction, accelerating the breakup of the Kipchak khanate and Transoxania.

Meanwhile, the spread of bubonic plague illustrated the dark side of global interconnection. Some time after the mid thirteenth century, when the Mongols invaded Southwest China and Burma, they may have transferred the fatal bacillus from its home to the rats of China and the steppe. Microparasites were fellow travelers of macroparasites. The germ-infected fleas traveled on the backs of rats along the land and sea routes of traders and armies. The plague, or Black Death, first appeared in North China in 1331. Map 13.2 shows how it spread. It appeared in the Crimea in 1346, and struck Western Europe at Marseilles in 1348. Death rates of up to 80 percent in cities ruined commerce and drove the survivors to the countryside. Europe was worst hit, losing up to one third of its population, and Russia 25 percent, but China and the Middle East suffered heavily. The Little Ice Age, an extended period of colder global climate beginning around the fourteenth century, damaged harvests too. Global population declined by approximately 10 million in the fourteenth century. Losses like this would not happen again until the twentieth century.

By 1400, certain areas began to recover. Some had been under Mongol control, some not. After Timur's destruction in 1402, the Ottomans continued to advance steadily, China established a new dynasty, and Russians began to throw off Mongol rule. Persia, India, Central Eurasia, Japan, and Europe, however, would remain disunited and unstable for another century or more. The fifteenth century was a darker, colder, more isolated world for many regions.

China's New Dynasty

By 1350, Yuan maladministration had driven China into an inglorious morass of corruption, natural disaster, and oppression. The Yellow River flooded repeatedly, famines struck yearly, and the inflation created by overissuing paper money had ruined the economy. Peasant rebel groups rose up all over the country, inspired by millenarian teachings that promised the advent of a new age led by the Buddha of the Future against the forces of darkness. Among them, **Zhu Yuanzhang** (1328–98), from a poor agricultural worker's family in South China, became the most successful military leader. In 1359 he occupied Nanjing ("Southern Capital"), which he made his main capital, and in 1368 he drove the Yuan out of Beijing and proclaimed himself emperor of a new dynasty: the Ming ("Bright"). Like the Yuan, he gave his dynasty a symbolic name, and many suspect that the imagery of light is a covert reference to his early millenarian origins, linked to the Manichaeanism of Central Eurasia.

For the first time in 1300 years, purely Han Chinese peasant armies had unified the empire. The base of the Ming state, unlike the Song and Yuan, would be agriculture, not commerce. Zhu first restored the agrarian economy with huge investments in dikes, canals, and land clearance. He built over 40,000 reservoirs all over China, and planted 50 million trees around Nanjing alone. Zhu's comprehensive survey gives us quite accurate figures for cultivated land and population. China's registered population was now down to only 60 million people, a catastrophic drop from the Song's 100 million. How much of the loss was due to plague, natural disaster, and warfare we do not know, but even the Mongols could not have killed this many by themselves.

The first Ming emperor liked peasants, but he distrusted scholars: most of them were wealthy landlords, they concealed taxes, and they asked uncomfortable questions. He purged thousands of high officials suspected of plotting against him, and by abolishing the office of prime minister, he placed all the six ministries and the armies under his absolute authority. He tried to set up rural schools everywhere, and he tried with heavy tax exactions to break landlord power, especially in the rich lower Yangtze Delta. Yet he could not control the commercial economy any better than the Yuan. Like them, he tried to enforce the value of paper money with government regulations, but paper lost out to lumps of silver as the preferred means of payment, as silver flowed in from Japan. Despite their efforts, the Ming emperors never really drove the Chinese economy back to pure agrarianism.

Ming China rejected the alien Mongols, but it still retained many Mongol institutions. The capital was moved back to Beijing so as to put the central government close to the northwest frontier. The military followed the Yuan model, many of the succession struggles looked familiar, and until the mid fifteenth century Ming emperors still tried to expand on all fronts. They forced Korea and Japan to pay tribute. Zhu's successor, the Yongle emperor (r. 1402–24), took power by military coup and launched five expeditions into Mongolia, dying during the last one.

Yongle also launched what is now one of the best-known world explorations, the great fleets led by the Muslim admiral **Zheng He**. He led seven expeditions into the Indian Ocean, as far as the coasts of Africa, from 1405 to 1433. On one voyage sixty-two colossal ships, weighing 1,500 tons and carrying 37,000 men, showed that China could dominate the seas if it chose. Nothing technological would have stopped the fleets from rounding Africa and proceeding across the Atlantic Ocean. But the next emperor called off the expeditions, and no more imperially sponsored ships went abroad. China's officially supported maritime age that began in the tenth century came to a close. However, civilian, non-official maritime expansion continued, spreading Chinese traders and settlers across Southeast Asia from the sixteenth to eighteenth centuries.

What inspired the voyages, and why did they end? Although the captains brought back valuable information about exotic lands, exploration and discovery were not the primary goals. Yongle, inheriting the Mongol dreams of universal empire, wanted to impose submission on tributary states, gain commercial profits, and make strategic alliances. But the Mongols had their revenge in the end. As the dispersed tribes continued to threaten the frontier, Ming rulers had to divert resources from the weak southeast to the powerful rivals in the northwest. Rational strategic decisions, not prejudice against trade, made the difference. Civilian Chinese shipping continued to dominate intra-Asian trade for several centuries, even though Chinese merchants overseas had no imperial protection. On the inland frontier, no subsequent emperor was as aggressive as Yongle, and one hapless ruler rashly marched out at the head of his troops and got himself captured by the Mongol khan in 1449. But life went on as usual back in Beijing, and the khan finally sent the emperor back.

By the mid fifteenth century, China was a more stable, but much more inward-looking and defensive empire than it ever had been before. Hostile Mongol tribes, whom the officials could not comprehend, cut most of its links with Central Eurasia. The restored examination system produced talented, educated scholar officials drilled in Neo-Confucian orthodoxy. Peasants paid lighter taxes, landlords evaded theirs, and merchants got along as best they could. China saw itself as the supremely civilized empire, graciously accepting submission from grateful tributaries. The wider world lay in obscurity.

The Rise of Muscovy

The protracted disintegration of the Mongol empire, followed by Timur's devastation, created a power vacuum in Central Eurasia. Upheaval and fragmentation offered new opportunities. In the Kipchak khanate, regional rulers broke away from the control of the khan at Sarai: Crimea in 1430, Kazan in 1436, and Astrakhan in 1466. Another regional power, Muscovy, formally cut tribute ties with the khan in 1480. By 1500, the Grand Princes of Muscovy had become the dominant new power in Western Eurasia. Co-operating eagerly with the khans, they steadily increased their possessions through purchase, inheritance, colonization, diplomacy, and conquest.

Russian historians have traditionally depicted Muscovy's rise as the "gathering of Russian lands" into a uniform Slavic

Map 13.2 Eurasian trade routes and spread of plague

civilization that threw off the barbarian "Tatar Yoke," but a closer look dispels these myths. Muscovy was no outsider, but an experienced player in Mongol–Tatar affairs. Moscow, its capital, controlled the headwaters of four major rivers: the Oka, Volga, Don, and Dnieper, where furs from the north met the major water routes leading south to the wealth of Byzantium and the Ottoman empire. It had strong commercial and diplomatic ties with Kazan, on the lower Volga, and later with the Crimean khanate on the Black Sea. Still, other more powerful rivals shared Muscovy's ambitions.

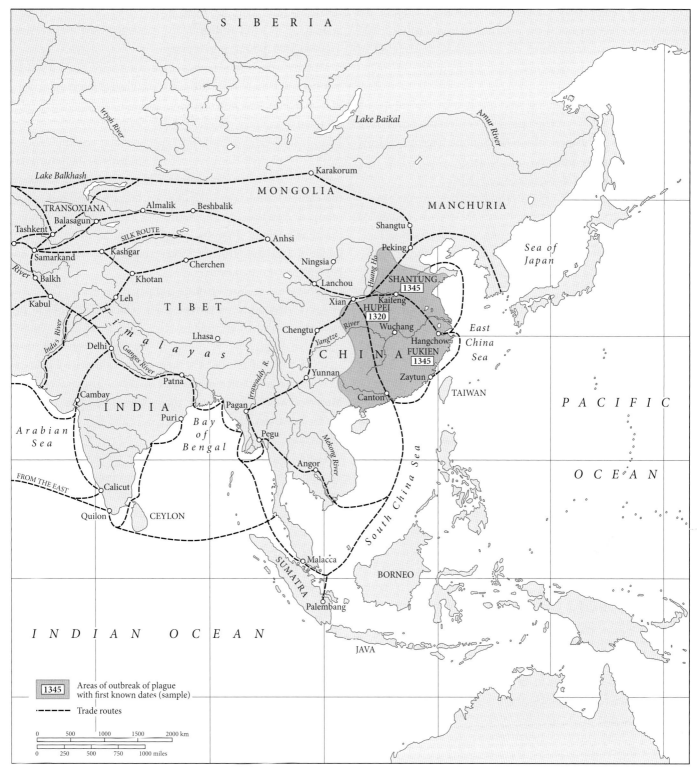

Map 13.2 (*cont.*)

Few thought that this minor frontier kingdom would become a huge empire.

The Russian princes, who traveled frequently to Sarai, adopted many institutions from the Mongols, whom they knew well. They kowtowed before the khan, like the Turks and Chinese, they implemented the Mongols' efficient postal system, they used Mongol-style tax collectors, modeled their military on the Mongols, and practiced similar kinds of clan rule. It was not despotism that Russians learned from the Mongols, but how to use family connections to control vast, poor lands.

Grand Duke Ivan III (the Great) of Moscow (r. 1462–1505) built his kingdom in an environment of ceaseless military and commercial competition. Over the previous century, his predecessors had expanded the principality from 600 to 15,000 square miles, but Ivan aimed for undisputed domination of all the Russian lands. Muscovy's size tripled during his reign. His first goal was to break the power of Novgorod. In Novgorod, Baltic Germans and Scandinavians dominated the fur trade. The city, with its own **veche** (assembly) of leading boyars and merchants, rose to its peak of influence in the fifteenth century. It was commercially powerful but militarily weak. When Ivan besieged the city in 1478, Novgorod surrendered without a fight. He abolished the veche, carried away the city bell, executed many top leaders, deported the leading boyars to Moscow, and exiled much of the population to the far north. After eliminating Tver, another serious rival, Muscovy faced no serious princely opposition. Ivan took the title of **gosudar**, or sovereign, staking his claim to rule all Russians.

Ivan actively pursued ties to the wealthy Middle East. His marriage to Sophia Paleologos of Byzantium brought in Greek and Italian architectural influences. Skilled builders turned Moscow's Kremlin from a crude wooden fort into a striking example of Italian Renaissance architecture. The thick brick walls, the cathedrals of the Dormition and Annunciation, the Palace of Facets, and the Bell Tower formed the colorful core of the Kremlin compound. By 1500 Moscow had about 100,000 people. It was still a fortress town, whose walls indicated the rise of the new gunpowder artillery form of warfare, but the growing power of the prince created a flourishing urban economy.

Ivan made a crucial alliance with the khan of the Crimea, Mengli Girei, who prospered from his position on the Black Sea between the Golden Horde, Byzantium, and the Ottomans. The Crimea split off from the Horde in 1430 and became a vassal of the Ottomans in 1475. In the century after its conquest by the Turks in 1453, Istanbul dominated the trade north of the Black Sea, and the Crimeans prospered by supplying the city with grain. This alliance allowed Ivan to reject tribute demands from the khan of the Golden Horde and resist pressures from the Lithuanian and Polish state to his west. The Lithuanians, in turn, allied with the khan of the Horde against Ivan and the Crimea. In 1480, the year of the final throwing off of the "Tatar Yoke," the khan's attack on Ivan failed because his Lithuanian allies never arrived. There was no clear-cut struggle between Christian and infidel, but many powers vying for the wealth of the remnants of the Mongol empire.

Gunpowder empires like Muscovy, China, Turkey, and India all needed large revenues. Ivan greedily sought resources for his state. He confiscated 2.7 million acres of church lands. State-promoted colonization of the northeast developed forest industries, salt extraction, fishing, and most important, the fur trade. To ensure that peasants paid their levies, Ivan began

restricting the right of peasants to leave the land. Serfdom grew hand-in-hand with military demands. New money taxes supported the postal courier system.

Muscovy, like the Manchus, a new state growing on a fluid frontier, did not have to face established internal rivals, like bourgeois and noble estates, autonomous religious establishments, military brotherhoods, or independent villages. Its primary focus was military expansion and accumulation of wealth. Ivan gave his boyars land (**pomestie**) in return for service to the ruler, very much like the Ottoman **timar** or the earlier Islamic iqta`. Unlike the boyar's hereditary patrimony, or **votchina**, the pomestie was subject to revocation at the ruler's whim. Pomestie provided income for cavalrymen under the Grand Prince's direct control, freeing him from dependence on the boyars.

Nobles in search of rewards competed vigorously for status at court, striving to occupy a "place" (**mesto**) as close to the tsar as possible. An elaborate system of ranks and titles (**mestnichestvo**), carefully recorded in registers, regulated their status. Except for the church, there was no alternative to court service, and no choice of princes to serve. The autocracy of Muscovy was a product of the pomestie land system and the lack of independent bases of power and legitimacy for the local elites.

The growing state needed an ideology. Unlike China, Persia, or France, for example, Muscovy had no indigenous imperial traditions. Muscovite rulers first built upon Mongolian political institutions, but these were not broad enough. The Russians borrowed Turkish and Mongolian words like *den'gi* (money), *bumaga* (paper), *yam* (postal courier), indicating Muscovy's links to Central Eurasia. Central Eurasians and Chinese called the tsar the "White [Western] Khan," but he needed a different, more universal basis of legitimation for his Russian Orthodox subjects. He surrounded Tatar administrative practices with Byzantine and Orthodox theories and symbols.

To legitimate the new state, Orthodox churchmen began to develop the theory of the "Third Rome." According to this theory, Rome had nurtured the early Christian church, but Byzantium inherited the true faith after the Great Schism of 1054. The conquest of **Constantinople** by the Turks in 1453 demonstrated that Byzantium had lost the grace of God, transferring the Christian mission to Moscow. In 1492, the year 7000 from the date of Creation, millenarian thinking flourished, but afterward, the dream of an all-powerful Orthodox leader held on. As one monk wrote, "The Russian Tsar will be elevated by God above other nations, and under his sway will be many heathen kings."[3] As the church stamped out heretics, its leaders exalted the unlimited power of the Grand Prince of Muscovy with more ambitious titles. Ivan III had occasionally used the title "tsar," which combined the Roman-Byzantine legacy of "Caesar" with the "khan" of Central Eurasia, making the Russian ruler the "Autocrat" (*Samoderzhavets*) and Defender of the Faith in one. Ivan IV assumed the formal title of tsar in 1547. Only a few clergymen genuinely endorsed the Third Rome theory at this time, but seventeenth-century tsars found it useful for justifying autocratic rule based on religion and power.

The Third Rome theory also reminded the ruler of his responsibilities to his Christian subjects, and, like the Chinese Mandate of Heaven, could imply limits to autocratic authority. One clergyman wrote, "If the Tsar who rules men is himself ruled by evil passions and sins ... such a Tsar is not God's servant but the Devil's, and he should not be considered a Tsar, but a tormentor."[4] The Confucian philosopher Mencius had invoked the same right to disobey an evil ruler. Later in the seventeenth century, Orthodox Old Believers attacked the tsar as Antichrist, as did rioters in Moscow in 1648.

The Muscovite bureaucracy was rudimentary. Provincial governors literally "fed" themselves by extracting their provisions from the local population. Muscovy needed literate clerks to draw up state documents, but structures of salaries, incentives, and promotions developed slowly. For quite a while, Kipchak Turkish remained the standard lingua franca for internal and external relations, but official Russian documentary language developed in the sixteenth century, while Old Church Slavonic endured in the religious hierarchy. Specialized ministries for finance, foreign relations, and other spheres worked out a technical language in voluminous documents, but Muscovy remained a nearly illiterate society. Church ritual relied on the brilliant imagery of icons, not on the word. Muscovy's many merchants had nothing like Ming China's vernacular printed culture.

By 1500, religious backing, commercial links, and military superiority had made Muscovy the predominant power of the Slavic lands, but its rulers had even more grandiose aims: cautious, but continuous expansion across Eurasia.

13.3 BEYOND THE MONGOLS' REACH

Regions that did not have to submit to the Mongols escaped either because they were far across the sea, like Japan or island Southeast Asia, or because of political luck, like Western Europe, or because they fought back successfully, like the Ottomans, Mamluks, and Vietnamese. In the long run, however, Mongol expansion had an impact even on those societies beyond their reach. India was the most vulnerable to Central Eurasian invasions by Turkic successors to the Mongols; Japan was the most isolated from the continent; the Ottoman Turks and Southeast Asians fell in between.

India: From Invasion to a New Empire

Beginning in the 1190s, Turkish warriors from Afghanistan took over North India, establishing a series of dynasties, known as the **Delhi** sultanates after their capital city, which lasted until the early sixteenth century. As devout Muslims, they called themselves lieutenants of the caliph in Baghdad, but they ruled as autocrats, much like the Japanese shogun. By the early fourteenth century, they had conquered nearly all of India and brought back great wealth from the temples of the south. They held off repeated Mongol attacks from the northwest, winning some battles, and avoiding destruction through adroit offers of submission. The Delhi rulers brought centralization and bureaucratic rule to the subcontinent, based on Persian techniques of administration, but regional lords still held substantial autonomy. They were given **iqta`**, or land grants, in return for military service. Their culture mixed Turkic, Islamic, Persian, and Hindu elements.

The sultans, their scribes, and officials, a tiny military elite ruling a large Hindu majority, still attempted to strengthen themselves by promoting conversion to Islam. They exempted converts from special taxes levied on non-Muslims, and sponsored mosques, schools, and publications. Islam spread most widely in Bengal, on the far eastern frontier. There the autonomous sultans incorporated many Hindu motifs into their rule, and immigrant **Sufi** sheikhs showed intense interest in tantric yoga texts (the Sufis were a mystical Islamic order seeking union with the divine through meditation and dance). Even so, Islam attracted mainly urban populations of soldiers, merchants, and administrators. Today Bengalis are, next to Arabs and Indonesians, the largest Muslim ethnic group, but mass conversion of the Bengali peasantry only took place after the sixteenth century.

One of the most remarkable, or strangest, of the Delhi rulers was **Muhammad bin Tughluq**, who ruled from 1325 to 1351. He was a generous, judicious scholar, knowledgeable in the sciences and in Persian poetry and medicine. The Arab traveler **Ibn Battuta**, who served as his chief judge, praised his strict enforcement of Islam. Yet he devastated the country with ambitious, impractical schemes. He tried to deport the population of Delhi to a new capital, which was better strategically situated, but located five hundred miles to the south. After ruining the old capital, he gave up the plan. Like the reckless Il-Khan before him, he admired Khubilai Khan's use of paper currency to enhance state revenue, and he tried to force the population to accept a new currency of copper tokens. This plan failed too, because the Indian population rapidly learned how to sabotage the markets with forged coins. Under **Firuz Shah** (r. 1351–88), who supported canal-building and charitable institutions, the population prospered but central control declined. After him, the sultans could not resist Timur's invasion in 1398. Timur inflicted more misery on India than any other invader, and Delhi suffered not only rape and pillage, but famine and pestilence after he left.

The sultanate then disintegrated into separate regional regimes, including one powerful Hindu empire, **Vijayanagar**, in the south, which lasted for over two centuries. Western visitors noticed the massive fortifications and splendor of its capital. Through ports on the Malabar coast, the empire established commercial relations across the Indian Ocean and as far as China, the Malay archipelago, and Portugal. In 1510, the king allowed the Portuguese to build a fort, after they had captured Goa. But at the Battle of Talikota, in 1565, the sultans of the Deccan defeated the Hindu army and destroyed the empire's capital, eliminating entirely the prospects for an independent Hindu kingdom in the south.

Despite wars and depredations by greedy rulers, India remained a wealthy country. The dense agricultural population, numbering nearly 90 million, fed itself and produced magnificent cotton textiles. Sea routes led to Arabia and the Spice Islands, and land routes led across Central Eurasia to Persia and Tibet. Peasants faced heavy taxation, however, and there were huge gaps between the luxuries of the military and noble elite and the poor farmer or artisan, probably greater than those of China. The sultans kept large slave households, and the seclusion of women, both Muslim and Hindu, spread even more widely.

The separate Hindu and Muslim communities absorbed characteristics from each other. Although Islam's militant monotheism seems far removed from Hindu polytheism, the two apparently alien religious traditions found common ground, just as Buddhism and Confucianism did in China. Hindu mystics endowed with special magical powers advocated the equality of all religions and the unity of all men with God. They looked very similar to the Sufi holy men, who possessed the magical power of **baraka** and likewise advocated mystical unity. Mutual admiration of each others' saints brought conversions in both directions. In Bengal, enthusiastic devotional cults concentrated around Sufi saints. The **Urdu** language, of Sanskritic origin, but written with the Persian script, and incorporating many Persian, Arabic, and Turkish words, became a major vehicle of poetic expression. Art and architecture also blended Indian and Islamic styles. **Nanak** (1469–1539), the founder of the Sikhs, preached toleration of all religions, adopting the good points of both Hinduism and Islam.

Babur (1483–1530), a Turkish descendant of Timur and Chinggis Khan, reunified India by conquest, founding the **Mughal** empire. Beginning in the small Central Eurasian principality of **Ferghana**, he embraced the bold ambition of his ancestors, and after failing to take Samarkand, set out to conquer Hindustan. At the historic Battle of Panipat northwest of Delhi in 1526, he defeated the sultan, whose army far outnumbered

him. Even more impressively, one year later he crushed the powerful Rajput army, and then defeated the Afghans. In these three victories, as a brilliant military leader, Babur laid the foundation for the long-lived empire that followed. He was the last of the great Turko-Mongolian conquerors who decisively affected the history of the world. He also wrote one of the great works of military memoir literature, the *Baburnama*, which expresses in forceful Turkish his literary skills and direct character.

Japan: A Warrior State Collapses, but Arts Flourish

The emperors of Japan established a centralized state in the seventh century CE, modeled on China's Tang dynasty, but this system coexisted uneasily with the power of aristocratic families and the rise of provincial governors. By the twelfth century, the court aristocracy had lost nearly all its power to the new military rulers, called **bushi** ("warriors"), in the provinces. For over two decades, the two most powerful military families, the **Taira** and the Minamoto, fought a vicious civil war. In 1185, in a great battle at Dannoura on the coast of the Inland Sea, fought by 280,000 men, the Taira, known for their sophisticated tastes and dedication to the elite Kyoto court culture, were annihilated by the rude provincial upstarts from eastern Japan. The tragic defeat of the Taira inspired nostalgic tales of military valor recounting the nobility of failure: "The proud Tairas endure but for a little time . . . In the end the brave are brought low and scattered like dust before the wind."[5] These tales attracted large popular audiences to the kabuki theater later on.

The victor, **Minamoto Yoritomo** (1147–99), established his seat of power in **Kamakura**, a small village south of modern Tokyo. The Kamakura period lasted from 1185 to 1333. Yoritomo called himself **shogun**, short for "barbarian-subduing generalissimo." He did not replace the emperor in Kyoto, but styled himself as the emperor's leading military officer. He called his government the **bakufu**, or "tent government." His followers, the **samurai**, vowed unconditional loyalty to their lords (see Chapter 11). Economic disintegration supported local military power, as independent manors, collecting their own revenues, broke away from the centralized bureaucratic administration.

Historians have called both Japan and Europe "feudal" because they have noticed striking similarities in this period. Many analysts have even made the dubious argument that the apparent parallels between Japanese and Western European feudalism, and the fact that they both escaped Mongol conquest, explains their successful industrialization in the late nineteenth century. How valid is this analogy? The simplest and broadest definition of feudalism is "a fusion of the civil, military, and judicial elements of government into a single authority."[6]

It implies fragmentation of political power, the dominance of military and religious institutions, and the construction of social bonds based on personal oaths and family alliances. Economically, it means the replacement of an imperial bureaucracy, Roman or Chinese in inspiration, with autonomous estates, and the binding of the peasant class to the land. Japan and Europe shared these features, but so did other places. The central institution that gave its name to "feudalism", the land grant (*feudum*) given in return for military service, was found all over Eurasia under many different names. On the other hand, Japan only partially resembled Europe. The Japanese equivalent, called *shiki*, was really an assemblage of tax collection rights, and not a consolidated estate. Japan's manors were fragmented landholdings rather than consolidated communities. And Japan did not suffer invasions from tribal warriors, as Europe did after the fall of the Roman empire. We can't push the analogy too far.

The bushi, rough provincial soldiers, developed their own code of values focused intensely on the cult of loyalty to one's lord. As samurai, they owed him total devotion; they should lead austere lives, and be prepared to commit suicide (**seppuku**, or **harakiri**) if the lord demanded it. Their central symbols were the cherry blossom, emblematic of the brief but beautiful span of a human life, and the sword. Japanese metallurgy was so advanced that even today scientists cannot reproduce the sharp, supple character of the finest swords. Samurai fought fiercely, but not for religious crusades; their primary loyalty was to their lord and their clan.

Once Yoritomo's military government established peace, the influence of civil administrators grew. Often the shoguns themselves abdicated when their heirs were only children, leaving real power in the hands of regents, who came from the **Hojo** family. During the thirteenth century, the Hojo regents, skilled bureaucrats, developed routine codes of procedure influenced by China, and carried out justice swiftly. "We have thus … the astonishing spectacle of a state at the head of which stands a titular emperor whose vestigial functions are usurped by an abdicated emperor, and whose real power is nominally delegated to a hereditary military dictator but actually wielded by a hereditary advisor of that dictator."[7] Japan's government looked like a hall of mirrors, but it worked. We should also note the role of the strong-minded woman, Hojo Masako (1156–1225), the "Nun General," who exerted considerable power behind the scenes. She joined with her brother to intervene decisively in many of the complicated succession disputes among the ruling elite.

Against this rickety structure the Mongol armies of Khubilai Khan launched their onslaughts in 1274 and 1281. Map 13.3 shows the Mongol invasion routes. Aided by the "divine wind," the kamikaze, the samurai held them off, but their victory

eventually tore Japan apart. Unlike the profitable civil wars of the previous century, driving off foreign invaders gave the warriors no opportunities to gather loot: despite their oaths, they fought for personal gain too. As one veteran stated in his petition for relief, "Why should I, who was wounded, have to wait empty for months and years and get nothing for my loyal service?"[8] Buddhist priests also claimed a great deal of credit for the victory, since their intensive recitation of sutras had brought down the divine wind.

Competition between rival factions at court, at the bakufu, and between the Buddhist sects began to tear the shogunate apart. Emperor **Go-Daigo**'s effort to restore imperial power split the country in half. From 1331 to 1392, two rival emperors and their followers fought each other all over the country. The shogunate recovered, but it moved to **Muromachi**, a district of Kyoto, from 1392 to 1573. Now the shogun himself had very little power; only his deputies, called **shugo**, controlled local authority. They began to turn themselves into genuinely autonomous territorially based lords, or **daimyo**. The shoguns lived in impotent elegance in Kyoto, heavily influenced by the highly aesthetic fashions of the court, while the daimyo divided the country. Akira Kurosawa, the great twentieth-century Japanese film director, set his most famous film, *Rashomon*, in this time of anxious uncertainty. The film demonstrates the complete incompatibility of each person's version of a story of rape, or love, or murder while a Buddhist priest comments on the vanity of human desire.

In the midst of this rough age, Japanese religion and art reached one of their most astonishing peaks of development. Buddhism, for the first time, now became a mass religion, spread through the country by activist priests. Three distinctive forms of Buddhism developed in Japan from Chinese roots: **Pure Land**, **Nichiren**, and **Zen**. Although the Buddha in principle offered salvation impartially to all human beings, the leading sects in Japan had established a strict hierarchy of access to nirvana, following esoteric and exclusive rituals. The Pure Land preachers, by contrast, offered rebirth in a land of bliss for anyone who recited fervently the phrase "Namu Amida Butsu," or "the name of the **Amida Buddha**," known as the **Nembutsu**. Amida, the Buddha of Boundless Light, would save anyone who called on him. Monks did not have to be celibate, and women had equal opportunities for salvation. The monk **Shinran** (1173–1263), banished from Kyoto for marrying, took his message to the townspeople. Large congregations sang hymns to Amida, saying: "Universally doth he send forth his endless, boundless, all-pervading, unrivaled, supreme Light, his Light of Purity, of Joy, of Wisdom. His changeless, unconceivable, unexplainable Light, brighter than the brightness of Sun or Moon … All sentient creatures enjoy it and are illuminated thereby."[9] Many laymen, including farmers, fishermen, and warriors,

Map 13.3 Japan and Mongol invasion routes

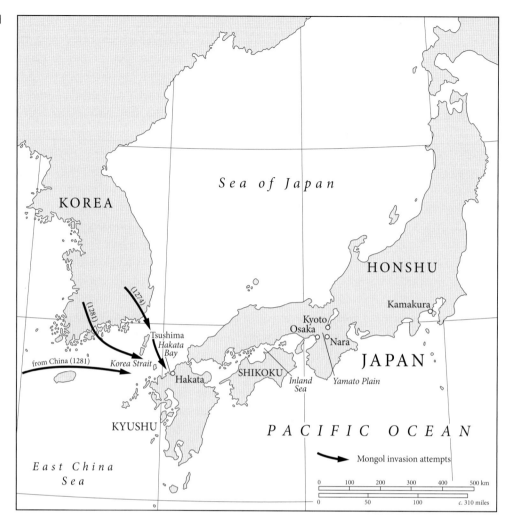

fervently recited the Nembutsu to release themselves from the daily world of pain and gain rebirth in Amida's holy land. Ecstatic mass singing and dancing attracted large crowds, supported by the apocalyptic belief that the world was coming to an end. By the thirteenth century, many believed that great changes were in the air. Pure Land believers inspired by this potent faith staged "Single-minded uprisings" (**ikko**) that resisted the heavy burdens of this world while expecting a glorious future.

Not all Buddhists are tolerant. The bellicose monk Nichiren (1222–82) also attracted enthusiastic devotees to a new sect based on the simple, repeated recitation of a phrase, "Myoho-Renge-Kyo" (Homage to the Scripture of the Lotus of the Good Law). He attributed all the calamities of his time, including the Mongol invasions, to corrupt religions that led people away from the truth, his truth. When Mongol envoys were executed, he remarked: "It is a great pity that they should have cut off the heads of the innocent Mongols and left unharmed the priests of Nembutsu [Amida], Shingon, Zen, and Ritsu, who are the enemies of Japan."[10] Nichiren narrowly escaped execution for his incessant attacks on his rivals, but he sternly disciplined his

followers in perseverance and self-sacrifice. The Nichiren sect collected millions of followers in the twentieth century, then fell into disgrace because it supported Japanese militarism. Revived in a different guise as the "new religion" of Soka Gakkai, it now proclaims its dedication to world peace, supports one of Japan's most powerful political parties, and sponsors new universities around the world.

Zen, the most famous of Japanese religions, rejected political action, or any attention to the outside world. Salvation could only be found within the individual soul, through deep, wordless meditation that would bring **satori**, or sudden enlightenment. It originated in China, where it was called *Chan*, meaning "concentration". Its principles were: "A special transmission outside the scriptures; no dependence on the written word; direct pointing at the soul of man; seeing one's nature and attaining Buddhahood." Zen teachers did not read sutras or conduct elaborate ceremonies; students could only gain enlightenment when they meditated on logical paradoxes (**koan**), or were literally beaten by their teachers. The texts of Zen consist not of scriptures, but of cryptic anecdotes about famous masters.

Box 13.4 The Tea Trade: Ceremonies, Profits, and Politics

Eisai (1141–1215), the pioneer of Zen in Japan, traveled to China twice and brought back two essential elements: a master's teachings, and tea. As he said, "The basis of life is the cultivation of health, and the secret of health lies in the well-being of the five organs. Among these five the heart is sovereign, and to build up the heart the drinking of tea is the finest method." The tea ceremony became an elaborate ritual that expressed the essence of Zen for the ordinary person: to assemble with close friends in a rude country hut and admire the plainness of rough pottery bowls. This deliberately simple practice attracted the wealthiest sponsors, driving up the prices of tea bowls to astronomical levels.

China produced the world's finest teas, but did not develop the elaborate rituals of Japan. Scholars, merchants, and politicians all used high quality teas, however, to impress their guests. Poor peasants had to make do with "white tea," or boiled water. The Chinese exchanged tea at frontier markets for horses in order to strengthen their defenses against the nomads. Tea from China likewise lubricated the wheels of trade throughout the Middle East. Tea traders served high politics, high culture, and high profits all at the same time.

Yet the enlightened soul need not leave the world; he can live as he did before, utterly transformed within. The simplicity and practicality of Zen appealed first of all, strangely enough, to the samurai. Supported by the shogun and local lords, they spread their teachings in local temple schools, which raised literacy in the countryside to a remarkably high level. Zen masters also served as important diplomatic envoys, and even as ship captains. Box 13.4 shows the close connection between the tea trade, Zen masters, and the elaborate rituals of the Japanese tea ceremony.

Zen was a product of newly restored contact with China. For nearly five centuries, Japan had little contact with the mainland, but the Mongol invasions had stimulated Japanese shipbuilding. Japan resumed official trade with Ming China in 1401 when China accepted the shogun as a tributary state. Shogun Yoshimitsu celebrated his new prosperity by establishing a great Zen monastery, and dressed himself in Ming clothing. In 1394 he built Japan's most beautiful secular structure, the Golden Pavilion in Kyoto, shown in Figure 13.4. This small three-storey building, with a Zen meditation room and a bronze phoenix at the top, harmonized effortlessly with the landscape garden and pond beneath it. The Silver Pavilion, built in 1482, displays the radical aesthetics of modesty, where beauty lies beneath the surface. It has no silver, but only a plain wooden structure overlooking a meticulously crafted small garden. The Japanese developed the Chinese landscape garden, a miniature portrayal of nature, into its ultimate refinement in the Ryoanji, which has no plants at all, only sand and rocks to depict the endless expanse of sea.

The Zen aesthetic which permeated Japanese society during these troubled times was responsible for many of the greatest masterpieces of the visual and architectural arts. Black and white brush paintings depicted a great landscape in a few well-defined strokes. Sesshu (1420–1506), like the English poet William Blake, saw "a world in a grain of sand, and eternity in a flower."[11] The extreme abstraction of his rough, splashed brush strokes only hints at a larger meaning. **No**, a slow ritual dance theater, also suggested spiritual worlds beyond the stage, and it attracted popular audiences by alternating with **kyogen**, the raucous, bawdy comedies. Popular picture scrolls displayed in bright colors the agonies of Buddhist hell. Perhaps the best-known piece of sculpture, the Great Buddha of Kamakura, is impressive only for its size, not its aesthetic quality. Much more striking are the vigorous realistic wooden statues of court nobles, military leaders, and Zen monks.

By the mid fifteenth century, contradictory pressures once again tore Japan apart. The economy grew, as farm technology improved, and the population increased to 17 million despite civil war. Powerful families in the towns offered protection to handicraft guilds, or **za**, which established far-reaching merchant networks like their German contemporaries in the Hanseatic league. Merchant elites controlled new towns, like Sakai on the Inland Sea, the gateway to Kyoto. Venetians would have felt right at home. Japan became a great exporter to China, supplying her with 37,000 swords in one year, and providing copper ore to meet the insatiable Chinese demand for cash currency. Japanese imports of copper coins in return spread a money economy, while Zen priests supervised the cargoes.

But peasants rebelled against heavy taxation and the abuses of brewers who milled their grain. They often succeeded in getting their taxes cancelled, after their headmen accepted execution. In a growing atmosphere of ceaseless intrigue, with no military leadership from the top, each family fought to protect its own, and men established domination over women. As the preservation of family property became paramount, law codes gave land to only one son, and no longer to women.

Figure 13.4 Shogun Yoshimitsu, a believer in Zen Buddhism, built this Golden Pavilion in the imperial city of Kyoto to display the aesthetics of severity, simplicity, and luxury characteristic of fourteenth-century Japan.

Beginning with the Onin War (1467–77), the country fell into incessant internecine warfare that lasted for over a century. Military factions destroyed nearly all of Kyoto, while poverty-stricken emperors had to peddle their calligraphy to survive. Ancient families and large armies were annihilated. As the haiku poet Basho later commented, viewing one of these battlefields: "The summer grasses! All that is left of the warriors' dreams!" The Japanese call this period the age of "Warring States daimyo", but "bastard feudalism," the European term for this period of social upheaval, also fits Japan.

Even after holding off the Mongol invasion, the Japanese were perfectly capable of committing collective social suicide. Nothing seemed to hold the country together in 1500, and its future looked bleak. The twilight of the true samurai had arrived. Yet the warring lords on their estates were laying the foundation for a new powerful state. Local political and administrative consolidation created the building blocks for much greater centralization in 1600 by the Tokugawa than the Kamakura shogunate had ever achieved.

Rise of the Ottomans

The Mongols indirectly brought about the end of Europe's oldest empire. The Byzantine empire had held on in Constantinople when the western Roman empire collapsed, but it faced heavy pressure from Turkish nomads to its east. The **Seljuk Turks**, who defeated the Byzantines at the Battle of **Manzikert** in 1071, opened the gates for further nomadic incursions (see Chapter 11). When the Mongol Il-Khans subordinated the Seljuks, they pushed other Turkic tribes westward across Anatolia. On the anarchic frontier between the Mongols, Seljuks, and Byzantines in western Anatolia, enterprising nomadic chieftains descended from their high summer pastures to raid the peasants below. One of these chiefs was **Osman**, founder of the Ottoman state. His "tribe" was not a collection of his relatives, but a confederation of nomads who banded together to wage war. Although they called themselves "warriors" for Islam (**ghazi**), the Ottomans were not primarily motivated by an Islamic "holy war" against Christendom; in fact, they included Greek Christians in their armies, and like the Mongols, in the early period they accommodated people of all faiths in their enterprise. They began to create a stable territorial regime in northwestern Turkey, or Bithynia. In 1301 they besieged Iznik and defeated the large Byzantine army, and took over the major cities of Bithynia in the next decades. Map 13.4 shows Ottoman expansion.

The Ottomans originated as a heterogeneous confederation of warriors much like the other Turkic and Mongolian "tribes," but they moved very quickly toward a settled state. By founding a new capital, **Yenisehir**, near Bursa, they stepped away from raiding and toward bureaucracy. Since agriculture could support

Map 13.4 Ottoman expansion

many more warriors than pastoralism, and the expansion of the state depended on siege warfare, not mounted archers, nomadism declined as scholars and bureaucrats rose. With the advent of Muslim schoolmen, the Ottomans indeed became an Islamic state, locked in struggle with the Christian Byzantines, but also with the Muslim Mamluks to the south. Going around Constantinople, they moved into the Balkans in the mid fourteenth century. There, they recognized the authority of the Orthodox Christian church, and tolerated the local nobility. They distributed timars, lands offered in exchange for military service, to all who joined them. Fending off local revolts and invasions from the east, and crushing the last efforts of the pope and Venetians to organize a crusade, Bayezid I (r. 1389–1402) decisively established Ottoman control of the Balkans. Just then, Timur captured him, allowing further revolts.

But the state did not disintegrate. From 1402 to 1453 the Ottomans staged an amazing recovery. They not only re-established rule over Anatolia and the Balkans, but they finally completed the capture of Constantinople. The key to their victory was the recruitment of slave-soldiers, many from Christian families, who became the backbone of the Ottoman military and administrative system. The fifty-four day siege of Constantinople, a crucial event for Western Europe, was almost a foregone conclusion. **Mehmed II** "the Conqueror" (r. 1451–81) used enormous cannon, the largest ever seen, to batter down the capital's vast walls. Under Mehmed, the empire now permanently straddled Europe and Asia, and could truly claim to be the heir to the Byzantines and the new power enacting the will of Allah. By the early sixteenth century, the Ottomans had taken the heart of the Middle East, including the holy cities of Mecca and Medina, and gained the authority to re-establish the Islamic caliphate. They were nearing their peak of power and prosperity.

Southeast Asia: States, Religions, and Traders Mix Together

The term "Southeast Asia" was created in the twentieth century to refer to the diverse cultures lying on the Asian continent

Figure 13.5 The great temple complex of Angkor Wat, built over centuries by the Khmer kingdom of Cambodia, included vast numbers of buildings, carefully arranged geometrically to form a mandala, a symbolic representation of the universe in the Hindu tradition.

between India and China, and the thousands of islands along the equator, plus the Philippines. The region contained a much smaller population than its giant neighbors, only about 14 million people in 1200, spread over the same area as South Asia. Settlers concentrated in low-lying areas that provided abundant rainfall and warm climates for excellent rice harvests, while dispersed groups of forest and hill peoples practiced slash-and-burn agriculture. Known throughout Eurasia for its valuable peppers and spices, Southeast Asia attracted maritime traders from Japan to Arabia. The new continental empires of this period built great temple complexes testifying to a flourishing mixed Hindu–Buddhist culture. Then, two powerful external forces struck: the Mongols and Chinese from the north, and Islam from the west.

Mongol invasions in 1287 severely damaged the Burmese kingdom of **Pagan**, established in the eleventh century. The Mongols left the lowland Burmese vulnerable to attacks from Shan highlanders, who finally destroyed Pagan and sacked the capital, Ava, in 1527. The Mongols also destroyed the Nanzhao kingdom in Southwest China, driving Tai groups further south into Siam. The Siamese (modern Thailand), by contrast, founded their first independent kingdom, **Sukhotai**, in the thirteenth century. Their rulers maintained friendly relations with Yuan China, bringing back skilled Chinese porcelain artisans with their tribute missions. Sukhotai declined quickly in the fourteenth century, as a new, more powerful kingdom rose further south, at **Ayutthaya**. This new expansive kingdom, still on good terms with Ming China after the Mongols fell, menaced the **Khmer** (Cambodian) kingdom of Angkor to its east.

The Angkor kingdom based its strength on its fertile rice fields. It also built giant reservoirs constructed with state-imposed labor dues. These reservoirs might have been purely ceremonial, but they could have stored water to supplement natural rainfall and flood irrigation. The imposing walled capital was abandoned in the fifteenth century. What remains are the temple complexes of **Angkor Wat**, the largest set of religious buildings in the world, mainly constructed in the twelfth century. Figure 13.5 gives one view of this huge complex. A moat 650 feet wide enclosed nearly one square mile of lofty golden towers, galleries, rich sculptures, and a golden statue of Vishnu in a majestic shrine at the center. The ruins of Angkor have miraculously survived Cambodia's devastating twentieth-century wars to inspire intrepid visitors today.

In the south of Vietnam, the very long-lived Hindu kingdom of **Champa**, founded in the seventh century CE, finally succumbed to attacks from the Khmer and especially to **Annam** in the north. Annam, or northern Vietnam, was the most powerful and centralized of the continental kingdoms. The Vietnamese throughout their history have effectively adapted Chinese bureaucratic and military structures to their small country and used them to ward off their powerful northern neighbor and exert dominance over much of the Indochina peninsula. The Vietnamese successfully rebelled against Chinese rule in the tenth century. The **Tran** dynasty which ruled northern Vietnam (1225–1400) had its capital, Hanoi, sacked by the Mongols in 1257, but their tenacious resistance forced the Mongol armies to retreat, and they successfully fought off two more Mongol invasions in the 1280s. Street signs all around Vietnam today commemorate the great general Tran Hungdao for his victories. But a new threat came from the north in 1407, when China sent an army to occupy Hanoi, supporting a usurper of the Vietnamese throne. The guerrilla commander **Le Lo'i**, a frontier hill chieftain of non-Vietnamese origin, led a mass uprising that threw off Chinese rule in 1428, ultimately establishing a new dynasty that lasted until the nineteenth century. Annam annexed Champa in 1471 and nearly eliminated its Hindu culture. Pieces of the state may have survived for a century, and the Cham people still exist as a minority in modern Vietnam. But like Angkor, only beautiful Cham ruins survive today as an architectural remnant of a once functioning state.

Island Southeast Asia produced its greatest empire in this period, the Javanese kingdom of **Majapahit** (1222–1451), which encompassed both the concentrated rice production of eastern Java and a far-reaching maritime empire. The Javanese kings drove out Mongol warships in 1293, after which they established prosperous commercial relations with Yuan China. At the capital,

> *people in vast numbers thronged the city . . . every kind of food was in great abundance. There was a ceaseless coming and going of people from the territories overseas which had submitted to the king . . . Everywhere one went there were gongs and drums being beaten, people dancing to the strains of all kinds of loud music, entertainments of many kinds like the living theatre, the shadow play, masked plays, step-dancing, and musical dramas.[12]*

Among Java's main commercial rivals was the upstart port-state of **Malacca**, founded in 1400 at a crucial location in the straits between Malaya and Singapore by a Sumatran prince who converted to Islam. The Chinese Muslim admiral Zheng He, taking his massive fleets through the straits, offered Malacca's ruler protection. The Muslim rulers of Malacca had a complementary relationship with Java. Java bought rice and Indian clothing from Malacca and sold them to the Spice Islands, then sold the spices back to Malacca. Majapahit collapsed in civil war and lost its authority over the coast and island ports in the fifteenth century.

Islam in Southeast Asia Unlike the core of Eurasia, Islam expanded here not through conquest, but through trade and assimilation, resembling the way it spread in East Africa (see Chapter 9). In the fifteenth century, as Malacca became the greatest commercial center of Southeast Asia, Muslim merchants and preachers built mosques and gathered believers throughout Java and the islands. Sufi mysticism was especially powerful in this form of Islam; the orthodox schools of law had much less authority. As in Bengal, the Sufi preachers adapted Islam to fit with traditions of multiplicity and quietism. Many saw Buddhism and Islam as "two in form, but one in essence."[13] As the Javanese gradually converted, Islam changed into versions unrecognizable either by Arabic legal specialists or Turkic warriors. When the Portuguese took Malacca in 1511, inaugurating Western colonialism, Islam was firmly enough established in Indonesia and Malaya to hold off the new militant Christian power. Indonesia now contains nearly as many Muslims as the entire Middle East.

Conclusion Beneath the confusing vicissitudes of empires, warriors, traders, and pilgrims, we can still discern common features of Eurasia. One central new element unified the continent's experiences: the Mongol conquests. Whether they held off the Mongols or submitted, everyone had to respond to them. The Silk Road land routes had already linked Eurasian regions; now, maritime routes across the Indian Ocean and up the coast of China definitely increased in prominence. The world's total population did not change much, growing only from about 360 million in 1200 to 425 million by 1500. India and China held over half of this population, and most of these people tilled the land.

New crops, bigger trade connections, and especially new supplies of currency generated higher productivity, allowing cities to grow. All rulers recognized the value of commercial wealth, but it was tricky to profit from these golden geese without killing them; those who tried to impose shortcut solutions (paper money, copper tokens) by force bungled the task. Nevertheless, the global trade networks and their canny participants survived even the worst depredations in the long run, although some cities collapsed forever, to be replaced by new arrivals. The overall structure of trade and cultural interaction remained remarkably durable, even though the mid fourteenth to fifteenth centuries strained it to the extremes. Disease, political collapse, and civil warfare marked much of the world in the latter part of this period. China escaped some of the turmoil by moving toward greater isolation. Eurasians experienced darker times than they had seen for a millennium.

Partly in response to such suffering, the great religious traditions gained many more mass followers. Let us briefly compare their fates. Buddhism was driven out of its homeland of India by Turkic conquerors, and in China Buddhists suffered persecution from Confucians and Daoists. Buddhists remained powerful in Sri Lanka and mainland Southeast Asia (Siam, Burma, and Vietnam), and found one of their greatest periods of renewal in Japan, where Zen, Pure Land, and the Nichiren sects dramatically changed politics, institutions, and the arts. In Tibet, Buddhists strengthened the power of state and noble protectors, and mixed their faith with magical shamanic rituals. Hindu states and populations lost ground to the encroachments of Vietnamese conquerors and Islamic preachers.

Christianity's sphere of influence shrank in some places and expanded in others. The Byzantine empire lost control of the Balkans and Middle East, but Orthodoxy gained the vast territories of Russia, and Moscow became its new center. Islands of Nestorian Christians kept the faith alive across Eurasia, and in Western Europe the high medieval period created a formalized philosophical version of orthodoxy under Thomas Aquinas, somewhat like Neo-Confucianism in China.

Islam, however, was still the most dynamic religion in the world. Mongol rulers promoted it in Persia and the Middle East. Turkish conquerors and Sufi mystics spread the faith through the Indian subcontinent, while traders brought Islam to West and East Africa and island Southeast Asia. Overall, it was Islam's adaptability, not its militancy, that brought it success. Containing multiple, decentralized communities, without a single authority at the center, this faith appealed to the most diverse peoples across the Old World.

This volume ends at 1500, the year in which historians conventionally begin the story of the early modern world. But we should not conclude that everything that happened before the last half millennium merely points backward to a vanished past. Much of the unprecedented dynamism of the world after 1500 was rooted in the military, political, and economic processes generated in these times. These processes were not unique to any region of the world: some places rose, some fell, but the interaction of all of them was essential for the peoples of the world to move forward.

Study Questions

(1) Why was Chinggis Khan so successful in war? What caused so many to follow him? Besides conquest, did he have any other goals?

(2) When the Mongols ruled other societies, what impact did they have on them? Where did they mix most with the local populations, and where the least? Which settled societies adopted the most new institutions from their Mongol rulers?

(3) How did the Mongols reshape global trade routes? What were the relative roles of the land and sea routes of Eurasia? Who benefited the most from the Mongol peace?

(4) Which religions did the Mongols support? How did religious figures gain influence under Mongol rule? Which religions profited the most?

(5) Compare the societies which the Mongols did not conquer, like Western Europe, Japan, and Java. How did their societies change after the threat of invasion ceased?

(6) You are the ruler of a state or empire, and you hear that a huge Mongol army is coming after you. What do you do: fight back, surrender, flee, or try to negotiate? Compare the responses of different states like Japan, Vietnam, Khwarazm Shah, and Kievan Russia to the Mongol conquests.

Suggested Reading

The Mongols JANET ABU-LUGHOD, *Before European Hegemony: The World System A.D. 1250–1350* (Oxford University Press, 1989). This work emphasizes the Mongol empire as a key moment of intercultural contact.

THOMAS ALLSEN, *Culture and Conquest in Mongol Eurasia* (Cambridge University Press, 2001). Allsen's book is a fascinating recent study of technological and cultural exchange across Eurasia.

ROSS DUNN, *The Adventures of Ibn Battuta, a Muslim Traveler of the Fourteenth Century* (Berkeley: University of California Press, 1986). Dunn describes in a lively narrative the wide-ranging travels of Ibn Battuta and the world he saw.

MORRIS ROSSABI, *Khubilai Khan: His Life and Times* (Berkeley: University of California Press, 1988). This is a very readable biography.

Voyager from Xanadu: Rabban Sauma and the First Journey from China to the West (New York: Kodansha, 1992). Rossabi narrates the story of Marco Polo's less well-known Chinese counterpart in a very readable account.

The Secret History of the Mongols: The Origin of Chinggis Khan, ed. and trans. PAUL KAHN (Boston, MA: Cheng & Tsui, 1998). This is the best primary source on the rise of Chinggis Khan.

China Under the Mongols JOHN D. LANGLOIS (ed.), *China Under Mongol Rule* (Princeton University Press, 1981). This collection of essays focuses on the Yuan dynasty in China.

MORRIS ROSSABI (ed.), *China Among Equals: The Middle Kingdom and its Neighbors, 10th–14th Centuries* (Berkeley: University of California Press, 1983). These essays cover Chinese and Central Eurasian states from the Song through Mongol periods.

Mongol Influences on Russia CHARLES HALPERIN, *Russia and the Golden Horde: The Mongol Impact on Medieval Russian History* (Bloomington: Indiana University Press, 1985). Halperin argues that the Mongol impact on Russia was limited.

Donald Ostrowski, *Muscovy and the Mongols: Cross-Cultural Influences on the Steppe Frontier, 1304–1589* (Cambridge University Press, 1998). In a contrasting argument to Halperin, Ostrowski stresses extensive Mongol influence.

Glossary

Amida Buddha: Buddha of Boundless Light worshipped by the masses in thirteenth-century Japan.

Angkor Wat: Temples built in central Cambodia in twelfth century, abandoned in 1430s.

Annam: Northern Vietnamese region, unified under Tran dynasty.

Assassins: Ismaili Islamic religious sect and warriors, centered in mountains of northern Persia.

Ayutthaya: Kingdom and capital city in central Thailand, fourteenth to eighteenth century.

Babur: Turkic warrior (1483–1530), and founder of Mughal empire in India.

bakufu: In Japanese, literally "tent government," term for government of the shogun.

baraka: Magical power said to be held by Sufi mystics.

Batu: Grandson of Chinggis Khan, and ruler of Kipchak khanate.

Bayezid I: Ottoman sultan (r. 1389–1402), captured by Timur.

Bukhara: Major Central Eurasian trading city; plundered by Mongols in the thirteenth century.

Bushi (or samurai): Japanese term for warrior class.

Champa: Hindu state in southern Vietnam, conquered by Vietnamese in the fifteenth century.

Changchun: Daoist priest who advised Chinggis Khan on secrets of long life.

Chinggis Khan: Founder of Mongol empire (*c.* 1162–1227), declared khan in 1206.

Christopher Marlowe: English playwright (1564–93), author of *Tamburlaine.*

Constantinople: Capital of Byzantine empire, renamed Istanbul by Ottomans.

daimyo: Japanese lords, owning landed estates and supported by military followers, or samurai.

Delhi: Indian city, capital of Delhi sultanates of the thirteenth century.

Ferghana: Home of Babur, a fertile valley in Central Eurasia, now divided between Kyrgystan, Tajikistan, and Uzbekistan.

Firuz Shah: Sultan of Delhi (r. 1351–88), builder of canals and founder of charitable institutions.

Ghazan: Il-Khanid ruler of Persia (r. 1295–1304).

ghazi: Warriors for Islam

Go-Daigo: Japanese emperor who attempted to restore imperial power in the fourteenth century, touching off civil war.

Golden Horde: See Kipchak khanate.

gosudar: Russian term for sovereign.

Hangzhou: Southern Chinese city, capital of Southern Song dynasty.

harakiri: Colloquial Japanese term for seppuku.

Herat: Prosperous city in Central Eurasia (modern Afghanistan), sacked by Timur.

Hojo: A family, members of which acted as regents controlling bakufu in Japan when shoguns were too young to rule.

Ibn Battuta: Muslim traveler (1304–69) who visited China, Spain, and Africa.

ikko: "Single-minded uprisings," or protest movements in Japan, often led by Buddhist believers.

Il-Khans: Mongolian viceroys, rulers of Persia in the fourteenth century.

iqta`: Land grants to regional lords in return for military service in the Delhi sultanates.

Ivan Kalita: First Grand Prince of Muscovy, named in 1328.

Jin: Empire ruling most of North China (1115–1234), founded by Jurchens of Manchuria.

Jurchen: People of Manchuria, founders of Jin dynasty.

Kamakura: A small village south of modern Tokyo which gives its name to a Japanese period of rule by shoguns (1185–1333).

kamikaze: Japanese for "divine wind," a typhoon credited with destroying a Mongol invasion fleet in the thirteenth century.

Karakhitai: Turkic people and empire of Central Eurasia, conquered by Chinggis Khan.

Karakorum: First capital of Mongol empire, founded in the thirteenth century in the Orkhon Valley.

Khitans: Manchurian people, founders of Liao dynasty.

Khmer: Cambodian people and name of empire, famous for building the temples at Angkor Wat.

Khubilai Khan: Grandson (1215–94) of Chinggis Khan, and Mongolian ruler of Yuan dynasty of China.

Khurasan: Region of northeastern Persia.

khuriltai: Acclamation ceremony for a khan.

Khwarazm Shah: (Sultan Mohammad) Islamic ruler of empire in Central Eurasia. His capital at Samarkand was destroyed by Chinggis Khan in 1220.

Kipchak khanate: Division of the Mongol empire which controlled Russia and western steppes of Central Eurasia.

koan: Logical paradoxes, used to stimulate enlightenment in Japanese Zen tradition.

kyogen: Japanese comic theater, performed in interludes between no rituals.

Le Lo'i: Leader of armies (1385–1433) who drove out Chinese. He established his own dynasty.

madrasas: Islamic schools.

Majapahit: Javanese kingdom (1222–1451).

Malacca: Port and city-state situated on the straits between Malaya and Singapore, founded in 1400, taken by Portuguese in 1511.

Mamluks: Egyptian slave-soldiers.

Manzikert: Battle (1071) in which Seljuk Turks defeated Byzantine army in modern Turkey.

Mehmed II: Ottoman sultan (r. 1451–81) who captured Constantinople in 1453.

mestnichestvo: An elaborate Russian system of noble ranks and titles.

mesto: A "place" as a courtier of the Russian tsar.

Minamoto Yoritomo: Japanese warrior leader (1147–99), founder of Kamakura shogunate.

Mughal: Indian empire (1526–1858) founded by Babur, finally conquered by British.

Muhammad bin Tughluq: Sultan of Delhi (r. 1325–51), a scholar and an ambitious, if impractical, ruler.

Muromachi: A district of Tokyo that gives its name to the period (1392–1573) when the Japanese shogunate was located there.

Nanak: Founder of the Sikhs (1469–1539), a militant offshoot of Hindu traditions.

Nembutsu: Name of the Amida Buddha, a phrase recited repeatedly by followers of Amida Buddhism in Japan in the thirteenth century.

Nichiren: A militant Buddhist sect attracting mass followers in thirteenth-century Japan, founded by the Japanese Buddhist monk Nichiren (1222–82).

no: Japanese genre of ritual sacred drama.

Osman: Turkic chieftain (c. 1280 – c. 1324), founder of the Ottoman state.

Pagan: Burmese state (1044–1527), with capital at Ava, destroyed in 1527.

pomestie: Lands given to Russian nobles in return for military service.

Pure Land: Buddhist sect of mass worship founded in thirteenth-century Japan.

Rashid al-Din: Persian world historian (1247–1318), chronicler of Mongol empire.

Samarkand: Central Eurasian city, capital of the empires of Khwarazm Shah and Timur.

samurai: Japanese warriors who owed unconditional loyalty to a lord, or daimyo.

Sarai: capital of Kipchak khanate, on lower Volga River.

satori: Japanese Buddhist term for sudden enlightenment, especially in Zen tradition.

Seljuk Turks: Turkish warriors from Central Eurasia.

seppuku: Japanese "cutting the belly": term for honorable suicide, demanded by samurai code of loyalty.

shariah: Islamic legal code, derived from interpretation of the Koran.

Shinran: Japanese monk (1173–1263), founder of Amida Buddhist sect.

shogun: Japanese term for leading general, the de facto ruler under the emperor.

shugo: Japanese deputies of the shogun, wielding local authority.

Sogdian: Language and people who were prominent traders throughout Central Eurasia.

Southern Song: Empire ruling South China (1127–1279), until conquered by Mongols.

Sufi: Mystical order of Islamic believers, seeking to attain union with the divine through meditation and dance.

Sukhotai: First independent kingdom in Thailand (1230–1376).

Sultan Mohammad: See Khwarazm Shah.

Taira: Japanese noble family, destroyed in the twelfth century by Minamoto warriors.

Tanguts: Tibetan-speaking people of northwest China, founders of Xi Xia dynasty.

Tatars: Common European name for many nomadic tribes.

Temujin: Personal name of Mongolian ruler later known as Chinggis Khan (*c*. 1162–1227).

timar: Land grant given by Ottoman rulers to military followers in exchange for service.

Timur: Turkic warrior and ruler (1336–1405) from Samarkand. He was known in Europe as Tamerlane.

Tran: Dynasty ruling Annam in northern Vietnam (1225–1400).

Transoxania: Region between Oxus (modern Amu Darya) and Jaxartes (modern Syr Darya) rivers, in Central Eurasia (modern Uzbekistan).

Turkestan: General term for Turkic regions of Central Eurasia, including the modern independent nations of Uzbekistan, Kazakhstan, Kirghizstan, Turkmenistan, and Tajikistan, and also Xinjiang in China.

Uighurs: Central Eurasian Turkic people, founders of an empire, conquered by Chinggis Khan.

Ulugh Beg: Timurid ruler (1394–1449), also a mathematician, astronomer, and scholar.

Urdu: Sanskritic language written in Persian alphabet, a product of the Mughal empire's conquest in the sixteenth century, and national language of modern Pakistan.

veche: Local city council in early Russian cities.

Vijayanagar: Hindu empire in South India (1335–1565).

votchina: Hereditary lands owned by Russian nobility.

yam: Mongol postal relay stations, adopted by Chinese and Russians.

Yenisehir: City near modern Bursa, and first capital of the Ottoman state, founded in the fourtenth century.

Yuan dynasty: Chinese dynasty (1279–1368) founded by Khubilai Khan.

za: Craft guilds in Japan with extensive merchant networks.

Zen (Chinese: chan): Buddhist sect stressing sudden enlightenment without rational causes, especially popular in Japan from the thirteenth century.

Zheng He: Chinese Muslim admiral (1371–1433), leader of expeditions to Indian Ocean from 1405–33.

Zhu Yuanzhang: Peasant military leader (1328–98), first emperor of the Ming dynasty.

Notes

1 Morris Rossabi, *Khubilai Khan: His Life and Times* (Berkeley: University of California Press, 1988), p. 138.
2 Edward Gibbon, *The History of the Decline and Fall of the Roman Empire* (London: Penguin, 1994), p. 800.
3 Janet Martin, *Medieval Russia, 980–1584* (Cambridge University Press, 1995), p. 260.
4 Martin, *Medieval Russia*, 264.
5 Ivan Morris, *The Nobility of Failure: Tragic Heroes in the History of Japan* (London: Secker & Warburg, 1975), p. 77.
6 John Whitney Hall, *Japan: From Prehistory to Modern Times* (London: Weidenfeld & Nicolson, 1970), p. 77.
7 George Sansom, *A Cultural History of Japan*, rev. edn. (London: Century Hutchinson, 1987), p. 297.
8 Sansom, *Cultural History of Japan*, p. 323.
9 Ryusaku Tsunoda, William Theodore de Bary, and Donald Keene, *Sources of Japanese Tradition* (New York: Columbia University Press, 1958), p. 207.
10 Sansom, *Cultural History of Japan*, p. 334.
11 Sansom, *Cultural History of Japan*, p. 393.
12 Nicholas Tarling (ed.), *The Cambridge History of Southeast Asia*, 2 vols. (Cambridge University Press, 1992), vol. I, p. 218.
13 Tarling (ed.), *Cambridge History of Southeast Asia*, vol. I, p. 333.

14 Europe and the world

Timeline

1203–04	Venetian conquest of Constantinople.
1208–29	French kings sponsor crusades against Albigensian heretics in the south.
c. 1225–74	Lifetime of Thomas Aquinas, theologian, later St. Thomas.
1240–55	Mongols conquer widely in Eastern Europe.
1265–1321	Lifetime of Dante Alighieri, Italian poet.
1271–95	Marco Polo's voyage to Asia.
1313–75	Lifetime of Giovanni Boccaccio, Italian author.
1320–82	Lifetime of Nicole Oresme, theologian and social analyst.
1332–1406	Lifetime of Ibn Khaldun, Muslim social analyst.
1337–1453	English–French wars, later called Hundred Years' War.
c. 1343–1400	Lifetime of Geoffrey Chaucer, English poet.
1347–52	Major plague epidemic across much of Mediterranean and Europe.
1350–1500	Major advances of Ottomans into Europe, including capture of Constantinople (1453).
1360–1405	Conquests of Timur (Tamerlane) in Eastern Europe and Asia.
1364–1430	Lifetime of Christine de Pisan, chronicler of women's history.
1391–1500	Intensifying Christian warfare and discrimination against Muslims and Jews in Iberia, ending with conquest, forced conversions, and expulsions in 1492–1500.
1412–31	Lifetime of Joan of Arc, French military leader and later saint.
1415	Portuguese expand navigation and conquest in Mediterranean and along Africa's Atlantic coast.
1444	Portuguese begin the Atlantic slave trade by capturing Africans for labor in Portugal.
1492	Sponsored by Spain, Genoese mariner Christopher Columbus reaches the Caribbean.
1498	Portuguese navigator Vasco da Gama sails around Africa to India.

The east coast of the Adriatic Sea runs from Italy's Trieste in the north to the Greek Peloponnesus in the south. Along that coast, not far north of Dubrovnik, the town and island of Korčula now belong to Croatia. During the thirteenth century, however, the trading city-state of Venice, at the Adriatic's very top, dominated most of the northern coast's islands, including Korčula. Among other local commercial activities, Korčula's shipyards built **galleys** – sleek, oared vessels used in trade and war – for the Venetian fleet. In 1254, according to Korčula's local lore, Marco Polo was born there. Venetians insist vehemently instead that he was born in Venice, where he certainly spent much of his youth. Wherever he was born, Marco belonged to a well-heeled Venetian merchant family that maintained trading posts in Korčula, Constantinople, the Crimea, and elsewhere. If we believe the stories he dictated to a fellow prisoner in 1298, he and his family made fabulous voyages to the East (see Map 14.1).

Marco Polo's father and uncle traveled widely in Persia and Central Asia. Then they went to the court of the great Mongol khan, Khubilai, grandson of Chinggis Khan. By that time, different groups of Mongols controlled most of the territory from Kiev to Korea, and Khubilai's forces were conquering South China as well. The Polos may have reached Shangdu (Xanadu to later Europeans), the khan's summer capital from 1264 onward. Khubilai asked the brothers to return home so they could encourage the pope to send back oil from the lamp at Jerusalem's Holy Sepulcher as well as a hundred men "acquainted with the Seven Arts" who would teach his people about Europe. As a safe conduct, the Polos carried a 12-inch-long golden tablet from the khan, inscribed "By the strength of the eternal Heaven, holy be the khan's name. Let him that pays him not reverence be killed." It worked. They reached Italy safely in 1269.

When the Polos set off again in 1271, 17-year-old Marco accompanied them. They originally planned to go east by ship from Hormuz on the Persian Gulf, a departure point for South and East Asia already well known to Arab seafarers. They abandoned that plan when they saw the leaky vessels that were supposed to carry them, "wretched affairs ... only stitched

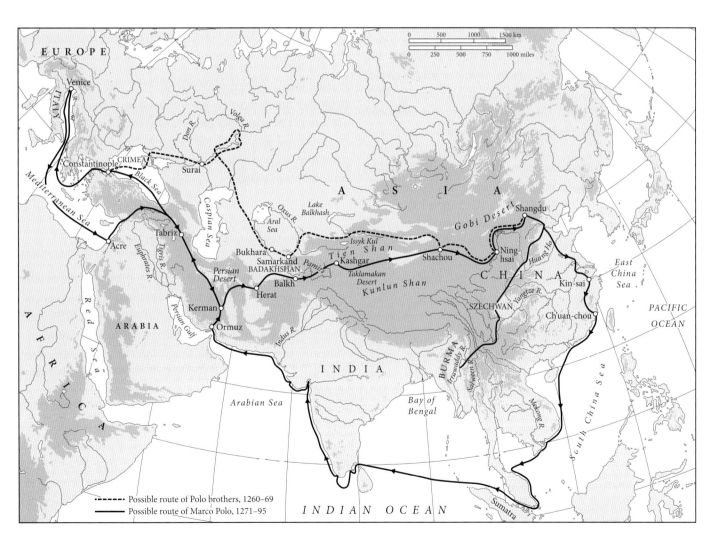

Map 14.1 Travels of Nicolò, Maffeo, and Marco Polo

together with twine made from the husk of the Indian nut." They shifted to an overland journey through Afghanistan, across Kashmir and Pamir, via the great Taklamakan Desert, then along the steppe's southern edge back to Shangdu.

The Polos traveled and traded widely in China, advised the khan, and accompanied him in his yearly migrations between Shangdu and the khan's winter residence in Cambulac, later known as Beijing. On their return trip to Venice, they traveled by sea to Indochina, Indonesia, India, and back to Hormuz. They lost most of their accumulated riches when officials in the Byzantine state of Trebizond, at the southeast corner of the Black Sea, seized their goods. After seventeen years in China plus seven years of long-distance travel, the Polos reached Venice in 1295. By that time, 41-year-old Marco had spent more than half his life on that momentous Asian journey.

In 1298, Venice again went to war against its great commercial rival, the city-state of Genoa. From the Venetian viewpoint, the war's worst moment arrived with the Battle of Korčula. After sacking Korčula, a Genoese fleet trounced its Venetian enemy and captured many galleys, including one outfitted and commanded by Marco Polo. The Genoese put Marco in prison, where a fellow captive, Rustichello, wrote down Marco's *Description of the World*, a mixture of memoir and travel guide. In his account, Marco offered vivid images of China's wealth and technical advancement over Europe. With wonder, he noted China's coal, paper currency, iron manufacturing, road networks, great canals, beautiful women, and magnificent cities.

At least the coal was less exotic than Polo said. When he dictated his recollections in 1298, blacksmiths in Amsterdam were already firing their forges with coal. Skeptics also point out that he (or maybe Rustichello) told some tall tales while failing to mention the Great Wall, Chinese calligraphy, tea, or women's footbinding. They likewise complain that no Chinese sources discovered so far mention the Polos. Still, much in Marco Polo's account of Chinese life has stood up to later criticism. Whether considered as fiction, fact, or stitching together of other travelers' reports, it circulated widely in manuscript copies. Two centuries later, Genoese sailor Christopher Columbus jotted notes in the margins of Marco Polo's travelogue in preparation for his third voyage to the New World, as he sought to reach China by sailing west. From Polo to Columbus, Asian connections strongly affected the fate of Europe.

During the three centuries from 1200 to 1500, Europe's increasing external connections combined with internal transformations to produce an economically and politically more powerful region. This chapter highlights several features of European changes in this period:

- Shift of Europe toward a more central position in Eurasian relations of trade and politics, accompanied by a shift within Europe from the Mediterranean toward the Atlantic.
- Growth of cities, population, manufacturing, trade, and agricultural productivity without fundamental changes in technology.
- Multiplication and competition of very different governmental and economic forms at the level of regions and countries.
- Growing impact of major wars on population, trade, and politics.
- Rising importance of Catholic and Orthodox churches as cultural connectors and political actors.
- Shocks to all these processes produced by the plague epidemic of 1347–52, later recurrences of plague in many parts of Europe, and the Mongol disruption of overland communication with Asia between 1360 and 1405, probably aggravated by general cooling of the climate during the fourteenth century, with resulting reduction of agricultural productivity.
- Toward 1500, energetic movement of European mariners, soldiers, traders, and priests into the Indian and Atlantic oceans.

In this light, the stories of Marco Polo and of Venice have important meanings for transformations of Europe between 1200 and 1500. The Polos grew rich not by drawing on European resources and technology but by connecting Europe with richer parts of Asia, near and far. Only later did the balance begin to turn in Europe's favor.

14.1 THE ASIAN CONNECTION

Chapter 11 described the interplay of Europe and the Muslim world between 900 and 1200. Remember how relations between Europe and Asia stood in 1200. All of Europe measures about 6 million square miles, roughly the same area as China. The whole of Asia covers about four times the space of Europe. Although Europe eventually produced the world's greatest concentration of economic and political power, in 1200 it was still a backwater. It then occupied the less developed northwestern edge within a vast, connected system of trade, political power, and culture. Muslim powers extended from southern Spain to North India, were moving southward in India, and were biting into the territory of Europe's only world-scale empire, the Byzantine. Mongols were then just uniting into the force that would over the next century conquer half of Asia and parts of Europe as well.

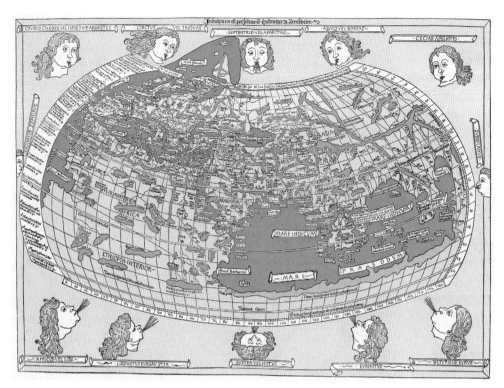

Figure 14.1 The 1482 world map. In 1482 Claudius Ptolemy (90–168) was the most famous geographer of the classical world. While medieval Europeans were familiar with his name, they were unfamiliar with his work until 1482 when a version of his world map was translated from Greek into Latin. There they found a map with actual geographic co-ordinates and lines of latitude and longitude. It used celestial observations to calculate terrestrial locations. The map was most accurate when dealing with the Mediterranean and the Indian Ocean as far as Malay. This was the height of Western geographic knowledge of the world in the classical era. While many of Ptolemy's co-ordinates were wrong, the attempt to correct them began a period of correction and measurement that would produce the maps we use today.

Venice and the Mediterranean

Marco Polo's Venice became rich and powerful as a hinge between Asia and the rest of Europe. The Lombard invasion of Italy in 568 had sent refugees to the Venetian islands. The islands long remained part of the Byzantine empire while Lombards and Franks successively occupied nearby mainland territory. Venice then served as a transfer station for goods shipped north from the Byzantine trading system. Eventually Venice became an independent power. Venetians traded Asian goods, salt, fish, slaves, and lumber to the rest of Europe, established colonies around the Adriatic, and managed much of Byzantium's own long-distance commerce. Venice profitably mixed trade, piracy, conquest, and participation in Crusades against Muslim lords of the Near East.

Venetian conquest of Constantinople in 1203–04 offers an object lesson in artful synthesis of greed and military might. Constantinople was still Europe's largest, richest city, but the Byzantine empire faced enormous pressure from Turks on the east, Normans on the west, and rivals for the crown within Byzantium. The last three emperors had all taken office by force. In 1201 a claimant to the throne asked the pope to authorize

diversion of the next Crusade to Constantinople and depose the sitting emperor on his behalf. The pope refused. Meanwhile, Venice contracted with prospective Crusaders to transport them to Egypt for 85,000 silver marks. Those who arrived in Venice could only raise 51,000. Since Venice had diverted its ships and money into preparations for the Crusade, the city faced a financial disaster. Doge (Duke) Dandolo of Venice proposed to postpone the balance of the debt if the Crusaders would retake the Adriatic island of Zara, which Hungarian forces had recently seized, for the city. The Crusaders obliged. Since they were seizing Zara from Hungary's king, who had also volunteered to join the Crusade, their action gave the pope a political headache. Unwilling to authorize Christians' killing of Christians but eager to recapture the Holy Land for his church, the pope excommunicated the Venetians, then forgave the Crusaders.

At that point the pretender to the Byzantine throne made the following offer: if the Crusaders would get him the emperorship, he would accept the pope's authority over the now independent Byzantine church, supply 10,000 soldiers for the coming Crusade to the Holy Land, and pay 200,000 marks to the Crusaders. Over

Figure 14.2 San Marco, Venice. With a population that never exceeded 200,000 in our period, Venice was one of the most powerful states in the Mediterranean world. It confronted coalitions of all the great European powers and even Islamic navies and as often as not emerged triumphant. The secret of Venice's power was its pivotal commercial role between East and West and the role of the Venetian state in shipbuilding and maritime commerce. San Marco was the great Venetian cathedral, the center of Venetian identity. To be a Venetian was to be loyal to St. Mark.

the pope's protests, and despite a Venetian treaty with the reigning emperor, Crusaders and Venetians accepted the offer.

In 1203–04 the invaders met their part of the bargain, but the new emperor found that he could only raise half the promised sum, and none of the troops. Another pretender took advantage of the turmoil by deposing and killing the newcomer. At that, Crusaders and Venetians captured Constantinople for themselves. Pillage of Constantinople gave the Crusaders enough to pay off their huge debts to Venice. A Venetian became the patriarch (religious leader) of Constantinople. The attack also brought the magnificent Byzantine bronze horses that now stand in the Piazza San Marco from Constantinople to Venice. Venice became overlord of many Greek islands, and a major maritime power throughout the Mediterranean. The city-state's merchants continued to play both sides, making huge profits by transporting Crusaders and pilgrims to the Holy Land, but also negotiating trading rights with the Ottoman Turks as those Muslim conquerors expanded into the Near East after 1280.

Venice faced intense rivalry from another great maritime city-state, Genoa. The two titanic cities competed throughout the Mediterranean, especially around its eastern end. But at the time when the Polos were touring China, Genoa controlled trade on the Black Sea, which blocked easy Venetian access to Central and East Asia. Genoese influence in Trebizond (where the returning Polos lost their riches) gave Genoa privileged connections to the Mongols, and therefore to China. In the background of Marco

Polo's stories we see flickers of a great commercial rivalry. Not until 1380, when Venetian galleys returned the Genoese favor of 1298 by smashing the Genoese fleet definitively, did Venice become supreme in the eastern Mediterranean.

After that, Venice maintained a major island and port empire (including, for example, Crete) until Ottoman expansion finally squeezed it out of the Aegean during the sixteenth and seventeenth centuries. Throughout the period from 1200 to 1500, Venice thrived on its connections with Asia. Even today, Venice overflows with reminders of the city's eastern orientation. In the splendid cathedral of San Marco (Figure 14.2), for example, the mosaics contain numerous Egyptian scenes, and the great domes echo designs from the Muslim world.

The Polos were not the first Europeans to return from Asia with fabulous news. The Polos' path to Beijing had long been known as the Silk Road. Silk, ceramics, cinnamon, tea, and other valuable goods started reaching Europe from East Asia around 200 BCE. Chinese and Middle Eastern adventurers started traveling the section of the road between China and Persia about the same time. Chinese chronicles record the arrival of merchants from the Roman empire in 166 CE. Europeans sent textiles, coral, pearls, amber, and glass toward China, usually through intermediaries, from that time on. Mediated by Muslims, such Chinese technological advances as paper, printing, and magnetic compasses also found their way into Europe during more recent centuries.

Mongol Impact on Europe

Mongol expansion made it easier for Europeans to bypass the barriers Muslim powers had set up between Europe and Asia. Among other things, Europeans who learned some version of the Mongols' Turkic languages could talk their way from Hungary to the Pacific. Just so long as merchants paid tribute, Mongols were happy to protect trade through their domains. Of course, influence ran in both directions; without caravans to tax and service, the towns and governments spread between Afghanistan and China could never have survived.

At first, Mongol expansion spurred Christian hopes that the new invaders would crush the Muslims who held the Holy Land. In 1219 the bishop of Acre (a Christian enclave within the Holy Land) announced that David, king of the Two Indies, was on his way to join Crusaders in driving out Saracens. Christian leaders soon learned otherwise. Fast-moving Mongol raiders took Kiev in 1240, sacked Krakow in 1241, and slashed their way through Croatia in 1242. Fearfully, the Catholic pope and the French king both sent emissaries to the Mongols between 1245 and 1255. The Mongols brought Europe's first gunpowder, a Chinese invention, with them on that devastating incursion, thus eventually increasing the deadliness of warfare among Europeans as well. Two centuries later, Europeans were building metal guns far more lethal than anything the Chinese or Mongols possessed. With mixed effects, from the 1250s onward Europe's connections with Asia as a whole grew steadily by land and sea.

14.2 AN OVERVIEW OF EUROPE, 1200–1500

In 1200, Europe was itself fragmented into hundreds of political units (see Map 14.2). Nominally larger states such as Poland, Hungary, the Holy Roman Empire, and France actually operated as multiple segments only weakly linked by military alliances and ruling dynasties. At almost every royal succession, competing claimants battled each other for the inheritance. Partly as a residue of the Roman empire, Europe did have a well-connected web of commercial and administrative cities. The roughly 800 bishoprics of the Roman Catholic church spread across those portions of the Roman empire's territory that Muslims had not conquered; most Catholic bishops presided over cathedrals in cities descending from Roman settlements. Urban areas were concentrated especially in northern Italy, Muslim southern Spain, and the zone from southeastern England across the Channel into France and the Low Countries. But Europe's largest cities were then Constantinople, Seville, Córdoba, Paris, Palermo, and Venice. All but one of them (Paris) were tied closely to the Mediterranean, while two of them (Seville and Córdoba) thrived under Muslim rule.

Mediterranean connections predominated because they gave Europeans access to Asian craft goods in exchange for gold, silver, precious stones, woolen cloth, linen textiles, and raw materials drawn from Europe and North Africa.

Notice two crucial implications of this description. First, taken as a whole, in 1200 the area we now call Europe had little coherence. Economically, politically, and ideologically, much of the southern third belonged to the Muslim world, while significant sections of the east maintained stronger ties with the Central Asian steppe than with Central, Southern, or Western Europe. A midsection identified roughly with the Catholic and Eastern Orthodox churches lived on the tattered remains of the Roman empire. Even those major segments left dozens of fringes and interstices.

Second, social organization varied enormously from one region to another. A band of relatively intense urban life organized around trade and manufacturing ran from southeastern England through northern France and the Low Countries, up the Rhine, across the Alps and down into northern Italy, including Venice. A second more prosperous band tied together cities of the northern Mediterranean and interacted intensely with nearby urban regions of Africa and Asia. In both these bands, zones of high-productivity agriculture supplied their urban populations. Nevertheless, the vast majority of Europe's population – very likely 95 percent – lived in rural areas dominated by agriculture, herding, fishing, or forestry. No country in today's world is nearly as rural as Europe was in 1200.

European Advances

By 1500, however, Europe was gaining visibly in both internal connectedness and world importance. Within the continent, a decisive shift toward the northwest was occurring. One sign is the arrival of Paris – by then some 225,000 inhabitants – as Europe's largest city. Constantinople (200,000) still followed closely. The next eight cities in order were Edirne (Adrianople, about 120 miles west of Constantinople), Naples, Venice, Milan, Bruges, Lyon, Ghent, and Rouen. Although the Mediterranean connection still kept Constantinople, Edirne, Naples, and Venice in play, Muslim power had disappeared from Spain, while northern Italy and the urban axis from Paris to the Low Countries were assuming major importance. Many of these cities wielded independent political power rather than being closely ruled by larger kingdoms or empires. As compared with 1200, furthermore, each of the European urban regions had produced important clusters of manufacturing backed by prosperous agricultural hinterlands.

To different forms of rule corresponded different kinds of military organization. Independent cities commonly created

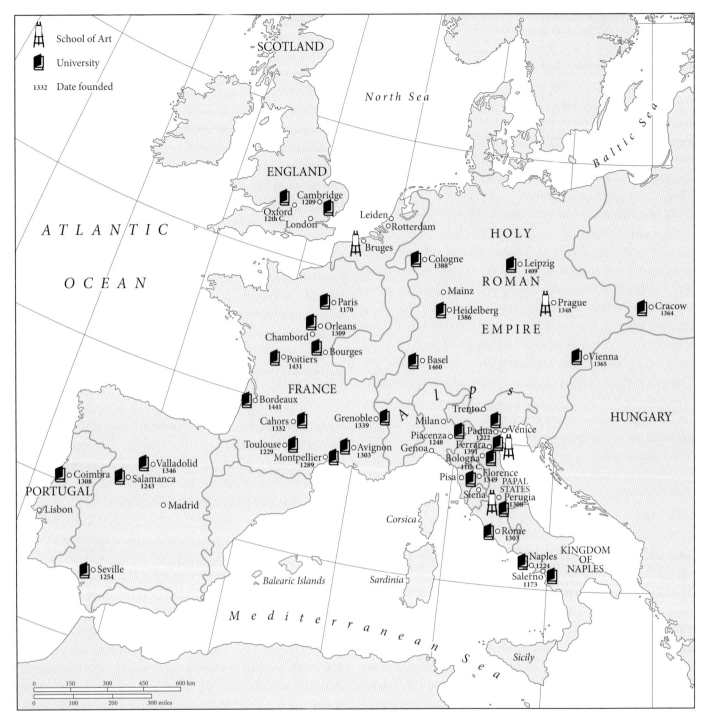

Map 14.2 Europe in 1200

their own militias and obliged citizens to serve. (Citizens never included all of the urban population, and were often limited to elected members of self-renewing guilds or councils.) In the case of Venice and many other maritime cities, military duties included not only militia but also naval service. In manorial systems, landlords often formed military units of their own vassals, tenants, and serfs, sometimes carrying on their own feuds and private wars, at other times joining an overlord's armies for a season of combat before returning to the country. Supposedly national armies actually consisted of aggregations of troops called up in this way, including a ruler's own personal followers.

Powers that had money but insufficient population commonly hired mercenaries, professional soldiers headed or recruited by military entrepreneurs. For centuries, Switzerland provided mercenaries to fight other people's wars when the Swiss themselves were not warring in and around the Alps. Only late in the period did rulers – France's kings prominent among them – start building regular, salaried national armies. Over the three centuries from 1200 to 1500, militias and feudal levies declined in military importance, while the expanding economy made mercenaries more feasible and attractive. By 1500, however, nuclei of national armies were also forming in many parts of Europe. Increasingly, troops in major wars combined small numbers of nationally recruited career soldiers with larger but variable numbers of mercenaries hired for the campaign.

The competing forms of military organization had different political consequences. Militias worked well for defense, but put serious strains on citizens' other activities when employed offensively. They empowered citizens who had the right and obligation to serve, but provided urban leaders with potent means of internal repression against non-citizens. Fighting wars with feudal levies reinforced the positions of vassals within their own domains while facilitating resistance to royal service or even military competition for royal power. Mercenaries frequently fought better than militias and feudal levies, but only so long as they received their pay; disbanded or unpaid mercenaries regularly turned to extortion, pillage, and banditry. Like mercenaries, however, genuine national armies depended on the ability of rulers to raise money and supplies to keep them going. Army-building rulers borrowed in the short run, seized vulnerable property in the medium run, and taxed in the long run. Choices of military organization and strategy therefore had fateful consequences for the character of states.

Within this world, both landlords and princes consolidated their power over peasants and town-dwellers whenever they could. From a master's perspective, the ideal arrangement imposed centralized control on farmers who produced surplus food and on merchants who shipped taxable goods. At a local scale, the manorial system embodied just such a logic: peasants tied to the land produced rents and supplies for landlords whose agents sold them for the lords' benefit. At a regional scale, a similar logic produced centralized, oppressive regimes. In periods and regions where demand for agricultural products was rising and rival political authorities were weak, both landlords and princes regularly attempted to build such systems of power.

The Holy Roman Emperors who seized grain-rich Sicily at the twelfth century's end built a repressive regime there at the cost of expelling or containing much of the island's Muslim population. Authoritarian successors of the Sicilian regime endured for centuries. Through much of Catalonia to the north of Barcelona, landlords of the eleventh to fourteenth centuries succeeded in making near-serfs of their peasants by usurping local and regional public power. Noble castles in northern Catalonia stood, on average, only 3.5 to 5 miles apart, an astonishing density.

Peasant producers supported those castles and their occupants. All this happened despite the fact – or, more accurately, because of the fact – that from the eleventh to fourteenth centuries Barcelona was one of the western Mediterranean's dominant trading cities. Landlords in Barcelona's hinterland who extracted food from their peasants had a ready market for that food. Catalonia's landlord-dominated system finally disappeared in a bloody civil war and peasant uprising between 1462 and 1486.

About the time of that struggle, in contrast, Polish landlords who benefited from the insatiable demand of Western Europeans for Polish wheat were creating their own versions of manors and serfs. Historians of Eastern Europe often call that process the Second Serfdom. Even cities, strange as it may seem, engaged in these forms of oppression. Despite priding themselves on self-government and independence from higher authorities, patricians of Swiss cities controlled the crafts and agriculture of their dependent rural territories ruthlessly. Although in the long run and on the average expanding markets eroded landlord power and promoted urban growth, in many instances landlords, princes, and patricians got to the markets first.

14.3 NEW INSTITUTIONS, OLD RELIGIONS

Between 1200 and 1500, the confrontation of bottom-up and top-down power produced the beginnings of representative institutions in important parts of Europe. Where kings faced rich churches, great landlords, and powerful merchants, the three frequently joined in periodic assemblies called Estates, with clergy the first estate, nobles the second estate, and commoners or representatives of cities the third estate. Cities often acted through the third estate. They also often established councils that both governed municipal affairs and negotiated directly with rulers over such matters as taxes, military defense, and the powers of royal courts.

In Iberia, the rulers of Christian kingdoms drew on cities and on great lords as they assembled armed forces to fight the Muslims who still controlled the south. Those cities and lords regularly created federations to negotiate grants and rights with the kings. The Castilian league of urban brotherhoods (*hermandades*), for example, began meeting regularly in 1282 to deal with Castile's demanding kings. Eventually leagues of Iberian cities and of nobles consolidated into national representative institutions under the name of Cortes. The great bulk of the population had no say in these institutions, but the assemblies did set limits to royal power.

Revival of Urban Life

When wealth accumulated and cities grew, the arts usually flourished. That happened for three main reasons. First, wealthy

Box 14.1 A Traveler from Tangier Sees Granada

Tangier-born traveler Ibn Battuta (born in 1304) reported of Granada, Spain, in 1355 that it was "capital of Andalusia and its most beautiful city. Its surroundings have no equal in the world: forty miles across, traversed by the famous river Genil and numerous other streams. The city is surrounded by gardens, orchards, terraces, palaces, and vineyards." Christian kings in Spain's northern regions had their eyes on that wealthy country, which they did not conquer until 1492, almost a century and a half later.

people and institutions broadcast their importance by building impressive monuments and patronizing the arts. Second, in urban regions artists and craft workers could find markets for their refined, specialized works. Third, city leaders competed with leaders of rival cities to embellish their cities and enhance the fame of their populations. Political leaders specialized in production of castles, fortresses, walls, monuments, triumphal arches, medals, and historical representations. Religious establishments fostered the production of churches, mosques, monasteries, sacred objects, and devotional art.

Merchants and bankers often supported the building of political or religious monuments to glorify their cities, but they also spent money on handsome guildhalls, exchanges, markets, portraits, and art works to decorate their private spaces. As Northwestern Europe prospered, its arts became more public, abundant, and distinctive. Its new arts included Gothic churches, public buildings, grand tapestries, religious paintings and sculpture, brilliant mosaics, portraits of city fathers, royal regalia, and elaborate hand-crafted objects.

Public intellectual activity everywhere divided between religious and secular institutions. In Catholic regions, literate people usually got their educations from the church, often in training for religious careers. The famous theologian St. Thomas Aquinas (c. 1224–74) came from a wealthy Italian family based near Rome, became a Dominican monk, taught in Paris, and served in the pope's court. Aquinas made his career reworking ideas from Aristotle, and Arab commentators on Aristotle, into a model of learned inquiry.

Among laymen, the commanding Italian poet Dante Alighieri (1265–1321) came from a patrician family of Florence, was banned from his city in 1302 for his opposition to papal influence there, and composed many of his greatest works, including the *Divine Comedy*, in exile. By writing in Florentine Italian instead of the usual literary Latin, Dante both made literature available outside the circle of classically trained scholars and established Florentine dialect (rather than, say, Roman or Venetian) as the medium for Italian literary production.

The fourteenth century brought a flowering of intellectual activity. The great social analyst Ibn Khaldun (1332–1406) was born in Tunis and educated in Fez, but also worked for the ruler of Granada (see Box 14.1), in Muslim Spain. His contemporaries included the English poet Geoffrey Chaucer (c. 1343–1400) and the Italian storyteller Giovanni Boccaccio (1313–75). Chaucer was a member of the gentry, a diplomat, and a London customs officer. Boccaccio, illegitimate son of a merchant, became a merchant himself. Chaucer's *Canterbury Tales* and Boccaccio's *Decameron* both tell earthy stories of daily life. That no sharp line separated religious and secular inquiry, however, we can see in the work of another contemporary, Nicole Oresme (1320–82). Oresme studied in Paris on a scholarship, took religious orders, ran a college, became a bishop, and advised two French kings. Oresme wrote theology in the rationalist mode inspired by Thomas Aquinas. But he also wrote one of the Middle Ages' outstanding analyses of economic processes: his *Treatise on the Origin, Nature, Law, and Transformations of Money*. He wrote the treatise at a time when France's monetary system had fallen into terrible disorder as a result of war, rebellion, and the king's own debasing of coinage.

Women in Art and Politics

Elite women took part in the revival of Europe's creative activity. The life of Christine de Pisan (1364–1430) illustrates opportunities for women, limits on those opportunities, and the importance of trans-European connections. Christine's father was the Venetian Tommaso de Pizzano, a famous physician and astrologer. Christine moved to Paris at the age of 5, when France's King Charles V invited her father to join his court. After receiving a fine education, she married a 25-year-old court secretary, Étienne du Castel, when she was 15. That same year King Charles died, leaving both father Tommaso and husband Étienne without the royal favors and income they had been receiving. Tommaso died soon after. After ten years of marriage and three children, Étienne also died, leaving Christine with her mother, her children, and a niece to support on Étienne's small, disputed inheritance.

Resourceful Christine began to earn her living as a writer. She wrote long poems, books of advice, a commissioned (and

Box 14.2 Bad News for Portugal's Jews

Isaac Abrabanel (1437–1508) was a renowned Jewish scholar who once served as treasurer for Portugal's King Alfonso V, but he, like all the other Jews, was forcibly expelled from Spain in 1492. In 1496 he wrote: "During these past thirty-two years, many terrible evils have come upon the Jewish people in all places such as no eye has seen nor has ever occurred previously, neither to them nor any other nation, from the time humankind was put on Earth until today."

flattering) biography of the late King Charles, and two widely read books about famous women: *The City of Ladies* and *The Treasure of the City of Ladies* (both 1405). These and other writings made a strong case for women's right to participate fully in public life. Later she wrote about France's wars, civil and international. In 1418 she retired to a convent, but continued to write. Her last known poem offered a tribute to Joan of Arc, who led a French army against English forces in 1429. Christine de Pisan died the following year.

Joan of Arc herself came from a very different background, but also made an important mark on French history. Daughter of prosperous peasants, Joan began hearing saints' voices in 1425, at the age of 13. Four years later, the voices told her to help the French armies that were defending Orléans (not far southwest of Paris) from an English siege. She not only led the city's successful relief but also took the uncrowned king to Reims cathedral for coronation as Charles VII. Jealous ministers soon cut Joan off from the king. In 1430, Burgundian forces that were allied with the English captured her in a battle north of Paris. The English bought Joan from the Burgundians, tried her as a witch, and had her burned in Rouen (1431). Christine de Pisan had not lived to learn about the disaster that befell the last of her heroines.

Religious Divisions and Warfare

Both Christine de Pisan and Joan of Arc died faithful to the Catholic church. Across the continent, religious identities loomed larger after 1200. Europe divided more clearly into zones of Muslim, Orthodox, and Catholic dominance, and Catholics themselves took to more active discrimination against Jews. Within Catholic regions, the papacy (despite a schism between Italian- and French-based popes from 1378 to 1417) acted as a major connector and secular power. New Catholic religious orders such as Franciscans (founded in 1209) and Dominicans (founded in 1216) preached Christianity to the masses and helped integrate them into the church. Prospering cities regularly marked their success by inviting religious orders to establish monasteries, churches, schools, and charitable establishments.

That organizational expansion coupled with the Crusaders' determination to extend the geographic range of Christendom. Conversion of non-Christians became a major activity of Europe's religious orders. Catholic monarchs declared their devotion by banning Jews, Muslims, and "false converts" from those faiths. The Catholic church's council of 1245 required Jews within its territory to wear skullcaps as distinguishing marks, French rulers banned Jews (only to recall them) four times between 1132 and 1321, while Edward I of England expelled Jews from his country in 1290. In 1348 and 1349, many Western Europeans blamed Jews' sins (and therefore, of course, God's vengeance) for the fast-moving epidemic of plague; Christians murdered thousands of Jews in response. After massacres of Jews in Spain during 1391, Spain's and Portugal's expulsions of Jews and Muslims between 1492 and 1500 simply culminated a century of state-backed intolerance. Still, it caused a great loss both to Iberia and to the victims, as seen in Box 14.2.

Not everyone, however, rejected Jews. Polish rulers welcomed Jews for their commercial skills and connections. Royal invitations to Poland's cities promoted a substantial movement of German-speaking Jews eastward. Yiddish (a dialect built largely on German) then became a common language in important parts of Northeastern Europe. Similarly, many Iberian Jews moved to North Africa and the Ottoman empire, where their Muslim hosts opened special niches for them. (Jews of Iberian origin were more likely to speak the dialect called Ladino than Yiddish.) A number of Jews also migrated to the more tolerant Italian city-states. Venice opened a new residential area for Jews, who had previously lived on the island of Giudecca – meaning "Jewish district" – in 1516. People called the new space Ghetto, meaning "foundry" in Venetian, for the metalworking industry already established there. Afterward, the word **ghetto** applied to any city's Jewish quarter. From the two movements toward Poland and the Mediterranean springs the still common distinction between Ashkenazi and Sephardic Jews.

Opposition to existing powers likewise often took religious forms. Albigensians of southern France (eleventh and twelfth centuries), Waldensians of the Alpine region (thirteenth to sixteenth centuries), Lollards of England (fourteenth and fifteenth centuries), and Hussites of Bohemia (fifteenth century) all combined heretical beliefs, programs of religious reform, and resistance to secular authority. Secular and ecclesiastical authorities alike took drastic steps to rid themselves of these threats; confiscation of property and burning at the stake were popular remedies. All these public displays of religious identity became more widespread as cities grew and the gains of commerce increased. Let us not exaggerate, however: In 1500, perhaps 8 percent of the total population lived in cities; 92 percent rural makes Europe of 1500 a little less urban than Burundi and Nepal in 2000. Only compared with the deeply rural baseline of 1200 does the growth of cities between then and 1500 look impressive.

Shocks to the Old Order

What produced the shift toward the northwest and the modest increase in the urban share of total population? Among other things, non-Muslim Europeans bullied their way through the barrier to sea traffic between Mediterranean and Atlantic ports that Muslim kingdoms had set down centuries earlier. In 1291, for example, a Genoese admiral defeated Moroccan forces blocking the Strait of Gibraltar for the first time. Meanwhile, cattle-tending and grain-growing Europeans had filled up much of the continent's cultivable land, converting forest to pasture and field. Merchants and manufacturers seized some of the resulting agricultural surplus and available population to expand town-based economies. Wielders of coercion – warlords, knights, and sometimes churchmen – found it profitable to grab control over the same surplus and population in return for providing a measure of protection. Trade in agricultural products and craft goods expanded, as the search for raw materials and labor extended up and down the Atlantic coasts. Although worsening climate slowed the whole process during the fourteenth century by depleting the agricultural base, in general European total population, urban population, trade, and manufacturing moved upward between 1200 and 1500.

Halfway through the three centuries, however, Europe took two punishing blows: the plague (or Black Death) and a new Mongol expansion. The first blow came from the plague epidemic that swept over almost the entire continent between 1347 and 1352 (see Map 14.3), then returned intermittently for another two centuries. The epidemic decimated the population and generated a serious labor shortage. New research in medical history, based on genetic analysis, has confirmed that the disease was bubonic **plague**, the bacterium *Yersinia pestis*, carried by rat-borne fleas. This microparasite worked fast, with devastating results. When it arrived, it often killed half or more of a local population within weeks.

Long before 1347, plague had spread recurrently into Eurasia's populations. In 1346 it struck the armies of a Mongol prince as they were besieging Caffa, a Genoese-controlled port in the Crimea, at the Black Sea's northern end. Brought by ship from Caffa, the dread disease reached the Greek islands, Sicily, southern Italy, and southern France in December 1347. A report from Egypt in 1347 reads as follows:

A ship arrived in Alexandria. Aboard it were thirty-two merchants and a total of three hundred people, among them traders and slaves. Nearly all of them had died. There was no one alive on the ship except four of the traders, one slave, and about forty sailors. These survivors soon died in Alexandria.

From southern Italy and southern France, the plague spread mainly overland, but at great speed. The lethal infection struck Paris by June 1348, London early in 1349, and Sweden by the end of 1350. Perhaps a quarter of Europe's entire population died in that plague epidemic. After the mid fourteenth century, plague flared up repeatedly in Europe without ever again reaching the epidemic proportions of 1347–52. Where it laid waste, farmers seem to have withdrawn cultivation from the marginal lands that had come under the plow during the previous two centuries of population growth. The result over Europe as a whole was probably regrowth of forests and heaths in thinly settled areas, plus net shifts toward herding where markets for wool, hides, meat, and dairy products existed.

Nomadic interventions in European history did not end with the plague of 1347. Between 1360 and 1405, the Turk Timur (or Tamerlane) conquered most of the territory from central Anatolia to central India and from the Persian Gulf to what is now southern Russia. Timur's conquests shook the Mongol Golden Horde's control over Muscovy, disrupted overland trade with Asia, and thus promoted seagoing contact between Europe and South and East Asia. The disintegration of Timur's temporary empire at his death in 1405 did not restore the old status quo. On the contrary, the fifteenth century brought consolidation of a powerful Ottoman empire on Europe's southeastern edge, the disappearance of Muslim states elsewhere in Europe, and intensive experimentation with different forms of rule, including city-states, dynastic kingdoms, urban federations, church-run domains, and loosely stitched empires. Timur's disruption of Asian trade, furthermore, drove the Ottoman empire into greater involvement with the European economy.

Ottoman expansion into Europe had further consequences. Until the fifteenth century, Europeans had drawn their sugar chiefly from Middle Eastern and eastern Mediterranean plantations that used slave labor. The Ottomans blocked that supply doubly: First they monopolized the flow of slaves captured in

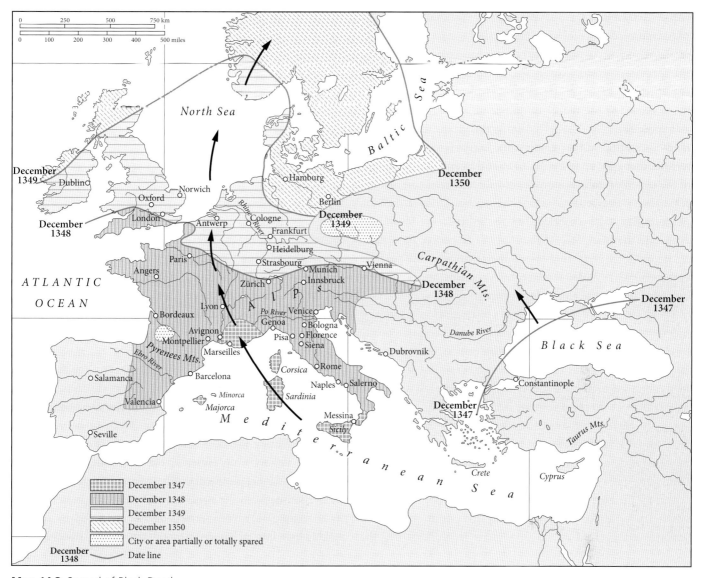

Map 14.3 Spread of Black Death

Southeastern Europe into the non-Muslim Mediterranean, then they took over many of the sugar-producing areas of the eastern Mediterranean. At that point, Iberian production of sugar in Spain, Portugal, the western Mediterranean, and nearby Atlantic islands using the labor of slaves captured in Africa began to increase rapidly. Portugal, already a significant presence on the West African coast by the 1440s, then began importing African slaves in earnest. Toward 1500 began a great age of European expansion, led by sailors of Portugal and Spain. Iberian colonizers soon began exporting their slave based plantation system to the Americas. They began with sugar, then added tobacco, coffee, and cotton for European consumption. Sea connections began to affect European lives as never before. Navigation of the Baltic, the North Sea, and the Atlantic exercised increasing influence over the whole continent's economics, politics, and culture.

14.4 A TOUR OF EUROPE

To get a sense of variation and change, let us tour Europe in a rough counter-clockwise circle before returning to the Atlantic. The tour will take us to very different cities and their regions: Dubrovnik and the Balkans; Krakow and the Central European plains; Stockholm and the thinly populated northeast; trading cities of the Baltic and North Sea coasts; Amsterdam and the Low Countries; Paris and northern France; Toulouse and southern France; the cities of Iberia; Palermo and Sicily.

Dubrovnik and the Balkans

Up to 1200, as we have seen, Southeastern Europe interacted with the rest of Eurasia far more intensively than other parts of

Europe did. Despite the Roman empire's expansion north of the Alps, before 1200 the lower southeast always sustained Europe's greatest concentrations of wealth and urban population. Within that maritime world, coastal regions had the lion's share of opulence and cities. Away from the Adriatic, the Mediterranean, the Aegean, and the Black Sea, people of the southeast's plains and mountains lived largely from grain production, forestry, herding, hunting, fishing, and mining. Except for weak manorial regimes that grew up in the plains of Poland and Hungary, most of the region's rural economy depended on peasant and pastoral populations. The Balkans include the southeast's lower half, the portion of the region bracketed by the Adriatic, the Mediterranean, and the Black Sea. At the start of our period, the Balkan territories of the Byzantine empire were shattering into separate kingdoms. The 1203–04 attack by Venetians and Crusaders unhinged the empire almost immediately.

The speed of the Byzantine empire's disintegration reminds us that for all their apparent magnificence the era's empires mostly took tribute from territories outside their centers, but let regional strongmen continue to rule in those territories just so long as they continued to pay and supply military support. A splintered empire did not simply disappear, but broke into its component parts. Elsewhere in the southeast, similarly segmented kingdoms and empires held precarious sway. Meanwhile, groups of mounted raiders repeatedly swooped in from the steppe to create temporary states north of the Black Sea.

During the next few centuries, the boundaries of southeastern states fluctuated endlessly, mainly as a result of incessant warfare. Venice held on to most of its territories along the Adriatic and in the eastern Mediterranean. But Venice also expanded north and west onto the mainland, up to the limits set by the Alps. Hungary grew almost to the Adriatic, blocked there by Venetian control of the coast. For a time, Serbia did the same further south. But after 1300 the big geopolitical news came from the far southeast: The Ottomans expanded from a small base in Anatolia to hegemony over most of the Balkans.

By 1350, Ottoman forces were conquering parts of the Balkans. In 1453, using cannon cast by Christian craftsmen, they captured Constantinople. They soon renamed the captured city Istanbul. A war with Venice from 1463 to 1479 consolidated Ottoman control over Albania and the Aegean, as well as requiring Venice to pay the Ottomans an annual fee for access to the Black Sea trade. By 1500 the northern perimeter of Ottoman control, including vassal states, ran from Bosnia across Serbia to Wallachia and Moldavia. That was, we have seen, a dual world, intensely commercial along seacoasts, deeply rural inland.

The two worlds met in Dubrovnik (Ragusa to Venetians), just down the Adriatic coast from Korčula. Dubrovnik was a trading port under successive Byzantine and Venetian rule; see the description of its merchants by a local schoolmaster in Box 14.3. During the late thirteenth century, the city housed a merchant colony from Florence, but also maintained its own colony in Ancona, on the opposite Italian coast. It thrived as a connection between the Balkans and Venice. In good Venetian style, Ragusa/Dubrovnik formed on islands joined by landfill, looking out into a harbor. Around the harbor stood a large

Box 14.3 Class and Food in Dubrovnik

Dubrovnik lived on commerce. A Dubrovnik schoolmaster of the 1430s left this description of Dubrovnik's merchants:

Some of the merchants are called plebei *[commoners], others are called* nobiles *[nobles]; among the first the lowest ones are the* perlabuchii, *who sell and buy the lowest goods: eggs, chicken and similar merchandise. Mediocre merchants are called* comardii *and they sell and buy cheese, salted meat, fresh meat and such. The supreme merchants buy and sell gold, silver, lead, wax, corals, pepper, textiles made of wool, silk, cotton . . . and similar merchandise of* great value. *The nobles also do all of this and I call them supreme merchants, although there are some who live only from rents, but those are few.*

Note a subtle implication of the schoolmaster's report. Cities like Dubrovnik depended not only on the maintenance of long-distance trade but also on guarantees of food supply. During the thirteenth century, Dubrovnik drew on seaborne supplies of grain for about ten months per year, as compared to the two months' worth of grain available from nearby farmers. (Despite access to the rich agricultural regions of northern Italy, even Venice counted on sea deliveries of grain for roughly half its annual consumption.) Everywhere in Europe, urban food supply remained precarious. In times of shortage, it therefore became a focus of struggle at both ends: Where merchants shipped grain out of producing areas toward higher-priced urban markets, and where urban authorities faced their own citizens in times of short supplies and high prices. More generally, urban authorities and rulers of city-states spent much of their energy establishing political arrangements to secure both their supply lines and their access to markets.

marketplace, several monasteries and churches, an arsenal, two forts (one on each side of the harbor), a customs house, and a governor's mansion. Dubrovnik contributed four galleys to the Venetian fleet for the disastrous Battle of Korčula (1298) that sent Marco Polo to prison. In 1358, Hungarian attacks on Venice's Dalmatian strongholds made Dubrovnik an essentially independent city-state.

During and after Venetian rule, Dubrovnik played a crucial part in the export of silver and other metals mined in the Balkan interior. It also handled the sale of slaves captured in the Balkans, especially young girls sold as concubines or domestic servants to traders from Western Europe. The general substitution of some version of the word "slave" for the Latin *servus* in Western European languages resulted, in fact, from the frequent capture and sale of Slavic-speaking people originating in the Balkans. Dubrovnik's contribution to the slave market, however, constituted only a small part of the Mediterranean's vast flow of captive labor. (During the later fourteenth century, for example, the Genoa-dominated Black Sea port of Caffa – through which the plague epidemic of 1347 reached Europe – was shipping 1,500 slaves a year to the Mediterranean.)

Dubrovnik's patricians struggled to maintain independence from their Venetian overlords, but also enjoyed Venice's military protection from potential competitors, pirates, and bandits while taking advantage of Venice's legal system to safeguard their commercial interests. That did not keep them, however, from seizing land that had once belonged to Venice. During the thirteenth to fifteenth centuries, they created a small republic including not only the city of Dubrovnik but also a substantial coastal strip and a number of nearby islands, stopping just short of Korčula. Their repeated fourteenth-century attempts to annex Korčula, however, all failed.

As the Ottoman empire expanded into the nearby Dalmatian mainland, Dubrovnik's leaders profited increasingly from their trade within the empire, but maintained their political separation. Like their former Venetian masters, they played both sides. During the fourteenth century, Ottoman frontier forces often helped Dubrovnik fight off would-be conquerors from the north and east, including Venice itself. Yet the city, whose residents were mainly Roman Catholic, joined the failed Crusade of 1443–44 against the Ottomans. At the same time, Dubrovnik's pragmatic citizens maintained their independence by means of judicious payments to Ottoman rulers. Between 1442 and 1482, Dubrovnik's annual payment to the sultan rose from 1,000 to 12,500 Venetian gold ducats per year. (That fact lends irony to a Latin inscription on one of Dubrovnik's two fortresses, which translates as "Freedom cannot be measured in gold.") Dubrovnik merchants became Ottoman tax farmers in Bosnia and Bulgaria. Living just at the edges of successive expanding Byzantine,

Venetian, Serbian, Croatian, and Ottoman powers between 1200 and 1500, Dubrovnik's citizens became adept at playing independent intermediary.

Krakow and the Central European Plains

A move north to Poland's Krakow reveals a very different relationship of political and economic power. In 1200, Polish government depended on an unstable set of competing duchies, one of them based at Krakow. Members of the Polish ruling family competed for control of the crown or for the independence of their own duchies. The region of Pomerania around Danzig (now Gdánsk) became independent of the Polish crown, for example, in 1227. Krakow itself occupied lowlands on the Vistula River, below the fortified hill that housed the duke's palace and the cathedral. Krakow ranged between 10,000 and 14,000 inhabitants over most of the three centuries from 1200 to 1500. For several centuries before 1200, the small city had serviced trade in amber, salt, and slaves at a crossroads between Kiev and Prague east to west, between the Balkans and the Baltic south to north. Later it became a major commercial center for Eastern Europe. Although Krakow served primarily as a redistribution center for cloth and other goods, its suburbs eventually developed big metal-processing shops.

The Mongol hit and run of 1241 smashed Krakow's feeble fortifications, burned many of its wooden buildings, and killed half its population. Toward 1300, Krakow's dukes made up for that vulnerability by building stone walls 30 feet high around the whole city. The duke's citadel, however, retained its own separate, formidable fortifications. The dukes who ruled Krakow often served simultaneously as kings of Poland, staging their coronations in the castle up the hill. They drew substantial revenues from fees and taxes in the city, but faced local opposition from the largely independent and self-selecting council of merchants. The patricians in turn drew important revenues from taxes, rents, and customs duties.

As was common in the regions east and south of Germany, thirteenth-century Krakow citizens received their duke's grant of **German law**, which meant a degree of self-government by the (largely German-speaking) merchant community and some protection for commercial contracts. When Krakow's Duke Casimir III (r. 1333–70) later began to expand his domains to Warsaw, Jaroslaw, and elsewhere in Poland, he regularly co-opted local urban leadership by granting them charters of German law. As Jews faced increasing discrimination in Western Europe during the thirteenth century and thereafter, dukes recruited Jewish merchants to Krakow, where they lived in segregated neighborhoods, engaging chiefly in banking and retail trade. Two big markets occupied the lower town center, which also contained a cloth hall, a merchants' church (with most sermons in German), a Franciscan monastery, and a Dominican monastery. In the surrounding countryside, nobles' large estates dominated the land. In contrast to Dubrovnik, Krakow lived in the long shadow of noble coercive power, and in the midst of impoverished, subordinated peasants. Yet its growing commercial significance, like that of Dubrovnik, gave it a measure of independence from surrounding systems of government.

East and north of Krakow, soldiers, priests, and merchants were actively seeking to integrate sparse populations into Christendom. Christian soldiers from further west took it as a right and duty to convert barbaric Eastern Europeans to their faith. The Teutonic Knights (an order of soldier-monks first formed to fight for Christian holy places in Palestine) fixed themselves in the southern Baltic during the 1220s. They immediately began military action against the pagan Lithuanians to their south. Inland, a parallel and more peaceful movement of German-speaking farmers promoted by religious orders or invited by local rulers colonized important parts of the region between Denmark and Russia. They established a pattern of free peasants and self-governing villages that lasted for centuries. By the fourteenth century, intensification of grain farming in Prussia, Lithuania, Poland, and the Ukraine made the Baltic a breadbasket for Central and Western Europe. Danzig became one of Europe's greatest grain-handling ports. Danzig and other Baltic ports also shipped Northeast European timber, tar, pitch, flax, and hemp for shipbuilding in the west. In return, Central and Western European ports sent wine, beer, salt and, especially, finished cloth to the Baltic.

Still further east, trade in furs, wax, and slaves loomed larger. Russian princes fought each other for control of thinly populated regions and their trade routes. For two centuries from the 1230s onward they also had to deal recurrently with Mongols who raided their territories, established overlordships at the eastern and southern edges of Russian power, and held their sons as hostages to the regular payment of tribute. Remember that Mongols seized Kiev, at Russia's western edge, in 1240, before moving on to Krakow. Only with Grand Prince Ivan III (or Ivan the Great, r. 1462–1505) did something like a continuous Russian kingdom form. The last Mongol attack on Moscow occurred in 1571. By that time, weakening of Mongol power on the steppe had combined with the rise of seaborne commerce (instead of overland and river trade from the Baltic to the Black Sea) to make Russia a less feasible target for Mongol control. That combination also diminished the importance of the trading network that had long connected Novgorod, Moscow, Smolensk, and Kiev. Novgorod, Russia's largest city, itself then began to make its major commercial connections through the Baltic rather than by road and river to the south or west.

In Russia and elsewhere, conquest's longer-term advantages depended on regular exploitation of agriculture, forestry, mining, and fishing. The very success of northern adventuring shifted the balance toward relatively settled forms of territorial rule. The opening of silver mines in northern Germany from 1160 onward gave German merchants and warlords a potent resource for entry into Eurasian markets and for financial support of governments. By 1200 a crazy-quilt Holy Roman Empire – with kings, princes, dukes, bishops, city leaders, and other dignitaries ruling its various segments – stretched over most of the space from the Rhine to the Elbe and down into Italy. Denmark, Norway, Sweden, Poland, and nearby territories were also consolidating into precarious kingdoms.

Stockholm and Northeastern Europe

In 1200, Europe's northeastern section was by far its most thinly populated major area. The further north and east a traveler went, the sparser the population and the fewer the urban settlements. Among the roughly 175 towns of any size in Scandinavia, for instance, almost every one hugged the southern coastal areas around the Baltic and the North Sea. More so than elsewhere in Europe, cities in the Nordic region first came into being as fortresses and political outposts. Only then did they develop their activities in trade, manufacturing, and agriculture. Typically rulers made agreements with merchants whose trade would give the rulers something to tax. The taxes paid for military equipment, mercenaries, and royal marriages.

Stockholm first grew into a city under royal patronage around 1250, then became Sweden's dominant export center for iron and copper during the first half of the fourteenth century. Characteristically, the city began on an island, now known to Stockholmers as the Old City. It centered on a market, a merchants' hall, a church, and a fort. Toward 1350 Stockholm's merchants (including many Germans) acquired a monopoly over shipping of goods from the coastal areas of the eastern Baltic. But away from the sea in Sweden and across the whole northeast the economy remained deeply rural. Pastoralists, hunters, fisherfolk, miners, and forest workers occupied much of the northeastern sector's northern tier.

Itinerant traders from the north, as earlier chapters have shown, shipped furs, captured slaves, honey, wax, and walrus ivory down the Volga and other rivers into Muslim territory from 800 or so onward. Scandinavian trader-adventurers probably founded Novgorod around that time, on their way to establishing a powerful connection between the Baltic and Constantinople. At that time, the word **Rus** meant, essentially, Viking. Only later did it come to designate Russian Slavs. Eventually north–south exchanges left major accumulations of

Mediterranean and Middle Eastern silver in Russia and Sweden. We have seen Krakow prospering further south as a crossroads in that trade.

Scandinavia's Vikings had also been trading and plundering in the Baltic and Atlantic. Erik the Red had made his first voyage to Iceland and Greenland between 983 and 986. During the next half-century Vikings had reached the North American mainland. They then continued hunting and trading in North America for the next three hundred years. Seafaring Norwegian forces took political control of Greenland in 1261 and of Iceland in 1262–64. Although the Greenland colony collapsed around 1450, people of Scandinavian stock have dominated Iceland since those early forays.

In the same period, Scandinavian adventurers were extending their power into the British Isles, down the North Sea coast, and into France. By 1200 their descendants dominated Normandy, England, southern Italy, and parts of the Mediterranean. Back in Scandinavia, kings were consolidating their power in Denmark, Sweden, and Norway, all of which became formidable presences in the north during the thirteenth century. Despite fighting off German merchants on one side and fiercely independent nobles on the other, the three crowns united into a fairly effective joint monarchy – the Union of Kalmar – in 1387, only to disintegrate again during the later fifteenth century.

The Hanse and Coastal Commerce

One reason Scandinavian monarchies had trouble maintaining centralized power was that the very mercantile activity they encouraged for the sake of revenue created a counter-current. Along the North Sea and Baltic coasts, a remarkable new form of organization developed during the thirteenth century: From lower Denmark along the Baltic to Novgorod, trading cities federated into the powerful, largely autonomous, and mainly German-speaking Hanseatic League, also known as the **Hanse**. From the north, League members shipped wood products, hides, fur, butter, fish, and metals west and south, while sending spices, liquor, silver, salt, and manufactured goods in the opposite directions. The urban league maintained its own armed forces to protect member cities and their trade. Often in alliance with local Slavic or Scandinavian rulers, Germans founded new trading towns all around the Baltic. Their cities followed a distinctive plan: walled and built largely in brick, with a central market flanked by a town hall and a merchants' church. The urban ruling classes, and sometimes the bulk of the population, became German. During the fourteenth century, 90 percent of Danzig's population was German, as was 80 percent of Riga's. Eventually about two hundred cities affiliated with the Hanse.

Hanse members generally adopted the law of Lübeck, one of the original Hanseatic cities and a pivotal point of entry for Baltic goods into Western and Central Europe. Lübeck had three immense advantages: (1) access to the Baltic through a navigable river that was fairly easy to defend against pirates; (2) location at the point where shipments between the Baltic and Western Europe shifted from water to land transportation or vice versa; and (3) overlords who were willing to offer protection in exchange for revenues from tolls. Pirates, bandits, warlords, and local rulers – the four often overlapped – regularly threatened the security of profitable long-distance trade. Anyone who guaranteed merchants secure passage could therefore command high fees for the service. Even non-member cities such as Stockholm had little choice but to deal seriously with the Hanse.

Within its zone, the Hanse established a much more effective monopoly over long-distance trade than Venice or Genoa was ever able to create in the Mediterranean. Of course, enhanced connections with the rest of Europe had their costs. They made commercial cities dependent on grain shipped in from elsewhere, and therefore at risk from bad weather and high prices. During the terrible stretch of bad weather and famine between 1315 and 1317, a chronicler of Baltic towns set down these equally terrible words:

> It is said that certain people . . . because of the excessive hunger devoured their very own children.

External connections also made the Baltic vulnerable to the plague. After ravaging the Mediterranean in 1347 and 1348, the disease was killing large shares of the population in Scandinavia and the Baltic rim during 1349 and 1350.

The federated cities became a major force not only in the commerce of Baltic goods but also of raw wool, woolen cloth, linen, and silver. The opening of seaborne trade from the Mediterranean around the Atlantic coast toward 1300 gave Baltic merchants a maritime connection with Southern Europe, Africa, and Asia in addition to the overland routes they had been using for hundreds of years. They enjoyed great leverage in bargaining with princes and kings. In 1347, for example, the Hanse cities struck a deal with England's King Edward III, who owed them large sums. Edward and his predecessors had borrowed money to pursue major wars, including his current war with France, eventually to be known as the Hundred Years' War. According to the bargain of 1347, while English merchants paid 1 shilling 2 pence export duty on each plain piece of cloth they exported and foreign merchants paid 2 shillings 9 pence per piece, Hanse merchants paid only 1 shilling. Hanse power continued to grow for another century. In 1474, the English government granted the Hanse virtual political autonomy within its own London enclave, the Steelyard.

The Hanse was not alone. Cities of the period often federated to defend their common interests both against territorial princes who would gladly have scooped up their surpluses and against bandits, pirates, or political marauders who threatened their mercantile connections. The urban League of Lower Saxony first linked the cities of Braunschweig, Magdeburg, and others nearby against their demanding Saxon prince during the later fourteenth century. Then the existence of their league provided a basis for those cities' joint entry into the Hanse.

A similar leaguing together produced a Swiss federation, starting with high mountain cantons in 1291. Rural Switzerland may seem an odd example of urban connection. In fact, the Swiss confederation grew rich from control of trade routes across the Alps, and generally expanded by incorporating a single commercial city – Zurich, Bern, and so on – plus its dependent rural territory at a time. When the Hanse did finally face major competition during the fifteenth century, it did not come from major territorial kingdoms but from city-state federations in southern Germany and the Low Countries. After 1500, consolidation of royal power around the Baltic and along the Atlantic coasts did weaken the collective grip of Hanseatic cities on maritime trade. Well past 1500, nevertheless, leagues of cities including the Hanse provided a heavy counterweight to princely expansion in Northeastern Europe.

Amsterdam and the Low Countries

Commerce did not flourish along the coasts alone. A band of commercial cities from southern England, through Flanders and the Rhineland, across the Alps, and into Italy carried major flows of trade from Roman times onward. We have already caught hints of that band's operation in Venice, Genoa, Dubrovnik, and Switzerland. In 1500 as in 1200, the cross-cutting region remained an area of intensive trade and fragmented sovereignty, as multiple powers, including city elders and church officials, tried to run their expensive enterprises with tolls and taxes on trade. Where merchants won, they typically set up self-governing city-states with their own militias, mercenaries, agricultural supply areas, churches, markets, producers' guilds, and oligarchies. The seaports among them also commonly maintained commercial fleets that doubled as (or included) military or pirate forces.

Take the case of a latecomer, Amsterdam. Some time after 1150, a village of farmers, fishing folk, and craft workers formed on marshy land with deep-water access to the North Sea via the sheltered but navigable Zuider Zee. Amsterdam did not become a significant commercial center until two things happened during the thirteenth century. First, as trade expanded along the Atlantic coast, inland waterways through the Low Countries, by which goods moving to and from the Hanse network traveled, became

more cumbersome because of heavy traffic, tricky navigation, and expensive tolls. Second, a big, new bulk-carrying ship, the **cog**, began to displace lighter, narrower, less maneuverable Scandinavian boats from the Atlantic and Baltic trades. (Frisians from the Dutch coast may well have invented the cog during the twelfth century and made the crucial substitution of a tiller for steering by oar during the thirteenth.) With the cog, Amsterdam's exposure to the sea turned from a threat into an opportunity. Sensing the promise, the Count of Holland incorporated Amsterdam into his territory in 1317. Instead of attempting to establish tolls, however, the Counts settled for collecting taxes from Amsterdam's merchants. That left the merchants much freer to ship their goods when and where they wanted.

Spurred by expanding trade, Dutch cities grew rapidly; by 1400, with close to half its population in Amsterdam and other cities, Holland became one of Europe's most urbanized regions. Still a muddy village in 1200, Amsterdam was one of Northern Europe's leading cities by 1400. Unlike Bruges and Antwerp, Amsterdam never hosted a major textile industry. Like Danzig, Stockholm, Dubrovnik, and Venice, it made its big money not from manufacturing, but from trade. Amsterdam came into its commercial own during the fourteenth century, as the city's merchant rulers allied closely with the Hanse and contributed ships to the Hanse's military operations. Once started, however, they competed with the Hanse. By the 1370s, Amsterdam was establishing its own commercial footholds around the Baltic, dealing directly with Scandinavians, sailing its big ships around Denmark, and bypassing Lübeck completely. As a result of that trading connection, Baltic herring remains a favorite snack in Amsterdam today.

During the later fifteenth century, an important Amsterdam firm brought together Symon Reyerszoon (that is, son of Reyer) and his nephew Reyer Dircszoon (son of Dirk, Symon's brother). The firm maintained a representative in Lübeck, but one or the other of the partners spent several months per year in Danzig. They bought talcum, wheat, rye, tar, pitch, wood, hemp, thread, potassium, and ash for shipping west. From Holland they exported salt, oil, fruit, wine, cloth, and herring – all produced elsewhere. Merchants with similar connections made the wealth of Amsterdam. Rather than the spices, silks, jewels, and other high-priced goods that southeastern cities had earlier imported from Asia in exchange for European raw materials and rough textiles, the traders of Amsterdam grew rich by exchanging staples. By the end of the fifteenth century, Amsterdam had become the dominant Western European port for connections with both the Baltic and the Mediterranean.

In Northwestern Europe we see both contradictions and syntheses of power based on trade, coercion, and religion driven further than elsewhere. Merchants and their cities prospered. In regions such as the Low Countries they acquired considerable political independence and power. In Flanders, the so-called Members that bargained with the Counts represented Bruges, Ghent, Ypres, and (as a cluster) Lille, Douai, Arras, and St. Omer. The States General representing Holland's major cities dealt confidently with their overlords, the formidable dukes of Burgundy. When Duke Charles the Bold died in battle with the French and Swiss at Nancy in 1477, the States General essentially took over Holland's government instead of meekly waiting for his successor to take office. The duke's outrage at the independence of the States General went back many years.

The dukes of Burgundy and their close relatives the Holy Roman Emperors failed in their efforts to build firmly centralized states. Yet the rival monarchies of Spain, France, and England extended their control over resources, including urban resources, enormously. Their expanded military activity shook the continent. At the same time, elements of the Catholic church, including the papacy and monastic orders, grew wealthy and powerful. The building of mighty, expensive city halls, royal castles, monasteries, and cathedrals through much of Northwestern Europe revealed an extraordinary concentration of mercantile, royal, and ecclesiastical power.

Paris and Northern France

Europe's fourth largest city of 1200, Paris, lived in rather a different world from the Hanse and Amsterdam. Paris owed its eminence directly to the growth of royal and ecclesiastical power in France after 1100 or so. King Philip Augustus (r. 1180–1223) fought off the claims of England's kings to much of northern France. Philip made Paris his major seat, and invested heavily in its physical improvement. At the same time the city's principal churches and abbeys became powerful landlords in the city and its surroundings. The heavily traveled River Seine connected Paris to Atlantic ports. Around the city, in the Île-de-France, developed one of Western Europe's most densely settled populations and richest agricultural regions. By 1200, Paris was also prospering from the expansion of manufacturing and trade in northern France and the Low Countries, to which it exported wine and other rural products.

Until the French Crown absorbed the nearby county of Champagne in 1285, the fairs of that region formed the bullseye of Western European commerce. Merchants from Genoa, Venice, and other Italian centers brought spices, silks, and other Asian goods to Champagne in exchange for woolen and linen cloth produced in textile cities far and wide. The Champagne fairs also featured extensive moneylending and financial exchange, with Jews and northern Italians actively involved. Bruges (now in Belgium) then took over as European center for both manufacture and sale of cloth. The financial side of the Champagne fairs migrated mainly to Paris. Meanwhile, Paris remained an important mercantile center, specializing in rural products such as wool, dyestuffs, meat, fish, cheese, wood, grain and, especially, wine. Its own manufacturing consisted of luxury items in gold, leather, and fine fabrics, all produced for its prosperous local population as well as for international markets.

The thirteenth century brought extensive new creation of municipal institutions. King Louis IX (the Crusader king, r. 1226–70, named St. Louis in 1297) established the college of the Sorbonne, for example, in 1257; it later became the nucleus for one of Europe's greatest universities. A few years later, Paris's Water Merchants – those who shipped goods by river and sea – created a corporation that effectively took over the Parisian municipal administration. (Even today the Paris coat of arms features a ship and a Latin motto declaring "it rolls but doesn't sink.") Until the eighteenth century, the head of the city's merchant guilds served as the equivalent of mayor. During the same period both the massive cathedral of Notre-Dame (begun in 1163, but under construction long after that) and St. Louis's exquisite Sainte-Chapelle (built rapidly between 1243 and 1248) went up on Paris's central island. They extended the new Gothic style that had first appeared in the nearby abbey of St. Denis during the twelfth century. Over the next two centuries Gothic became the standard church architectural style throughout Western Europe (see Map 14.4).

Later Parisian history gives an idea of the vast processes that transformed the whole of Europe between 1200 and 1500. Over the period as a whole, Europe's successful states were greatly expanding their geographic scale and their control over people, resources, and armed forces within their territories. They sometimes expanded by their rulers' canny marriages, but mostly by war. It was not easy. War called up new taxes and new demands on a country's subject population, which in turn commonly incited popular rebellions and armed resistance by regional power-holders. The largest single French international conflict of the period was the Hundred Years' War, the war depicted by Christine de Pisan and fought briefly by Joan of Arc. Actually a whole series of wars extending from 1337 to 1453 with large intervals of truce and regrouping, it pitted French against English over English claims to continental lands. At times, in fact, English forces dominated most of the territory we now think of as France. If the war had gone somewhat differently, a single Franco-English empire could easily have become the dominant power in Western Europe.

Meanwhile, the overlap of war, plague, and the global cooling of the later fourteenth century seriously cramped the activity of Paris as an agricultural market. Whenever English armies or their French collaborators entered the Paris region, they

Map 14.4 Distribution of Gothic cathedrals c. 1500

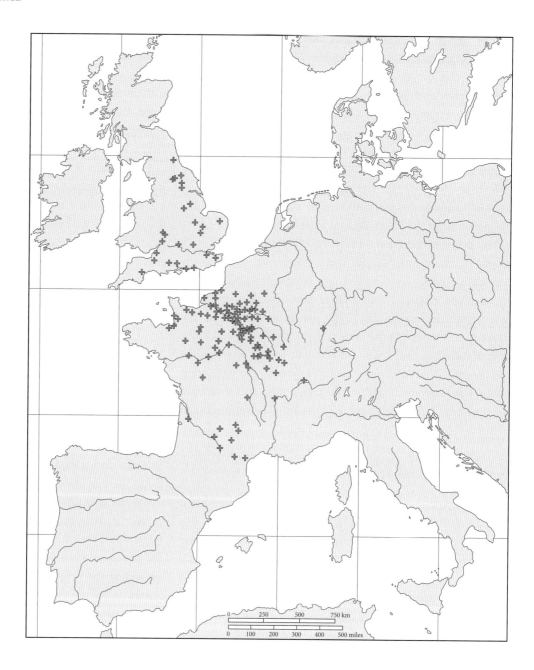

threatened not only the market, but the food supply of the large Parisian population as well, just when refugees from the countryside were swelling that population. When battles ceased, demobilized but unpaid troops often became bandits, preying on peasants and merchants alike. In the midst of these troubles, a brief civil war of 1358 allied the Parisian militia with armed peasants from the Île-de-France against the regional nobility and royal forces. Royal victory in the civil war brought bloody repression down on the popular side. As a result of incessant struggle and royal advance, the fourteenth century ended with Paris surrounded by royal fortresses: the Louvre, the Bastille, Vincennes Castle, and still others further from the center.

For another half-century, civil wars, rebellions, and realignments of factions marked the history of Paris and of France as a whole. Followers of the French king's enemy, the powerful duke of Burgundy, actually occupied Paris for eighteen years, from 1418 to 1436. Even Joan of Arc, who led an attack on the city in 1429, was unable to dislodge the Burgundians. Only a precarious peace with the English permitted the French king, Charles VII (r. 1422–61), to re-enter Paris in 1436. Then a period of rebuilding began. The first creation of a regular army in 1445 and 1446 advanced royal power as well as French advantage in the struggle with England and its French allies. French forces adopted new cast cannon that overwhelmed the English just as the Ottomans were using similar weapons to blast Constantinople. By 1453 the French Crown had won back all but a small space on the English Channel.

The war's end in 1461 consolidated the king's position and began a round of centralization, soon complicated by new wars with rebellious nobles and with the ambitious dukes of Burgundy. An alliance with the Swiss, who had created some of Europe's most advanced military units, helped King Louis XI (r. 1461–83) beat down the Burgundians. A famous battle at Nancy (1477) ended Burgundy's threat to France and to Paris. In general the last half of the fifteenth century brought military, economic, and political recovery to Paris and France. France was soon expanding its territory aggressively, with Parisians paying ever more taxes to support an increasingly expensive royal government. Away from Paris, that governmental expansion paradoxically fortified the positions of regional strongmen. In the short run, at least, the Crown depended on them for collaboration in collecting taxes (from which nobles enjoyed considerable exemptions), in governing their regions, and in putting down rebellion. In that way, formation of a demanding central state reinforced "feudal" features of French life outside the capital.

Toulouse and Southern France

To see that top-down process more clearly, we can move to the region of Toulouse, not far from the Pyrenees Mountains in southern France. After a long period of stagnation, the old Roman city of Toulouse had begun to grow again during the eleventh century. Agriculture was reviving through much of its province, Languedoc. As landlords offered incentives for farmers to settle in their newly founded villages and cultivate the land more intensely, the manorial system and serfdom gave way to peasant agriculture. Shepherds in the nearby plains drove their flocks up and across the Pyrenees into Spain. They thus established communication lines linking Toulouse with people and ideas beyond the mountains. Toulouse became a significant regional center for crafts and grain-milling as well as a link in trade routes running from the Mediterranean to the Atlantic.

In 1200, the Consuls who ran the city of perhaps 30,000 people enjoyed near-autonomy. They fended for themselves because the kings and great lords who claimed rights to rule them continued to battle each other. Their nominal overlord, the Count of Toulouse, needed their revenues and military support far more than they needed his protection. At that point both France's King Philip Augustus and England's King John, with their vassals, claimed Toulouse and its surroundings. The king of Aragon, based across the mountains, also intermittently demanded recognition as the city's true ruler. But he was busy elsewhere, joining wars against Muslim powers in southern Spain.

Internally, the city divided sharply between its church-dominated central city and its commercial suburb. Suburban Toulouse leaned toward the populist heresy of Catharism, a set of beliefs and practices that was then spreading widely in southern France and eastern Spain. Cathar activity concentrated in the old kingdom of Aragon, which stretched along the Mediterranean and across the Pyrenees from Nice to Barcelona. Many people in the Pyrenees followed the heresy. Toulouse became one of its major centers. Led by ascetic traveling preachers and counselors called Perfects, its followers rejected the Catholic church and much of the secular world as Satan's work. In 1207, the pope's representative in the region excommunicated the Count of Toulouse for tolerating heretics in his domain. The great preacher Dominique de Guzman, later to be known as St. Dominic, railed against heresy in Toulouse between 1210 and 1215. In 1215 he founded the first chapter of what became the Dominican order in Toulouse as a bulwark of the faith. About the same time, the archbishop of Toulouse began construction of the city's great Gothic cathedral. Through top-down measures, the Catholic church reasserted its authority over wayward members.

The French king, in contrast, sought to extirpate heresy by means of armed force. Three times between 1211 and 1219 soldiers of the Albigensian Crusade against the Cathars besieged Toulouse. The city's militia joined with forces of the Count of Toulouse and Aragon's king to defend the city. King Peter of Aragon died defending Toulouse in the Battle of Muret (1213). The city's women, according to local legend, operated the rock-throwing machine that killed the Crusaders' leader, Simon de Montfort, as he led the siege of June 1218. Crusaders returned a year later, but rapidly abandoned the effort to subdue Toulouse. Under renewed military pressure, nevertheless, the Consuls and the Count of Toulouse finally signed a treaty with the king, the young man who would eventually become St. Louis, in April 1229. In collaboration with the king, the papacy soon established a university and a branch of the Inquisition, an institution the church had established in 1215 to root out heresy. In 1245 and 1246 alone, Toulouse's inquisitors questioned more than 5,000 people from Languedoc about the heresy. The church drove its heretics underground, although it never quite succeeded in purging Cathars from the villages and hill towns on the Pyrenees' French and Spanish flanks.

During the next two centuries, Toulouse prospered as a merchandiser and processor of agricultural products, a seat of landlords with large holdings in the surrounding countryside, and an administrative base for church and state. With English-held Aquitaine not far to the west, Toulouse's rulers enjoyed a measure of political leverage. The distant king had to worry about whether Toulouse could get better treatment from his English enemies. But when King Louis's brother Alphonse inherited the County of Toulouse in 1251, the royal presence came closer. Starting in 1319, the Estates of Languedoc – with separate assemblies for nobility, clergy, and rich commoners – began sitting in Toulouse. On one side, the Estates served as a protector of provincial rights. On the other, they became the principal means by which the king extracted taxes from the province. Popular rebellions and noble plots abounded in Languedoc as they did elsewhere in France during the fourteenth and fifteenth centuries. In 1320, some of Toulouse's inhabitants joined an unauthorized anti-Semitic crusade from the north in massacring local Jews. When the plague and English invaders arrived more or less simultaneously between 1348 and 1361, the stricken city destroyed all settlements that had grown up outside the walls and retreated within the walls. Yet through the great wars that brought English forces repeatedly into Languedoc, Toulouse remained a bastion of French royal power.

Iberian Cities

Between 1200 and 1500, France provided one of Europe's extreme cases of royal centralization, matched in its scale only by England. The experience of Iberia (now Spain and Portugal) shows more clearly the limits of centralizing processes during the period. In 1200 the northern three fifths or so of Iberia divided into the Christian kingdoms of Portugal, Léon, Castile, Navarre, and Aragon, the last an extremely fragmented set of territories scattered across the Pyrenees from Barcelona to Nice. Two Muslim regimes – the kingdom of Valencia and a segment of the North African Almohad empire – divided the mainland's remainder. Other Muslim powers held a number of nearby islands. It was a rich land.

For two centuries, all of Iberia's Christian kings had been battling their way south into Muslim territory, which in 1037 had covered some three quarters of the peninsula. As Chapter 10 explains, Spanish historians call the whole process "la Reconquista" – the **Reconquest**. Organizationally, it resembled the Crusades, with similar rewards and rights being offered to those who joined the military effort. As kings moved south, they typically offered grants to lords and municipalities that would raise their own military forces for anti-Muslim war. The result was a distinctive regime in which warrior-nobles and municipalities alike held royal charters guaranteeing them extensive rights. Often the rights included control over land newly taken from Muslims.

Once those practices fell into place, kings used the same devices to raise armies against each other. The distinction between richer horsemen (*caballeros*) and poorer foot-soldiers (*peones*) in that effort crystallized into a major Iberian class division. Before that crystallization, a peon could become a knight by the simple expedient of acquiring enough money to buy a horse and arms, then volunteering to fight. Later, to be a knight meant honor, privilege, and exemption from many taxes ordinary peons had to pay.

The whole Reconquest continued for another three centuries. The great Muslim city of Córdoba fell to Castile in 1236, followed by Seville in 1248. Christian conquerors installed Catholic institutions and suppressed their Muslim counterparts. When Aragonese forces took Valencia in 1238, for example, they immediately converted the city's chief mosque into a cathedral. Castilian forces did the same in Seville when they arrived there. By 1284 the militarization of Christian kingdoms had both solidified their frontiers and left Castile the only one with Muslim territories on its borders.

Castilian kings continued to battle Muslim forces to their south until the defeat of Granada, the last Iberian Muslim kingdom, in 1492. In the meantime, the earlier empowerment of nobles and municipalities profoundly affected Iberian political life. Kings attempting to raise military forces frequently faced resistance from well-entrenched nobles, and often forged alliances with municipal leaders in return for confirmation of urban privileges and defense against aristocrats' bids for power over the cities. As the northerners moved south, their kings generally granted charters to the newly incorporated cities resembling the charters of their own cities. As of the early fifteenth century, for instance, Andalusia (by then a property of Castile) had nine chartered cities including Córdoba and Seville. Even though charters resembled each other in many regards, each one gave the city independent bargaining power. As a result, kings of Castile found themselves negotiating incessantly with cities and great lords, as well as frequently facing rebellions from each of them or both together.

The marriage of Isabella (Castilian heiress) to Ferdinand (heir of Aragon) in 1469 started a partial reversal of that devolution. Aligning themselves with towns against aristocrats, conquering Granada, commissioning voyages of discovery, arranging a concordat with the pope, adapting the Inquisition to royal purposes, persecuting Jews and Muslims before expelling them, energetic Ferdinand and Isabella pushed their dual kingdoms in the direction of centralization. But at Ferdinand's death in 1516 Spain remained a composite realm, far more so than neighboring France. The arrival of Ferdinand's Dutch-born successor Charles I, soon to become Holy Roman Emperor Charles V as well, drew Aragon and Castile further into European political affairs and Atlantic conquest, but maintained their composite character.

Palermo, Sicily, and the Mediterranean

In 1200, Italy and Muslim Spain were by far the wealthiest and most urban regions of Western Europe. Recall that Europe's largest cities were then Constantinople, Seville, Córdoba, Paris, Palermo, and Venice. Constantinople and Venice we already

Box 14.4 Muslim Culture and Connections in Sicily

When Normans conquered Sicily at the end of the eleventh century, western Mediterranean culture bore the heavy imprint of Islam. Spanish Muslim intellectual Ibn Jubayr (1145–1217) lived in Valencia, Granada, Malaga, Ceuta, and Fez, on both sides of what were then Muslim waters at the Mediterranean's western exit. When Ibn Jubayr suffered a shipwreck off Sicily while returning from Mecca in 1184, he discovered that many of the Sicilian king's staff, servants, and harem women passed for Christian but were secretly Muslim. Ibn Jubayr described Palermo's women in these terms:

The Christian women of this city dressed like Muslims. Speaking freely, covered and veiled, they came out for Christmas day. They had put on silken robes embroidered in gold, with lovely draperies. Faces covered by colored veils, their feet in golden slippers, they sashayed as they went to church, or rather their gazelles' den, decorated like Muslim women: jewels, cosmetics, and perfume.

Palermo connected closely with Constantinople, Seville, Córdoba, and Venice in a world for which Islam and Arabic meant high culture. A century after the Norman conquest, Sicily's Norman and Holy Roman rulers regularly learned Arabic.

know well. Seville and Córdoba were, respectively, the chief port and the capital of Muslim Spain. Cosmopolitan Palermo served as capital of the kingdom of Sicily. Norman invaders first attacked Sicily in 1061, not long before some of them also took part in the momentous 1066 Norman invasion of England. They established a Sicilian foothold at Messina, then captured Palermo in 1071. They immediately began conquest of the whole grain-rich island from its Muslim rulers. Long after the conquest of Sicily, Muslim traditions remained strong, as Box 14.4 shows.

Palermo's later history registers Europe's reorientation between 1200 and 1500. France's house of Anjou seized Sicily and southern Italy (the kingdom of Naples) after killing the king, illegitimate son of the Holy Roman Emperor, in a battle of 1266. The new Angevin king of Sicily and Naples soon had the 16-year-old heir of the defeated king beheaded, an act that lost his regime support both in Sicily and abroad. A bloody internationally backed rebellion called the Sicilian Vespers (1282) ousted the Angevins, with 2,000 French deaths in Palermo alone during a single night and morning. The island's barons offered its crown to King Peter of Aragon, a descendant of the King Peter who died defending Toulouse in 1213. Sicily remained a property of Aragon – and therefore maintained a close connection with the trading city of Barcelona – for centuries. Nevertheless, the French made repeated attempts to reconquer Sicily. From being Muslim territory, Sicily had become a pawn in Europe's dynastic struggles.

Conclusion Mongols and Muslims, we have seen, repeatedly shaped the lives of Europeans between 1200 and 1500. It is not just that they provided influential models of culture, technique, war-making, and social organization. They did, but over the long run they influenced Europe even more profoundly by connecting Europeans with other parts of the world and providing Europeans with models, means, and incentives for making their own connections outside the continent. Wealthy Venetians of the thirteenth and fourteenth centuries regularly sent their young sons to live in Middle Eastern cities as part of their education. Those sojourns prepared the sons for commercial careers that would carry them mostly south and east. Even Vikings carried their furs, captured slaves, honey, wax, and walrus ivory down past the Mongols and into Muslim territory as they made their early connections with the major Eurasian trading systems.

European maritime expansion outside of Europe both responded to Mongols and followed Muslims. It responded to Mongols because Timur's occupation of the steppe blocked overland traffic to Asia and thus made the sea route more attractive to Muslims and other Europeans alike. It followed Muslims because Muslim mariners had done the pioneer work of navigating and mapping the Indian Ocean, because Muslims had revealed the possibilities of profitable trade in Africa, and because fourteenth-century Iberians sought to outflank Muslim navigators by finding a new sea route to Asia around Africa or across the Atlantic. The Portuguese began their maritime adventures with twelfth-century attacks on Muslim-held North African territory, continued to raid North Africa during the thirteenth and fourteenth centuries, and finally took Ceuta (just opposite Gibraltar) in 1415. To some extent even the great Portuguese exploitation of Africa simply continued the Reconquista. But it had enormous consequences: When a Portuguese expedition of 1444 brought back 200 captured Africans for sale as slaves in Portugal, it started an Atlantic slave trade that was to affect work and inequality in the Americas profoundly over the next four centuries (see Volume 2, Chapter 3).

Portuguese recognition of differences in wind patterns at various latitudes helped enormously. Portuguese sailors working the African coast during the fourteenth century discovered, to oversimplify, that winds blow mainly from the east 20 degrees or so from the equator, but mainly from the west 40 degrees or so from the equator. Today New York, Lisbon, and Beijing lie in the vicinity of 40 degrees north; the line 20 degrees north runs near Santiago de Cuba, Dakar, Oman, Bombay, and Hanoi. That discovery made circular voyages easier to plan: for example, from Lisbon south to Dakar, west toward the Caribbean, north from there, then back to Lisbon. Columbus completed the transatlantic version of the circuit first, but Portuguese mariners had been practicing smaller circles along the African coast for eighty years before 1492. Vasco da Gama used similar knowledge in 1498 when his fleet sailed around Africa to India. Soon Portuguese soldier-merchants were muscling their way into the Indian Ocean trade.

They learned some of their power plays from Venetian and Genoan entrepreneurs, who had been using them (often against each other) in the Mediterranean and Black Sea for four centuries. Yet in navigation they outdid Venetian galleys. Portuguese sailors first reached São Tomé in 1474, entered the Congo River in 1482, touched the Cape of Good Hope in 1488, and got all the way to Calicut in 1498. Soon they were gunning their way into the Indian Ocean spice trade. By 1550 they came close to controlling the movement of spices among its major ports and to Europe. Meanwhile, on the Atlantic side, another expedition to India swung too wide in 1500, touching Brazil for the first time. Portuguese conquest and settlement in South America was to come. Similarly, this chapter's final date leaves Spain in possession of the Canary Islands and with no more than garbled news of the Caribbean from Columbus' voyages of 1492, 1493, and 1498. Columbus made one more voyage in 1502. The great age of European expansion and conquest was just beginning.

Study Questions

(1) What does Marco Polo's voyage tell us about changing relations between Europe and Asia?

(2) What caused Europe's shift of political power, economic activity, and cultural creativity toward the northwest between 1200 and 1500?

(3) Did the Roman Catholic church gain or lose power within Europe during this period? Why and how?

(4) Which had a larger impact on European life between 1200 and 1500: the Black Death or major wars? How and why?

(5) How did invasions from Asia (for example, the Mongols, the Ottomans, and Timur) affect European trade, politics, and culture?

Suggested Reading

GIORGIO CHITTOLINI (ed.), *Two Thousand Years of Warfare* (Danbury, CT: Grolier Educational Corporation, 1994). Since war loomed so large in Europe from 1200 to 1500, this beautifully illustrated history of warfare in Europe places the period in context.

GEORGES DUBY (ed.), *A History of Private Life: Revelations of the Medieval World* (Cambridge, MA: Belknap Press, 1993). Instead of concentrating on kings, wars, and doctrines, European historians study the bedrooms, kitchens, and wardrobes of everyday life.

UMBERTO ECO, *The Search for the Perfect Language* (Oxford: Blackwell, 1995). Eco tells how Dante and other Europeans sought the origins of their civilization in a single primeval language from which they thought the contemporary Babel had sprung.

JOSEPH GIES AND FRANCES GIES, *Life in a Medieval City* (New York: HarperCollins, 1981). The city is Troyes, but nicely displays the intersection of trade, politics, and culture in many cities of Northwestern Europe during our period. You can also consult the Gieses for other readable books on social life in villages, castles, and elsewhere during the Middle Ages.

BARIŠA KREKIĆ (ed.), *Urban Society of Eastern Europe in Premodern Times* (Berkeley: University of California Press, 1987). Europe's medieval histories commonly pay plenty of attention to cities in Western Europe, but here you can learn about what was going on in cities of the continent's other half.

EILEEN POWER, *Medieval Women* (Cambridge University Press, 1997). The lady, the peasant, the city woman, and the nun, are portrayed by a great medievalist historian.

CHARLES TILLY, *Coercion, Capital, and European States, 990–1992*, rev. edn. (Oxford: Blackwell, 1992). Tilly gives an overview of processes that transformed European politics before, during, and after this chapter's period.

Glossary

cog: Large cargo-carrying ship introduced into international trade by Dutch during the thirteenth century.

galley: swift rowed ship used widely in trade and warfare in the Mediterranean.

German law: Codes of rights and obligations originating in German cities but widely adopted in merchant or peasant settlements of Eastern and Northern Europe.

ghetto: The Jewish quarter of any city.

Hanse: The Hanseatic League, a federation of trading cities powerful in Northern Europe from the thirteenth century into the sixteenth.

khan: Mongol term for king or emperor.

plague: Devastating disease that killed widely in Europe, especially in 1347–52 and later; also known as the Black Death.

Reconquest: The Spanish Reconquista, a drive of Iberian kingdoms to recapture Muslim territories, culminating in conquest of Granada (1492).

Rus: Long a European term for Vikings, but eventually applied to Russian Slavs.

INDEX